ADVERTISING &
INTEGRATED BRAND PROMOTION

Ninth Edition

Angeline Close Scheinbaum

Associate Professor of Marketing/Dan Duncan Professor of Sports Marketing
Clemson University
Wilbur O. and Ann Powers College of Business

Thomas Clayton O'Guinn

Professor of Marketing/Irwin Maier Distinguished Chair in Business
University of Wisconsin—Madison

Richard J. Semenik

Professor Emeritus of Marketing
Montana State University

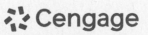
Cengage

Australia • Brazil • Canada • Mexico • Singapore • United Kingdom • United States

Advertising & Integrated Brand Promotion, **Ninth Edition**

Angeline Close Scheinbaum, Thomas Clayton O'Guinn, Richard J. Semenik

SVP, Product: Erin Joyner

VP, Product: Thais Alencar

Product Director: Joe Sabatino

Product Manager: Heather Thompson

Product Assistant: Hannah May

Learning Designer: Megan Guiliani

Content Manager: Amanda White

Digital Delivery Quality Partner: Jessica Witczak

VP, Product Marketing: Jason Sakos

Director, Product Marketing: April Danaë

Portfolio Marketing Manager: Anthony Winslow

IP Analyst: Diane Garrity

IP Project Coordinator: Tennessee Sundermeyer

Production Service: Lumina Datamatics, Inc.

Designer: Felicia Bennett

Cover Image Source: Cafe Racer/Shutterstock.com
CSA-Printstock/gettyimages.com

For product information and technology assistance, contact us at **Cengage Customer & Sales Support, 1-800-354-9706** or **support.cengage.com.**

For permission to use material from this text or product, submit all requests online at **www.copyright.com.**

Library of Congress Control Number: 2022904620

ISBN: 978-0-357-72140-7

Cengage
200 Pier 4 Boulevard
Boston, MA 02210
USA

Cengage is a leading provider of customized learning solutions with employees residing in nearly 40 different countries and sales in more than 125 countries around the world. Find your local representative at **www.cengage.com.**

To learn more about Cengage platforms and services, register or access your online learning solution, or purchase materials for your course, visit **www.cengage.com.**

Printed in the United States of America
Print Number: 01   Print Year: 2022

To my son Corbyn, who I love so much.

Angeline Close Scheinbaum

To my dear late friend, Steven Hale Steward.

Thomas Clayton O'Guinn

To Molly, the best partner I could ever hope to have. To Andi, you have done so much, so well, so quickly—you inspire me.

Rich Semenik

About the Authors

Dr. Angeline Close Scheinbaum is the Dan Duncan Professor of Sports Marketing and Associate Professor of Marketing in the Wilbur O. and Ann Powers College of Business at Clemson University. Her research interest is in the areas of branding, online consumer behavior and sponsorship/event marketing—namely, how consumers' experiences at sponsored events influence attitudes and consumer behavior. Her research explains e-commerce behaviors and motivations as well as how to engage consumers with events, how to uncover drivers of effective sponsorships, how entertainment impacts affect toward events/purchase intention toward sponsors, what the role of sponsor-event congruity is, and why consumers may resist events. Professor Close Scheinbaum also researches consumers' experiences with electronic marketplaces in social media and e-commerce. She has contributed over thirty-five peer-reviewed journal articles and edited three scholarly books on these topics. They have appeared in rigorous journals such as the *Journal of the Academy of Marketing Science, Advances in Consumer Research, Journal of Advertising Research,* and *Journal of Business Research,* among others. This research has been featured on CBS and in the New York Times, Washington Post, the Los Angeles Times, and Forbes. Angeline also brings industry experience as she has contributed research projects for Dodge, Ford, Cingular, AT&T, Fashion Show Mall, Suzuki, Tour de GA, Road Atlanta, Lexus, Shell, Volkswagen, and the United States Tennis Association among others. Prior to joining Clemson, she was a tenured associate professor in the Stan Richards School of Advertising & Public Relations at The University of Texas at Austin. Her education is in both advertising and marketing at the University of Georgia's Grady College of Journalism & Mass Communication and the Terry College of Business. Raised in Georgia, Close Scheinbaum has gained global experience while studying abroad in Spain and France.

Dr. Thomas Clayton O'Guinn is a Professor of Marketing and the Irwin Maier Distinguished Chair in Business. He received his Ph.D. from the University of Texas at Austin. Prior to coming to Wisconsin, he was at The University of Illinois Urbana-Champaign. He has also taught at UCLA and Duke and was a visiting professor at Georgetown University. Professor O'Guinn's research is broadly sociological and is widely published in the field's top journals, such as *Journal of Marketing, Journal of Consumer Research,* and *Journal of the Academy of Marketing Science.* His work is often near the intersection of sociology and social psychology, or microsociology. Among his most notable works are several multi-method pieces, including survey data, content analysis, and ethnography. His work is sociologically and theoretical substantive.

His work began with studies of special groups of consumers, such as Mexican-American immigrants, then moved to those consumers who used consumption in a compulsive manner, and then to how various strata were affected by television viewing in terms of their beliefs about others, or economic and consumption norms. He then co-founded (along with then doctoral student, Albert Muniz, Jr.), a research stream on consumption and brand-centered communities. Their seminal paper in *Journal of Consumer Research* on brand community is high impact with over 8,000 citations. More recently his work explores social strata, particularly social class, as it relates to the use and value of physical space within commercial settings, and the value of objects and services delivered with them. He is also currently working on social class and consumption within New American Urban neighborhoods, institutional responses by marketers to social disruption, and a sociological model of brands. Tom has served on many editorial and advisory boards, and his research has won several awards. He has assisted several major marketers with their advertising and marketing.

© Richard J. Semenik

Dr. Richard J. Semenik is Professor Emeritus of Marketing and former Dean of the College of Business at Montana State University-Bozeman. He was also founder and Executive Director of the College's Center for Entrepreneurship for the New West which facilitated the launch of multiple start-up firms in Montana and other western states. In 2005, he was named Educator of the Year in Montana by the Office of the Governor. Before coming to Montana State, Rich served variously as Professor Marketing, head of the Marketing Department and Associate Dean for Research at the Eccles School of Business at the University of Utah. He also has co-founded two companies. With expertise in marketing strategy, advertising, and branding, he has given numerous speeches and seminars across the United States, as well as in Ireland, Italy, the Netherlands, Finland, Mexico, Germany, France, Belgium, and Scotland. He has been a visiting research scholar at the Vrije Universiteit in Amsterdam, the Netherlands, visiting scholar at Anahuac Universidad in Mexico City, Mexico and visiting professor at Ecole Superieure de Commerce et de Management Tours, France. His research has appeared in the *Journal of Advertising, Journal of Consumer Research,* and *Journal of International Advertising*, as well as the proceedings of the American Marketing Association and Association for Consumer Research conferences. He has consulted with major corporations, advertising agencies, and early stage start-up companies including IBM, Premier Resorts International, SFX Entertainment, the Van Gogh Museum (Netherlands), American Investment Bank, Printingforless.com, Info-Gears, Scientific Materials, and LigoCyte Pharmaceuticals. Professor Semenik served on the National Board of Directors of the American Advertising Museum and the Industry Relations Board of the American Academy of Advertising. He was a judge for the American Marketing Dissertation competition three times. He received his undergraduate degree from the University of Michigan, an MBA from Michigan State University, and Ph.D. from The Ohio State University.

Brief Contents

Part 1

Advertising and Integrated Brand Promotion in Business and Society 3

1 The World of Advertising and Integrated Brand Promotion 4
2 The Structure of the Advertising and Promotion Industry: Advertisers, Agencies, Media, and Support Organizations 28
3 The History of Advertising and Brand Promotion 52
4 Social, Ethical, and Regulatory Aspects of Advertising and Promotion 78

Part 2

Analyzing the Environment for Advertising and Integrated Brand Promotion 105

5 Advertising, Integrated Brand Promotion, and Consumer Behavior 106
6 Market Segmentation, Positioning, and the Value Proposition 126
7 Advertising Research 142
8 Planning Advertising and Integrated Brand Promotion 164

Part 3

The Creative Process 185

9 Managing Creativity in Advertising and IBP 186
10 Creative Message Strategy 204
11 Executing the Creative 228

Part 4

The Media Process 255

12 Media Planning Essentials 256
13 Media Planning: Newspapers, Magazines, TV, and Radio 276
14 Media Planning: Advertising and IBP in Digital, Social, & Mobile Media 298

Part
5

Integrated Brand Promotion   321

15   Sales Promotion, Point-of-Purchase Advertising, and Support Media   322

16   Event Sponsorship, Product Placements, and Branded Entertainment   350

17   Integrating Direct Marketing and Personal Selling   370

18   Public Relations, Influencer Marketing, and Corporate Advertising   394

Glossary   420

Name/Brand/Company Index   435

Subject Index   441

Contents

About the Authors   iv
Preface   xv

Part 1

Advertising and Integrated Brand Promotion in Business and Society   3

Chapter 1   The World of Advertising and Integrated Brand Promotion   4

1-1   The New World of Advertising and Integrated Brand Promotion   5
1-1a   Old Media/New Digital Media—It's All about the Brand   6

1-2   What Advertising, Advertising Campaigns, and Integrated Brand Promotion Are and What They Can Do   7
1-2a   Advertising Defined   8
1-2b   Integrated Brand Promotion Defined   8
1-2c   Advertisements, Advertising Campaigns, and Integrated Brand Promotion   9
1-2d   A Focus on Advertising   10

1-3   Advertising as a Communication Process: A Model of Mass-Mediated Communication   10

1-4   Different Ways of Classifying Audiences for Advertising and IBP   12
1-4a   Audience Categories   12
1-4b   Audience Geography   14

1-5   Advertising as a Business Process   14
1-5a   The Role of Advertising in the Marketing Mix   15

1-6   Types of Advertising and the Economic Effects of Advertising   20
1-6a   Types of Advertising   20
1-6b   The Economic Effects of Advertising   21

1-7   From Advertising to Integrated Marketing Communications to Integrated Brand Promotion   22

Summary   24
Key Terms   25
Endnotes   26

Chapter 2   The Structure of the Advertising and Promotion Industry: Advertisers, Agencies, Media, and Support Organizations   28

2-1   The Advertising Industry in Constant Transition   28

2-2   Trends Affecting the Advertising and Promotion Industry   31
2-2a   Consumer Control: Social Media, On-Demand Streaming, and Cutting the Cord   31
2-2b   Media Proliferation, Consolidation, and "Multiplatform" Media Organizations   32
2-2c   Media Clutter and Fragmentation Means More IBP   32
2-2d   Crowdsourcing   33
2-2e   Mobile Marketing/Mobile Media   34

2-3   The Scope and Structure of the Advertising and Promotion Industry   34
2-3a   Structure of the Advertising and Promotion Industry   34
2-3b   Advertisers   36
2-3c   The Role of the Advertiser in IBP   37

2-4   Advertising and Promotion Agencies   38
2-4a   Advertising Agencies   38
2-4b   Agency Services   42
2-4c   Agency Compensation   44

2-5   External Facilitators   45

2-6   Media Organizations   46
2-6a   Target Audiences and Content Marketing   48

Summary   48
Key Terms   49
Endnotes   50

Chapter 3   The History of Advertising and Brand Promotion   52

3-1   Factors Behind The Rise of Advertising   53
3-1a   The Rise of Capitalism   53
3-1b   The Industrial Revolution   53
3-1c   The Emergence of Modern Branding   54
3-1d   The Rise of Modern Mass Media   55

3-2   The Eras of Advertising   55
3-2a   The Preindustrialization Era (Pre 1800)   55
3-2b   The Era of Industrialization (1800 to 1875)   55
3-2c   The "P.T. Barnum Era" (1875–1918)   56
3-2d   The 1920s (1918–1929)   57
3-2e   The Depression (1929–1941)   59
3-2f   World War II and the 1950s (1942 to 1960)   60
3-2g   Peace, Love, and the Creative Revolution (1960–1972)   63

3-2h   The 1970s (1973–1980)   66
3-2i   The Designer Era (1980 to 1992)   68
3-2j   The E-Revolution Begins (1993 to 2000)   70
3-2k   Consumer Access, Connections, Branded Entertainment, and the Rise of Ad Blockers (2000 to 2020)   71
3-2l   Business and Advertising in a COVID Era (2020–Current)   73

3-3   Forces Affecting the Evolution of Advertising and IBP   74

Summary   74

Key Terms   75

Endnotes   75

Chapter 4   Social, Ethical, and Regulatory Aspects of Advertising and Promotion   78

4-1   The Social Aspects of Advertising   79
4-1a   Advertising Educates Consumers   79
4-1b   Advertising Improves the Standard of Living   80
4-1c   Advertising Affects Happiness and General Well-Being   80
4-1d   Advertising: Demeaning and Deceitful or Liberating and Artful?   82
4-1e   Advertising Has a Powerful Effect on the Mass Media   86

4-2   The Ethical Aspects of Advertising   87
4-2a   Truth in Advertising   87
4-2b   Advertising to Children   87
4-2c   Advertising Controversial Products   88

4-3   The Regulatory Aspects of Advertising   89
4-3a   Areas of Advertising Regulation   89
4-3b   Regulatory Agents   90

4-4   The Regulation of Other Promotional Tools   95
4-4a   Regulatory Issues in Direct Marketing and the Internet   95
4-4b   Regulatory Issues in Sales Promotion   96
4-4c   Regulatory Issues in Public Relations   98

Summary   99

Key Terms   99

Endnotes   100

Part 2

Analyzing the Environment for Advertising and Integrated Brand Promotion   105

Chapter 5   Advertising, Integrated Brand Promotion, and Consumer Behavior   106

5-1   Consumer Behavior Perspective One: The Consumer as a Decision Maker   108
5-1a   The Consumer Decision-Making Process   108
5-1b   Four Modes of Consumer Decision-Making   110
5-1c   Advertising, Consumer Behavior, and Memory   113

5-2   Consumer Behavior Perspective Two: The Consumer as a Social Being   115

5-2a   Consuming in the Real World   115
5-2b   Cultural Branding and Advertising   121

5-3   How Ads Transmit Meaning   121

Summary   123

Key Terms   124

Endnotes   124

Chapter 6   Market Segmentation, Positioning, and the Value Proposition   126

6-1   STP Marketing and Advertising   127

6-2   Segmenting Markets   128
6-2a   Usage and Commitment Level   128
6-2b   Switchers and Variety Seekers   129
6-2c   Emergent Consumers   130
6-2d   Demographics   131
6-2e   Geographic Location   131

6-2f   Psychographics and Lifestyle   132
6-2g   Benefit Segmentation   132
6-2h   Segmenting Business-to-Business Markets   133

6-3   Prioritizing Segments   133

6-4   Targeting   135
6-4a   Positioning and Repositioning   135
6-4b   Positioning Opportunity   136

6-4c Essentials for Effective Positioning Strategies   137

6-5 Working with a Value Proposition and a Brand Platform   138
6-5a Now, Making It Happen   138

Summary   140
Key Terms   140
Endnotes   141

Chapter 7   Advertising Research   142

7-1 Stage One: Developmental Advertising and IBP Research   143
7-1a Design Thinking   144
7-1b Concept Testing   144
7-1c Audience Profiling   144
7-1d Focus Groups   144
7-1e Projective Techniques   146
7-1f Method: Fieldwork/Long Interviews   149

7-2 Sources of Secondary Data   150
7-2a Netnography and Big Data   150
7-2b Internal Company Sources   150
7-2c Government Sources   150
7-2d Commercial, Industry, and Nonprofit Sources   151

7-3 Stage Two: Copy Research   151
7-3a Evaluative Criteria and Methods   151
7-3b Common Methods for Assessing Cognitive Impact   152

7-4 Stage Three: Results Research   157
7-4a Method: Tracking Studies   157
7-4b Method: Direct Response   158
7-4c Method: Estimating Sales Derived from Advertising   158
7-4d Method: All-in-One Single-Source Data   159
7-4e Account Planning versus Advertising Research   159
7-4f Future of Advertising Research   159

Summary   160
Key Terms   160
Endnotes   161

Chapter 8   Planning Advertising and Integrated Brand Promotion   164

8-1 The Advertising Plan and Marketing Context   165

8-2 Introduction   166

8-3 Situation Analysis   166
8-3a Cultural Context   167
8-3b Historical Context   168
8-3c Industry Analysis   168
8-3d Market Analysis   169
8-3e Competitor Analysis   169

8-4 Objectives   169
8-4a Communications versus Sales Objectives   172

8-5 Budgeting   173
8-5a Percentage of Sales   173
8-5b Share of Market/Share of Voice   174
8-5c Response Models   174

8-5d Objective and Task   174
8-5e Implementing the Objective-and-Task Budgeting Method   175

8-6 Strategy   176

8-7 Execution   177
8-7a Copy Strategy   177
8-7b Media Plan   177
8-7c Integrated Brand Promotion   177

8-8 Evaluation   178

8-9 The Role of the Agency in Planning Advertising and IBP   178

Summary   179
Key Terms   180
Endnotes   181

Part 3   The Creative Process   185

Chapter 9   Managing Creativity in Advertising and IBP   186

9-1 Why Does Advertising Thrive on Creativity?   186

9-2 Creativity across Domains   187
9-2a Creative Genius in the Advertising Business   188
9-2b Creativity in the Business World   190
9-2c Can You Become Creative?   190
9-2d Notes of Caution   190

9-3 Agencies, Clients, and the Creative Process   191
9-3a Oil and Water: Conflicts and Tensions in the Creative/Management Interface   192

9-4 Making Beautiful Music Together: Coordination, Collaboration, and Creativity   196
9-4a What We Know about Teams   196
9-4b When Sparks Fly: Igniting Creativity through Teams   199
9-4c Final Thoughts on Teams and Creativity   199

9-5 Have You Decided to Become More Creative?   201

Summary   201
Key Terms   202
Endnotes   202

Chapter 10   Creative Message Strategy   204

10-1   Creative Message Strategy   204

10-2   Ten Essential Message Objectives and Strategies   205
10-2a Objective #1: Promote Brand Recall   205
10-2b Objective #2: Link Key Attribute(s) to the Brand Name   208
10-2c Objective #3: Persuade the Consumer   210
10-2d Objective #4: Affective Association: Get the Consumer to Feel Good about the Brand   215
10-2e Objective #5: Scare the Consumer into Action   218
10-2f Objective #6: Change Behavior by Inducing Anxiety   218

10-2g Objective #7: Define the Brand Image   219
10-2h Objective #8: Give the Brand the Desired Social Meaning   221
10-2i Objective #9: Leverage Social Disruption and Cultural Contradictions   222
10-2j Objective #10: Transform Consumption Experiences   223

Summary   225

Key Terms   225

Endnotes   226

Chapter 11   Executing the Creative   228

11-1   The Creative Team and the Creative Brief   229
11-1a The Creative Team   229
11-1b Copywriters and Art Directors   229
11-1c The Creative Brief   230

11-2   Copywriting for Print Advertising   230
11-2a The Headline   231
11-2b The Subhead   231
11-2c The Body Copy   231

11-3   Copywriting for Television and Video   232
11-3a Writing Copy for Television (Video)   232
11-3b Guidelines for Writing Television Copy   233

11-4   Writing Copy for Radio and Podcast Advertising   234
11-4a Guidelines for Writing Radio Copy   234

11-5   Copywriting for Digital/Interactive Media   235

11-5a Copywriting Approaches to Digital/Interactive Advertising   235

11-6   Slogans/Taglines   236
11-6a The Copy Approval Process   236

11-7   Art Direction   238
11-7a Illustration, Design, and Layout   238
11-7b Art Direction and Production in Digital/Interactive/ Mobile Media   244
11-7c Art Direction and Production in Television Advertising   245

11-8   The Production Process in Television Advertising   246
11-8a Preproduction   246

Summary   250

Key Terms   251

Endnotes   251

Part 4   The Media Process   255

Chapter 12   Media Planning Essentials   256

12-1   Measured and Unmeasured Media   257
12-1a Media Investment Allocations   258

12-2   Media Investment Terminology   260
12-2a Media Strategies, Objectives, and Data   260
12-2b Continuity and the Forgetting Function   265
12-2c Length or Size of Advertisements   265

12-3   Competitive Media Assessment and Share of Voice   266

12-4   Media Efficiency   266
12-4a Digital/Internet Media   267

12-5   Social Media: A Media Planning Perspective   267
12-5a Social Networks and Integrated Brand Promotions   267

12-6   Branded Entertainment as a Media Choice   268
12-6a Branded Entertainment   268

12-7   Media Planning Models: Benefits and Realities   269

12-8   Media Buying and Programmatic Media Buying   271

Summary   273

Key Terms   274

Endnotes   274

Chapter 13   Media Planning: Newspapers, Magazines, TV, and Radio   276

13-1   The Present and Future of Traditional Mass Media   278

13-2   Newspapers and Digital Newspapers   279
13-2a Advantages of Newspapers   280

13-2b Disadvantages of Newspapers   281
13-2c Categories of Newspaper Advertising   281
13-2d The Future of Newspapers   281

13-3 Magazines 282
13-3a Advantages of Magazines 282
13-3b Disadvantages of Magazines 284
13-3c The Future of Magazines 285

13-4 Television 285
13-4a Television Categories 285
13-4b Advantages of Television 287
13-4c Disadvantages of Television 288
13-4d Measuring Television Audiences 289
13-4e The Future of Television 290

13-5 Radio 290
13-5a Radio Categories 290
13-5b Types of Radio Advertising 291
13-5c Advantages of Radio 291
13-5d Disadvantages of Radio 292
13-5e The Future of Radio 292

Summary 293
Key Terms 294
Endnotes 294

Chapter 14   Media Planning: Advertising and IBP in Digital, Social, and Mobile Media   298

14-1 The Role of Digital, Social, and Mobile Media for IBP Synergy 298
14-1a Social Media and Web 3.0 299
14-1b Media Types in Social Media 300
14-1c Options via Digital or Social Media: Definitions and Categories 302

14-2 Consumer and Brand Virtual Identity 303
14-2a Consumer Virtual Identity 303
14-2b Social Media as a Brand Management Tool: Brand Image and Visibility 304

14-3 Basics of Digital Advertising and Online Search 307
14-3a Digital Advertising Investments 307
14-3b Search 308

14-4 Importance of IBP in E-Tail: Emergence of Social E-Commerce and Big Data 309

14-5 Advantages of Digital, Social, and Mobile Media for Implementing Advertising and IBP Campaigns, as Well as the Dark Side 310
14-5a Advantages of Digital, Social, and Mobile Media 310
14-5b Privacy Issues and the Dark Side of Digital, Social, and Mobile Media 311

14-6 Synergizing with Other IBP Tools 313
14-6a Video Games and Advergaming 313
14-6b Sales Promotion 314
14-6c Public Relations and Publicity 314
14-6d Direct Marketing and E-Commerce 314
14-6e Mobile Marketing and M-Commerce 315

Summary 316
Key Terms 317
Endnotes 317

Part 5   Integrated Brand Promotion   321

Chapter 15   Sales Promotion, Point-of-Purchase Advertising, and Support Media   322

15-1 Sales Promotion Defined and Types of Sales Promotion 324

15-2 The Importance and Growth of Sales Promotion 325
15-2a The Importance of Sales Promotion 326
15-2b Growth in the Use of Sales Promotion 327

15-3 Sales Promotion Directed at Consumers 330
15-3a Objectives for Consumer-Market Sales Promotion 330
15-3b Consumer-Market Sales Promotion Techniques 332

15-4 Sales Promotion Directed at the Trade Channel and Business Markets 338
15-4a Objectives for Promotions in the Trade Channel 338
15-4b Trade-Market Sales Promotion Techniques 339
15-4c Business-Market Sales Promotion Techniques 340

15-5 The Risks of Sales Promotion 341
15-5a Creating a Price Orientation 341
15-5b Borrowing from Future Sales 341
15-5c Alienating Customers 341
15-5d Managerial Time and Expense 341

15-5e Legal Considerations 341

15-6 Point-of-Purchase Advertising 342
15-6a Point-of-Purchase Advertising Defined 342
15-6b Objectives for Point-of-Purchase Advertising 342
15-6c Types of Point-of-Purchase Advertising and Displays 342
15-6d P-O-P Advertising and Mobile or Location Marketing 343
15-6e P-O-P Advertising and the Trade and Business Markets 343

15-7 The Role of Support Media in a Comprehensive IBP Strategy 343
15-7a Outdoor Signage and Billboard Advertising 344
15-7b Out-of-Home Media Advertising: Transit, Aerial, Cinema 345
15-7c Packaging 346

Summary 347
Key Terms 348
Endnotes 348

Chapter 16   Event Sponsorship, Product Placements, and Branded Entertainment 350

16-1 The Role of Event Sponsorship, Product Placements, and Branded Entertainment in IBP: Experiential Marketing and the Convergence of Advertising and Entertainment 350
16-1a Experiential Marketing 352
16-1b Brand-Building and the Convergence of Advertising and Entertainment 352

16-2 Event Sponsorship: Who Uses It, Measurement, Benefits, and Leveraging 353
16-2a Who Uses Event Sponsorship? 354
16-2b Finding the Sweet Spot for Event Sponsorship 356
16-2c Assessing the Benefits of Event Sponsorship 357
16-2d Leveraging Event Sponsorship 359

16-3 Product Placements 359
16-3a On Television 360
16-3b At the Movies 360
16-3c In Video Games 361
16-3d What We Know about Product Placement 361

16-4 Branded Entertainment 362
16-4a Where Are Product Placement and Branded Entertainment Headed? 364
16-4b What's Old is New Again 364

16-5 The Coordination Challenge 365

Summary 366

Key Terms 366

Endnotes 367

Chapter 17   Integrating Direct Marketing and Personal Selling 370

17-1 Direct Marketing: Definition and Purposes 372

17-2 The Evolution of Direct Marketing and Direct Marketing Today 374
17-2a Origins in Catalog Marketing 374
17-2b Direct Marketing Today 374

17-3 Advantages of Direct Marketing 378

17-4 Database Marketing 380
17-4a Mailing Lists/Email Lists 380
17-4b List Enhancement 381
17-4c The Marketing Database 381
17-4d Marketing Database Applications 382

17-5 The Privacy Concern 382

17-6 Media Applications in Direct Marketing 384
17-6a Direct Mail 385
17-6b Email 385
17-6c Telemarketing 387
17-6d Direct Response Advertising in Other Media 387
17-6e Infomercials 387

17-7 Closing the Sale with Direct Marketing and/or Personal Selling 388
17-7a Personal Selling 388
17-7b Customer Relationship Management 390

Summary 391

Key Terms 392

Endnotes 392

Chapter 18   Public Relations, Influencer Marketing, and Corporate Advertising 394

18-1 Public Relations 396
18-1a Public Relations, Social Media, and Brand Conversations 397
18-1b Public Relations and Damage Control 399

18-2 Objectives for Public Relations 400

18-3 The Tools of Public Relations 401
18-3a Press Releases 401
18-3b Feature Stories 403
18-3c Company Newsletters/E-Newsletters 403
18-3d Interviews and Press Conferences 403
18-3e Sponsored Events and Event Marketing 403
18-3f Publicity 404

18-4 Proactive and Reactive Public Relations Strategies 404
18-4a Proactive Strategy 405
18-4b Reactive Strategy 406

18-5 Influencer Marketing and Social Media for PR Strategy 408
18-5a Professional Influencer Programs 408
18-5b Peer-to-Peer Influencer Programs 409

18-6 Corporate Advertising 414
18-6a The Scope and Objectives of Corporate Advertising 414
18-6b Types of Corporate Advertising 415

Summary 417

Key Terms 418

Endnotes 418

Glossary 420

Name/Brand/Company Index 435

Subject Index 441

Preface

David Ogilvy, named by Advertising Age as one of the 100 most influential people in advertising history, said this: "It takes a big idea to attract the attention of consumers and get them to buy your product. Unless your advertising contains a big idea, it will pass like a ship in the night." Our big idea for *Advertising and Integrated Brand Promotion 9e* remains the longstanding commitment to focus on the role of **branding** (rather than the mere integrated marketing communications) while highlighting the concept of **integration** and **synergy** among branding efforts.

We present a **balanced perspective** of branding and include both the positive side of branding and marketing as well as a critical lens. We acknowledge that sometimes there is a dark side to advertising and marketing, and that sometimes there are unintended consequences to consumers, businesses, or society. Importantly, we offer a balanced perspective on critical issues such as privacy in the digital and mobile age, diversity/equity/inclusivity, and social responsibility.

Some brands flourish, some brands face hardships, and some brands are cancelled due to not being in touch with modern consumer expectations (being "tone deaf") or not considering those (often unintended) consequences of the brand or campaign on consumers or society. Some brand managers are good at considering various stakeholders and perspective gathering and very in tune, while others miss the mark at times. The same is true of advertising executives. This is because branding is complicated, and it takes considering various perspectives and potential outcomes for every creative and media decision. Thus, in this book, we write about how companies and marketing or advertising professionals read the market environment, evolve their brands effectively, use technology to their advantage, communicate with their target markets, and nurture brand equity and loyalty.

And we have done the same thing with *Advertising and Integrated Brand Promotion.* We have evolved our book's brand along with the evolving and increasingly digital advertising and marketing environment. We have also evolved it to consider aspects of diversity and social justice, and how brands can be and often should be voices of advocacy. We have also evolved the book to consider some changes to consumer behavior and branding in an era that has been hit by a global pandemic. We have made extensive updates to advertising and integrated brand promotion processes, increasing the emphasis on leveraging synergy among all elements for planning and implementing successful campaigns in modern times. This book is based on extensive feedback from faculty, students, and practitioners.

Advertising and Integrated Brand Promotion 9e focuses on integration of various brand communication tools and strategies. It is not just a book on advertising or branding; we emphasize the importance of synergy for advertising with public relations, social media, digital, mobile, experiential marketing, event marketing, influencer marketing, branded entertainment, sponsorship, and celebrity endorsement among others.

Advertising and Integrated Brand Promotion 9e is full of social, digital, and mobile media content. You can find this in both the definitions as well as multiple from real brands that represent both timeless campaigns as well as newer ones. You will notice many new key terms, coverage of automated media buying, social media strategy for brands, mobile marketing, and new disruptive product categories and brands. The book is direct while remaining comprehensive. *Advertising and Integrated Brand Promotion 9e* represents the world of advertising and integrated brand promotion as it is evolving over time.

Despite all the updates and the tighter focus, there is one point we want to make emphatically: *Advertising and Integrated Brand Promotion 9e* remains the most current and forward-thinking book on the market. Since the launch of the first edition in 1998, we have alerted students to leading-edge issues and challenges facing the advertising and marketing industries. We were the first to devote an entire chapter to the Internet as an advertising medium (1998), the first to alert students to the "dot-com" agency incursion on traditional advertising structure (2000), the first to raise the issue of consumers seeking and seizing control of their personal communications environment (2003), and the first to highlight blogs and DVRs and the role they played in disseminating (or blocking) information about brands (2006). Also, we were the first to alert students to the emergence and growing potential of the early social networking sites (2009). In the past three editions, we pioneered coverage of branded entertainment, the rise of influencer marketing, and the challenges of modern media strategies. *Advertising and Integrated Brand Promotion 9e* continues the tradition of breaking new ground, with an innovative framework diagramming the context, environment, and steps in the overall process of advertising and integrated brand promotion in digital and traditional media environments. There is a newer focus on the streaming revolution, post COVID-19 consumer behavior and mindsets, automated media buying, design thinking, mobile media, diversity, and all things social and digital.

There is a deep commitment among the authors to seek out a balance of the best traditional and progressive thinking about advertising and integrated brand promotion from a wide array of both peer-reviewed scholarly and trade publications. You will see this commitment manifest in the breadth, depth, and currency of the references in each chapter. We are confident you will find the content and perspective of this new edition a worthy addition to students' classroom experience.

Why We Write This Book

When we introduced the first edition of *Advertising and Integrated Brand Promotion*, we summed up our attitude and passion about advertising in this way:

Advertising is a lot of things. It's democratic pop culture, capitalist tool, oppressor, liberator, art, and theater, all rolled into one. It's free speech, it's creative flow, it's information, and it helps businesses get things sold. Above all, it's fun.

We still feel the same way. Advertising and promotion are fun, and this book reflects it. Advertising and promotion are also important businesses, and this edition carries forward a perspective that clearly conveys that message as well. Like other aspects of business, advertising and integrated brand promotion stem from arduous work and careful planning. Creating good advertising is an enormous challenge. We understand that and give homage and profound respect to the creative process. We understand advertising and promotion in its business, marketing, and creative context. But we also feel that other books on the market do not emphasize enough a focus on the *brand* and *integration* in the advertising and promotional effort. Brands are the reasons advertising exists. While most books of this type have IMC (integrated marketing communication) in the title, we choose to emphasize the brand in the title and throughout the topics in the book.

This book is written by professors with ample experience in both academic and professional settings. We have collectively been consultants for many firms and their agencies. Thus, this book is grounded in real-world experience. It is not, however, a book that seeks to sell you a "show-and-tell coffee-table book" version of the advertising and promotion industries. Rather, we highlight a balanced perspective along with the challenges facing advertisers and offer complete treatment of the tools they use to meet those challenges.

We respect our academic and practitioner colleagues. This book is completely real world, but the real world is also explained in terms of very rigorous and relevant peer-reviewed academic scholarship. You will notice many current theory-based insights from leading journals in marketing and advertising. This book copies no one yet pays homage to many. More than anything, we seek to be honest, thoughtful, and imaginative. We acknowledge the complexity of human communication and consumer behavior.

Students love this book—they tell us so over and over. We've spent considerable time reviewing student and instructor likes and dislikes of other advertising and marketing textbooks, in addition to examining their reactions to our own book. With this feedback, we have devoted pages and pictures, ideas, and intelligence to creating a place for student and

professor to meet and discuss one of the most important and intrinsically interesting phenomena of contemporary times: advertising and promotion in the service of brands.

Unique Framework Diagram Highlights Relevant, Intelligent Organization

This book has a unique framework diagram that guides students through the background, environment, and steps of advertising and integrated brand promotion. This valuable new diagram showcases the thoughtful and well-paced five-part organization, helping students understand the way each part and chapter of the book fits with other parts and chapters. As a result, students are able to visualize exactly how each topic builds on the previous topic to provide a well-rounded, practical picture of advertising and marketing today.

Over the years, we have found that the organization of the text is so popular because it lays out the advertising and integrated brand promotion process the same way it unfolds in practice and application:

Part 1: Advertising and Integrated Brand Promotion in Business and Society. Part 1 recognizes that students need to understand just what advertising and IBP all are about and how the process works. This section contains the core fundamentals. It describes the entire landscape of advertising and promotion and provides a look at the structure of the industry and a historical perspective on the evolution of the process. But we have infused this part of the book with extensive coverage of the challenges and opportunities being presented by social networks and the mobile devices (smartphones, tablets, mobile marketing communications) that are changing the landscape for advertising and promotion. Again, it is not just technological changes, but societal and cultural changes as well. This part concludes with the key social, ethical, and regulatory issues facing practitioners and consumers.

Part 2: Analyzing the Environment for Advertising and Integrated Brand Promotion. Part 2 provides all the essential perspectives needed to understand how to plan and carry out effective advertising and IBP. Key strategic concepts related to the overall process, including consumer behavior analysis, market segmentation, brand differentiation, and brand positioning, are considered. Then this section proceeds to a discussion of the types of research advertising and promotion planners rely on to develop effective advertising and IBP. Additionally, there is special emphasis on "consuming in the real world" and how advertising and IBP can adapt to consumer lifestyles and consumer adoption of innovative technologies and mindsets to facilitate those lifestyles.

Whether you are teaching or studying advertising and marketing in a business school curriculum or an advertising/journalism curriculum, the first two parts of the book provide the background and perspective that show how advertising and IBP have become even more powerful business and societal forces in the 21st century.

Part 3: The Creative Process. Part 3 is all about creativity: creativity itself, as a managerial issue, and as a part of art direction, copywriting, and message strategy. Most adopters in advertising and communication programs use this section and put focus on Chapter 10, in which the tensions between the creative and management processes are highlighted. Some business school adopters skip some of the creative chapters in Part 3. We believe everyone will find Chapter 11, which offers a highly integrated discussion of the overall creative effort, a useful and realistic perspective on the process.

Part 4: The Media Process. Part 4 focuses on the use and application of all media—including traditional and social, mobile, and digital media—to reach target audiences. These chapters are key to understanding many of the execution aspects of good advertising and integrated brand promotion strategies. Programmatic media buying is an industry game changer for companies, and streaming is a game changer especially for consumers and how they consume content. It is in this section that you will learn not just about the traditional mass media but also about the array of emerging media options and consumers' new-found power in managing their information environments through these options. Of note is the recognition of the opportunities now offered by mobile devices as another way to reach consumers through "second screens".

Part 5: Integrated Brand Promotion. Part 5 covers the many tools of integrated brand promotion. We bundled these four chapters together, since our business school adopters often place much emphasis on them as business tools. Here you will find the best coverage of sales promotion, event sponsorship, product placement, direct marketing, personal selling, branded entertainment, influencer marketing, public relations, and corporate advertising. A sizable percentage of the book's pages are devoted to IBP tools beyond advertising because of the opportunities to leverage multiple tools for synergy in communicating with, engaging, and influencing consumers and business customers.

Integrated Brand Promotion in Action

The most successful brands understand that effective campaigns must leverage multiple elements for synergy and optimal impact. That's why we include "Integrated Brand Promotion in Action," demonstrating how 18 advertisers use different promotional

presentations to reach target audiences. Chapter by chapter, here are the advertisers showcased in this feature:

Chapter 1	Panera
Chapter 2	Colorado (tourism)
Chapter 3	Coca-Cola
Chapter 4	REI
Chapter 5	Target
Chapter 6	Hilton
Chapter 7	IKEA
Chapter 8	KitKat
Chapter 9	Hotels.com
Chapter 10	Blendtec
Chapter 11	Mountain Dew
Chapter 12	Graeter's
Chapter 13	Absolut
Chapter 14	Zappos
Chapter 15	M&M's
Chapter 16	Monster Energy
Chapter 17	L.L.Bean
Chapter 18	Gatorade

Compelling Fundamentals

We fully expect our book to continue to set the standard for coverage of new branding topics and industry issues. It is loaded with features, insights, and commonsense advertising perspectives about the ever-changing nature of the advertising and promotion industry, and we continue to incorporate coverage of new examples in *every* chapter.

That said, we feel a truly distinguishing strength of this book is that we do not abandon complete and high-level treatment of the fundamentals of advertising and promotion. We simply cannot appreciate the role of the emerging media or technologies without a solid understanding of the fundamentals from traditional media. If you doubt our commitment to the fundamentals, take a good look at Chapters 2 through 8. This is where we, once again, part company with other books on the market. *Advertising and Integrated Brand Promotion 9e* is the only book on the market that ensures the deep economic roots of advertising and promotion are fully understood in the context of brand integration in today's social media and digital business environment (e.g., the economic effects of advertising, primary vs. selective demand). Also, we take the time to be certain that not just the business but also the social and psychological contexts of advertising are clear. Check out just how completely the foundational aspects are covered.

Also, notice that we don't wait until the end of the book to bring the legal, ethical, and social issues (Chapter 4) into mainstream thinking about advertising and IBP. While most books put these issues as one of the last chapters—as if they are an afterthought—we feel strongly that they are mainstream to the development of high-quality and responsible advertising and promotional efforts. In fact, we introduce some of these issues starting in Chapter 1 and integrate coverage throughout for an unusually well-rounded examination of priorities, challenges, and trends. In the modern environment, ethics and "better marketing for a better world" movements are paramount, as the purpose of advertising and marketing goes much beyond sales and profits. We show how advertising and marketing can be and should be a force for good and at times prosocial persuasion.

Extensive Social and Digital Media Coverage

It is paramount for brands to have a synergistic social media presence and strategy that reinforces their advertising and brand image. We give you the tools to understand social media from a theoretical lens as well as some industry best practices with social media. In-depth consideration of new media vehicles is provided throughout Part 1 but is truly highlighted in Part 4 of the book, "The Media Process." Media is the main area in which the industry has changed. Chapter 14 is all about advertising and marketing in the social and digital media era, and it reviews many technical considerations for working with this—now not-so-new but still challenging and evolving—method for reaching and affecting consumers. Chapter 15 highlights all the modern ways advertising and promotion can provide an experiential encounter with the brand. Brands benefit from sponsorships of fitting events and other consumer experiences; we show the importance of integrating social media with experiential/event marketing as well as via influencers. But these sections are not the only place new media coverage is prominent. Chapters 1 and 2 highlight how consumers use new social media options to control their information flow, and Chapter 5 considers the effects of new media on consumer decision making.

Student Engagement and Learning

You will find that this book provides a clear and sophisticated examination of advertising fundamentals and contemporary issues in lively, concise language. We don't avoid controversies, and we're not shy about challenging conventions. In addition, the book features a stylish internal design and many current ads, tables, and figures. Reading this book is an engaging experience.

The markers of our commitment to student learning are easily identified throughout the book. Every chapter begins with a statement of the *learning objectives* for that chapter. (For a quick appreciation of the coverage provided by this book, take a pass through it and read the learning objectives on the first page of each chapter.) Chapters are organized to deliver content that responds to each learning objective, and the *Chapter Summaries* are written to reflect what the chapter has offered with respect to each learning objective. After the chapter summaries, students will find *Key Terms* from the chapter that appear in bold type throughout the chapter. Full definitions of these terms are provided at the end of the book.

We also believe that students must be challenged to go beyond their reading to think about the issues raised in the book. We provide paths for thoughtful analysis rather than mere regurgitation, and additional exercises will help students put their learning to use in ways that will help them take more away from the course than just textbook learning. Complete use of this text will yield a dramatic and engaging learning experience for students of all ages who are studying advertising at various levels.

A Closer Look at Some Ninth-Edition Features

In Every Chapter:

Learning Objectives and a Built-In Integrated Learning System. The text is organized around the learning objectives that appear at the beginning of each chapter to provide you and your students with an easy-to-use, integrated learning system. A numbered icon identifies each chapter objective and appears next to its related material throughout the chapter. This integrated learning system can provide you with a structure for creating lesson plans as well as tests.

The integrated system also gives structure to students as they prepare for tests. The icons identify all the material in the text that fulfills each learning objective. Students can easily check their grasp of each objective by reading the text sections and reviewing the corresponding summary sections. They can also return to appropriate text sections for further review if they have difficulty with end-of-chapter questions.

Framework Diagram. Each part and each chapter open with an integrative framework diagram, as discussed earlier in this preface. The purpose is to indicate how topics fit within the overall book, so students have a clear and specific context for understanding the background and relevance of each chapter. Students can also use the diagram to follow the flow of individual chapters and review the relationship among chapter concepts as they study.

Concise Chapter Summaries. Each chapter ends with a summary that distills the main points of the chapter. Chapter summaries are organized around the learning objectives so that students can use them as a quick check on their achievement of learning goals.

Key Terms. Each chapter ends with a listing of the key terms found in the chapter. Key terms also appear in boldface in the text. Students can prepare for exams by scanning these lists to be sure they can define or explain each term. Just a few of the key terms introduced in this revised edition are: ad blocker, Big Data, click fraud, geofencing, greenwashing, event social responsibility, event sponsorship measurement, and programmatic media buying.

MindTap

The *Advertising and Integrated Brand Promotion* ninth edition MindTap is a teaching and learning experience with relevant assignments that guide students to analyze, apply, and improve thinking, allowing you to measure skills and outcomes with ease. Key features in the MindTap include:

- *Learn It: Concept Check Quizzes:* Students complete the Concept Check Quizzes after reading the chapter content. Learn It: Concept Check Quizzes encourage students to concentrate on smaller amounts of material at a time and move at their own pace. These quizzes are designed to build a foundation of knowledge that students can then apply in later exercises, leading to a gradual, scaffolded learning experience.
- *Chapter Assignments:* Students complete the Chapter Assignment activities after learning chapter concepts. Chapter Assignments are designed to test students' understanding and application of learned concepts.
- *Case Activities:* Students use their understanding of key concepts from the chapter and apply them to real company scenarios. These Case Activities are meant to build critical thinking and problem-solving skills, while also allowing students to learn in context and build marketing and business acumen.

By combining readings, multimedia, activities, and assessments into a singular learning experience, MindTap guides students through their course with ease and engagement. Instructors can personalize the learning experience by customizing Cengage Learning resources and adding their own content via apps that integrate into the MindTap framework seamlessly.

Instructor Supplements

The Cengage Instructor Center provides a full array of teaching and learning supplementary materials to complement the *Advertising and Integrated Brand Promotion* ninth edition. Key supplements include:

Instructor's Manual. The instructor's manual has been thoroughly revised to reflect all updated learning content, including comprehensive lecture outlines; discussion questions; additional class activities; and suggested answers for all exercises found within the text.

PowerPoint®. Teach with ease using this edition's PowerPoint® lecture slides. The lecture slides outline key chapter concepts and topics and include supplemental lecture notes allowing you to expand your discussion with your class and students. Activities like knowledge checks, discussion activities, and group activities are also included to help keep your students engaged in learning the course material.

Test Bank. This comprehensive test bank is organized around the main text's learning objectives. Each question is labeled according to the learning objective that is covered, the difficulty level of the question, and A-heads. Each question is also tagged to interdisciplinary learning outcomes, marketing disciplinary learning outcomes, and Bloom's taxonomy. Grouping the questions according to type allows for maximum flexibility in creating tests that are customized to individual classroom needs and preferences. The test bank includes true/false, multiple-choice, scenario application, and essay questions. All questions have been carefully reviewed for clarity and accuracy.

Cognero Testing Software. The Cognero Testing system is a full-featured, online assessment system that allows you to manage content, create and assign tests, deliver tests through a secure online test center, and have complete reporting and data dissemination at your fingertips. The following are some of the features of the Cognero Testing System:

- Access from anywhere. Web-based software that runs in a Web browser. No installs are required to start using Cognero. Works in Windows, Mac, and Linux browsers.
- Desktop-like interface. Looks and feels like a desktop application. Uses the latest Web functionality to imitate desktop usability features like drag-and-drop and wizards.
- Full-featured test generator. Author and manage your assessment content as well as build tests using the only online test generator that supports all the major functionality of its desktop competitors. Cognero is complete with a full-featured word processor, multilanguage support, Math-ML-compliant equation editor, algorithmic content support, native support for 15 question types (true/false, modified true/false, yes/no, multiple choice, multiple response, numeric response, completion, matching, objective short answer, subjective short answer, multimode, ordering, opinion scale/Likert, essay, and custom), unlimited metadata, ability to print professional paper tests with multiple styles and versions, and more.
- Class Management and Assignments. Manage your students, classes, and assignments with the ease of simple drag-and-drop. You can build or import rosters, have students self-register for a class, and move students easily from class to class. Once your roster is set, simply drag a test to a class to schedule and put your students to work.
- Secure Online Testing. Cognero has an integrated secure online testing center for your students. Along with delivering traditional tests, your students can receive immediate feedback on each question and/or receive a detailed end-of-assignment report to help them know exactly how they are doing.
- Complete Reporting System. What is the use of assessment without being able to disseminate the data derived from it? Cognero allows you to analyze how your students are performing on a real-time basis and from multiple approaches to allow for immediate intervention. You can also quickly analyze your questions and perform a gap analysis of student testing.

- Content Management System. Cognero has a unique set of tools to allow for the creation of products (groups of question sets and tests) for distribution to other users. This system includes workflow management for the shared authoring environment, the ability to authorize specific users to access your content, and the ability to edit content and push changes through to subscribers. There are also several design features to make high-volume authoring within Cognero very efficient. All content created in this system has built-in digital rights management, meaning that your content is protected against unauthorized use.

Acknowledgments

The most pleasant task in writing a textbook is expressing gratitude to people and institutions that have helped the authors. We appreciate the support and encouragement we received from many individuals, including the following:

- Thank you to Product Manager Heather Thompson, Learning Designer Megan Guiliani, and Content Manager Amanda White at Cengage for their dedicated efforts on this project.
- Katie Gilstrap and Marian Burk Wood who served as consultants for developmental and editorial assistance.
- David Moore, Vice President/Executive Producer at Leo Burnett, who gave us invaluable insights on the broadcast production process and helped us secure key materials for the text.
- Matt Smith of Arnold Finnegan & Martin, for providing us with the Watermark ad and sketches in Chapter 11.
- Connie M. Johnson, for years and years of great and loving observations about the human condition.
- Patrick Gavin Quinlan, for years of great advice and best friendship.
- Marilyn A. Boland, for her love, creativity, smart suggestions, great questions, support, and wonderful images.
- David Bryan Teets, University of Illinois, for help with the TV-commercial-director-becomes-movie-director lists and references. Dave knows film.
- Professor John Murphy II, Joe C. Thompson Centennial Professor Emeritus & Distinguished University Teaching Professor Emeritus at the Stan Richards School of Advertising & Public Relations (The University of Texas at Austin), who has given us great feedback and continued support.
- Steve Hall, who supports, critiques, and gives his all to his students at the University of Illinois.
- Rance Crain, Allison Arden, and Ann Marie Kerwin of *Advertising Age* for their help in bringing a rich set of content to students.

We are also grateful to the following individuals from the business/advertising community:

Chris Aaronholt
Medalist Sports

Dick Antoine
President of the National Academy of Human Resources and the President of AO Consulting

Nate Carney
Bridge Worldwide

Jack Cassidy
Cincinnati Bell

Lauren Dickson
Saatchi & Saatchi

Patricia Dimichele
Procter & Gamble

Dixon Douglas
GMR Marketing

Denise Garcia
Conill Advertising Inc.

Mike Gold
Flying Horse Communications

Jacques Hagopian
Procter & Gamble

Lisa Hillenbrand
Procter & Gamble

Karen Klei
Procter & Gamble

Dave Knox
Rockfish Interactive

Fred Krupp
Environmental Defense

Greg Lechner
Luxottica Retail

Liv Lewis
DeVries-pr

Marsha Lindsay
Lindsay, Stone & Briggs

Dave Linne
ConAgra

Brian Lipman
ConAgra

Mike Loyson
Procter & Gamble

James Moorhead
Procter & Gamble

Emily Morrison
GMR Marketing

Emily Neidhardt
Grey

Jim Neupert
Isthmus Partners

Bill Ogle
Motorola

Mason Page
imc²

Kavya Peerbhoy
StrawberryFrog

Jackie Reau
Game Day Communications

Kathy Selker
Northlich

Jim Stengel
The Jim Stengel Company

John Stichweh
Bridge Worldwide

Meghan Sturges
Saatchi & Saatchi

Candace Thomas
Jack Morton Worldwide

Mauricio Troncoso
Procter & Gamble

Jackie Tyson
Peloton Sports

Ted Woehrle
Newell Rubbermaid

We are particularly indebted to our reviewers—past and present—and the following individuals whose thoughtful comments, suggestions, and specific feedback shaped the content of *Advertising and Integrated Brand Promotion*. Our thanks go to:

Wendi L. Achey
Northampton Community College

Edward E. Ackerley
University of Arizona

Robert B. Affe
Indiana University

Ron Bernthal
Sullivan County Community College

Claudia M. Bridges
California State University, Sacramento

Jeff W. Bruns
Bacone College

Dr. Janice Bukovac Phelps
Michigan State University

Kelli S. Burns
University of South Florida

Trini Callava
Miami Dade College

Joshua Coplen
Santa Monica College

Anne Cunningham
University of Tennessee

Deborah S. David
Fashion Institute of Technology

John Davies
University of North Florida

Dr. De'Arno De'Armond
West Texas A&M University

Federico deGregorio
University of Akron

Raj Devasagayam
Siena College

John Dinsmore
University of Cincinnati

Susan Dobscha
Bentley University

Anthony Dudo
The University of Texas at Austin

Jeffrey E. Durgee
Rensselaer Polytechnic Institute

Mary Edrington
Drake University

Brendan P. Ferrara
Savannah Technical College

Aubrey R. Fowler III
Valdosta State University

Jon Freiden
Florida State University

Cynthia Frisby
University of Missouri–Columbia

George J. Gannage Jr.
West Georgia Technical College

Michael Giebelhausen
Clemson University

Katie Gilstrap
Virginia Commonwealth University

Gary E. Golden
Muskingum College

Corliss L. Green
Georgia State University

Cynthia Grether
Delta College

Thomas Groth
University of West Florida

Scott Hamula
Keuka College

Michael Hanley
Ball State University

Joseph P. Helgert
Grand Valley State University

Wayne Hilinski
Penn State University

David C. Houghton
Charleston Southern University

Wayne Hoyer
The University of Texas at Austin

E. Lincoln James
Washington State University

Karen James
Louisiana State University–Shreveport

Melissa St. James
CSU Dominguez Hills

Michelle Jasso
New Mexico State University

Ed Johnson
Campbell University

Donald Jugenheimer
Southern Illinois University

George Kelley
Erie Community College–City Campus

Patricia Kennedy
University of Nebraska–Lincoln

Robert Kent
University of Delaware

Kirk D. Kern
Bowling Green State University

Kacy Kim
Elon University

Marshall R. Kohr, II
Northwestern University

Priscilla LaBarbera
New York University

Barbara Lafferty
University of South Florida

William LaFief
Frostburg State University

Jacquie Lamer
Northwest Missouri State University

David H. Lange
Grand Rapids Community College

Debbie Laverie
Texas Tech

Mary Alice LoCicero
Oakland Community College

Gail Love
California State University, Fullerton

Eina M. Lowrey
University of Texas at San Antonio

Deanna Mader
Marshall University

Mike Marn
University of Nebraska at Kearney

Marty Matthews
University of Washington

John A. McCarty
The College of New Jersey

Norman D. McElvany
Johnston State College

Nancy Mitchell
University of Nebraska–Lincoln

Elizabeth Moore
University of Notre Dame

Deborah Morrison
University of Oregon

Cynthia R. Morton
University of Florida

Darrel Muehling
Washington State University

John H. Murphy, II
The University of Texas at Austin

Andrew E. Norman
Iowa State

Marcella M. Norwood
University of Houston

James Pokrywczynski
Marquette University

Linda Price
University of Wyoming

John Purcell
Castleton State College

William E. Rice
CSU Fresno

Maria del Pilar Rivera
The University of Texas at Austin

Ann H. Rodriguez
Texas Tech University

Jim Rose
Bauder College

Marla Royne
University of Memphis

Dana K. Saewitz
Temple University

Minita Sanghvi
Skidmore College

Debra Scammon
University of Utah

Allen D. Schaefer
Missouri State University

Carol Schibi
State Fair Community College

Erina Sego
Boise State University

Andrea Semenik
Simon Fraser University

Kim Sheehan
University of Oregon

Daniel A. Sheinin
University of Rhode Island

Alan Shields
Suffolk County Community College

Sloane Signal
University of Nebraska-Lincoln

Jan Slater
Syracuse University

Lewis F. Small
York College of Pennsylvania

Barry Solomon
Florida State University

Melissa St. James
CSU Dominguez Hills

Laurel Steinfield
Bentley University

Patricia Stout
The University of Texas at Austin

Annette Tower
Clemson University

Lynn Walters
Texas A&M

Jon P. Wardrip
University of South Carolina

Robert O. Watson
Quinnipiac University

Marc Weinberger
University of Georgia

Professor Joan R. Weiss
Bucks County Community College

Gary B. Wilcox
The University of Texas at Austin

Kurt Wildermuth
University of Missouri–Columbia

Dr. Janice K. Williams
University of Central Oklahoma

Patti Williams
Wharton

Dr. Amy Wojciechowski
West Shore Community College

Doreen (DW) Wood
Rogue Community College

Courtney Worsham
University of South Carolina

Christine Wright-Isak
Florida Gulf Coast University

Adrienne Zaitz
University of Memphis

Molly Ziske
Michigan State University

Lara Zwarun
The University of Texas at Arlington

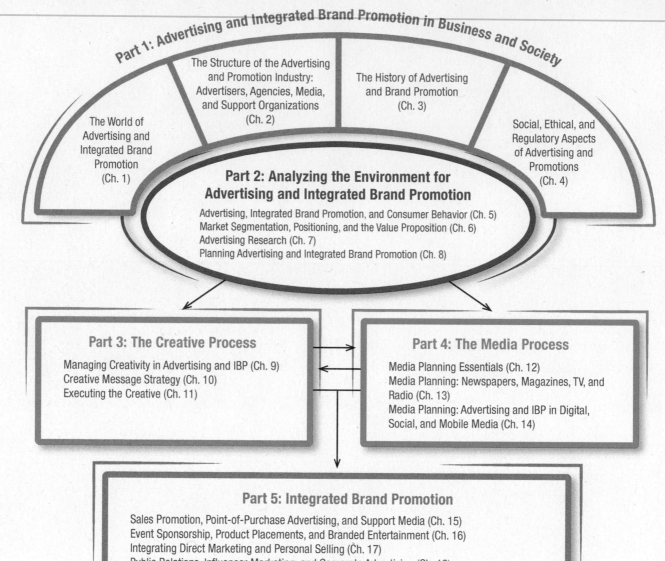

Part 1: Advertising and Integrated Brand Promotion in Business and Society

The World of Advertising and Integrated Brand Promotion (Ch. 1)

The Structure of the Advertising and Promotion Industry: Advertisers, Agencies, Media, and Support Organizations (Ch. 2)

The History of Advertising and Brand Promotion (Ch. 3)

Social, Ethical, and Regulatory Aspects of Advertising and Promotions (Ch. 4)

Part 2: Analyzing the Environment for Advertising and Integrated Brand Promotion

Advertising, Integrated Brand Promotion, and Consumer Behavior (Ch. 5)
Market Segmentation, Positioning, and the Value Proposition (Ch. 6)
Advertising Research (Ch. 7)
Planning Advertising and Integrated Brand Promotion (Ch. 8)

Part 3: The Creative Process

Managing Creativity in Advertising and IBP (Ch. 9)
Creative Message Strategy (Ch. 10)
Executing the Creative (Ch. 11)

Part 4: The Media Process

Media Planning Essentials (Ch. 12)
Media Planning: Newspapers, Magazines, TV, and Radio (Ch. 13)
Media Planning: Advertising and IBP in Digital, Social, and Mobile Media (Ch. 14)

Part 5: Integrated Brand Promotion

Sales Promotion, Point-of-Purchase Advertising, and Support Media (Ch. 15)
Event Sponsorship, Product Placements, and Branded Entertainment (Ch. 16)
Integrating Direct Marketing and Personal Selling (Ch. 17)
Public Relations, Influencer Marketing, and Corporate Advertising (Ch. 18)

As the framework indicates, the first part of the book introduces the broad landscape of the advertising and IBP processes that expose us to brands and what they have to offer, starting with an overview of the world of advertising and IBP (Chapter 1). Next, you'll learn about the people and organizations that make up the structure of the advertising and promotion industry (Chapter 2). Understanding the history of advertising and brand promotion (Chapter 3) will give you a practical foundation for applying concepts today. Finally, you'll be introduced to key social, ethical, and regulatory aspects of advertising and promotion, including balanced perspectives that examine both the positive elements and the darker sides of advertising (Chapter 4).

Part 1

Advertising and Integrated Brand Promotion in Business and Society

1 The World of Advertising and Integrated Brand Promotion *4*

2 The Structure of the Advertising and Promotion Industry: Advertisers, Agencies, Media, and Support Organizations *28*

3 The History of Advertising and Brand Promotion *52*

4 Social, Ethical, and Regulatory Aspects of Advertising and Promotion *78*

Advertising has evolved from the traditional mass media messages of the past; today's advertising is more diverse and dynamic and is a key component of integrated brand promotion (IBP). IBP is the process of using a variety of promotional techniques and tools—from television ads and billboards to digital/social media and influencer marketing to sponsorships and celebrity endorsements—to communicate with consumers about brands. In turn, advertising and IBP communications are part of a broader social communication process that has transformed over time with changes in culture, technology, and business strategies. Advertising is on the upswing: it's big business, with big career opportunities working with some fascinating brands that are a reflection of the world around us.

The framework depicted here shows how we will address advertising and IBP from a broad lens—and from a very important economic perspective. Chapter by chapter, you can use this framework to understand how each aspect of advertising and IBP fits within the big picture. Remember, no aspect of advertising or IBP stands alone—each is connected to the environment, under the larger umbrella of business and society, and each plays a role in communicating with consumers about brands.

The World of Advertising and Integrated Brand Promotion

CSA-Printstock/DigitalVision Vectors/Getty Images

Learning Objectives

After reading and thinking about this chapter, you will be able to do the following:

1. Describe the new world of branding.

2. Define what advertising, advertising campaigns, and integrated brand promotion (IBP) are and what they can do.

3. Explain advertising as a communication process via a model of mass mediated communication.

4. Describe the different ways of classifying audiences for advertising and IBP.

5. Explain advertising as a business process.

6. Identify the various types of advertising and the economic effects of advertising.

7. Identify the shift from advertising to integrated marketing communications to IBP.

The framework in Exhibit 1.1 illustrates the complexity of the new world of advertising and integrated brand promotion (IBP). IBP is the modern form of IMC, or *integrated marketing communications*. The central issue with the IMC thinking of the past is that it is not brand centric, whereas building and maintaining strong brands in the competitive and global marketplace is central to the IBP approach, making it more relevant and meaningful in the modern era.

Why IBP? Well, as a consumer, you're a real challenge for companies. You like to get your information from friends and through social media instead of from newspaper advertising and television commercials. So how are companies supposed to reach you with their advertising and brand messages? Well, that is a very real challenge. Companies *are* using traditional mass media advertising, but they are also integrating newer and more interactive forms of communication to try to get their brand messages across and to influence your brand attitudes and decisions.[1] At the same time, companies are struggling to measure exactly how many people they're reaching and how advertising and IBP activities influence brand attitudes and purchasing behavior in today's cluttered communications environment.[2]

You'll still see advertising during your favorite television show or in your favorite magazine—a lot of advertising, in fact. But if you're a smartphone user, you may have noticed advertising within apps, or you may be using branded apps for fun and shopping. If you're one of the 213 million U.S. consumers who enjoy smartphone games, you've probably noticed ads in the cyberscenery, between game screens, or on reward screens.[3] Welcome to the new and increasingly dynamic world of advertising and IBP.

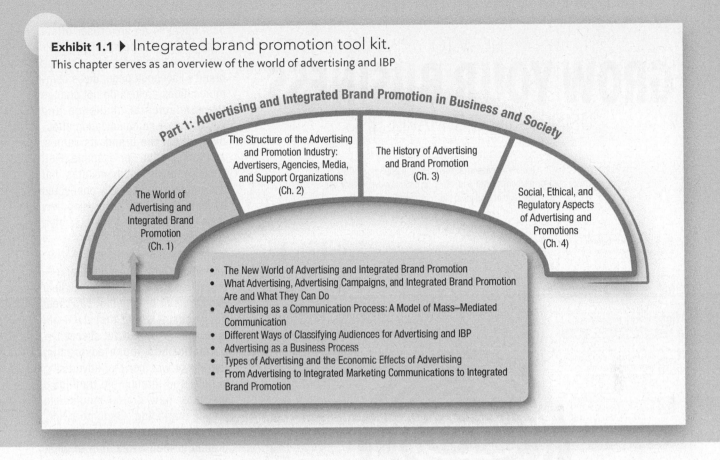

Exhibit 1.1 ▶ Integrated brand promotion tool kit.
This chapter serves as an overview of the world of advertising and IBP

Part 1: Advertising and Integrated Brand Promotion in Business and Society

The World of Advertising and Integrated Brand Promotion (Ch. 1)

The Structure of the Advertising and Promotion Industry: Advertisers, Agencies, Media, and Support Organizations (Ch. 2)

The History of Advertising and Brand Promotion (Ch. 3)

Social, Ethical, and Regulatory Aspects of Advertising and Promotions (Ch. 4)

- The New World of Advertising and Integrated Brand Promotion
- What Advertising, Advertising Campaigns, and Integrated Brand Promotion Are and What They Can Do
- Advertising as a Communication Process: A Model of Mass–Mediated Communication
- Different Ways of Classifying Audiences for Advertising and IBP
- Advertising as a Business Process
- Types of Advertising and the Economic Effects of Advertising
- From Advertising to Integrated Marketing Communications to Integrated Brand Promotion

LO **1**

1-1 The New World of Advertising and Integrated Brand Promotion

The world of branding is going through enormous change. Marketing has become much more experiential, as seen in the sustained growth of the sponsorship and event marketing industry. Artificial intelligence–based algorithms help place ads via behavioral targeting and retargeting consumers with ads they have clicked on in the past. In short, consumer preferences and new technologies are reshaping the communication environment and the future of advertising.[4]

Because of this, we can't stress measurement and research enough. Firms expect a real return on their advertising investment. Advertising investments total both the creative and the media aspects of making and placing the content of IBP tools, respectively. Every brand-related or communication investment must be measured; IBP tools that are not yet measured as precisely as they should be will have to find ways to measure audiences and responses. For instance, *content marketing* is a hot industry term that collectively refers to the marketing of informational content such as videos or posts for target audiences online and on social

media. How can firms measure their return on investment in content marketing? As Exhibit 1.2 indicates, businesses use content marketing in a variety of ways to support growth, so the ability to gauge results is important.

Measurement is crucial for the field of marketing and, in particular, for the vitality of advertising and IBP, in the context of how organizations finance and evaluate their investments in marketing activities. Also critical is the ability to understand how to measure the wider scope of social shifting that events, sponsorships, or ad campaigns can bring. For instance, organizations may want to evaluate event sponsorship effectiveness on the basis of event social responsibility as well as on the economic impact to local communities.

The lines between information, entertainment, networking, and commercial messages are blurring. Content marketing and influencer marketing have changed digital marketing environments. Now companies are turning to these techniques in addition to branded entertainment, digital marketing, and other communication tactics to reach consumers and get their brand messages integrated into consumers' lifestyles.

Advertising, IBP, and marketing overall are rapidly becoming more digital, more interactive, and more social. If you're among the 81 percent of American consumers who use a smartphone, you're a prime target audience for **mobile marketing**, communicating branded messages via mobile devices like smartphones and tablet devices.[5] But for now, the "new world of advertising" is still in transition and still has some fundamentals that will not change, no matter what, as the next section describes.

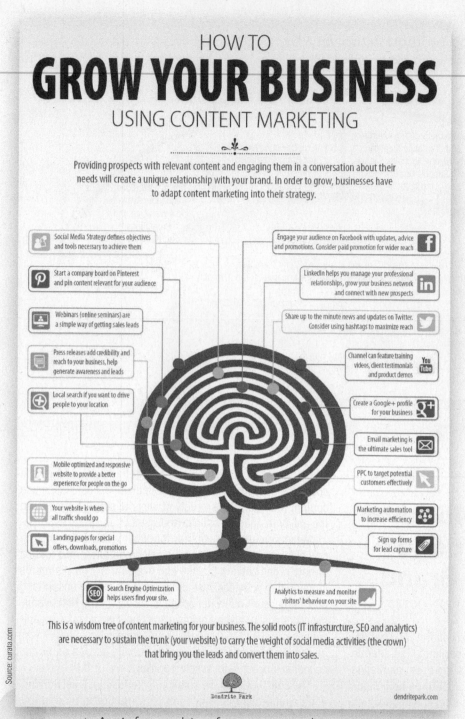

HOW TO
GROW YOUR BUSINESS
USING CONTENT MARKETING

Providing prospects with relevant content and engaging them in a conversation about their needs will create a unique relationship with your brand. In order to grow, businesses have to adapt content marketing into their strategy.

Social Media Strategy defines objectives and tools necessary to achieve them

Start a company board on Pinterest and pin content relevant for your audience

Webinars (online seminars) are a simple way of getting sales leads

Press releases add credibility and reach to your business, help generate awareness and leads

Local search if you want to drive people to your location

Mobile optimized and responsive website to provide a better experience for people on the go

Your website is where all traffic should go

Landing pages for special offers, downloads, promotions

Engage your audience on Facebook with updates, advice and promotions. Consider paid promotion for wider reach

LinkedIn helps you manage your professional relationships, grow your business network and connect with new prospects

Share up to the minute news and updates on Twitter. Consider using hashtags to maximize reach

Channel can feature training videos, client testimonials and product demos

Create a Google+ profile for your business

Email marketing is the ultimate sales tool

PPC to target potential customers effectively

Marketing automation to increase efficiency

Sign up forms for lead capture

Search Engine Optimization helps users find your site.

Analytics to measure and monitor visitors' behaviour on your site

This is a wisdom tree of content marketing for your business. The solid roots (IT infrastructure, SEO and analytics) are necessary to sustain the trunk (your website) to carry the weight of social media activities (the crown) that bring you the leads and convert them into sales.

Dendrite Park

dendritepark.com

Source: curata.com

Exhibit 1.2 ▶ An infographic of content marketing.

1-1a Old Media/New Digital Media—It's All about the Brand

No matter how much technology changes or how many new media options and opportunities are available for delivering messages, advertising and IBP are still all about the brand![6]

Just because an advertiser offers consumers the opportunity to "follow" it on Instagram or visit the brand's Facebook page, these communications options do not change the fundamental challenge and opportunity—communicating effectively about the brand, its values, and its benefits. For example, Fiat, a car company, communicates that it is modern and socially connected by featuring in their advertising how their cars can offer voice-activated social media updates.[7]

As consumers, we know what we like and want, and advertising—regardless of the method—can help expose us to brands that can meet our needs. A brand that does *not* meet our needs will not succeed—no matter how much advertising there is or whether that advertising is delivered through old traditional media or new digital media and mobile marketing. Remember, too, how much consumers emphasize brands in their evaluation of what offering will best meet their needs. Consumers are irresistibly drawn to brands to fulfill their needs and desires and also for the social symbolism that brands represent. This creates an opportunity for brands to communicate how they are able to meet the multidimensional, comprehensive needs of their audiences.

However, established brands in particular face the challenge of maintaining an updated market-driven image and communicating the brand's contemporary identity to the target audience. Consider the complex case of Cadillac, an American luxury car brand that is part of the General Motors (GM) company. In the early 1950s, when there was little competition, Cadillac was a stronghold in the U.S. car market and was a leading advertiser in the automobile market year after year. But by 2005, the U.S. market share had fallen to about 1.31 percent; it dropped just below 1 percent in 2014 and to 0.88 percent in 2020.[7]

What happened to the Cadillac brand? It wasn't the advertising. The competition became more global and the need had arisen to have very clear product positioning of its products and brand image. A series of product missteps confused

Exhibit 1.3 ▶ In 2021, Cars.com named the Cadillac Escalade winner for Luxury Car of the Year.

Exhibit 1.4 ▶ Small Business Saturday, founded by American Express, is a day promoting the idea of buying from small and local businesses, using the hashtag #ShopSmall as a unifying slogan.

the market's perception of the upscale brand: the 1986 Cimarron, for example, used a Chevy chassis and did not look luxurious. Formidable competitors like Lexus and Infiniti entered the market with powerful and stylish alternatives that were effectively advertised in the luxury space. To regain momentum, GM has been spending heavily to reshape perceptions of Cadillac as a modern, high-end, high-tech brand. The company has redesigned its vehicles, introducing new features and special options for today's car buyers. It has also boosted spending on digital platforms and launched a "Dare Greatly" campaign in multiple media to connect the brand with bold, creative people and places (see Exhibit 1.3). And Cadillac's efforts have paid off! Its 2021 Escalade was named Cars.com's Luxury Vehicle of the Year.[7]

LO 2

1-2 What Advertising, Advertising Campaigns, and Integrated Brand Promotion Are and What They Can Do

Now that we've set the new and dynamic context for communication, let's consider the tools companies use: advertising and IBP. We'll start with advertising. You have your own ideas about advertising because you see some advertising every day—even if you try to avoid most of it.

You need to know that advertising means different things to different people, though. It's a business, an art form, an institution, and a cultural phenomenon. To the CEO of a multinational corporation, like Visa, advertising is an essential marketing tool that helps create brand awareness and brand loyalty. To the owner of a small retail shop, advertising is a way to bring people into the store, as shown in Exhibit 1.4. To the art director in an advertising agency, advertising is the creative expression of a concept. To a media planner, advertising is the way a firm uses the media to communicate with current and potential customers. To a website manager, it's a way to drive traffic to the URL. To scholars and museum curators, advertising is an important cultural artifact, text, and historical record. Advertising means something different to all these people. In fact, sometimes determining just what is and what is not advertising is a difficult task.

Even though companies believe in and rely heavily on advertising, some people have significant misperceptions about advertising and what it's supposed to do, what it can do, and what it can't do. The average person sees advertising as amusing, informative, somewhat annoying, sort of helpful, and occasionally hip.[8] The truth about advertising lies somewhere between the extremes.

Sometimes advertising is economically and socially impactful and powerful; at other times, it's irritating. Advertising plays a pivotal role in world commerce and in the way we experience and live our lives. It is part of our language and our culture. It is a complex communication process, a dynamic business process, and now a part of the social interaction process.

1-2a Advertising Defined

Keeping in mind that different people in different contexts see advertising so differently and that advertising suffers from some controversies, we offer this straightforward definition:

> **Advertising** is a paid, mass-mediated attempt to inform, persuade, or remind.

First, as this definition states, advertising is *paid* communication by a company or organization that wants its information disseminated. In advertising language, the company or organization that pays for advertising is called the **client** or **sponsor**. Although other definitions have proposed that paid not be a part of the definition with the reasoning that media can also be owned or earned, we contend that the paid media aspect is important to distinguish advertising from the many other related forms of integrated brand promotion that will be detailed in this book. Again, if a communication is *not paid for,* it's not advertising. For example, a form of public relations promotion called *publicity* is not advertising because it is not paid for. Let's say Bella Thorne appears on a talk show to promote her newest movie. Is this advertising? No, because the producer or film studio did not pay the talk show for airtime. In this example, the show gets an interesting and popular guest, the guest star gets exposure, and the film gets plugged. This is public relations, not advertising. But when the movie studio creates and runs ads for the newest movie, this is advertising because the studio is paying for the messages. For the same reason, public service announcements (PSAs) are not advertising either.

Second, advertising is *mass mediated,* delivered through a communication medium designed to reach more than one person, typically a large number—or mass—of people. Advertising is widely disseminated through television, radio, newspapers, magazines, direct mail, billboards, video games, social media, and other media. The mass-mediated nature of advertising creates a communication environment in which the message is not delivered in a face-to-face manner. This distinguishes advertising from personal selling as a form of communication.

Third, all advertising includes an *attempt to persuade, inform, or remind.* Even an advertisement with a stated objective of being purely informational or intended to remind consumers about the product or service still has persuasion at its core. The ad informs the consumer for some purpose, and that purpose is to get the consumer to like the brand and, because of that liking, to eventually buy the brand. Advertising can also help remind consumers about the brand, to help keep it on their minds especially when they may be ready to buy.

It is important to note here that advertising can be persuasive communication not only about a product or service but also about an idea, a person, or an entire organization. When

Exhibit 1.5 ▶ Apple Watch as an example of showcasing an innovative product.

Source: Alexey Boldin/Shutterstock.com

Ford and Kia use advertising, this is product advertising and meets all three criteria (paid, mass mediated, persuasive). When Southwest Air Lines and lawyers run advertisements about their services, these advertisements also meet all three criteria. When political candidates run ads on television or in newspapers, these (people) ads meet all three criteria as well. And when Apple advertises, it usually means the launch of an innovation, such as its Apple Watch, part of the ever-expanding wearable-technology category (see Exhibit 1.5).

1-2b Integrated Brand Promotion Defined

Integrated brand promotion is related to and yet distinct from advertising. Here is how it is defined:

> **Integrated brand promotion (IBP)** is the process of using a wide range of promotional tools that work together to create widespread brand exposure. It is brand focused.

Just as the definition of advertising is loaded with meaning, so too is the definition of IBP. First, IBP is a process and needs to be managed in an integrated fashion. Second, IBP uses a wide range of promotional tools that have to be evaluated and scheduled. IBP creates exposure for the *brand.* Whether it is a branded product or an overall corporate brand, the IBP process is squarely focused on brand exposure. You can find a list of the most prominent tools marketers use for IBP in Exhibit 1.6.

Exhibit 1.6 ▶ IBP tool kit checklist.

INTEGRATED BRAND PROMOTION (IBP) TOOL KIT	* DIGITAL - TRADITIONAL # BOTH/EITHER
Advertising in traditional media (television, radio, newspapers, magazines, billboards)	-
Advertising in digital media (mobile, websites, social media)	*
Sponsorship (cash or in-kind partnerships or sponsored content)	#
Event marketing/experiential marketing	#
Sales promotions (coupons, premiums, discounts, gift cards, contests, samples, trial offers, rebates, frequent user affinity programs, trade shows)	#
Point-of-purchase (in-store) advertising	#
Direct marketing (catalogs, telemarketing, email offers, infomercials)	#
Personal selling/professional sales	-
Internet advertising (banners, pop-ups/pop-unders, websites)	*
Social media or digital media sponsored content	*
Podcasting/smartphone messaging	*
Video advertising/blogs	*
Branded entertainment (product placement/insertion in television programming, apps, video games, and films), also referred to as "advertainment"	#
Outdoor signage	-
Billboard, transit, and aerial advertising	-
Public relations	-
Influencer marketing (peer-to-peer persuasion often through social networks)	#
Corporate advertising	-
Guerilla marketing/street-level marketing/ambush sponsorship	-
Advergaming (advertising embedded in video games)	*
Celebrity endorsement	#
Content marketing	#

Source: Adidas AG

Exhibit 1.7 ▶ Adidas has an ad that incorporates IBP within it.

Notice that this long list of IBP tools includes various types of advertising, but it also goes well beyond traditional advertising forms. All of these tools allow a marketer to reach target customers in different ways with different kinds of messages to achieve broad exposure for a brand. The best advertising can accomplish integration *within an ad.* For instance, if Adidas is able to feature the celebrity endorsement IBP tool and reinforce this or activate a sponsorship or endorsement within an image as seen in Exhibit 1.7, that integration adds to the power.

Third, the definition of IBP highlights that these tools need to work together to create a consistent and compelling impression of the brand. The brand will suffer if its image is presented one way in a magazine ad and not authentically, differently, in a TikTok post. We, as consumers, can spot authenticity in a brand, and one signal of that is if the brand seems true to its roots and its core across all types of media. For effectiveness and efficiency, all the messages and all the tools must be integrated to support a clear and coordinated brand impression. The integration brings synergy.

Finally, the definition of IBP emphasizes that the advertising and promotional effort undertaken by a firm is designed to create widespread exposure for a brand. Unless consumers are reached by these various forms of messages, they will have a difficult time understanding the brand and deciding whether to use it regularly.

1-2c Advertisements, Advertising Campaigns, and Integrated Brand Promotion

Now that we have working definitions of advertising and IBP, we can turn our attention to some other important distinctions and definitions. Let's start with the basics. An **advertisement** refers to a specific message that an organization has created to persuade an audience. An **advertising campaign** is a series of coordinated advertisements that communicates a reasonably cohesive and integrated theme about a brand. The theme may be made up of several claims or points but should advance an essentially singular theme. Successful advertising campaigns can be developed around a single advertisement placed in multiple media, or they can be made up of several different advertisements with a similar look, feel, and message.

How does IBP fit in with advertisements and advertising campaigns? As we discussed earlier, IBP is the use of many promotional tools, including advertising, in a coordinated manner to build and then maintain brand awareness, identity, and preference. When marketers combine contests, a website, event sponsorship, and point-of-purchase displays with advertisements and advertising campaigns or other tools, for example, they create an IBP. Integrated brand promotion, by definition, requires careful coordination and sequencing of different promotional efforts.[9]

Popeyes has recently had some well-coordinated IBP. The fast-food brand uses television commercials and other advertisements to reach mass audiences, showcasing the brand, new menu items, and, in some cases integrating celebrity endorsement. As can be seen in Exhibit 1.8, Popeyes has worked with musician Megan Thee Stallion to promote "Hottie Sauce" as one of their sauce options, and integrated her name, image, or likeness into their IBP. As another creative execution of their IBP, Popeyes had some fun poking at their competitor McDonald's over the "chicken sandwich wars." Popeyes launched a very fried successful chicken sandwich, and to help promote it, they launched a contest where they challenged customers to misspell a website URL for a chance for a free chicken sandwich. This IBP execution not only helped promote their signature product while also calling attention to the difficult to spell website URL that McDonald's had used for their revamped fried chicken sandwich.[10]

The executive who is especially interested in IBP is the **chief marketing officer (CMO)**. Advertisers and marketers (especially CMOs) evaluate the results of advertising and IBP efforts by analyzing sales, brand awareness, and other marketing metrics that are relevant to their brand.

1-2d A Focus on Advertising

Integrated brand promotion will be a key concept throughout our discussion of advertising because of its importance to the contemporary marketing effort. As consumers encounter a daily blitz of commercial messages, brands and the images they project allow consumers to quickly identify and evaluate the relevance of a brand to their lives and value systems. The marketer who does *not* use advertising and IBP as a way to build brand identity and meaning for consumers will, frankly, be ignored.

Exhibit 1.8 ▶ Popeyes uses their Twitter account to Promote their "Hottie Sauce."

We will develop the concept and describe the execution of IBP throughout the text and demonstrate how advertising is central to the process. The encounters between consumers and advertising, advertisements, and advertising campaigns, specifically, are the focus of our next discussion. You will learn more about the features and application of other IBP tools in Part 5 of the text.

1-3 Advertising as a Communication Process: A Model of Mass-Mediated Communication

Communication is a fundamental aspect of human existence, and advertising is one of those communications. To understand advertising at all, you must understand something about communication in general and about mass communication in particular.

Because advertising is mass-mediated communication, it often occurs not face to face but through a medium (such as television, on the side of a building, or on your smartphone). Although there are many valuable models of mass communication, a contemporary model of mass-mediated communication

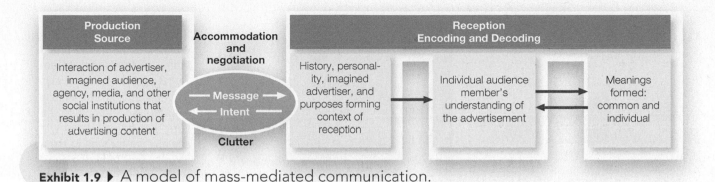

Production Source	Accommodation and negotiation	Reception Encoding and Decoding		
Interaction of advertiser, imagined audience, agency, media, and other social institutions that results in production of advertising content	Message → ← Intent Clutter	History, personality, imagined advertiser, and purposes forming context of reception	Individual audience member's understanding of the advertisement	Meanings formed: common and individual

Exhibit 1.9 ▶ A model of mass-mediated communication.

is presented in Exhibit 1.9. This model shows mass communication as a process through which people, institutions, and messages interact. It has two major components: production (by the sender of a message) and reception (by the receiver of a message). Between production and reception are the mediating (interpretation) processes of accommodation and negotiation.

The first point about the model is that it is fluid and not unidirectional. Notice the feedback loop from meanings formed back to the audience, illustrating how we gain understanding of a brand or an ad. Moving from left to right in the model, you first see the process of communication production, where the content of a mass communication is created.

The **source** is the originator or creator of the content. An advertisement, like other forms of mass communication, is the product of institutions (such as corporations, organizations, advertising agencies, and governments) interacting to create content (what is developed for a digital ad, print ad, television ad, radio ad, podcast, Pinterest image, or the company's website). The creation of the advertisement is a complex interaction of the company's brand message, the company's expectations about the target audience's desire for information, the company's assumptions about how members of an audience will interpret the words and images in an ad, and the rules and regulations of the medium that transmits the message.

Continuing to the right, notice that the mediating processes of **accommodation** and **negotiation** lie between the production and reception phases. Accommodation and negotiation are the ways in which consumers interpret ads, *decoding* what the source has *encoded*. Individual audience members have some ideas about how the company wants them to interpret the ad (we all know the rules of advertising—somebody is trying to persuade us to buy something or like that brand or idea). And each consumer has needs, agendas, and preferred interpretations based on history, experience, and individual value systems. Given all this, every consumer who sees an ad arrives at an interpretation of the ad that makes sense to that person individually, serves their needs, and fits their personal history with a product category and a set of brands.

Reception also takes place in the context of potential interference such as "clutter"—the sheer number and diversity of brand messages to which you're exposed every day in every medium.[10] In fact, digital advertisers consider clutter the biggest challenge they face in trying to get messages across to consumers.[11] You'll learn more about the wide range of influences on each consumer in Chapter 5—"Advertising, Integrated Brand Promotion, and Consumer Behavior."

What's interesting about the whole progression of consumer receipt and then interpretation of a communication is that it is often wholly *incompatible* with the way the company wants consumers to see an ad. In other words, the receivers of the communication must *accommodate* their perceived multiple meanings and personal agendas and then *negotiate* a meaning—that is, an interpretation—of the ad according to their individual life experiences and value systems. That's why communication is inherently a *social* process: What a message means to any given consumer is a function not of an isolated thinker but of an inherently social being responding to what they know about the producers of the message (the companies), other receivers (peer groups, for example), and the social world in which the brand and the message exists. Now, admittedly, all this interpretation happens very fast and without much contemplation. The level of conscious interpretation by each receiver might be minimal (mere recognition) or it might be extensive (thoughtful, elaborate processing of an ad), but there is *always* interpretation.

Consider what a receiver might think and feel about the Panera messages in Exhibit 1.10 (Integrated Brand Promotion in Action). To demonstrate the vital importance of IBP, each chapter has a modern "Integrated Brand Promotion in Action" featuring a brand that is using strategic IBP. We present two examples of an advertiser's IBP activities and pose a question for you to consider.

The communication model underscores a critical point: No ad contains a single meaning or even the same meaning for each audience member. Ads are interpreted by each audience member according to their unique set of experiences, values, and beliefs. An ad for a pair of women's shoes means something different for women than it does for men. Each audience member decides what meaning to take away from a communication.[12]

Exhibit 1.10 ▶ Integrated Brand Promotion in Action: Panera.
Panera Bread includes its green and white brand logo with mouth-watering food photos in its advertising and integrated brand promotions. *How does the logo's color combination help associate the brand with its message of "clean food" with no preservation of artificial additives?*

> " *No ad contains a single meaning or even the same meaning for each audience member.*
> *Ads are interpreted by each audience member according to their unique set of experiences, values, and beliefs.* "

LO 4

1-4 Different Ways of Classifying Audiences for Advertising and IBP

In the language of advertising, an **audience** is a group of individuals who receive and interpret messages sent from companies or organizations. The audience could be made up of household consumers, college students, or business-people, for example. Any large group of people can be an audience. A **target audience** is a particular group of consumers singled out by an organization for an advertising or IBP campaign. These target audiences are selected because the firm has discovered that these specific audience members like the product category and might prefer their particular brand amongst the competition. Target audiences are always *potential* audiences because a company can never be sure that the message will actually get through to them as intended. Targeting audiences means that a company wants to reach individuals or groups with a message. Even though companies can identify dozens of different target audiences, many specifically target these categories: household consumers, members of business organizations, members of a trade channel, professionals, and government officials and employees.

1-4a Audience Categories

Household consumers are the most conspicuous audience in that most mass media advertising is directed at them. McDonald's, Tesla, Target, Progressive Insurance, and Apple have products and services designed for the consumer market, and so their advertising targets household consumers.

According to the U.S. Census Bureau, there are more than 321 million household consumers who spend trillions of dollars a year on retail goods and services.[13] Under the very broad heading of "consumer advertising," very fine audience distinctions can be made by advertisers. A target audience definition such as men, 25 to 45, in professional occupations, living in metropolitan areas, with incomes greater than $50,000 per year would be the kind of target audience description an advertiser might develop.

Members of business organizations are the focus of advertising for firms that produce business and industrial goods and services, such as office equipment, production machinery, supplies, and software. Although products and services targeted to this audience often require personal selling, advertising is used to create awareness and a favorable attitude among potential buyers. IBM has used advertising during the U.S. Open tennis tournament to reach chief marketing officers within organizations, because this audience is becoming more influential regarding hardware and software decisions within corporations. The company is also targeting decision makers at businesses like Campbell's Soup and Unilever with messages about Watson Ads, branded advertising for consumer products designed for interactivity powered by IBM's Watson.[14] Not-for-profit businesses such as universities, some research laboratories, philanthropic groups, and cultural organizations also represent an important and separate business audience for advertising.

Exhibit 1.11 ▶ Absolut nights.

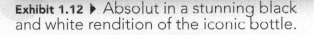

Exhibit 1.12 ▶ Absolut in a stunning black and white rendition of the iconic bottle.

Absolut is an icon in advertising, with stylish messages targeting consumers. There has been very little change to the overarching strategy of the ads over the years. See examples in Exhibits 1.11, 1.12, and 1.13 of this classic campaign.

Members of a trade channel include retailers (like Best Buy for consumer electronics), wholesalers (like Castle Wholesalers for construction tools), and distributors (like Sysco Food Services for restaurant supplies). These members of the trade channel are a target audience for producers of both household and business goods and services. The promotional tool used most often to communicate with this group is personal selling, because this audience represents a relatively small, easily identifiable group. Other IBP tools, including sales promotion, are also used when targeting this audience. When advertising is directed at this target audience, it can serve an extremely useful purpose, as we will see later in the section on advertising as a business process.

Professionals form a special target audience and are defined as doctors, lawyers, accountants, teachers, electricians, or any other professional group that has special training or certification. This audience warrants a separate classification because its members have specialized needs and interests. Advertising directed to professionals typically highlights products and services uniquely designed to serve their more narrowly defined needs. The language and images used in advertising to this target audience often rely on esoteric terminology and unique circumstances that members of professions readily recognize. Advertising to professionals is predominantly carried out through trade publications. **Trade journals,** like *Food Technology*, are magazines (in digital and/or print format) published specifically for members of a trade and carry technical articles of interest to that audience.

Government officials and employees constitute an audience in themselves due to the large dollar volume of buying that federal, state, and local governments do. Government organizations from universities to road maintenance operations buy huge amounts of various types of products. Producers of items such as office furniture, construction materials and equipment, vehicles, fertilizers, computers, and business services all target government organizations with advertising. Advertising to this target audience is dominated by direct mail, catalogs, personal selling, and digital advertising.

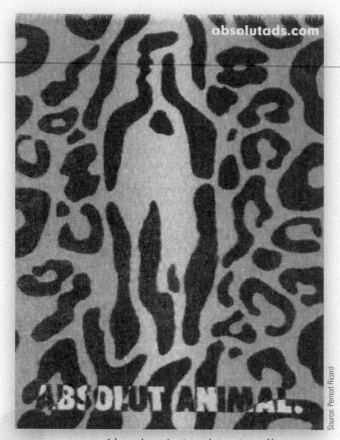

absolutads.com

Source: Pernod Ricard

Exhibit 1.13 ▶ Absolut Animal is visually stunning.

1-4b Audience Geography

Audiences can also be broken down by geographic location. Because of the cultural differences and practical needs often associated with geographic location, very few ads can be effective for all consumers worldwide.

Global advertising is advertising that is used worldwide with only minor changes in the visual and message content. Very few brands can use global advertising. These are typically brands that are considered "citizens of the world" and whose manner of use does not vary tremendously by culture or location. Using a Samsung television or taking a trip on Singapore Airlines doesn't change much from culture to culture and geographic location to geographic location. Firms that market brands with global appeal, like IBM, Apple, and Pirelli Tires, try to develop and place advertisements with a common theme and presentation in all markets around the world where the firm's brands are sold. Global placement is effective *only* when a brand and the messages about that brand have a common appeal across diverse cultures.

International advertising occurs when firms prepare and place different advertising in different national markets for the same brand outside their home market. Each international market might require unique advertising due to product adaptations or message appeals tailored specifically for that market. Unilever prepares different versions of ads for its laundry products for nearly every international market because consumers in different cultures don't have the same needs or household situations. Consumers in the United States use large and powerful washers and dryers and a lot of hot water. Households in Brazil use very little hot water and hang clothes out to dry. Few firms enjoy the luxury of having a brand with truly cross-cultural appeal and global recognition, as is necessary for global advertising as described in the previous section. International advertising differs from global advertising in that different ads for the same brand are tailored for each market.

National advertising reaches all geographic areas of a single nation. National advertising is the term typically used to describe the kind of advertising we see most often in the mass media in the domestic U.S. market.

Regional advertising is carried out by producers, wholesalers, distributors, and retailers that concentrate their efforts in a relatively large but not national geographic region, to reach customers and potential customers. Finally, **local advertising** is directed at an audience in a single trading area, either a city or a state. Under special circumstances, national companies will share advertising expenses in a market with local dealers to achieve specific advertising objectives. This sharing of advertising expenses between national companies and local merchants is called **cooperative advertising** (or **co-op advertising**). As more companies step up their online branded advertising and support co-op advertising for their retail partners, coordinating these efforts is vital for both efficiency and effectiveness.[15]

LO 5

1-5 Advertising as a Business Process

Advertising is very much a business process as well as a communication process. For multinational organizations like Proctor & Gamble and Johnson & Johnson, as well as for small local retailers, advertising is a basic business tool that is essential to retaining current customers and attracting new ones. We need to understand that advertising functions as a business process in three ways. First, we'll consider the role advertising plays in the overall marketing and brand development programs in firms. Second, we will look at the types of advertising used by firms. Finally, we will take a broader look at advertising by identifying the economic effects of the process.

The role of advertising relates to four important aspects of the marketing process undertaken by every organization: (1) contributing to the marketing mix, (2) developing and managing the brand, (3) achieving effective market segmentation, differentiation, and positioning, and (4) contributing to revenue and profit generation.

1-5a The Role of Advertising in the Marketing Mix

As you can see from this formal definition, advertising (as a part of communication) plays a vital role in marketing:

Marketing is the activity, set of institutions, and processes for creating, communicating, delivering, and exchanging offerings that have value for customers, clients, partners, and society at large.[16]

Within an organization, the four main areas of responsibility and decision making in marketing are developing, pricing, promoting, and distributing goods and services. This set of activities is referred to as the **marketing mix.** The word *mix* describes the blend of strategic emphasis on the product versus its price versus its promotion (including advertising) versus its distribution when a brand is marketed to consumers—a mix that results in the overall marketing program for a brand. Advertising is important, but it is only *one* of the major areas of marketing responsibility *and* only one of many IBP tools relied on in the marketing mix. Under Armour unleashed "an audacious $25 million campaign" with the slogan "The future is ours!" to introduce its noncleated shoe line. Under Armour sales in that category did not grow the following year—competition from Nike, Adidas, and Reebok proved too formidable. Advertising alone, no matter how "audacious," could not overcome the strength of the competition's product features and distribution.[17]

Exhibit 1.14 lists the strategic decision factors typically considered in each area of the marketing mix. You can see that decisions under each of the marketing mix areas can directly affect the advertising message. The important point is that a firm's advertising effort must be consistent with and complement the overall marketing mix strategy. It must also support the organization's broader social purpose, as you'll see later in this section.

Exhibit 1.14 ▶ These are the factors that an organization needs to consider in creating a marketing mix. Advertising messages, media placement, and IBP techniques must be consistent with and complement strategies in all other areas of the marketing mix.

PRODUCT	PROMOTION
Functional features	Amount and type of advertising
Aesthetic design	Number and qualifications of salespeople
Accompanying services	Extent and type of personal selling program
Instructions for use	Sales promotion—coupons, contests, sweepstakes
Warranty	Trade shows
Product differentiation	Public relations activities
Product positioning	Direct mail or telemarketing
	Event sponsorships
	Internet communications/mobile marketing
PRICE	**DISTRIBUTION**
Level:	Number of retail outlets
Top of the line	Location of retail outlets
Competitive, average prices	Types of retail outlets
Low-price policy	Catalog sales
Terms offered:	Other nonstore retail methods—Internet
Cash/PayPal/Apple Pay	Number and type of wholesalers
Credit:	Inventories—extent and location
Extended	Services provided by distribution:
Restricted	Credit
Interest charges	Delivery
Lease/rental	Installation
	Training

The Role of Advertising in Brand Management

Advertising also plays a critical role in brand development and management. A formal definition of **brand** is a name, term, sign, symbol, or any other feature that identifies one seller's good or service as distinct from those of other sellers.[18] A brand is in many ways the most precious business asset owned by a firm.[19] It allows a firm to communicate consistently and efficiently with the market. Is it really worth investing all that time, effort, and money in building a brand name and image? Yes, because a brand name is often worth much more than the annual sales of the brand. Coca-Cola, one of the world's most valuable brands, is estimated to be worth about $84 billion even though the Coca-Cola company's annual revenues amount to only about $33 billion. Within the portfolio of the Coca-Cola company are 20 brands that *each* generate more than $1 billion in annual sales, including Coca-Cola Zero, Dasani, Fanta, Sprite, and Minute Maid.[20] Using advertising and IBP to build and maintain those brands is a good investment for Coca-Cola, as it is for other businesses.

For every organization, advertising affects brand development and management in five important ways

Information and Persuasion

Target audiences can learn about a brand's features and benefits through advertising and, to a lesser extent, other IBP tools (most other promotional tools, except digital marketing and personal selling, are not heavy on content). But advertising has the best ability to inform or persuade target audiences about the value a brand has to offer. No other variable in the marketing mix is designed to accomplish this communication.

For example, branding is crucially important in the multibillion-dollar soft-drink industry, where Coca-Cola and Pepsi compete with Dr Pepper and many other brands. Advertising, with its ability to use images and emotionally appealing messages, can distinguish a brand like Dr Pepper from competing brands even when there are few true functional differences—because consumers have taste and brand preferences. Advertising helps brands stand out by providing information such as caloric content and persuading consumers based on tangible or intangible benefits.

Introduction of New Brand or Brand Extensions (Variants)

Advertising is absolutely critical when organizations introduce a new brand or extensions of existing brands. Consider Peacock, a new streaming service that Comcast Corporation's NBCUniversal launched on July 15, 2020. It was advertised heavily on its parent company's TV networks and websites in the months leading up to the debut; and the strategy paid off, with the streaming service earning $80 million in revenue in its first four months.[21]

A **brand extension** (also referred to as a **brand variant**) is an adaptation of an existing brand to a new product area. For example, the line of Ben & Jerry's nondairy frozen desserts is a brand extension of the original Ben & Jerry's ice cream product line. When brand extensions are brought to market, advertising and IBP play a key role in attracting attention to the brand—so much so that researchers now suggest "managers should favor the brand extension with a greater allocation of the ad budget."[22] This is often accomplished with advertising working in conjunction with other promotional activities such as sales promotions and point-of-purchase displays.

Building and Maintaining Brand Loyalty among Consumers

Loyalty to a brand is one of the most important assets a firm can have. **Brand loyalty** occurs when a consumer repeatedly purchases the same brand to the exclusion of competitors' brands. This loyalty can result because of habit, because brand names are prominent in the consumer's memory, because of barely conscious associations with brand images, or because consumers have attached some fairly deep meanings to the brands they buy.

Even though brand features are the most important influence on building and maintaining brand loyalty, advertising plays a key role in the process as well. Advertising reminds consumers of those brand features—tangible and intangible. Other promotional tools can offer similarly valuable communications that help build and strengthen lasting and positive associations with a brand—such as a frequent-flyer or frequent-buyer program. When a firm creates and maintains positive associations with the brand in the mind of consumers and builds brand loyalty, the firm goes on to develop what is called brand equity. **Brand equity** is a set of brand assets linked to a brand, its name, and symbol.[23] Advertising activities and integrated communications are both very important for long-term success in building brand equity.[24] A brand such as Nike can leverage its brand equity—backed by advertising and IBP—to achieve ambitious goals such as ringing up $50 billion in worldwide revenues within only a few years. Also adding to the brand equity is the unique retail environment created and fully controlled by Nike in its flagship stores. Here, Nike offers *branded experiences*, such as seen in Exhibit 1.15. The brand is inviting consumers to test products, walk or run on treadmills, participate in sports drills, and shop while surrounded by brand cues such as the famous Nike swoosh.[25]

Creating an Image and Meaning for a Brand

As we discussed in the marketing mix section, advertising can communicate how a brand fulfills needs and desires and therefore plays an important role in attracting customers to brands that appear to be useful and satisfying. But advertising can go further. It can help link a brand's image and meaning to a consumer's social environment and to the larger culture; and in this way, advertising can actually deliver a sense of personal connection for the consumer.

Building and Maintaining Brand Loyalty within the Trade

It might not seem as if wholesalers, retailers, distributors, and brokers would be brand loyal, but they can indeed favor one brand over others given the proper support from a manufacturer. Advertising and particularly advertising integrated with other brand promotions is an area where support can be given. Marketers can provide the trade with sales training programs, collateral advertising materials (e.g., brochures, banners, posters), point-of-purchase advertising displays, premiums (giveaways like T-shirts or free app downloads), Web traffic–building advertising, and foot traffic–building special events. Exide, the battery company, pays to be the official battery of NASCAR racing. Exide's vice president of marketing and product

Exhibit 1.15 ▶ At the Nike flagship store in New York, customers can try out apparel and sporting equipment prior to purchasing.

management explains: "Both our distributors and our distributors' customers, for the most part, are race fans, so it's the place we want to be."[26]

Also, remember that trade buyers (retailers, wholesalers, distributors, brokers) can be key to the success of new brands or brand extensions, as we pointed out earlier in the discussion of the trade market as a target audience. Marketers have little hope of successfully introducing a brand if there is no cooperation in the trade channel among wholesalers and retailers. This is where IBP as a factor in advertising becomes prominent. Trade buyers are generally less responsive to advertising messages than they are to other forms of promotion. Direct support to the trade in terms of displays, contests, increased margins, and personal selling combined with advertising in an IBP program helps ensure the success of a brand. Retailer acceptance of a brand extension is key to the success of the new product, and advertising and IBP, in turn, help achieve retailer acceptance.[27]

The Role of Advertising in Market Segmentation, Differentiation, and Positioning

Another role for advertising in marketing is helping the firm implement the important market strategies of market segmentation, differentiation, and positioning.

Market segmentation is the process of breaking down a large, widely varied (*heterogeneous*) market into submarkets, or segments, that are more similar (*homogeneous*) than dissimilar in terms of consumer characteristics. Underlying the strategy of market segmentation are the facts that consumers differ in their wants and that the wants of one person can differ under various circumstances.[28] The automobile market, for example, can be divided into submarkets for different types

of automobiles based on the needs and desires of various groups of buyers: large or small, luxury or economy, sedan or SUV, or pickup or minivan.

In addition to needs or desires, markets are also segmented based on characteristics of consumers related to **demographics** (such as age, marital status, education, gender, and income) or **psychographics** (attitudes, beliefs, personality, lifestyle, and values). These data are widely available and tend to relate to product preference and use. Advertising's role in the market segmentation process is to develop messages that appeal to the needs and desires of different segments and then to transmit those messages via appropriate media.

Ford, for example, targets different segments for different vehicles and creates advertising and IBP messages suited to each segment's needs and wants. It paid to have its F-series Super Duty pickup trucks named "Official Truck of the NFL" as a way to link its "Built Ford Tough" trucks with the toughness of football—reaching a key target audience while reinforcing a key benefit. For Ford's sporty Mustang car, the company targeted buyers interested in performance and design with its "Powerful, By Design" ads.[29] These ads are reinforced by Ford's interactive social media as seen in Exhibit 1.16.

Differentiation is the process of creating a perceived difference, in the mind of the consumer, between a brand and its competition. Notice that this definition emphasizes that brand differentiation is based on *consumer perception.* The perceived differences can be tangible differences, or they may be based on image or style factors. The critical issue in differentiation is that consumers *perceive* a difference between brands. If consumers do not perceive a difference, then any actual differences do not matter. Further, if a firm's brand is not perceived as distinctive *and attractive* by consumers, then consumers will have no reason to choose that brand over one from the competition or to pay higher prices for the

Ford Motor Company @Ford · Oct 8

Built for more extreme adventures - the Expedition Timberline Off-Grid concept vehicle, based on the 2022 #FordExpedition Timberline series is upfitted to help adventurers confidently trek to hard-to-reach mountainside trailheads, remote lakes and distant desert dunes.

 36   78   429

Source: Ford Motor Company

Exhibit 1.16 ▶   In this ad, Ford captures the toughness of the new Expedition Timberline Off-Grid vehicle, targeting adventure seekers.

"better" or "more meaningful" brand. Think about bottled water (Coca-Cola's Dasani and PepsiCo's Aquafina) and other formerly undifferentiated product categories, in which marketers are using advertising and IBP strategies to highlight points of differentiation.

In order for advertising to help create a difference in the mind of the consumer between a brand and its competitors' brands, the ad may emphasize performance features, or it may create a distinctive image for the brand. The essential task for advertising is to develop a message that is different and unmistakably linked to a company's brand. **Positioning** is the process of designing a brand so that it can occupy a distinct and valued place in the target consumer's mind relative to other brands. This distinctiveness can be communicated through advertising. Positioning, like differentiation, depends on a perceived image of tangible or intangible features. The importance of positioning can be understood by recognizing that consumers create a *perceptual space* in their minds for all the brands they might consider purchasing. A perceptual space is how one brand is seen on any number of dimensions—such as quality, taste, price, or social display value—in relation to those same dimensions in other brands.

There are really three positioning strategic decisions to be made. First, a firm must decide on the **external position** for a brand—that is, the niche the brand will pursue relative to all the competitive brands on the market. Next, an **internal position** must be achieved with regard to the other, similar brands the firm itself markets. With the external-positioning decision, a firm tries to create a distinctive *competitive* position based on design features, pricing, distribution, or promotion or advertising strategy. Some brands are positioned at the top of their competitive product category, such as Acura's NSX, among the costliest cars built in America, starting at about $157,000. Other brands seek a position at the low end, such as the Nissan Versa sedan, with a base price below $15,000.[30]

Effective external positioning is achieved when the firm carefully segments the market, develops brand features and values that are distinctive from the competition, and follows through with advertising and IBP messages that highlight the distinctions.

Effective internal positioning is accomplished by developing vastly different products *within* the firm's own product line. Ben & Jerry's ice cream, for example, offers plenty of distinctive flavors. Ben & Jerry's has a somewhat easier task in meeting this challenge, since each of the ice creams it needs to internally position has a tangible feature to highlight (flavor, ingredients, and so on). A more challenging approach to internal position is creating advertising messages that appeal to different consumer needs and desires when there are few conspicuously tangible differences.

Procter & Gamble (P&G) successfully positions its many laundry detergent brands both internally and externally using a combination of product design and effective advertising. Although some of these brands assume different positions within P&G's line due to substantive differences (a liquid soap versus a powder soap, for example), others with minor differences achieve distinctive positioning through advertising. One P&G brand is advertised as being effective on kids' dirty clothes, whereas another brand is portrayed as effective for preventing colors from running. In this way, advertising helps create a distinctive position, both internally and externally.

Finally, **repositioning** occurs when a firm believes that a brand needs to be revived or updated to address changing market or competitive conditions. Repositioning is aided by a variety of advertising and IBP tactics. An advertising message can be altered to appeal to consumer behavior trends. Packaging can be changed to attract attention, or the brand's logo can be updated to provide a more powerful visual brand representation. Some analysts refer to the process of repositioning with such visual elements of IBP as "the best way into a consumer's mind is not with verbal nails, but with a visual hammer."[31] The methods and strategic options available to an organization with respect to market segmentation, product differentiation, and positioning will be discussed in Chapter 6, "Market Segmentation, Positioning, and the Value Proposition."

The Role of Advertising in Contributing to Revenue and Profit Generation

There are many who believe that the fundamental purpose of marketing (and advertising) is to generate revenue. Marketing is the only part of an organization that has revenue generation as its primary purpose. In the words of highly regarded management consultant and scholar Peter Drucker, "Marketing and innovation produce results: all the rest are 'costs.'"[32] The "results" Drucker refers to are revenues. The marketing process is designed to generate sales and therefore revenues for the firm. Now take that one step further: publicly traded companies are concerned not just with revenues but also with customer satisfaction—because higher satisfaction is linked to higher stock prices.[33]

Helping create sales to generate revenue is where advertising plays a significant role. As we have seen, advertising communicates persuasive information to audiences based on the value created in the marketing mix related to the product attributes, its price, or its distribution. This advertising communication then highlights brand features—performance, price, emotion, values, or availability—and then attracts a target market. In this way, advertising makes a direct contribution to the marketing goal of revenue generation. Notice that advertising *contributes* to the process of creating sales and revenue. It cannot be solely responsible for creating sales and revenue—it's not that powerful. Sales occur when a brand has a well-conceived and complete marketing mix—including good advertising.

The effect of advertising on profits is a bit more involved and complicated. Its effect on profits comes about when advertising gives an organization greater flexibility in the price it *charges* for a product or service. Advertising can help create pricing flexibility by (1) contributing to economies of scale and (2) helping create inelasticity (insensitivity) of demand to price changes. When an organization creates large-scale demand for its brand, the quantity of product produced is increased, and **economies of scale** lead to lower unit production costs. Cost of production decreases because fixed costs (such as rent and equipment costs) are spread over a greater number of units produced.

How does advertising play a role in helping create economies of scale? When Colgate manufactures hundreds of thousands of tubes of its Colgate Total toothpaste and ships them to warehouses, the fixed costs of production and shipping per unit are greatly reduced. With lower fixed costs per unit, Colgate can realize greater profits on each toothpaste sold. Advertising contributes to demand stimulation by communicating the features and availability of a brand to the market. This, in turn, contributes to the process of creating these economies of scale, which ultimately translates into higher profits per unit for the organization.

Remember the concept of brand loyalty we discussed earlier? Well, brand loyalty and advertising work together to create another important economic effect related to pricing flexibility and profits. When consumers are brand loyal, they are generally less sensitive to price increases for the brand. In economic terms, this is known as **inelasticity of demand**. When consumers are less price sensitive, firms have the flexibility to maintain higher prices and increase profit margins. Advertising contributes directly to brand loyalty, and thus to inelasticity of demand, by persuading and reminding consumers of the satisfaction and value related to a brand and why they want to choose that brand over competitors' brands.

These arguments related to the positive business effects of advertising were recently supported by a large research study. The study found that companies that build strong brands and raise prices are more profitable than companies that cut costs as a way to increase profits—by nearly twice the profit percentage. Luxury brands are a good example. Hermes, which makes premium clothing and accessories ($1200 per handbag or more), enjoys an operating margin of 31 percent supported by the brand image created and maintained via advertising.[34]

The Role of Advertising in Contributing to Social Purpose

Advertising is trending toward having more social purpose and can reinforce aspects of corporate or event social responsibility. More than ever before, consumers are looking carefully at the differences among brands—and seeking out brands with a purpose, as illustrated in Exhibit 1.17.[35] Advertising, as part of the broader marketing effort, can help organizations make a difference to society. So **purpose-driven marketing** is marketing (including advertising and IBP) that helps the organization achieve its long-term social purpose.[36] Doing good can actually help a company do well, as businesses like Unilever have found. Unilever is taking concrete steps, through its brands and through corporate actions, to save the planet. This social purpose appeals to consumers interested in environmental causes. "For our brands, we are seeing particular growth in sales for those that have built purpose and sustainability into their brand mixes," confirms Unilever's chief marketing and communications officer. Another business benefit of purpose-driven marketing is the ability to recruit and motivate talented employees. A Unilever sustainability executive explains, "We know that one reason young people want to join us is that we are a business with a clearly defined purpose," as reflected in the company's advertising and IBP messages.[37]

Source: World Wildlife Fund

WHAT
ON EARTH
ARE WE DOING
TO OUR PLANET?

Exhibit 1.17 ▶ Notice the purpose in this WWF ad featuring a polar bear asking us, "What on earth are we doing to our planet?"

For organizations that have tried to stimulate primary demand in mature product categories (including milk, orange juice, beef, and pork), the results have been dismal. The National Fluid Milk Processor Promotion Board has tried for years to use advertising to stimulate primary demand for the entire product category of milk. Do you remember the iconic Got Milk? Campaign? In terms of recognition, popularity, reach, recall, and many other measures, Got Milk? continues to be regarded as an iconic success. Yet after more than 20 years of consistent ad buys, milk sales have continued to suffer; in fact, people are drinking less milk than they were at the start of the campaign.[38] Only broad influences on society, like demographics, cultural values, or technology, can affect primary demand for a long-established product category such as milk.

The true power of advertising is realized when it functions to stimulate demand for a particular company's brand. This is known as selective demand stimulation. The purpose of **selective demand stimulation** advertising is to point out a brand's unique benefits compared to the competition. This is the proper role for advertising and IBP, and it is effective for individual brands, even those within mature product categories. For example, Trickling Springs Creamery in Pennsylvania is building sales for its ice cream and milk products by promoting the local nature of its dairy farms and the organic ingredients. The creamery's marketing director observes, "Customers want to learn the story behind the food to see if it's the values they hold."[39] Advertising and IBP are excellent ways to communicate the story behind specific brands and products.

LO 6

1-6 Types of Advertising and the Economic Effects of Advertising

To understand advertising, it is important to be familiar with the basic typologies that categorize advertising according to fundamental approaches to communication.

1-6a Types of Advertising

Primary versus Selective Demand Stimulation

In primary demand stimulation, a company would be trying to create demand for an entire *product category*. **Primary demand stimulation** is challenging and costly, and research evidence suggests that it is likely to have an impact only for totally new products—not brand extensions or product categories that have been around a long time (known as mature products).

Direct- versus Delayed-Response Advertising

Another important type of advertising involves how quickly we want consumers to respond. **Direct-response advertising** asks consumers to act immediately. All those ads you see that suggest you "call this toll-free number" or "click here to order NOW" are examples of direct-response advertising. In most cases, direct-response advertising is used for products that consumers are familiar with, that do not require inspection at the point of purchase, and that are relatively low cost. However, the proliferation of toll-free numbers and websites or mobile marketing campaigns that provide detailed information and direct online ordering, coupled with the widespread use of credit cards and *mobile payment methods* like Apple Pay, have been a boon to direct response for higher-priced products as well.

Delayed-response advertising relies on imagery and message themes that emphasize the benefits and satisfying characteristics of a brand. Rather than trying to stimulate an immediate action from an audience, delayed-response advertising attempts to develop awareness and preference for a brand over time. In general, delayed-response advertising attempts to create brand awareness, reinforce the benefits of using a brand (that is, brand loyalty), develop a general liking for the brand, and create an image for a brand. When a consumer enters the purchase process, the information from delayed-response advertising comes into play. Most advertisements we see on television and in magazines are of the delayed-response type.

Corporate versus Brand Advertising

Corporate advertising is not designed to promote a specific brand but is meant to create a favorable attitude toward a company as a whole. Prominent users of corporate advertising include Apple, BP, and General Electric. **Brand advertising**, as we have seen throughout this chapter, communicates the specific features, values, and benefits of a particular brand marketed by a particular organization. By contrast, the firms that have long-established corporate campaigns have designed them to generate favorable public opinion toward the corporation as a whole. When shareholders see good corporate advertising, it instills confidence and, ideally, long-term commitment to the firm and its stock. We'll consider this type of advertising in detail in Chapter 18.

Another form of corporate advertising is carried out by members of a trade channel—mostly retailers. When corporate advertising takes place in a trade channel, it is referred to as **institutional advertising**. Retailers such as Ross, Target, and Old Navy advertise to persuade consumers to shop at their stores or buy on their websites. Although these retailers may feature a particular manufacturer's brand in the advertising (Nordstrom often features Clinique cosmetics, for example), the main purpose of the advertising is to attract shoppers. Sometimes Nordstrom uses its advertising and IBP to show appreciation to its customers, as shown in this holiday headline on the store's YouTube channel (see Exhibit 1.18).

1-6b The Economic Effects of Advertising

Advertising can have a powerful influence across the entire economic system of a country—the macro effects.

Source: Nordstrom, Inc.

Exhibit 1.18 ▶ At holiday time, Nordstrom thanks its customers on YouTube.

Advertising's Effect on Gross Domestic Product

Gross domestic product (GDP) is the measure of the total value of goods and services produced within an economic system. Earlier, we discussed advertising's role in the marketing mix. Recall that as advertising contributes to marketing mix strategy, it can contribute to sales along with the right product, the right price, and the right distribution. Because of this role, advertising is related to GDP in that it can contribute to levels of overall consumer demand when it helps introduce new products, such as alternative energy sources. As demand for these new products grows, this consumer spending fuels retail sales, housing starts, and corporate investment in finished goods and capital equipment—all part of a nation's GDP.[40]

Advertising's Effect on Competition

Can advertising stimulate competition, motivating firms to develop better products, better production methods, and other competitive advantages that benefit the economy as a whole? Certainly, when advertising serves as a way to enter new markets, competition across the economic system is fostered. However, advertising is not universally hailed as a way to stimulate competition. Critics point out that the amount of advertising dollars needed to compete effectively in many industries can act as a barrier to entry. In other words, a firm may have the capability to compete in an industry in every way *except* being unable to afford the advertising expense needed to really compete. Thus, some argue that advertising can decrease competition.

Advertising's Effect on Prices

One of the widely debated effects of advertising has to do with its impact on the prices consumers pay for products and services. Firms like GM and Procter & Gamble spend billions of dollars on advertising products and services. Would these products and services cost a lot less if firms did no advertising? Not necessarily.

First, across all industries, advertising costs incurred by firms range from about 2 percent of sales in the automobile and certain retail industries up to 20 percent of sales for luxury products like perfume. Remember that there is no consistent and predictable relationship between advertising spending and sales—it all depends on the product category, competition, size of market, and complexity of the message. Procter & Gamble, with total annual revenues of almost $65 billion, spends upward of $8 billion every year to advertise its diverse brands, which face fierce competition in the global marketplace.[41] P&G's advertising outlay is more than ten times that of Luxottica, the global maker and retailer of eyewear. Luxottica spends less than $700 million on advertising (and rings up more than $9 billion in annual revenue).[42] Different products and different market conditions demand that firms spend different amounts of money on advertising. These same conditions make it difficult to identify a predictable relationship between advertising and sales.

It is true that the cost of advertising is woven into product costs, which may be ultimately passed on to consumers. But this effect on price must be judged against a couple of cost savings that *lower* the price consumers pay. First, there is the reduced time and effort a consumer must spend in searching for a product or service. Second, economies of scale, as discussed earlier, have a direct impact on the cost of goods produced and then on prices. Recall that economies of scale serve to lower the cost of production by spreading fixed costs over a large number of units produced. This lower cost can be passed on to consumers in terms of lower prices, as firms search for competitive advantage with lower prices.

Advertising's Effect on Value

Value is the password for successful marketing. **Value**, in modern marketing and advertising, refers to a perception by consumers that a brand provides satisfaction beyond the cost incurred to obtain that brand. The value perspective of the modern consumer is based on wanting every purchase to be a "good deal." Value can be added to the consumption experience by advertising.

Advertising also affects a consumer's perception of value by contributing to the symbolic value and the social meaning of a brand. **Symbolic value** refers to what a product or service means to consumers in a nonliteral way. For example, branded clothing such as Lululemon, Ralph Lauren, or The North Face can symbolize self-concept for some consumers. In reality, all branded products rely to some extent on symbolic value; otherwise, they would not be brands but just unmarked commodities (like potatoes).

Social meaning refers to what a product or service means in a societal context. For example, social class is marked by any number of products, such as cars, beverages, and clothes, that are used and displayed to signify class membership. Often, the brand's connection to social class values addresses a need within consumers to move up in class.

Researchers have long argued that objects (brands included) are never just objects. They take on meaning from culture, society, and consumers.[43] It is important to remember that these meanings often become just as much a part of the brand as the physical features. Because advertising is an essential way in which the image of a brand is developed, it contributes directly to consumers' perception of the value of the brand. The more value consumers see in a brand, the more they are willing to pay to acquire the brand. If the image of a Gucci watch, a Toyota Prius, or a Four Seasons hotel is valued by consumers, then consumers will pay a premium to acquire that value.

LO 7

1-7 From Advertising to Integrated Marketing Communications to Integrated Brand Promotion

As we discussed at the beginning of your introduction to the world of advertising and IBP, it is important to recognize that advertising is only one of many promotional tools available to impress and persuade consumers. There is another distinction that is important for you to recognize as you embark on learning about advertising and IBP.

Beginning in about 1990, the concept of mixing various promotional tools was referred to as **integrated marketing communications (IMC)**. But as the discussions throughout this chapter have highlighted, the reality of promotional strategies in the 21st century demands that the emphasis on *communication* give way to an emphasis on the *brand*. Organizations of all types are not interested in merely communicating with potential and existing customers through advertising and promotion. They want to build brand awareness, identity, and preference through advertising and promotion.

Recall from the definition earlier in the chapter that IBP is the use of various communication tools, including advertising, in a coordinated manner to build and maintain brand awareness, identity, and preference. The distinction between IBP and IMC is that IBP is explicitly brand centric. IMC emphasizes the communication effort per se and the need for coordinated and synergistic messages. IBP retains the emphasis on coordination and synergy of communication but goes beyond the parameters of IMC. In IBP, the emphasis is on the brand and not just the communication. With a focus on building brand awareness, identity, and ultimately preference, the IBP perspective recognizes that coordinated promotional messages need to have both brand-building and communication effects.

The future of advertising and IBP is exciting. Content will be more personal and, ideally, more useful to target audiences. Onscreen ads will seem to "magically" appear for things you really

Google AdWords   SIGN IN   START NOW ▾

Home   How it Works   Pricing   Marketing Goals   Tools   Resources

Overview   **Search Ads**   Display Ads   Video Ads   App Ads

Be just a Google search away.

Search ads appear next to Google search results when people look for products and services you offer. And, you only pay when people click to visit your website or call your business.

▼◢ 📶 🔋 10:50

Google

🔍 Kids' furniture   🎤

WEB   APPS   IMAGES   VIDEOS   NEWS

Kids' Bunk Beds   ⓘ
Ad www.casakids.com

Custom kids room and furniture   📞
with stairs, desk, crib and storage.   Call

Source: Google

Exhibit 1.19 ▶ An overview of Google AdWords.

are interested in because you have previously searched online for them (*retargeting*). It is common with digital marketing and Web and mobile platforms for brands such as Nordstrom to employ retargeting ads based on previous online consumer behavior. Eyeballs and clicks represent money as advertising incorporates innovative pricing models based on bidding wars for key search words and cost-per-click models as well as those still based on more traditional measures like how many people were exposed to an ad. While we get deeper into digital and content marketing in Chapter 14, which covers digital and social media, Exhibit 1.19 introduces the concept by illustrating how Google AdWords operates.

The industry structure will also change, as you'll see in Chapter 2. Most change relates with technological advances. For instance, virtual agencies will be on the rise. Freelance work is going to be crowdsourced. Advertising revenue models are also in transition, as many must coexist with other business models such as subscriptions to digital services or online communities. Constants are that advertising and IBP, along with marketing, will continually change. A need for strategic and creative brand messaging, such as seen in the creative McDonald's ad in Exhibit 1.20 will also remain constant.

However the greatest constant in advertising and marketing is having a strong brand and brand strategy—hence the brand-centric nature of this book. As examples of strong (and global) brands, brands like Apple, Amazon, Google, Visa, McDonald's, and Mastercard have mastered the power of a strong and integrated brand[44]. Check out Kantar's top brands (Exhibit 1.21),

Real Good. M

Source: McDonald's

Exhibit 1.20 ▶ This is a creative example literally reminding us that french fries are potato products.

Kantar BrandZ Top 10 Most Valuable Global Brands 2021

Rank 2021	Brand	Brand Value 2021 ($Mil)	% Increase 2021 vs 2020
1	Amazon	683,852	64%
2	Apple	611,997	74%
3	Google	457,998	42%
4	Microsoft	410,271	26%
5	Tencent	240,931	60%
6	Facebook	226,744	54%
7	Alibaba	196,912	29%
8	Visa	191,285	2%
9	McDonald's	154,921	20%
10	MasterCard	112,876	4%

Exhibit 1.21 ▶ This list shows some of the top Global brands, as measured by Kantar Media. The first column shows the brand rank, then the brand, as well as the estimated brand valuation as of 202 in millions (US$). The last column is of note because it shows the percentage increase from the previous year (in other words, it suggests brand valuation growth). One thing these brands have in common is strong integrated brand promotion strategy.

and ask yourself what they have in common—and that seems to be strong products/services, global reach or accessibility such as through e-commerce, and of course powerful integrated brand promotion. For instance, Amazon, Apple, Google, Microsoft, Facebook, and Alibaba offer strong online services, wide accessibility via digital means, and an identifiable brand. Other brands on the list, such as Visa, McDonald's, and MasterCard are known for reliable products and services,

and their integrated brand promotion messaging reinforces the accessibility and reliability position. As can be seen in the table, the brands rankings are a function of the brand value (in millions) and also in consideration of any percentage increase from the previous year. Notice how some brands, such as Apple and Amazon had a massive increase in value, whereas other strong brands, such as Visa and MasterCard remained strong with more subtle brand valuation increases.

Summary

1. Describe the new world of advertising and integrated brand promotion (IBP).

The new world around advertising and IBP centers around the need for measuring these marketing tools and knowing that the lines among information, entertainment, networking, and commercial messages are blurring. The new world of advertising and IBP is also more digital, more interactive, and more social. Brands are integrating digital marketing and content marketing such as branded entertainment, social media, influencer marketing, and other communication techniques to reach consumers and get their brand integrated into consumers' lifestyles.

2. Define what advertising, advertising campaigns, and integrated brand promotion (IBP) are and what they can do.

Since advertising has become so pervasive, it would be reasonable to expect that you might have your own working definition for this critical term. But an informed perspective on advertising goes beyond what is obvious and can be seen daily. Advertising is distinctive and recognizable as a form of communication by its three essential elements: its paid sponsorship, its use of mass media, and its intent to persuade. An advertisement is a specific message that a company has placed to persuade an audience. An advertising campaign is a series of ads and other promotional efforts with a common theme also placed to persuade an audience over a specified period of time. Integrated brand promotion (IBP) is the use of many promotional tools, including advertising, in a coordinated manner to build and maintain brand awareness, identity, and preference.

3. Explain advertising as a communication process via a model of mass mediated communication.

Advertising cannot be effective unless some form of communication takes place between the company and the audience. But advertising is about mass communication. The model introduced in this chapter features basic considerations such as the message-production process versus the message-reception process, and this model says that consumers create their own meanings when they interpret advertisements. A message has a source, and the audience (consumer) accommodates and negotiates the message and its intent. The model includes encoding and decoding of the message, with meanings formed during the interplay with the individual person's comprehension of the content. Reception takes place in the context of potential interference such as clutter that might disturb the process.

4. Describe the different ways of classifying audiences for advertising and IBP.

Although it is possible to provide a simple and clear definition of what advertising is, it is also true that advertising takes many forms and serves different purposes from one application to another. One way to appreciate the complexity and diversity of advertising is to classify it by audience category or by geographic focus. For example, advertising might be directed at households or government officials. Using another perspective, it can be global or local in its focus.

5. Explain advertising as a business process.

Many different types of organizations use advertising to achieve their business purposes. For major multinational corporations, such as Procter & Gamble, and for smaller, more localized businesses, such as the San Diego Zoo, advertising is one part of a critical business process known as marketing. Advertising is one element of the promotional piece of the marketing mix; the other key elements are the firm's products, their prices, and the distribution network. Advertising must work in conjunction with these other marketing mix elements if the organization's marketing objectives are to be achieved. It is important to recognize that of all the roles played by advertising in the marketing process, none is more important than contributing to building brand awareness and brand equity. Similarly, firms have turned to more diverse methods of communication beyond advertising that we have referred to as IBP. That is, firms are using communication tools such as public relations, sponsorship, direct marketing, and sales promotion along with advertising to achieve communication goals. Organizations also use advertising and IBP as part of their plans for purpose-driven marketing.

6. Identify the various types of advertising and the economic effects of advertising.

There are six fundamental types of advertising described in contrasting pairs:

a. Primary versus selective demand stimulation: Primary demand stimulation is the attempt to stimulate demand for an entire product category. Selective demand stimulation is the attempt to stimulate demand for a particular brand within a product category. Advertising is not powerful enough to stimulate demand for a product category—only broad influences like demographics, cultural values, or technology can stimulate primary demand. Selective demand is what advertising does and can be very effective for building brand awareness and preference.

b. Direct-response versus delayed-response advertising: Direct-response advertising asks consumers to act immediately upon receipt of the advertising message. Delayed-response advertising develops awareness, preference, and an image for a brand that takes much longer to affect consumer choice.

c. Corporate versus brand advertising: Corporate advertising features an entire corporation rather than focusing on any one brand marketed by that corporation.

The economic effects of advertising are the macro effects of advertising on GDP, competition, prices, and value. In short, advertising and IBP are very important drivers of the economy.

7. Identify the evolution from advertising to integrated marketing communications to IBP.

Advertising originated first as a mass-mediated attempt to inform, persuade, or remind consumers about a product or service. Then, the term IMC emerged to show the importance of integrating a variety of marketing tools. In modern times, now the role of the brand is more prominent, and hence the more new-age shift to IBP that puts the brand front and center.

Key Terms

accommodation	audience	brand extension (variant)
advertisement	brand	brand loyalty
advertising	brand advertising	chief marketing officer
advertising campaign	brand equity	client, or sponsor

cooperative advertising, or co-op
   advertising
corporate advertising
delayed-response advertising
demographics
differentiation
direct-response advertising
economies of scale
external position
global advertising
government officials and employees
gross domestic product (GDP)
household consumers
inelasticity of demand
institutional advertising

integrated brand promotion (IBP)
integrated marketing communications
   (IMC)
internal position
international advertising
local advertising
marketing
marketing mix
market segmentation
members of a trade channel
members of business organizations
mobile marketing
national advertising
negotiation
positioning

primary demand stimulation
professionals
psychographics
purpose-driven marketing
regional advertising
repositioning
selective demand stimulation
social meaning
source
symbolic value
target audience
trade journals
value

Endnotes

1. For more about the synergistic effect of advertising and IBP, see Rajeev Batra and Kevin Lane Keller, "Integrating Marketing Communications: New Findings, New Lessons, and New Ideas," *Journal of Marketing* 80, no. 6 (November 2016), 122–145; and Rodrigo Uribe, "Separate and Joint Effects of Advertising and Placement," *Journal of Business Research* 69, no. 2 (2016), 459–465; and "Number of Mobile Users in The United States From 2011 to 2020," *Statista*, July, 2020, https://www.statista.com/statistics/455601/digital-game-users-category-digital-market-outlook-usa/

2. German Zenetti and Daniel Klapper, "Advertising Effects Under Consumer Heterogeneity—the Moderating Role of Brand Experience, Advertising Recall and Attitude," *Journal of Retailing* 92, no. 3 (September 2016), 352–372; and Gita Venkataramani Johar, "Mistaken Inferences from Advertising Conversations: A Modest Research Agenda," *Journal of Advertising* 45, no. 3 (2016), 318–325.

3. Tathagata Ghosh, "Winning Versus Not Losing: Exploring the Effects of In-Game Advertising Outcome on Its Effectiveness," *Journal of Interactive Marketing* 36 (2016), 134–147; and *Statista*, (2020); and "Number of Mobile Game Users in The United States From 2011 to 2020," https://www.statista.com/statistics/455601/digital-game-users-category-digital-market-outlook-usa/

4. V. Kumar and Shaphali Gupta, "Conceptualizing the Evolution and Future of Advertising," *Journal of Advertising* 45, no. 3 (2016), 302–317; and Jisu Huh, "Comment: Advertising Won't Die, But Defining It Will Continue to Be Challenging," *Journal of Advertising* 45, no. 3 (2016), 356–358.

5. Shiri Melumad and Michael Tuan Pham, "The Smartphone as Pacifying Technology," *Journal of Consumer Research* 47, no. 2, (2020); and Shelly Rodgers, "Themed Issue Introduction: Promises and Perils of Artificial Intelligence and Advertising," *Journal of Advertising* 50, no. 1, 22 Feb. 2021, 1–10.

6. Micael Dahlen and Sara Rosengren, "If Advertising Won't Die, What Will It Be? Toward a Working Definition of Advertising," *Journal of Advertising* 45, no. 3 (2016), 334–345.

7. Tom Huddleston Jr., "Fiat's New Google-Branded Cars Let You Talk to Your Car Remotely with 'Hey Google'— Take a Look" *CNBC Make It*, April 3, 2021, https://www.cnbc.com/2021/04/03/photos-see-fiats-hey-google-family-of-cars-with-voice-assistant.html; and Good Car Bad Car, "Cadillac US Sales Figures," https://www.goodcarbadcar.net/cadillac-us-sales-figures/#share; and Arjun Kharpal, "We're Better at Car Tech Than Silicon Valley: Cadillac President," CNBC, November 8, 2016, http://www.cnbc.com/2016/11/08/were-better-at-car-tech-than-silicon-valley-cadillac-president.html; and Hannah Keshishian, "Luxury Vehicles-US-March 2021," *Mintel*, March 2021, https://reports-mintel-com.proxy.library.vcu.edu/display/1044729/?fromSearch=%3Ffreetext%3DCADILLAC%26sortBy%3Drecent#

8. Marc Pritchard, "Half my *Digital* Advertising is Wasted...," *Journal of Marketing* 85, no. 1, (2021), 26–29.

9. For more about the importance of integration and promotion, see Kevin Lane Keller, "Unlocking the Power of Integrated Marketing Communications: How Integrated Is Your IMC Program?" *Journal of Advertising* 45, no. 3 (2016), 286–301.

10. Linda Zavoral, "Popeyes Throws Shade at McDonalds New Crispy Chicken Campaign," The Mercury News, February 18, 2021, https://www.mercurynews.com/2021/02/18/popeyes-throws-shade-at-mcdonalds-new-crispy-chicken-campaign-and-gives-out-free-sandwiches/.

11. "How Many Ads Do You See Each Day?" *GradSchools* 2020, https://www.gradschools.com/degree-guide/how-many-ads-do-you-see-each-day.

12. Azzouz Essamiri, Sally McKechnie, and Heidi Winklhofer, "Co-Creating Corporate Brand Identity with Online Brand Communities," *Journal of Business Research* 96 (March 2019), 366-375

13. U.S. Census Bureau, "Quick Facts," 2019 population estimate, https://www.census.gov/quickfacts/table/PST045215/00.

14. Christopher Heine, "IBM Watson Is Now Offering AI-Powered Digital Ads That Answer Consumers' Questions," *Adweek*, June 2, 2016, http://www.adweek.com/news/technology/ibm-watson-now-offering-ai-powered-digital-ads-answer-consumers-questions-171783; and Natalie Zmuda, "IBM Uses U.S. Open to Debut TV Ads Targeting CMOs," *AdAge*, August 27, 2012, https://adage.com/article/cmo-strategy/ibm-u-s-open-debut-tv-ads-targeting-cmos/236845.

15. Ruiliang Yan, Zixia Cao, and Zhi Pei, "Manufacturer's Cooperative Advertising, Demand Uncertainty, and Information Sharing," *Journal of Business Research* 69, no. 2 (2016), 709–717.

16. This definition of marketing was approved in 2013 by the American Marketing Association (www.ama.org).

17. Jeremy Mullman, "Under Armour Can't Live Up to Own Hype," *Advertising Age,* November 2, 2009, 3, 51.

18. Peter D. Bennett, *Dictionary of Marketing Terms,* 2nd ed. (Chicago: American Marketing Association, 1995), 4.

19. "Your Brand is Your Greatest Asset." Forbes, February 20, 2020, https://www.forbes.com/sites/forbesagencycouncil/2020/02/24/your-brand-is-your-greatest-asset/?sh=6542d7fb63b7.

20. Data drawn from "Coca-Cola's Brand Value From 2006-2020," *Statista*, January 14, 2021, https://www.statista.com/statistics/326065/coca-cola-brand; and Azzouz Essamiri, Sally McKechnie, and Heidi Winklhofer, "Co-Creating Corporate Brand Identity with Online Brand Communities," *Journal of Business Research* 96 (March 2019), 366–375.

21. Nina Goetzen, "Ad Revenues for AVOD streaming services Grew By Almost A Third In Q2," *Business Insider*, August 17, 2020, https://www.businessinsider.com/ad-supported-streaming-services-were-bright-spot-in-q2-2020-8; and Sahil Patel, "NBC's Peacock Enlists Advertisers and Cable Companies In Marketing Push," *The Wall Street Journal*, January 16, 2020, https://www.wsj.com/articles/nbcs-peacock-enlists-advertisers-and-cable-companies-in-marketing-push-11579208400.

22. Douglas W. Vorhies, "Brand Extension Helps Parent Gain Influence," *Marketing News,* January 20, 2003, 25. This concept was verified in academic research as well. See Franziska Volckner and Henrik Sattler, "Drivers of Brand Extension Success," *Journal of Marketing* 70 (April 2006), 18–34.

23. David A. Aaker, *Managing Brand Equity* (New York: The Free Press, 1991), 15.

24. Kevin L. Keller, "Conceptualizing, Measuring, and Managing Customer-Based Brand Equity," *Journal of Marketing* 57 (January 1993), 4; and Streedhar Madhavaram, Vishag Badrinarayanan, and Robert E. McDonald, "Integrated Marketing Communication (IMC) and Brand Identity as Critical Components of Brand Equity Strategy," *Journal of Advertising* 34, no. 4 (Winter 2005), 69–80.

25. Marc Bain, "Nike's New Store in New York Is Like Legoland for People Who Love Sports," *Quartz,* November 14, 2016, http://qz.com/836671/nikes-new-store-in-new-york-has-a-basketball-court-where-you-can-test-drive-their-shoes/.

26. Beth Snyder Bulik, "The Company You Keep," *Sales & Marketing Management,* November 2003, 14.

27. Franziska Volckner and Henrik Sattler, "Drivers of Brand Extension Success," *Journal of Marketing* 70 (April 2006), 18–34.

28. Jiapeng Liu, Wei Huang, Xiuwu Liao, and Xianzhao Liao, "Market Segmentation: a Multiple Criteria Approach Combining Preference Analysis and Segmentation Decision," *Omega* 83, March 2019, 1–13.

29. Terry Troy, "Ford F-Series Super Duty Named 'Official Truck of the NFL,'" *Cleveland.com,* September 14, 2016, http://www.cleveland.com/automotive/plaindealer/index.ssf/2016/09/ford_f-series_super_duty_named_official_truck_of_the_nfl.html; "Best Integrated Campaign: Ford 'By Design,'" *MediaPost,* March 10, 2016, http://www.mediapost.com/publications/article/270991/best-integrated-campaign-ford-by-design.html.

30. Dan Eaton, "Acura NSX: The Most Expensive Car Made in the USA Coming Out of Ohio," *Columbus Business First,* March 17, 2016, http://www.bizjournals.com/columbus/news/2016/03/17/acura-nsx-the-most-expensive-car-made-in-the-usa.html; and "2021 Nissan Versa" Nissan, 2021 https://www.nissanusa.com/vehicles/cars/versa-sedan.html.

31. Laura Ries, "Repositioning 'Positioning': The Best Way into a Consumer's Mind Is Not with Verbal Nails, but with a Visual Hammer," *Advertising Age,* March 12, 2012, 12–13.

32. Peter F. Drucker, *People and Performance: The Best of Peter Drucker* (New York: HarperCollins, 1997), 90.

33. Claes Fornell, Forrest V. Morgeson III, and G. Tomas M. Hult, "An Abnormally Abnormal Intangible: Stock Returns on Customer Satisfaction," *Journal of Marketing* 80, no. 5 (2016), 122–125.

34. The research study is reported in Robert G. Docters, Michael R. Reopel, Jeanne-Mey Sun, and Stephen M. Tanney, *Winning the Profit Game: Smarter Pricing, Smarter Branding* (New York: McGraw-Hill, 2004); information on Hermes is from "Hermes International (RMS)" *Market Screener*, December 2020, https://www.marketscreener.com/quote/stock/HERMES-INTERNATIONAL-4657/financials/.

35. Bryan Usrey, et al. "How Downplaying Product Greenness Affects Performance Evaluations: Examining the Effects of Implicit and Explicit Green Signals in Advertising," *Journal of Advertising* 49, no. 2, 6 February 2020, 125–140.

36. Bonnie Simpson, et al. "Making the World a Better Place: How Crowdfunding Increases Consumer Demand for Social-Good Products," *Journal of Marketing Research* 58, no. 2, 22 December 2020, 363 376.

37. Nicola Kemp, "Unilever's Keith Weed: Brands with Purpose Deliver Growth," *Campaign Live (UK),* April 27, 2015, http://www.campaignlive.co.uk/article/1344079/unilevers-keith-weed-brands-purpose-deliver-growth; and Terry Slavin, "Nestlé, Unilever, FedEx, and WBCSD on Finding Profit in Social Purpose," *Ethical Corporation,* October 31, 2016, http://www.ethicalcorp.com/nestle-unilever-fedex-and-wbcsd-finding-profit-social-purpose.

38. Ian Berry and Kelsey Gee, "The U.S. Milk Business Is in 'Crisis,'" *Wall Street Journal,* December 11, 2012, B1; and Kirk Kardashian, "The End of Got Milk?" *The New Yorker*, February 28, 2014, https://www.newyorker.com/business/currency/the-end-of-got-milk

39. Kevin Pang, "Milk Jumps Onto the Small-Batch Bandwagon," *New York Times,* April 12, 2016, http://www.nytimes.com/2016/04/13/dining/milk-dairy-locavore.html?_r=0.

40. There are several highly sophisticated historical treatments of how advertising is related to demand and overall GDP. See, for example, Neil H. Borden, *The Economic Effects of Advertising* (Chicago: Richard D. Irwin, 1942), 187–189; and John Kenneth Galbraith, *The New Industrial State* (Boston: Houghton Mifflin, 1967), 203–207.

41. Barrett J. Brunsman, "P&G Reclaims Role as World's Largest Advertiser," *Cincinnati Business Courier,* December 30, 2019, https://www.bizjournals.com/cincinnati/news/2019/12/30/p-g-reclaims-role-as-world-s-largest-advertiser.html

42. Tugba Sabanoglu, "Global Revenues of Luxottica From 2007 to 2020," *Statista,* May 11, 2021, https://www.statista.com/statistics/241567/global-net-sales-of-luxottica/; and "Luxottica Annual Report 2018," *Luxottica*, March 26, 2019, https://www.luxottica.com/sites/luxottica.com/files/luxottica_group_relazione_finanziaria_annuale_2018_eng_20190410.pdf

43. For a historical perspective on culture, consumers, and the meaning of goods, see Ernest Ditcher, *Handbook of Consumer Motivations* (New York: McGraw-Hill, 1964), 6. For a more contemporary view, see David Glen Mick and Claus Buhl, "A Meaning-Based Model of Advertising Experiences," *Journal of Consumer Research* 19 (December 1992), 312–338.

44. Kantar Media, "What are the Most Valuable Global Brands in 2021?", June 20, 2021, https://www.kantar.com/inspiration/brands/what-are-the-most-valuable-global-brands-in-2021.

Chapter 2

The Structure of the Advertising and Promotion Industry: Advertisers, Agencies, Media, and Support Organizations

Learning Objectives

After reading and thinking about this chapter, you will be able to do the following:

1 Identify how the advertising industry is in constant transition.

2 Discuss five broad trends transforming the advertising and promotion industry.

3 Describe the advertising and promotion industry's size, structure, and participants.

4 Discuss the role played by advertising and promotion agencies/consolidated agency networks, the services provided by these agencies, and how the agencies are compensated.

5 Identify key external facilitators who assist in planning and executing advertising and integrated brand promotion campaigns.

6 Discuss the role played by media organizations in executing effective advertising and integrated brand promotion campaigns.

CSA-Printstock/DigitalVision Vectors/Getty Images

LO 1

2-1 The Advertising Industry in Constant Transition

The framework for this chapter (see Exhibit 2.1) examines several key dimensions of the advertising and promotion industry, including its dynamic nature, the broad trends that directly impact it, and its unique scope and structure. To help illuminate the most current state of the advertising industry, which was understandably volatile during the COVID-19 pandemic, consider these very telling statistics from the 2021 Ad Age Datacenter that show advertising is on the rebound—largely due to digital.[1]

- Global advertising revenue will rise by more than 10 percent to $651 billion in 2021 (after falling 4.1 percent in 2020 during the COVID pandemic).

Exhibit 2.1 ▶ The framework of this chapter diagram shows now that the World of Advertising Overview is complete, we are focusing on the industry's structure. There are two perspectives. One is industry transition and trends. The other perspective is industry scope and structure.

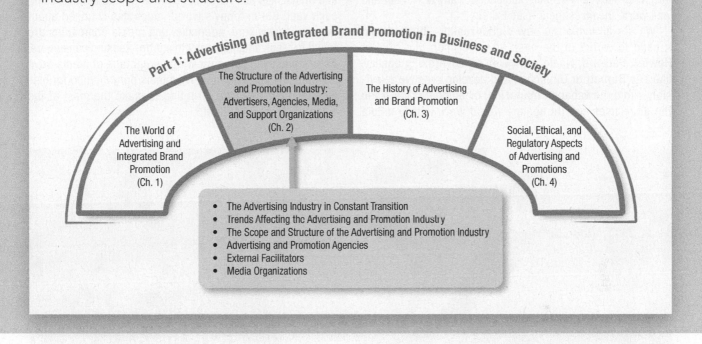

- Advertising spending in the United States will rise by at least 3 percent, to $237 billion, in 2021 (after experiencing a 5.4 percent drop in 2020).

- Worldwide advertising revenue for digital media companies, including Google and Facebook, will rise by more than 14 percent to $397 billion in 2021.

- 61 percent of global ad revenue will be in digital.

- Digital ad spending in the United States will grow by 9.6 percent to $136 billion in 2021, with the Internet capturing 58 percent of U.S. advertising dollars.

- Globally, 114 marketers spent more than $1 billion on global advertising.

- In the United States, 47 marketers spent more than $1 billion on their domestic advertising spending.

- The world's biggest advertiser is Amazon; they spent $11 billion in ad and promotion spending worldwide in 2019 (latest available data).

- The United States' biggest advertiser is also Amazon; of their $11 billion ad/promotion spend, $6.9 billion was for campaigns in the United States in 2019 (latest available data).

Now, let's consider how the advertising industry is both changing and needs to remain flexible. There have always been power struggles in this space: brand versus brand, one agency competing against another, agency versus media company, big advertiser with lots of money versus big retailer with lots of money. But those old-style power struggles are child's play compared with the 21st-century tensions. Consumers are tired of the barrage of ads on every screen, in every store, in every inbox; and they are actively looking for ways to avoid most of them. So the power struggle now is focused on how the advertising industry can successfully adapt to the new technologies that consumers are willing and, in many cases, eager to use as they seek more control over their information environment.[2] The solution, in part, seems to be that advertisers must integrate advertising investments more into targeted digital media, online advertising, social media, and mobile marketing—and synergize the social media and digital content with appropriate traditional mass media like television, magazines, and radio.

Consumers are discovering technologies and media options that give them more control over the communications they see and hear. From Facebook and Twitter to TikTok and specialty websites, consumers are seeking out information ecosystems, with digital and mobile information access, where *they* control their exposure to information rather than an advertiser or media company being in control. And the effects are widespread. Back in 2009, advertising in traditional media plunged by nearly 15 percent, with most advertisers surveyed saying they shifted more than 70 percent of their savings from traditional media to digital alternatives, including social network media and online advertising.[3]

Today, U.S. advertisers are continuing to increase their use of digital media, including online display ads, paid search ads, branded video content, social media ads, and mobile marketing. Why? Because digital media are attracting and engaging ever-growing audiences, increasing efficiency and providing better possibilities for target marketing and retargeting customers who may have searched for a product, service, or brand online.[4] Qatar Airways, whose Facebook followers increased by 4 million during the pandemic, says it can reach 26 million Facebook users through careful targeting—that's a sizeable audience for any advertiser and well worth the investment[5] (see Exhibit 2.2).

We are all living the new digital reality—but how did it used to work? In the past, an advertiser, like Nike or Hewlett-Packard, would work with an advertising agency, like Leo Burnett or Omnicom, and develop creative television, radio, newspaper, magazine, or billboard ads. Then the advertiser and its agency would work with a media

company, like NBC television or Hearst newspapers, and buy time or space to place the ad so that you, as the consumer, would see it when you watched television or read a newspaper. This still happens. Major media like television, radio, and magazines still rake in billions of dollars in advertising each year. But in today's world, much has changed about the way advertisers, agencies, and media companies are trying to reach and engage with control-seeking consumers. As just one example, a growing percentage of media buys are made by software-driven systems programmed for pinpointed, cost-effective targeting to make the most of the advertiser's media budget.[6]

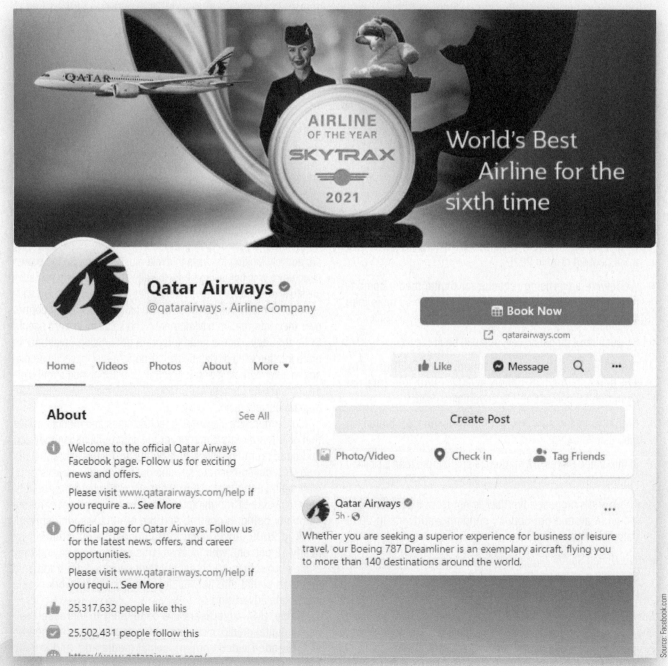

Exhibit 2.2 ▶ As seen in this screenshot of the Qatar Airways Facebook page, more than 25 million consumers digitally engage with the company.

Let's explore the industry structure from the consumer's perspective first. With the large number of digital media options available for news, information, and entertainment, "media fragmentation" is a boon to consumers and a huge headache for advertisers and their advertising agencies. The new generation of consumers, many of whom have multiple streaming subscriptions, is behaving very differently from the cable-TV generation that preceded it. Today's consumers are insisting on the convenience and appeal of a laptop, tablet computer, smartphone, or various on-demand streaming media services.

There is some irony in the control that consumers are starting to exert, however. Even though the traditional structure of the advertising and media industry may be changed forever, the *goal* of that old traditional structure remains the same—the brand and its value proposition still need to be highlighted with persuasive communications.[7] In fact, the change in consumer orientation and the myriad of available media choices have made the combination of advertising and integrated brand promotion even *more* important as consumers choose which persuasive messages or content they want to be exposed to and where/when they want to access and engage with them.[8]

The pace and complexity of the changes happening today are resulting in challenges more significant than anything the industry has ever faced. This chapter examines the structure in the industry and all the "players" that are creating and being affected by the changes and trends over time. Remember that the fundamental *process* of advertising and promotion and the role they play in organizations remains the same: persuasive communications directed at target audiences—no matter what is happening with technology, economic conditions, society, or business philosophies. Later in the chapter, we will turn our attention to understanding how advertising and other promotional tools are managed in the communications industry. Along the way, we'll consider the different participants in the process, particularly advertisers and their advertising and promotion agencies.

LO**2**

2-2 Trends Affecting the Advertising and Promotion Industry

Many of the trends affecting the advertising and promotion industry have to do with new technologies and how their application has changed the structure and the very nature of the way communications occur. Other trends have to do

with consumer culture and what sort of communication makes sense to today's consumers. But in the end, what is important is the critical need to focus on the brand, its image, its value proposition, and a persuasive, integrated presentation of that brand to the target market.

Let's consider five broad trends in the marketplace that directly impact the advertising and promotion industry.

2-2a Consumer Control: Social Media, On-Demand Streaming, and Cutting the Cord

As featured at the outset of the chapter, consumers are now in greater control of the information they receive about product categories and brands—making this the top trend on our list. Collectively, individuals sharing and creating content through social media and video sites like YouTube are referred to as Web 2.0—the second generation of Web-based use and services that emphasize online collaboration and sharing among users. Consider how YouTube, for example, also has ads; you may be enjoying watching video content but in between videos you may be delivered ads (see Exhibit 2.3). Web 3.0 (largely focused on artificial intelligence and machine learning) is still in its infancy and will manifest itself more fully when computers, tablets, and smartphones have the ability to understand and interpret digital data as quickly and accurately as humans can.

One indicator of Web 2.0 is when consumers log on to the Internet and visit sites *they* choose to visit for either information or shopping. **Social media**, those highly accessible Web-based media that allow the sharing of information between individuals and between individuals and groups (like TikTok, Pinterest, Instagram, Snapchat, Facebook, YouTube, and Yelp), have emerged as the most significant form of consumer control over information creation and communication. You will examine the breadth and intensity of use of social media in Chapter 14, "Media Planning: Advertising and IBP in Digital, Social, and Mobile Media;" but for now, it is important to have a perspective on the digital side of advertising and communications and the power of these communications to make an impression and influence consumer behavior.[9]

Exhibit 2.3 ▶ YouTube generates significant revenue with ads. See the top content in the screenshot of YouTube—that one is an ad.

Almost 2.8 billion users worldwide log on to Facebook every month, 1 billion log on to Instagram every month, and 700 million users log on to TikTok.[10] You can be sure the next new thing in social media is being developed at this very minute; and it will gain users quickly, although how long it will remain popular is anyone's guess. Meanwhile, even though firms are not always *exactly* sure of the value and impact of engaging consumers through current and emerging social media sites, no firm wants to be absent from the digital scene. General Motors tested advertising on Facebook for a while, stopped advertising there for several years, and is once again using the site to reach millions of users with integrated promotions. As one example, it video-streamed the product introduction of its Chevy Bolt EV via Facebook Live.[11]

Another way consumers control their information is through blogs. **Blogs**, websites frequented by individuals with common interests where they can post facts, opinions, and personal experiences, have emerged as sophisticated (although typically not very objective) sources of product and brand information. Once criticized as the "ephemeral scribble" of 13-year-old girls and the babble of techno-geeks, blogs are gaining greater recognition and organization with two-thirds of U.S. Internet users reading blogs on a regular basis. Web-based service firms like WordPress are making blogs easier to create, use, and make accessible to the masses. Advertisers should pay attention not only to the popularity of social media sites and blogs but also to the power of their communications. Research has shown that such "word-of-mouth" communication among consumers results in longer lasting brand impressions and stronger **new customer acquisition** than traditional marketing efforts.[12]

Another example of increasing consumer control is the growth in use of on-demand streaming services like Hulu, Netflix, Disney +, and Amazon Prime. Consumers want to watch programs at *their* convenience, sometimes with the option of skipping commercials. According to one study, almost 60 percent of all U.S. households are not paying for TV access—many of these have "cut the cord" by using entertainment-streaming sites as a substitute for cable TV. This trend is sending advertisers, agencies, and media firms back to the drawing board to adapt to a world in which consumers have control over the information they choose to receive and when they choose to receive it.[13]

How will the advertising industry adapt? Creativity is one answer. The more entertaining and informative an ad is, the more likely consumers will want to watch it. Another technique, less creative but certainly effective, is to run advertising messages along the bottom of the programming screen.[14] This way, even the ad-skipping streaming users must see messages since they are embedded in the broadcast. In fact, the concept of what is considered "advertising" is already evolving in this new environment.[15]

2-2b Media Proliferation, Consolidation, and "Multiplatform" Media Organizations

At another level of the industry, the media level, proliferation and consolidation have been taking place simultaneously. The exponential growth of cable television channels, direct marketing technology, Web options, and alternative media (mobile marketing, for example) have created a visible explosion of media possibilities. Diversity of media options and the advertising dollars they can attract has always been a driving force for many media companies.

Media companies of all types tend to pursue more and more "properties" if they are allowed to legally, thus creating "multiplatform" media organizations.[16] Consider Walt Disney Co., which owns the ABC broadcasting network and the ESPN cable network group, plus multiple other cable TV stations, radio stations, websites, video-on-demand operations, TV and movie studios, digital game operations, plus books, comic books, and magazines. Brand integration is key to Disney's success. You name a medium, and Disney uses it to reach audiences, generating $58 billion in worldwide revenue in the process.[17]

Not to be outdone, the Web has its own media conglomerates. InterActiveCorp (IAC) has amassed a media empire of Internet sites that are as diverse as they are successful. IAC is an Internet conglomerate with a grab bag of online offerings, including search engine Ask.com, dating service Match.com, and various start-ups and smaller properties. Together, these sites generate about $3 billion in worldwide revenue. Other Internet giants like Alphabet, parent of Google, are even bigger at about $182.5 billion in worldwide revenue and even more diversified with all sorts of systems (Chrome), entertainment (YouTube), and service sites (like Blogger).[18] One commercial service offered by Google is DoubleClick, which provides advertisers and agencies with services designed to simplify complex online campaigns using a proprietary digital ad management platform.

The point is that media companies, to effectively "cover all the bases" in reaching audiences, have been wheeling and dealing to engage consumers in as many ways as possible, from traditional media—broadcast television, newspapers, radio, and magazines—to cable and satellite broadcast and all forms of Internet-based and mobile communication.

2-2c Media Clutter and Fragmentation Means More IBP

Even though the media and agency levels of the industry may be consolidating into fewer and fewer large firms, this does not mean that there are fewer media options. Quite the contrary is true. There are *more* ways to try to reach consumers than ever before. In 1994, the consumer had access to about 27 television channels. Today, the average U.S. household has access to more than 175 channels—yet each household tends to watch only 12 of them.[19] In 1995, it took three well-placed TV spots to reach 80 percent of women television viewers! Today, it takes multiple times more spots across a variety of media to achieve the same effect.

From television ads to virtual billboards to banner ads on the Internet to advertising messages in podcasts, new and increased media options have resulted in so much clutter that the probability of any one advertisement breaking through and making a real difference continues to diminish. Promotion options such as online communication, brand placement in film and television, point-of-purchase displays, and sponsorships are becoming increasingly attractive to advertisers.[20] For example, advertisers during the Super Bowl, notorious for its clutter and stratospheric ad prices ($5.5 million for a 30-second spot), have turned instead to promotional tie-ins to enhance the effect of the advertising. To combat the clutter and expense at one Super Bowl, Miller Brewing distributed thousands of inflatable Miller Lite chairs by game day. The chairs were a tie-in with a national advertising campaign that began during the regular season before the Super Bowl. Integrated promotion is the key to making an impact, as advertisers look beyond the 100+ million Super Bowl viewers to break through clutter, generate buzz, and increase involvement through tactics like encouraging viral sharing and using campaign hashtags in social media conversations.[21]

Given the backlash against advertising that clutter can cause and the trends in consumers' use of media, advertisers and their agencies are rethinking the way they try to communicate with consumers, with digital buys on the rise.[22] Advertisers are shifting spending out of traditional media and are looking to the full complement of integrated promotional opportunities in sales promotions (like the Miller chairs), event sponsorships, new media options, and public relations as means to support and enhance the primary advertising effort for brands. Advertisers like Mountain Dew and Toyota are also incorporating costly new technologies like **virtual reality**, because the novelty can help break through clutter

and attract consumer interest in an integrated promotional campaign.[23] Advertisers are also pursuing product/brand placements and advertising in digital games to engage consumers and reinforce brand recall.[24]

2-2d Crowdsourcing

Crowdsourcing (and the related concept of user-generated content) involves the online distribution of certain tasks to groups (crowds) of experts, enthusiasts, or even consumers.[25] Glossier's Milk Jelly product is the result of the company's founder asking customers via her blog to imagine their dream face wash. Starbucks' "My Starbucks Idea" asks Starbucks customers to recommend new products and services for Starbucks outlets (see Exhibit 2.4). The strategy behind crowdsourcing is to get consumers more involved with and committed to a brand in a way that passive, intrusive advertising simply cannot. Consumers help "build the brand" with recommendations for features or even advertising campaign images. They also can communicate about the brand to audiences in ways that seem natural and credible—something corporate-launched advertising sometimes struggles with. Just as important, products identified as crowdsourced tend to do better in the marketplace, because consumers perceive that these products will effectively address their needs.[26]

The frozen food company McCain has used crowdsourced videos to create timely commercials with authentic emotional appeal. Every day for a week, the brand invited UK consumers to submit short videos of their families enjoying dinner that evening. Within two hours, McCain and its UK agency, Adam & Eve/DDB, edited clips from the videos into one commercial that aired later the same day. This crowdsourcing effort generated buzz not only because it involved consumers and

Exhibit 2.4 ▶ As an example of crowdsourcing via social media, Starbucks launched more than 300 ideas for products and services from concepts originally submitted by consumers.

Source: Starbucks

reflected familiar, warm-hearted situations but also because of the whirlwind of production needed to edit the videos into a cohesive commercial within a matter of hours.[27]

2-2e Mobile Marketing/ Mobile Media

Technology has created significant opportunities for advertisers to reach their target audiences with messages directed to consumers' mobile devices—primarily smartphones and tablets like Apple's iPad and Microsoft's Surface. To develop relevant messages for appropriate audiences, advertisers and agencies must have a true understanding of consumer behavior, the technologies preferred by consumers, and the context in which messages are received and interpreted.[28] Consumers are so intent on controlling the information flow that 22 percent of mobile users worldwide have installed ad blockers to screen out ads, posing a challenge to advertisers seeking to reach this audience.[29] As you can see, it is important for advertisers to ask permission to send messages to mobile devices, to avoid appearing intrusive and running counter to consumers' desires for information control. Even then, overt sales messages may not be well received, so advertisers must understand how to appeal to digital audiences. "If we misstep with certain audiences, they'll unplug," notes eBay's chief marketing officer.[30]

Still, knowing how much time consumers spend with their mobile devices, for everything from communications and driving directions to price comparisons and purchases, it's not surprising that advertisers are eager to jump on board. Investments in mobile advertisement worldwide is forecasted to exceed $240 billion annually by the end of 2022. Some experts, in fact, argue that advertisers are not yet investing enough in mobile media.[31] And the amount invested in mobile advertising is expected to continue increasing year after year. Advertisers are trying **branded apps**, placing advertising inside message apps widely adopted by consumers, and testing creative content such as branded games and entertainment that can be accessed via mobile devices in hopes of digital engagement. For example, Mondelez International, maker of Oreos and other branded snacks, offers branded mobile game apps and branded video content for digital engagement. "Consumers are consuming more media in more places than ever before, and it's more difficult than ever to reach them," explains Mondelez's global head of content and media monetization. "The audience is in the driver's seat choosing when, how, and where to watch content."[32]

For decades to come, these trends, new technology, and the changes they bring will force advertisers to think differently about advertising and IBP. Similarly, advertising agencies and media firms will need to think about the way they serve their clients and the way communications are delivered to audiences. The goal of creating effective communication remains intact—attract attention and develop preference for a brand—and so the dynamics of the communications environment just

discussed all directly impact that overall goal. Mondelez, for example, doesn't want to simply advertise: It wants to make money from as much as 10 percent of its promotional investments by packaging branded entertainment content for wider audiences via media partners like Fox.[33]

2-3 The Scope and Structure of the Advertising and Promotion Industry

To fully appreciate the structure of the advertising and promotion industry, let's first consider its absolute size. The advertising industry is huge: worldwide, nearly $580 billion is spent on various categories of advertising. Spending on other forms of IBP is no less impressive. Spending on all forms of IBP worldwide, including advertising, exceeds a trillion dollars a year.[34] The combined ad spending of the top ten U.S. advertisers alone—including corporate giants like Procter & Gamble and Ford—exceeds $32 billion annually.[35] Another perspective on the scope of advertising and promotion is the amount spent on advertising by individual firms. Hundreds of millions of dollars a year and, in the case of the largest spenders, billions of dollars a year is a huge amount of money to invest in advertising. But remember that the $2.95 billion spent by General Motors on advertising is only a small fraction of GM's annual sales. Similarly, Ford spends $2.5 billion yearly, which represents a sliver of its overall sales revenues.[36] So even though the absolute dollars seem huge, the relative spending is often much more modest.

2-3a Structure of the Advertising and Promotion Industry

Beyond the scope of spending, the *structure* of the industry is really the key issue. When we understand how the advertising and promotion industry works, we know *who* does *what*, *in what order*, during the process. The industry is a collection of a wide range of talented people, all of whom have special expertise and perform a wide variety of tasks in planning, preparing, and placing advertising content. Exhibit 2.5 shows the structure of the advertising and promotion industry by illustrating who the different participants are.

This exhibit demonstrates that *advertisers* (such as Kellogg) can employ the services of advertising and promotion *agencies* (such as Grey Group) that may (or may not) contract for specialized services with various *external facilitators* (such as comScore), which results in advertising and promotion being directed with the help of various *media organizations* (such as the TBS cable network and Google) to one or more *target audiences* (like you!).

Note the dashed line on the left side of Exhibit 2.5. This indicates that advertisers do not always need to employ the services of agencies. Nor do advertisers or agencies always seek the services of external facilitators. Some advertisers deal directly with media organizations or online content publishers for placement of their advertisements or implementation of their promotions. This happens either when an advertiser has an internal advertising/promotions department that prepares all the materials for the process, or when media organizations provide technical assistance in the preparation of materials. The newer interactive and mobile media formats also allow advertisers the opportunity to work directly with entertainment

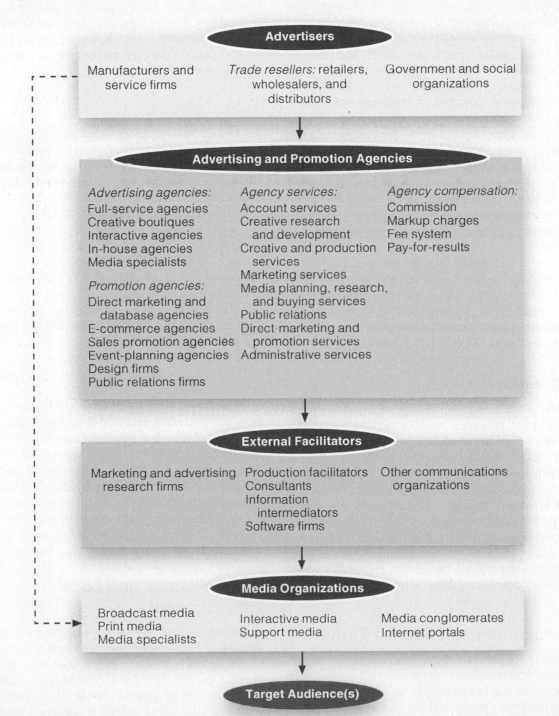

Exhibit 2.5 ▶ The structure of the advertising and promotion industry and participants in the process.

programming firms, such as Walt Disney and Sony, to provide integrated programming and brand placements in films, television programs, and entertainment events. And, as you will see, many of the new media agencies provide the creative and technical assistance advertisers need to implement campaigns through new media.

Another emerging trend is a much closer relationship between advertisers and their agencies—so close, in fact, that sometimes the advertiser's employees work side by side with their agency counterparts. Here's an interesting example: When McDonald's chose Omnicom as its lead U.S. creative agency, advertiser and agency agreed to set up a separate dedicated agency office staffed by both McDonald's and Omnicom personnel. The idea is to have knowledgeable McDonald's marketing managers working closely with the agency's advertising and promotion experts on the development of television commercials, in-store promotions, and social media campaigns. "This agency of the future really has digital and data at the heart, which allows us to be customer obsessed at a whole new level in everything that we do," notes McDonald's CMO.[37] The trend reinforces a very important point: Creativity is not confined to the realm of agencies or external facilitators alone. Advertisers are deeply involved in the creative process of developing advertising and IBP solutions for targeted audiences.[38]

Each level in the structure of the industry is complex. So let's take a look at each rung, with particular emphasis on the nature and activities of agencies, which provide creative firepower and represent a critical link in the structure. When you need to devise advertising or a fully integrated brand promotion, no source will be more valuable than your advertising or promotion agency.

2-3b Advertisers

First in the structure of advertising are the advertisers themselves. From your local pet store to multinational corporations, organizations of all types and sizes seek to benefit from the effects of advertising. **Advertisers** are business, not-for-profit, and government organizations that use advertising and other promotional techniques to communicate with target markets and to stimulate awareness and demand for their brands. Advertisers are also referred to as **clients** by their advertising and promotion agency partners. Different types of advertisers use advertising and promotion somewhat differently depending on the type of product or service they market. The following categories describe the different types of advertisers and the role advertising plays for them.

Manufacturers and Service Firms

Large national manufacturers of consumer products and services are the most prominent users of advertising and promotion, often spending billions of dollars annually to reach targeted audiences and to support IBP at the retail level.[39] Procter & Gamble, PepsiCo, and Verizon all have national or global markets for their products and services. The use of advertising, particularly mass media advertising, by these firms is essential in creating awareness and

preference for their brands, although they also use regional and local media.[40] Regional and local producers of household goods and services also rely heavily on advertising. For example, regional dairy companies sell milk, cheese, and other dairy products in regions usually comprising a few states. These firms often use ads placed in newspapers and regional editions of magazines, as well as partnering with regional retailers to feature brands in store ads. Further, couponing and sampling are methods of communicating with target markets using the tools of IBP that are well suited to regional application. Local producers of products are relatively rare, but local service organizations are common. Medical facilities, hair salons, restaurants, auto dealers, and arts organizations are examples of local service providers that use advertising to create awareness and stimulate demand.

Trade Resellers

The term **trade reseller** includes organizations in the marketing channel of distribution that buy products to resell to customers. As Exhibit 2.5 showed, resellers can be retailers, wholesalers, or distributors, operating online or at physical locations or both. These resellers deal with both household consumers and business buyers at all geographic market levels.

Retailers that sell in national or global markets are the most visible reseller advertisers and promotion users. Target, Dunkin', and H&M are examples of national and global retail companies that use various forms of IBP, traditional and digital, to communicate with customers. Regional retail chains, typically grocery chains such as Safeway or department stores such as Dillard's, serve multistate markets and use advertising suited to their regional customers. At the local level, small retail shops of all sorts rely on newspaper, radio, television, and billboard advertising as well as special promotional events to reach a relatively small geographic area.

Wholesalers and distributors such as AmerisourceBergen are a completely different breed of reseller. Technically, these types of companies deal only with business customers, since their position in the distribution channel dictates that they sell products either to producers (who buy goods to produce other goods) or to retailers (who resell goods to household consumers). Wholesalers and distributors have little need for advertising in mass media, such as television and radio, because they tend to focus on relationships with clients via communication channels such as the sales force and direct marketing.

Federal, State, and Local Governments

Government bodies invest millions of dollars in advertising annually. The U.S. government often ranks as one of the 100 largest spenders on advertising in the United States, with expenditures typically in the range of $1 billion each year.[41] If you add in other IBP expenses like brochures, recruiting fairs, and the personal selling expense of recruiting offices, the U.S. government easily spends more than $2 billion in IBP annually. The federal government's spending on advertising and promotion is concentrated in two areas: armed forces recruiting and social issues. As an example, the U.S. government regularly uses broad-based advertising campaigns for military recruiting, including traditional media such as magazines and TV, plus special events that attract potential recruits. It is also active online (www.goarmy.com) and on social media sites such as Facebook, Pinterest, Snapchat, and YouTube, using hashtags like #ArmyTeam and #GoArmy. Individual states and regions invest in IBP to attract tourists (consumer audiences) and employers (business audiences). See Integrated Brand Promotion in Action (Exhibit 2.6) for a good example of state tourism promotion. Thanks to such promotional activities, Colorado is drawing record numbers of tourists each year and increasing the amount that tourists spend in the state.[42]

> *The advertising used by social organizations has the same fundamental purpose as the advertising carried out by major multinational corporations: to stimulate demand and disseminate information.*

Social and Not-for-Profit Organizations

Advertising by social organizations at the national, state, and local levels is common. The Nature Conservancy, United Way, American Red Cross, and arts organizations use advertising to raise awareness of their organizations, seek donations, and attempt to shape behavior (deter drug use or encourage breast self-examinations, for example). Organizations such as these use both the mass media and direct mail to promote their causes and services. In addition to

major national organizations like the Red Cross, every state has its own unique state-wide organizations, such as Citizens Against Hunger, a state arts council, a tourism office, an economic development office, and/or a historical society. While big multinational organizations might use national or even global advertising, local organizations rely on advertising through local media and community events and promotions to reach neighboring audiences with messages about serving local needs or raising money for good causes.

2-3c The Role of the Advertiser in IBP

Very few of the advertisers just discussed have the employees or the financial resources to strategically plan and then totally prepare effective advertising and IBP programs. This is why advertising and promotion agencies play such an important role in the structure of the advertising industry. But there is an important role played by the advertiser *before* the services of an agency are enlisted. Advertisers of all sizes and types must be prepared for their interaction with an agency for the agency to do *its* job effectively. That is, it is the advertiser's role to:

- Fully understand and describe the value that the firm's brand(s) provides to users.

- Understand and describe the brand's position in the market relative to the competition.

- Describe the firm's objectives for the brand in the near term and long term (for example, brand extensions, international market launches).

- Identify the target market(s) that are most likely to respond favorably to the brand.

- Identify and manage the supply chain/distribution system that will most effectively reach the target market(s).

- Be committed to integrating advertising, event sponsorship, and other promotional tools as part of the organization's overall marketing strategy to grow the brand via both digital and traditional channels.

Exhibit 2.6 ▶ Integrated Brand Promotion in Action: Colorado

Colorado encourages tourism by focusing much of its advertising, website content, and social media messages on vivid images of the state's natural beauty. *How should Colorado, or any state, measure the results of its investment in integrated brand promotion?*

Once an advertiser has done its job with respect to the six factors listed, then and *only* then is it time to enlist the services of an agency to help effectively and creatively develop the market for the brand. Doing this homework is vital so the advertiser is prepared for a productive partnership with its agency and/or specialty firms.

LO 4

2-4 Advertising and Promotion Agencies

Advertisers are fortunate to have a full complement of agencies that specialize in literally every detail of advertising and promotion. Let's take a closer look at the types of agencies advertisers can rely on to help create their advertising and IBP campaigns.

2-4a Advertising Agencies

Most advertisers choose to enlist the services of an advertising agency. An **advertising agency** is an organization of professionals who provide creative and business services to clients in planning, preparing, and placing advertisements. The reason so many firms rely on advertising agencies is that agencies house a collection of professionals with very specialized talent, experience, and expertise that simply cannot be matched by in-house capabilities.

Most big cities and even small towns in the United States have advertising agencies. Each year since 1945, Ad Age publishes an agency report (Exhibit 2.7) that shows the yearly ranking and analysis of advertising and marketing agencies, based on their revenue (both United States and worldwide). In the United States, 2020 agency revenue experienced the second largest drop since 1945 to 6.8 percent.[43] Agencies, like many other business service industries, were impacted by the pandemic; however, the advertising market is expected to recover.

Examples of top ad agencies in the United States include: Ogilvy, BBDO, Omnicom Group, McCann, AKQA, TBWA Worldwide, Grey, Edelman, J. Walter Thompson, Havas, Leo Burnett, Droga5, Interbrand, and Wieden + Kennedy. Notably, many are based in New York City, and specifically located on Madison Avenue, which is regarded as the epicenter of much American advertising.

Many of these American agencies are also international agencies, and other top agencies are headquartered in other countries, namely in Europe. Among the largest international agencies are Dentsu (based in Tokyo), WPP (London), and Publicis (Paris). Advertising agencies often are global businesses, especially given the number of megamergers among agencies that have occurred over the years. Not long ago, Publicis and Omnicom (New York) considered a megamerger that would have created the world's largest ad agency, but they soon called the whole thing off. Instead, Publicis pursued other

acquisitions, including buying Sapient, an agency known for its digital marketing and technology expertise.[44] Omnicom, meanwhile, has been acquiring specialized and full-service firms like the London-based agency Portland.[45] Exhibit 2.8 shows part of the Publicis website, featuring the global firm's emphasis on staying ahead of the ever-changing environment surrounding advertising and IBP.

While some are advertising agency companies, others are **consolidated agency networks**. Consolidated agency networks refer to large holding companies that consist of many agencies or marketing groups. Examples include Accenture Interactive, Deloitte Digital, PwC Digital Services, IBM iX, Blue Focus, McCann Worldgroup, Wunderman Thompson, and Dentsu Aegis Network. It is of note how some traditional business consulting firms are dominating here and serve as a real threat to the more traditional ad agencies. These are very powerful as evidenced by the fact that the top 25 consolidated agency networks' key holdings brought in $70 billion in revenue according to the 2020 Ad Age Agency report.[46]

Advertisers can also use a mixture of work done "in-house" (that is, by their own employees) and by agencies. For instance, Pepsi has an agency for digital advertising, while its social media (which was once more agency-oriented work, perhaps) recently moved in-house. In other words, brand employees are now likely the ones doing their social media—not brand representatives from agencies. There are benefits to both agency and in-house approaches, and a blend may often be best.

The types of agency professionals who help advertisers in the planning, preparation, and placement of advertising and other promotional activities include the following:

Account planners	Creative directors
Marketing specialists	Sales promotion and event planners
Account executives	Copywriters
Media buyers/planners	Direct marketing specialists
Art directors	Radio and television producers
Graphic designers	Web developers
Lead account planners	Researchers
Chief executive officers (CEOs)	Interactive media planners
Chief financial officers (CFOs)	Artists
Chief technology officers (CTOs)	Social media experts
Chief marketing officers (CMOs)	Public relations specialists

Exhibit 2.7 ▶ shows the 2020 Ranking of the Top 25 Global Agencies, along with their revenues in US $ in Billions.

[2020] Global Ad Agency Top 25 (source: Ad Age Agency Report)

Rank	Company	HQ	Country	Revenue ($, B)
1	WPP	London	UK	15.4
2	Omnicom Group	New York	US	13.2
3	Publicis Groupe	Paris	France	12.3
4	Accenture's Accenture Interactive	New York	US	10.7
5	Interpublic Group of Cos.	New York	US	9.1
6	Dentsu Group	Tokyo	Japan	8.8
7	Deloitte's Deloitte Digital	New York	US	8.0
8	PwC's PwC Digital Services	New York	US	7.7
9	BlueFocus Communication Group	Beijing	China	5.9
10	IBM Corp.'s IBMiX*	Armonk, N.Y.	US	5.5
11	Vivendi's Havas	Puteaux	France	2.4
12	Hakuhodo DY Holdings*	Tokyo	Japan	2.4
13	Cheil Worldwide	Seoul	Korea	2.3
14	MDC Partners	New York	US	1.2
15	Quad	Sussex, Wis.	US	1.1
16	R.R. Donnelley's RRD Marketing Solutions	Chicago	US	1.1
17	Innocean Worldwide	Seoul	Korea	1.0
18	Advantage Marketing Partners	Irvine, Calif	US	1.0
19	DJE Holdings*	Chicago	US	0.9
20	The Stagwell Group	Washington	US	0.9
21	Serviceplan Group	Munich	Germany	0.7
22	EPAM Systems' EPAM Continuum*	Boston	US	0.7
23	mc Group (media consulta)	Berlin	Germany	0.6
24	Horizon Media*	New York	US	0.5
25	S4Capital	London	UK	0.4
	Top 25 Total			114

As this list suggests, some advertising agencies can provide advertisers with a host of services, from campaign planning and developing creative concepts to architecting interactive campaigns and measuring effectiveness. It is also important to note from this discussion that an agency is indeed a business. Agencies have **chief executive officers (CEOs)**, **chief financial officers (CFOs)**, and **chief technology officers (CTOs)** just like any other business. Salaries in the positions listed here range from about several million a year for a big agency CEO to about $100,000 a year for an experienced media planner and more than $200,000 for experienced production directors.[47] Of course, entry-level salaries are more modest, and those salaries change depending on job performance and whether you're in a big urban market or a small regional or local market.

Here is a short description of the major different types of agencies available to advertisers.

Full-Service Agencies A **full-service agency** typically includes an array of advertising professionals to meet virtually all the promotional needs of clients. Often, such an agency will also offer a client global contacts and services, the way Omnicom Group, Publicis, and Dentsu do. Full-service agencies are not necessarily large organizations employing hundreds or even thousands of people. Smaller shops can be full service with just a few dozen employees serving clients of various sizes. In a world filled with specialists, a full-service agency has advantages, says the CEO of The S3 Agency in New Jersey: "That mix of strategic planning and creative execution remains the stronghold of traditional agencies."[48]

Creative Boutiques A **creative boutique** typically emphasizes creative concept development, copywriting, and artistic services to clients. An advertiser can employ this alternative for the strict purpose of infusing greater creativity into the message theme or individual advertisement. Advertisers

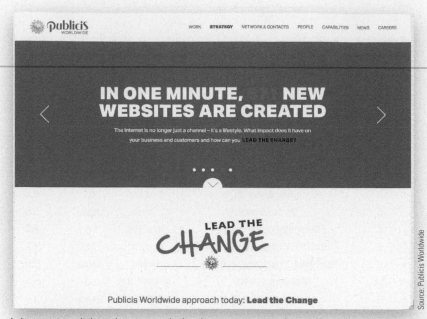

Source: Publicis Worldwide

Exhibit 2.8 ▶ Publicis Worldwide is a global agency with expertise in many aspects of advertising and integrated brand promotion, including digital advertising.

find that boutique agencies can bring deep expertise in trying to reach special target segments, such as older consumers or manufacturing companies. Creative boutiques are idea factories, functioning as independent agencies or, on occasion, established inside large full-service agencies.

The creative boutique's greatest advantage, niche expertise, may be its greatest liability as well. As firms search for IBP programs and make a commitment to IBP campaigns, the creative boutique may be an extra expense and step that advertisers simply don't feel they can afford. But, as you will learn in Chapter 9, "Managing Creativity in Advertising and IBP," the creative effort is so valuable to effective brand building that creativity often rises to prominence in the process; and creative boutiques are well positioned to deliver that value.

Digital/Interactive Agencies   These agencies help advertisers prepare communications for new media such as the Internet, mobile marketing, and interactive television. **Digital/interactive agencies** focus on ways to use online, mobile, and social media solutions for direct marketing and target market communications. Interactive agencies do work for BMW, Oracle, Nintendo, and the U.S. Army. Today, even a midsize full-service agency will offer digital and interactive services to clients. This being the case, many firms have consolidated all their IBP needs, including interactive media, with their main full-service agency. In fact, digital agencies like DigitasLBi and Organic are owned by large full-service agencies Publicis and Omnicom. That doesn't mean there are not hundreds of highly creative smaller shops that produce leading-edge digital campaigns. Digital and interactive agencies have also taken over a wide range of e-commerce activities that formerly required specialized agency services. The agency

24/7 Media used to specialize in e-commerce solutions and now provides a full range of services through digital/interactive programs and consulting.

An **in-house agency** is often referred to as the advertising department within a firm that takes responsibility for the planning and preparation of some or all advertising materials. This option has the advantage of greater coordination and control in all phases of the advertising and promotion process, including control over customer information and marketing analyses—an important point in this era of Big Data.[47] The advertiser's personnel have control over and knowledge of marketing activities, such as product development and distribution tactics that can provide unique insights into target markets. Another advantage is that the firm can keep all commissions that an external agency would have earned. Even though the advantages of doing advertising work in-house are attractive, there are limitations. First, there may be a lack of objectivity, thereby constraining the execution of all phases of the advertising process. Second, it is highly unlikely that an in-house agency could ever match the breadth and depth of talent and experience available in an external agency. Note that some advertisers both rely on in-house agency expertise and hire outside agencies or specialists. Coty, which markets beauty products, purchased the digital and social media agency Beamly as its in-house agency and looked outside to hire Publicis Media as its lead media agency.[49]

Media Specialists   Although not technically agencies, **media specialists** are organizations that specialize in buying media time and space and offer media strategy consulting to advertising agencies and advertisers. The task of strategic coordination of media and promotional efforts has become more complex because of the proliferation of media options and extensive use of promotional tools beyond advertising. One additional advantage of using media specialists is that since they buy media in large quantities, they often acquire media time and/or space at a much lower cost than an agency or advertiser could. Also, media specialists often have time and/or space in inventory and can offer last-minute placement to advertisers. Media-buying services have been part of the advertising industry structure for many years, even as technology has changed. Increasingly, media services are automatically programming buys, based on bids for key words or other criteria, for better targeting and for budget reasons.[50] Moreover, media firms can do a lot more than make buys—they can also provide keen insights to support and develop the media strategy throughout the process.

Promotion Agencies

Although advertisers often rely on an advertising agency as a **steering organization** for their promotional efforts, many specialized agencies often enter the process and are referred to as **promotion agencies**. This is because advertising agencies, even full-service agencies, will concentrate more on the advertising efforts and often provide only a few key ancillary services for other promotional initiatives. This is particularly true in the current era, in which new media are offering so many different ways to communicate to target markets. Promotion agencies can handle everything from sampling to event promotions to retail promotional tie-ins. But we also have to remember that consolidation is also a trend among agencies; so many full-service agencies do, in fact, provide specialized promotion services. Descriptions of different types of promotional agencies and their services follow.

Direct Marketing and Database Agencies   These agencies (sometimes also called **direct-response agencies**) provide a variety of direct marketing services. **Direct marketing agencies** and **database agencies** maintain and manage large databases of mailing lists as one of their services. These firms can design direct marketing campaigns that use either (1) mail or telemarketing or (2) direct-response campaigns using all forms of media. These agencies help advertisers construct databases of target customers, merge databases, develop promotional materials, and then execute the campaign. In many cases, these agencies maintain **fulfillment centers**, which ensure that customers receive the product ordered through direct mail.

Many of these agencies are set up to provide creative and production services to clients. These firms will design and help execute direct-response advertising campaigns using traditional media such as radio, television, magazines, and newspapers. Also, some firms can prepare **infomercials** for clients: 5- to 60-minute information programs that promote a brand and offer direct purchase to viewers.

Sales Promotion Agencies   These specialists design and then operate contests, sweepstakes, special displays, or coupon campaigns for advertisers. It is important to recognize that these agencies can specialize in **consumer sales promotions** and will focus on price-off deals, coupons, sampling, rebates, and premiums. Other firms specialize in **trade-market sales promotions** designed to help advertisers use promotions aimed at wholesalers, retailers, vendors, and trade resellers. These agencies are experts in designing incentive programs, trade shows, sales force contests, in-store merchandising, and point-of-purchase materials.

Event-Planning Agencies   Event sponsorship can also be targeted to household consumers or the trade market. **Event-planning agencies** and organizers are experts in finding locations, securing dates, and putting together a team of people to pull off a promotional event: audio/visual people, caterers, security experts, entertainers, celebrity participants, or whoever is necessary to make the event a success. The event-planning organization will also often assume the task of advertising the event and ensuring the press provides coverage (publicity) of the event. When an advertiser sponsors an entire event, such as a PGA golf tournament, managers will work closely with the event-planning agencies. If an advertiser is just one of several sponsors of an event, such as a NASCAR race, then it has less control over planning and execution.

Design Firms   Designers and graphics specialists do not get nearly enough credit in the advertising and promotion process. If you take a job in advertising or promotion, your designer will be one of your first and most important partners. Even though designers are rarely involved in strategy planning, they are intimately involved in the execution of the advertising or IBP effort. In the most basic sense, **designers** help a firm create the visual impression of a firm's advertising materials—particularly print, in-store display, or Web graphics. Designers are also enlisted to create a firm's **logo**—the graphic mark that identifies a company—and other visual representations that promote an identity for a firm. This mark will appear on everything from advertising to packaging to the company stationery, business cards, and signage (think Nike swoosh). But beyond the logo, graphic designers will also design most of the materials used in supportive communications such as the package design, coupons, in-store displays, brochures, outdoor banners for events, newsletters, and direct mail pieces. One of the world's largest consumer package goods firms, Procter & Gamble, long ago made a large commitment to design across all aspects of marketing and promotion, saying that design was critical to "winning customers in the store with packaging and displays [being] major factors in the outcome (referring to consumer brand choice)."[51] PepsiCo created the position of chief design officer because of the company's emphasis on integrated promotions for its brands. "Our work covers each brand's visual identity, from the product itself all the way to the marketing and merchandising activities that bring a brand to life across different platforms—music, sports, fashion, and so forth," explains the CDO.[52]

Public Relations Firms **Public relations firms** manage an organization's relationships with the media, the local community, competitors, industry associations, and government organizations. The tools of public relations include press releases, feature stories, lobbying, spokespersons, and company newsletters. Most advertisers do not like to handle their own public relations tasks for two reasons. First, public relations require highly specialized skills and talent not normally found within the company ranks. Second, managers are too close to public relations problems and may not be capable of handling a situation, particularly a negative situation, with measured public responses. For these reasons, advertisers and even advertising agencies turn to outside public relations firms. In keeping with the movement to incorporate the Internet across all forms of promotion, there are even organizations that will handle putting all of a firm's news releases online. One such firm is PR Newswire.

In a search for more and distinctive visibility for their brands, advertisers have been turning to public relations firms and film companies to achieve a wide range of film and television placements. One film-making venture that began by sprinkling films with brands and brand images ultimately grew into a company that shot ads for brands such as Revlon and Activision.[53]

2-4b Agency Services

Advertising and promotion agencies offer a wide range of services. The advertiser may need a large, global, full-service advertising agency to plan, prepare, and execute its advertising and IBP campaigns. On the other hand, a creative boutique or digital/interactive agency may offer the right combination of specialized services. Similarly, a large promotion firm might be needed to manage events and retail promotions, while a design firm is enlisted for design work, but nothing else. The most important issue, however, is for the advertiser and the agency to negotiate and reach an agreement on the services being provided before any agency is hired. Exhibit 2.9 shows one typical version of the organizational structure of a full-service advertising agency that also provides a significant number of IBP services.

A word of caution here. Many agencies, large and small, have been flattened—literally and figuratively. In response to downturns in consumer spending and corporate revenues, many advertisers have cut advertising and promotion budgets over the last seven to ten years. In turn, many agencies have seen large, lucrative accounts shrink or disappear completely as corporations consolidate and consumer behavior changes, leading to changes in IBP strategy and budgets. Although

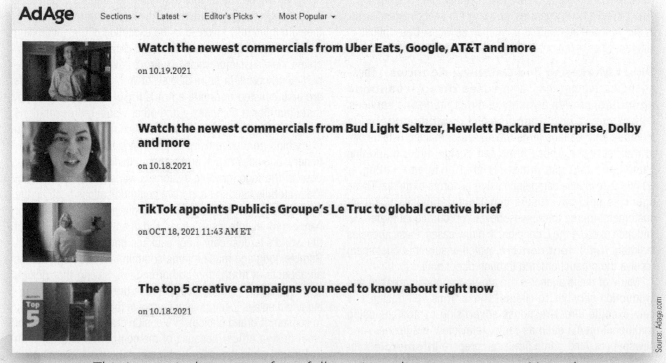

Exhibit 2.9 ▶ This is a typical structure for a full-service advertising agency. Note that this structure includes significant IBP services as well as strict advertising services and functions. Be aware that many agencies, in response to the changing technological environment, have added more digital and interactive services to their structure.

shuttering an entire office is a dramatic example of agencies' responses to economic downturns, other radical changes have occurred as well. Many big agencies have consolidated all forms of production under one manager. Where there used to be print production, film/video production, radio production, and retail advertising, now there is just "production." Other structural changes have occurred as well. Omnicom group's TBWA created the position of chief compensation officer because financial discussions between clients and agencies had deteriorated to the point that neither side was satisfied.[54]

Moreover, a growing number of advertisers want and expect 24/7 IBP representation because consumers have 24/7 exposure to brand information. Advertisers "need partners that are built on that marketplace of speed," in the words of the CEO of DDB North America. At the same time, clients are pressing for higher efficiency and changes in how they pay for agency services. As a result, agencies are evolving new organizational structures and working with clients to develop different compensation systems that reflect the value added and yet fit within advertisers' budget constraints.[55] So while the services discussed in what follows are still relevant and the organizational structure presented here is still generally representative, be aware that any one agency's structure and menu of services might be quite different from the one shown.

Account Services

These services are offered by managers who have titles such as account executive, account supervisor, or account manager and who work with clients to determine how the brand can benefit most from advertising and IBP. **Account services** entail identifying the benefits a brand offers, its target audiences, and the best competitive positioning and then developing a complete plan. In some cases, account services in an agency can provide basic marketing and consumer behavior research; but in general, the client should bring this information to the table, as noted earlier in the chapter. Knowing the target segment, the brand's value, and the positioning strategy are really the responsibility of the advertiser (more on this in Chapter 5, "Advertising, Integrated Brand Promotion, and Consumer Behavior," and Chapter 6, "Market Segmentation, Positioning, and the Value Proposition").

Account services managers also work with the client in translating cultural and consumer values into advertising and promotional messages through the creative services in the agency. Finally, they work with media services (both internal and external) to develop an effective media strategy for determining the best vehicles for reaching the targeted audiences. One of the primary tasks in account services is to keep the various agency teams' creativity, production, and media efforts on schedule and within budget.

Marketing Research Services

Research conducted by an agency for a client usually consists of the agency locating studies (conducted by commercial research organizations) that have bearing on a client's market

or advertising and IBP objectives. The research group will help the client interpret the research and communicate these interpretations to the creative and media teams. If existing studies are not sufficient, research may be conducted by the agency itself. As mentioned in the account services discussion, some agencies can assemble consumers from the target audience to evaluate different versions of proposed advertising and determine whether messages are being communicated effectively. These are usually done in a focus group format—something you will learn about in Chapter 7, "Advertising Research."

Many agencies have established the position of **account planner** to coordinate the research effort. An account planner's stature in the organization is on par with that of an account executive. The account planner is assigned to clients to ensure that research input is included at each stage of development of campaign materials. Agencies understand that research, signaled by the appointment of an account planner, is key to successful promotional campaigns.

Creative and Production Services

The **creative services** group in an agency develops concepts that express the value of a company's brand in interesting and memorable ways. In simple terms, the creative services group develops the message that will be delivered through advertising, sales promotion, direct marketing, social networks, mobile marketing, event sponsorship, or public relations. The creative group in an agency will typically include a creative director, art director, illustrators or designers, and copywriters. In specialized promotion agencies, event planners, contest experts, and interactive media specialists will join the core group. **Production services** include producers (and sometimes directors) who take creative ideas and turn them into advertisements, direct mail pieces, and other IBP materials. Producers generally oversee and manage the many details of the production of the advertisement and/or other promotion efforts. Advertising agencies maintain the largest and most sophisticated creative and production staffs.

Media Planning and Buying Services

This service was discussed earlier as a specialized agency effort through which advertisers can contract for media buying and planning. Advertising agencies themselves provide **media planning and buying services** like those of the specialized agencies. The central challenge is to determine how a client's message can most effectively and efficiently reach the target audience. Media planners and buyers examine an enormous number of options to build an effective media plan within the client's budget. But media planning and buying is much more than simply buying ad space, timing a coupon distribution, launching a mobile media effort, or scheduling an event. A wide range of media strategies can be implemented to enhance the impact of the message. As mentioned earlier, most large agencies, such as Omnicom Group, set up their own digital/interactive media teams years ago in response to client needs. The three positions typically found in the media area are media planner, media buyer, and media researcher. This is where much of the client's money is spent, because it's very important.

Administrative Services

Like other businesses, agencies must manage their business affairs. Agencies have personnel departments, accounting and billing teams, and sales staffs that go out and sell the agency to clients. Most important to clients is the traffic department, which has the responsibility of monitoring projects to be sure that deadlines are met. Traffic managers make sure the creative group and media services are coordinated so that deadlines for getting promotional materials to printers, Web designers, retailers, and media organizations are met. The job requires tremendous organizational skills and is critical to delivering the other services to clients.

2-4c Agency Compensation

The way agencies get paid is somewhat different from the way other professional organizations are compensated. While accountants, doctors, lawyers, and consultants often work on a fee basis, advertising agencies have historically based compensation on a commission or markup system. Promotion agencies occasionally work on a commission basis but more often work on a fee or contract basis. The atmosphere surrounding agency compensation has been tense for several years. Clients are demanding more services at lower cost. Clients are including "procurement officers" in planning meetings with agencies, and in response, agencies are bringing their own financial executives (thus the chief compensation officer of TBWA discussed earlier). Agencies are starting to push back on clients who are demanding a fee structure for services that is lower than the cost to produce the services.[56]

We will examine the four most prevalent agency compensation methods: commissions, markup charges, fee systems, and the now prevalent pay-for-results plans. Realize that while these are common methods, all aspects of client–agency compensation are up for negotiation.

Commissions

The traditional method of agency compensation is the **commission system**, which is based on the amount of money the advertiser spends on media. Under this method, 15 percent of the total amount billed by a media organization is retained by the advertising or promotion agency as compensation for all costs in creating advertising/promotion for the advertiser. The only variation is that the rate typically changes to 16 percent for outdoor media. This is a conservative commission rate, and it may be higher (as much as 30 percent). Clients should make sure to ask if the agency or consultant is paid per commission of the media spend and at what percent, as it could be negotiable. Exhibit 2.10 shows a simple example of how the commission system works. The agency bills the client (the company is who is paying the agency for their services) $1,000,000 for television airtime. The agency pays the television media company $850,000 for the television airtime. The agency earns 15 percent commission—$150,000.

During the past 25 years, and particularly in the past five years with the changes in consumer media use, the wisdom of the commission system has been questioned by both advertisers and agencies themselves. Many advertisers compensate their agencies using a commission system based on media cost, but fewer use the traditional 15 percent commission. More advertisers are using other percentage levels of commission, often negotiated levels, as the basis for agency compensation. But even the use of media-based commissions is under fire. The global marketing officer for Procter & Gamble laid the foundation for change several years ago when he told American Association of Advertising Agencies (AAAA) members that the media-based model dependent on the 30-second TV spot is "broken" and that the industry needs to understand the complexity of media use by contemporary consumers.[57] This message indirectly calls into question the whole issue of basing compensation on media billings at all.

Markup Charges

Another method of agency compensation is to add a percentage **markup charge** (sometimes referred to as cost-plus) to a variety of services the agency purchases from outside suppliers. In many cases, an agency will turn to outside contractors for art, illustration, photography, printing, research, and production. The agency then, in agreement with the client, adds a markup charge to these services. The reason markup charges became prevalent in the industry is that many promotion agencies began providing services that did not use traditional media. Since the traditional commission method was based on media charges, there was no way for these agencies to receive payment for their work. This being the case, the markup system was developed. A typical markup on outside services has traditionally been 17.65 to 20 percent.

Fee Systems

A **fee system** is much like that used by consultants or attorneys, whereby the advertiser and the agency agree on an hourly rate for different

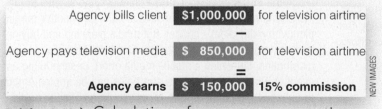

Agency bills client	**$1,000,000**	for television airtime
Agency pays television media	**$ 850,000**	for television airtime
Agency earns	**$ 150,000**	**15% commission**

NEW IMAGES

Exhibit 2.10 ▶ Calculation of agency compensation using a traditional commission-based compensation system.

services provided. The hourly rate can be based on average salaries within departments or on some agreed-on hourly rate across all services. This is the most common basis for promotion agency compensation.

Another version of the fee system is a contracted fixed-fee set for a project between the client and the agency. It is imperative that the agency and the advertiser agree on precisely what services will be provided, by what departments in the agency, over what specified period of time. In addition, the parties must agree on which supplies, materials, travel costs, and other expenses will be reimbursed beyond the fixed fee. Fixed-fee systems have the potential for causing serious rifts in the client–agency relationship, because out-of-scope work can easily spiral out of control when so many variables are at play.

Agencies have generally been opposed to the fee system approach. They argue that creative impact cannot be measured in "work hours" but rather must be measured in "the value of the materials the agency is creating for the client."[58] Analysts agree. They refer to the fee system as "very flawed" and believe that the proper compensation model is performance based, as described in the next section.[59]

Pay-for-Results

Many advertisers and agencies alike have been working on compensation programs called **pay-for-results** or incentive-based compensation that base the agency's fee on the achievement of agreed-upon results. Historically, agencies would not (rightly so) agree to be evaluated on results because results were often narrowly defined as "sales." The key effects on sales are related to factors outside the agency's control such as brand features, pricing strategy, and distribution programs (i.e., the overall marketing mix, not just advertising or IBP). An agency might agree to be compensated based on achievement of sales levels, but more often (and more appropriately), communications objectives such as awareness, brand identification, or brand feature knowledge among target audiences will serve as the main results criteria. When DDB North America won the McDonald's account, it agreed to pay-for-results compensation based on the fast-food company's brand and business performance. "We feel positively about the potential to be measured in a way that's more correlated with the impact we will create," the agency's CEO said.[60]

LO 5

2-5 External Facilitators

Even though agencies offer clients a variety of services and continue to add more, advertisers often need to rely on specialized external facilitators for planning, preparing, and executing promotional campaigns. **External facilitators** are organizations or individuals that provide specialized services to

advertisers and agencies. The most important of these external facilitators are discussed in the following sections.

Marketing and Advertising Research Firms

Many firms rely on outside assistance during the planning phase of advertising. Research firms such as Burke can perform original research for advertisers using focus groups, surveys, or experiments to assist in understanding the potential market or consumer perceptions of a product or service. Other research firms, such as IRI, routinely collect data (from grocery store scanners, for example) and provide insights from these data for a fee, also offering sophisticated analyses that can reveal meaningful patterns in consumer behavior.

Advertisers and their agencies also seek measures of promotional program effectiveness after a campaign has run. After an advertisement or promotion has been active for a reasonable amount of time, firms such as Starch Advertising Research will run recognition tests on print advertisements. Other firms such as Burke offer day-after recall tests of broadcast advertisements. Some firms specialize in message testing to determine whether consumers find advertising messages appealing and understandable.

Consultants

A variety of **consultants** specialize in areas related to the promotional process. Advertisers can seek out marketing consultants for assistance in the planning stage regarding market segment behaviors and macro-economic and cultural trends. Creative and communications consultants provide insights on issues related to message strategy and message themes. Consultants in event planning and sponsorships offer their expertise to both advertisers and agencies. Public relations consultants often work with top management. Media experts can help an advertiser determine the proper media mix and efficient media placement.

Three new types of consultants have emerged in recent years. One is a database consultant, who works with both advertisers and agencies. Organizations of this type help firms identify and then manage databases that allow for the development of integrated marketing communications programs. Diverse databases from research sources discussed earlier can be merged or cross-referenced in developing effective communications programs. Database consultants are particularly useful in planning couponing or direct mail (email) campaigns. Another new type of consultant specializes in website development and management. These consultants typically have the creative skills to develop websites and corporate home pages and the technical skills to advise advertisers on managing the technical aspects of the **user interface**. The third type of consultant works with a firm to integrate information across a wide variety of customer contacts (including social media activities) and to organize all this information to achieve customer relationship management (CRM). In recent years, traditional management consultants— such as IBM, Accenture, and McKinsey—have started to work with agencies on structure and business strategy. These sorts of consultants can also advise on image strategy, market research procedure, and process and account planning. But the combination of traditional consulting and advertising has not always produced compelling results, and the typical role of consultants—focusing on marketing, creative, or technical issues—is the more likely role for consultants in the future.

Production Facilitators

External **production facilitators** offer essential services both during and after the production process. Production is the area in which advertisers and their agencies rely most heavily on external facilitators. All forms of media advertising require special expertise that even the largest full-service agency, much less an advertiser, typically does not retain on staff. In broadcast production, directors, production managers, songwriters, camera operators, audio and lighting technicians, and performers are all essential to preparing a professional, high-quality radio, television, or video ad. Production houses can provide the physical facilities, including sets, stages, equipment, and crews, needed for broadcast production. Similarly, in preparing print advertising, brochures, and direct mail pieces, graphic artists, photographers, models, directors, and producers may be hired from outside the advertising agency or firm to provide the specialized skills and facilities needed in preparing advertisements. In-store promotions and trade show booths are other areas in which designing and producing materials requires the skills of a specialty organization.

Just as there are digital agencies, there are also digital production houses that assist both agencies and advertisers with the development of video and animation for both online and traditional media applications. These digital production houses are the ones that come up with the digital special effects that can make both online and broadcast production ads much more interesting. One such production company, B-Reel, has entered the mainstream of production and helps advertisers incorporate digital technology across many different media applications.[61]

The specific activities performed by external facilitators and the techniques employed by the personnel in these firms will be covered in greater detail in Part 3 of the text. For now, it is sufficient to recognize the role these firms play in the advertising and promotions industry.

Software Firms

Increasingly, software firms are helping advertisers and agencies make the best use of evolving media and technology. Some of these firms are well established and well known, such

as Microsoft and Oracle. Database management software can assist advertisers in making strategic decisions. Databases offer the opportunity to gatherer and analyze data related to Web surfing behavior, streaming audio and video, and managing relationships with trade partners. These firms offer such specialized expertise that many ad agencies seek their assistance.

2-6 Media Organizations

The next level in the industry structure, shown separately in Exhibit 2.11, comprises the media available to advertisers. The media available for placing advertising, such as broadcast and print media, are well known to most of us simply because we're exposed to them daily. In addition, advertisers can direct and distribute their advertising and promotional messages in digital, interactive, and social media—with or without agency help.

In traditional media, major television networks such as NBC and CBS, as well as national magazines such as *Coastal Living* and *Vogue*, provide advertisers with time and space for their messages at considerable cost. Other media options are useful for reaching narrowly defined target audiences. Specialty programming on cable television, tightly focused direct mail pieces, and a well-designed online campaign, social media campaign, or mobile marketing campaign may be better ways to reach a specific audience.

Note the inclusion of media conglomerates in the list shown in Exhibit 2.11. This category is included because organizations such as Viacom and Comcast own and operate companies in broadcast, print, and interactive media. Viacom brings you cable networks such as Nickelodeon, BET, MTV, Comedy Central, VH1, and TV Land. Thanks to this diverse portfolio of networks, Viacom can offer advertisers access to diverse audiences in global markets, with sophisticated data analysis tools for better targeting. The company is also experimenting with ways to engage TV viewers by bringing the excitement of mobile-accessed live streaming to programming on cable channels.[62] Newer emphasis on this area of consumer media is on streaming subscriptions, such as Netflix and Disney +.

Some advertisers want to place their messages outside mainstream traditional or interactive media. Often referred to as out-of-home media, these support media organizations include transit companies (bus and taxi boards), billboard organizations, specialized directory companies, and sports and performance arenas for sponsorships, display materials, and premium items.

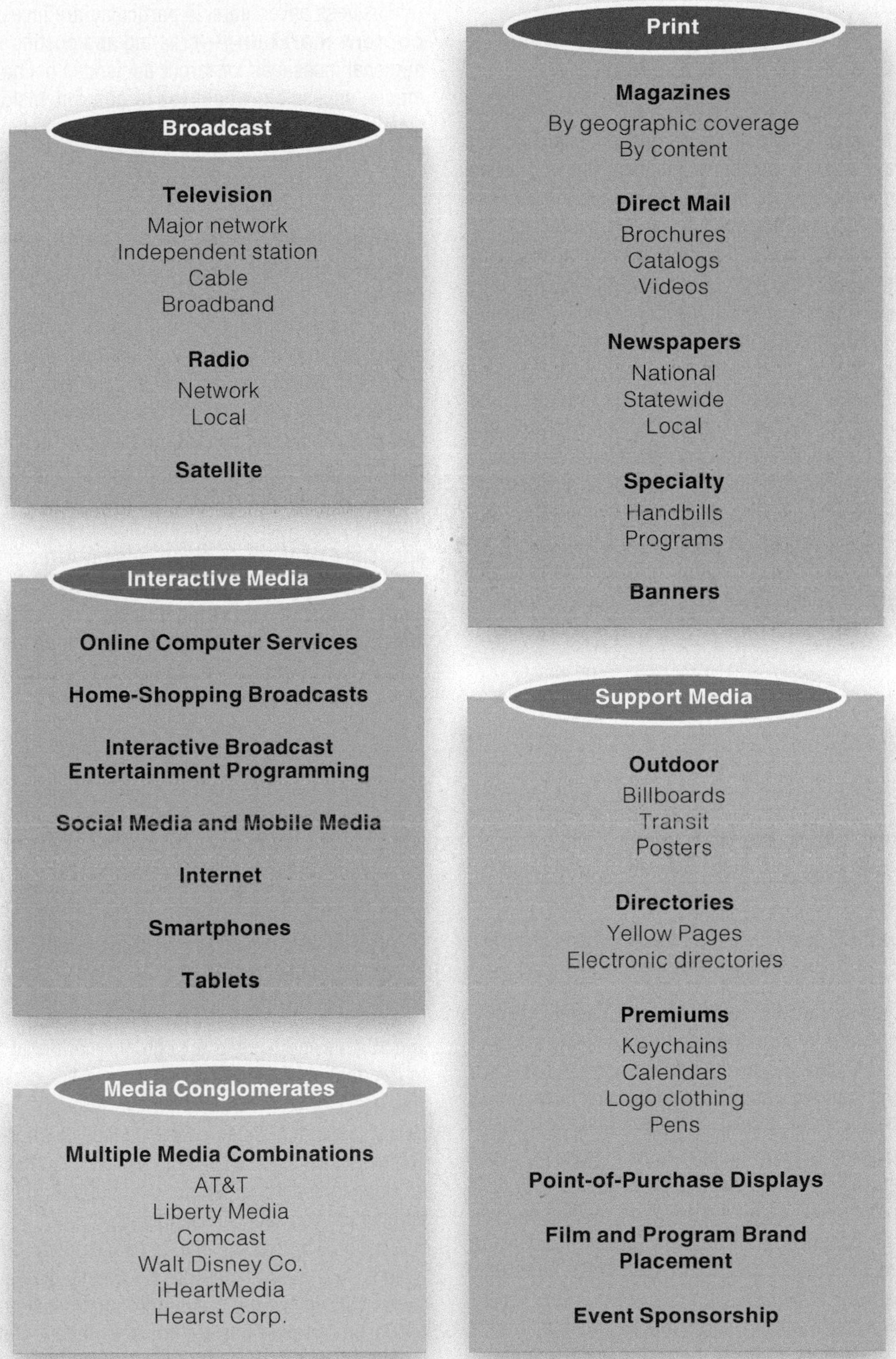

Broadcast

Television
Major network
Independent station
Cable
Broadband

Radio
Network
Local

Satellite

Print

Magazines
By geographic coverage
By content

Direct Mail
Brochures
Catalogs
Videos

Newspapers
National
Statewide
Local

Specialty
Handbills
Programs

Banners

Interactive Media

Online Computer Services

Home-Shopping Broadcasts

**Interactive Broadcast
Entertainment Programming**

Social Media and Mobile Media

Internet

Smartphones

Tablets

Support Media

Outdoor
Billboards
Transit
Posters

Directories
Yellow Pages
Electronic directories

Premiums
Keychains
Calendars
Logo clothing
Pens

Point-of-Purchase Displays

**Film and Program Brand
Placement**

Event Sponsorship

Media Conglomerates

Multiple Media Combinations
AT&T
Liberty Media
Comcast
Walt Disney Co.
iHeartMedia
Hearst Corp.

Exhibit 2.11 ▶ Advertisers have an array of media organizations available to them. This illustration shows only some of the possibilities. Notice that the choices range from traditional print and broadcast media to interactive media to media conglomerates.

2-6a Target Audiences and Content Marketing

The structure of the advertising and promotion industry and the flow of communication would obviously be incomplete without an audience: no audience, no communication. One interesting thing about the audiences for promotional communications is that, with the exception of household consumers, they are also the *advertisers* who use advertising and IBP communications. We are all familiar with the type of advertising directed at us in our role as consumers: entertainment, tourism, toothpaste, window cleaner, sport-utility vehicles, soft drinks, insurance, and so on.

But business and government audiences are key to the success of a large number of firms that sell only to business and government buyers. While many of these firms rely heavily on personal selling, many also use a variety of advertising and IBP tools. Accenture Consulting uses high-profile television, magazine advertising, sponsored events, and online and social media campaigns. Many business and trade sellers regularly need public relations, and most use direct mail to communicate with potential customers as a prelude to a personal selling call.

Business advertisers, in particular, are investing heavily in **content marketing**—creating and posting relevant informational messages for target audiences online and on social media, accessible whenever targeted decision makers are considering a purchase. The focus is on making and sharing value-added content of interest to the target audience of decision makers, whether it's a presentation of facts and figures, a product demonstration, or background details about how to solve a particular problem. Content can be presented to target audiences in multiple media through integration of promotional efforts.

For example, Philips, traditionally known for consumer products like light bulbs, has staked out a strong position as a provider of sophisticated health-care equipment to hospitals and medical centers. The company's definition of content marketing is "delivering consistent and high-quality content that provides value or utility to the end-user." For World Sleep Day, Philips used multimedia content marketing to educate and inform target audiences of medical center decision makers about the dangers of sleep apnea. After this integrated campaign began, Philips noted higher sales of its sleep apnea products.[63] However, do note that modern advertising effectiveness now transcends so much more than sales.

Summary

1. Identify how the advertising industry is in constant transition.

Refer back to the key statistics on the state of the industry provided at the beginning of this chapter. They illustrate the pace of change and how the complexity of the changes today are more challenging than any change the advertising industry has ever faced. The advertising industry is successfully adapting to the new technologies that consumers are willing or even eager to use because consumers are seeking more control over their information environment (vs. an advertiser or media company being in control). Consumers are actively looking for ways to avoid advertising at times. To best adapt, advertisers must integrate traditional advertising investments more with targeted digital media, online advertising, social media, and mobile marketing. The industry is in midst of the digital reality; however, it is crucial to note that major traditional media like television, radio, and magazines still rake in billions of advertising dollars worldwide in a year. Despite this constant transition, the goal of the traditional structure remains—the brand and its differentiation need to be highlighted with persuasive communications.

2. Discuss five broad trends transforming the advertising and promotion industry.

One major trend affecting advertisers, agencies, and the media is that consumers are now in greater control of their exposure to information. Collectively, individuals are gravitating toward sharing and creating information through websites, social media, apps, and video sites. Another example of consumer control is the increased use of on-demand streaming and digital video recorders, with a growing number of households cutting the cord on cable subscriptions.

The proliferation of media has created new advertising options, and media firms are becoming multiplatform media giants with television, radio, print, and/or Internet properties. Media proliferation has led to more media clutter and fragmentation, reducing the effectiveness of advertisements; as a result, advertisers are using more IBP tools and digital buys to enhance the primary advertising effort. Through crowdsourcing, advertisers get consumers more involved with and committed to a brand. Technology enables advertisers to reach consumers with messages directed to consumers' mobile devices, despite the growing use of ad blockers as consumers seek to retain control over information flow.

3. Describe the advertising and promotion industry's size, structure, and participants.

Many different types of organizations make up this large industry. The process begins with an organization (the advertiser) that has a message to communicate to a target audience. The advertiser typically hires advertising and promotion agencies to launch and manage a campaign, but other external facilitators are often brought in to perform specialized functions, such as digital/interactive agencies for mobile marketing and social media campaigns. To reach target markets, advertisers and their agencies work with media organizations.

4. Discuss the role played by advertising and promotion agencies, the services provided by these agencies, and how the agencies are compensated.

Advertising and promotion agencies come in many varieties and offer services such as market research and marketing planning, the creation and production of ad materials, the planning and purchase of media time or space for ads, and traffic management to keep production on schedule. Some advertising agencies offer a full array of services under one roof; others, such as creative boutiques, develop a particular expertise with specialized skills. Promotion agencies specialize in one or more of the other forms of promotion beyond advertising. The four most prevalent ways to compensate an agency for services are commissions, markups, fee systems, and the pay-for-results programs. Agency compensation is changing as the industry changes and agencies face more competition from digital media companies and consulting companies.

5. Identify key external facilitators who assist in planning and executing advertising and integrated brand promotion campaigns.

Marketing and advertising research firms assist advertisers and their agencies in understanding the market environment. Consultants of all sorts from marketing strategy through event planning and retail display are also external facilitators. External production facilitators offer services during and after the production process. In promotions, designers and planners are called on to assist in creation and execution of promotional mix tools. Software firms fill a growing role in the industry by offering specialized expertise in tracking and analyzing consumer behavior and media usage.

6. Discuss the role played by media organizations in executing effective advertising and integrated brand promotion campaigns.

Media organizations are the essential link in delivering advertising and IBP communications to target audiences. In addition to traditional media organizations, advertisers can reach audiences through interactive media options (online, mobile, social media) and support media. The media industry is geared toward target audiences of consumers and of businesses and government agencies. Business advertisers are investing heavily in content marketing to appeal to decision makers.

Key Terms

account planner
account services
advertiser
advertising agency
blog
branded apps
chief executive officers (CEOs)
chief financial officers (CFOs)
chief technology officers (CTOs)
client
commission system
consolidated agency networks
consultant
consumer sales promotion
content marketing
creative boutique

creative services
crowdsourcing
customer acquisition
database agency
designer
digital/interactive agency
direct-response agency
direct marketing agency
event-planning agency
external facilitator
fee system
fulfillment center
full-service agency
in-house agency
infomercial
logo

markup charge
media planning and buying services
media specialist
pay-for-results
production facilitator
production services
promotion agency
public relations firm
social media
steering organization
trade-market sales promotion
trade reseller
user interface
virtual reality

Endnotes

1. Bradley Johnson, "Global Advertising Forecast to Set a New Record in 2021: Five Key Takeaways from Ad Age Marketing Factpack 2021," *Ad Age*, December 21, 2020, https://adage.com/article/datacenter/global-advertising-forecast-set-new-record-2021/2302256; and Ad Agency Report Rankings and Analysis 2021, *Ad Age*, May 20, 2021, https://adage.com/article/datacenter/ad-age-agency-report-2021-rankings-and-analysis/2332371.

2. See Suzanne Vranica, "Advertisers Try New Tactics to Break Through to Consumers," *Wall Street Journal*, June 19, 2016, http://www.wsj.com/articles/advertisers-try-new-tactics-to-break-through-to-consumers-1466328601.

3. "Ad Spending Heads into Tepid Recovery," *Advertising Age*, Annual 2010, December 28, 2009, 8; and Brian Steinberg, "Marketers Say TV Spending Will Drop. Nets Stay Bullish. Let the Deals Begin," *Advertising Age*, February 8, 2010.

4. Bradley Johnson, "How Nation's Top 200 Marketers Are Honing Digital Strategies," *Advertising Age*, June 27, 2016, http://adage.com/article/advertising/top-200-u-s-advertisers-spend-smarter/304625/; and Steven Park and Byungho Park, "Advertising on Mobile Apps," *Journal of Advertising Research* 60, (December 1, 2020), 381.

5. "Qatar Airlines Becomes the Only Global Airline in The World to Surpass 20 Million Followers on Facebook," *Qatar Airlines*, October 20, 2020, https://www.qatarairways.com/en/press-releases/2020/october/fb20million.html.

6. Thomas H. Davenport and Judah Phillips, "The Future of Marketing Automation," *Applied Marketing Analytics* 2, no. 3 (2016), 213–224.

7. Leigh McAlister, Raji Srinivasan, Niket Jindal, and Albert A. Cannella, "Advertising Effectiveness: The Moderating Effect of Firm Strategy," *Journal of Marketing Research* 53, no. 2 (2016), 207–224.

8. See Rodrigo Uribe, "Separate and Joint Effects of Advertising and Placement," *Journal of Business Research* 69, no. 2 (2016), 459–465; and Rajeev Batra and Kevin Lane Keller, "Integrating Marketing Communications: New Findings, New Lessons, and New Ideas," *Journal of Marketing* 80, no. 6 (November 2016), 122–145.

9. Michael Trusov, Randolph E. Bucklin, and Koen Pauwels, "Effects of Word-of-Mouth versus Traditional Marketing: Findings from an Internet Social Networking Site," *Journal of Marketing* 73 (September 2009), 90–102.

10. H. Tankovska,"Number of Monthly Active Facebook Users Worldwide as of 4th Quarter 2020," *Statista*, February 2, 2021, https://www.statista.com/statistics/264810/number-of-monthly-active-facebook-users-worldwide/; and H. Tankovska, "Number of Monthly Active Instagram Users from January 2013 to June 2018," *Statista*, January 27, 2021, https://www.statista.com/statistics/253577/number-of-monthly-active-instagram-users/; and Alex Sherman, "TikTok Reveals Detailed User Numbers For the First Time," *CNBC*, August 24, 2020, https://www.cnbc.com/2020/08/24/tiktok-reveals-us-global-user-growth-numbers-for-first-time.html.

11. Jack Neff, "P&G, GM and Facebook Agree: Big Is Beautiful," *Advertising Age*, September 27, 2016, http://adage.com/article/special-report-advertising-week/p-g-gm-facebook-agree-big-beautiful/306057/.

12. Michael Liedtke, "Periscope Extends Beyond Phones as Twitter Ups Ante on Video," *ABC News*, October 13, 2016, http://abcnews.go.com/Entertainment/wireStory/periscope-extends-phones-twitter-ups-ante-video-42778882.

13. Andy Meek, "Surprising No One, Almost 60% of Americans Have Ditched Cable TV," *BGR*, January 29, 2019, https://bgr.com/business/cord-cutting-news-60-%-cancel-cable-5693092/.

14. Chingching Chang, "How Branded Videos Can Inspire," *Journal of Advertising* 49, (October 19, 2020), 613-632.

15. Micael Dahlen and Sara Rosengren, "If Advertising Won't Die, What Will It Be? Toward a Working Definition of Advertising," *Journal of Advertising* 45, no. 3 (2016), 334-345.

16. Nat Ives, "Special Report: More Than Magazines," *Advertising Age*, March 12, 2007, s1–s6.

17. "Disney Revenues 2006-2021," *MacroTrends*, https://www.macrotrends.net/stocks/charts/DIS/disney/revenue.

18. H. Tankovska, "Annual Revenue Generated by IAC from 2004 to 2020," *Statista*, February 10, 2021, https://www.statista.com/statistics/266398/annual-revenue-of-iac/; and Joseph Johnson, "Annual Revenue of Alphabet from 2006 to 2020," *Statista*, February 5, 2021, https://www.statista.com/statistics/507742/alphabet-annual-global-revenue/.

19. Daniel Frankel, "TV Channels Received by U.S. Households dropped 6.4% in 2019," *NextTV*, February 13, 2021, https://www.nexttv.com/news/tv-channels-received-by-us-households-dropped-64-in-2019-report.

20. Duane Varan, Magda Nenycz-Thiel, Rachel Kennedy, and Steven Bellman, "The Effects of Commercial Length on Advertising Impact," *Journal of Advertising Research* 60, (March 2020), 54.

21. Chris Woodyard, "Super Bowl Ad Costs Soar—But So Does Buzz," *USA Today*, February 7, 2016, http://www.usatoday.com/story/money/2016/02/07/super-bowl-ad-costs-soar----but-so-does-buzz/79903058/.

22. "TV and Digital Are in a Dead Heat for US Media Dollars," *eMarketer*, October 4, 2016, https://www.emarketer.com/Article/TV-Digital-Dead-Heat-US-Media-Dollars/1014552; and Jack Neff, "J&J Jolts 'Old Media' with $250M Spend Shift," *Advertising Age*, March 19, 2007, 1, 29.

23. Marty Swant, "Will Virtual Reality Experiences for Brands Rival Super Bowl Ads? Quality VR Can Reach a Massive Audience," *Adweek*, October 18, 2016, http://www.adweek.com/news/technology/will-virtual-reality-experiences-brands-rival-super-bowl-ads-174105.

24. Tathagata Ghosh, "Winning Versus Not Losing: Exploring the Effects of In-Game Advertising Outcome on Its Effectiveness," *Journal of Interactive Marketing* 36 (2016), 134–147.

25. Garrik Schmitt, "Can Creativity Be Crowdsourced?" *Ad Age*, Digital Next, April 16, 2009, https://adage.com/article/digitalnext/tools-technology-force-big-ad-industry/136019.

26. Martin Schreier, Hidehiko Nishikawa, Christoph Fuchs, and Susumu Ogawa, "Crowdsourced Products Sell Better When They're Marketed That Way," *Harvard Business Review*, November 8, 2016, https://hbr.org/2016/11/crowdsourced-products-sell-better-when-theyre-marketed-that-way; see also Anna S. Cui and Fang Wu, "Utilizing Customer Knowledge in Innovation: Antecedents and Impact Of Customer Involvement on New Product Performance," *Journal of the Academy of Marketing Science* 44, no. 4 (July 2016), 516–538.

27. Alexandra Jardine, "McCain's Airs Crowdsourced Ads Less Than Two Hours After They're Made," *Creativity*, October 6, 2015, http://creativity-online.com/work/mccain-nations-teatime/43628.

28. Dhruv Grewal, Yakov Bart, Martin Spann, and Peter Pal Zubcsek, "Mobile Advertising: A Framework and Research Agenda," *Journal of Interactive Marketing* 34 (2016), 3–14.

29. Laurie Sullivan, "Mobile App Ad Blocking Skyrocketing, Forcing Brands to Rethink Advertising," *MediaPost*, May 31, 2016, http://www.mediapost.com/publications/article/277011/mobile-app-ad-blocking-skyrocketing-forcing-brand.html.

30. Quoted in Robert D. Hof, "As Messaging Apps Boom, Brands Tiptoe In," *New York Times*, April 4, 2016, http://www.nytimes.com/2016/04/04/business/media/as-messaging-apps-boom-brands-tiptoe-in.html?_r=0.

31. "Mobile advertising spending worldwide from 2007 to 2022," *Statista*, August 6, 2021, https://www.statista.com/statistics/303817/mobile-internet-advertising-revenue-worldwide/; and Davey Alba, "Mary Meeker Says Advertisers Aren't Spending Enough on Mobile," *Wired*, June 1, 2016, https://www.wired.com/2016/06/mary-meeker-says-advertisers-arent-spending-enough-mobile/.

32. Nathalie Tadena, "Mondelez Makes Moves to Look More Like a Media Company," *Wall Street Journal*, May 31, 2016, http://www.wsj.com/articles/mondelez-makes-moves-to-look-more-like-a-media-company-1464692402.

33. Ibid.

34. A. Guttmann, "Advertising Media Owners Revenue Worldwide from 2012 to 2024," *Statista*, March 1, 2021, https://www.statista.com/statistics/236943/global-advertising-spending/.

35. Neil Patel, "Which US Brands Are Spending the Most on Advertising?" *NeilPatel*, June 2018, https://neilpatel.com/blog/top-ad-spenders/

36. "General Motors Company's Advertising Spending in The United States from 2007 to 2019," *Statista*, January 14, 2021, https://www.statista.com/statistics/261531/general-motors-advertising-spending-in-the-us/; and "Ford Motors Company's Advertising Spending in the United States From 2007-2019," *Statista*, January 12, 2021, https://www.statista.com/statistics/261535/ford-motors-advertising-spending-in-the-us/#:~:text=In%202019%2C%20Ford%20Motors%20spent,had%20a%20turbulent%20path%20since; and I. Wagner, "Ford — Statistics and Facts," *Statista*, March 29, 2021, https://www.statista.com/topics/1886/ford/.

37. Quoted in: Jessica Wohl, "McDonald's Picks Omnicom as Winner of U.S. Creative Review," *Advertising Age*, August 29, 2016, http://adage.com/article/cmo-strategy/mcdonald-s-picks-omnicom-winner-creative-review/305635/; also: Patrick Coffee, "McDonald's and Omnicom Refer to Their Dedicated Unit as an 'Agency of the Present,'" *Adweek*, September 26, 2016, http://www.adweek.com/news/advertising-branding/mcdonalds-and-omnicom-refer-their-dedicated-unit-agency-present-173726.

38. See, for example, C. Page Moreau and Marit Gundersen Engeset, "The Downstream Consequences of Problem-Solving Mindsets: How Playing with LEGO Influences Creativity," *Journal of Marketing Research* 53, no. 1 (2016), 18–30.

39. Guiomar Martín-Herrán and Simon P. Sigué, "An Integrative Framework of Cooperative Advertising: Should Manufacturers Continuously Support Retailer Advertising?" *Journal of Business Research* 70, (January 2017), 67–73.

40. Shrihari Sridhar, Frank Germann, Charles Kang, and Rajdeep Grewal, "Relating Online, Regional, and National Advertising to Firm Value," *Journal of Marketing* 80, no. 4 (July 2016), 39–55.

41. The 2011 ranking for the U.S. Government ad spending was 56th in the United States at $738 million annual spending, "100 Leading National Advertisers," *Advertising Age*, June 25, 2012, 16.

42. Jason Blevins, "Colorado Breaks Tourism Record with 77.7 Million Visitors Spending $19.1 billion," *Denver Post*, July 20, 2016, http://www.denverpost.com/2016/07/20/record-colorado-tourism-2015/.

43. Bradley Johnson, "For Agencies, It's Morning Again in America… Maybe: Ad Agency Report 2021," *Advertising Age*, May 3, 2021, https://adage.com/article/datacenter/agencies-its-morning-again-america-maybe-ad-age-agency-report-2021/2331576.

44. Nathalie Tadena, "Publicis Says It Is 'Confident' About Sapient's Growth," *Wall Street Journal*, February 11, 2016, http://www.wsj.com/articles/publicis-says-it-is-confident-about-sapients-growth-1455214879.

45. John Harrington, "Omnicom Set to Take Full Ownership of London Agency Portland," *Advertising Age*, October 21, 2016, http://www.prweek.com/article/1412990/omnicom-set-full-ownership-london-agency-portland.

46. Shareen Pathak, "Looking for New Hires? Be Prepared to Pay Up," *Advertising Age*, April 30, 2012, 9.

47. Tessa Wegert, "Can Accenture Take Over Advertising?" *Contently*, July 29, 2016, https://contently.com/strategist/2016/07/29/can-accenture-take-over-advertising/.

48. See Mark W. Schaefer, "6 Reasons Marketing Is Moving In-House," *Harvard Business Review*, July 30, 2015, https://hbr.org/2015/07/6-reasons-marketing-is-moving-in-house.

49. "Coty Appoints Publicis as Lead Media Agency," *Cosmetics Business*, September 19, 2016, http://www.cosmeticsbusiness.com/news/article_page/Coty_appoints_Publicis_as_lead_media_agency/121166.

50. Davenport and Phillips, "The Future of Marketing Automation."

51. James de Vries, "PepsiCo's Chief Design Officer on Creating an Organization Where Design Can Thrive," *Harvard Business Review*, August 11, 2015, https://hbr.org/2015/08/pepsicos-chief-design-officer-on-creating-an-organization-where-design-can-thrive; and Jack Neff, "P&G Boosts Design's Role in Marketing," *Advertising Age*, February 9, 2004, 1, 52.

52. Natalie Zumda, "Pepsi Creates Chief Design Officer Role," *Advertising Age*, June 2012, http://adage.com/article/global-news/pepsico-adds-chief-design-officer-role-taps-3m-s-porcini/235264/.

53. Burt Helm, "Hollywood's Ad Auteur," *Bloomberg BusinessWeek*, January 18, 2010, 50–51.

54. Rupal Parekh, "TBWA's Answer to Client Squeeze: Anoint a Chief Compensation Officer," *Advertising Age*, February 8, 2010, 1, 21.

55. Nathalie Tadena, "Creative Ad Agencies Shake Up Legacy Model," *Wall Street Journal*, June 22, 2016, http://www.wsj.com/articles/creative-ad-agencies-shake-up-legacy-model-1466568061.

56. Rupal Parekh, "Fed-Up Shops Pitch a Fit at Procurement," *Advertising Age*, October 26, 2009, 1, 55.

57. Jeff Neff and Lisa Sanders, "It's Broken," *Advertising Age*, February 16, 2004, 75 (7), 1–30.

58. Lisa Sanders and Alice Z. Cuneo, "Fed-Up Agencies Quit Punching the Clock," *Advertising Age*, January 27, 2007.

59. Matthew Creamer, "Marketing's Five-Year Plan," *Advertising Age*, October 8, 2012, 22.

60. Lara O'Reilly, "McDonald's Is Paying Its New Ad Agency in an Unusual Way, but the Agency's Boss Explains Why Pay-for-Performance Is a Good Thing," *Business Insider*, September 1, 2016, http://www.businessinsider.com/ddb-ceo-wendy-clark-mcdonalds-2016-9.

61. Ann-Christine Diaz, "Production Company A-List 2015: B-Reel," *Advertising Age*, September 15, 2015, http://adage.com/article/creativity/creativity-production-company-a-list-2015-b-reel/300585/; and Ann-Christine Diaz, "Production Company of the Year: B-Reel," *Advertising Age*, February 20, 2012, 10.

62. Sahil Patel, "How Viacom Is Experimenting with New Tech to Engage Viewers," *DigiDay*, July 21, 2016, http://digiday.com/publishers/fans-first-inside-viacoms-emerging-tech-innovation-lab/; and Janine Poggi, "Viacom Aims to Make Data Accessible to All Marketers," *Advertising Age*, March 8, 2016, http://adage.com/article/special-report-tv-upfront/viacom-make-data-accessible-marketers/303007/.

63. Jonathan Bacon, "How Content Marketing Is Helping Philips Move into Healthcare," *Marketing Week*, October 18, 2016, https://www.marketingweek.com/2016/10/18/how-content-marketing-is-helping-philips-move-into-healthcare/.

The History of Advertising and Brand Promotion

Chapter 3

CSA-Printstock/DigitalVision Vectors/Getty Images

Some of the best advertising of all time has something in common: it leverages existing anxiety; it seeks to resolve cultural contradictions; it tugs on our heart strings or makes us think; it seeks to calm the individual consumer, and reinforces a marketer-friendly vision of society. Today the same basic dynamics persist; only the specifics differ. Knowing the past makes you much better in the present.

First, ads are part of their times. Great advertising uses consumer culture and current events to its advantage. To understand advertising and succeed in the advertising and integrated brand promotion business, you must understand that successful advertisements convey a particular version of contemporary culture and society. *If you are in the advertising business, you are in the culture and society business.*

We can best see the workings of culture at a distance. This is why there are such valuable lessons to be found in advertising's history. Most of us are too close to our own contemporary culture to see culture's consequences as easily as we can when separated by time. The idea is to get good at doing that: understanding your culture in the moment, in the present. The great advertising professionals have that ability. But to learn how to do that, most of us need lessons from the past. So when the sands of culture and society shift beneath consumers' feet, opportunities for advertisers present themselves, if one can see them. History helps one to see them.

Exhibit 3.1 ▶ This framework shows that the history of advertising is part of the overall environment of business and society, within which integrated brand promotion operates. The chapter covers the history of advertising from three perspectives, as illustrated here.

This chapter serves as an overview of the world of advertising and IBP

See the chapter framework in Exhibit 3.1. This chapter covers three perspectives of advertising history—practical lessons learned in the past that can be applied today and tomorrow. Throughout the decades, advertisers have tried many different strategies and approaches, and you can learn from their successes and failures. Most (but not all) ad strategies used today were invented decades ago—only specifics have changed, and sometimes not even those. In fact, some organizations actively archive and preserve advertising materials of the past so that advertising professionals can gain insights that will help them prepare new advertisements and brand promotions.[1] Studying advertising history will allow you to know when a given advertising technique is something new, and when and why it worked. You can see how particular advertising strategies leveraged the social forces of their day—and how you can leverage the ones of your day.

LO 1

3-1 Factors Behind The Rise of Advertising

Advertising is sometimes said to have had its origins in ancient times. However, actually advertising is a product of more modern times and media. Before we get into an overview of history of advertising in the Western world, let's first consider some of the key factors that gave rise to advertising. Advertising came into being as a result of at least four major factors:

1. The rise of capitalism
2. The Industrial Revolution
3. The emergence of modern branding
4. The rise of modern mass media

3-1a The Rise of Capitalism

The tenets of capitalism warrant that organizations compete for resources, called *capital*, in a free-market environment. Part of the competition for resources involves stimulating demand for the organization's goods or services. When an individual organization successfully stimulates demand, it attracts capital to the organization in the form of money (or other goods) as payment. One of the tools used to stimulate demand is advertising. So as the Western world turned to capitalism as the foundation of economic systems, the foundation was laid for advertising to become a prominent part of the business environment.

3-1b The Industrial Revolution

The **Industrial Revolution** was an economic force that yielded the need for advertising. Beginning about 1750 in England, the revolution spread to North America and progressed slowly until the early 1800s, when the War of 1812 in the United States boosted domestic production. The emergence of the principle of interchangeable parts and the perfection of the sewing machine, both in 1850, coupled with the American Civil War a decade later, set the scene for widespread industrialization. The Industrial Revolution took Western societies away from household self-sufficiency as a method of fulfilling material needs to dependency on a marketplace as a way of life. The Industrial Revolution was a force behind the increase in mass-produced goods that required stimulation of demand—something that advertising is good at. By providing a need for advertising, the Industrial Revolution was an influence in its emergence and growth in Western economies.

> ❝
> *Brands command a higher price than commodities (think Starbucks vs. coffee).*
> ❞

Part of the Industrial Revolution was a revolution in transportation, dramatically symbolized by the east–west connection of the United States in 1869 by the railroad. This connection represented the beginnings of the distribution network needed to move the mass quantities of goods for which advertising would help stimulate demand.

In the 1840s, the **principle of limited liability**, which restricts an investor's risk in a business venture to only his or her shares in a corporation rather than all personal assets, gained acceptance and resulted in the accumulation of large amounts of capital to finance the Industrial Revolution. Finally, rapid population growth and urbanization began taking place in the 1800s. From 1830 to 1860, the population of the United States nearly tripled, from 12.8 million to 31.4 million. During the same period, the number of cities with more than 20,000 inhabitants grew to 43. Historically, there is a strong relationship between per-capita outlays for advertising and an increase in the size of cities.[2] Modernity gave rise to both urbanism and advertising. Overall, the growth and concentration of population provided the marketplaces that were essential to the widespread use of advertising. As the potential grew for goods to be produced, delivered, and introduced to large numbers of people residing in concentrated areas, the stage was set for advertising to emerge and flourish.

3-1c The Emergence of Modern Branding

Modern capitalism required **branding**. Manufacturers had to develop brand names so that consumers could focus their attention on a clearly identified item. Manufacturers began branding previously unmarked commodities, such as work clothes and package goods. In the late 1800s, Ivory (1882), Coca-Cola (1886), Budweiser (1891), and Maxwell House (1892) were among the first branded consumer products to show up on shopkeepers' shelves (see Exhibit 3.2).

Source: Coca-Cola

Mauritius Images GmbH/Alamy Stock Photo

Exhibit 3.2 ▶ Integrated brand promotion in action: Coca-Cola.
Note the progression of branding for Coca-Cola from historic to modern times.

Coca-Cola's iconic bottle and well-known logo have been featured in the brand's integrated brand promotions for decades. *How is the company's long history of advertising likely to affect audiences for these two messages?*

Once a product had a brand mark and name that consumers could identify, marketers gained power. Brands command a higher price than commodities (think Ivory vs. soap). Branding required advertising. It's no accident of history that modern branding and modern advertising agencies appeared at exactly the same time in the late 19th century. Brand demand also gives marketers added power over retailers: if consumers demand Tide, the retailer better stock Tide.[3]

3-1d The Rise of Modern Mass Media

Advertising is also tied to the rise of mass communication. With the invention of the telegraph in 1844, a communication revolution was set in motion. The telegraph not only allowed nations to benefit from the inherent efficiencies of rapid communication but also did a great deal to engender a sense of national identity. People began to know and care about people and things going on thousands of miles away. This changed not only commerce but society as well.[4] Also, during this period, many new magazines designed for larger and less socially privileged audiences made magazines a viable mass advertising medium.[5] Through advertising in these mass-circulation magazines, brands could be projected into national consciousness. National magazines made national advertising possible; national advertising made national brands possible. Without the rise of mass media, there would be no national brands and no advertising.

It is critical to realize that for the most part, mass media are supported by advertising. Television networks, radio stations, newspapers, magazines, and websites produce shows, articles, films, programs, and Web content not for the ultimate goal of entertaining or informing, but to profit from selling brands through advertising and branded entertainment. Media vehicles sell audiences to make money.

3-2 The Eras of Advertising

So far, our discussion of the evolution of advertising has identified the fundamental social and economic influences that fostered advertising's rise. Now we'll turn our focus to the evolution of advertising in practice. A few important periods can be identified and considered. In each are valuable lessons on how and why advertising operates as it does.

3-2a The Preindustrialization Era (Pre 1800)

In the 17th century, printed advertisements appeared in newsbooks (the precursor to the newspaper).[6] The messages were informational in nature and appeared on the last pages of the tabloid. In America, the first newspaper advertisement is said to have appeared in 1704 in the *Boston News Letter.* Two notices were printed under the heading "Advertising" and offered rewards for the return of merchandise stolen from an apparel shop and a wharf.[7]

Advertising grew in popularity during the 18th century in both Britain and the American colonies. The *Pennsylvania Gazette* printed advertisements and was the first newspaper to separate ads with blank lines, which made the ads both easier to read and more prominent.[8] As far as we know, it was also the first newspaper to use illustrations in advertisements. But advertising changed little during the next 70 years. Even though the early 1800s saw the advent of the penny newspaper, which resulted in widespread distribution of the news media, advertisements in penny newspapers were dominated by simple announcements by skilled laborers. As one historian notes, "Advertising was closer to the classified notices in newspapers than to product promotions in our media today."[9] Advertising was about to change dramatically, however.

3-2b The Era of Industrialization (1800 to 1875)

In practice, users of advertising in the mid- to late 1800s were trying to cultivate markets for growing production in the context of an increasing urban population. A middle class, spawned by the rise of wages from factory jobs, was beginning to emerge. This newly developing population with the economic means to consume was concentrated in cities.

By 1850, circulation of the **dailies**, as newspapers were then called, was estimated at 1 million copies per day. The first advertising agent—thought to be Volney Palmer, who opened shop in Philadelphia—basically worked for the newspapers by soliciting orders for advertising and collecting payment from advertisers.[10] This new opportunity to reach consumers was embraced readily by merchants, and newspaper advertising volume soared.[11]

With the expansion of newspaper circulation fostered by the railroads and growing urban centers, a new era of opportunity emerged for advertising. Further, there were virtually no laws or regulations to restrict advertisers from saying or doing anything they cared to. Advertisers could outright lie, deceive, and otherwise cheat with little or no threat of being punished by government. Many advertisers took advantage of the situation, and advertising was commonly considered an embarrassment by some segments of society. At one point, firms even risked their credit ratings if they used advertising—banks considered the practice a sign of financial weakness. Advertising for patent medicines reinforced this tawdry reputation. These advertisements promised a cure for everything from rheumatism and arthritis to cancer. They were also one of the very first large categories of consumer packaged goods advertised on a mass scale. Exhibit 3.3 shows a typical ad of this period. It is for Bull's Sarsaparilla, and if you look closely at the ad's copy, you will read that Bull's will cure liver problems, kidney problems, syphilis, and that "faint gnawing feeling at the pit of the stomach."

3-2c The "P.T. Barnum Era" (1875–1918)

Shortly after the Civil War in the United States, modern advertising began. This is advertising that we would recognize as advertising. Even though advertising existed during the era of industrialization, it wasn't until America was well on its way to being an urban, industrialized nation that advertising became a vital and integral part of the social landscape. From 1875 to 1918, advertising ushered in what has come to be known as **consumer culture**, or a way of life centered on consumption. True, consumer culture was advancing prior to this period, but during this age, it took hold, and the rise of modern advertising had a lot to do with it. Advertising became a full-fledged industry in this period.

It was the time of advertising legends: Albert Lasker, head of Lord and Thomas in Chicago, possibly the most influential agency of its day; Francis W. Ayer, founder of N. W. Ayer; John E. Powers, the most important copywriter of the period; Earnest Elmo Calkins, champion of advertising design; Claude Hopkins, influential in promoting ads as "dramatic salesmanship;" and John E. Kennedy, creator of "reason why" advertising.[12] These were some of the founders, the visionaries, and the artists who played principal roles in the establishment of the advertising business. One interesting note is that several of the founders of this industry had fathers who shared the very same occupation: minister. This industry was founded in part by the sons of preachers. More than a coincidence, these young men would have been exposed to public speaking and the passionate selling of ideas, as well as to the need of 19th-century clergy to adapt to modernity: city life, science, progress, and public consumption. Sons of preachers were the ideal apostles of advertising and consumer culture.

By 1900, total sales of patent medicines in the United States had reached $75 million—an early demonstration

Exhibit 3.3 ▶ The expansion of newspapers fostered widespread use of advertising. Unfortunately, some of this advertising helped give advertising a bad name. Ads like this one promised cures for just about everything. At that time, there were no laws to prevent advertisers from saying anything they wanted. So the next time people ask who needs regulation, remind them of what advertisers did before the government stepped in.

of the power of advertising.[13] In this period, the first advertising agencies were founded, and the practice of branding became the norm. Advertising was motivated by the need to sell the vastly increased supply of goods brought on by mass production and by the demands of an increasingly urban population seeking social identity through branded products among other things. In earlier times, when shoppers went to the general store and bought soap sliced from a large, locally produced cake, advertising had no real place. But with advertising's ability to create meaningful differences between near-identical soaps, advertising suddenly became critical. Advertising made unmarked commodities into social symbols and identity markers, and it allowed marketers to charge far more money for them. Consumers were quite willing to pay more money for brands (e.g., Ivory) than for unmarked commodities (generic soap wrapped in plain paper), even if they were otherwise identical. This is the power of brands: the power of advertising—helping bestow desired meanings on things for sale.

Advertising was completely unregulated in the United States until 1906. In that year, Congress passed the **Pure Food and Drug Act**, which required manufacturers to list the active ingredients of their products on their labels. You could still put various ingredients in products; you just had to now tell the consumer. The direct effect of this federal act on advertising was minimal; advertisers could continue to say just about anything—and usually did. Many advertisements still took on the style of a "snake oil" sales pitch. The tone and spirit of advertising of this period owed more to P. T. Barnum—"There's a sucker born every minute"—than to any other influence. Of course, Barnum was the famous showman and circus entrepreneur (Barnum and Bailey Circus) of his day. So it's no surprise that ads of this period were bold, carnivalesque, garish, and often full of dense copy that hurled incredible claims at prototype modern consumers.

Several things are notable about these ads: more copy (words) than in today's ads; very little color, very little photography, and plenty of exaggeration and even some lies. During this period, there was variation and steady evolution, but this is what ads were generally like up until around World War I.

Consider the world in which these ads existed. It was a period of rapid urbanization, massive immigration, labor unrest, and significant concerns about the abuses of capitalism. Some of capitalism's excesses and abuses, in the form of deceptive and misleading advertising, were the targets of early reformers. It was also the age of the suffrage movement, the progressive movement, silent motion pictures, and mass culture. The world changed rapidly in this period, and it was no doubt disruptive and unsettling to many—but advertising was there to offer solutions to the stresses of modern life, no matter how real, imagined, or ad created. Advertisers had something to solve just about any problem. Social and cultural changes opened up opportunities for advertisers. Further, had World War I not occurred and diverted attention, it is very possible that there would have been more meaningful and earlier regulation of advertising. Just before World War I, there was a real and growing movement to significantly limit and regulate advertising, but that didn't happen. Exhibit 3.4 shows an ad that tries to use patriotism for the war effort by urging readers to either join the Armed Forces or buy war bonds. As a result of World War I, advertising became an often-used instrument of government policy and action.

3-2d The 1920s (1918–1929)

In many ways, the Roaring Twenties began a couple of years early. After World War I, advertising found respectability, fame, and even glamour. Working in an advertising agency was the most modern of all professions; it was, short of being in the movies, one of the most fashionable. According to popular perception, it was where the young, smart, and sophisticated worked and played. During the 1920s, advertising was also a place of very few restrictions. The prewar movement to reform and regulate advertising was pretty much dissipated by the distractions of the war and advertising's role in the war effort. During World War I, the advertising industry learned a valuable

Exhibit 3.4 ▶ The ad shown here illustrates cooperation between the American advertising industry and the U.S. government. As a result of its efforts in World War I, advertising became an often-used instrument of government policy and action.

lesson: Donating time and personnel to the common good is not only good civics (make your own judgment on war) but also smart business.

The 1920s were generally prosperous times. Most (but not nearly all) enjoyed a significantly improved standard of living. It was an age in which public pleasure was a lesser sin than in the Victorian era. Most importantly, a great social experiment in the joys of consumption was underway. Victorian repression and modesty gave way to a somewhat more open sexuality and to pleasure in general and a love affair with modernity. Advertising was made for this burgeoning hedonism; advertising gave people permission to enjoy and to enjoy now. The 1920s and advertising were made for each other. Ads of the era exhorted consumers to have a good time and instructed them how to do it. Consumption and advertising were becoming respectable.

During these relatively good economic times, advertising instructed consumers how to be thoroughly modern and how to avoid the pitfalls or side effects of this new age.

An important advertising logic is that good times always come with side effects and then a product to remedy the side effect. Consumers learned of halitosis from Listerine advertising and about body odor from Lifebuoy advertising. See the ad in Exhibit 3.5, a Lifebuoy ad from 1926. Notice the expression on the face of the man on the right—body odor alert. The other guy is not going to get a raise; he may get fired—for body odor.

Not too surprisingly, there just happened to be a product with a cure for just about any social anxiety and personal failing one could imagine, many of which had supposedly been brought on as side effects of modernity. This was perfect for the growth and entrenchment of advertising as an institution: Modern times bring on many wonderful new things, but the new way of life has side effects that, in turn, have to be remedied by even more modern goods and services, and on and on. For example, modern canned food replaced fresh fruit and vegetables, thus "weakening the gums," causing dental problems—which could be cured by a modern toothbrush. But the new toothbrush would require a new toothpaste— which then needed ever-better ingredients and additives. Thus, an endless consumption chain was created: Needs

lead to products; new needs are created by the unintended side effects of modern times and new products; even newer products solve even newer needs, and on and on. This **chain of needs** is essential to a capitalist economy, which must continue to expand in order to survive. This makes a necessity of advertising.

Other ads from the 1920s emphasized other modernity themes, such as the division between public workspace, the male domain of the office, and the private, "feminine" space of the home. Thus, two separate consumption domains were created, with women placed in charge of the latter— the one advertisers especially cared about. Advertisers soon figured out that women were responsible for as much as 90 percent of household purchases. While 1920s men were out in the jungle of the work world, women made most purchase decisions. So from this time forward, women became advertising's primary targets.

Another very important aspect of advertising in the 1920s and beyond was the role that science and technology began to play. Science and technology were in many ways the new religion of the modern era. The modern way was the scientific way. So one saw ads appealing to the popularity of science in virtually all product categories of advertising during this period. Ads stressed the latest scientific offerings. The style of 1920s ads was more visual than in the past. Twenties ads showed slices of life, or carefully constructed "snapshots" of social life with the brand. In these ads, the relative position, background, and dress of the people using or needing the advertised product were carefully crafted, as they are today. These visual lessons were generally about how to fit in with the "smart" crowd, how to be urbane and modern by using the newest conveniences, and how not to fall victim to the perils and pressure of the new fast-paced modern world. The social context of product use became critical. This is when and where "slice-of-life" advertising came from. It remains one of advertising's most popular and successful message forms. Reasons for its power are its inherently social nature and its ability to place brands in a carefully constructed social setting or moment in which ongoing social tensions and cultural contradictions can be resolved by merely purchasing the advertised brand.

During the 1920s, advertising began regularly constructing relationships between people and branded products by depicting the social settings and circumstances into which people and things fit, and what that fit yielded in terms of the consumer's life satisfaction. Consider Exhibit 3.6. Here is an advertiser trying to sell plumbing. The ad doesn't say a word about the plumbing, its physical qualities, its price, or anything else. But look at the attention paid to the era; it was the 1920s, when showing hygiene was important because in 1918 the great influenza epidemic killed millions of Americans. The ad works because it demonstrates plumbing in a social context that works for both advertiser and consumer: it soothes anxieties and resolves tensions and contradictions.

Source: Unilever U.S.A.

Exhibit 3.5 ▶ Here is a man with a limited future—if only he had used Lifebuoy.

J. Walter Thompson was the dominant agency of the period. Stanley Resor, Helen Resor, and James Webb Young brought this agency to a leadership position through management, vision, and great advertising. Helen Resor was the first prominent female advertising executive and was instrumental in J. Walter Thompson's success. Still, the most famous ad person of the era was a very interesting man named Bruce Barton. He was not only the leader of BBDO but also a best-selling author, most notably of a 1924 book called *The Man Nobody Knows*.[14] The book was about Jesus and portrayed him as the archetypal ad man. This was a best-selling book, indicating the popularity of reconciling things people feel conflicted about—cultural contradictions. Remember, brands and content that can resolve (even wishfully or partially) cultural contradictions and soothe social disruptions will often be effective.

Source: American Standard

Exhibit 3.6 ▶ Look at this ad: it is selling plumbing and never says a word about plumbing. It doesn't have to. The slice-of-life technique is used to perfection here. People in the 1920s knew why the baby was being weighed and why the modern bath looked so uncluttered and almost sterile.

3-2e The Depression (1929–1941)

By 1932, a quarter of American workers were unemployed. But matters were worse than this suggests, for three-quarters of those who had jobs were working part time—either working short hours or faced with chronic and repeated layoffs. . . . Perhaps half the working population at one time or another knew what it was like to lose a job. Millions went hungry, not once but again and again. Millions knew what it was like to eat bread and water for supper, sometimes for days at a stretch. A million people were drifting around the country begging, among them thousands of children, including numbers of girls disguised as boys. People lived in shanty towns on the fields at edges of cities, their food sometimes weeds plucked from the roadside.[15]

The Great Depression was brutal, crushing, and mean. It killed people; it broke lives. Those who lived through it and kept their dignity are to be deeply admired. Many of this greatest generation went on to fight in World War II. They gave of themselves for the common good; they may have been the last truly unselfish generation of Americans. The way people thought about work, money, and consumption would change forever after World War II. The change would be profitable for the advertising industry; whether it was good for society and its citizens is another question.

The **Great Depression** forever changed the way people thought about a great many things: their government, business, money, spending, saving, credit, and, not coincidentally, advertising. Just as sure as advertising was glamorous in the 1920s, it was suspect in the 1930s. Advertising was part of big business, and big business, big greed, and big lust had gotten America into the great economic depression beginning in 1929—or so the simple story goes. The public now saw advertising as something more suspect, something that had tempted and seduced people into the excesses for which they were being punished. The advertising industry's collective response only made things worse.

Advertisers responded to the depression by adopting a tough, no-frills advertising style. The stylish ads of the 1920s gave way to harsher, more cluttered, inappropriately sexual, and often egregiously unethical advertising. As one historian said, "The new hard-boiled advertising mystique brought a proliferation of 'ugly' attention-grabbing, picture-dominated copy in the style of the tabloid newspaper."[16] Clients wanted their money's worth, and agencies responded by cramming every bit of copy and image they could into their ads or using obviously inappropriate sex appeals. Advertisers played on the anxieties and vulnerabilities of troubled people. In the short run, these ads may have worked more often than not because they leveraged the social disruptions and cultural contradictions of the times. But their long-term effect was not positive

This type of advertising made the relationship between the public and the institution of advertising worse. It hurt advertising's public image; the public was getting wise to the opportunistic techniques and resented them, even when they worked. Regrettably, doing exactly the same thing is still an industry impulse in bad economic times today. The themes in advertisements traded on the anxieties of the day; losing one's job meant being a bad provider, spouse, or parent, unable to give the family what it needed—or, when nothing else came to mind: sex. The ad in Exhibit 3.7 is stylish, and done in the pin-up girl style.

Another notable event during these early years was the emergence of radio as a significant advertising medium. During the 1930s, the number of radio stations rose from a handful to 814 by the end of the decade, and the number of radio sets in use more than quadrupled to 51 million, slightly more than one radio set per household. Radio was in its heyday as a news and entertainment medium, and it would remain so until the 1950s when television emerged. An important aspect of radio was its ability to create a sense of community in which people thousands of miles apart listened to and became involved with their favorite radio soap opera, so named in reference to the soap sponsors of these shows. Radio's contribution to advertising history should not be underestimated. It not only ushered in the idea of broadcasting, but it also socialized consumers to depend on a connection to distant characters, programs, brands, and the idea that there were other people "out there" who shared this connection—a mass audience. Voices of radio friends from afar made good company, particularly during hard times.

The advertising industry, like the rest of the country, suffered during this period. Agencies cut salaries and forced staff to work four-day weeks without being paid for the mandatory extra day off. Clients demanded frequent review of work, and agencies were compelled to provide more and more free services to keep accounts. Advertising would emerge from this depression, just as the economy itself did, during World War II. However, the advertising industry would never again reach its pre-Depression cultural status.

The U.S. Congress passed real advertising reform in this period. In 1938, the Wheeler–Lea Amendments to the Federal Trade Commission Act declared "deceptive acts of commerce" to be against the law; this was interpreted to include advertising. This changed the entire game: Now individual advertisers could be held liable for deceptive practices. Between 1938 and 1940, the FTC issued 18 injunctions against advertisers, including "forcing Fleischmann's Yeast to stop claiming that it cured crooked teeth, bad skin, constipation and halitosis."[17] Believe it or not, eating yeast was successfully promoted by Fleishman's as a healthy practice. Government agencies soon used their new powers against a few large national advertisers, including Lifebuoy and Lux soaps. Advertisers would have to be at least a little more careful.

3-2f World War II and the 1950s (1942 to 1960)

In the 1950s,

Almost one-half of all women married while they were still teenagers. Two out of three white women in college dropped out before they graduated. In 1955, 41 percent of women "thought the ideal number of children was four."[18]

Many people mark the end of the Great Depression with the start of America's involvement in World War II in December 1941. During the war, advertising often made direct reference to the war effort, linking the advertised brand with patriotism and further helping to rehabilitate the tarnished image of advertising. During the war, advertisers sold war bonds and

Thomas O'Guinn

Exhibit 3.7 ▶ Look closely at this 1935 ad. It is done by famed pin-up artist George Petty (1894 to 1975) for Old Gold Cigarettes. It is so 1930s. Sex appeal, cigarettes, and a stretch in terms of the brand's promise: 1930s advertising at its best.

encouraged conservation. Of all companies, Coca-Cola probably both contributed to and benefited the most from its amazingly successful efforts to get Coca-Cola to the front lines.[19] Its World War II–period ads are classics; they create a social world in which Coca-Cola is expected, natural, and always welcoming. Examine the ad in Exhibit 3.8 showing U.S. soldiers sharing Cokes with Parisians, a goodwill gesture that also symbolizes the globalization of the soft-drink brand.

In addition, women joined the workforce in what were nontraditional roles, as seen in the so-called Rosie the Riveter ads. The ad in Exhibit 3.9 for the Penn Railroad is an example of this style. *Again, a smart advertiser leverages a social change.*

Following World War II, the economy continued (with a few notable starts and stops) to improve, and the consumption spree was on again. The first shopping malls were built in the suburbs to follow affluent populations and to create a more "feminine" shopping environment. It is during this

period that consumer culture became the new normal, a permanent central feature of society. Historian Liz Cohen terms it "a consumer's republic."

This time, however, public sentiment toward advertising itself was different from what it had been in the 1920s, following World War I. Public attitudes toward advertising were more negative, more skeptical, and the public largely assumed that it was very powerful. But why? Advertisers had been so patriotic during the war.

The reason is fairly simple. After World War II, there was widespread belief that America's successful propaganda experts at the War Department simply moved over to Madison Avenue and started manipulating consumer minds. At the same time, there was great concern about the rise of communism and its use of "mind control" in the Cold War. Perhaps it was only natural to believe that advertising was involved in the same type of pursuit. The United States was filled with suspicion related to McCarthyism, the bomb, repressed sexual thoughts (witness a resurgence of Freudian

Exhibit 3.8 ▶ Study this ad. In it you will see an illustration by the artist Louis Bouche (1886 to 1969) in which the newly liberated Paris is cast through the prism of one of the world's very first global brands: Coca-Cola. Think about how the ad uses the moment (the end of World War II in 1945) to sell Coke.

Exhibit 3.9 ▶ During the war, advertisers encouraged women to work outside the home, as this ad for Penn Railroad illustrates. The advertiser served the interests of government and promoted itself.

thought), and creatures from atomic science gone bad: *The Fifty-Foot Woman* (Exhibit 3.10), *Pods, Blob, The Un-Dead,* and *Body-Snatchers*, to name a few movies of the time. One of the common themes of these films was that it was hard to know who was "one of them" and who was "one of us." This was often said to be an allegory to not knowing who was working to subvert American ideals while looking, acting, and sounding just like "us." People were building bomb shelters in their backyards, wondering whether listening to rock 'n roll would make their daughters less virtuous.

The 1950s were about fear, and advertisers again leveraged the accompanying disruption. Fearful people might be coaxed into anything that made them feel more secure. But at the same time, that fear of being manipulated by "modern science" and "mind control" made them very wary of advertising. Like other times, advertisers would turn these anxieties, contradictions, and social disruptions into advertising strategies.

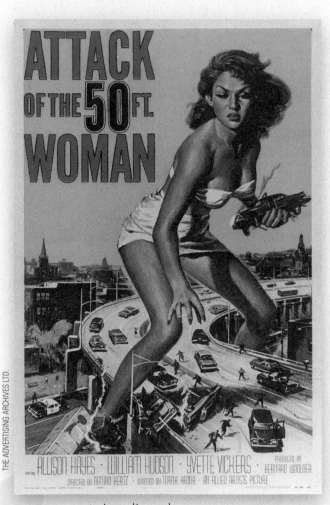

Exhibit 3.10 ▶ Irradiated women were part of the 1950s culture of titillation and great ambivalence to modern science. This was the culture; and ads were the culture—no wonder 1950s ads, including this movie ad, were sometimes weird.

In this environment of mass fear, stories began circulating in the 1950s that advertising agencies were doing motivation research and using the "psychological sell," which served only to fuel an underlying suspicion of advertising. It was also during this period that Americans began to fear they were being seduced by **subliminal advertising** (subconscious advertising) to buy all sorts of things they didn't want or need. There had to be a reason that homes and garages were filling up with so much stuff; it must be all that powerful advertising—what a great excuse. In fact, a best-selling 1957 book, *The Hidden Persuaders*, offered the answer: Slick advertising worked on the subconscious.[20] This very popular book made a lot of sense to 1950s consumers, and suspicions about slick advertising's power persist to this day.

The most incredible story of the period involved a man named James Vicary. According to historian Stuart Rogers, in 1957, Vicary convinced the advertising world, and most of the U.S. population, that he had successfully demonstrated a technique to get consumers to do exactly what advertisers wanted. He claimed to have placed subliminal messages in a motion picture, brought in audiences, and recorded the results. He claimed that the embedded messages of "Eat Popcorn" and "Drink Coca-Cola" had increased sales of popcorn by 57.5 percent and Coca-Cola by 18.1 percent. He held press conferences and took retainer fees from advertising agencies. According to later research, he then skipped town, just ahead of reporters who had figured out that none of his claims had ever happened. He completely disappeared, leaving no bank accounts and no forwarding address. He left town with about $4.5 million (around $28 million in today's dollars) in advertising agency and client money.[21] The bigger problem is that a lot of people still believe in the hype Vicary was selling and that advertisers can actually do such things—and easily.

The 1950s were also about sex, and sex in a very paradoxical and conflicting way. On the one hand, the 1950s were about conformity, chastity, the nuclear family, and very strict gender roles and sexual norms. On the other, this was the time of neo-Freudian pop psychology and presexploitation films dripping with sexual innuendo and titillation. Sexual desire is everywhere in 1950s popular culture, but so is the countervailing message: chastity for women; a tempered "boys-will-be-boys" for young men. Double standards for adult sexual behavior were common—men couldn't help themselves, but women had to. In fact, it was during the latter part of this period that ad consultant Ernest Dichter actually advised one of the big three U.S. carmakers to remember: think of the family car (station wagon; big sedan) as a man's wife; the sports car his "mistress." Now there is one large cultural contradiction to exploit—and they did. This was not advertising's finest hour.

What's more, the kids of the 1950s would be advertised to with a singular focus and force never seen before, becoming, as a result, the first TV-kid market and then the first teen ad targets. Because of their sheer numbers, they would ultimately constitute an unstoppable youth culture, one that everyone else had to deal with and try to please—the baby boomers. They would, over their parents' objections, buy rock 'n roll records in numbers large enough to revolutionize the music industry. Now they buy SUVs, mutual funds, and $15,000 bicycles and will retire with you in the wake (and debt) of their consumption.

And then there was TV. Nothing like it had happened before. Its rise from pre-World War II science experiment to 90 percent penetration in U.S. households occurred during this period. At first, advertisers didn't know what to do with it and produced two- and three-minute commercials, typically demonstrations. Of course, they soon began to learn TV's look and language.

This era also saw growth in the U.S. economy and in household incomes. The suburbs emerged, and along with them, there was an explosion of consumption. Technological change was relentless and was a national obsession. The television, the telephone, and the automatic washer and dryer became common to the American lifestyle. Advertisements of this era were characterized by scenes of modern life, social promises, and reliance on science and technology. Chemicals, all kinds of chemicals, were good, and good for you. The ad in Exhibit 3.11 is real. That's right: "DDT IS GOOD FOR ME." This ad ran in 1947. Yes, a chemical that has been banned in the United States since the 1970s was sold as being "good for you."

Essentially, 1950s advertising projected a confused, often harsh, while at other times sappy, presence. It is rarely remembered as advertising's golden age. Two of the most significant advertising personalities of the period were Rosser Reeves of the Ted Bates agency, who is best remembered for his ultra-hard-sell style (see Exhibit 3.13), and consultant Ernest Dichter, best remembered for his motivational research, which focused on the subconscious and symbolic elements of consumer desire. *Mad Men* watchers, do you recognize these characters? Exhibit 3.12 is representative of the advertising from this contradictory and jumbled period in American advertising. Can you see why advertising (and the culture) needed a revolution?

Fifties ads show mythic nuclear families, well-behaved children, our "buddy" the atom, an uneasy faith in science, and rigid (but about to break loose) gender roles, while the rumblings of the sexual revolution of the 1960s were just audible. In a few short years, the atom would no longer be our friend (as it is in Exhibit 3.13); we would question science; youth would rebel and become a hugely important market; women and people of color would demand inclusion and fairness; and bullet bras would be replaced with no bras. Oral birth control's introduction in 1960 would change the culture's view of appropriate sexual behavior, or at least consequences. A period of great social change would occur, which is usually a very good time for advertisers: new needs, new liberties, new anxieties, new goods and services, and new brands. Again, social disruption and cultural

Source: Penn Salt

An ad for Penn Salt Chemicals boasts "DDT is good for me!" and "The great expectations held for DDT have been realized."

Exhibit 3.11 ▶ Yes, DDT is "a benefactor of all humanity." And you thought it was just another banned toxic chemical. It was not uncommon then, nor now, for industrial products or practices to be advertised in this style.

contradictions in need of resolution; it is in this space that many great brands and great advertising emerged.

3-2g Peace, Love, and the Creative Revolution (1960–1972)

As you probably know, there was a cultural revolution in the 1960s. It affected just about everything—including advertising. Ads started to take on the themes, the language, and the look of the 1960s. But as an institution, advertising during the 1960s was actually slow to respond to the massive social revolution going on all around it. While the world was struggling with civil rights, the Vietnam War, the sexual revolution, and the youth revolution, advertising was, for the most part,

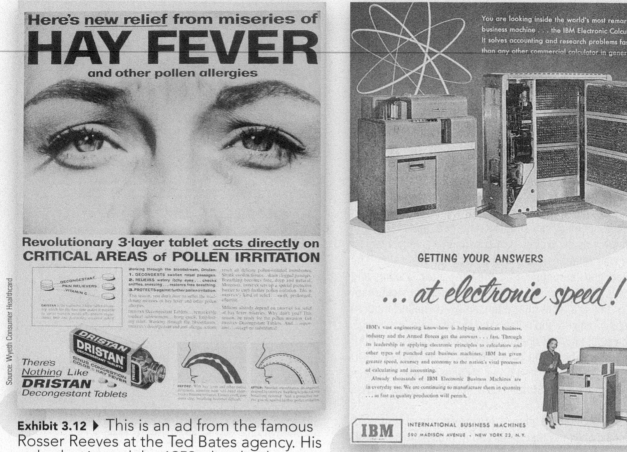

Exhibit 3.12 ▶ This is an ad from the famous Rosser Reeves at the Ted Bates agency. His style dominated the 1950s: harsh, abrasive, repetitive, and diagrammatic. He believed that selling the brand had virtually nothing to do with art or winning creative awards. His style of advertising is what the creative revolution revolted against.

Exhibit 3.13 ▶ Check out the atomic symbol next to this early computer from IBM. That would be very odd to see today, but it made perfect sense in the 1950s, when atomic power was new and considered cutting edge.

still portraying women and other minorities in subservient roles (see Exhibit 3.14). As writer Thomas Frank has pointed out, advertising leveraged the trappings and the revolutionary impulse of the decade to sell things, yet it remained a fairly conservative capitalist institution. Advertising agencies remained one of the whitest industries in America. People who went against the heteronormative lifestyle, as far as advertising was concerned, didn't exist. And in ads, much of the sexual revolution wasn't exactly liberating for everyone.

The thing that stood out about 1960s advertising was the creativity. This creative revolution was characterized by the "creatives" (art directors and copywriters) having a bigger say in the management of their agencies, and the look and feel of the ads. The emphasis in advertising turned "from ancillary services to the creative product; from science and research to art, inspiration, and intuition."[22] At first, the look of this revolutionary advertising was clean and minimalist, with

simple copy and a sense of self-effacing humor. Later (around 1968 or so), it became something more. In the late 1960s, advertising had finally changed in meaningful ways. For one, it became fairly self-aware. Advertising admitted being advertising, and sometimes even poked fun at itself. Ads during the late 1960s and into the early 1970s conveyed the sentiment, "okay, here's an ad, you know it's an ad—and so do we." That was something new. Advertising began to trade on insider status—making fun of the straight and now silly ads of the 1950s and by playing to a sense of irony. This insider ironic orientation made advertising occasionally hip. The 1960s was when advertising began to understand that it was all about hip, cool, youth, and rebellion. From that point on, defining and chasing cool was a prime advertising directive. But as is typically the case, the 1960s cultural revolution soon became ad copy. Everything became rebellion; even an unhip brand like Dodge tried to cash in with the "Dodge Rebellion."[23] Once

Exhibit 3.14 ▶ Something special in the air. This ad from American Airlines shows that not everyone got the memo on the revolution. What is this ad about?

Exhibit 3.15 ▶ Doyle Dane Bernbach made VW in the United States a reality. The agency did it by self-effacing and very cool advertising. This ad is from one of the most famous U.S. campaigns of all time.

advertising learned that it could successfully attach itself to youth, hipness, and revolution, it never went back. Even hip anti-advertising sentiment could be used to help sell stuff through advertising. That is ironic.

The creative revolution, and the look it produced, is most often associated with four famous advertising agencies: Leo Burnett in Chicago, Ogilvy & Mather in New York, Doyle Dane Bernbach in New York (DDB), and Wells Rich and Green in New York. They were led in this revolution by agency heads Leo Burnett, David Ogilvy, Bill Bernbach, and Mary Wells. Recall the image of advertising professionals in the hit series *Mad Men*? A great deal of the story line and characters come from here. The Volkswagen and Braniff ads pictured in Exhibits 3.15 and 3.16 are 1960s ads prepared by Bernbach and Wells, respectively. Note how the ad in Exhibit 3.16 is sexist because it features a woman in a bikini for an airline ad; it is incongruent with sex or nudity and has no place other than to use a scantily clad woman for attention. Thankfully, there is less tolerance for such sexist ads today—in part due to the control that consumers have in expressing distaste for sexist or racist ads via social media.

Of course, not all 1960s ads were revolutionary. Plenty of ads in the 1960s still reflected traditional values and relied on relatively worn-out executions. Pepsi may have taken better advantage of the disruptions of the 1960s than any other advertiser. As late as the mid-1950s, Coke had an enormous lead over Pepsi. Up until the 1960s, Pepsi kept trying to sell Pepsi as a product based on taste. It was only when the company switched from trying to sell the product (a cola) to selling the consumers who drank it, "those who think young," that it began to eat up Coke's lead. As noted by Thomas Frank and others, it was Pepsi's new strategy to "name and claim the youth revolution as their own." There was a growing generation gap/war; Pepsi leveraged that beautifully. Coke is for old un-hip people; Pepsi is for us cool kids (Exhibit 3.17), traded on youth and the idea of youth. Within a few short years, Pepsi had pulled almost even with Coke, erasing a 3-to-1 lead coming out of World War II. Again, the company did it by leveraging the contractions, anxieties, and social dislocations of the day—cultural marketing and advertising at work.

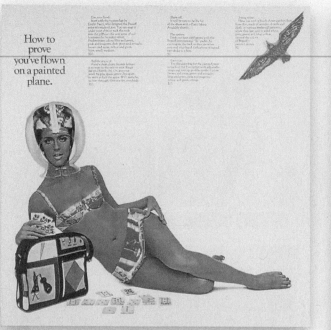

Exhibit 3.16 ▶ Mary Wells was one of the giants of the creative revolution. Here, she sells Braniff Airlines (now defunct) through the space bikini motif. This is very 1960s.

Exhibit 3.17 ▶ Pepsi "created" a generation and traded on the discovery of the vast youth market. Pepsi claimed youth as its own. www.pepsi.com

A final point: The era from 1960 to 1972 was a period when advertising as an institution became generally aware of its own role in consumer culture. While advertising played a role in encouraging consumption, it had become a symbol of consumption itself. Musicians (think Bob Dylan, The Who, the Rolling Stones), artists (think Warhol, Lichtenstein), filmmakers, poets, and authors were all very aware that advertising, consuming, youth, revolution, sex, satisfaction, and identity were all jumbled up together. The paradox of advertising/marketing/consuming had gone public. The love/hate relationship was now being celebrated in art (Warhol, Lichtenstein) and in movies and in songs. Advertisers learned that people (particularly youth) play out their revolutionary impulse *through* consumption—even when it's an anticonsumption revolution, you've got to have the right look, the right clothes, the right revolutionary garb. In a very significant way, advertising learned how to forever dodge the harshest criticism of the very thing that advanced capitalism: Hide in plain sight. Paradox is good business.

Thomas Frank suggested that since the 1960s nothing has been particularly new—just another branded faux-revolution. Every few years, it seems, the cycles of the 60s repeat themselves on a smaller scale, with new rebel youth cultures bubbling their way to a happy replenishing of the various culture industries' depleted arsenal of cool. New generations obsolete the old, new celebrities render old ones ridiculous, and on and on in an ever-ascending spiral of hip upon hip.

As ad-man Merle Steir wrote back in 1967, "Youth has won. Youth must always win. The new naturally replaces the old." And we will have new generations of youth rebellion as certainly as we will have generations of mufflers or toothpaste or footwear.[24]

3-2h The 1970s (1973–1980)

Mr. Blutarski, fat, drunk, and stupid is no way to go through life.

—Dean Vernon Wormer (John Vernon) in National Lampoon's *Animal House*, 1978

Dean Wormer's advice to John Belushi's character in *Animal House* captured essential aspects of the 1970s, a time of excess and self-induced numbness. It was the end of the cultural revolution.

The reelection of Richard Nixon in 1972 marked the real start of the 1970s. The 1970s was the age of polyester, disco, and drugs. But more than anything else, it was America's age of self-doubt. America had just suffered through its first lost war, the memory of four student protesters shot and killed by the National Guard at Kent State University in the spring of 1970 was still vivid, Mideast nations appeared to be dictating the energy policy of the United States, and the Americans were, as President Jimmy Carter suggested late in this period, in a national malaise. In this environment, advertising retreated a bit from the creative revolution. The ads of this period took sexuality in advertising bit further, seemed a little less artistic, were a little more racially integrated, and used a bit more hard-sell.

The major social shifts of the decade were the second wave of American feminism, the self-doubt of Western democracies, and a mass identity/authenticity question "Who am I; What is real?" (See how the Coca-Cola company smartly answered the question in Exhibit 3.18.) "What can I believe in?" Part of this was the rise of the self-help-therapy industry; the philosophy and advice that seemed to sell the best was "it's okay to be selfish." "Me" became the biggest word in the 1970s, implying that it was not only OK to be selfish, but it was the right thing to do. Selfishness was said to be natural and good. Many ads implied that being good to oneself

often meant self-indulgence, self-gifting, and buying material things—which can be good for advertising.

Still, most periods have countercurrents: the 1970s saw added regulation for the protection of special audiences. First, there was growing concern over what effect $200 million a year in advertising had on children. A group of women in Boston formed **Action for Children's Television**, which lobbied the government to limit the amount and content of advertising directed at children. Established regulatory bodies, in particular the **Federal Trade Commission (FTC)** and the industry's **National Advertising Review Board**, demanded higher standards of honesty and disclosure from the advertising industry. A clever end-run around this was the advent of what were essentially program-length commercials (PLCs), particularly in children's television. Another term for this type of programming is infomercials. Product/show blends for toys like Barbie made regulation more difficult: If it's a show about a product, then it's not technically an ad (and can't be regulated as an ad)—or is it? This drove regulators crazy, but program-length commercials were here to stay, at least in the United States.[25] They were generally treated by regulators as shows (with some degree of First Amendment protection) and opened the door for countless imitators. So in a real sense, what is now being called the "new" branded entertainment had its start in the 1970s.

Several firms were subjected to legislative mandates and fines because their advertising was judged to be misleading. Most notable among these firms were Warner-Lambert (for advertising that Listerine mouthwash could cure and prevent colds), Campbell's (for putting marbles in the bottom of a soup bowl to bolster its look), and Anacin (for advertising that its aspirin could help relieve tension).

During the 1970s, advertising agency hiring and promotion practices with respect to minorities were formally challenged in the courts. The industry remained very white. In what is to this day an odd segregation, "specialty" agencies emerged for serving various ethnic groups. Two important agencies owned and managed by Black Americans thrived: Thomas J. Burrell founded Burrell Advertising, and Byron Lewis founded Uniworld. Burrell is perhaps best known for ads that rely on the principle of "positive realism." Positive realism is "people working productively; people engaging in family life . . . people being well-rounded . . . and thoughtful; people caring about other people; good neighbors, good parents . . . people with dreams and aspirations; people with ambition." Burrell once said, "in 30 seconds you can build a brand and break a stereotype." He also believed that "whites are easier to reach through black advertising than vice versa."[26] "The idea was that we don't have to be the same as white people to be equal to white people; that we should celebrate our differences while not shying away from demanding our rights."[27]

One of Burrell's ads is shown in Exhibit 3.19. Another very important person was John H. Johnson, founder of *Ebony* magazine, and in many ways the man who made the Black

Source: The Coca-Cola Company

Exhibit 3.18 ▶ Claiming authenticity is tried and true branding, particularly when it is at the center of cultural conversations and social disruption. It was during the 1960s and 1970s. Is it now?

American experience in publishing, marketing, and advertising possible. He opened up enormous opportunities for black entrepreneurs, advertisers, and artists. His funeral was attended by a former U.S. president, U.S. senators, celebrities, and a lot of people who simply adored him. He was very important in advertising and beyond.

The 1970s also signaled a period of growth in communications technology. Consumers began to surround themselves with devices related to communication. The VCR, cable television, and the laser disc player were all developed during the 1970s. Cable TV claimed 20 million subscribers by the end of the decade. Similarly, cable programming grew in quality with viewing options such as ESPN, CNN, TBS, and Nickelodeon. As cable subscribers and their viewing options increased, advertisers learned how to reach more specific audiences through the diversity of programming on cable systems.

There was, as always, a youth undercurrent of revolution (with a small "r") in the 1970s. This one was more cynical and ambivalent about consumption and advertising than the one a decade earlier. Their anticonsumption thesis was set to music by hundreds of British punk and American alternative bands. Although notably more ironic and cynical than their 1960s counterparts, it was still about finding authenticity, identity, and meaning in a sea of consumption and ads. The ad in Exhibit 3.20 is pretty typical of the period. As you can see from this ad, there was more inclusion by the 1970s. It was not, however, even across categories. You can also see a pretty typical 1970s visual style, a bit crowded, somewhat reminiscent of the 1930s. The headline "Have it your way" was one of Burger King's most famous slogans. It noted BK's willingness to customize your burger, a rare thing at the time.

3-2i The Designer Era (1980 to 1992)

Greed, for a lack of a better word, is good.
—Gordon Gekko (Michael Douglas) in
Wall Street, 1987

Exhibit 3.19 ▶ Although a bad economy and a national malaise caused a retreat to the tried-and-true styles of decades before, a bright spot of 1970s advertising was the portrayal of people of color. Thomas Burrell created ads that portrayed Black people with "positive realism."

Exhibit 3.20 ▶ This Burger King ad was appropriate for the period and also foreshadowed the coming trend of customization.

"In 1980, the average American had twice as much real income as his parents had had at the end of WWII."[28] The political, social, business, and advertising landscape changed in 1980 with the election of Ronald Reagan. The country made a right, and conservative politics were the order of the day. There was, of course, some backlash and many countercurrents, but the conservatives were in the mainstream. Greed was good, stuff was good, and advertising was good. American, Britain, and the West generally experienced a profound political and consumption shift. In the fall of 1989, the Berlin Wall fell, and those in the East were now free to buy. Mass-market capitalism and consumerism experienced some glory days.

In the 1980s, we witnessed the label moving from inside the shirt to the outside. Although it had started in the 1970s, the 1980s saw the explosion of designer goods: everything became about public consumption, status, and their markers. Not surprisingly, many ads from the designer era are particularly social-class conscious and values conscious. They openly promote consumption but in a conservative way, wrapped up in "traditional American values." The quintessential 1980s ad may be the 1984 television ad for President Ronald Reagan's reelection campaign,

"Morning in America." The storyboard for this ad is shown in Exhibit 3.21. This ad is soft in texture, but it is a firm reaffirmation of family and country—and capitalism. Other advertisers quickly followed with ads that looked similar to "Morning in America." The 1980s were also about designer labels, social-class consciousness, and having stuff. Television advertising of the 1980s period was influenced by the rapid-cut editing style of MTV: rapid cuts with a very self-conscious character.

The advertising of the 1980s had a few other changes. One was the growth and creative impact of British agencies, particularly Saatchi and Saatchi. One of the things Saatchi and Saatchi realized earlier than most was that politics, culture, and products all resonate together. The Saatchi and Saatchi ads of this period were often sophisticated and politically nonneutral. In the United Kingdom, they more openly blended politics and advertising. They worked, and they began to be copied (at least the sensibility) in other places, including the United States. Exhibit 3.22 is pretty typical of 1980s North American ads. Please look at its visual composition and the relatively small number of words (copy). Eighties ads were visually a bit "in your face."

Exhibit 3.21 ▶ An ad that embodied the tone and style of 1980s advertising was Ronald Reagan's 1984 reelection campaign ad "Morning in America." The ad is soft in texture but firm in its affirmation of the conservative values of family and country.

Imitation is the sincerest form of flattery.

Tanqueray. A singular experience.

Exhibit 3.22 ▶ Look over the ad below. Tight visual focus, edgy for its day, and few words, all are pretty typical of the 1980s print ad style.

3-2j The E-Revolution Begins (1993 to 2000)

Some say that Internet advertising became truly viable around 1993. One can argue with the exact date, but somewhere near the mid-1990s is the point where it became clear that Internet adverting and other e-brand promotions were not only here to stay but were going to change the entire advertising landscape. From that date until the dot-com meltdown in 2000, advertising was struggling with all sorts of new possibilities and challenges. Ads in traditional media were getting edgier while e-ads were still trying to define themselves: find their best form.

There were scary moments for those heavily vested in traditional advertising. In May 1994, Edwin L. Artzt, then chairman and CEO of Procter & Gamble (P&G), the then $40 billion-a-year marketer of consumer packaged goods, dropped a bomb on the advertising industry. During an address to participants at the American Association of Advertising Agencies (4As) annual conference, he warned that agencies must confront a "new media" future that won't be driven by traditional advertising. Although at that time P&G was spending about $1 billion a year on television advertising, Artzt told the 4As audience, "From where we stand today, we can't be sure that ad-supported TV programming will have a future in the world being created—a world of video-on-demand, pay-per-view, and subscription TV. These are designed to carry no advertising at all."[29] This was not good news to those who preferred business as usual.

Then, just when the industry had almost recovered from Artzt's dire proclamation, William T. Esrey, chairman and CEO of Sprint, gave it another jolt a year later at the same annual conference. Esrey's point was somewhat different but equally challenging to the industry. He said that clients are "going to hold ad agencies more closely accountable for results than ever before. That's not just because we're going to be more demanding in getting value for our advertising dollars. It's also because we know the technology is there to measure advertising impact more precisely than you have done in the past."[30] Esrey's point: new **interactive media** will allow direct measurement of ad exposure and impact, quickly revealing those ads that perform well and those that do not. Secondly, the agency will be held accountable for results. The saga continues. Still unsure of what could be delivered and what could be counted, in August 1998, P&G hosted an Internet "summit," due to "what is widely perceived as the poky pace of efforts to eliminate the difficulties confronted by marketers using online media to pitch products."[31] Some of these problems were technological: incompatible standards, limited bandwidth, and disappointing measurement of both audience and return on investment. Others were the result of naïveté. Advertisers such as P&G want to know what they were getting and what it costs when they place an Internet ad. Does anyone notice these ads, or do people click right past them? What would "exposure" in this environment mean? Is "exposure" even a meaningful term in the new media ad world? How do you use these new media to build brands? At the end of this summit, P&G reaffirmed its commitment to the Internet.

But history again showed that measurement of bang for buck (return on investment, ROI) in advertising (Internet or not) is very elusive. Although better than TV, the Internet was fundamentally unable to yield precise measurements of return on investment in advertisement due to too many variables, too much noise in the system, too many delayed effects, and too many uncertainties about who is online. But advertisers still became more demanding in terms of "results." This has been largely the case throughout advertising's history. Ad agencies are now operating with fewer staff and smaller margins than before. Clients are more tightfisted these days and at least try to demand accountability. Things have certainly changed, particularly in print advertising, but not all old media are sick, much less dead.

Another change has come in the form of a significant challenge to New York's claim as the center of the advertising universe. In the United States, the center moved west, with the ascendancy of agencies in California, Minnesota, Oregon, and Washington, not to mention international hot spots such as London and Singapore. In the 1990s, these agencies tended to be more creatively oriented and less interested in numbers-oriented research than those in New York. Other important advertising markets include Minneapolis, Austin, Atlanta, Houston, and Dallas. Outside the United States, London emerged as the key player, with Singapore and Seoul as close seconds.

In terms of style and cultural connections, the 1990s was (like most eras) a mixed bag. But one clear trend was what some have referred to as an abundance of irony and soft cynicism. In the 1990s, self-parody of advertising was the inside joke, except everyone was "inside." Winks and nods to the media-savvy audience were pretty common. Ads said in a sense, "This is an ad . . . you know it, we know it, but we are still going to try to sell you something." This was said to be a product of the Generation-X mindset. This was slacker cynicism: laid-back cool; no ladder climbing; just hanging out; having heard it all before. These words from 1999's *Fight Club* say it well:

> *Advertising has us chasing cars and clothes, working jobs we hate so we can buy **** we don't need. We're the middle children of history, man. No purpose or place. We have no Great War. No Great Depression. Our Great War's a spiritual war . . . our Great Depression is our lives. We've all been raised on television to believe that one day we'd all be millionaires and movie gods and rock stars. But we won't. And we're slowly learning that fact. And we're, very p ***ed off.*

Fight Club and Nirvana were examples of touchstones of cutting-edge 1990s culture. Advertising was fast, and it was self-consciously hip. Exhibit 3.23 is a good example of this period's print style.

Source: Susan Van Etten

Exhibit 3.23 ▶ This ad leverages the well-known mom–teenager language problem. The visual style is a cool, pen-drawn look.

3-2k Consumer Access, Connections, Branded Entertainment, and the Rise of Ad Blockers (2000 to 2020)

When the dot-com bubble burst in 2000, many online companies that never turned a profit went out of business. Part of the problem was that pop-up ads and easy-to-avoid Internet ads had not generated enough advertising revenue. Online buying continued to grow, but online advertising couldn't catch up until companies became more sophisticated at using new media to generate sales. The corner seems to have been turned around 2002. Phase II of the digital advertising revolution (tied to Web 2.0) has been much more successful. One major difference between Web 2.0 and what came before is the basic consumer-advertising/brand promotion model—it is now much more about pull than push. Consumers still have to hear about your brand in the first place, but that's where the integration of media comes in: one medium makes you

aware, another pulls you, and another engages you (more in Chapters 14 and 15).

Consumers can now communicate with each other, enter into a dialogue with advertisers, and even make their own ads and distribute them on social media such as YouTube. Consumers now "cocreate" brand messages and brands in a meaningful way. Consumers' reactions (particularly young people's) are fused with agency "professional" creatives to make ads that are one step from homemade, or in some cases completely homemade. This is typically called **consumer-generated content (CGC)**. As a result of these industry changes, *Advertising Age* has declared this the "post-advertising age."

Other observers point to the rise of the **ad blocker**—software that consumers install to prevent advertising messages from being visible—as another reason for the post-advertising age. Millions of consumers around the world use ad blockers to keep potentially distracting or annoying ad messages out of sight on a laptop, tablet computer, desktop computer, or smartphone. With consumers in charge of whether to view messages, advertisers have to work harder and smarter to attract attention, engage consumers, and make any integrated brand promotion a great experience.[32]

Although it may be premature to declare that we are in the post-advertising age, things have changed a lot, and greater consumer connectivity and control are key reasons. Major changes such as these can be leveraged to create compelling advertising campaigns. Do you see any of these conditions being leveraged in this ad (Exhibit 3.24), or do you just see pretty traditional product-based pitches, or maybe cool images that get attention? Check them out.

There was also a proliferation of business-to-business promotion online, in which companies selling to business customers (rather than to household consumers) began to rely on the Internet to send messages and close sales. Because of advances in technology, firms like Harley-Davidson and P&G continue to invest heavily in newer means of connecting with consumers, not just for efficiency but also for the opportunity to develop more relevant and engaging branded experiences. For instances, businesses such as IBM are leveraging multiple promotions to keep their brands in front of target audiences. Exhibit 3.25 shows the Harley Owners Group website, a branded community for Harley owners. As another example, P&G maintains a heavy schedule of product sampling and in-store promotions, as well as operating dozens of websites for the company's brands to serve and interact with customers worldwide. The company is very active on social media, particularly on Facebook, where it can reach large audiences or, when needed, target more precisely for specific brands and products. At the same time, P&G has "made a choice to raise the bar on creativity, and that's the key to our market growth," says the chief brand officer. So campaigns like "Like a Girl" (for the Always feminine hygiene brand, identified as #LikeAGirl), which run both online and in traditional media, have not only earned industry awards but have also had a positive effect on market share and brand profitability.[33]

Source: Pepsi Cola Company

Exhibit 3.24 ▶ "Drink up, Rock Out"—really? Is this ad as simpleminded as it seems? Are we missing some greater meaning, or is it just Rock Out = Pepsi?

Branded entertainment is the blending of advertising and integrated brand promotion with entertainment, primarily film, music, and television programming. A subset of branded entertainment is *product placement*, the significant placement of brands within films or television programs. When the CW Network's teen drama *Riverdale* featured characters with Doritos, and when singer Lizzo's music video showed

her holding a bag of Cheetos, audiences took notice. Branded entertainment takes product placement a quantum leap forward. With branded entertainment, a brand is not just featured at times, but it is a star of the program (see Exhibit 3.26). BMW is an early participant in branded entertainment and still a standout in using the technique. BMW launched the BMW Web film series in 2001 and has featured the work of well-known directors, including Neill Blomkamp, Wong Kar-Wai, Ang Lee, John Frankenheimer, Guy Ritchie, and Alejandro Gonzalez Inärritu. Other sites featuring entertainment by featuring the brand include Pepsi (www.pepsi.com) and the U.S. Army, with its Web-based computer games, ringtones, and comics app (www.goarmy.com).

There are many advantages to branded entertainment—among them, not running into the consumer's resistance to ads and not having to go through all the ad regulations. In an ad, BMW has to use a disclaimer ("closed track, professional driver") when it shows its cars tearing around, but in movies, like *The Italian Job*, no such disclaimer is required. Also, movies have been seen by the courts as artistic speech, not as the less protected "commercial speech." Branded entertainment, therefore, gets more First Amendment protection than ordinary advertising does. This is an important distinction, since regulation and legal fights surrounding ads represent a large cost of doing business.

As you can imagine, advertisers love the exposure that branded entertainment can provide. It seems not all consumers are wildly enthusiastic about the blurring line between advertising and entertainment. But aren't real brands visible and being used in the real world? Personally, we don't think today's consumers find it particularly distracting to have brands embedded in entertainment, particularly if it's done well.

Source: HOG Members

Exhibit 3.25 ▶ The HOG—the Harley Davidson Owners Group—is one of the best examples of a brand community.

Bryan Bedder/Getty Images Entertainment/Getty Images

Exhibit 3.26 ▶ Look at the brands on the stage. It is crucial to measure event sponsorship, just as it is crucial to measure any other type of advertising or marketing efforts in integrated brand promotion.

3-2l Business and Advertising in a COVID Era (2020–Current)

While current business and advertising is currently still linked with digital and branded entertainment as in the previous era, there was an event that changed business and advertising overnight—a global pandemic (COVID-19). All over the world, consumers often wore masks if in public and avoided the marketplace (and hence exposure to most in-person marketing) due to government shutdowns or personal choice to stay home. In fact, in the United States, there was a national campaign focused on staying home. Business migrated online or went hybrid, including restaurants moving to contactless delivery of food and curb side pick-up. The new emphasis on hygiene drove businesses to revamp their cleaning protocols and to have less direct contact with customers and their credit cards. It also meant the focus of advertising messages changed. Many brands moved from product promotion to functional messages, promoting their pandemic-related cleaning and service protocols and commitment to customer and employee health and safety.

Themes of ads were often uplifting. Some humor-based ads seemed tamer than in the pre-COVID era, as advertisers needed to be mindful of the somber environment the pandemic created across the world and the fear it instilled in many customers. While some ads tried and even did very well (e.g., the "it wasn't me" Cheetos ad featuring celebrities), it was important not to be *too* funny and cheerful as that would not acknowledge the severity of the situation. Interestingly, there were a lot of celebrity cameos in ads, especially the Super Bowl ads in 2020 and 2021; this suggests it was a smart strategy to bring an entertainment component to balance out the more informative appeals consumers were getting that related to hygiene and the pandemic/health communication. Simultaneously, creative messages also became more prosocial, connected to social movements such as Black Lives Matter, and marketers embedded social justice messages in their ads (e.g., Nike).

Along with the creative changes that took place, media evolved as well. Some entire industries were shut down, like live entertainment and sporting events, and that halted message placements in those industries. When professional sport games were not played, the sponsorships couldn't be activated. And when sports returned to empty arenas, there may have been more attention on sponsor placement as there were not fans drawing the eye. Media shifted even more online, as many consumers changed to more e-shopping rather than taking the health and safety risks of shopping in person. For many brands, media budgets were reduced to account for lost sales, and as a result many sponsor or advertising deals were cut or postponed.

At the industry level, the ad agency or business unit structure changed to become more flexible for remote workers.

A sort of virtual agency became more prominent, in that a team of employees served consumer needs virtually from various locations. It is not yet known if this shift was a temporary change or the beginning of a **new normal**. In fact, the world heard that term a lot as COVID-19 approached. It referred to how people and industries alike have made some big shifts in how things operate, and routines and standards became disrupted perhaps for good.

3-3 Forces Affecting the Evolution of Advertising and IBP

There are various forces that will continue to affect how advertising and IBP evolves; three broad forces are the cyclical nature of history, technology, and the leveraging of contemporary culture. For one, is the cyclical nature of history; it is valuable to understand history as it could repeat itself. For instance, we covered how hygiene appeals were used in advertising during a flu pandemic in the 1920s, and this again emerged as important during the COVID-19 pandemic that was in place by 2020.

A second main force affecting the evolution of advertising and IBP is technology. Technology (particularly e-commerce and m-commerce, or mobile commerce) is reshaping the way people shop, gather information, attend events, and make purchases. And although the advance in digital advertising continues, net TV revenues are still attractive, because advertisers still find it a good way to reach enormous audiences with sight and sound. As intriguing as new technology may be for advertisers and consumers alike, we shouldn't jump to the conclusion that everything about advertising will change due to technological advances.

A third force affecting the evolution of advertising and IBP is the contemporary culture. Some of the most effective and creative advertising and branding comes out of leveraging contemporary culture to its advantage, no matter what changes our society is experiencing. So far, persuasion hasn't fundamentally changed even with recent social/political integrations in contemporary culture. Advertising remains a paid, mass-mediated attempt to persuade, inform, or remind. As a business process, advertising will still be one of the primary marketing mix tools that leverages modern culture and contributes to revenues and profits by stimulating demand and nurturing brand loyalty. It is also safe to argue that consumers will still be highly involved in some product decisions and not so involved in others, so that some messages delivered along with contemporary culture will be particularly relevant and others will be completely irrelevant to forming and maintaining beliefs and feelings about brands.

In this chapter, we offered a historical perspective on advertising. As a lot of smart people know, history is important as a means to help inform future decisions. You don't have to make the same mistakes over and over. Learn what works and doesn't work from the past. But don't get so focused on the past that you lose sight of the present and future.

Summary

1. Describe the main factors that gave rise to advertising.

Although some might contend that the practice of advertising began thousands of years ago, it is more meaningful to connect advertising as we know it today with the emergence of modernity and capitalism. The explosion in production capacity that marked the Industrial Revolution gave demand-stimulation tools added importance. Mass moves of consumers to cities and modern times helped create, along with advertising, consumer culture.

2. Discuss eras in the evolution of advertising in the United States and relate changes in advertising practice to fundamental changes in society and culture—noting how successful ads leverage the social and cultural forces of their day.

Before the Industrial Revolution, advertising's presence in the United States was barely noticeable. With an explosion in economic growth around the turn of the century, modern advertising was born: The "P.T. Barnum era" and the 1920s established advertising as a major force in the U.S. economic system but was harsh, unregulated, and often unethical. It was carnivalesque. Advertising's heyday may have been the 1920s. In this period, advertising was stylish, and many of the techniques used today were invented. With the Great Depression and World War II, cynicism toward and distrust of advertising began to grow. This concern led to refinements in practice and more careful regulation of advertising in the 1960s and 1970s. The 1960s saw advertisers truly refine their skills in terms of resolving seemingly contradictory things: advertising could now sell a revolution against un-hip consumption. Consumption was once again in vogue during the designer era of the 1980s. The new communication technologies that emerged in the 1990s gave rise to greater consumer connectivity (with each other) and access to relevant consumer information.

From then until the current period, we have seen advertisers adjust to new media, the greatest economic upheaval since the Great Depression, and the merging of advertising with other entertainment and communication technologies. In all of this change, the constant is that advertisers rely on familiar strategies to react to a changing culture and society.

The 2000s brought greater consumer access to information and connectivity, the rise of ad blockers, and branded entertainment. Consumers are able to communicate with each other, have two-way communication with advertisers, and create their own ads (consumer-generated content) for posting on social media and websites. Consumers have more control over access to information, and many use ad blockers to screen out unwanted ads. Technology enables advertisers to reach consumers efficiently and with relevant, engaging branded experiences. Branded entertainment blends advertising and integrated brand promotion with entertainment such as film and television programming.

Most recently (2020–current), a COVID-19 era brought changes to the industry structure, business at large, and advertising. For advertising, the changes were seen in agency structure, creative tone, and message placement.

3. **Identify forces continuing to affect the evolution of advertising and integrated brand promotion.**

There are various forces that will continue to affect how advertising and IBP evolves; three broad forces are the cyclical nature of history, technology, and the leveraging of contemporary culture. Even with these forces affecting constant change, advertising will always be a paid, mass-mediated attempt to inform, persuade, or remind. Understanding history and its cyclical nature can help advertisers and everyone in the advertising industry understand what works and avoid making the same mistakes again. Technology is reshaping the way people shop, gather information, attend events, and make purchases. Consumers will continue to be affected by social and cultural change and provide opportunities for advertisers, thus leveraging of contemporary culture will continue to impact the constant evolution of advertising and IBP.

Key Terms

Action for Children's Television
ad blocker
branded entertainment
branding
chain of needs
consumer-generated content (CGC)

consumer culture
dailies
Federal Trade Commission (FTC)
Great Depression
Industrial Revolution
interactive media

National Advertising Review Board
new normal
principle of limited liability
Pure Food and Drug Act
subliminal advertising

Endnotes

1. John Tylee, "Pictures: Ad Industry Celebrates Campaign Archive Launch," *Campaign,* October 17, 2016, http://www.campaignlive .co.uk/article/pictures-ad-industry-celebrates-campaign-archive -launch/1412395#6Dp3wEAswuriKckd.99.

2. Julian Simon, *Issues in the Economics of Advertising* (Urbana: University of Illinois Press, 1970), 41–51.

3. Vincent P. Norris, "Advertising History—According to the Textbooks," *Journal of Advertising* 9, no. 3 (1980), 3–12.

4. James W. Carey, *Communication as Culture: Essays on Media and Society* (Winchester, MA: Unwin Hyman, 1989).

5. Christopher P. Wilson, "The Rhetoric of Consumption: Mass-Market Magazines and the Demise of the Gentle Reader, 1880–1920," in Richard Weightman Fox and T. J. Jackson Lears (Eds.), *The Culture of Consumption: Critical Essays in American History, 1880–1980* (New York: Pantheon, 1983), 39–65.

6. Frank Presbrey, *The History and Development of Advertising* (Garden City, NY: Doubleday, Doran & Co., 1929), 7.

7. Ibid., 11.

8. Ibid., 40.

9. James P. Wood, *The Story of Advertising* (New York: Ronald, 1958), 45–46.

10. Daniel Pope, *The Making of Modern Advertising and Its Creators* (New York: William Morrow, 1984), 14.

11. Cited in Stephen Fox, *The Mirror Makers: A History of American Advertising and Its Creators* (New York: William Morrow, 1984), 14.

12. Ibid., 14.

13. Presbrey, *The History and Development of Advertising,* 16.

14. Bruce Barton, *The Man Nobody Knows* (New York: Bobbs-Merrill, 1924).

15. James Lincoln Collier, *The Rise of Selfishness in America* (New York: Oxford University Press, 1991), 162.

16. Ibid., 303–304.

17. Fox, *The Mirror Makers,* 168.

18. Wini Breines, *Young, White and Miserable: Growing Up Female in the Fifties* (Boston: Beacon, 1992).

19. Mark Pendergrast, *For God, Country & Coca-Cola: The Definitive History of the Great American Soft Drink and the Company That Makes It* (New York: Basic Books, 2003).

20. Vance Packard, *The Hidden Persuaders* (New York: D. McKay, 1957). Researchers have shown that although subliminal *communication* is possible, subliminal *persuasion*, in the typical real-world environment, remains all but impossible. As it was discussed, as mind control, in the 1950s, it remains a joke. See Timothy E. Moore, "Subliminal Advertising: What You See Is What You Get," *Journal of Marketing* 46 (Spring 1982), 38–47.

21. Stuart Rogers, "How a Publicity Blitz Created the Myth of Subliminal Advertising," *Public Relations Quarterly* (Winter 1992–1993), 12–17.

22. Fox, *The Mirror Makers*, 218.

23. Thomas Frank, *The Conquest of Cool: Business Culture, Counterculture, and the Rise of Hip Consumerism* (Chicago: University of Chicago Press, 1997).

24. Ibid., 235.

25. Tom Engelhardt, "The Shortcake Strategy," in Todd Gitlin (Ed.), *Watching Television* (New York: Pantheon, 1986), 68–110.

26. http://www.ciadvertising.org/studies/student/99_fall/theory/cal/aainadvertising/folder/burrell.html.

27. http://blackmbamagazine.net/articles/docs/2005-2_an%20advertising%20legend%20leads%20with%20passion%20purpose%20and%20power.pdf.

28. Collier, *The Rise of Selfishness in America*, 230.

29. This quote and information from this section can be found in Steve Yahn, "Advertising's Grave New World," *Advertising Age*, May 16, 1994, 53.

30. Kevin Goodman, "Sprint Chief Lectures Agencies on Future," *The Wall Street Journal*, April 28, 1995, B6.

31. Stuart Elliot, "Procter & Gamble Calls Internet Marketing Executives to Cincinnati for a Summit Meeting," *The New York Times*, August 19, 1998, D3, http://www.nytimes.com.

32. Adam Broitman, "Three Reasons Why Ad Blockers Are Good for Advertising," *Advertising Age*, March 22, 2016, http://adage.com/article/digitalnext/reasons-ad-blockers-good-advertising/303190/; and Ayal Stainer, "How Ad Blockers Are Hurling Us into a Post-Advertising Age," *Marketing Magazine,* September 28, 2015, https://www.marketingmag.com.au/hubs-c/ad-blockers-hurling-us-post-advertising-age/.

33. Christine Birkner, "7 Ads That Pulled P&G Out of the Content 'Crap Trap,'" *Adweek,* October 20, 2016, http://www.adweek.com/news/advertising-branding/7-ads-pulled-pg-out-content-crap-trap-174164; and Sarah Vizard, "P&G Admits Marketing Cuts Hit Growth as It Refocuses on Brand Investment," *Marketing Week*, August 2, 2016, https://www.marketingweek.com/2016/08/02/pg-admits-marketing-cuts-hit-growth-as-it-refocuses-on-brand-investement/.

Social, Ethical, and Regulatory Aspects of Advertising and Promotion

Learning Objectives

After reading and thinking about this chapter, you will be able to do the following:

1 Understand a balanced perspective of advertising and IBP by identifying both benefits and problems of advertising and promotion and debating key issues concerning their effects on society's well-being.

2 Explain how ethical considerations affect the development and implementation of advertising and IBP campaigns.

3 Explain the role of government agencies, consumers, and industry self-regulation for the regulation of advertising and promotion.

4 Discuss the regulation of the full range of techniques used in the IBP process.

CSA-Printstock/DigitalVision Vectors/Getty Images

As you can see from the framework in Exhibit 4.1, in this chapter we consider a wide range of social, ethical, and legal issues related to advertising and the many tools of integrated brand promotion—part of the influence of business and society. What is socially responsible or irresponsible, ethically acceptable, politically correct, or legal? As technology, cultural trends, and consumer behavior change, the answers to these questions are constantly changing as well. As a society changes, so do its perspectives and values. Like anything else with social roots and implications, advertising and promotion will affect and be affected by these changes.

Exhibit 4.1 ▶ Advertising and promotion within business and society are examined in the context of social, ethical, and regulatory aspects.

Part 1: Advertising and Integrated Brand Promotion in Business and Society

- The World of Advertising and Integrated Brand Promotion (Ch. 1)
- The Structure of the Advertising and Promotion Industry: Advertisers, Agencies, Media, and Support Organizations (Ch. 2)
- The History of Advertising and Brand Promotion (Ch. 3)
- Social, Ethical, and Regulatory Aspects of Advertising and Promotions (Ch. 4)

- The Social Aspects of Advertising
- The Ethical Aspects of Advertising
- The Regulatory Aspects of Advertising
- The Regulation of Other Promotional Tools

LO **1**

4-1 The Social Aspects of Advertising

For those who feel that advertising is intrusive, crass, and manipulative, the social aspects usually provide the most fuel for debate. In this chapter, we will examine both the positive and negative social aspects of advertising. On the positive side, we'll consider advertising's effect on consumers' knowledge, standard of living, and feelings of happiness and well-being, as well as its potential influences on media. On the negative side, we'll examine a variety of social criticisms ranging from the claim that advertising wastes resources and promotes materialism to the argument that advertising perpetuates stereotypes.

Our approach is to offer the pros and cons on several issues about which critics and advertisers commonly argue. Please note that some are matters of opinion, with no clear right and wrong answers. We will present what the experts on both sides have to say. Keep in mind that some of the cons of advertising can be overcome by using other forms of IBP instead, such as event sponsorship or experiential marketing.

4-1a Advertising Educates Consumers

Does advertising provide valuable information to consumers, or is it pervasive and intrusive rather than informative?

Pro: Advertising Informs

- Advertising educates consumers, equipping them with the information needed to make informed purchase decisions. By assessing information and advertising claims, consumers become more educated regarding the features, benefits, functions, and value of products.

- Better-educated consumers enhance their lifestyles and economic power through astute marketplace decision making.

- Consumers may become more aware of their own tendencies toward being persuaded by certain types of product information. Advertising is "an immensely powerful instrument for the elimination of ignorance."[1]

- Advertising reduces product search time. The large amount of information readily available through advertising and websites allows consumers to easily assess information about the potential value of brands without spending time and effort traveling from retail store to retail store trying to evaluate the alternatives. The information contained in an advertisement "reduces drastically the cost of search."[2]

- Advertising is good for storytelling. Consumers welcome the creativity and storytelling aspects of branded entertainment—and will seek and watch the best.[3]

- Advertising can elevate important issues such as environmental protection and healthy lifestyles. Advertisers can play a role in influencing public attitudes and actions with respect to important matters facing society, like the environment.[4] Green advertising, for example, can help showcase products and services that are better for the environment or consumer health. And despite the potential informational benefits, ads featuring food products that are branded as healthy may actually encourage some health-conscious consumers to eat more of these foods and exercise less.[5] Thus, many advertising messages aim to appeal to a healthier lifestyle.

Con: Advertising Is Superficial and Intrusive

- Many ads don't carry enough actual product information; the information they contain is biased toward that brand. Critics of advertising believe that ads should contain information that relates to functional features and performance results—things that can be measured and tested brand by brand.

- Advertising can be intrusive.[6] In 2020, approximately 73 million Internet users in the United States have installed ad blockers on their devices.[7] Similarly, consumers are getting frustrated with brands working their way into entertainment and information programming. As an example, in 2020 NBCUniversal announced that it will be have less commercial time and more uninterrupted content with integrated product placement.[8]

- Advertising can be clutter.[9] It has become so ubiquitous that consumers have developed market resistance. In the words of Patagonia's vice president of marketing, "Brands talk a lot about cutting through the clutter, but a lot of times they're creating that clutter."[10] Another industry expert suggests, "New media have more potential to deliver even more saturation, clutter, and intrusiveness than traditional media, in which case the new media will only worsen marketing resistance."[11]

4-1b Advertising Improves the Standard of Living

Whether advertising improves the standard of living is also being debated.

Pro: The Economic Effects of Advertising Lower the Cost of Products

Four aspects of the nature of advertising help lower the cost of products:

- Due to economies of scale (it costs less to produce products in large quantities), partly due to advertising's contribution to stimulating demand, products cost less than if there were no advertising. Stronger demand results in lower production and administrative costs per unit produced, and lower prices are passed on to consumers.

- Consumers have more choice in products and services because advertising increases the probability of success that new products will succeed. The more products that succeed, the fewer losses firms incur from failed product introductions. In the end, this should make products cost less.

- The pressures of competition and the desire to have fresh, marketable brands motivate firms to produce improved products and to introduce lower-priced brands.

- The speed and reach of the advertising process facilitate the flow of innovations. This means that new discoveries can be delivered to a large percentage of the marketplace very quickly. Innovations succeed when advertising communicates the offerings' benefits to the customer.

All four of these factors can contribute positively to the standard of living and quality of life in a society. Advertising may be instrumental in bringing about these effects because it serves an important role in demand stimulation and keeping customers informed, as well as playing a role in supporting the economy.

Con: Advertising Wastes Resources and Raises the Standard of Living Only for Some

- Advertising can be an inefficient, wasteful process that does little more than "shuffling of existing total demand" rather than contributing to the expansion of total demand.[12] Advertising can therefore drive economic stagnation and a foster a lower standard of living.

- Critics argue that brand differences are trivial and that the proliferation of brands does not offer a greater variety of choice but instead results in a meaningless waste of resources and creates confusion and frustration for the consumer.

- Finally, critics argue that advertising only helps widen the gap between rich and poor, creating greater inequity among social classes.

4-1c Advertising Affects Happiness and General Well-Being

Does advertising affect consumers' happiness and well-being? Here are both sides of this argument.

Con: Advertising Creates Needs

- A common complaint among critics is that advertising invents unnecessary needs and drives people to buy things they don't really need or even want. The argument is that consumers are relatively easy to seduce into wanting the next shiny bauble offered by marketers.

- Advertising could even create perceived "needs" that are designed to strive toward unobtainable standards. For instance, young consumers especially may feel a perceived need to look like models in advertising who are airbrushed and photoshopped. Fashion advertising may be teaching young people to covet slim bodies. An upscale fitness chain sparked outrage when it ran an ad featuring "waif-like women languishing around a mansion in sexually suggestive positions" without a single workout machine in sight.[13] Similarly, cosmetics giants like Estée Lauder and Revlon typically spend from 15 to 30 cents from every dollar of sales to promote their brands as the ultimate beauty solution.

Pro: Advertising Addresses a Wide Variety of Basic Human Needs

- *While advertising does not create basic human needs, individuals turn to goods and services to satisfy needs, such as hunger (see Exhibit 4.2).* That is, the need exists as a human motivation, and advertised products offer a means to pursue that motivation.

- Advertising of certain products can remind us of five types of needs that we all share, no matter what we look like, how old we are, or how much money we have. Abraham Maslow, a pioneer in the study of human motivation, conceived that human behavior progresses through the following hierarchy of need states:[14]

- *Physiological needs:* Biological needs that require the satisfaction of hunger, thirst, and basic bodily functions. Food and health-care product advertising, for example, relates to physiological needs.

- *Safety needs:* The need to provide shelter and protection for the body and to maintain a comfortable existence. Home security systems and smoke detector ads help remind us of our safety needs, for instance.

- *Love and belonging needs:* The need for affiliation and affection. A person will strive for both the giving and receiving of love. Advertising during Valentine's Day (which also brings some market resistance due to the perception that buying things is "required" if you are in a romantic relationship) reminds us that giving gifts such as flowers or jewelry can symbolize love.

- *Esteem needs:* The need for recognition, status, and prestige. In addition to the respect of others, there is a need and desire for self-respect. Much personal-care product marketing can promote feelings of self-esteem, confidence, and romance. In the pursuit of esteem, many consumers buy products they perceive to have status and prestige: expensive clothing, cars, and homes are examples.

- *Self-actualization needs:* This is the highest of all the need states and is achieved by only a small percentage of people, according to Maslow. The individual strives for maximum fulfilment of individual capabilities. Although it is difficult to buy **self-actualization** (the highest level of Maslow's hierarchy), educational pursuits and high-intensity leisure activities can foster pride and accomplishments that contribute to self-actualization.

Source: McDonald

Exhibit 4.2 ▶ McDonald's ad creatively reminding us we are hungry.

Con: Advertising Promotes Materialism

- Individuals' wants and aspirations may be distorted by advertising.

- In societies characterized by heavy advertising, there is a tendency for conformity and status-seeking behavior, both of which are considered materialistic and superficial.[15] Material goods are placed ahead of spiritual and intellectual pursuits.

■ Advertising, which portrays brands as symbols of status, success, and happiness, contributes to materialism and superficiality. It creates wants and aspirations that are artificial and self-centered. This, in turn, results in an overemphasis on the production of private goods, to the detriment of public goods (such as highways, parks, schools, social services, and infrastructure).[16]

It is important to note, however, that these criticisms aren't always justified; some advertisers are taking a different approach. The outdoor retailer REI, for example, has, for a few years, remained closed on Black Friday, traditionally the busiest shopping day of the year. The advertiser encourages consumers and employees alike to #OptOutside and enjoy nature rather than participating in the usual holiday shopping frenzy (see Exhibit 4.3, Integrated Brand Promotion in Action: REI).[17]

Pro: Advertising Only Reflects Society's Priorities

Advertising of some products reflects our love for special events, plays significant roles in rituals such as Thanksgiving dinner and football, and serves as vessels of special meaning. The "consumption culture" in America started long before there was modern advertising. Advertising did not *create* the American emphasis on consumption. For example, in the United States, major holidays such as Christmas (gifts), Thanksgiving (food), and Easter (candy and clothing) have traditionally been festivals of consumption. Historian and social observer Stephen Fox explains why advertising is not to blame. He says,

> *American culture is … money-mad, hedonistic, superficial, rushing heedlessly down a railroad track called*

progress. Tocqueville and other observers of the young republic described America in these terms in the early 1800s, decades before the development of national advertising. To blame advertising now for these most basic tendencies in American history is to miss the point. . . . The people who have created modern advertising are not hidden persuaders pushing our buttons in the service of some malevolent purpose. They are just producing an especially visible manifestation, good and bad, of the American way of life.[18]

4-1d Advertising: Demeaning and Deceitful or Liberating and Artful?

Critics and supporters disagree about whether advertising is demeaning and offensive or artful and liberating.

Con: Advertising Perpetuates Stereotypes

■ *Advertisers often feature people in advertisements who look like members of their target audience with the hope that those who see the ad will be more prone to relate to the ad and respond to its message.* Critics charge that this practice yields a very negative effect, in that it perpetuates stereotypes.

■ *The portrayals of older people, people of color, and women are of particular concern.* Older adults are often shown as helpless or ill, even though many enjoy an active and rich lifestyle; and advertisers' propensity to feature Black and

Exhibit 4.3 ▶ Integrated Brand Promotion in Action: REI.
The outdoor retailer REI has been closing its stores on the Friday after Thanksgiving, promoting the idea of enjoying nature rather than going shopping. *What are the pros and cons of REI's message running counter to the materialism that often accompanies the traditional start of the holiday shopping season?*

Latin Americans as athletes and women in domestic roles could be seen as a contemporary form of stereotyping

- *Another criticism is that women are too often cast as objects of desire or depicted unrealistically (such as in ads that have been airbrushed and photoshopped), reinforcing stereotypes and affecting personal body image.*[19]

Pro: Advertisers Are Showing Much More Sensitivity

- Advertisers are realizing that a diverse world requires diversity in the social reality that ads represent and help construct. However, many remain dissatisfied with the pace of change.

- Advocates of advertising say that the stereotyping described here is less prevalent and is on its way to becoming part of the past.

- Advertisers can help change stereotypes about older people. Ads ranging from financial services to retirement communities to cruise lines now show older adults in fulfilling, active lifestyles.

- Advertisers can help change stereotypes about people with disabilities. Ads in many product categories are becoming more inclusive here.

- Advertisers are becoming more inclusive of LGBTQ+ consumers. Looking at LGBTQ+ people in advertising, a growing number of advertisers are avoiding stereotypical depictions—such as McDonald's, which ran a commercial in Taiwan featuring a son coming out to his father while at a McCafé.[20] Tiffany & Co. and Wells Fargo have also developed inclusive advertising designed to highlight this community (see Exhibits 4.4 and 4.5). Wells Fargo, for example, featured a lesbian couple as they navigated their adoption journey and transitioned into their new home with their baby, showcasing how the banking brand can be there for life's changing financial needs. This evolution in representation is important, because despite the legalization of marriage equality, the advertising community has been slow to incorporate people who identify as LGBTQ+ in advertising.[21]

- *Beauty advertisers are becoming more inclusive to people besides women.* Beauty ads from L'Oréal and Cover Girl now feature young men, because a growing number of males are using some form of cosmetics.[22] Cover Girl's latest "cover boy" happens to be a big influencer on makeup in social media.

- Some advertisers are helping to counteract gender stereotypes. Dove's parent company, Unilever, continues to counteract gender stereotypes with its #Unstereotype campaign. The goal is to bring the way it depicts men and women in its advertising "much closer to the reality of gender and people today."[23] Over time, women's attitudes toward sexual themes in advertising are also changing.

> **Cosmopolitan** ✓
> @Cosmopolitan
>
> Tiffany's gorgeous new engagement ring ad is EVERYTHING:
> cosm.ag/6013a43W
>
> 7:45 PM - 9 Jan 2015
>
> **410** RETWEETS **779** FAVORITES

Source: Tiffany & Co.

Exhibit 4.4 ▶ Tiffany & Co.'s first ad featuring a gay couple in the firm's very long brand history came in 2015.

Exhibit 4.5 ▶ Wells Fargo print ads in "When Two Accounts Become One" campaign.

Exhibit 4.6 ▶ Advertisers today realize the diverse reality of consumers' lives. This Dove ad is a beautiful example of advertisers' efforts to represent diversity.

A recent study found that some women have a more positive view of ads containing nudity than they did even a few years ago.[24]

■ Some advertisers can help us redefine constructs like beauty. Dove launched its "Campaign for Real Beauty" with ads featuring real women (not models) whose appearances do not conform to the relatively narrow, stereotypical beauty norms (see Exhibit 4.6). The way consumers respond to an ad featuring a model with a larger body type depends, in part, on their reactions to the advertised product and their perceived similarity to the model.[25] Dove's short video called "Evolution" is worth seeing.

Con: Advertising Is Often Offensive

■ Advertising can be offensive, and the appeals are sometimes in poor taste.

■ Moreover, some would say that one trend in American advertising is to be rude, crude, and sometimes lewd. GoDaddy made its mark in the highly competitive market of Web hosting with a series of crude (but attention-getting) ad campaigns featuring race-car driver Danica Patrick. After years of criticism, the company finally stopped running those campaigns.[26]

■ As taste is a personal and inherently subjective evaluation, it isn't always easy to ensure some ads don't offend anyone. What is offensive to one person is merely satiric to another. What should we call an ad prepared for the Australian market that showed the owner of an older Honda Accord admiring a newer model? In the ad, the old Honda reacts by locking its doors, revving its motor, and driving off a cliff—with the owner still inside. Critics decried the ad as trivializing suicide—an acute problem among young people, who were the ad's target audience.[27]

But not all advertising deemed offensive has to be as extreme as these examples.

■ Many times, advertisers get caught in a firestorm of controversy because certain and sometimes relatively small segments of the population are offended. The history of advertising is loaded with examples of companies that were surprised by negative reactions to their messages. For example, a public-service spot developed by Aetna Life & Casualty insurance for a measles vaccine showed a wicked witch with green skin and a wart. This ad was challenged by a witches' rights group. As another example, a commercial for Black Flag bug spray had to be altered after a war veterans' group objected to the playing of "Taps" over dead bugs.

■ It can be difficult for advertisers who mess up to stop or pull offensive ads as they get leaked online. And even though government may move to provide a legal remedy to deter offensive broadcasts—whether advertising messages or programming—the fact is that what is acceptable and what is offensive changes over time in a culture. Note how some really old ads are now seemingly horrific.

Pro: Advertising Is a Source of Fulfillment and Liberation

- The consumption that advertising glorifies can be quite good for society. Most people sincerely appreciate modern conveniences that liberate us from the fouler facets of everyday life, such as body odor, close contact with dirty diapers, and washing clothes by hand.

- Modern advertising has helped give rise to a "democratization" of goods. Before the modern consumer age, consumption of many goods was restricted by social class. Observers argue that there is a liberating quality to advertising and consumption that should be appreciated

and encouraged. Sometimes a chocolate McDonald's milkshake is just what you need (see Exhibit 4.7).

Con: Advertisers Deceive via Subliminal Stimulation

- There is much controversy and confusion that persists about the issue of subliminal (below the threshold of consciousness) communication and advertising.[28] Let us clarify: No one ever sold anything by putting images of breasts in ice cubes or the word *sex* in the background of an ad. We realize it makes for a great story, but hiding pictures in other pictures doesn't work to get anyone to buy anything.

- Advertisers can benefit from unconscious ad processing. Note that these effects are very short-lived and found only in laboratories.[29] If the rumors are true that some advertisers are actually trying to use subliminal messages in their ads, the best research on the topic would conclude that they're wasting their money.[30]

Pro: Advertising Is Democratic Art

- Advertising is art just as much as it is business in some cases. Some argue that one of the best aspects of advertising is its artistic nature. The pop art movement of the late 1950s and 1960s, particularly in London and New York, was characterized by a fascination with commercial culture.

- Some of this art critiqued consumer culture and simultaneously celebrated it. Above all, Andy Warhol, himself a commercial illustrator, demonstrated that art was for the people and that the most accessible art was advertising. Art was not restricted to museum walls; it was on Campbell's soup cans, LifeSavers candy rolls, and Brillo pads. Advertising is anti-elitist, prodemocratic, widely accessible art. Warhol said this about America, democracy, and Coke:

    What's great about this country is that America started the tradition where the richest consumers buy essentially the same things as the poorest. You can be watching TV and see Coca-Cola, and you can know that the President drinks Coke, Liz Taylor drinks Coke, and just think, you can drink Coke, too. A Coke is a Coke and no amount of money can get you a better Coke than the one the bum on the corner is drinking. All the Cokes are the same and all the Cokes are good. Liz Taylor knows it, the President knows it, the bum knows it, and you know it.[31]

- Some recent integrated brand promotions are combining art with a bit of the democratic process. Patrón Tequila, for example, invites submission of artworks inspired by the brand's iconic bottle and allows consumers to vote online for their favorites.[32] For more examples of artistic ads, see Exhibits 4.8 and 4.9.

Source: McDonald

**happy family
happy me**

Keeping everyone in the family satisfied can be easy. With a little help from us. It can be fun too. There's a Family Hostess to lend a hand, so you can enjoy a much-deserved break while your kids play in the Playland and join in on the fun activities. And to make it extra special, you can treat them with the new Chicken Burger Happy Meal. It comes with a free toy for a discounted price of only RM5.95**, and there's a new toy every week! So for great food in a friendly atmosphere, warm service and a wonderful day out that will put a smile on your family's faces, we're here to make it happen for you.

with FREE TOY

HAPPY MEAL FROM **5.95** 7.15

Exhibit 4.7 ▶ McDonald's shows a happy family, as happiness is a core of its brand and integrated into "Happy Meals."

Source: McDonalds

Exhibit 4.8 ▶ Note the artistic tone of this McDonalds ad.

Source: Trendhunterstatic

Exhibit 4.9 ▶ Advertising is art in creative transit advertising.

4-1e Advertising Has a Powerful Effect on the Mass Media

One final issue that advertisers and their critics debate is the matter of advertising's influence on the mass media.

Pro: Advertising Fosters a Diverse and Affordable Mass Media

■ *Advertising can be good for a more informed democracy because it is often the financial mechanism for purportedly unbiased media.* Magazines, newspapers, television, radio stations, and many websites are supported by advertising expenditures, allowing consumers access to a variety of information and entertainment sources at a low cost. Advertisers are reaching out to consumers through social media sites such as Snapchat, Twitter, TikTok, and Facebook, which means social media channels are benefitting from advertising dollars as well.

■ Without advertising support, network television, radio broadcasts, websites, and social media would not be free; and newspapers and magazines would have to drastically increase their prices or significantly cut content. Basic Gmail accounts or Pandora online radio accounts, for instance, are free because of advertising. Already, with global spending on printed newspaper ads down to $42.8 billion annually, newspapers are cutting costs by reducing the number of printed sections and letting employees go.[33]

■ Advertising provides invaluable exposure to issues. When noncommercial organizations (such as social service organizations) use advertising, members of society receive information on important social and political issues. An example of the noncommercial use of advertising is the ongoing multimedia campaign launched by a national nonprofit to remind the public of dangers of drugs.[34] The Partnership for Drug-Free Kids uses television commercials, print advertising, and digital messages to reach target audiences, especially parents.[35]

Con: Advertising Affects Programming

■ Advertisers can shape the content of the information they promote, sometimes in unethical ways. The CEO of a firm headed for prosecution was accused of hiring a public relations firm to turn out a series of newspaper articles sympathetic to the CEO's firm.[36] Similarly, there have been instances of "stealth sponsorship" of newspaper opinion editorials in which the journalists were being paid by corporations who were receiving favorable treatment in the editorials.[37]

- Advertisers tend to buy airtime on programs that draw large audiences. Critics argue that these mass-market programs lower television quality because cultural and educational programs, which draw smaller and more selective markets, are dropped in favor of mass-market programs.

- Furthermore, television programs that deal with controversial issues, such as abortion, sexual abuse, or AIDS might have trouble drawing advertisers who fear the consequences of any association with controversial issues.

─────────── LO 2 ───────────

4-2 The Ethical Aspects of Advertising

Many of the ethical aspects of advertising interact with both the social and legal considerations of the advertising process. **Ethics** are moral standards and principles against which behavior is judged. Honesty, integrity, fairness, and sensitivity are all included in a broad definition of ethics. Much comes down to personal judgment. We will discuss the ethical aspects of advertising in three areas: truth in advertising, advertising to children, and advertising controversial products.

4-2a Truth in Advertising

Although truth in advertising is a key legal issue, it has ethical dimensions as well. The most fundamental ethical issue has to do with **deception**—making false or misleading statements in an advertisement. The difficulty regarding this issue is in determining what is deceptive. A manufacturer who claims a laundry product can remove grass stains is exposed to legal sanctions if the product cannot perform the task.

Another manufacturer who claims to have "The Best Laundry Detergent in the World," however, is within its rights to employ superlatives. The use of absolute superlatives such as "Number One" or "Best in the World" is called **puffery** and is legal (remember the World's Best Coffee in the movie *Elf?*). The courts have long held that superlatives are understood by consumers as simply the exaggerated commercial language of advertising and are interpreted by consumers as such.

Besides advertising, other promotional tools used in integrated branding are often challenged as being deceptive.[38] The "**small print**" that accompanies many contests or sweepstakes is often challenged by consumers. Bloggers or influencers on digital media often receive free products in exchange for featuring the brand in their content, and not all influencers choose to disclose the partnership. This is seen in product placement in movies, video games, and shows.[39]

Consumer watchdog groups try and help bring attention and solutions to these issues. One such group, Public Citizen's Commercial Alert, has argued for years that U.S. television networks are deceiving consumers by not disclosing that they are taking money for highlighting brands within shows and films. The organization states that, "Product placements are inherently deceptive, because many people do not realize that they are, in fact, advertisements."[40] But product placement rules differ from country to country. For example, U.K. television programs must show a "P" before and after every show containing any product placements, as well as after every commercial break, to alert viewers that brands have paid for placement.[41]

Another area of debate regarding truth in advertising relates to emotional appeals. It is impossible to legislate against emotional appeals such as those made about the beauty- or prestige-enhancing qualities of a brand, because these claims are unquantifiable.[42] Since these types of appeals are legal, the ethics of such appeals fall into a gray area. Beauty and prestige, it is argued, are in the eye of the beholder, and such appeals are neither illegal nor unethical. As you can see, there is nothing clear-cut about the issue of ethics in advertising.

4-2b Advertising to Children

Children are vulnerable consumers, and the desire to restrict advertising aimed at children is based on a wide range of concerns, not the least of which is that children between 2 and 11 years old see around 25,600 ads in a year.[43] One concern about this heavy volume of advertising directed at children is that advertising promotes superficiality and creates values founded in material goods and consumption.[44] We also don't want to compromise children's innocence by exposing them to adult topics or graphic scenes, such as violence or sex in advertising.

Another concern is that children are inexperienced consumers and lack the cognitive capabilities to critically analyze ad messages.[45] Then there's product placement, which has a positive effect on children's affinity for those brands (but a negative effect on mothers' affinity for the same brands).[46] Children are therefore easy prey for the sophisticated persuasions of advertisers in traditional and digital media—all of which can influence children's demands for everything from toys to snack foods.[47]

These demands, in turn, create an environment of child–parent conflict. Parents find themselves having to say no over and over again to children whose desires are piqued by effective advertising. This is called **pester power**, which notes the strong influence kids can have on adult's purchases even when they have no money. Add to that, the historical view held by child psychologists who contend that advertising advocates violence, is responsible for child obesity, creates a breakdown in early learning skills, and results in a destruction of parental authority.[48] Researchers have found that food advertising does, in fact, affect the eating behavior of children, which is why many are concerned, as obesity continues to be problematic.[49]

There is also concern that many television programs, videos, and films aimed at children constitute program-length commercials. This movement began in 1990 when critics argued that 70 programs airing at the time were based on commercial products such as He-Man, the Smurfs, and the Muppets.[50] Today's "commercial" stars include SpongeBob, Elmo, and Peppa Pig. Over the years, there have been attempts by special-interest groups to strictly regulate program-length commercials aimed at children.

One of the earliest efforts to restrict the amount of advertising children might see was due to the efforts of the special-interest group Action for Children's Television that helped get the Children's Television Act passed in 1990. This U.S. regulation restricts advertising on children's programming to 10.5 minutes per hour on weekends and 12 minutes per hour on weekdays, and mandates the airing of informational and educational programming for children.[51] Voluntary efforts are also underway. The Council of Better Business Bureaus and 18 large food marketers—such as McDonald's, Kraft, Pepsi, and General Mills—have signed the Children's Food and Beverage Advertising Initiative, a voluntary commitment to address the issue of obesity among children. These food and beverage marketers have pledged to devote half of their advertising dollars to messages promoting healthier eating alternatives for children.[52]

Yet consider the other side of the ethical debate about advertising to children. Children grow up in a system in which consumption is a part of everyday life. They learn the rules of "commerce" early and understand full well that people are trying to sell them "stuff." At a fairly young age, children understand what advertising is, gain a healthy skepticism for advertising, and clearly recognize its intent.[53]

4-2c Advertising Controversial Products

Some people question the allowing of advertising for controversial products and services, such as tobacco, alcoholic beverages, gambling and lotteries, and firearms. Critics charge that tobacco and alcoholic beverage firms target adolescents and make dangerous and addictive products appealing.[54] Some research has debunked the claim that advertising causes more alcohol consumption, while other research says that advertising increases cigarette and alcohol consumption—particularly among teenagers.[55] The controversy over alcohol has moved to the forefront as loosening restrictions by

networks have caused a spike in spending and ad placement on television by alcoholic beverage marketers.[56]

Some alcohol advertising studies contradict research conducted since the 1950s carried out by marketing, communications, psychology, and economics researchers—including assessments of all the available research by the Federal Trade Commission.[57] These studies (as well as Gallup polls during the 1990s) found that family, friends, and peers—not advertising—are the primary influences on the use of tobacco and alcohol products. Later studies reaffirmed the findings.[58] Although children at a very early age recognize tobacco advertising characters like the now defunct Joe Camel, they also recognize the Energizer Bunny (batteries) and the Jolly Green Giant (canned vegetables), which are characters associated with other products aimed at adults. Kids are also aware that cigarettes cause disease and know that they are intended for adults. Research in Europe offers the same conclusion: "Every study on the subject of advertising effects on the use of tobacco and alcohol finds that children are more influenced by parents and playmates than by the mass media."[59] Despite this research however, Congress and various public interest groups found that the use of the character blurred an important line between the child and adult market segments and pressured RJR, the parent company of Camel cigarettes, to end its use of the Joe Camel character.[60]

Why doesn't advertising *cause* people to smoke and drink? Because advertising generally isn't powerful enough to create primary demand in mature product categories such as milk, automobiles, toothpaste, tobacco, and alcohol. **Primary demand** is demand for an entire product category. Advertising does not create primary demand for tobacco or alcohol or any other mature product category.[61] Advertising is, however, capable of stimulating demand for a brand within a product category and shifting brand preference (say to Budweiser from Coors). Product category demand is the result of social and cultural trends, economic conditions, technological change, and other broad influences on consumers' needs and lifestyles. And advertising plays its most important role in consumers' choice of brands (e.g., Camel, Heineken) after consumers have decided to use a product category (e.g., cigarettes, beer).

Gambling and state-run lotteries represent another controversial product area with respect to advertising. What is the purpose of this advertising? Is it meant to inform gamblers and lottery players of the choices of games and places to play? This would be selective (i.e., brand) demand stimulation. Or is such advertising designed to stimulate demand for engaging in wagering behavior? This would be primary demand stimulation. What about compulsive gamblers? What is the state's obligation to protect "vulnerable" citizens by restricting the placement or content of lottery advertising?

The issue of advertising controversial products can indeed be complex. One would not normally put food in the "controversial products" category. But as people began suing companies, claiming that their advertising caused them to eat unhealthy food and made them obese—suddenly there was a controversy. McDonald's and other food companies had to defend themselves against lawsuits from people who have claimed food providers "made them obese." The U.S. government passed legislation barring people from suing food companies for their obesity, with one of the bill's sponsors arguing that the law was about "common sense and personal responsibility."[62]

Although we can group these ethical issues of advertising into some reasonable categories—truth in advertising, advertising to children, and advertising controversial products—it is not as easy to make definitive statements about the status of ethics in advertising. Ethics will always be a matter of personal values and personal interpretation. And as long as there are unethical people in the world, there will be ethical problems in advertising just like in every other phase of business and life.

LO 3

4-3 The Regulatory Aspects of Advertising

Three primary groups—consumers, industry organizations, and government bodies—regulate advertising in the truest sense: Together they shape and restrict the process. The government relies on legal restrictions, while consumers and industry groups use less-formal controls. Like the other topics in this chapter, regulation of advertising can be controversial, and opinions about what does and doesn't need to be regulated can be highly variable.

4-3a Areas of Advertising Regulation

There are three basic areas of advertising regulation: deception and unfairness in advertising, competitive issues, and advertising to children. Each area is a focal point for regulatory action.

Deception and Unfairness

It is a shared belief that that deception in advertising is completely unacceptable. The problem is that it is as difficult to determine what is deceptive from a regulatory standpoint as it is from an ethical standpoint. The Federal Trade Commission's (FTC's) policy statement on deception is the authoritative source when it comes to defining deceptive

advertising. It specifies the following three elements as essential in declaring an ad deceptive:[63]

1. There must be a representation, omission, or practice that is likely to mislead the consumer.
2. This representation, omission, or practice must be judged from the perspective of a consumer acting reasonably in the circumstance.
3. The representation, omission, or practice must be a "material" one. Is the act or the practice likely to affect the consumer's conduct or decision with regard to the product or service? If so, the practice is material, and therefore consumer harm is likely, because consumers are likely to have chosen differently if not for the deception.

If this definition of deception sounds like carefully worded legal jargon, that's because it is. It is also a definition that can lead to diverse interpretations when it is applied to advertisements in real life. One critical point about the FTC's approach to deception is that both implied claims and *missing* information can be bases for deeming an ad deceptive. The FTC expects any explicit claim made in an ad to be truthful, but it also is on the lookout for ads that deceive through allusion and innuendo or ads that deceive by not telling the whole story.

Although the FTC and the courts have been reasonably specific about what constitutes deception, the definition of unfairness in advertising has been left relatively vague. In 1994, Congress ended a long-running dispute in the courts and in the advertising industry by approving legislation that defines **unfair advertising** as "acts or practices that cause or are likely to cause substantial injury to consumers, which is not reasonably avoidable by consumers themselves, and not outweighed by the countervailing benefits to consumers or competition."[64] This definition obligates the FTC to assess both the benefits and costs of advertising, and rules out reckless acts on the part of consumers, before a judgment can be rendered that an advertiser has been unfair.

Competitive Issues

Because the large dollar amounts spent on advertising may foster inequities that literally can destroy competition, several advertising practices relating to maintaining fair competition are regulated. Among these practices are vertical cooperative advertising, comparison advertising, and the use of monopoly power.

Vertical cooperative advertising is an advertising technique whereby a manufacturer and a wholesaler or retailer share the expense of advertising. This technique is commonly used in regional or local markets where a manufacturer wants a brand to benefit from promotions run by local dealers. Cooperative advertising is legal and has been used widely and regularly for many years, even expanding to the Internet as manufacturers partner with online retailers.[65]

The competitive concern, however, is that dealers might receive bogus cooperative advertising allowances from manufacturers. These allowances require little or no effort or expenditure on the part of the dealer/retailer and thus represent hidden price concessions, which is illegal because it results in unfair competition. If a dealer receives an advertising allowance, it must demonstrate that the funds are applied specifically to advertising.

Next, the potential exists for firms to engage in unfair competition if they use comparison ads inappropriately. **Comparison advertisements** are those in which an advertiser makes a comparison between the firm's brand and competitors' brands. The comparison may or may not explicitly identify the competition. Again, comparison ads are legal, are used frequently by all sorts of organizations, and are typically an effective technique.[66] But such campaigns can get quite aggressive and might attract regulatory scrutiny. The advertiser must convey a fair comparison in the ad, be ready to substantiate its claims, and show that its assertions are not intended to deceive. Also remember that different countries have specific regulations regarding comparison ads, a point to keep in mind when targeting customers across borders.

Finally, some firms are so powerful in their use of advertising that **monopoly power** by virtue of their advertising spending can become a problem. This issue sometimes arises in the context of mergers and acquisitions.

Advertising to Children

As we discussed earlier, critics worry about advertising targeting children. Even though government organizations, such as the FTC, have been actively trying to regulate such advertising, industry and consumer groups have also been vocal about restrictions. One area of regulation where the FTC has recently reduced its efforts is the attempt to restrict the advertising of food products to children. Despite pressure from consumer organizations[67] that say food advertising contributes to the problem of childhood obesity, the FTC has stated that "the commission does not support legislation restricting food advertising to children."

The Council of Better Business Bureaus established a Children's Advertising Review Unit and has issued a set of guidelines for advertising directed at children. These guidelines emphasize that advertisers should be sensitive to the level of knowledge and sophistication of children as decision makers. The guidelines also urge advertisers to make a constructive contribution to the social development of children by emphasizing positive social standards in advertising, such as friendship, kindness, honesty, and generosity.

The Internet era has raised additional concerns about privacy and children. In response, Congress passed the Children's Online Privacy Protection Act (COPPA), under which the FTC regulates websites directed at children under 13. Any such site that gathers information must obtain parent or guardian consent before doing so. After watchdog groups asked the FTC to strengthen aspects of COPPA, the agency added new regulatory safeguards.[68] Now regulators around the world are implementing similar safeguards.[69]

4-3b Regulatory Agents

Earlier in this section, we noted that consumer and industry groups as well as government agencies all participate in the regulation of advertising. We will now discuss examples of each of these agents along with the kind of influence they exert. Given the multiple participants, this turns out to be a highly complex activity that we can only examine at a high level here. Note that our discussion focuses on regulatory activities in the United States, but it is important to mention that advertising regulations can vary dramatically from country to country.

Government Regulation

Governments have a powerful tool available for regulating advertising: the threat of legal action. In the United States, several different government agencies have been given the power and responsibility to regulate the advertising process. Exhibit 4.10 identifies seven agencies that have legal mandates concerning advertising and their areas of regulatory responsibility. Most active among these agencies is the Federal Trade Commission (see below).

Several other agencies have minor powers in the regulation of advertising, such as the Civil Aeronautics Board (advertising by air carriers), the Patent Office (trademark infringement), and the Library of Congress (copyright protection).

The FTC Legislative Mandates.   The Federal Trade Commission was created by the Federal Trade Commission Act in 1914 to prohibit unfair methods of competition. In 1916, the FTC concluded that false advertising was one way in which a firm could take unfair advantage of another, and advertising was established as a primary concern of the agency. The Wheeler-Lea Amendment (1938) broadened the FTC's powers to include regulation of advertising that was misleading to the public (regardless of the effect on competition).

Several other acts provide the FTC with legal powers over advertising. The Robinson-Patman Act (1936) prohibits firms from providing phantom cooperative-advertising allowances as a way to court important dealers. Consumer protection legislation, which seeks to increase the ability of consumers to make more-informed product comparisons, includes the Fair Packaging and Labeling Act (1966), the Truth in Lending Act (1969), and the Fair Credit Reporting Act (1970). The FTC Improvement Act (1975) expanded the authority of the commission by giving it the power to issue trade regulation rules. Many of these acts have been updated over the years to continue protecting consumers. The Fair Packaging and Labeling Act, for instance, was

Exhibit 4.10 ▶ Primary government agencies regulating advertising.

GOVERNMENT AGENCY	AREAS OF ADVERTISING REGULATION
Federal Trade Commission (FTC)	Controls unfair methods of competition, regulates deceptive advertising, and has various programs for controlling the advertising process.
Federal Communications Commission (FCC)	Prohibits obscenity, fraud, and lotteries on radio and television. Ultimate power lies in the ability to deny or revoke broadcast licenses.
Food and Drug Administration (FDA)	Regulates the advertising and labeling of food, drug, cosmetic, and medical products. Can require special labeling for hazardous products such as household cleaners. Prohibits false labeling and packaging.
Securities and Exchange Commission (SEC)	Regulates the advertising of securities and the disclosure of information in corporate annual reports.
U.S. Postal Service (USPS)	Responsible for regulating direct mail advertising and prohibiting lotteries, fraud, and misrepresentation. It can also regulate and impose fines for mailed materials deemed to be obscene.
Bureau of Alcohol, Tobacco, Firearms, and Explosives (ATF)	Most direct influence has been on regulation of advertising for alcoholic beverages. This agency was responsible for putting warning labels on alcoholic beverage advertising and banning active athletes as celebrities in beer ads. It has the power to determine what constitutes misleading advertising in these product areas.
Consumer Finance Protection Agency (CFPA)	Broad oversight over consumer financial products such as credit cards, debit cards, prepaid cards, mortgages, money transfers, and payday loans. It requires that detailed disclosures for financial products are clearly presented to consumers and protects against abuse and fraud.

updated not long ago to help consumers compare the cost of household commodities and to prevent deceptive packaging or labeling.

The FTC's Regulatory Programs and Remedies. The application of legislation has evolved as the FTC exercises its powers and expands its role as a regulatory agency. This evolution of the FTC has spawned several regulatory programs and remedies to help enforce legislative mandates in specific situations.

The **advertising substantiation program** of the FTC was initiated in 1971 with the intention of ensuring that advertisers make supporting evidence for their claims available to consumers. The program was strengthened in 1972 when the commission forwarded the notion of "reasonable basis" for the substantiation of advertising. This extension suggests not only that advertisers should substantiate their claims but also that the substantiation should provide a reasonable basis for believing the claims are true.[70] Simply put, before a company runs an ad, it must have documented evidence that supports the claim it wants to make in that ad. The kind of evidence required depends on the kind of claim being

made. For example, health and safety claims will require competent and reliable scientific evidence that has been examined and validated by experts in the field (see www .ftc.gov). The FTC also has issued guidelines with respect to "green" claims being made by companies, requiring more concrete substantiation regarding products' "sustainability" and "environmental impact."[71]

The consent order and the cease-and-desist order are the most basic remedies used by the FTC in dealing with deceptive or unfair advertising. In a **consent order**, an advertiser accused of running deceptive or unfair advertising agrees to stop running the advertisements in question without admitting guilt. For advertisers who do not comply voluntarily, the FTC can issue a **cease-and-desist order**, which generally requires that the advertising in question be stopped within 30 days so that a hearing can be held to determine whether the advertising is deceptive or unfair. For products that have a direct effect on consumers' health or safety (e.g., foods), the FTC can issue an immediate cease-and-desist order.

Affirmative disclosure is another remedy available to the FTC. An advertisement that fails to disclose important material facts about a product can be deemed deceptive, and the FTC may require **affirmative disclosure**, whereby the important material absent from prior ads must be included in subsequent advertisements. The absence of important material information might cause consumers to make false assumptions about products in comparison to the competition.

The most extensive remedy for advertising determined to be misleading is **corrective advertising**.[72] In cases where evidence suggests that consumers have developed incorrect beliefs about a brand based on deceptive or unfair advertising, the firm may be required to run corrective ads in an attempt to dispel those faulty beliefs. The goal of corrective advertising is to rectify erroneous beliefs created by deceptive advertising, but it hasn't always worked as intended. During its long history, the corrective advertising remedy has been required of ads ranging from Listerine mouthwash in the 1970s claiming that it could "cure and prevent colds" (which it couldn't) to more recent ad campaigns for pain relievers.

Another area of FTC regulation and remedy involves *celebrity endorsements, testimonials, and bloggers.* The FTC has specific rules for advertisements that use an expert or celebrity as a spokesperson for a product and guidelines for bloggers who feature brands in their blogs. In the case of experts (those whose experience or training provides them with credibility), the endorser's actual qualifications must justify his or her status as an expert, like a doctor recommending a cold remedy or surgical procedure. In the case of "average consumer" endorsements, the ad must reveal whether the results being portrayed are "typical." Also, FTC guidelines state that a celebrity endorser must be an actual user of the product, or the ad is considered deceptive. Finally, the FTC requires clear disclosure when a popular blogger or other social media star receives cash or in-kind payments (e.g., free products) in exchange for mentioning a brand or product. On Twitter, for example, endorsers are using hashtags such as #paid, #ad, or #sponsored to alert the public to their relationship with a sponsor.[73]

State Regulation.   State governments do not have extensive policing powers over the promotional activities of firms. Since the vast majority of companies are involved in interstate marketing of goods and services, any violation of fair practice or existing regulation is a federal government issue. There is typically one state government organization, the attorney general's office, that is responsible for investigating questionable promotional practices. In addition, the National Association of Attorneys General, whose members include the attorneys general from all 50 states, has been active as a group in monitoring advertising and sharing its findings.

Industry Self-Regulation

Self-regulation is the promotion industry's attempt to police itself. Supporters say it shows that government intervention is unnecessary.[74] Critics say meaningful self-regulation occurs only when the threat of government action is imminent. Several industry and trade associations and public service organizations have voluntarily established guidelines for promotion within their industries, reasoning that this is good for the promotion community as a whole and creates credibility for the effectiveness of promotion itself. Exhibit 4.11 lists only a few of the many organizations that have adopted self-regulation of promotional activities. The effectiveness of industry self-regulation depends, of course, on the cooperation of members and the policing mechanisms used.

But self-regulation is not just the result of efforts by industry organizations. Firms themselves often voluntarily regulate their behavior. The Walt Disney Company, in an attempt to respond to consumers' concerns about child obesity, decided to carefully monitor all products advertised on the firm's child-focused television channels to ensure that all ads complied with strict new nutritional standards.[75]

The National Advertising Review Board.   One important self-regulation organization is the **National Advertising Review Board (NARB)**. The NARB is the operations arm of the Advertising Self-Regulatory Council (ASRC), which establishes the policies and procedures for advertising industry self-regulation, including the National Advertising Division (NAD), Children's Advertising Review Unit (CARU), National Advertising Review Board (NARB), Electronic Retailing Self-Regulation Program (ERSP), and Online Interest-Based Advertising Accountability Program (Accountability Program). Complaints received from consumers, competitors, or local branches of the Better Business Bureau (BBB) are forwarded to the NAD. Most such complaints come from competitors. After a full review of the complaint, the issue may be forwarded to the NARB and evaluated by a panel. The general procedure for dealing with complaints is detailed in Exhibit 4.12. Note in particular that the NARB process starts with a recommendation from the NAD that an advertising or promotional campaign complaint be fully evaluated. Some examples of the types of complaints received and processed include:

- Hardee's sued rival Jack in the Box to stop TV ads that it says suggest that Hardee's uses cow anuses to make Angus beef burgers.

- The Sugar Association sued Johnson & Johnson over a marketing campaign related to J&J's artificial sweetener Splenda, accusing the company of misleading buyers into believing that Splenda is a natural product.

Exhibit 4.11 ▶ Selected business organizations and industry associations with advertising self-regulation programs.

ORGANIZATION	CODE ESTABLISHED
ADVERTISING ASSOCIATIONS	
American Advertising Federation	1965
American Association of Advertising Agencies	1924
Association of National Advertisers	1972
Business/Professional Advertising Association	1975
SPECIAL INDUSTRY GROUPS	
Council of Better Business Bureaus	1912
Household furniture	1978
Automobiles and trucks	1978
Carpet and rugs	1978
Home improvement	1975
Charitable solicitations	1974
Children's Advertising Review Unit	1974
National Advertising Division/National Advertising Review Board	1971
Network Advertising Initiative	2000
Digital Advertising Alliance Self-Regulatory Program for Online	
Behavioral Advertising	2010
MEDIA ASSOCIATIONS	
American Business Press	1910
Direct Mail Marketing Association	1960
Direct Selling Association	1970
National Association of Broadcasters	
Radio	1937
Television	1952
Outdoor Advertising Association of America	1950
SELECTED TRADE ASSOCIATIONS	
American Wine Association	1949
Wine Institute	1949
Distilled Spirits Association	1934
United States Brewers Association	1955
Pharmaceutical Manufacturers Association	1958
Proprietary Association	1934
Bank Marketing Association	1976
Motion Picture Association of America	1930
National Swimming Pool Institute	1970
Toy Manufacturers Association	1962

■ Procter & Gamble sued McLane Company, Salado Sales, and Consumer Value Products, charging that the companies are selling products in packages that copy P&G's packaging for Bounty, Charmin, and Vicks NyQuil and DayQuil.[76]

■ MillerCoors sued Anheuser-Busch over its 2019 Super Bowl ad, claiming that it purposely misled consumers into believing there is corn syrup in Coors Light and Miller Lite, when there is not.[77]

The NAD maintains a permanent professional staff that works to resolve complaints with the advertiser and its agency before the issue gets to the NARB. If no resolution is achieved, the complaint is appealed to the NARB, which appoints a panel made up of three advertiser representatives, one agency representative, and one public representative. This panel then holds hearings regarding the advertising in question. The advertiser is allowed to present its case. If no agreement can be reached by the panel either to dismiss the case or to persuade the advertiser to change the advertising, then the NARB initiates two actions. First, the NARB publicly identifies the advertiser, the complaint against them, and the panel's findings. Second, the case is forwarded to an appropriate government regulatory agency (usually the FTC). The NAD and the NARB are not empowered to impose penalties on advertisers, but the threat of going before the board acts as a deterrent to deceptive and questionable advertising practices.

State and Local Better Business Bureaus. Aside from the national BBB, there are more than 140 separate local bureaus. Each local organization is supported by membership dues paid by area businesses. The three divisions of a local BBB—merchandise, financial, and solicitations—investigate the advertising and selling practices of firms in their areas. A local BBB has the power to forward a complaint to the NAD for evaluation.

Beyond its regulatory activities, the BBB tries to avert problems associated with advertising by counseling new businesses and providing information to advertisers and agencies regarding legislation, potential problem areas, and industry standards.

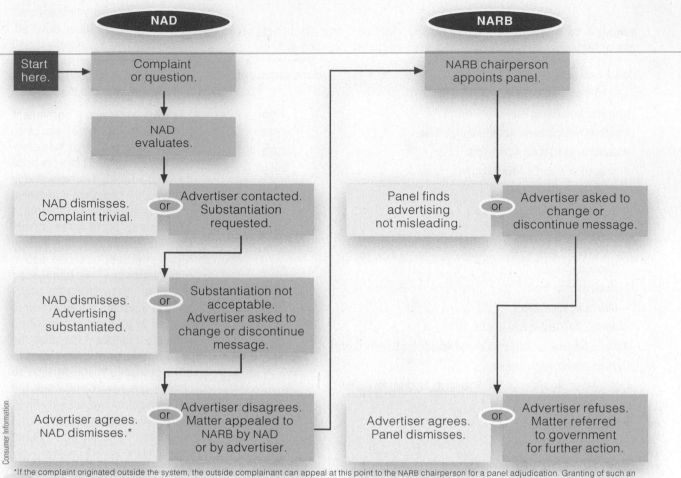

*If the complaint originated outside the system, the outside complainant can appeal at this point to the NARB chairperson for a panel adjudication. Granting of such an appeal is at the chairperson's discretion.

Exhibit 4.12 ▶ The NAD and NARB regulatory process.

Advertising Agencies and Associations. . It makes sense that advertising agencies and their industry associations would engage in self-regulation. An individual agency is legally responsible for the advertising it produces and is subject to reprisal for deceptive claims. The agency is in a difficult position in that it must monitor not only the activities of its own people but also the information that clients provide to the agency. Should a client direct an agency to use a product appeal that turns out to be untruthful, the agency is still responsible.

The American Association of Advertising Agencies (4As) has no legal or binding power over its agency members, but it can apply pressure when its board feels that industry standards are not being upheld. The 4As also publishes guidelines regarding various aspects of advertising messages. One of the most widely recognized industry standards is the 4As' Creative Code, outlining the responsibilities and social impact of advertising and promoting high ethical standards of honesty and decency.

Media Organizations.   Individual media organizations evaluate the advertising they receive for broadcast and publication. The National Association of Broadcasters (NAB) has a

policing arm known as the Code Authority, which implements separate radio and television codes regarding truth, fairness, and good taste in broadcast advertising. Newspapers have historically been rigorous in their screening of advertising, and many individual magazines have very high standards for advertising acceptance.

The Direct Marketing Association (DMA) is active in promoting ethical behavior and standards among its members. It has published guidelines for ethical business practices and has, for more than four decades, maintained a database for consumers who want their names removed from most phone, direct email, and snail-mail lists.

A review of all aspects of industry self-regulation suggests not only that a variety of programs and organizations are designed to monitor advertising but also that many of these programs are effective. Those whose livelihoods depend on advertising are just as interested as consumers and legislators in maintaining high standards. If advertising is perceived by consumers as an unethical and untrustworthy business activity, the economic vitality of many organizations will be compromised. Self-regulation can be helpful in this regard.

Internet Self-Regulation

A growing number of industry groups are involved in self-regulation. The Network Alliance Initiative has set up a voluntary code covering the responsible collection and use of digital data for online advertising. The Digital Advertising Alliance (DAA) maintains Self-Regulatory Principles for Online Behavioral Advertising, applying consumer-friendly standards to online behavioral advertising across the Internet. The Center for Digital Democracy focuses on research, public education, and advocacy designed to protect consumers in the digital age.

Consumers as Regulatory Agents

Consumers themselves are motivated to act as regulatory agents based on a variety of interests, including product safety, reasonable choice, the right to information, and privacy. Advertising tends to be a focus of consumer regulatory activities because of its conspicuousness. **Consumerism**, the actions of individual consumers or groups of consumers designed to exert power in the marketplace, is by no means a recent phenomenon. The earliest consumerism efforts can be traced back to 17th-century England. In general, consumerism movements have focused on the same issue: Consumers want a greater voice in the process of product development, distribution, and information dissemination. Consumers try to create pressure on firms by posting critical comments on social media channels or spreading negative word of mouth, sometimes attempting to seriously damage the image of the targeted brands.[78] Others withhold patronage through boycotts. Firms as powerful as Procter & Gamble, Kimberly-Clark, and General Mills have historically responded to threatened or actual boycotts by pulling advertising consumers found offensive.

Consumer Organizations. The other major consumer effort to bring about regulation is through established consumer organizations. The following are the most prominent consumer organizations and their prime activities:

- *Consumer Federation of America (CFA).* This organization, founded in 1968, now includes roughly 300 national, state, and local consumer groups and labor unions as affiliate members. The goals of the CFA are to encourage the creation of consumer organizations, provide services to consumer groups, and act as a voice for consumers at the state and federal legislative levels (www.consumerfed.org).

- *Consumers Union.* This nonprofit consumer organization is best known for its publication of *Consumer Reports*, both in print and online (www.consumersunion.org). Established in 1936, Consumers Union "is dedicated to one enduring idea: Unleashing the world-changing power of consumers."[79]

These two consumer organizations are the most active, widely known, and potent of the consumer groups, but there are hundreds of such groups organized by geographic

location or product category. Consumers have proven that when faced with an organized effort, corporations can and will change their practices. In one of the most publicized events in the history of marketing, consumers applied pressure to Coca-Cola and, in part, were responsible for forcing the firm to return to the original formula of Coca-Cola only 79 days after the introduction of "New" Coke.[80] If consumers are able to exert such a powerful influence on a firm such as Coca-Cola, imagine what other changes they might influence in the marketplace.

4-4 The Regulation of Other Promotional Tools

As firms integrate promotional tools for synergistic effects beyond those of advertising alone, it is important to understand the regulatory environment for direct marketing and e-commerce, sales promotion, and public relations.

4-4a Regulatory Issues in Direct Marketing and the Internet

Privacy and spam are two of the most pressing regulatory issues facing direct marketing and e-commerce today. Other regulatory issues for advertisers include contests, sweepstakes, coupons, and click fraud, as well as the use of telemarketing, all discussed here.

Privacy

Privacy in both direct marketing and online marketing contexts encompasses a wide range of issues, with behavioral targeting concerns emerging from technological advances. **Behavioral targeting** is the process of database development facilitated by online tracking markers that advertisers place on an Internet user's devices in order to track that person's online behavior. Big online content providers, such as Facebook and Google, don't charge users a fee for access to a variety of data and information services. Instead, to generate revenue from these services, they sell their online behavior patterns to advertisers (although people can "opt out" by changing their user settings).[81] Another technological advance that has created the potential for invasion of a user's privacy is the capability to track consumers' physical whereabouts via their smartphones. Advertisers can use **geofencing** to identify smartphone users within a given geographic area (such as inside a hotel or near a restaurant) and then offer these nearby consumers special deals or monitor their social media posts. With geofencing, Marriott, for example, knows when guests at its hotels and resorts post photos or comment on social media channels—and the company can immediately respond with a personalized offer or a customized customer service message.[82]

However, there is some hope for improved privacy. Twitter and Pinterest, among other sites, have adopted a "do-not-track" policy option. Many Web browsers have settings that allow users to avoid being tracked by sites they visit, and users can also install specialized software to prevent tracking by online advertisers.[83]

Spam

Few of us would argue with the allegation that **spam**, unsolicited commercial messages sent through the email system, is the scourge of the Internet. A particularly insidious version of spam is **phishing**, through which spammers try to entice Web users to enter personal information on a fake website that is forged to look like it is from a bank, the IRS, or another organization that could garner the email user's attention-and ultimately, their personal information. To cope with the onslaught, individuals and companies are turning to spam-filtering software to stem the flow and take back control of their email systems. In 2003, the CAN SPAM Act (Controlling the Assault of Non-Solicited Pornography and Marketing) was enacted. This legislation targets fraudulent, deceptive, and pornographic email messages and has resulted in some prosecutions, with violators spending time in jail.

Contests, Sweepstakes, Coupons, Click Fraud

Even though privacy and spam are huge direct marketing and e-commerce concerns, they are not the only ones. The next biggest legal issue has to do with sweepstakes, contests, and coupons. Because of the success and widespread use of sweepstakes in direct marketing (such as the Publishers Clearing House sweepstakes), Congress imposed limits on such promotions. Now direct mail sweepstakes must include the phrases "No purchase is necessary to win" and "A purchase will not improve an individual's chance of winning," repeated three times in letters to consumers and again on the entry form. In addition, penalties can be imposed on marketers who do not promptly remove consumers' names from mailing lists at the consumer's request.

Coupons distributed through direct mail, newspapers, magazines, or the Internet require legal protection for the *marketer* more than anything else. Phony coupons can easily be reproduced and redeemed well after the firm's planned promotional campaign ends. Safeguards like stating strict limitations on redemption, geographic limitations, or encrypted bar codes that can be scanned to detect fraud are

all ways to reduce problems with contests, sweepstakes, and coupons. **Click fraud** is a $7 billion problem for companies that pay "by the click" for digital advertising.[84] Fraud occurs when a company's ads are clicked not by actual humans but by bots designed to mimic what Internet users do, causing the advertiser to overpay. To combat click fraud, advertisers are closely monitoring click patterns and installing antibot software.[85]

Telemarketing

Another important legal issue in direct marketing has to do with telemarketing practices. The first restriction on telemarketing was the Telephone Consumer Fraud and Abuse Prevention Act of 1994 (later strengthened by the FTC), which requires telemarketers to state their name and company, as well as the purpose of the call. The act prohibits telemarketers from calling before 8 a.m. and after 9 p.m., and they cannot call the same customer more than once every three months. Consumers who wish to avoid telemarketers can sign up for the FTC's Do Not Call Registry (www.donotcall.gov; see Exhibit 4.13). Even if you have registered with the Do Not Call Registry, calls are still allowed from charities, political groups, market research firms, companies you do business with, and companies that have sold you something during the previous 18 months. Telemarketing regulations bar the use of automatic dialing machines, which make so-called robocalls containing recorded messages, but illegal scammers often find ways around these restrictions.[86]

4-4b Regulatory Issues in Sales Promotion

Regulatory issues in sales promotion focus on three areas: premium offers, trade allowances, and contests and sweepstakes. (See Exhibit 4.14 for an example of "free" in sales promotion.)

Premium Offers

With respect to **premiums** (an item offered for "free" or at a greatly reduced price with the purchase of another item), the main area of regulation has to do with requiring marketers to state the fair retail value of the item offered as a premium.

Trade Allowances

Marketers need to be familiar with the guidelines for trade allowances mentioned in the original Robinson-Patman Act of 1936. The Robinson-Patman Act, which applies to contemporary practices, requires marketers to offer similar customers (particularly wholesalers and retailers) similar prices on similar merchandise and quantities. So a marketer cannot use

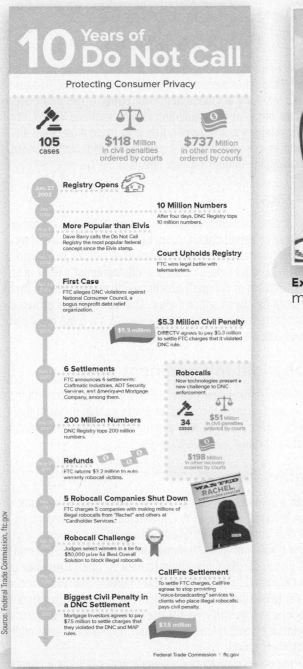

Source: Federal Trade Commission, ftc.gov

Exhibit 4.13 ▶ The Do Not Call Registry allows consumers to prevent a wide variety of telemarketers from calling with sales pitches.

Source: McDonald

Exhibit 4.14 ▶ The word FREE is very powerful in marketing.

special allowances as a way to discount the price to highly attractive customers.

Contests and Sweepstakes

In the area of sweepstakes and contests, the issues discussed in the previous section under direct marketing and e-commerce also apply, but there are other issues as well. The FTC has specified four violations of regulations that marketers must avoid in carrying out sweepstakes and contests:

- Misrepresentations about the value (e.g., stating an inflated retail price) of the prizes being offered.

- Failure to provide complete disclosure about the conditions necessary to win (are there behaviors required on the part of the contestant?).

- Failure to disclose the conditions necessary to obtain a prize (are there behaviors required of the contestant after the contestant is designated a "winner"?).

- Failure to ensure that a contest or sweepstakes is not classified as a lottery, which is considered gambling—a contest or sweepstakes is a lottery if a prize is offered based on chance and the contestant has to give up something of value in order to play.

Product/Brand Placement (Insertion)

The area of sales promotion receiving attention most recently in the regulatory arena is brand/product placement in television programs and films. As discussed earlier, consumer groups feel that unless television networks and film producers reveal that brands are placed in a program or film for a fee, consumers could mistakenly believe that the product use is natural and real. The industry counterclaim is, "There is a paranoia about our business that shouldn't be there. We don't control the storyline or the brands that are included. The writers and producers do." There are, of course, exceptions to this industry claim. Note the 2020 industry statistics and see how *content marketing* or marketing of one's unique content to be sold or shared via social and digital media is a trend. As such, new legal issues will be developed with respect to online brand placements and insertions. Exhibit 4.15 shows a modern example of digital media.

Source: Instagram

Exhibit 4.15 ▸ Many digital ads, such as those on social media, are designed to fit in so they look like other posts or content in a person's social media feed. This example from L'Oreal Paris is an ad on Instagram, and this is denoted with a "Sponsored" disclosure.

4-4c Regulatory Issues in Public Relations

Public relations is not bound by the same set of laws that govern the other elements of the promotional mix. Because public relations activities deal with public press and public figures, much of the regulation relates to these issues. The public relations activities of a firm may place it on either side of legal issues with respect to privacy, copyright infringement, or defamation through slander and libel.

Privacy

The privacy problems facing a public relations firm center on the issue of appropriation. **Appropriation** is the use of pictures or images owned by someone else without permission. If a firm uses a model's photo or a photographer's work in an advertisement or company brochure without permission, then the work has been appropriated. The same is true of public relations materials prepared for release to the press or as part of a company's public relations kit.

Copyright Infringement

Copyright infringement can occur when a public relations effort uses written, recorded, or photographic material from others' works. Much as with appropriation, written permission must be obtained to use such works.

Defamation

When a communication occurs that damages the reputation of an individual because the information in the communication was untrue, this is called **defamation** (you may have heard it referred to as "defamation of character"). Defamation can occur through either slander or libel. **Slander** is oral defamation and in the context of promotion would occur during television or radio broadcast of an event involving a company and its employees. **Libel** is defamation that occurs in print and would relate to magazine, newspaper, direct mail, or Internet reports.

The public relations practitioner's job is to protect clients from slanderous or libelous reports about a company's activities. Inflammatory TV "investigative" news programs are often sued for slander and are challenged to prove the allegations they make about a company and personnel working for a company. The issues revolve around whether negative comments can be fully substantiated. Erroneous reports in websites, magazines, and newspapers about a firm can result in a defamation lawsuit as well. Less frequently, public relations experts need to defend a client accused of making defamatory remarks.

Summary

1. **Understand a balanced perspective of advertising and IBP by identifying both benefits and problems of advertising and promotion and debating key issues concerning their effects on society's well-being.**

Advocates of advertising argue that it offers benefits for individual consumers and society at large, including educating consumers, promoting a higher standard of living, affecting happiness and general well-being, democratizing goods and art, and fostering diverse and affordable mass media. Critics argue that advertising is superficial and intrusive, wastes resources and widens the gap between rich and poor, encourages people to buy what they don't really need, promotes materialism, perpetuates superficial stereotypes, is offensive and even manipulative, and affects entertainment programming.

2. **Explain how ethical considerations affect the development and implementation of advertising and IBP campaigns.**

Ethical considerations are a concern when creating advertising and promotion. Deception in advertising and promotion is never acceptable or defendable. The ethical considerations get more complex, especially when advertising is targeted to children or involves controversial products such as firearms, gambling, alcohol, or cigarettes. Although ethical standards are a matter for personal reflection, unethical people can create unethical advertising. But there are also many safeguards against such behavior, including the corporate and personal integrity of advertisers.

3. **Explain the role of government agencies, consumers, and industry self-regulation for the regulation of advertising and promotion.**

Governments typically are involved in the regulation of advertising and promotion to combat deception and unfairness, deter unfair competition, and protect children. However, regulations can vary dramatically from one country to the next.

In the United States, the seven primary government agencies regulating advertising are the Federal Trade Commission; the Federal Communications Commission; the Food and Drug Administration; the U.S. Postal Service; the Bureau of Alcohol, Tobacco, Firearms, and Explosives; the Securities and Exchange Commission; and the Consumer Finance Protection Agency. State governments in the United States have limited powers due to the interstate nature of most advertising and promotion, thereby making any legal issues federal in nature. Consumerism and consumer organizations can also be regulatory agents.

Some of the most important controls on advertising and promotion are voluntary; that is, they are a matter of self-regulation by advertising and marketing professionals (i.e., industry self-regulation). For example, the American Association of Advertising Agencies has issued guidelines for promoting fairness and accuracy when using comparative advertisements. Many other organizations, such as the Better Business Bureau, the National Association of Broadcasters, and the Direct Marketing Association, participate in the process to help ensure fairness and assess consumer complaints about advertising and promotion. One important self-regulation organization is the National Advertising Review Board.

4. **Discuss the regulation of the full range of techniques used in the IBP process.**

The regulation of other tools in the IBP process focuses on direct marketing, e-commerce, sales promotions, and public relations. In direct marketing and e-commerce, areas of concern include consumer privacy, spam, contests and sweepstakes, coupon fraud, click fraud, and telemarketing. In sales promotions, premium offers, trade allowances, and offline contests and sweepstakes are subject to regulation, as is product/brand placement. The regulation of public relations efforts has to do with privacy, copyright infringement, and defamation.

Key Terms

advertising substantiation program
affirmative disclosure
appropriation
behavioral targeting
cease-and-desist order

click fraud
comparison advertisements
consent order
consumerism
consumer watchdog groups

corrective advertising
deception
defamation
ethics
geofencing

libel
monopoly power
National Advertising Review Board
    (NARB)
pester power
phishing

premiums
primary demand
puffery
self-actualization
self-regulation
slander

small print
spam
unfair advertising
vertical cooperative advertising

Endnotes

1. George J. Stigler, "The Economics of Information," *Journal of Political Economy* (June 1961), 213–220.

2. Ibid., 220.

3. Scott Donaton, "Why Brands Need to Skip the Ads and Start Telling Stories," *AdWeek,* April 19, 2016, http://www.adweek.com/news/advertising-branding/why-brands-need-skip-ads-and-start-telling-stories-170905.

4. Saurabh Mishra and Sachin B. Modi, "Corporate Social Responsibility and Shareholder Wealth: The Role of Marketing Capability," *Journal of Marketing* 80, no. 1 (2016), 26–46. For a perspective on how the environmental advertising agendas of nonprofits and for-profit organizations can be better aligned with the micro-agendas of consumers, see Aubrey R. Fowler III and Angeline G. Close, "It Ain't Easy Being Green: Macro, Meso, and Micro Green Advertising Agendas," *Journal of Advertising* 41, no. 4 (2012), 119–132.

5. Joerg Koenigstorfer and Hans Baumgartner, "The Effect of Fitness Branding on Restrained Eaters' Food Consumption and Postconsumption Physical Activity," *Journal of Marketing Research* 53, no. 1 (2016), 124–138.

6. Marc Pritchard, "Half my Digital Advertising is Wasted...," *Journal of Marketing* 85, no. 1, (2021), 26–29.

7. "Ad blocking user penetration rate in the United States from 2014 to 2021," *Statista,* March 22, 2021, https://www.statista.com/statistics/804008/ad-blocking-reach-usage-us/.

8. Jill Goldsmith, "NBCUniversal Is Reducing Commercials as Advertisers Scale Back and Shift Messaging; Hello, Family Movie Night with Limited Ads," *Deadline,* April 6, 2020, https://deadline.com/2020/04/nbcuniversal-reducing-commercials-as-advertisers-scale-back-shift-message-family-movie-night-limited-ads-1202901703/#!.

9. Nicholas De Canha, et al., "The Impact of Advertising on Market Share," *Journal of Advertising Research* 60, no. 1, March 29, 2019, 87–103, EBSCOhost, doi:10.2501/JAR-2019-011.

10. Jeff Beer, "It Might Get Loud: Patagonia's New VP of Marketing Doubles Down on Brand Mission," *Fast Company Create,* October 18, 2016, https://www.fastcocreate.com/3064745/creative-conversations/it-might-get-loud-patagonias-new-vp-of-marketing-doubles-down-on-its.

11. Matthew Creamer, "Caught in the Clutter Crossfire: Your Brand," *Advertising Age, April 2,* 2007, 1, 35.

12. Richard Caves, *American Industry: Structure, Conduct, Performance* (Upper Saddle River, NJ: Prentice Hall, 1964), 102.

13. Piper Weiss, "Outrage over Gym's Skinny Model Campaign. Members Want More Muscle," *Healthy Living,* January 5, 2012, www.shine.yahoo.com/healthy-living.

14. A. H. Maslow, *Motivation and Personality* (New York: Harper & Row, 1970).

15. Vance Packard, *The Status Seekers* (New York: David McKay, 1959).

16. This argument was first offered by authors George Katona, *The Mass Consumption Society* (New York: McGraw-Hill, 1964), 54–61, and John Kenneth Galbraith, *The Affluent Society* (Boston: Houghton Mifflin, 1958).

17. John Kell, "Why REI Is Opting Out of Black Friday Again This Year," *Fortune,* October 24, 2016, http://fortune.com/2016/10/24/rei-closing-black-friday-again/.

18. Stephen Fox, *The Mirror Makers: A History of American Advertising and Its Creators* (New York: William Morrow, 1984), 330.

19. See, for example, Melissa D. Cinelli and Lifeng Yang, "The Role of Implicit Theories in Evaluations of 'Plus-Size' Advertising," *Journal of Advertising* (2016), 1–10.

20. Drew Sheldrick, "Gay Coffee Ad Causes a Stir in Taiwan," *Special Broadcasting Service (Australia),* March 9, 2016, http://www.sbs.com.au/topics/sexuality/article/2016/03/09/gay-coffee-ad-causes-stir-taiwan.

21. See, for example, Blaine Branchik and Bay O'Leary, "Funny, Scary, Dead: Negative Depictions of Male Homosexuality in American Advertising," *Journal of Historical Research in Marketing* 8, no. 4 (2016).

22. Valeriya Safronova, "Meet CoverGirl's New Cover Boy," *New York Times,* October 12, 2016, http://www.nytimes.com/2016/10/16/fashion/meet-covergirls-new-cover-boy.html?_r=0; Rachel Gee, "L'Oréal Targets Men for the First Time as It Evolves Strapline to Embrace Diversity," *Marketing Week,* August 26, 2016, https://www.marketingweek.com/2016/08/26/loreal-targets-men-for-the-first-time-as-it-evolves-strapline-to-embrace-diversity/.

23. Christine Birkner, "Q&A: Unilever's Global Marketing Chief on Busting Gender Stereotypes in Advertising," *Adweek,* October 24, 2016, http://www.adweek.com/news/advertising-branding/qa-unilevers-global-marketing-chief-busting-gender-stereotypes-advertising-174242.

24. Hojoon Choi, Kyunga Yoo, Tom Reichert, and Michael S. LaTour, "Do Feminists Still Respond Negatively to Female Nudity in Advertising? Investigating the Influence of Feminist Attitudes on Reactions to Sexual Appeals," *International Journal of Advertising* (2016), 1–23.

25. See Melissa D. Cinelli and Lifeng Yang, "The Role of Implicit Theories in Evaluations of 'Plus-Size' Advertising," *Journal of Advertising* (2016), 1–10.

26. Tim Calkins and Derek D. Rucker, "Why GoDaddy's Offensive Super Bowl Ads Worked," *Fortune,* February 4, 2016, http://fortune.com/2016/02/04/godaddy-super-bowl-50/.

27. Normandy Madden, "Honda Pulls Suicide Car Ad from Australian TV Market," *Advertising Age,* September 22, 2003, 3.

28. Don E. Schultz, "Subliminal Ad Notions Still Resonate Today," *Marketing News,* March 15, 2007, 5, 9.

29. Murphy, Monahan, and Zajonc, "Additivity of Nonconscious Affect: Combined Effects of Priming and Exposure," *Journal of Personality and Social Psychology* 69 (1995), 589–602. For a more recent discussion and real-world test, see "Does Subliminal Advertising Actually Work?" *BBC Magazine,* January 20, 2015, http://www.bbc.com/news/magazine-30878843.

30. Timothy E. Moore, "Subliminal Advertising: What You See Is What You Get," *Journal of Marketing* 46 (Spring 1982), 38–47; and Timothy E. Moore, "The Case Against Subliminal Manipulation," *Psychology and Marketing* 5, no. 4 (Winter 1988), 297–317.

31. Andy Warhol, *The Philosophy of Andy Warhol: From A to B and Back Again* (New York: Harcourt Brace Jovanovich, 1975), 101.

32. Fred Schonenberg, "Art Thinking: Why More Brands Should Ask 'Wouldn't It Be Cool If...'" *Campaign US,* October 11, 2016, http://www.campaignlive.com/article/art-thinking-why-brands-ask-wouldnt-cool-if/1411909.

33. A. Guttmann, "Newspaper advertising expenditure worldwide from 2000 to 2022," *Statista,* June 2, 2021, https://www.statista.com/statistics/273708/global-newspaper-advertising-expenditure/.

34. B. G. Gregg, "Tax Funds Bankroll New Anti-Drug Ads," *Cincinnati Enquirer,* July 10, 1998, A1, A17.

35. Kristina Monllos, "Iconic Anti-Drug 'Fried Egg' Spot Returns by Targeting Parents With New Messaging," *Ad Week,* August 8, 2016, http://www.adweek.com/news/advertising-branding/iconic-anti-drug-fried-egg-spot-returns-new-messaging-todays-landscape-172867.

36. Jay Reeves, "Scrushy Said to Pay for Positive Stories," *Associated Press,* January 19, 2006, www.news.yahoo.com, accessed January 20, 2006.

37. Eamon Javers, "This Opinion Brought to You By ..." *BusinessWeek,* January 30, 2006, 35.

38. Aribarg, Anocha, and Eric M. Schwartz, "Native Advertising in Online News: Trade-Offs Among Clicks, Brand Recognition, and Website Trustworthiness," *Journal of Marketing Research* 57, no. 1, November 10, 2019, 20–34. *SAGE* journals, doi:10.1177/0022243719879711.

39. Daniela Andreini, et al., "How a CEO's Personality, Performance, and Leadership Predict Advertising Credibility," *Journal of Advertising Research* 61, no. 1, July 23, 2020, 110–124. *EBSCOhost,* doi:10.2501/jar-2020-003.

40. This quote is taken from the Commercial Alert website and is part of the organization's discussion of the deceptive nature of product placement within television shows, videos, video games, and a process they refer to as "adversongs," January 6, 2013, http://www.commercialalert.org/issues/culture/product placement.

41. Paul Revoir, "ITV Has Shown Over 4,000 Hours of Programming Featuring Product Placement," *Radio Times,* November 26, 2015, http://www.radiotimes.com/news/2015-11-26/itv-has-shown-over-4000-hours-of-programming-featuring-product-placement.

42. Wu, Linwan, and Naa Amponsah Dodoo. "Being accepted or ostracized: how social experience influences consumer responses to advertisements with different regulatory focus." *Journal of Advertising* 49.3 (2020): 234–249.

43. "Children Not Seeing More Food Ads on Television," *Federal Trade Commission Report,* www.ftc.gov, released June 1, 2007.

44. "Survey: Most Americans Believe Advertising to Children Is Unethical and Advertisers Should Stop Marketing to Kids Under 8 Years Old," *Marketing News Weekly,* December 12, 2020, 44.

45. Agnes Nairn and Cordelia Fine, "Who's Messing with My Mind? The Implications of Dual-Process Models for the Ethics of Advertising to Children," *International Journal of Advertising* 27, no. 3 (2008), 447–470.

46. Kacy K. Kim, Jerome D. Williams, and Gary B. Wilcox, "'Kid Tested, Mother Approved': The Relationship Between Advertising Expenditures and 'Most-Loved' Brands," *International Journal of Advertising* 35, no. 1 (2016), 42–60.

47. For more about parents' concerns relative to Internet advertising aimed at children, see Akshaya Vijayalakshmi, Meng-Hsien Lin (Jenny), and Russell N. Laczniak, "Parental Mediation of Internet Advertising and Children's Persuasion Knowledge," *American Academy of Advertising Conference Proceedings* (2016), 147–149.

48. Richard Linnett, "Psychologists Protest Kids' Ads," *Advertising Age,* September 11, 2000, 4.

49. See Frans Folkvord, Doeschka J. Anschütz, Emma Boyland, Bridget Kelly, and Moniek Buijzen, "Food Advertising and Eating Behavior in Children," *Current Opinion in Behavioral Sciences* 9 (June 2016), 26–31.

50. Patrick J. Sheridan, "FCC Sets Children's Ad Limits," *1990 Information Access Company* 119, no. 20 (1990), 33.

51. Sandra L. Calvert and Jennifer A. Kotler, "Lessons from Children's Television: The Impact of the Children's Television Act on Children's Learning," *Applied Developmental Psychology* 24 (2003), 275–335; for more detail, see the FCC website, https://www.fcc.gov/consumers/guides/childrens-educational-television.

52. Current information about this initiative can be found at https://www.bbb.org/council/the-national-partner-program/national-advertising-review-services/childrens-food-and-beverage-advertising-initiative/.

53. J. Goldstein, "Children and Advertising—the Research," *Commercial Communications,* July 1998, 4–7; and Tina Mangelburg and Terry Bristol, "Socialization and Adolescent's Skepticism toward Advertising," *Journal of Advertising* 27, no. 3 (Fall 1998), 11–21.

54. While a lot of articles were written alleging this practice by the tobacco industry, a representative piece during the height of the argument is: Kathleen Deveny, "Joe Camel Ads Reach Children, Research Finds," *The Wall Street Journal,* December 11, 1991, B1, B6.

55. As an example of this type of research, see Joseph R. DiFranza et al., "RJR Nabisco's Cartoon Camel Promotes Camel Cigarettes to Children," *Journal of the American Medical Association* 266, no. 22 (1991), 3168–3153.

56. E. J. Schultz, "Liquor Advertising Pours into TV," *Advertising Age,* May 14, 2012, 1, 41.

57. For a summary of more than 60 articles dating back to the 1960s that address the issue of alcohol and cigarette advertising and the lack of a relationship between advertising and cigarette and alcohol industry demand, see Mark Frankena et al.., "Alcohol, Consumption, and Abuse," *Bureau of Economics, Federal Trade Commission,* March 5, 1985. For a similar listing of research articles in which the same conclusions were drawn during congressional hearings on the topic, see "Advertising of Tobacco Products," Hearings before the Subcommittee on Health and the Environment, Committee on Energy and Commerce, House of Representatives, 99th Congress, July 18 and August 1, 1986, 99–167. The findings of these early articles were recently reaffirmed: Michael L. Capella, Charles R. Taylor, and Cynthia Webster, "The Effect of Cigarette Advertising Bans on Consumption: A Meta-Analysis," *Journal of Advertising* 37, no. 2 (Summer 2008), 7–18.

58. For additional studies that reaffirm peers and family rather than advertising as the basis for smoking initiation, see Charles R. Taylor and P. Greg Bonner, "Comment on 'American Media and the Smoking-Related Behaviors of Asian Adolescents,'" *Journal of Advertising Research* (December 2003), 419–430; Bruce Simons Morton,

"Peer and Parent Influences on Smoking and Drinking Among Early Adolescents," *Journal of Health Education and Behavior* (February 2000); and Karen H. Smith and Mary Ann Stutz, "Factors that Influence Adolescents to Smoke," *Journal of Consumer Affairs* 33, no. 2 (Winter 1999), 321–357.

59.   With regard to cartoon characters see, for example, Lucy L. Henke, "Young Children's Perceptions of Cigarette Brand Advertising: Awareness, Affect and Target Market Identification," *Journal of Advertising* 24, no. 4 (Winter 1995), 13–27, and Richard Mizerski, "The Relationship between Cartoon Trade Character Recognition and Attitude toward the Product Category," *Journal of Marketing* 59 (October 1995), 58–70. The evidence in Europe is provided by Jeffrey Goldstein, "Children and Advertising—the Research," *Commercial Communications*, July 1998, 4–8.

60.   Mary Cross, *A Century of American Icons: 100 Products and Slogans from the 20th-Century Consumer Culture* (Westport: Greenwood Press, 2002), 204–206.

61.   For research on this topic across several decades, see Richard Schmalensee, *The Economics of Advertising* (Amsterdam and London: North-Holland, 1972); Mark S. Albion and Paul W. Farris, *The Advertising Controversy* (Boston: Auburn House, 1981); Michael J. Waterson, "Advertising and Tobacco Consumption: An Analysis of the Two Major Aspects of the Debate," *International Journal of Advertising* 9 (1990), 59–72; and Michael L. Capella, Charles R. Taylor, and Cynthia Webster, "The Effect of Cigarette Advertising Bans on Consumption: A Meta-Analysis," *Journal of Advertising* 37, no. 2 (Summer 2008), 7–18.

62.   Rep. Ric Keller (R-Florida), quoted in Joanne Kenen, "U.S. House Backs Ban on Obesity Lawsuits," *Reuters*, Reuters.com, published March 10, 2004, accessed March 14, 2004.

63.   The definition of deception and the FTC criteria can be found at https://www.ftc.gov/public-statements/1983/10/ftc -policy-statement-deception.

64.   Christy Fisher, "How Congress Broke Unfair Ad Impasse," *Advertising Age*, August 22, 1994, 34. For additional discussion of the FTC's definition of unfairness, see Ivan Preston, "Unfairness Developments in FTC Advertising Cases," *Journal of Public Policy and Marketing* 14, no. 2 (1995), 318–321.

65.   See Guiomar Martín-Herrán and Simon P. Sigué, "An Integrative Framework of Cooperative Advertising: Should Manufacturers Continuously Support Retailer Advertising?" *Journal of Business Research* 70 (January 2017), 67–73; and Ruiliang Yan, Zixia Cao, and Zhi Pei, "Manufacturer's Cooperative Advertising, Demand Uncertainty, and Information Sharing," *Journal of Business Research* 69, no. 2 (2016), 709–717.

66.   Paul W. Miniard, Michael J. Barone, Randall L. Rose, and Kenneth C. Manning, "A Further Assessment of Indirect Comparative Advertising Claims of Superiority over All Competitors," *Journal of Advertising* 35, no. 4 (Winter 2006), 53–64.

67.   E. J. Schultz, "FTC's Attempt to Limit Food Marketing to Kids Peters Out," *Advertising Age*, May 7, 2012, 3, 103.

68.   Anthony D. Miyazaki, Andrea J. S. Stanaland, and May O. Lwin, "Self-Regulatory Safeguards and the Online Privacy of Preteen Children," *Journal of Advertising* 38, no. 4 (Winter 2009), 80.

69.   See Bryan Cave, "Guidelines for Collecting Information From Children: A Comparison of US Law, EU Law, and Soon-to-Be EU Law," *Lexology*, October 26, 2016, http://www.lexology.com/library /detail.aspx?g=86cc44f3-2dc6-4c0d-ad4e -947d280278d5.

70.   For a discussion of the origins and intent of the FTC's advertising substantiation program and its extension to require reasonable basis, see Debra L. Scammon and Richard J. Semenik, "The FTC's 'Reasonable Basis' for Substantiation of Advertising: Expanded Standards and Implications," *Journal of Advertising* 12, no. 1 (1983), 4–11.

71.   "Are Green Labels Legitimate or Just Greenwashing?" *Scientific American*, April 18, 2016, https://www.scientificamerican.com /article/are-green-labels-legitimate-or-just-greenwashing/.

72.   The history and intent of the corrective advertising concept and several of its applications are provided by Debra L. Scammon and Richard J. Semenik, "Corrective Advertising: Evolution of the Legal Theory and Application of the Remedy," *Journal of Advertising* 11, no. 1 (1982), 10–20.

73.   Lauren Johnson, "Snapchat Influencers Start Labeling Social Endorsements as Paid Ads," *Adweek*, August 3, 2016, http://www .adweek.com/news/technology/snapchat-influencers-start-labeling -social-endorsements-paid-ads-172775; "FTC Publishes Final Guides Governing Endorsements, Bloggers, Testimonials," Federal Trade Commission, October 5, 2009, www.ftc.gov.

74.   Christopher Graham, "Advertising self-regulation," Brand Strategy; London (Dec 2003), 12. https://www.proquest.com /docview/224164459

75.   Brooks Barnes, "Promoting Nutrition, Disney to Restrict Junk-Food Ads," *The New York Times*, June 5, 2012, www.nytimes.com.

76.   Gary Gentile, "Jack in the Box Ads Called Misleading," *Associated Press*, May 25, 2007, biz.yahoo.com; Sophie Walker, "J&J Sued Over Splenda Ad Campaign," *Reuters News Service*, January 31, 2005, story.news.yahoo.com; and Bizjournals.com, "P&G Sues Companies Over Product Packaging," December 22, 2005, biz.yahoo.com/bizj.

77.   Concepción de León, "MillerCoors Sues Anheuser-Busch Over 'Mis-leading' Bud Light Ad," *New York Times*, March 21, 2019, https:// www.nytimes.com/2019/03/21/business/miller-lite-bud-light -lawsuit.html.

78.   Andrea Kähr, Bettina Nyffenegger, Harley Krohmer, and Wayne D. Hoyer, "When Hostile Consumers Wreak Havoc on Your Brand: The Phenomenon of Consumer Brand Sabotage," *Journal of Marketing* 80, no. 3 (May 2016), 25–41.

79.   Quoted from the Consumers Union website, www.consumersunion .org.

80.   "The Real Story of New Coke," November 14, 2013, Coca-Cola corporate website, http://www.coca-colacompany.com/stories /coke-lore-new-coke.

81.   Kate Cox, "New Google Accounts Now Opted-In to Ad Tracking Features by Default," *The Consumerist*, October 25, 2016, https:// consumerist.com/2016/10/25/new-google-accounts-now-opted -in-to-ad-tracking-features-by-default/.

82.   Jessica Golden and Michelle Caruso-Cabrera, "Why Marriott Is So Interested in Your Social Media," *CNBC*, August 3, 2016, http://www .cnbc.com/2016/08/02/why-marriott-looks-at-what-you-post-on -social-media-from-your-room.html.

83.   Roger A. Grimes, "17 Essential Tools to Protect Your Online Identity, Privacy," *InfoWorld*, October 31, 2016, http://www.infoworld .com/article/3135324/security/17-essential-tools-to-protect-your -online-identity-and-privacy.html.

84.   Gian M. Fulgoni, "Fraud in Digital Advertising: A Multibillion-Dollar Black Hole," *Journal of Advertising Research* 56, no. 2 (June 2016).

85.   Paul Rubens, "Why CIOs Should Care About Click Fraud," *CIO*, June 29, 2016, http://www.cio.com/article/3088996/security/why-cios -should-care-about-click-fraud.html.

86.   Helaine Olen, "Congratulations! You Lost," *Slate*, May 24, 2016, http://www.slate.com/articles/business/the_bills/2016/05 /robocalls_have_triumphed_over_the_do_not_call_list_whose _fault_is_it.html.

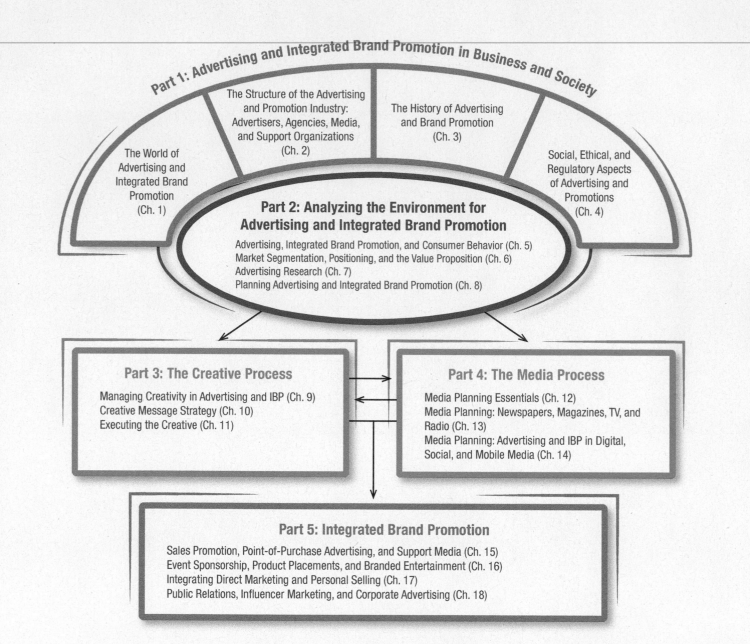

Part 1: Advertising and Integrated Brand Promotion in Business and Society

The Structure of the Advertising and Promotion Industry: Advertisers, Agencies, Media, and Support Organizations (Ch. 2)

The History of Advertising and Brand Promotion (Ch. 3)

The World of Advertising and Integrated Brand Promotion (Ch. 1)

Social, Ethical, and Regulatory Aspects of Advertising and Promotions (Ch. 4)

Part 2: Analyzing the Environment for Advertising and Integrated Brand Promotion

Advertising, Integrated Brand Promotion, and Consumer Behavior (Ch. 5)
Market Segmentation, Positioning, and the Value Proposition (Ch. 6)
Advertising Research (Ch. 7)
Planning Advertising and Integrated Brand Promotion (Ch. 8)

Part 3: The Creative Process

Managing Creativity in Advertising and IBP (Ch. 9)
Creative Message Strategy (Ch. 10)
Executing the Creative (Ch. 11)

Part 4: The Media Process

Media Planning Essentials (Ch. 12)
Media Planning: Newspapers, Magazines, TV, and Radio (Ch. 13)
Media Planning: Advertising and IBP in Digital, Social, and Mobile Media (Ch. 14)

Part 5: Integrated Brand Promotion

Sales Promotion, Point-of-Purchase Advertising, and Support Media (Ch. 15)
Event Sponsorship, Product Placements, and Branded Entertainment (Ch. 16)
Integrating Direct Marketing and Personal Selling (Ch. 17)
Public Relations, Influencer Marketing, and Corporate Advertising (Ch. 18)

Now with Part 1 complete and the knowledge of how advertising and integrated brand promotion operate in the macro-environment of business and society, we move to Part 2, which entails analyzing the environment for advertising and integrated brand promotion. The framework shows how the aspects of analyzing the environment are considered under the umbrella of business and society as a whole. As shown in the framework for Part 2, we will develop the topics of advertising and integrated brand promotion related to: consumer behavior, segmentation and positioning, research, and planning.

Part 2

Analyzing the Environment for Advertising and Integrated Brand Promotion

5 Advertising, Integrated Brand Promotion, and Consumer Behavior *106*

6 Market Segmentation, Positioning, and the Value Proposition *126*

7 Advertising Research *142*

8 Planning Advertising and Integrated Brand Promotion *164*

Successful advertising and integrated brand promotion rely on a clear understanding of how and why consumers make purchase decisions. Successful advertising and brand communication are rooted in sound marketing strategies and research about a brand's market environment. This understanding of consumers and the market, strategy, and research are brought together in an advertising and IBP plan. The chapters in Part 2, "Analyzing the Environment for Advertising and Integrated Brand Promotion," discuss the many important ways to assess the environment in the development of an advertising and IBP plan. Consumer behavior (Chapter 5) must be understood, market segments must be analyzed, brand positioning decisions must be made (Chapter 6), and research must be carried out in a systematic and analytical manner (Chapter 7). This part concludes with an examination of the advertising and IBP planning process (Chapter 8).

Chapter 5

Advertising, Integrated Brand Promotion, and Consumer Behavior

Learning Objectives

After reading and thinking about this chapter, you will be able to do the following:

1 Describe consumer behavior from a decision-making perspective and the four stages of the consumer decision-making process along with the roles of involvement, experience, memory, and emotion.

2 Discuss consumer behavior from a social and cultural perspective and the role of social class, taste, and cultural capital that influence consumer behavior.

3 Explain how meaning is derived from advertising and how effective advertising uses sociocultural meaning.

As you can see from the framework in Exhibit 5.1, we have completed Part 1 (the macro-environment) and are beginning Part 2, first focusing on two complementary perspectives of consumer behavior as it relates to advertising and IBP. **Consumer behavior** is defined as all things related to how humans operate as consumers—from need recognition and acquisition to use and disposal of a good, an idea, or a service. It is far better for advertisers to understand consumer behavior than not. Due to simply being the first, the biggest, or the luckiest, some companies do well with only a thin understanding of how and why their customers choose their brands. This is especially true in the case of the so-called low-involvement goods, such as **consumer packaged goods (CPG)**—think trash bags, paper towels, laundry detergent, canned soup, chips.

Can you imagine a new company having enough money to launch a new brand that would successfully unseat a market leader like Doritos chips? It's possible but not very likely. CPG consumer behavior, like most low-involvement examples, is about memory and habit. Invest enough advertising for a brand name such as Doritos, and you can get people to remember it. This may even lead to habit, with consumers buying the same brand time after time in part due to habit.

But, marketers can transform CPG or other low-involvement brands from simple memory-based ones into more culturally and socially meaningful ones through advertising. When you are dealing with more high-involvement categories, such as automobiles or clothing, then the advertising, integrated brand promotion, and related consumer behavior are more multi-dimensional. Some brands can actually be **self-transformative** or used by the consumer to help create or transform their sense of self.

Exhibit 5.1 ▶ A framework of analyzing the external environment: Complementary perspectives.

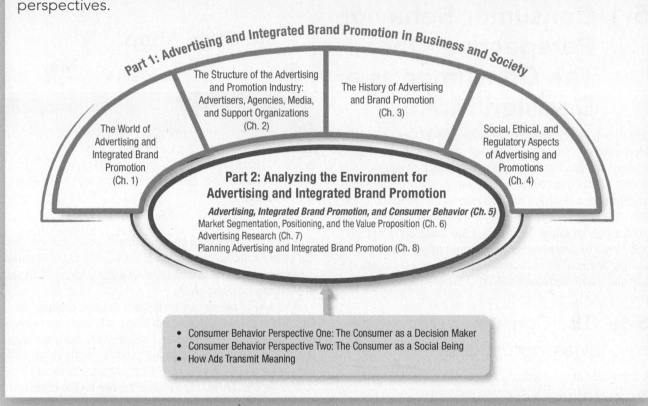

For instance, a person who wants to see themself as more rugged, adventurous, and outdoorsy chooses to buy a Jeep Wrangler or Ford Bronco because those brands/models are known for their offroading capabilities and for being suited to trails and adventure. The bottom line is this: all advertisers could significantly improve their profits and society at large by better understanding their consumers and their wants, needs, desires, and well-being.

This chapter summarizes the concepts and frameworks most helpful in trying to understand consumer behavior as it relates to advertising and integrated brand promotion. In this chapter, we examine examples from Doritos and Target, because both are strong brands that base their integrated brand promotion around and an understanding of consumer behavior principles. We explain consumer behavior from two different perspectives, one psychological and two sociocultural.

The psychological is what happens in consumers' minds (cognition). It portrays consumers as systematic (but not always rational) information seekers, processors, and decision makers. The psychological perspective is useful for either high-involvement or low-involvement goods. But typically, this perspective is most relevant when discussing low-cost, low-involvement goods. This type of brand advertising is often called "mindshare" marketing because it is hugely dependent on how easily the brand name and a small set of attributes are retrieved from memory. Easily remembered brands, such as Target, are considered to have a high mindshare and are **mindshare brands.**

The second perspective views consumers as social beings who operate in their societies and cultures and thus behave largely as a function of social circumstance and cultural forces. This is where advertising and brand management can create truly great, sustainable brands, rather than just reinforcing memory or encouraging habitual buying. This second type of brand advertising is often referred to as "cultural branding," because it leverages social and cultural forces. It is typically used for more expensive and high-involvement categories, although some great low-cost brands such as Doritos are brilliant users of cultural marketing. Although differing in assumptions and focus, both of these perspectives offer something valuable to the process of creating effective advertising and brand promotion.

5-1 Consumer Behavior Perspective One: The Consumer as a Decision Maker

One way to view consumer behavior is as a fairly predictable sequential process culminating with the individual's reaping a set of benefits from a product or service that satisfies that person's perceived needs. In this view, we think of individuals as purposeful decision makers who either weigh and balance alternatives or resort to simple decision rules of thumb (heuristics) to make decisions if the decision is complex and they are overwhelmed with information. Often but not always, the consumer decision-making process occurs in a straightforward sequence, shown in Exhibit 5.2.

5-1a The Consumer Decision-Making Process

A discussion of what typically happens at each stage will give us a foundation for understanding consumers from a psychological perspective, and it can also illuminate opportunities for developing effective advertising for integrative branding.

Need Recognition

From the psychological perspective, the consumption process begins when people perceive they have a need. A **need state** arises when one's desired state of affairs differs from one's actual state of affairs. Need states are accompanied by a mental discomfort or anxiety that motivates action; the severity of this discomfort can be widely variable depending on the genesis of the need. For example, the need state that arises when one runs out of toothpaste would involve very mild discomfort for most people, whereas the need state that accompanies the breakdown of one's automobile can approach desperation.

One way advertising works is to point to and thereby activate needs that will motivate consumers to buy a product or service. For instance, because consumers are often busy, a motivating factor for shopping at a place like Target is being able to shop for many categories instead of going to different

Source: target brands, inc.

Exhibit 5.3 ▶ Target uses billboard advertising with recognizable brand symbols like the bulls-eye to catch the eye of shoppers.

specialty retailers, such as pet stores to buy dog food. See the ad in Exhibit 5.3 and think about how Target communicates that the brand is a welcoming place to meet the need of shopping for many goods.

A variety of needs can be fulfilled through consumption, and it is reasonable to suggest that consumers' needs are often sufficiently recognized and motivating to many consumers. Products and services should provide benefits that fulfill consumers' needs; hence, one of the advertiser's primary jobs is to make the connection between the two for the consumer. Marketers are sometimes said to turn wants into needs; but in reality, if the consumer thinks of it as a need, then it's a need. Advertising can sometimes help this along; but in the world of advertising, everything is a need.[1]

Information Search and Alternative Evaluation

Once a consumer has recognized a need, the best way to satisfy that need is not always obvious. Need recognition sets a process in motion that may involve extensive information search and careful evaluation of alternatives prior to purchase. During this search and evaluation phase, there are numerous opportunities for the advertiser to influence the final purchase decision. The consumer's first option for information is to draw on personal experience and prior knowledge. This **internal search** for information may be all that is required. When a consumer has considerable prior experience with the products in question, thoughts and feelings about the alternatives may be well established and determine choice.

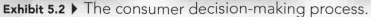

Exhibit 5.2 ▶ The consumer decision-making process.

LEE SNIDER PHOTO IMAGES/Shutterstock.com

An internal search can also tap into information that has accumulated in one's memory as a result of repeated advertising exposures, such as Dorito's "For the Bold," or from stored judgments, for example, "Shopping at Target is awesome." Advertisers want the outcome of internal search to result in their brand being in the "**evoked set**," that is, the set of brands (usually two to five) that come to mind when a category is mentioned. I say "chips," and you say "Doritos" or "For the Bold." Here, the evoked set consists of the brands, all stored internally, found through internal search, and probably the product of the integration of the brands via advertising, sponsorships, exposure to brands in stores, actual use, and habit. The evoked set is usually highly related to the **consideration set**, the set of the brands the consumer will evaluate for purchase.

If your brand is the first mentioned, you have achieved something even better: **top of mind awareness**. Top-of-mind awareness is a pretty good predictor of fairly inexpensive and low-risk CPG purchases. Affecting people's beliefs about a brand before their actual use of it, or merely establishing the existence of the brand in the consumer's consciousness, is a critical function of advertising and other integrated brand promotion. As noted in Chapter 1, the purpose of delayed-response advertising is to generate recognition of and a favorable predisposition toward a brand so that when consumers enter search mode, that brand will be one they immediately consider as a possible solution to their needs. If the consumer has not used a brand previously and has no recollection that it even exists, then that brand probably will not be the brand of choice. Good retailing (such as point-of-purchase displays and visibility on the shelf) can help, but prior awareness is a very good thing and something advertising can help establish.

It is possible that an internal search will not turn up enough information to yield a decision. In this instance, the consumer then engages in an **external search**. An external search typically involves visiting retail stores or looking online to examine the alternatives, seeking input from friends and relatives about their product experiences, or reading product evaluations.[2] In addition, when consumers are in an active information-gathering mode, they may be receptive to detailed, informative advertisements delivered through both traditional and digital/social media channels. For instance, in digital consumer behavior, online customer reviews can be critical in this phase of the decision-making process.

During an internal or external search, consumers have some need that is propelling them through the process, and their goal is to make a decision that yields benefits for them. The consumer searches for and is simultaneously forming thoughts and opinions about possible alternatives. This is the **alternative-evaluation** stage of the decision process, and it is another key phase for the advertiser to manage. Advertisers should also consider the consumer's mindset and how frame of mind might influence information selection, processing, and evaluation during this search process.[3]

Alternative evaluation will be structured by the consumer's consideration set and evaluative criteria. The **consideration set** is the subset of brands from a particular product category that becomes the focal point of the consumer's evaluation. Most product categories contain too many brands for all to be carefully considered, so the consumer finds some way to synthesize the search and evaluation. For example, for autos, consumers may only consider cars priced less than $30,000, or only cars that have rear backup cameras or only electric cars, or only cars sold at dealerships within a 20-mile radius of their work or home. A critical function of advertising is to make consumers aware of the brand and keep them aware so that the brand has a chance to be part of the consideration set.

As the search-and-evaluation process proceeds, consumers form evaluations based on the characteristics or attributes of those brands in their consideration set. These product attributes or performance characteristics are referred to as **evaluative criteria**. Evaluative criteria differ from one product category to the next and can include many factors, such as price, texture, warranty terms, service support, color, scent, or carb content.

It is critical for advertisers to understand the evaluative criteria that consumers use to make their buying decisions. They should also know how consumers rate their brand in comparison with others from the consideration set. Understanding consumers' evaluative criteria furnishes a powerful starting point for any advertising campaign.

Purchase

At the third stage, **purchase** occurs. The consumer has made their decision, and a sale is made. However, it would be a big mistake to view purchase as the culmination of the decision-making process. No matter what the product or service category, the consumer is likely to buy from it again in the future. So what happens after the sale is very important to advertisers. Advertisers want trial; they then want **conversion** (repeat purchase). They want brand loyalty, even though competitors will be working to attract customers. Some want to create **brand ambassadors**, users who will become apostles for the brand, spreading the brand gospel. As shown in Exhibit 5.4, Target features brand ambassadors in its YouTube features about how to decorate a college dorm room.

Postpurchase Use and Evaluation

The goal for marketers and advertisers must not be simply to generate a sale; it must be to create satisfied and, ultimately, loyal customers. The data to support this position are quite

Source: target brands, inc.

Exhibit 5.4 ▶ The Target College Haul "how to" videos offer suggestions about different ways to decorate a college dorm room, featuring products available at Target.

undivided attention of the consumer and to provide information and advice about product use that will increase customer satisfaction. Without satisfied customers, it is very difficult to have a successful business. Nowadays, consumers often seek reassurance about their purchase by reading what other purchasers say in online reviews or in brand communities. Some advertisers provide this type of postpurchase information to make you a satisfied customer.

astounding.[4] About 65 percent of the average company's business comes from its present, satisfied customers, and 91 percent of dissatisfied customers will never buy again from the company that disappointed them.[5] Thus, consumers' evaluations of products in use become a major determinant of which brands will be in the consideration set the next time around.

Customer satisfaction stems from a favorable **postpurchase experience**. It may emerge after a single use, but more likely it will require sustained exposures and experiences. Advertising can play an important role in inducing customer satisfaction by creating appropriate expectations for a brand's performance or by helping the consumer who has already bought the advertised brand to feel good about doing so.

Advertising plays an important role in alleviating the **cognitive dissonance** that can occur after a purchase. Cognitive dissonance is the anxiety or regret that lingers after a difficult decision, sometimes called "buyer's remorse." Often, rejected alternatives have attractive features that lead people to second-guess their own decisions. If the goal is to generate satisfied customers, this dissonance must be resolved in a way that leads consumers to conclude that they did make the right decision after all. Purchasing high-cost items or choosing from categories that include many desirable and comparable brands can yield high levels of cognitive dissonance.

When dissonance is expected, it makes good sense for the advertiser to reassure buyers with detailed information about its brands. Postpurchase reinforcement programs might involve direct mail, email, or other types of personalized contacts with the customer. This postpurchase period represents a great opportunity for the advertiser to have the

5-1b Four Modes of Consumer Decision-Making

As you know from your own experience, consumers aren't always deliberate and systematic; sometimes they are hasty, impulsive, or even irrational. Do they always go through these four stages in a slow and deliberate manner? No, not always. The search time that people invest in their purchases can vary drastically for different types of products. Some purchase decisions are just more engaging than others. In the following sections, we will elaborate on the view of the consumer as the decision maker by explaining four decision-making modes that help advertisers appreciate the richness and complexity of consumer behavior. These four modes are determined by a consumer's involvement and prior experiences with the product or service in question.

Sources of Involvement

To accommodate the complexity of consumption decisions, those who study consumer behavior typically examine the involvement level associated with any particular decision. **Involvement** is the degree of perceived relevance and personal importance accompanying the choice of a certain product or service within a particular context: How much it matters to you. Many things affect an individual's level of involvement with a consumption decision. People can develop interests and avocations in many different areas, such as cooking, photography, pet ownership, and exercise and fitness. Such ongoing personal interests can enhance involvement levels in a variety of product categories. Also, any time a great deal of risk is associated with a purchase—perhaps as a result of the high price of the item or because the consumer will have to live with the decision for a long period of time—one should also expect heightened involvement. So cars are usually high-involvement purchases, and things like chips are typically low involvement. There are exceptions, but most CPG (e.g., laundry detergent, paper towels) are low involvement. Sometimes, advertisers try to make an otherwise low-involvement choice into a high-involvement one.

Consumers can derive symbolic meaning from products and brands. Ownership or use of some products can help people reinforce some aspect of their self-image or make a statement to other people.[6] If a purchase carries great symbolic and real consequences—such as choosing the right gift for a special someone on Valentine's Day—it will be highly involving. If a brand expresses your preferred identity to the world, then it is probably high involvement. Think about clothing. Think about cars. Think about smartphones.

Higher involvement may be a function of a **consumer–brand relationship**.[7] By relationship, we do not mean that the consumer sees the brand as their best friend, their father, or anything like that. It just means that the consumer has come to have some sort of emotional attachment to the brand or even the category. Maybe the consumer is a cyclist; and the entire category is meaningful, but their first nice road bike was a Trek brand. They now have a consumer–brand relationship that brings with it high involvement. Brand relationships are formed by all sorts of things, including serendipity. But if you can get consumers to develop strong brand relationships, you have evolved the brand into the high-involvement side of things, and you are generally much better off.

Involvement levels vary not only among product categories for any given individual but also among individuals for any given product category. Snacks are not generally a high-involvement category, but many consumers feel strongly about their favorite brands. Doritos leveraged that involvement not long ago when it added a "Rock the Vote" message to vending machines selling its products and posted a video about it on the Doritos brand website (see Exhibit 5.5).

Now we will use the ideas of involvement and prior experience to help conceive four different types or modes of consumer decision making. These four modes are shown in Exhibit 5.6. Any specific consumption decision is based on a high or low level of previous experience with the product or service in question and a high or low level of involvement.

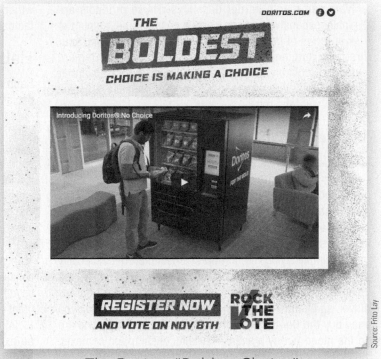

Exhibit 5.5 ▶ The Doritos "Boldest Choice" campaign encouraged brand fans to vote, using messages on vending machines and online.

Source: Frito Lay

Exhibit 5.6 ▶ Four modes of consumer decision-making.

This yields the four modes of decision making: (1) extended problem solving, (2) limited problem solving, (3) habit or variety seeking, and (4) brand loyalty. Each is described in the following sections.

Extended Problem Solving

When consumers are inexperienced in a particular consumption setting, yet find the setting highly involving, they are likely to engage in **extended problem solving**. In this mode, consumers go through a deliberate decision-making process that begins with explicit need recognition, proceeds with careful internal and external search, continues through alternative evaluation and purchase, and ends with a lengthy postpurchase evaluation. Examples of extended problem solving come with harder decisions. These products are typically expensive and can carry a considerable amount of risk in terms of making an uneducated choice. Buying your first new automobile and selecting a college may require extended problem solving. But it is important to remember that while extended problem solving is possible, it is the exception, not the rule.

Limited Problem Solving

In this decision-making mode, experience and involvement are both low. **Limited problem solving** is a more common mode of decision-making. In this mode, a consumer is less systematic in his/her/their decision-making. The consumer has a new problem to solve, but it is not a problem that is interesting or engaging, so the information search is limited to simply trying the first brand encountered—especially when the "problem" is minor. For example, you perceive a need for a snack. You have seen many ads for a new Doritos flavor, and you tasted an in-store sample. If acceptable, you may buy the Doritos then or wait until the next time you are in the mood to buy a snack. Certain consumption contexts, such as watching the Super Bowl, are prime for snacking, and Doritos reminds us of this with the integrative branding shown in Exhibit 5.7.

In the limited-problem-solving mode, we often see consumers simply seeking adequate solutions to mundane problems. It is also a mode in which just trying a brand or two may be the most efficient way of collecting information about one's options. Smart marketers realize that trial offers can be a preferred means of collecting information, and they facilitate trial of their brands through free samples, inexpensive "trial sizes," or discount coupons. It is in this mode that integrated advertising and brand promotion often occurs

within CPG categories, where consumer memory is a huge factor in purchase decisions.

Habit or Variety Seeking

Habit and variety seeking are common in settings where a decision isn't involving and a consumer purchases from the category repeatedly. In terms of sheer numbers, habitual purchases are probably the most common decision-making mode.[8] Consumers find a brand of snacks or shampoo that suits their needs, they run out of the product, and they buy it again. The cycle repeats itself many times per year in an almost mindless fashion. Getting in the habit of buying only one brand can be a way to simplify life and minimize the time invested in routine or "nuisance" purchases. When a consumer perceives little difference among the various competitive brands, it is easier to buy the same brand repeatedly. A lot of consumption decisions are boring but necessary. Habits help us minimize the inconvenience of having to make low-involvement purchase decisions.

In some product categories where a buying habit would be expected, an interesting phenomenon called **variety seeking** may be observed instead. Remember, **habit** refers to buying a single brand repeatedly as a solution to a simple consumption problem. It is not the same as brand loyalty. This habitual purchasing can be very boring however, and some consumers fight the boredom through variety seeking, which happens in many areas of life. **Variety seeking** refers to the tendency of consumers to switch their selection among various brands in a given category in a seemingly random pattern. This is not to say that a consumer will buy just any brand; he/she/they probably have two to five brands that all provide similar levels of satisfaction to a particular consumption problem. However, from one purchase occasion to the next, the individual will switch brands from within this set, just for the sake of variety.

Variety seeking is most likely to occur in frequently purchased categories in which sensory experience, such as taste or smell, accompanies product use. In such categories, no amount of ad spending can overcome the consumer's basic desire for a fresh sensory experience.[9] Satiation occurs after repeated use and leaves the consumer looking for a change of pace. Product categories such as oral care, sports drinks and alcoholic beverages, salty snacks, and haircare are prone to variety seeking, so marketers in these categories must constantly be introducing new possibilities to feed consumers' craving for variety. One day, you may decide you're ready for a new snack—especially

Source: Frito Lay

Exhibit 5.7 ▶ Year after year, Doritos invited consumer involvement in creating ads for the Super Bowl, reinforcing the association between its snack brands and watching the big game.

Source: Twitter.com

Exhibit 5.8 ▶ Consumers seeking variety are the target audience for this Lay's tweet.

if a marketer has presented you with a fresh new choice that appeals to your taste buds (see Exhibit 5.8).

Brand Loyalty

The final decision-making mode is characterized by high involvement and rich prior experience. In this mode, brand loyalty becomes a major consideration in the purchase decision. Consumers demonstrate brand loyalty when they repeatedly purchase a single brand as their choice to fulfill a specific need and have some degree of emotional connection to the brand.[10] In one sense, brand-loyal purchasers may look as if they have developed a simple buying habit; however, it is important to distinguish brand loyalty from pure habit. Brand loyalty is based on an emotional connection toward the brand and a conscious commitment to find this brand each time the consumer purchases from this category. Conversely, habits are merely consumption simplifiers that are not based on the power of an emotional relationship, however minor, with the brand. Habits can be disrupted through a synergistic combination of advertising and sales promotions. Spending advertising dollars to persuade truly brand-loyal consumers to try an alternative can be a great waste of resources.

Brands such as Amazon, Netflix, Home Depot, Samsung, Disney, Pepsi, Heineken, IKEA, Jeep, and Harley-Davidson have inspired very loyal consumers. Brand loyalty is something that any marketer aspires to have, but in a world filled with more-savvy consumers and endless product (and advertising) proliferation, it is becoming harder and harder to attain. Brand loyalty may emerge because the consumer perceives that one brand simply outperforms all others in providing some critical benefit.

Perhaps even more important, brand loyalty can stem from the emotional benefits that accompany certain brands.

One of the strongest indicators of brand loyalty has to be the tendency on the part of some loyal consumers to tattoo their bodies with the insignia of their favorite brand. It is claimed that the worldwide leader in brand-name tattoos is Harley-Davidson. What accounts for Harley's fervent following? Is Harley's brand loyalty simply a function of performing better than its competitors? Or does a Harley rider derive some deep emotional benefit from taking that big bike out on the open road and leaving civilization far behind? Is part of the Harley loyalty due to membership in a brand community and buying into the-mythology of the slightly outlaw nature of the Harley mystique? Harley's ads often try to leverage these feelings and connections.

Research shows that when consumers have an emotional connection to a brand, they actually distort information in a positive way to favor that brand and distort information in a negative way to diminish competing brands. This is called **predecisional distortion** and has been shown at the brain level to be very important in brand selection.[11] This suggests that one way to create true brand loyalty is through emotional advertising, ads that link a certain emotion with the brand.

5-1c Advertising, Consumer Behavior, and Memory

Memory is of obvious importance to advertisers because consumers need to remember an ad or brand placement for it to really resonate. It is thus helpful to understand just a few basics of human memory.

Semantic (Word) Memory

Semantic memory is very important where advertising is concerned. This is the kind of memory through which names, words, and concepts are stored and retrieved from our minds. It is the type of memory that drives a great deal of low-involvement or mindshare brands. CPG (consumer packaged goods) are the most common users of semantic memory–based advertising, for example, laundry detergent, canned foods, and paper goods such as paper towels and toilet paper. It is a relatively well understood form of human memory and is easily used by advertisers in an integrated brand promotion context.

The more easily you can retrieve something from semantic memory, the more accessible it is. Greater **accessibility** is a good thing for advertised brand names for at least two reasons. The first is obvious; you are more likely to buy a low-involvement good for a brand you remember than one you don't. The second reason is a bit more complicated; but suffice it to say that the more easily (or more quickly) one retrieves something from memory, the more frequent or popular one believes it to be. So if I ask for the name of a laundry detergent and you quickly say Tide, odds are you also will overestimate Tide's market share and believe it to be a more popular brand than it actually is. This is called the **accessibility bonus**.[12] So easily recalled brands are a very good thing. That is why advertisers for so-called mindshare brands spend so much money getting you to remember them. Anything that can be done to promote better recall is important in advertising.

Episodic Memory

Episodic memory is just like it sounds: memories of episodes. It is your memory of events, what you did last night, your friend's party, and so on. It could also be a consumption experience like eating at a certain restaurant or having your hair cut at a particular salon. It could also be an ad, most likely a video ad from TV, computer, or smartphone. Episodic memory is not as well understood as semantic memory. It is also true that episodic memory is much more fluid and less fixed than we had thought. We no longer think of this type of memory as a mental video recorder that makes a perfect record of everything we experience. Instead, we now view it as a system driven as much by motivation and how we choose to remember as anything else. The fact that these memories are so easily altered makes opportunities for advertisers to shape them in ways that benefit the brand.

Emotion

We have come to appreciate that emotion is incredibly important in consumer behavior. Researchers have shown that if a brand is associated with a positive emotion or feeling, the subsequent information about the brand is actually distorted in favor of the emotion-linked brand and against others. By this, we mean that consumers actually change the nature of incoming information to favor this emotional brand connection. It then affects subsequent consumer decisions in favor of the emotion-linked brand. This power clearly favors the use of emotional branding techniques and brand relationship building, including advertising.

Information Overload and Simplification

As you know, there is a lot of advertising in our lives—an enormous amount of information, presented in print, on TV, on digital devices, in the movies, and in other media. Two things are almost always true in this context: (1) consumers will say the more information, the better and (2) that is not always true. Consumers appear to have a strong desire to

have as much information as possible; they have always been told that good consumer decisions are based on having the most data. Some people particularly enjoy mulling over such details, not only what they can learn from ads but also from promotions including sponsorship of events, for example—another reason why message integration is so vital.[13]

Yet research has revealed the threat of information overload. Consumers simply get too much information and confront too many choices to be able to comprehensively and effectively apply all information to the choice task. What they do then is use a decision heuristic, or a way of simplifying the task. Common heuristics include buying the most popular brand, the least expensive, the most expensive, the one you have heard the most about, or the one you bought most recently. Advertisers understand this problem, but in the escalating war of advertising, saying less is hard to do, even when saying less is really saying more.

Clutter and Attention

Advertising clutter emerges from the context in which ads are processed.[14] Even if a person wanted to, it would be impossible to process and integrate every advertising message that he/she/they is/are exposed to each day. The clutter problem is further magnified by competitive brands making very similar performance claims.[15] Was it Crest, Colgate, Sensodyne, or Arm & Hammer that promised you healthier gums? Each of us is exposed to thousands of ads each day, and no one has the time or inclination to sort through them all. Some industry experts and researchers believe that the simple mass of advertising, the enormous number of ads, is now working very hard against the institution of advertising itself. Ironic as it is, advertising might be the death of advertising.

Advertisers use a variety of tactics to gain attention and reinforce recognition. Target, for example, highlights its eye-catching bulls-eye logo in ads, promotional materials, and store signage (see this chapter's Integrated Brand Promotion in Action [Exhibit 5.9]). This not only identifies Target to the audience, it captures attention across integrated promotions.

Popular music, celebrity spokespersons, sexy models, rapid scene changes, and anything that is novel are devices for combating selective attention.[16] Remember, as we discussed in Chapter 4, advertisers constantly walk that fine line between novel and obnoxious in their never-ending battle for the attention of the consumer. They really don't want to insult you or anyone else; they just want to be noticed.

The battle for consumers' attention poses another dilemma for advertisers. Without attention, there is little chance that an advertiser's message will have its desired impact; however, the provocative, attention-attracting devices used to engage consumers often become the focal point of consumers' ad processing. They remember seeing an ad featuring Elvis Presley impersonators, but they can't recall what brand was being promoted or what claims were

Exhibit 5.9 ▶ Integrated Brand Promotion in Action: Target
Target plans its IBP efforts to cut through clutter.
Target includes the bulls' eye logo in its ads and store signage to cut through the clutter and capture consumer's attention. *What effect is this repetition and recognition likely to have on memory, given the possibility of information overload?*

being made. If advertisers must entertain consumers to win their attention, they must also be careful that the brand and message don't get lost in the shuffle.

LO **2**

5-2 Consumer Behavior Perspective Two: The Consumer as a Social Being

In this section, we present a second perspective on consumer behavior, branding, and advertising, a perspective based on social and cultural factors. It should be considered another part of the larger story of how advertising works. Remember, we are still talking about the same consumers discussed in the preceding section; we are just viewing their behavior from a different vantage point. Ad professionals have long been believers in culturally and socially based advertising and branding.

Consumers are more than information processors, and ads are more than socially isolated attempts at **attitude** manipulation with this approach, **meaning** is the focus, and consumer behavior is meaningfully social. The social meaning-based approach centers on knowing how to connect with human beings around their lives and consumption practices with advertising and other brand promotion tactics. That's why advertising agencies commonly hire people who know about material culture (anthropology), demography and social forces (sociology), the history of brands and consumption practices (history), communication, text (literature), and art. So if you want to make great advertising, pay attention to culture and society.

5-2a Consuming in the Real World

Let's consider some major components of consumers' real lives:

Culture

If you are in the ad business, you are in the culture business.

>
> *The social meaning-based approach centers on knowing how to connect with human beings around their lives and consumption practices with advertising and other brand promotion tactics.*

Culture is what a people do, or "the total life ways of a people, the social legacy the individual acquires from his (her) group."[17] It is the way we eat, groom, celebrate, travel, play, get together, communicate, and otherwise express feelings. Cultures may be national, regional, local, or cross geographic borders: *urban hipster culture, teen tech-nerd, Junior League,* and so on. It's usually easier to see and note culture when it's more distant and unfamiliar. Members of a culture often find the ways they do things to be perfectly natural and normal. If everyone around us behaves in a similar fashion, we do not easily think about the existence of some larger force acting on us all. But it's there; this constant background force is the force of culture, and it's powerful.

In some cultures, people place particular emphasis on money and material goods, a cultural value known as **materialism**. Materialistic consumers tend to be more interested in brands and products that signal status or wealth within the culture.[18] As discussed in Chapter 4, advertising has been criticized for promoting materialism, although its defenders say it only reflects the values of the society.

Culture surrounds the creation, transmission, reception, and interpretation of ads and brands, just as it touches every aspect of consumption. Culture is about as "real world" as it gets. Whether you are doing advertising for Jersey Mike's or Jimmy Choo, Listerine or lululemon, you have a very good reason to understand why people do things a certain way (e.g., buy things for one holiday but not for another, or eat certain things for breakfast in a certain way, or drive a convertible on sunny days).

Rituals, "often-repeated formalized behaviors involving symbols," are core elements of culture.[19] Cultures affirm, express, and maintain themselves through rituals. They are a way in which individuals are made part of the culture and a method by which the culture constantly renews and perpetuates itself. For example, ritual-laden holidays such as Thanksgiving, Christmas, Hanukah, and the Fourth of July help perpetuate aspects of American culture through their repeated re-enactment (tradition). Globally, there are a myriad of very important cultural rituals, all involving consumption (e.g., feasts and gift giving). This is true around the world, and rituals help intertwine culture and consumption practices in a very real way. If you are a consumer packaged goods manufacturer, understanding these types of rituals is a key concern. Exhibit 5.10 shows that some brands are very aware of the role of consumption rituals. Even packing school lunches can be a ritual, as Target Stores indicates in its "how to" updated for today's emoji generation.

Rituals also occur every day in millions of other contexts. For instance, when someone buys a new car or a new home, they do all sorts of "unnecessary" things to make it theirs. They clean the carpets even if they were just cleaned, they hang things from the mirror of the used car they just bought, they change oil that was just changed—all to make the new possession theirs and remove any trace of the former owner. These behaviors are important not only to anthropologists but also to those making and trying to sell products such as paint, rug shampoos, household disinfectants, lawn and garden equipment, auto accessories, and on and on.

There are everyday rituals, such as the way we eat, groom ourselves, and prepare for work. Think about all the habitual things you do from the time you get up in the morning until you crawl into bed at night. These things are done in a certain way; they are not random.[20] Members of a common culture tend to do them one way, and members of other cultures do them other ways. Daily rituals seem inconsequential because they are habitual and routine and thus "invisible." If, however, someone tried to get you to significantly alter the way you do these things, he/she/they would quickly learn just how important and resistant to change these rituals are. If a product or service cannot be incorporated into an already-existing ritual, it is very difficult and expensive for advertisers to initiate change. On the other hand, if an advertiser can successfully incorporate the consumption of its good or service into an existing ritual, then success is much more likely. Imagine how important rituals are to the global beauty industry. Cleaning and beauty practices and breakfast habits are highly ritualized, for instance.

Stratification

Stratification refers to systematic inequalities in things such as wealth, income, education, power, and status. For example, some members of society exist within a wealthier group (stratum), others within a less affluent stratum. Race and gender are also unequally distributed across income; for example, men tend to have higher incomes than women. Thus a cross-section, or slice, of American society would reveal many different levels (or strata) of the population along these different dimensions. Some combination of these inequalities is what we think of when we say "social class." Social class is hard to pin down in some contemporary societies, easier in others. In America, a very large number of folks with a huge range in income, wealth, and education call themselves "middle class."

Source: target brands, inc.

Exhibit 5.10 ▶ Target's video plays off the school-day ritual of packing lunches for children.

In North America and much of the world, social class was most strongly determined by income: high-income Americans were generally seen as being in a higher social class, and low-income Americans were considered to be in a lower class. But that is an imperfect relationship. For example, successful plumbers often had higher incomes than some types of lawyers (the United States has lots of lawyers), but their occupation was seen (to some) as less prestigious, and thus their social class designation was lower. So the prestige of one's occupation also entered into what we called "social class." Education also has something to do with social class, but a person with a little college experience and a lot of inherited wealth would probably rank higher than an insurance agent with an MBA. Thus, income, education, and occupation are three important variables for indicating social class but are still individually, or even collectively, inadequate at capturing its full meaning.

Important to marketers is the belief that members of the same social strata tend to live in similar ways, have similar views and philosophies, and, most critically, tend to consume in somewhat similar ways.[21] You could supposedly tell "social class" from what people consume and how they consume; at least, that's what lots of marketers and advertisers believed. Social class and stratification were supposed to be reflected in a consumer's taste and thus their consumption. The traditional view was that advertisers cared about social class and stratification because consumers used their choices to reflect their class. But this assumption has recently been challenged. Some believe that traditional social class–consumption taste hierarchies have collapsed or at least become much less stable and reliable. What do you think—can you tell someone's social standing by their consumption patterns? Are tastes related to social stratification a thing of the past? We see this situation as fluid but believe that class, social status, and taste indicators remain and still matter to consumers and, therefore, to advertisers.

We are also living in a time of great and increasing income inequality. In the United States, for example, the wealthy are pulling away from the rest at a very sharp clip. There has been no or very little real income growth for most Americans lately. Upward mobility in the United States is nowhere near what it once was. This, some fear, will become the new normal, an economy and a society of lowered expectations and possibilities, but with the wealthy doing very well, and better and better. If this is the case, how will it affect consumption and advertising? Will luxury brands flourish for the upper 1 or 2 percent and the rest seek greater and greater value? Look at the ad in Exhibit 5.11; here is an example of Target, a discount retailer, communicating style and luxury.

How will this increasing income inequality affect the various ways advertising attempts to link social status to brands? Brands tend to suffer when their prices and profit margins decline. If they go too low, they become commodities, sold on price. When that happens, advertising tends to be a smaller

Exhibit 5.11 ▶ Target appeals to consumers not only on the basis of value but also on the basis of luxury and style.

Source: Target brands, inc

player, because the only meaning you are trying to convey is related to everyday low prices and value. That frequently means more coupon codes, more point-of-purchase displays, and more price promotions. Some advertising is geared toward price-sensitive consumers at any income level who are interested in special deals. Here, social pressure ("hundreds of people have already purchased this product") and time pressure ("available today only") can have an effect on consumer behavior.[22]

Taste

This brings us to taste. **Taste** refers to a generalized set of or orientation to consumer aesthetic preferences. If social class affects consumption through taste, it also affects media preferences. We think of golf more than bowling, and brie more than Velveeta, as belonging to the upper classes. Ordering wine instead of beer has social significance, as does driving a luxury car brand. We believe social stratification and taste are intertwined while acknowledging that consumption preferences and strata are a little less dependable than in the past. Some smart advertisers have successfully leveraged the "democratization" of taste. Target has done a good job of this, as shown in Exhibit 5.11. Another important concept is *cultural capital*, the value that cultures place on certain consumption practices and objects. For example, a certain consumption practice, say snowboarding, has a certain capital or value (like money) for some segment of the population. If you own a snowboard (a certain amount of cultural capital) and can actually use it (more cultural capital) and look good while using it (even more capital), then this activity is like cultural currency or cultural money in the bank. A pair of Hunter boots has cultural capital, as do Land Rover SUVs and Kendra Scott earrings. By ownership, the consumer gets a little cultural capital, points if you will, in the culture. Capital is by definition worth something. It gets you things you want. A Maserati has a certain cultural capital among some groups, as does wearing khakis, ordering the right pinot noir, knowing how to hail a cab, flying first class, or knowing about the latest band or cool video trend on TikTok. This capital may exist within a hipster culture, or a 40-something wine culture, or a biker culture—it's still cultural capital.

In all of these cultures, certain consumer practices are favored or valued. Advertisers try to figure out which ones are valued more and why, and how to make their product sought after because it has higher cultural capital and can therefore be sold at a higher price. Does Target have more cultural capital than Walmart? To whom? In which culture and market segment(s)? Having good "taste" helps you know which things have high cultural capital. Ads try to emphasize the cultural capital, style, and taste to be found in the product and then transferred to the consumer.

The interaction of social stratification and cultural capital becomes apparent when a person moves from one stratum into another. Consider this example: Kiara grew up in lower-middle-class surroundings and she was promoted into a high-paying job after graduate school. She has now moved into an upscale neighborhood, composed mostly of "old money." One weekend, Kiara goes out to her driveway and begins to do something she has done since she started driving: change the oil in her car. One of her neighbors comes over and chats, subtly suggesting that people in this neighborhood hire "someone else" do "that sort of thing." Kiara gets the message: It's not cool to change your oil in your own driveway in this neighborhood. To her, paying someone else to do this simple job seems wasteful. She is a bit offended and a little embarrassed. But, over time, she decides it's better to go along with the other people in the neighborhood, and she changes her attitudes and resulting consumer behavior due mainly to the socio-cultural influences.

This is an example of the effect of stratification and (negative) cultural capital on consumer behavior. Kiara will no longer be a good target for AutoZone, or any other product or service used to change oil at home. On the other hand, she is now a perfect candidate for quick-oil-change businesses such as Valvoline.

Family

The consumer behavior of families is also of great interest to advertisers. Advertisers want not only to discern the needs of different kinds of families but also to discover how decisions are made within families. The first is possible, the latter much more difficult. For a while, consumer researchers tried to determine who in the traditional nuclear family (i.e., mom, dad, and the kids) made various purchasing decisions. This was largely an exercise in futility. Due to errors in reporting and conflicting perceptions between partners, it became clear that the family purchasing process is anything but clear. Even though some types of purchases are handled by one family member, many decisions are actually non decisions, arrived via a "muddling-through" process.[23] These "decisions" just get made, and no one is really sure who made them or even when. For an advertiser to influence such a scattered and vague process is indeed a challenge. The consumer behavior of the family is a complex and often subtle type of social negotiation. Sometimes specific purchases fall along gender or age lines, but sometimes they don't. Some advertisers capitalize on the flexibility of this social system by suggesting in their ads who *should* take charge of a given consumption task and then arming that person with the appearance of expertise so that whoever wants the job can take it and defend their purchases. Even though they may not be the buyer in many instances, children can play important roles as initiators, influencers, and users in many categories, such as cereals, clothing, vacation destinations, fast-food restaurants, and technology (like computers). In fact, Target recently invited children to direct some of the retailer's back-to-school ads, as shown in Exhibit 5.12.

Advertisers often focus on the major or gross differences in types of families, because different families have different needs, buy different things, and are reached by different media. Family roles often change when both parents (or a single parent) are employed outside the home. For instance, a teenage son or a daughter may be given the role of initiator and buyer, while the parent or parents serve merely as influencers. There are a lot of single parents and quite a few second and even third marriages. The point is that *family* is an open concept, especially now that gay marriage is legal across the United States. Families are not defined as much by marriage as in the past. Plenty of cohabitating but not married families exist and are just as legitimate as any other—certainly from the business perspective of a company trying to sell them branded

Kids Run the Show: Behind the Scenes of Target's Back to School Campaign

Source: target brands, inc.

Exhibit 5.12 ▶ Target has involved children in creating back-to-school ads because parents are influenced by what their children request.

goods and services. In addition to the "traditional" nuclear family and the single-parent household, there is the extended family (nuclear family plus grandparents, cousins, and others), including single parents and same-sex households with and without children.

Advertisers are often interested in knowing things like the age of the youngest child, the size of the family, and the family income. The age of the youngest child at home tells an advertiser where the family is in terms of its needs and obligations (i.e., toys, investments for college savings, clothing, and vacations). When the youngest child leaves home, the family's consumption patterns change. Advertisers like to track the age of the youngest child living at home and use it as a planning criterion. This is called a **life-stage** variable and is used frequently in advertising and promotion planning.

Identity is a sociological concept; it matters a great deal to advertisers. There is no sense of identity outside the social context. All humans think of themselves relative to others. Our very idea of self is meaningless in the absence of others. Across the life-course, there are several times when identity is particularly in play. The most obvious era is adolescence. One reason that teenagers are such a targeted market segment is that their identity is in constant flux; and to express identity, they constantly consume things: clothing, music, electronics, sports and recreational goods and services, jewelry, and so on. With each identity they try on, they spend money on branded goods.[24] Later in life, identity is also challenged occasionally: birth of first child, retirement, last child moves out of the house, and so on. At these pressure points, consumption changes, and advertisers are there to help consumers work out their identity issues. It is also worth saying that when consumers

are identity challenged, a strong ethical orientation is really important. You can do harm.

Race and Ethnicity

Race and ethnicity provide other ways to think about important social groups. Answering the question of how race and ethnicity figure into consumer behavior is very difficult. Our discomfort stems from having, on the one hand, the desire to say, "Race doesn't matter, we're all the same," and on the other hand, not being able to deny the significance of race and ethnicity in terms of reaching ethnic cultures and influencing a wide variety of behaviors, including consumer behavior. The truth is we are less and less sure what *race* is and what it means. Obviously, a person's pigmentation, in and of itself, has almost nothing to do with preferences for one type of product over another. But because race and ethnicity have mattered in culture, they do still matter in consumer behavior. To effectively communicate with consumers in America, advertisers cannot ignore demographic trends, including the increasing diversity of the population.

But race does affect one's social identity to varying degrees. One is not unaware of one's own ethnicity. Black Americans, Latinos, and other ethnic groups have culturally related consumption preferences. It is not enough, however, for advertisers to say one group is different from another or that they prefer one brand over another simply because they are members of a racial or an ethnic category. If advertisers really want a good, long-term relationship with their customers, they must acquire, through good consumer research, a deeper understanding of who their customers are and how this identity is affected by culture, felt ethnicity, and race. In short, advertisers must ask why groups of consumers are different, or prefer different brands, and not settle for an easy answer. It wasn't until the mid- to late 1980s that most American corporations made a concerted effort to court African-American consumers.[25]

Politics

First, it might seem odd to mention politics in the same breath as consumer behavior. It shouldn't. There are many places in the world where religious–ethnic–political strife is abundant, and this strife is then played out in consumption contexts. This is done for many reasons, including a company's labor history (e.g., Coors, Walmart), its connection to a colonial power (think old British brands in Ireland and India), its perceived working-class status (Pabst Blue Ribbon), or its degree of greenness. In many parts of the world, consumption and branding have a long political history, so brand–political associations are commonplace. That is happening more now in the United States as well.

Gender

Obviously, gender matters in consumption. But is the consumption behavior of men and women really that different in any meaningful way, beyond the obvious? Again, to the extent that gender informs a "culture of gender," the answer is yes. As long as men and women are the products of differential socialization, then they will continue to be different in some significant ways.[26] There is, however, no definitive list of gender differences in consumption, because the expression of gender, just like anything else social, depends on the situation and the social circumstances. In the 1920s, advertisers openly referred to women as less logical, more emotional, and the cultural stewards of beauty.[27] (Some critics complain that the same soft, irrational, emotional feminine persona is still invoked in advertising.) Advertising helps construct a social reality in which gender is a predominant feature. Obviously, gender's impact on consumer behavior is not limited to heterosexual men and women. LGBTQ+ consumers comprise significant market segments.[28] Again, these are markets that desire to be acknowledged and served but not stereotyped and patronized. Johnson & Johnson's Clean & Clear skin-care brand is one of a growing number of brands targeting transgender consumers, for instance, with advertising and social media messages.[29] Exhibit 5.13 shows how Doritos partners with the LGBTQ+ community to promote understanding and, in the process, promote its brand.

In the late 1970s, advertisers began targeting working women. In the 1980s, marketers targeted Black Americans and Hispanic consumers at more of a mainstream level. Soon after, more marketers targeted Asian Americans, and more recently, advertisers target LGBTQ+ consumers. Inclusiveness and authentic representation are important aspects of advertising.

Community

Community is a powerful and traditional sociological concept. Its meaning extends well beyond the idea of a specific geographic place. Communities can be imagined or even virtual. Community members believe that they belong to a group of people who are similar to them in some important way and different from those not in the community. Members of communities often share rituals and traditions and feel some sort of responsibility to one another and the community.

Advertisers are becoming increasingly aware of the power of community, particularly as it relates to social media. Products have social meanings, and community is the

Exhibit 5.13 ▶ Doritos celebrated diversity and inclusion with the limited-edition Rainbows chips.

Source: Frito Lay

quintessential social domain, so consumption is inseparable from the notion of where we live and with whom we feel a kinship or a sense of belonging. Communities often exert a great deal of power. A community may be your neighborhood, or it may be people like you with whom you feel a kinship, such as members of social clubs, other consumers who collect the same things you do, or people who have, use, or admire the same brands you do.

Brand communities are groups of consumers who feel a commonality and a shared purpose attached to a consumer good or service.[30] When owners of Tesla, Apple, or Mountain Dew experience a sense of connectedness by virtue of their common ownership or usage, a brand community exists. When two perfect strangers stand in a parking lot and act like old friends simply because they both own a Subaru, a type of community emerges. Most of these communities exist online, and some reveal a certain level of brand fanaticism. Other times, these communities expose an important and more "mainstream" connection among owners, users, or admirers of brands who, with the rise of the Internet, have made these communities important to marketers. Brands matter socially, so brands matter. Social media make brand communities very important.

5-2b Cultural Branding and Advertising

Cultural branding is a type of branding that leverages sociocultural forces to create and maintain great brands. It is often dependent on advertising. Cultural branding has been championed by Harvard Business School professor Doug Holt and a few others.[31] Interestingly, people in the real world were using this approach, maybe without knowing it in certain terms, for the last 100 years or so. But sometimes it takes a Harvard professor to give it a good name and endorse it. The basic idea is to find some rift or stress in the seams of society and culture and then use this to offer a solution in the form of a branded good. Again, the Doritos example that uses the brand to celebrate diversity and inclusion with the limited-edition Rainbow chips product is an example of cultural branding and advertising that can be integrated through both traditional and digital/social media.

Rebellion and Advertising

Scholars have noted that consumers sometimes use their consumption choices to stake out a position in a "revolution" of sorts. Author Thomas Frank traces this to the 1960s cultural revolution (discussed in Chapter 3) and sees it as an opportunity, particularly for youth markets, to provide the costumes and consumable accessories for these "revolutionaries." More generally, it must be remembered that anytime there is a significant social movement, a time of rapid change, opportunities galore are opened up to the advertiser.

When the earth moves under our feet, we feel off balance and in need of reassurance, and advertised products often promise that reassurance. Some of these were mentioned in Chapter 3: how Pepsi used the youth revolution to tear into Coca-Cola's market share lead in the 1960s or Apple giving those who chose not to see themselves as corporate a "computer for the rest of us." These were advertising's home runs—brands turned into cultural icons—by leveraging rifts or disruptions in the social sphere. Even today, brands such as Harley-Davidson continue to ride the wave of a feeling of rebellion, creating integrated brand promotions emphasizing themes such as adventure and freedom.[32]

Authenticity and Opinion Leaders

Among the attributes advertising can give to a brand, authenticity (in the eyes of others) is one of the very most powerful. If an advertiser can convince consumers that its brand is the "real," the authentic choice of those in the know, the original, then it is often seen as the best. This is a simple but very powerful brand statement. Harley-Davidson, for example, is perceived to be so authentic that celebrities like Rihanna choose to wear its branded clothing.[33] In turn, these **opinion leaders** influence the opinions and behaviors of consumers, which reinforces Harley-Davidson's authenticity and multiplies the effect of its advertising and integrated brand promotions. Note that some companies just claim to be real so long that it eventually becomes true—at times.

LO **3**

5-3 How Ads Transmit Meaning

Start work in an ad agency and the first thing they teach you is the difference between a product and a brand. That is because it is advertising's job to turn one into another.[34]

—Martin Davidson

In order to "get" ads, you have to know something of the cultural code, or the ads would make no sense. In order to really understand a movie, to really get it, you have to know something about the culture that created it. Sometimes when you see a foreign film (even in your native tongue), you just don't quite get all the jokes and references, because you don't possess the cultural knowledge necessary. How does this work in advertising? Ads try to turn already meaningful things into things with a very special meaning, a crafted connotation with the purpose of selling. Consumers are free to accept, reject, or adjust that meaning to suit their taste. Likewise, consumers determine what is or is not cool, what has cultural value (capital) to them, and how much. But advertisers are a big part of that conversation.

Yes, ads turn products into brands, and sometimes successful ones. They do this, in large part, by trying to wrap material objects or marketed services with a certain meaning—a meaning that comes from culture. The link between culture and advertising is key. Anthropologist Grant McCracken has offered the model in Exhibit 5.14 to explain how advertising (along with other cultural agents) functions in the transmission of meaning.[35] To understand advertising as a mechanism of cultural meaning transfer is to understand a great deal about advertising. In fact, one could legitimately say that advertisers are really in the meaning-transfer business. You take meaning that exists in the culture and massage it, shape it, and try to transfer it onto your brand.

Think about McCracken's model as you examine the social media post by Doritos in Exhibit 5.15. The product—in this case, Doritos snacks—exists in the culturally constituted world, but it needs IBP to link it to certain social scenes, certain slices of life, such as a music venue. The advertiser places the advertised product and the slice of social life in a promotional setting to get the two to rub off on each other, to intermingle, and to become part of the same social scene. In other words, the product is given social meaning by being placed within an ad or integrated branding promotion that represents an idealized context. This slice of life is the type of social setting in which potential customers might find or desire to find themselves.

According to McCracken's model, meaning has moved from the world to the product (snack) by virtue of its sharing space within the frame of the advertisement. When advertisers put things within the frame of an ad, they want the reader of the ad to put them together seamlessly, to take them

We're taking gaming & music to the next level at E3. Check out our 6-story #MixArcade that doubles as a music venue.

RETWEETS 131   LIKES 524

1:28 PM - 8 Jun 2016

Source: Doritos

Exhibit 5.15 ▶ Look closely at how Doritos helps the audience associate the snack brand with a slice of life—here, at a concert.

together as part of each other. When a consumer purchases or otherwise incorporates that good or service into their own life, the meaning is then transferred to the individual consumer. Meaning is thus moved from the world to the product (via advertising) to the individual. When the individual uses the product, that person conveys to others the meaning they and the advertisement have now given it. Their use incorporates various rituals that facilitate the movement of meaning from good to consumer. The rituals aren't central to this discussion, but they would be the kinds of things discussed earlier in the section on rituals. For example, one of the first things you probably do when you move into a new apartment or home is to make it more "yours" by vacuuming, scrubbing, and painting it, even if you are completely happy with the paint and are convinced it is clean. You put your stuff on the walls partly to make it yours (possession rituals).

Ads also become part of consumers' everyday landscape, language, and reality. Characters, lines, and references all become part of conversations, thoughts, and—coming full circle—the culture. Children, coworkers, family members, and talk-show hosts all pick up phrases, ideas, slogans, and agendas from ads and then replay them, adapt them, and recirculate them just like things from movies and TV shows, books, and other content. Ads, in many ways, don't exist just within the sociocultural context; they *are* the sociocultural context of our time. If you want to do well in the real ad world, it's a very good idea to understand that getting the contemporary culture and knowing how to translate it into ads and attach it to brands is how you make great advertising. It is how advertising works.

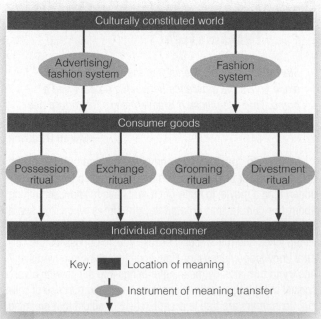

Exhibit 5.14 ▶ The movement of meaning: how fashion and advertising move meaning to sell things.

Summary

1. Describe the four basic stages of consumer decision-making.

Advertisers need a keen understanding of their consumers as a basis for developing effective advertising. This understanding begins with a view of consumers as systematic decision makers who follow a fairly predictable process in making their choices among products and brands. The process begins when consumers perceive a need, and it proceeds with a search for information that will help in making an informed choice. The search-and-evaluation stage is followed by purchase. Postpurchase use and evaluation then become critical as the stage in which customer satisfaction is ultimately determined.

2. Explain how consumers adapt their decision-making processes as a function of involvement and experience.

Some purchases are more important to people than others, and this fact adds complexity to any analysis of consumer behavior. To accommodate this complexity, advertisers often think about the level of involvement that attends any given purchase. Involvement and prior experience with a product or service category can lead to four diverse modes of consumer decision making. These modes are extended problem solving, limited problem solving, habit or variety seeking, and brand loyalty.

3. Discuss the role of memory and emotion in how advertising may influence consumer behavior.

Advertisements are developed to influence the way people think about products and brands. More specifically, advertising is designed to affect consumers' beliefs and brand attitudes. Advertisers use attitude models to help them ascertain the beliefs and attitudes of target consumers. However, consumers have perceptual defenses that allow them to ignore or distort most of the commercial messages to which they are exposed. When consumers are not motivated to thoughtfully process an advertiser's message, it may be in that advertiser's best interest to feature one or more peripheral cues as part of the message.

4. Discuss the role of culture in consumer behavior and in creating good advertising.

Advertisers who overlook the influence of culture are bound to struggle in their attempt to communicate with the target audience. For example, rituals are patterns of behavior shared by individuals from a common culture. Violating cultural values and rituals is a sure way to squander advertising dollars. Advertising and integrated brand promotion help turn products into brands. They do this by infusing brands with cultural meaning. Brands with high cultural capital are worth more. Brands are co-created by consumers and advertisers.

5. Discuss the role of social class, taste, and cultural capital in consumer behavior and advertising.

Consumer behavior is an activity that each of us undertakes before a broad audience of other consumers. Advertising helps the transfer of meaning. Gender, ethnicity, and race are important influences on consumption. Who consumers are—their identity—is changeable; consumers can change aspects of who they are rapidly and frequently through what they buy and use. Celebrities are particularly important in this regard.

6. Discuss the role of family, identity, gender, and community in consumer behavior and advertising.

All four of these sociological factors influence how consumers see themselves and others. It affects why and what they buy.

7. Describe the basic idea underlying cultural branding.

Cultural branding is a type of branding that leverages sociocultural forces to create and maintain great brands. The basic idea is to find some rift or stress in society and culture and then use this to offer a solution in the form of a branded good.

8. Discuss how effective advertising uses sociocultural meaning in order to sell things.

Advertising transfers a desired meaning to the brand by placing it within a carefully constructed social world represented in an ad, or "slice of life." Advertisers paint a picture of the ideal social world, with all the meanings they want to impart to their brand. Then the brand is carefully placed in that picture, and the two (the constructed social world and the brand) rub off on each other, becoming a part of each other. Meaning is thus transferred from the carefully constructed social world within the ad to the brand.

Key Terms

accessibility
accessibility bonus
advertising clutter
attitude
brand ambassadors
brand communities
cognitive dissonance
community
consideration set
consumer behavior
consumer package goods (CPG)
consumer–brand relationship
conversion

culture
customer satisfaction
evaluative criteria
evoked set
extended problem solving
external search
habit
identity
internal search
involvement
life-stage
limited problem solving
materialism

meaning
mindshare brands
need state
opinion leaders
predecisional distortion
rituals
self-transformative
stratification
taste
top of mind
variety seeking

Endnotes

1. Walter Herzog, et al., "Marketers Project Their Personal Preferences onto Consumers: Overcoming the Threat of Egocentric Decision Making," *Journal of Marketing Research* 58, no. 3 (2021), in press.

2. Hengchen Dai, et al., "People Rely Less on Consumer Reviews for Experiential than Material Purchases," *Journal of Consumer Research* 4, no. 6 (2020), 1052–1075.

3. See Derek D. Rucker and Adam D. Galinsky, "Growing Beyond Growth: Why Multiple Mindsets Matter for Consumer Behavior," *Journal of Consumer Psychology* 26, no. 1 (2016), 161–164; and Yunhui Huang and Jaideep Sengupta, "The Influence of Disease Cues on Preference for Typical versus Atypical Products," *Journal of Consumer Research* 47, no. 3 (2020), 393–411.

4. Wajid Hussain Rizvi, Salman Bashir Mmon, and Dahrl Samad, "Brand Experience Clustering and Depiction of Brand Satisfaction, Brand Loyalty and Emotional Confidence," *Foundations of Management* 12, no. 1 (2020), 111–124.

5. Terry G. Vavra, *Aftermarketing: How to Keep Customers for Life through Relationship Marketing* (Homewood, IL: Business One Irwin, 1992), 13.

6. Linwan Wu, et al., "Being Accepted or Ostracized: How Social Experience Influences Consumer Responses to Advertisements with Different Regulatory Focus," *Journal of Advertising* 49, no. 3 (2019), 234–249.

7. Mansur Khamitov, et al., "How Well Do Consumer-Brand Relationships Drive Customer Brand Loyalty? Generalizations from a Meta-Analysis of Brand Relationship Elasticities," *Journal of Consumer Research* 46, no. 3 (October 2019), 435–459.

8. Kelley Gullo, et al., "Does Time of Day Affect Variety Seeking?," *Journal of Consumer Research* 46, no. 1 (June 2019), 20–35.

9. Shirley Leung, "Fast-Food Firms Budgets Don't Buy Consumer Loyalty," *The Wall Street Journal*, July 24, 2003, B4.

10. Atefeh Yazdanparast and Omer Bayar, "Olympic Sponsorships and Brand Value: An Empirical Analysis," *Journal of Advertising* 50, no. 2 (2021), 139–159.

11. Gordon Marshall (Ed.), *The Concise Oxford Dictionary of Sociology* (New York: Oxford University Press, 1994), 104–105.

12. Baba Shiv and Antoine Bechara, "Revisiting the Customer Value Proposition," in Barbara Loken, Rohini Ahluwalia, and Michael J. Houston (Eds.), *Brands and Brand Management: Contemporary Research Perspectives* (New York and London: Routledge, 2010), 189–206.

13. Angeline Close Scheinbaum and Russell Lacey, "Event Social Responsibility: A Note to Improve Outcomes for Sponsors and Events," *Journal of Business Research* 68, no. 9 (2015), 1982–1986.

14. Marc Pritchard, "Half my Digital Advertising is Wasted...," *Journal of Marketing* 85, no. 1 (2021), 26–29.

15. Research has shown that clutter interferes with basic memory functions, inhibiting a person's ability to keep straight which brands are making what claims. For more details, see Anand Kumar and Shanker Krishnan, "Memory Interference in Advertising: A Replication and Extension," *Journal of Consumer Research* 30 (March 2004), 602–612.

16. Yongdan Lui, et al., "Big Star Undercover: The Reinforcing Effect of Attenuated Celebrity Endorsers' Faces on Consumers' Brand Memory," *Journal of Advertising* 49, no. 2 (2020), 185–194.

17. Gordon Marshall (Ed.), *The Concise Oxford Dictionary of Sociology* (New York: Oxford University Press, 1994), 104–105.

18. Naomi Mandel, Derek D. Rucker, Jonathan Levav, and Adam D. Galinsky, "The Compensatory Consumer Behavior Model: How Self-discrepancies Drive Consumer Behavior," *Journal of Consumer Psychology* 27, no. 1 (January 2017), 133–146.

19. Marshall (Ed.), *The Concise Oxford Dictionary of Sociology*, 452.

20. For a review, see Cele C. Otnes and Tina M. Lowrey (Eds.), *Contemporary Consumption Rituals: A Research Anthology* (Mahwah, NJ: Lawrence Erlbaum, 2004).

21. Sharon Shavitt, Duo Jiang, and Hyewon Cho, "Stratification and Segmentation: Social Class in Consumer Behavior," *Journal of Consumer Psychology* 26, no. 4 (2016), 583–593; and Jennifer J. Sun, et al., "Buy Less, Buy Luxury: Understanding and Overcoming Product Durability Neglect for Sustainable Consumption," *Journal of Marketing* 85, no. 3 (2021), 28–43.

22. See, for example, Monika Kukar-Kinney, Angeline Close Scheinbaum, and Tobias Schaefers, "Compulsive Buying in Online Daily Deal Settings: An Investigation of Motivations and Contextual Elements," *Journal of Business Research* 69, no. 2 (2016), 691–699.

23. C. Whan Park, "Joint Decisions in Home Purchasing: A Muddling-Through Process," *Journal of Consumer Research* 9 (September 1982), 151–162.

24. Richard Elliot and Andrea Davies, "Symbolic Brands and Authenticity of Identity Performance," in Jonathan E. Schroeder and Miriam Salzer-Morling (Eds.), *Brand Culture* (London: Routledge, 2006), 155–170.

25. Jannette L. Dates, "Advertising," in Jannette L. Dates and William Barlow (Eds.), *Split Image: African Americans in Mass Media* (Washington, DC: Howard University Press, 1990), 421–454.

26. Karina T. Liljedal, et al., "Effects of Nonstereotyped Occupational Gender Role Portrayal in Advertising," *Journal of Advertising Research* 60, no. 2 (2020), 179–196.

27. Roland Marchand, *Advertising: The American Dream* (Berkeley: University of California Press, 1984), 25.

28. Bradley J. Bond and Justine Rapp Farrell, "Does Depicting Gay Couples in Ads Influence Behavioral Intentions?," *Journal of Advertising Research* 60, no. 2 (2020), 208–221.

29. Chris Daniels, "Marketing to the T: Brands Get Inclusive of Transgender Consumers in LGBT Marketing," *PR Week,* February 24, 2016, www.prweek.com/article/1384780/marketing-t-brands -inclusive-transgender-consumers-lgbt-marketing.

30. Albert Muniz Jr. and Thomas O'Guinn, "Brand Community," *Journal of Consumer Research* 27 (2001), 412–432.

31. Douglas B. Holt, *How Brands Become Icons* (Cambridge, MA: Harvard Business School Press, 2004).

32. Kristina Monllos, "5 Ways Historically Male Brands Are Now Reaching Out to Women," *Adweek,* April 24, 2016, www.adweek .com/news/advertising-branding/5-ways-historically-male -brands-are-now-reaching-out-women-170995.

33. Debra Borchardt, "Harley-Davidson's Authenticity Is a Hit With Stylists," *WWD,* April 26, 2016, http://wwd.com/business-news /marketing-promotion/harley-davidson-apparel-10417875/.

34. Martin Davidson, "Objects of Desire: How Advertising Works," in Martin Davidson (Ed.), *The Consumerist Manifesto: Advertising in Postmodern Times* (London: Routledge, 1992), 23–60.

35. Grant McCracken, "Culture and Consumption: A Theoretical Account of the Structure and Movement of the Cultural Meaning of Consumer Goods," *Journal of Consumer Research* 13 (June 1986), 71–84.

Chapter 6

Market Segmentation, Positioning, and the Value Proposition

Learning Objectives

After reading and thinking about this chapter, you will be able to do the following:

1. Explain the process known as STP marketing.

2. Describe different bases that marketers use to identify segments.

3. Identify the criteria used to target a segment.

4. Identify the essential elements of an effective positioning strategy.

5. Define the necessary ingredients for creating a brand's value proposition.

In the previous chapter, you learned about analyzing consumer behavior as part of the environment for advertising and integrated brand promotion (IBP). This chapter focuses on another set of elements to be analyzed within the environment: the interconnected processes of segmentation, targeting, positioning, and the value proposition, as shown in the framework diagram (Exhibit 6.1). Understanding these processes is essential for effective integrated brand promotion.

Exhibit 6.1 ▶ Framework diagram for Chapter 6 shows some key focal areas for analyzing the environment.

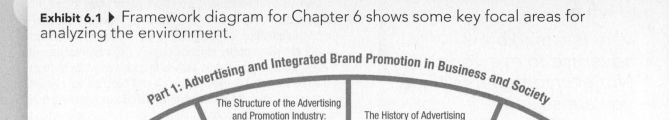

Part 1: Advertising and Integrated Brand Promotion in Business and Society

The World of Advertising and Integrated Brand Promotion (Ch. 1)

The Structure of the Advertising and Promotion Industry: Advertisers, Agencies, Media, and Support Organizations (Ch. 2)

The History of Advertising and Brand Promotion (Ch. 3)

Social, Ethical, and Regulatory Aspects of Advertising and Promotions (Ch. 4)

Part 2: Analyzing the Environment for Advertising and Integrated Brand Promotion

Advertising, Integrated Brand Promotion, and Consumer Behavior (Ch. 5)
Market Segmentation, Positioning, and the Value Proposition (Ch. 6)
Advertising Research (Ch. 7)
Planning Advertising and Integrated Brand Promotion (Ch. 8)

- STP Marketing and Advertising
- Segmenting Markets
- Prioritizing Segments
- Targeting
- Working with a Value Proposition and a Brand Platform

LO 1

6-1 STP Marketing and Advertising

Very few marketers advertise to everyone. It is impossible to reach all consumers. It is far too expensive and wasteful because not everyone wants what you are selling. So advertisers usually have to **segment** the market—that is, cut a broader market into groups of potential customers and focus on these groups (segments) that make the most sense for the brand. Marketers/advertisers then decide to **target** (focus advertising and IBP for delivery to) that segment or segments with advertising and integrated brand promotion. These decisions are best made based on marketing research. Then marketers/advertisers strategically **position** their brand for that/those segment/s. Positioning is an attempt to give a brand a certain meaning relative to its competitors. Managing the three efforts together is called **STP marketing.** Defined, this is a strategy where markets are segmented; segments of markets (groups of potential customers) are targeted, and brands are positioned. While some of this work

is done primarily by the marketer, increasingly advertising and IBP professionals collaborate on this strategy. Ultimately, advertising and IBP professionals create the messages and advertisements to help give the brand the meaning the advertiser desires to best position the product or service in the marketplace against its competitors.

In most product or service categories, marketers find that different consumers are looking for different things, and the only way for a company to take advantage of the sales potential represented by different customer segments is to develop and market a different brand for each segment. An example of this is Hilton, which markets more than a dozen hotel brands and one vacation brand, each of which is aimed at specific segments of the consumer and business markets for lodgings and meeting space. Its Tru by Hilton brand targets travelers who want affordable accommodations and who have a "millennial mindset," meaning those who are younger than 35 or *feel* like they're in that age bracket. Hilton's Waldorf Astoria hotel brand targets affluent travelers who desire a luxurious experience with personalized service. The Hilton Hotel brand stands for full-service accommodations (restaurants, room service, spas, meeting rooms). The Hilton Hotels Worldwide website describes each brand in the portfolio and what it offers the targeted segment.[1]

"
Very few marketers advertise to everyone. Not everyone wants what you are selling.
"

LO 2

6-2 Segmenting Markets

The first step in STP marketing involves breaking down large, broader markets into more manageable submarkets or customer segments. This activity is known as *market segmentation*. It can be accomplished in many ways, but keep in mind that advertisers need to identify a segment with common characteristics that will lead the members of that segment to respond distinctively to a marketing program. For a segment to be really useful, advertisers also must be able to reach that segment with information about the brand. Typically this means that advertisers must be able to identify the media the segment uses so they can most effectively deliver messages to it. In this section, we will examine how consumer markets are commonly segmented.

Markets can be segmented on the basis of many things, but usage patterns and commitment levels, demographic and geographic information, psychographics and lifestyles, or benefits sought are some of the most commonly used approaches. In the real world, segmentation evolves in such a way that multiple variables are actually used to identify and describe the chosen segment(s). Dove, for instance, in Exhibit 6.2 is speaking to a segment of women who are older than the younger women more commonly featured in advertising.

6-2a Usage and Commitment Level

One of the most common ways to segment markets is by consumers' brand commitment or usage levels.[2] With respect to usage, it is important to recognize that for most products and services, some users will purchase much more, and more frequently, than others. These consumers are called **heavy users**, **committed users**, or **lead users**. Sometimes, by convention, they are defined as the top quintile, or 20 percent of users by volume, but this is not a hard-and-fast rule. In fact, it is not uncommon to find that heavy users in a category account for the majority of a product's sales and thus become the preferred or primary target segment.[3] Note that users are, in general, more likely to remember the brand's advertising than nonusers.[4]

Yet targeting casual users—those who are not yet committed—can be a way to start customers on the path to loyalty by inviting them to try the product or service. Citi Bike, the bicycle-sharing service in New York City, has a loyal following of

too many age spots to be in an anti-aging ad

but this isn't an anti-aging ad. this is pro-age.
a new line of skin care from dove. beauty has no age limit.

Source: Unilever United States

Exhibit 6.2 ▶ Dove is good at market segmentation; in this ad, note how it segments by age and targets older women along with featuring them in the ad.

customers who buy annual memberships to use its bikes around the city. But Citi Bike also wanted to increase the number of casual users who might want to share a bike for a day or a week, hoping they might become regular users. Citi Bike changed the "usage" decals that appear on each bike kiosk, simplifying the instructions and including "how to" graphics for first-time users. Casual usage increased by 14 percent in the first month after this change. Now Citi Bike is monitoring usage to determine the effect on growth in annual memberships.[5]

It is important to keep in mind that, perhaps counter intuitively, the heavy-user–focused segmentation plan has some potential downsides. For one, devoted users may need no encouragement at all to keep consuming. In addition, a heavy-user focus takes attention and resources away from those who do need encouragement to purchase the marketer's brand. Heavy users differ significantly from average or infrequent users in terms of their motivations to consume, their approach to the brand, or their image of the brand. They may be heavy users because of the inherent value seen in the brand and/or because the brand has a social function. For instance, Coors Light (and other beer brands) tend to be known for having strong brand loyalty among their heavy-user segment.

6-2b Switchers and Variety Seekers

Switchers are consumers who often buy whatever is on sale or choose brands that offer discounts, coupons, or other price incentives. Whether they are pursued through price incentives, high-profile advertising campaigns, or both, switchers can be a costly target segment for competing brands and affect category profitability.[6] Much can be spent in getting their business merely to have it disappear just as quickly as it was won; for instance, consumers may purchase as a result of playing a promotional game (and plausibly switch to another brand that has the latest promotion).[7]

Variety seekers simply enjoy new experiences and switch brands or products for that reason, not necessarily for lower prices or another incentive. Understanding the behavior of variety seekers, some companies deliberately provide variety within a brand (think of all the new Doritos flavors introduced every year, such as seen in Exhibit 6.3). This enables variety seekers to try something new and different without actually switching away to a competitor.

Source: Twitter.com

Exhibit 6.3 ▶ Doritos addresses the consumer need for variety with flavor variety and related IBP; this strategy helps prevent consumers from switching away from the Doritos brand when they want a change from flagship flavors like Nacho Cheese and Cool Ranch.

Note the IBP strategy is different for brands that have distinct segments they target, such as Hilton, which uses a multibrand portfolio IBP strategy. For companies that target multiple segments, multibrand portfolios also offer opportunities for variety seekers (see Exhibit 6.4).

Exhibit 6.4 ▶ Integrated brand promotion in action: Hilton.

Hilton, which uses a multibrand strategy along with market segmentation, understands the power of advertising and IBP.

Hilton runs campaigns for individual brands as well for its portfolio of brands. *How do both of these messages appeal to variety seekers who stay at hotels for business or fun getaways?*

6-2c Emergent Consumers

These consumers offer the organization an important business opportunity. In most product categories, there is a gradual but constant influx of first-time buyers. The reasons for this influx vary by product category and include purchase triggers such as college graduation, marriage, a new baby, divorce, a new job, a big raise, or retirement. Immigration can also be a source of new customers in many product categories.

Emergent consumers are motivated by many different factors, but they share one notable characteristic: Their brand preferences are still developing. Targeting emergents with messages that fit their age or social circumstances may produce modest effects in the short run, but it eventually may yield a brand loyalty that pays handsome rewards for the discerning organization.[8] Developing advertising campaigns to win with first-time users is often referred to as **point-of-entry marketing**. As a case in point, the marketers of Folgers want to appeal specifically to the next generation of coffee drinkers. Attracted by coffee titans like Starbucks and Dunkin', many people get to know coffee in their teens. But when it's time to start brewing coffee at home, Folgers sees a big opportunity to get into your cupboard.

The Folgers brand team launched an advertising initiative to attract millennials who are primed to develop the coffee habit. Folgers aspires to be the brand of choice as these customers develop a brew-it-yourself morning coffee ritual. But how does Folgers, your grandparents' brand, make a connection with a new generation of coffee drinkers? Working with its ad agency, the Folgers brand team started with the premise that mornings are hard, filled with emails and bosses making demands and those annoying "morning people." The agency created a short film to show Folgers as a coffee drinker's first line of defense when confronted with "morning people." The film was designed to steer traffic to a branded website, part of a campaign supported by print ads.

Folgers spent zero dollars on media for this film. Rather, it was submitted to three websites. As chatter about the film filled social media, website hits increased, and the film received hundreds of thousands of viewings on YouTube. The brand team has followed up with new ads and other IBP tools, including a handy Amazon Dash button that orders Folgers coffee from Amazon as easily as pressing the button (see Exhibit 6.5).[9]

Source: The J.M. Smucker Company

Exhibit 6.5 ▶ See the great example of innovation with the Amazon Dash Folgers Button.

6-2d Demographics

Demographic segmentation is widely used in selecting target segments and includes descriptors such as age, gender, race, marital status, income, education, and occupation (see examples of American demographics at www.factfinder .census.gov). Demographic information has special value in market segmentation because if an advertiser knows the demographic characteristics of the target segment, choosing media to efficiently reach that segment is much easier.[10] In this age of Big Data, advertisers can identify the needs and characteristics of specific groups—even those of individual consumers—for more precise segmentation and targeting than can be achieved with demographics.[11]

Demographics are commonly used to describe or profile segments that have been identified with some other variable. If an organization had first segmented its market in terms of product usage rates, as an example, the next step would be to describe or profile its users in terms of demographic characteristics such as age or income. Hilton, for example, knows that millennials are frequent travelers, making them an excellent demographic segment to target for hotel accommodations. But Hilton also combines other variables to better understand this segment's needs and wants. Aware that millennials tend to rely heavily on mobile devices, Hilton offers a branded app for selecting individual rooms and checking in, a convenience appreciated by this segment.[12]

In addition, demographic filters are used frequently as the starting point in market segmentation. Since families commonly plan vacations together, demographics will also be a major consideration for targeting by the tourism industry, where families with children are often the marketer's focus. For instance, the Outback Queensland Tourism Association, which promotes tourism to Australia's Queensland region, launched a social and digital media campaign targeting families. The campaign, which includes a tourism website and other digital content, focuses on the shared outdoor experience of parents and children being on the road together to explore the outback country.[13]

Another demographic group receiving renewed attention from advertisers is the "woopies," or well-off older people. In the United States, Baby Boomers (who are all over the age of 50) contribute to more than 50 percent of the country's consumer expenditures.[14] No wonder ads for fashion brands and beauty brands like L'Oréal are featuring models or people in this age group.[15] Like any other age segment, older consumers are a diverse group, and the temptation to stereotype must be resisted. When consumers are **stigmatized**, which is defined as when someone's personal attribute is a source of devaluation in the marketplace or by other people, they perceive marketing differently which can be an obstacle to marketers in a variety of industries.[16]

6-2e Geographic Location

Geographic segmentation needs little explanation other than to emphasize how useful geography is in segmenting markets. Geographic segmentation may be conducted within a country by region, by state or province, by city, or even by neighborhood. Climate and topographical features yield dramatic differences in consumption by region for products such as snow tires and surfboards, but geography can also correlate with other differences that are not so obvious. Eating and food preparation habits, entertainment preferences, recreational activities, and other aspects of lifestyle have been shown to vary dramatically along geographic lines. Reactions to well-known global brands and advertising also vary from one country to another.[17]

In recent years, skillful marketers have merged information on where people live with the U.S. Census Bureau's demographic data to produce a form of market segmentation known as geodemographic segmentation. **Geodemographic segmentation** identifies neighborhoods (by zip codes) around the country that share common demographic characteristics. One such system, known as PRIZM, identifies 68 market segments that encompass all the zip codes in the United States. Each of these segments has similar lifestyle characteristics and can be found throughout the country. Prizm also documents Lifestage Groups and Social Groups to help marketers segment audiences or consumers by their lifestage and social habits.

For example, the American Dreams segment of upper middle-income families is found in many urban areas, and more than half of these households are multilingual.

This segment's brand preferences are different from those of the low-income families belonging to the Young & Rustic segment, which mainly consists of singles and young families that live in rural America. Systems such as PRIZM are popular because of the depth of segment description they provide, along with their ability to precisely identify where the segment can be found.[18]

6-2f Psychographics and Lifestyle

Psychographics is a term that advertisers created in the mid-1960s to refer to a form of research that emphasizes the understanding of consumers' activities, interests, and opinions (AIOs). Many advertising agencies were using demographic variables for segmentation purposes; but they wanted insights into consumers' motivations, which demographic variables did not offer. Psychographics were created as a tool to supplement the use of demographic data. Because a focus on consumers' activities, interests, and opinions often produces insights into differences in the lifestyles of various segments, this approach usually results in **lifestyle segmentation**. Knowing details about the lifestyle of a target segment can be valuable for creating advertising messages that ring true to the consumer. For instance, the brand Samsung appeals to sports enthusiasts in some of their past advertising as a way to connect to the lifestyles of their global customers.

Lifestyle or psychographic segmentation can be customized with a focus on the issues germane to a single product category, or it may be pursued so that the resulting segments have general applicability to many different product or service categories. The footwear brand Vans uses psychographics to segment the market for its casual shoes. Skateboarders and surfers have traditionally been the brand's primary segments, targeted by lifestyle rather than solely by age. Vans also uses the psychographic variable of creative expression to identify consumers of any age who buy shoes as an expression of their personality. With these psychographic segments in mind, Vans develops different marketing and advertising programs to appeal to each group. For example, it creates limited-edition artistically inspired shoes (for the creative expression segment), reissues classic skate shoes (for skateboarder segment), and so on. Thanks to its successful segmentation, Vans has surpassed $9 billion in global sales.[19] See Exhibit 6.6 that represents some consumer love for the Vans brand.

6-2g Benefit Segmentation

Another segmentation approach developed by advertising researchers is **benefit segmentation**. In benefit segmentation, target segments are delineated by the various benefit packages that different consumers want from competing products and brands (i.e., the benefits sought by consumers). For instance, different people want different benefits from their vehicles. Some consumers want efficient and reliable transportation; others want speed, excitement, and glamour; and still others want luxury, comfort, and prestige. One product could not possibly serve such diverse benefit segments. As an example, Toyota promotes the sustainability benefits and money-saving features of its Prius cars, pursuing the segment of people who want to save the planet and save money at the same time. Toyota uses multiple variables to

Source: Vans, A VF Company

Exhibit 6.6 ▶ Known as a loved brand, Vans leverages the originality of its sneakers and the heart symbolism in its branding.

identify Prius buyers, including age, income, environmental consciousness, and technology usage.[20] Other Toyota vehicles are geared toward different benefit segments, such as rugged driving or luxury. Each vehicle's marketing has synergistic IBP activities appropriate for the targeted segment. Check out how Toyota speaks to environmentally conscious or "green" consumers while also taking a humorous approach in Exhibit 6.7.

6-2h Segmenting Business-to-Business Markets

Thus far, our discussion of segmentation options has focused on ways to segment **consumer markets**. Consumer markets are the markets for products and services purchased by individuals or households to satisfy their specific needs. Consumer marketing is often compared and contrasted with business-to-business marketing. **Business markets** are the institutional buyers who purchase items to be used in other products and services or to be resold to other businesses or households. Although advertising is more prevalent in consumer markets, products and services such as smartphones, overnight delivery, Web hosting, consulting services, and a wide array of technology and computer-support services are commonly promoted to business customers around the world. Hence, segmentation strategies are also valuable for **business-to-business** (B2B) marketers.

Business markets can be segmented using several of the options already discussed. Business customers differ in their usage rates and geographic locations, so these variables may be productive bases for segmenting business markets. In addition, one of the most common approaches uses the North American Industry Classification System (NAICS) prepared by the U.S. Census Bureau. NAICS information is helpful for identifying categories of businesses and then pinpointing the precise locations of these organizations.

For example, the Hilton Hotel in downtown Chicago segmented the market for business meetings and group events held in hotels, as identified by industry. It then sets up separate digital content for decision makers in five targeted industries: financial services, technology, athletics, pharmaceuticals, and unions. Each page of content uses wording particular to that industry and emphasizes the features and benefits sought by that industry, such as healthy menu options for group meals (of interest to pharmaceutical and medical groups) and availability of high-speed Wi-Fi for groups (of interest to the technology industry).[21]

6-3 Prioritizing Segments

Whether it is done through usage patterns, demographic characteristics, geographic location, benefit packages, or any combination of options, segmenting markets typically yields a mix of segments that vary in their attractiveness to

Source: Toyota Motor Corporation

Exhibit 6.7 ▶ In this Prius ad, Toyota compares emissions to those of a sheep in a comical approach that also speaks nicely to the green consumer segment.

the advertiser. In pursuing STP marketing, the advertiser must get beyond this potentially confusing mixture of segments and select a subset that will become the target for its marketing and advertising programs.

Perhaps the most fundamental criterion in segment selection revolves around what the members of the segment want versus the organization's ability to provide it. Every organization has distinctive strengths and weaknesses that must be acknowledged when choosing its target segment. The organization may be particularly strong in some aspect of manufacturing or customer service. To serve a target segment, an organization may have to commit substantial resources to acquire or develop the capabilities to provide what that segment wants. If the price tag for these new capabilities is too high, the organization must find another segment.

Another major consideration in segment selection entails the size and growth potential of the segment. Segment size is a function of the number of people, households, or institutions in the segment, plus their willingness to spend in the product category. When assessing size, advertisers must keep in mind that the number of people in a segment of heavy users may be relatively small, but the extraordinary usage rates of these consumers can more than make up for their small numbers. In addition, it is not enough to simply assess a segment's size as of today. Segments are dynamic, and it is common to find marketers most interested in devoting resources to segments projected for dramatic growth. As we have already seen, the purchasing power and growth projections for people aged 50 and older have made this a segment that many companies are targeting.

A second consideration is the forecasted return on investment (ROI) for the segment. While this is difficult to calculate precisely, good estimates can be made; with better and better marketing analytics, the accuracy of this key metric has improved.

A third selection criterion is the **competitive field**—companies that compete for the segment's business. Advertisers must first look at the competitive field and then decide whether it has a particular expertise, or perhaps just a bigger budget, that would allow it to serve the segment more effectively. This is often discussed in terms of who "owns" a certain segment of the market. Oftentimes marketers are afraid or unwilling to make a move against a competitor who is already successfully mining a strong segment. And while it is understandable that it could be an uphill battle to successfully earn a meaningful stake in a segment that is well served, it also means that a lot of good opportunities can be missed.

The smaller-is-better segmentation principle applies to **niche marketing**. A market niche is a relatively small group of consumers within a segment that has a distinctive set of needs or that seeks very specific benefits; even if the customers are loyal, a small market size is concerning hence the adage of targeting small yet very loyal groups of customers has recently shown to be a myth.[22] The small size of a market niche often means it would not be profitable for many organizations to serve it. Thus, when a firm identifies and develops products for market niches, the threat of competitors developing imitative products to attack the niche is reduced.

Niche marketing will continue to grow in popularity as the mass media splinter into a series of complex and narrowly defined array of specialized vehicles, and advertisers target audiences more precisely with social and digital media. A niche may be small in the beginning; but over time, it can grow into a substantial segment that attracts more consumers and more competition. When Chobani first began selling Greek yogurt in 2007, the product's niche

Source: Chobani, LLC

Exhibit 6.8 ▶ This Chobani ad truly gets the power of integration for great branding; note the leveraging of the sports sponsorship with the Olympics as well as savvy social media integration.

was small. But as Chobani secured shelf space in major U.S. supermarket chains and introduced new products, competitors saw how consumers responded, and they launched their own products. Now Greek yogurt accounts for roughly half of all U.S. yogurt sales—even though it was a tiny niche when it started.[23] In Exhibit 6.8, note Chobani's integration of the sport sponsorship with the Olympics as a great example of how to have an integrated brand promotion strategy. Brilliantly, the company also remembered to integrate social media with #nobadstuff. Greek yogurt is no longer a niche marketing category, partly due to the exposure from this and competing brands' heavy advertising and IBP investments.

LO **4**

6-4 Targeting

Now that a company has decided on which segment or segments to focus, next comes the question of how to target them. Although this is a media-planning question and will be covered in Chapter 12, targeting cannot be completely separated from segmenting or positioning. For now, remember that the main idea of targeting is to efficiently deliver the branding effort to the chosen segments.

6-4a Positioning and Repositioning

For most professionals, positioning or repositioning is where the fun is. It is where the advertiser and IBP pros work on crafting the meaning of the desired brand. Consumers are going to have something to say about that. For a minute, think about the relative positions of Apple and Samsung. How do their brand positions differ? As shown in Exhibit 6.9, Apple is positioning around the concept of privacy, which is an important concern that consumers have about their data and photos. With this ad, Apple wants us to associate their brand with privacy.

Meanwhile, competitor Samsung is also positioning its brand with IBP by integrating celebrity, social media, and advertising. Samsung positions itself as authentic with the #BeWhoYouAre. Where Apple is focusing on privacy, such as the one seen in Exhibit 6.9, Samsung (see Exhibit 6.10) leverages its official partnerships and offers a one-year warranty on its products. In light of Samsung's 2016 scandal with a recall of exploding phones, holding a brand position of product quality backed by a warranty is a smart strategy.

At the heart of any good positioning method is the quest to secure and shape the brand's meaning relative to other

Exhibit 6.9 ▶ To keep its modern and innovative brand position, Apple holds a focus on privacy, which is a crucial value to many users of smartphones and personal technology.

Source: Samsung Group

project that positioning (relative meaning) to consumers. For example, brands that position as healthy or in preventative health could target customers with a personalized advertising system that is based on heart rate variability measured on customers' wearable technology.[24] Even brands in more mundane sectors such as orange juice must dynamically evolve their brand position. For instance, Tropicana has reduced the sugar content of its products and repositioned the brand as healthier.

Exhibit 6.10 ▶ Samsung seeks to look more modern and also takes a position of high-tech with more individuality.

brands. In the case of a new brand: What is the landscape of the brand meaning? In the case of repositioning or significantly changing the meaning of an existing brand, the same basic question applies: What should our brand mean relative to other brands? Once this is determined, the advertising and integrated branded promotion tactics are deployed in order to

6-4b Positioning Opportunity

InterBrand is among the world's largest brand consultancies, well known for its annual ranking of global brands by value. The company's former head of consulting, Anne Bahr Thompson, offers the positioning model in Exhibit 6.11.[25] It has four factors represented by overlapping circles.

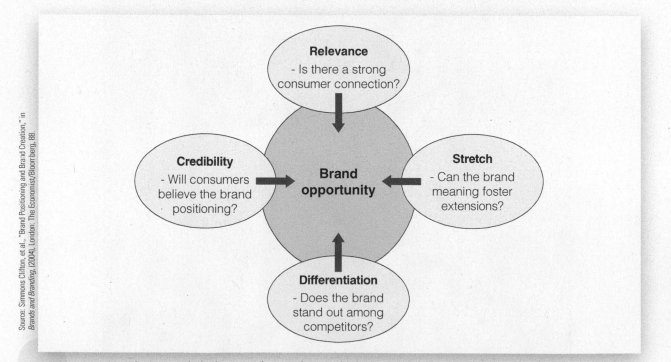

Source: Simmons Clifton, et al., "Brand Positioning and Brand Creation," in *Brands and Branding*, (2004), London: The Economist/Bloomberg, 88.

Exhibit 6.11 ▶ This model shows that a brand's best opportunity for success involves the overlapping of four important factors: current relevance to the consumer, credibility or consumer belief in the brand, differentiation or a recognition of uniqueness, and "stretch" or the potential for consumer relevance over time.

The point where they intersect is considered the best opportunity, the brand's best position. They are:

- **Relevance:** Where is the strong consumer connection? What is the revealed need(s) of consumers?

- **Differentiation:** Can the brand stand out as significantly different from the others?

- **Credibility:** Will consumers believe it?

- **Stretch:** Will the brand's meaning have sustainable relevance in changing times? Will it foster brand extensions?

To identify a brand's best positioning strategy, find the place where the answer to all four questions is "yes." Then you know that your positioning is strong and viable.[26] For instance, Giorgio Armani takes a position of luxury and as a market leader in the long-lasting lip color category in a relevant, credible way that stands apart from regular lipstick (see Exhibit 6.12).

Now notice a competitor, Chanel, that also takes a luxury position, but without a call to the product (lipstick) features/benefits here (see Exhibit 6.13). Chanel is very good at showcasing the brand image, often without the need to address product features and benefits.

6-4c Essentials for Effective Positioning Strategies

Any sound **positioning strategy** includes several essential elements. Effective positioning strategies are based on meaningful commitments of organizational resources to produce substantive value for the target segment. They also are consistent internally and over time, and they feature simple and distinctive themes. Each of these essential elements is described in the following sections.

Source: Giorgio Armani S.P.A.

Exhibit 6.12 ▶ In this Armani ad, it is rare to see a brand with a true luxury position also showcase product benefits, as shown here with the long-lasting matte lip color.

Source: Chanel S.A.

Exhibit 6.13 ▶ Chanel, in contrast to Armani, showcases the high-end luxury brand position with image-based advertising while leaving out any features or benefits of the powder and lipstick shown in this ad.

Deliver on the Promise

For a positioning strategy to be effective and remain effective over time, the organization must be committed to creating substantive value for the customer. Again, consider the Toyota Prius, well known for its positioning as a "green" car, as established earlier in this chapter with respect to the brand positioning. Originally, the Prius was a hybrid car, with a combination of gasoline-electric engine. The promise of that positioning still applies today, as Toyota introduces additional models that are earth friendly, including the Prius Prime, a plug-in hybrid with excellent gas mileage. Year after year, Toyota uses both advertising and IBP to demonstrate how it delivers on the promise of a "green car," keeping the brand in the public eye to maintain its competitive edge over newer brand entries in the "green" category.

There's Magic in Consistency

A positioning strategy also must be consistent internally and over time. Regarding internal consistency, all elements of the strategy must work in concert to reinforce a distinct perception in the consumer's eyes about what a brand stands for. The Prius has never changed its positioning, remaining firmly in the "green" lane no matter how many models are introduced under that brand.[27] Even the distinctive look of the Prius vehicles communicates differentiation and sets the brand apart from competitors.

Consistency in positioning is important because consumers have perceptual defenses that allow them to screen or ignore most of the ad messages they are exposed to. Breaking through the clutter and establishing what a brand stands for is a tremendous challenge made easier by consistent positioning. If, year in and year out, an advertiser communicates the same basic themes, then the message may get through and shape the way consumers perceive the brand, as it has for the Prius. Another example of a consistent approach in the automotive category is the long-running BMW ad slogan, "Ultimate Driving Machine." BMW consistently uses that slogan to convey the brand's positioning on the basis of luxury, performance, and driving pleasure.

Make It Different Simply

Simplicity and distinctiveness are essential to the advertising task. No matter how distinctive, effective, and helpful a product is, it will fail in the marketplace if the consumer doesn't understand what it can do. In a world of harried consumers who can be expected to ignore, distort, or forget most of the ads they are exposed to, complicated, imitative messages simply have no chance of resonating. The basic premise of a positioning strategy must be simple and distinctive if it is to be communicated effectively to the target segment.

6-5 Working with a Value Proposition and a Brand Platform

Brand positioning is often also referred to as a value proposition, a brand promise, or a brand platform, which are three ways of saying (almost) the same thing. In this chapter, we have presented several important concepts for understanding how marketers develop strategies for their brands that then have major implications for the integrated advertising campaigns that are executed to build and maintain those brands. Marketers have to assess customer segments and target markets along with the competitive field to make decisions about various positioning themes that might be appropriate for their brand's advertising and IBP campaign.

A **value proposition** consolidates the emphasis on customer benefits that has been featured in this chapter into one or two sentences that state what value the brand will offer to the customer. Below are value propositions for McDonald's.[28] The **brand promise** is another name for this idea, and it articulates what it is that the brand promises the customer.

McDonald's Value Propositions

- *Functional benefits:* Good-tasting hamburgers, fries, and drinks served fast; extras such as playgrounds, prizes, premiums, and games.

- *Emotional benefits:* Kids—fun via excitement at birthday parties; a feeling of special family times. Adults—warmth via time spent enjoying a meal with the kids; admiration of McDonald's social involvement with charities.

Another way of summarizing or "putting it all together" is known as the **brand platform**:

The **brand platform** *is a core idea that frames an ambition or aspiration for the brand that will be relevant to target audiences over time.*[29]

6-5a Now, Making It Happen

The strategic planning triangle proposed by advertising researchers Esther Thorson and Jeri Moore is a practical model that brings together the key concepts presented in

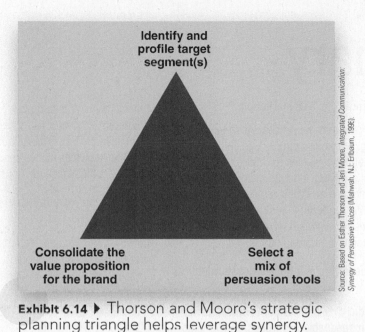

Source: Based on Esther Thorson and Jeri Moore, *Integrated Communication: Synergy of Persuasive Voices* (Mahwah, NJ: Erlbaum, 1996)

Exhibit 6.14 ▶ Thorson and Moore's strategic planning triangle helps leverage synergy.

this chapter.[30] As reflected in Exhibit 6.14, the apexes of the planning triangle entail the segment(s) selected as targets for the campaign, the brand's value proposition, and the array of persuasion tools that will be deployed to achieve campaign goals.

As we have seen, the starting point of STP marketing is identifying who the customers or prospects are and what they want. Hence, Thorson and Moore place identification and specification of the target segment as the paramount apex in their model. Building a consensus between the client and the agency about which segments will be targeted is essential to the campaign's effectiveness. Compelling advertising begins with insights about one's target segment that are both personal and precise.

The second important apex in the planning triangle entails specification of the brand's value proposition. A brand's value proposition is a statement of the functional, emotional, and/or self-expressive benefits delivered by the brand. In formulating the value proposition, consider both what a brand has stood for or communicated to consumers

in the past and what new types of value or additional benefits one wants to claim for the brand going forward. For mature, successful brands, reaffirming the existing value proposition may be the primary objective for advertising and IBP activities. When launching a new brand, there is an opportunity to start from scratch in establishing the value proposition through integrated message content.

The final apex of the planning triangle considers the various persuasion tools that may be deployed as part of the campaign, all described in Parts 4 and 5 of this book. Chapters 12 and 13 emphasize traditional mass media tools, Chapter 14 looks at digital, social, and mobile options, Chapter 15 considers support media and sales promotions, Chapter 16 examines events, placements, and branded entertainment, Chapter 17 covers direct marketing and personal selling, and Chapter 18 discusses public relations, influencer marketing, and corporate advertising. You must know the target segment and the value proposition to plan the appropriate tools and implement an effective integrated brand promotion campaign.

Summary

1. Explain the process known as STP marketing.

The term *STP marketing* refers to the process of segmenting, targeting, and positioning. Marketers pursue this set of activities in formulating marketing strategies for their brands. STP marketing also provides a strong foundation for the development of advertising campaigns. While no single approach can guarantee success in marketing and advertising, STP marketing should always be considered when consumers in a category have heterogeneous wants and needs.

2. Describe different bases that marketers use to identify segments.

In market segmentation, the goal is to break down a heterogeneous market into more manageable subgroups or segments. Many different bases can be used for this purpose. Markets can be segmented on the basis of usage patterns and commitment levels, demographics, geography, psychographics, lifestyles, benefits sought, NAICS business categories, or stages in the purchase process. Different bases are typically applied for segmenting consumer versus business-to-business markets.

3. Identify the criteria to target a segment.

In pursuing STP marketing, an organization must get beyond the stage of segment identification and settle on one or more segments as a target for its marketing and advertising efforts. Several criteria are useful in establishing the organization's target segment. First, the organization must decide whether it has the proper skills to serve the segment in question. The size of the segment and its growth potential must also be taken into consideration. Another key criterion involves the intensity of the competition the firm is likely to face in the segment. Often, small segments known as niches can be attractive because they have few if any competitors and may have significant growth potential.

4. Identify the essential elements of an effective positioning strategy.

The *P* in *STP marketing* refers to the positioning strategy that must be developed as a guide for all marketing and advertising activities that will be undertaken in pursuit of the target segment. Effective positioning strategies should be linked to the substantive benefits offered by the brand. They are also consistent internally and over time, and they feature simple and distinctive themes. Benefit positioning, user positioning, and competitive positioning are options that should be considered when formulating a positioning strategy.

5. Define the necessary ingredients for creating a brand's value proposition.

Many complex considerations underlie marketing and advertising strategies, so the value proposition is a useful way of summarizing the essence of the brand's strategy. A value proposition is a statement of the various benefits (functional, emotional, and self-expressive) offered by a brand that create value for the customer. These benefits as a set justify the price of the product or service. Clarity in expression of the value proposition is critical for development of advertising that sells.

Key Terms

benefit segmentation
brand platform
brand promise
business markets
competitive field
consumer markets
demographic segmentation
emergent consumers

geodemographic segmentation
heavy users, committed users, lead users
lifestyle segmentation
niche marketing
point-of-entry marketing
position
positioning strategy

psychographics
segment
stigmatized
STP marketing
switchers
target
value proposition
variety seekers

Endnotes

1. Nancy Trejos, "Hilton Launches a New Brand, Its 14th," *USA Today,* January 23, 2017, http://www.usatoday.com/story/travel /roadwarriorvoices/2017/01/23/hilton-launches-new-brand-its -14th/96938920/; and Lindsay Stein, "Hilton Introduces New Hotel Brand with Millennial Mindset," *Advertising Age,* January 25, 2016, http://adage.com/article/cmo-strategy/hilton-introduces-hotel -brand-millennial-mindset/302310/; http://www.hiltonworldwide .com/portfolio.

2. Harsh Taneja, "The Myth of Targeting Small, But Loyal Niche Audiences," *Journal of Advertising Research* 60, no. 3 (2019), 239–250.

3. Don E. Schultz, "Pareto Pared," *Marketing News,* November 15, 2009, 24; and Steve Hughes, "Small Segments, Big Payoff," *Advertising Age,* January 15, 2007, 17.

4. Kelly Vaughan, Virginia Beal, and Jenni Romaniuk, "Can Brand Users Really Remember Advertising More Than Nonusers?" *Journal of Advertising Research* 56, no. 3 (2016), 311–320.

5. Rob Walker, "Makeover Mania," *New York Times Magazine,* November 10, 2016, http://www.nytimes.com/interactive/2016/11/13/magazine /design-issue-redesign-craze.html?_r=0.

6. See Sudhir Voleti, Manish Gangwar, and Praveen K. Kopalle, "Why the Dynamics of Competition Matter for Category Profitability," *Journal of Marketing* 81, no. 1 (2017), 1–16.

7. Stefan J. Hock, Rajesh Bagchi, and Thomas M. Anderson, "Promotional Games Increase Consumer Conversion Rates and Spending," *Journal of Consumer Research* 47, no. 1 (2019), 79–99.

8. Lei Su, Alokparna (Sonia) Basu Monga, and Yuwei Jiang, "How Life-Role Transitions Shape Consumer Responses to Brand Extensions," *Journal of Marketing Research* 58, no. 3 (2021), 579–594.

9. Angela Moscaritolo, "Order More Folgers, Cheez-Its With the Press of a Dash Button," *PC Magazine,* October 25, 2016, http://www.pcmag.com/news/349004/order-more-folgers -cheez-its-with-the-press-of-a-dash-butto.

10. J.P. James and Tyrha M. Lindsey-Warren, "An Examination of Television Consumption by Racial and Ethnic Audiences in the U.S.: Implications for Multicultural Media Planning and Media Measurement," *Journal of Advertising Research* 61, no. 2 (2018), 40–52.

11. See Niraj Dawar, "Labels Like 'Millennial' and 'Boomer' Are Obsolete," *Harvard Business Review,* November 18, 2016, https ://hbr.org/2016/11/labels-like-millennial-and-boomer-are-obsolete.

12. Natalie Mortimer, "Inside Hilton's Plan to Stay Ahead of the Tech Curve, and the Competition," *The Drum,* October 7, 2016, http ://www.thedrum.com/news/2016/10/07/inside-hilton-s-plan-stay -ahead-the-tech-curve-and-the-competition; and Felicia Greiff, "Millennials, Now Bigger than Boomers, Offer Hotels Challenge," *Advertising Age,* July 24, 2015, http://adage.com/article/advertising /appeal-millennial-traveler/298989/.

13. Kathleen Calderwood, "Outback Tourism Group Renews Push to Get More Families on the Road," *ABC.net,* March 21, 2016, http://www .abc.net.au/news/2016-03-21/outback-tourism-family-holidays -marketing-push/7264014; http://www.outbackqueensland .com.au.

14. Vaughan Emsley, "Don't Underestimate the Power of the 50+ Crowd," *Harvard Business Review*, January 9, 2020, https://hbr.org/2020/01 /dont-underestimate-the-market-power-of-the-50-crowd.

15. Emma Bazilian, "Why Older Women Are the New It-Girls of Fashion," *Adweek,* April 6, 2015, http://www.adweek.com/news/advertising -branding/why-older-women-are-new-it-girls-fashion-163871.

16. Colleen M. Harmeling, et al. "Marketing, Through the Eyes of the Stigmatized," *Journal of Marketing Research* 58, no. 2 (2021), 223–245.

17. Jae-Eun Kim, Stephen Lloyd, and Marie-Cécile Cervellon, "Narrative-Transportation Storylines in Luxury Brand Advertising: Motivating Consumer Engagement," *Journal of Business Research* 69, no. 1 (2016), 304–313.

18. For more information, see https://segmentationsolutions.nielsen .com/mybestsegments/.

19. CNBC, "Vans Sneaker Maker's Revenue, Profit Forecast Disappoints on Pandemic Hit," January 27, 2021, https://www.cnbc .com/2021/01/27/vans-sneaker-makers-revenue-profit-forecast -disappoints-on-pandemic-hit.html.

20. E. J. Schultz, "Toyota Turns to Addressable TV to Sell the Prius Prime," *Advertising Age,* November 8, 2016, http://adage .com/article/cmo-strategy/toyota-turns-addressable-tv-sell -prius-prime/306668/.

21. Matt Alderton, "Segmented for Success," *Successful Meetings,* July 28, 2016, https://www.successfulmeetings.com/Strategy /Meetings-Events/Segmented-for-Success-Meetings-Verticals -and-Hotels.

22. Philip Kotler and Kevin Lane Keller, *Framework for Marketing Management,* 6th ed. (Upper Saddle River, NJ: Pearson Prentice Hall, 2016), 102; see also Harsh Taneja, "The Myth of Targeting Small, But Loyal Niche Audiences" *Journal of Advertising Research* 60, no. 3 (2019), 239–250.

23. Elaine Watson, "Chobani Notched Up Double-digit US Growth in 2016," *Food Navigator USA,* January 13, 2017, http://www .foodnavigator-usa.com/Manufacturers/Chobani-has-record -year-in-US-has-no-plans-to-go-back-to-Europe; and Roberto A. Ferdman, "Goodbye, Good Old Greek Yogurt," *Washington Post,* December 18, 2015, https://www.washingtonpost.com/news/wonk /wp/2015/12/18/goodbye-good-old-greek-yogurt/.

24. Davide Christian Orazi and Greg Nyilasi, "Straight to the Heart of Your Target Audience: Personalized Advertising Systems Based On Wearable Technology and Heart-Rate Variability," *Journal of Advertising Research* 59, no. 2 (2019), 137–141.

25. Anne Bahr Thompson, "Brand Positioning and Brand Creation," in *Brands and Branding* (London: The Economist in Association with Profile Books, 2003), 79–95.

26. Hannes Gurzki, Nadia Schlatter, and David M. Woisetschläger, "Crafting Extraordinary Stories: Decoding Luxury Brand Communications," *Journal of Advertising* 48, no. 4 (2019), 404–414.

27. Ali Tezer and H. Onur Bodur, "The Greenconsumption Effect: How Using Green Products Improves Consumption Experience," *Journal of Consumer Research* 47, no. 1 (2019), 25–39.

28. This definition is adapted from David Aaker, *Building Strong Brands* (New York: Free Press, 1996), ch. 3.

29. Anne Bahr Thompson, "Brand Positioning and Brand Creation," in *Brands and Branding* (2003), 79–95.

30. Esther Thorson and Jeri Moore, *Integrated Communication: Synergy of Persuasive Voices* (Mahwah, NJ: Erlbaum, 1996).

Advertising Research

Advertising and brand promotion research is research that aids in the development, execution, or evaluation of advertising and promotion. Research is an essential element in analyzing the environment, as shown in Exhibit 7.1.

Here is a brief historical overview of the role of research in advertising and IBP. Although some advertising agencies have had research specialists or even formal research departments for more than 100 years, their real growth occurred in the mid-20th century, with the 1950s being their heyday. During this period, agencies began collaborating with research companies, as it became apparent that there was a need to better understand how ads work. Advertising agencies became susceptible to feeling that they could not afford to get behind in the modern consumer psychology race to better understand consumers through scientific advertising research. There was also an economic boom in consumption happening at the same time, meaning that agencies could afford to build their own in-house research departments. Then the 1960s saw the creative revolution; the 1970s still had a focus on creative—along with some backing by consumer psychology. But by the early 1980s, advertising agencies again began to openly voice their distrust for some of the research methods used in earlier times. In the past 20 years, several advertising agencies have come to believe that stand-alone research departments are a luxury that they can no longer afford, given the increased demands for accountability, profit, and relevance. As such, much advertising research comes from consultants, professors, and other vendors for agencies without in-house research departments.

Exhibit 7.1 ▶ Advertising research is a key element in the environment for advertising and IBP.

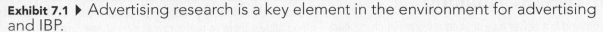

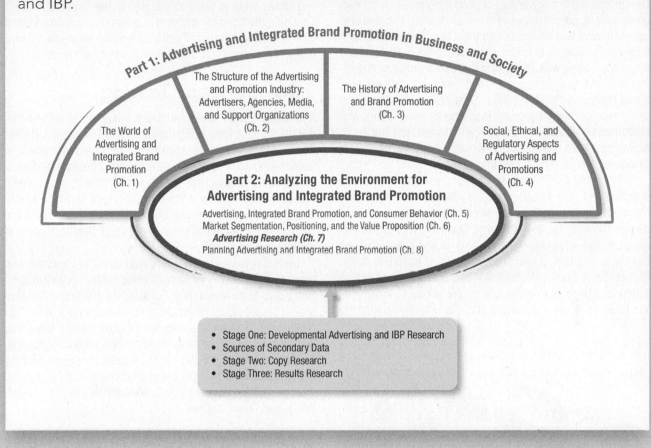

Part 1: Advertising and Integrated Brand Promotion in Business and Society

The Structure of the Advertising and Promotion Industry: Advertisers, Agencies, Media, and Support Organizations (Ch. 2)

The History of Advertising and Brand Promotion (Ch. 3)

The World of Advertising and Integrated Brand Promotion (Ch. 1)

Social, Ethical, and Regulatory Aspects of Advertising and Promotions (Ch. 4)

Part 2: Analyzing the Environment for Advertising and Integrated Brand Promotion

Advertising, Integrated Brand Promotion, and Consumer Behavior (Ch. 5)
Market Segmentation, Positioning, and the Value Proposition (Ch. 6)
Advertising Research (Ch. 7)
Planning Advertising and Integrated Brand Promotion (Ch. 8)

- Stage One: Developmental Advertising and IBP Research
- Sources of Secondary Data
- Stage Two: Copy Research
- Stage Three: Results Research

Currently, marketers conduct three types of research to support advertising and brand promotion activities: (1) developmental advertising and promotion research (before ads are made); (2) copy research (as the ads are being finished or are finished); and (3) results-oriented research (after the ads are in the marketplace).

LO **1**

7-1 Stage One: Developmental Advertising and IBP Research

Developmental advertising and promotion research is used to generate opportunities and messages. It helps creatives, account planners, digital strategists, and brand managers discern the target audience's identity, perceived needs, usage expectations, history, and context, among other things. Developmental research provides critical information—**consumer insights**—early in the process so creatives can apply what they learn when actually producing ads and

branded promotions. Related to consumer insight generation is **trendspotting**—identifying new trends in the marketplace. For example, a top ad agency (J. Walter Thompson) has a director of trend forecasting to lead its trendspotting research. Some recent trends that JWT has identified include branding together, new gaming frontiers, live commerce, fin-fluencers (finance influencers), immunity wellness, ethical branding, micropreneurs (entrepreneurs at a small level), intersectional beauty, calmtainment, and delivery-based dining. In past years, they had top takeaways in augmented reality (such as Pokémon Go and branded social media selfie "masks"), machine learning, person to person payments, cryptocurrency, halal tourism (travel geared for Muslim travelers), cannabusiness (the legal marijuana industry), and retail naturalism (more natural, friendly retail environments).[1] Trendspotting and consumer insight generation help marketers think big, using tools like the design thinking methodology.

7-1a Design Thinking

Design thinking is a newer way of integrating research, product development, advertising, and brand promotion. The idea is to get marketers and advertisers to think like designers. Design thinking digs deeper to reveal what consumers really need and want, proceeding with an ongoing process of prototyping, testing, feedback, prototyping again, and communicating what the brand really does (or could do) for real consumers. Designers use a type of thought process that ignores assumptions and preconceived notions of a good or service and replaces it with a process where designers partner with users/potential users to develop the good or service from scratch.

Why should a wallet look like existing wallets? Why should a laptop look like existing laptops? Maybe they shouldn't. Maybe there is a better way. Microsoft, for instance, used design thinking for the Microsoft Surface Pro, resulting in an innovative integration of both a tablet and a laptop in one device. In addition to Microsoft, companies including Apple, Target, Coca-Cola, Tide, and IBM are champions of design thinking. IBM is also using the methodology to differentiate itself as it develops branded digital experiences for its customers.[2] Design thinking can help advertisers figure out what the brand really means (or could mean) to consumers and allows them to better create and shape brand meaning.[3] Changing the "design" of liquid or powder laundry detergent to less messy detergent "pods" is another example of how design thinking can drive sustainable, effective branding.

7-1b Concept Testing

A **concept test** seeks feedback designed to screen the quality of a new idea, using consumers as the judge and jury. Concept testing may be used to vet new ideas for specific advertisements or to assess new product concepts. Before a new product is launched, the advertiser should have a deep understanding of how it fits current needs and how much consumers are willing to pay. Concept tests of many kinds are commonly conducted in order to get quick feedback on new product or brand ideas.

Especially when a brand is very established, doing something new can be risky; and as such, the new product or design concept needs to be researched. For instance, the brand Tide has been a household name for decades, as shown in Exhibit 7.2. Historically, Tide depicted women as homemakers using the detergent to get a deep clean. Now the new product concept is the detergent pods; Exhibit 7.3 showcases the newer product concept and more modern brand positioning that likely went through rigorous concept testing to examine the product and the "Pop of Clean" tagline.

7-1c Audience Profiling

Perhaps the most important service provided by developmental advertising research is the profiling of target audiences. Creatives need to know as much as they can about the people who will see, hear, and interact with their branded communications. This research is done in a variety of ways, including **lifestyle research**, also known as **AIO** (activities, interests, and opinions) research, which uses survey data from consumers who have answered questions about themselves. From the responses given to a wide variety of survey questions, advertisers can develop a meaningful profile of their targeted consumers, their motivations and needs, and their consumption patterns. For example, it may turn out that the target market for an automobile brand consists of male consumers, age 35 to 45, living in larger cities who have to deal with difficult parallel parking and parking in tight spots. As such, companies such as Volkswagen (VW) generally profile the target audience psychographically and use lifestyle research to generate ads such as the one in Exhibit 7.4, which focuses on the car's park-assist features.

7-1d Focus Groups

Qualitative research entails research that has data that is descriptive and entails phenomena that are observed

Exhibit 7.2 ▶ This is an old-school ad from Tide. Before concept testing, advertisers ran ads that might not have resonated with the target market—or could even be offensive, so testing before airing ads is very important.

Source: Procter & Gamble

Source: Procter & Gamble

Exhibit 7.3 ▶ This is a modern ad from Tide that likely benefited from copy-testing to ensure that consumers understood the concept of laundry detergent "pods."

rather than measured. This is in contrast to **quantitative research**, which uses data that have information about quantities or numbers, and are measured. Examples of qualitative research are in-depth interviews and focus group interviews. **In-depth interviews** with consumers are often used to supplement the findings from AIO research and vice versa. A **focus group** is a type of qualitative research. It is a discussion session with (typically) 6 to 10 target customers who have been brought together to generate new insights about a good or service. With a professional moderator guiding the discussion, the consumers first answer some general questions; then, as the session progresses, they answer more focused questions and discuss brand issues in detail. Advertisers tend to like focus groups because they can understand them and observe the participants as their feedback is being collected. In fact, the actual ad copy may, in the end, come from the mouths of focus group members.

However, even multiple focus groups represent a very small sample of the target audience. And focus groups may be prone to problems associated with group dynamics and the desire to please the researcher. Neither Procter & Gamble nor Unilever, two giants in the world of consumer products, rely as heavily on traditional focus groups as they once did.[4] Instead, some advertisers combine focus groups with other research methods to obtain more focused feedback for developing specific message or media decisions. For instance, when Nestlé decided to air a Super Bowl commercial for Butterfinger candy bars, it hired researchers to examine potential creative approaches. The researchers convened two large focus groups to react to the creative ideas and help Nestlé tweak the creative concept it chose for the final commercial (see the screenshot of the TV spot in Exhibit 7.5), "Bolder than Bold."[5] The focus groups helped

Source: Volkswagen of America, Inc.

Exhibit 7.4 ▶ VW has likely benefited from AIO or lifestyle research to understand consumers' sentiments about parking to develop this Precision Parking ad highlighting the parking-assist features in a creative way.

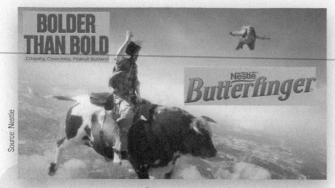

Source: Nestle

Exhibit 7.5 ▶ Butterfinger benefited from focus groups to help create its Super Bowl TV spot, "Bolder than Bold."

the company understand what bold means and chose a flying cowboy and a skydiver to represent bold people who could be even bolder with the candy bar.

7-1e Projective Techniques

When combined with some quantitative data (such as consumers' online shopping data), the qualitative approach is especially helpful when seeking to access deep consumer insights. Projective techniques are another qualitative research method. **Projective techniques** are designed to allow consumers to "project" their thoughts, but mostly their feelings (conscious or unconscious), onto a "blank" or neutral "surface," like an inkblot or benign painting or scene. It's like seeing zoo animals in clouds or faces in ice cubes. Projective techniques often consist of offering consumers fragments of pictures or words and asking them to complete the fragment. The most common projective techniques are association tests, dialogue balloons, story construction, and sentence or picture completion. As an example of a classic projective technique, consider interpreting inkblots as a psychologist (Rorschach) did. Exhibit 7.6 shows the Rorschach inkblot test; consumers interpret the ink, and it helps give insights about how the person thinks and interprets things. Note this specific projective technique is suited to help diagnose anxiety disorders or depression more so than to offer insights on specific brands. However, dialogue balloons are a projective technique well suited to brand research.

Dialogue balloons offer consumers the chance to fill in the dialogue of cartoon-like stories. The story usually has to do with a product use situation. The idea is that the consumers will "project" their thoughts, feelings, and attitudes thoughts into the balloons. For instance, see how the soft-drink brand Fanta can use dialogue balloons in Exhibit 7.7.

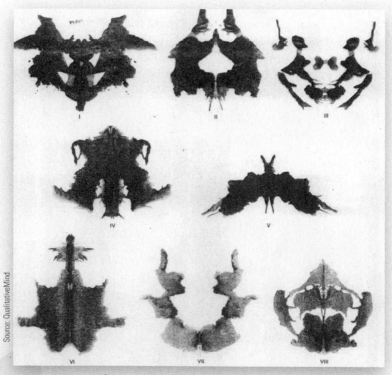

Source: QualitativeMind

Exhibit 7.6 ▶ The most classic example of projective techniques in psychology (not in branding research however) is the Rorschach Inkblot Projective Test. What do you see in these images?

Exhibit 7.7 ▶ Here is an example of what dialogue balloons look like; this projective technique can help brands such as Fanta soft drink to understand what consumers see as its brand personality.

Story construction is a related projective technique well suited for brand research. It asks consumers to tell a story about people depicted in a scene or picture. Respondents might be asked to tell a story about the personalities of the people in the scene, what they are doing, what they were doing just before this scene, what type of car they drive, and what type of house they live in.

The **Zaltman Metaphor Elicitation Technique (ZMET)** is also projective in nature. A metaphor simply involves defining one thing in terms of another. ZMET draws metaphors from consumers by asking them to spend time thinking about how they would visually represent their experiences with a particular product or service. Participants are asked to develop a collection of photographs and pictures from magazines that reflect their experience. In-depth interviews with several dozen of these metaphor-collecting consumers can reveal insights about consumers' consumption motives, which may be useful in the creation of appropriate products and targeted ad campaigns. Examine Exhibit 7.8; images like these are used in the ZMET to understand consumers' connections, particularly their unconscious ones.

As another example of ZMET style work, consider what luxury means. Exhibit 7.9 shows a collage of things a consumer chose as "luxurious"—namely sports cars, air travel, and designer fashions. In turn, Exhibit 7.10 shows a resulting mind map that lists the words associated with luxury in this projective exercise; key words include "cars," "gold," "travel," "holiday," "status," and "indulgence," to name a few.

Exhibit 7.8 ▶ The ZMET has been a successful way of getting consumers to reveal their thoughts and feelings by using our ability to think visually and use metaphors.

Valentino Ristevski/Shutterstock.com, Patrick Poendl/Shutterstock.com, iStock.com/StudioThreeDots

Exhibit 7.9 ▶ Here is an example of a collage done in ZMET style research; it depicts photos of things consumers perceive as "luxurious" in this example.

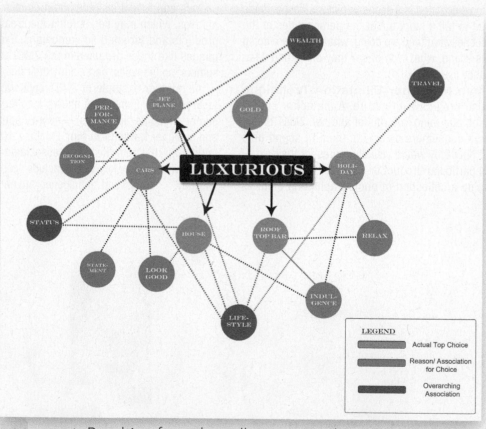

Exhibit 7.10 ▶ Resulting from the collage, researchers can create a mind map such as this one that visually shows and links key terms that emerged from projective research with consumers in the target market.

7-1f   Method: Fieldwork/ Long Interviews

Consumers live real lives, and their behavior as consumers is intertwined throughout their day-to-day activities. Their consumption practices are **embedded**; that is, they are tightly connected to their social context. Two methods of obtaining information about the specific details of consumer behavior are through fieldwork and in-depth interviews.

Fieldwork

Fieldwork is conducted outside the agency (i.e., in the "field"), usually in the home or site of consumption. It is sometimes called a field study, or piece of research or data collection that was done not in a lab, but typically along with a company or organization and the data represents actual consumer or marketplace behaviors. It can be a qualitative or quantitative (i.e., numbers-based) approach. Its purpose is to learn from the experiences of the consumer, usually from direct observation, sampling, or conducting surveys at a sponsored event to assess its **advertising effectiveness**, or how effective a particular ad or marketing approach is in meeting its goal. While there may be less researcher control in the field, hosting surveys or experiments at live events, for example, provide a realness that studies "in the lab" can never duplicate.

Through **ethnographic research**, researchers observe and interview consumers in real-world settings to understand needs and product or consumption usage. In some cases, advertisers, their agencies, or specialized researchers make video recordings or have consumers video themselves to assess the real usage opportunities and consumption practices of actual consumers in actual settings. Advertising researchers can create better targeting, messaging, and media decisions if they understand the lives of their target audiences and how various products fit in actual usage context.

For example, the home furnishings company IKEA recently invited a group of consumers to video themselves at home, answering questions about their "dream home" and the IKEA brand. Its researchers also interviewed consumers at length to better understand what they value and how the brand aligns with those values. Based on insights gained from this and other research, IKEA's ad agency created an integrated campaign focused on helping targeted consumers achieve their dream of a comfortable home that fits their lifestyle and their budget. After testing the message with target audiences, IKEA launched the campaign on television, in print, and on social media (see Exhibit 7.11).[6]

Long Interview

The **long interview** (also called *in-depth interview*) is another qualitative method of accessing insights about the real lives of consumers and the way they think about the brand, the category, and how its consumption fits (or doesn't) into their lives. Long interviews usually last about an hour. They often are semi-structured, with an interview guide. A successful interview has the interviewee doing most of the talking, with the interviewer (researcher) listening and probing for further or deeper responses. The researcher then transcribes the interview data and constructs themes that emerge from multiple interviews. A disadvantage is the time it takes (mainly in transcribing, coding, and making themes); yet the crucial advantage is the depth of the insights about the phenomenon being studied.

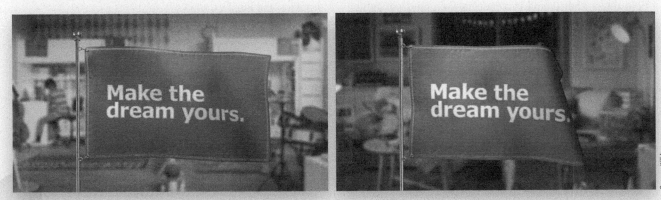

Exhibit 7.11 ▶ Integrated brand promotion in action: IKEA

Consider how IKEA uses IBP; the Swedish brand is a strong example of sound integration of social media messaging and traditional media.

IKEA, which markets home furnishings, reposts commercials on its social media sites to reach more brand fans and reinforce its campaign slogan. *What methods can IKEA use to evaluate the results of such integrated brand promotions?*

7-2 Sources of Secondary Data

7-2a Netnography and Big Data

Often in **secondary research**, data points already exist or the research has already been done by another party. Secondary research is when the researcher does not collect the data, but acquires it from another source. In contrast, **primary research** is when the researcher designs their own study and/or collects their own original research. The lines between secondary research and primary research are blurring, especially as the Internet has revolutionized developmental research. **Big Data** is data in a very large dataset that researchers find patterns in using computer algorithms. Big Data is often analyzed by artificial intelligence, as these algorithms detect the patterns or trends, rather than the researcher. The downside is that Big Data tells researchers what consumers did in the past without knowing why the behavior happened. For instance, a child clicked on an ad because it looked like a video game. The online behavior is recorded as it happened, but it would be incorrect to assume that the ad was clicked on out of interest.

While Big Data refers to large data sets, **netnography** is a method of understanding online communities or online cultures. It is an ethnography conducted online; the term comes from the words "network" and "ethnography." In netnography, the researcher observes and collects data from online communities. At the same time, the researcher actively seeks answers from online informants, the way a field researcher would in a face-to-face physical setting (only at far lower expense).

Online and mobile surveys of key groups are also employed. These are similar to the kinds of surveys one gets in the mail or on the phone, but these are conducted on a website or by sending questions or a link to consumers' mobile devices.[7] Although researchers are getting better at online and mobile sampling, issues of generalizability and representativeness are still present. They are, however, gaining popularity as a method of getting critical information from targeted brand users. Some researchers systematically analyze brand-talk (conversations about their brands and competitors) by searching and sampling online chatter and analyzing words that co-occur, such as a brand and a descriptive term like "cool" or "authentic." Over time this can be a good source of unobtrusively gathered brand information that can be used to develop new ads and other brand messaging.

7-2b Internal Company Sources

Some of the most valuable data are available within a firm itself. Commonly available information within a company includes strategic marketing plans, research reports, customer service records, warranty registration cards, letters from customers, customer complaints, and various sales data (broken down by region, by customer type, or by product line). All of this information provides a wealth of insights relating to the proficiency of the company's advertising programs and, more generally, changing consumer tastes and preferences. When planning new advertising or IBP activities, advertisers should carefully examine the results of previous campaigns, as well, for lessons learned that can be applied to future efforts. In this era of big data, internal databases are particularly rich sources of details about individual buyers and buying trends that occur in the context of the advertiser's IBP activities.[8]

7-2c Government Sources

Various local, state, and federal government organizations in the United States collect and report data on factors of interest to advertising planners, such as population and housing trends, transportation, consumer spending, and recreational activities. The Census Bureau has a great website with access to numerous demographic tables and analyses. The American Community Survey (ACS) provides estimates of demographic, housing, social, and economic characteristics every year for states, cities, counties, metropolitan areas, and population groups. Demographic changes are key to so many advertising and branding opportunities, especially when combined with psychographics and lifestyle analysis.

The Current Population Survey, a national survey conducted monthly since 1940, provides information on unemployment, occupation, income, and sources of income, as well as a rotating set of topics such as health, work schedules, school enrollment, fertility, households, immigration, and language. Population trends rapidly change, affecting consumer tastes, needs, and preferences.

For European brands, Eurobarometer is a good source of survey data among European consumers. The International Social Survey Programme has data on feelings of consumers from dozens of nations on a variety of topics, including environmental issues (quite a find for companies trying to market "green products"). In short, even a small business owner can access large amounts of information for advertising planning purposes at little or no cost by looking for government sources.

7-2d Commercial, Industry, and Nonprofit Sources

Because information has become such a critical resource in marketing and advertising decision-making, commercial data services have emerged to provide data of various types and to package existing data. Some firms specialize in data-gathering efforts at the household or neighborhood level, while others specialize in particular market segments or technologies. Forrester Research, for example, is known for its research of consumer use of tech products and digital media. Advertisers are interested in the firm's research about consumers' use of mobile devices for a variety of functions, as a foundation for preparing messages and selecting media for target markets. The NPD Group maintains a large, nationwide consumer panel of people who answer questions about purchasing, consumption, and lifestyle subjects—again, areas of great interest to advertisers and agencies.

The Pew Center, a widely respected nonprofit public opinion survey center, is particularly good at tracking general consumer attitudes toward major social issues, media trends, and other key topics. Advertisers who want a broad understanding of consumer sentiment can visit the Pew Research Center's online resource collection for regularly updated insights. Industry groups also conduct or commission research for the benefit of members. The National Retail Federation, as another example, maintains links to research useful for retailers of all sizes.

Information from commercial data vendors and many trade and nonprofit groups is generally gathered using sound methods. Many offer consumer surveys (one-shot attempts: one person answers the survey one time) and consumer panels (surveys in which the same members stay on the panel and are asked questions numerous times over months or years). Other studies address specific issues or trace ongoing changes that affect consumers.

Another secondary data source is professional publications (in print and online) in which marketing and advertising professionals report significant information related to industry trends or new research findings. Examples include *Progressive Grocer, American Banker,* and *Beverage.* Every industry has at least one professional publication covering the news, the companies, and the latest developments.

LO **3**

7-3 Stage Two: Copy Research

The second major type of advertising and promotion research is known as copy research, or **evaluative research**. It is an old term that was created when ads were mostly text.

Now it means research on the actual ads or promotional language, finished or unfinished. Copy research is used to judge or *evaluate* ads and promotions, usually right before or after the ad is finalized. Advertisers may be interested in **normative test scores** to understand how well a particular ad scores against average commercials of its type that have been tested previously. Yet agencies also recognize the difficulty of assessing the intangible quality and emotional impact of creative advertising and IBP messages through quantitative scoring.

Another factor to be examined is speed, as advertisers and agencies race to stay ahead of emerging market trends and react quickly to changes in consumer behavior. Unilever, which owns Dove, Axe, and other consumer brands, says it is creating so many digital messages and personalizing so many of them that copy-testing doesn't always make sense in today's fast-paced digital environment. Yogurt marketer Chobani doesn't copy-test its advertising messages, and major advertisers like Procter & Gamble sometimes pick and choose what to test. P&G's initial ad for the Old Spice campaign "The Man Your Man Could Smell Like" wasn't copy-tested, yet it led to an enormously popular campaign with a positive effect on sales.[9]

Despite the potential challenges, copy research that is properly conceived, correctly conducted, and appropriately applied can yield important data that management can then use to determine the suitability of an ad. Frito-Lay usually copy-tests major media campaigns before implementation, for example, because of the investment involved. But it doesn't always copy-test the small percentage of digital advertising efforts considered experimental, preferring to implement quickly and watch what happens.[10] The following section discusses different tests to use, and when to test at all.

7-3a Evaluative Criteria and Methods

Traditionally, ads have been judged according to communication tests and tests of what people remember. Again, these "tests" are usually done right as the ad is being finished or is finished.

Communication Tests

A **communication test** simply seeks to discover whether a message is communicating something close to what the advertiser desired. Sometimes advertisers just want to know if audience members "get" the ad. In other words, do they generally understand it, get the joke, see the connection, or get the main point?

Communication tests are usually done in a group setting, with data coming from a combination of questionnaires and group discussion. Members of the target audience are shown the ad, or some preliminary or rough version of it, possibly seeing it several times, and are then asked to discuss it. One reason communication tests are performed is to prevent communicating something completely wrong, something the creators of the ad are too close to see but that is entirely obvious to consumers. With more transnational or global advertising, an unexpected interpretation of the imagery might emerge as that ad is moved from country to country around the world. Another question research can answer is how often a message should be repeated to get the point across without the audience tuning out.[11] These are all instances in which well-trained and experienced researchers are needed to draw a proper conclusion from the testing.

What Do They Remember?

It is assumed that if the consumer was exposed to the ad, something of that ad remains in the consumer's mind: cognitive residue, pieces of the ads mixed with the consumer's own thoughts and reactions. It might be a memory of the headline, the brand name, the joke in a TV spot, a stray piece of copy, a vague memory trace of an executional element in the ad, or just about anything else. So for decades advertisers have tried to quantify this cognitive residue, or the things left in consumers' minds from the ads. However, memory measures of ads (not brands) don't tend to predict actual sales very well. Why? Well, for one thing, consumers may remember all sorts of things in ads and not care for the advertised brand at all. Or they remember things that are completely irrelevant to the advertiser's intended message, or some of their thoughts actually interfere with associating the advertiser's brand name with the ad itself. Humorous ads are great examples of this. The consumer remembers what is funny but not the brand name—or worse yet, remembers the competitor's brand name instead. Now some companies are insisting on recall measures for branded entertainment.[12]

Memory now appears to be much more of an interpretive act than previously thought. It is actually fairly easy to get a person to remember brands that don't exist and consumption experiences that never happened.[13] This work is a reminder not to rely heavily on memory as a measure of advertising effectiveness. There are certainly times when such measures are appropriate, like memory of a brand name or a key attribute, but nowhere near as much as they are used.

7-3b Common Methods for Assessing Cognitive Impact

Thought Listings

It is commonly assumed that advertising and promotions generate some thoughts during and following exposure. Copy research that tries to identify specific thoughts that were generated by an ad is referred to as **thought listing**, or **cognitive response analysis**. These are tests of knowledge, cognitive impact, and to a lesser degree feelings and emotions. Thought-listing tests are either conducted in-house or obtained from a commercial-testing service. They are most often used with television ads, although they can be applied to all ads. Here the researcher is interested in the thoughts that an ad or promotion generates in the mind of the audience. This research is conducted by having individuals watch the commercial in groups and, as soon as it is over, asking them to write down all the thoughts that were in their minds while watching. Researchers then ask about these thoughts, probing for further explanation or amplification.

These verbatim responses can then be analyzed in a number of ways. Usually simple percentages or box scores of word counts are used, such as the ratio of favorable to unfavorable thoughts. The idea itself is appealing: capturing people's stream of thoughts about an ad at the time of exposure. But in its actual practice, problems arise. These thoughts are in reality more retrospective than in the moment, self-edited, and obtained in artificial environments, unlike in the real world where ads are actually experienced. Still, there is some value in capturing these thoughts. The trick, of course, is to know what is valuable and what is just "noise." A lot has to do with how well matched the ad and the method are. Some ads, for example, are designed in such a way that the last thing the advertiser really wants is a lot of deep thought (more on this in Chapter 10). For other ads (those in which certain conclusions are the desired goal), it can be a good test.

Recall Tests

Recall tests, designed to determine how much, if anything, an audience member remembers of an ad, are among both the most commonly used tests in advertising and the most controversial. Their purpose is to assess the cognitive residue associated with ads. The basic idea is that if the ad is to work, it has to be remembered. Following on this premise is the further assumption that the ads best remembered are the ones most likely to work. If brand awareness is the goal, recall would be an appropriate way to measure whether advertising has accomplished that aim.[14] Recall is commonly used for television advertising, **recognition** for print. Recognition simply means that the audience members indicate that they have seen an ad before (i.e., they recognize it), whereas recall requires that they retrieve the ad from memory. Digital ads and branded video tend to use both recall and recognition tests.

In television, the basic recall procedure is to recruit a group of individuals from the target market who will be watching a certain channel during a certain time on a test date. They are asked to participate ahead of time and are simply told to watch the show. A day after exposure, the testing company calls the individuals on the phone and determines, of those who actually saw the ad, how much they can recall. The day-after-recall (DAR) procedure generally starts with questions such as, "Do you remember seeing a commercial for any laundry detergents? If not, do you remember seeing a commercial for Tide?" If the respondents remember, they are asked what the commercial said about the product: "What did the commercial show? What did the commercial look like?" The interview is recorded and transcribed. The verbatim interview is coded into various categories representing different levels of recall, typically reported as a percentage. *Unaided recall* is when the respondent demonstrates that he/she/they saw the commercial and remembered the brand name without having it mentioned. If the person had to be asked about a Tide commercial, it would be scored as *aided recall*.

Recognition Tests

Recognition tests are the standard memory test for print ads and promotions. Rather than asking you if you recall something, they ask if you *recognize* an ad or something in an ad. This type of testing attempts to get a little more than evidence of exposure residue. Recognition tests ask magazine readers (and sometimes television viewers) whether they remember having seen particular advertisements and whether they can name the company sponsoring the ad. For print advertising, the actual advertisement is shown to respondents; and for television advertising, a script with accompanying photos is shown. For instance, a recognition test might ask, "Do you remember seeing the laundry detergent ad earlier in this chapter?" This is a much easier task than recall in that respondents are cued by the very stimulus they are supposed to remember, and they aren't asked to do anything more than say yes or no. Also, this question is tougher than "Do you remember seeing the Tide ad earlier in this chapter?"

Companies that do this kind of research follow some general procedures. Subscribers to a relevant magazine are contacted and asked if an interview can be set up in their home. The readers must have at least glanced at the issue to qualify. Then each target ad is shown, and the readers are asked if they remember seeing the ad (if they *noted* it), if they read or saw enough of the ad to notice the brand name (if they *associated* it), if they *read any* part of the ad copy, or if they claim to have read at least 50 percent of the copy *(read most)*. This testing is usually conducted just a few days after the current issue becomes available. The *noted*, *associated*, and *read most* scores are then calculated. Starch is a company that conducts online testing to get results more quickly for specific magazine issues.

For TV ads, research companies first select a sample of television viewers and send them a photoboard (a board with still frames from the actual ad) of the TV commercial with the brand name obscured. Then researchers ask recognition questions such as "Do you remember seeing this commercial on TV?" The respondent is asked to identify the brand and answer some attitude questions. From these responses, researchers compile a recognition score, along with attitude data, for the advertiser to consider. This method is fairly inexpensive and, because brand names are obscured, may provide a better measure of recognition.

Recognition scores have been collected for a long time, which allows advertisers to compare their current ads with similar ones done last week, last month, or 50 years ago. This is part of the attraction to recognition scores as a metric. The biggest problem with this practice is that many people say they recognize an ad that in fact they've never seen. After a few days, do you really think you could correctly remember which of the three ads in Exhibits 7.12 through 7.14 you really saw, if you saw the ads under natural viewing conditions? Still, on a relative basis, these tests may tell which ads are significantly better or worse than others.

But here's the rub: Considerable research indicates that there is little relation between recall or recognition scores and actual sales.[15] As ads become more and more visual, recall of words and claims is more and more irrelevant except, usually, for simple brand names. The fact is that, as measured, the level of recall for an ad seems to have relatively little (if anything) to do with sales. This may be due to highly inflated and artificial recall scores. It may also be that ads that were never designed to elicit recall are being tested as if they were. Doing this—applying this test so widely and so indiscriminately—makes the test itself look bad. When recall or recognition is the desired result, these tests are clearly appropriate and worthwhile.

A recall measurement does make sense when simple memory goals are the aim of the commercial. But as advertising moves to fewer words and more pictures, recognition tests, good recognition tests, may become much more valuable than recall. And for most ads or branded entertainment that operate at far more sophisticated and advanced levels than either recall or recognition, these measures are very likely insufficient.

Implicit Memory Measures

What we have been discussing up to this point are explicit memory measures, measures and procedures that require the research subject to recall the actual exposure. In contrast, **implicit memory measures** do not refer to the ad or exposure but instead try to access memory by using tasks like word fragments: say, part of a brand name, like INTL for Intel. Subjects are asked to complete the brand name (which the researcher scores) along with other recollections. The idea is that this is a much more sensitive, less demanding (artificial), and perhaps more meaningful measure of advertising. It is being used occasionally in actual practice, but its intensive procedure and instrumentation make it more of an academic pursuit than an applied one. Some promising research indicates that implicit attitude measures can be very meaningful indicators of closely held attitudes rather than those reported to researchers.

Exhibits 7.12, 7.13, and 7.14 ▶ All of these ads, so strikingly similar, do little to (1) differentiate the product, (2) make it memorable for the consumer, or (3) promote the brand, although presumably GM and Ford had intended to do all three with these ads. Compare and contrast the new Cadillac models (www.cadillac.com) with the Ford luxury models (www .lincoln.com). Has either company broken any new ground in its approach to advertising these vehicles? Do you think in a few days you could distinguish between these models or remember the message of these websites?

Brand Knowledge

Brand Knowledge is a big step up from cognitive residue. To have **brand knowledge** that could have come only from an ad is a much more meaningful measure of advertising effectiveness. This knowledge may take several forms. It could be a brand claim or a belief about the brand. For example, the consumer may believe that Brand X cleans twice as well as Brand Y. If Brand X's advertising and promotion activities have been stressing this very fact, then we may generally assume that the consumer has learned something from the promotion and advertising efforts and that brand knowledge has been created. But with the explosion in available information for consumers, it's becoming increasingly difficult to determine exactly where some piece of knowledge came from.

Attitude Change

Attitudes suggest where a brand stands in the consumer's mind. Attitudes can be influenced both by what people know and by how people feel about a brand. In this sense, attitude or preference is a summary evaluation that ties together the influences of many different factors.

Common sense tells us that attitudes would be worthwhile in assessing ads. Did the ads change the consumers' attitudes in the right direction? Although the usefulness of the attitude concept itself has come under fire, attitude studies are still used, though more often at the results stage. One of the big problems is getting advertisers to run true scientific field experiments with tight controls.[16] Also, advertisers cannot assume that a favorable attitude toward the ad will always lead to a favorable and meaningful attitude toward the brand. Furthermore, attitudes are not very strong predictors of actual behavior and are subject to all kinds of social desirability bias and other measurement problems. Still, in the right circumstance, when the correct attitude dimensions are defined, assessing summary evaluations makes sense.

Attitude Studies

The typical industry **attitude study** measures consumer attitudes after exposure to an ad. Surveys are a popular research tool for understanding attitudes. Essentially, people from the target market are recruited, and their attitudes toward the advertised brand as well as toward competitors' brands are noted. Ideally, there would be pre- and post-exposure attitude measurement so that one could see the change related to seeing the ad in question. Unfortunately, financial constraints mean that often only post-exposure measures are applied. True pre–post tests are becoming increasingly rare.

To the extent that attitudes reflect something meaningful and something important, these tests may be very useful. Their validity is typically premised on a single ad exposure in an unnatural viewing environment. Many advertisers believe that commercials don't register their impact until after three or four exposures in a real environment; others believe the number is much higher. Still, a significant swing in attitude scores with a single exposure suggests that something is going on and that some of this effect might be expected when the ad reaches real consumers in the comfort of their homes. The bottom line is that attitude studies have proven not to been very predictive of actual behavior, even under the best of conditions—conditions that almost never exist in commercial advertising research.

Feelings and Emotions

Advertisers have always had a special interest in feelings and emotions. Research by business professor Michel Pham and others[17] has shown that feelings have three distinct properties that create a very powerful influence over how consumers react to advertisements and the advertised goods and services: (1) Consumers monitor and access feelings very quickly—consumers often know how they feel before they know what they think; (2) there is much more agreement in how consumers feel about ads and brands than in what they think about them;[18] and (3) feelings are very good predictors of thoughts. This research adds a great deal of support to the argument that, in many ways, feelings are more important than thoughts when it comes to advertising. It also appears that ads that use feelings produce stronger and more lasting effects than those that try to persuade by thought alone.[19]

Resonance Tests

In a **resonance test**, the goal is to determine to what extent the message resonates or rings true with target audience members. The question becomes: Does this ad match consumers' own experiences? Does it produce an affinity reaction? Do consumers who view it say, "Yeah, that's right; I feel just like that"? Do consumers read the ad and make it their own? The method is pretty much the same as a communication test. Consumers see an ad in a group several times and then discuss it, prompted by questions like: How do you feel about this ad? How does it make you feel?

Frame-by-Frame Tests

Frame-by-frame tests are typically used when the emotional component of an ad is key, although they may also be used to obtain thought listing as well. These tests typically work by getting consumers to turn dials (like/dislike) while viewing television commercials in a theater setting. The data from these dials are then collected, averaged, and later superimposed over the commercial for the researchers in the form of a line graph. The height of the line reflects the level of interest in the ad. The high points in the line represent periods of higher interest in the ad, and the dips show where the audience had less interest in a particular part of the ad. Whereas some research companies do ask consumers what they were thinking or feeling at certain points along the trace—and sometimes these responses are diagnostic—others do not. In those cases, what the trace line really does then is measure the levels of interest at each specific moment in the execution—it does not explain whether or why consumers' reactions were positive or negative. The downside of frame-by-frame tests is that they involve somewhat higher costs than other methods, and there are some validity concerns in that you are asking consumers to do something they do not normally do while watching television. But even with these issues, the method does have some fans. In general, assessment of feelings evoked by ads is becoming an increasingly important goal of the advertising industry.

Physiological Assessment and Neuroscience

The technology of **physiological assessment** of advertising enables researchers to use brain imaging and other *neuroscience* techniques to measure consumers' reactions to advertising and IBP messages and media. For example, researchers are using functional magnetic resonance imaging (fMRI) both to see which parts of the brain "light up" during exposure to various stimuli, or during certain tasks, and to understand what is happening when they light up. (Exhibit 7.15 shows an fMRI test.)

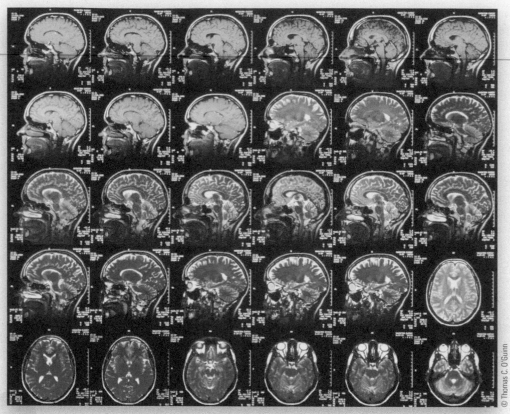

Exhibit 7.15 ▶ These are examples of fMRIs from an advertising study about celebrity appeal in ads. The researchers can see what parts of the brain activate upon exposure to the ads.

As neuroscience develops, researchers expect to be able to help advertisers and agencies make informed decisions about the content and length of a commercial by tracking what happens in consumers' brains as they watch.[20] Samsung, for example, teamed up with a neuroscience research firm to study the brain reactions of Apple and Samsung smartphone users, hoping to design ads that would appeal to Apple users in particular.[21] Further, recent studies have revealed fMRI research to be a valuable predictor of which ad messages will actually influence buying behavior.[22]

Eye Tracking

Eye-tracking systems have been developed to monitor eye movements across print and online ads. With one such system, respondents wear a goggle-like device that records (on a computer system) pupil dilations, eye movements, and length of time each sector of an advertisement is viewed. Individual advertisers commission eye-tracking studies to answer questions like what part of an ad will attract attention, what elements hold attention, and for how long. Broader studies are helping advertisers understand the nuances of digital messages, such as how long an ad must be visible to attract attention on a

computer screen cluttered with content.[23] See Exhibit 7.16 for an example of eye-tracking in research; the green represents less visual attention and the red represents more visual attention. Interestingly, you can compare differences in men's and women's visual attention patterns in Exhibit 7.16.

Behavioral Intent

Behavioral Intent is essentially what consumers say they intend to do. If, after exposure to Brand X's advertising, consumers' stated intent to purchase Brand X goes up, there is some reason to believe that the tested advertising had something to do with it. Of course, intentions aren't the same as actual actions, which is why intended behavior is not a great substitute for actual behavior. On a relative basis (say, percentage who intend to buy Pepsi versus percentage who intend to buy Coke, or at least who tell some researcher that), these measures can be meaningful and helpful, particularly if the changes are substantial. When Baileys and its ad agency were working on IBP activities to encourage year-round consumption, their research found that consumers exposed to messages about adding the liqueur to coffee reported an 80 percent future purchase intent. With that research in hand,

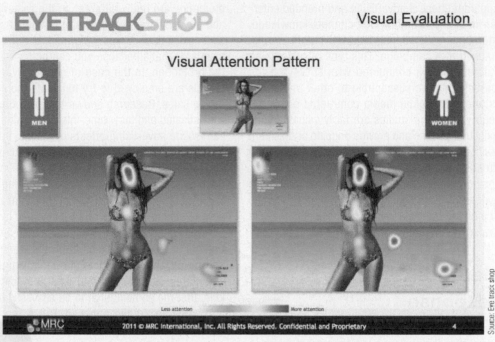

Exhibit 7.16 ▶ Consider this example of visual processing research using eye-tracking software; especially interesting are any differences between men and women's visual attention. Do you notice any differences?

Baileys invested in an ongoing, integrated campaign of advertising, social media messages, and sampling focusing on taste.[24] As seen in Exhibit 7.17, Baileys uses a hashtag (#DontBlushBaby) in its print ads for a good example of integrated brand promotion featuring the product as a great gift.

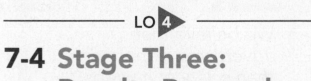

7-4 Stage Three: Results Research

At this stage, the ads are already out in the world, and the advertisers are trying to assess whether they are working. Here, it's important to note the difficulty of determining the exact connection between advertising and sales, in part because consumers are exposed to many IBP activities over time (and at the point of sale).[25]

7-4a Method: Tracking Studies

Tracking studies are one of the most commonly used advertising and promotion research methods. Basically, they

Exhibit 7.17 ▶ Another great example of integration in branding, Baileys uses a measurable hashtag for social media. What research would you suggest to improve this message strategy or execution?

"track" the apparent effect of advertising and branded entertainment over time, assessing attitude change, knowledge, behavioral intent, and self-reported behavior before, during, or after the launch of a campaign. This type of advertising research is almost always conducted with surveys. Even though the participants are susceptible to other influences (e.g., news stories and social media comments about the brand or category), tracking studies are fairly valuable tests because they occur over time and provide ongoing assessment rather than taking a one-time, one-shot approach. The method has been extended to tracking advertising within gaming, which presents new ethical issues given that most gamers are young. However, advertisers should be aware that sometimes attitudes shift a bit but translate into no noticeable increase in sales and no return on investment (ROI).

7-4b Method: Direct Response

Direct response advertisements in print, the Internet, and broadcast media offer the audience the opportunity to place an inquiry or respond directly through a website, reply card, or toll-free phone number. These ads produce **inquiry/direct response measures**.

These measures are quite straightforward in the sense that advertisements that generate a high number of inquiries or direct responses, compared to historical benchmarks, are deemed effective. Additional analyses may compare the number of inquiries or responses to the number of sales generated. For example, some print ads will use different 800 numbers for different versions of the ad so that the agency can compute which ad is generating more inquiries. These measures are not relevant for all types of advertising, however. Ads designed to have long-term image building or brand identity effects should not be judged using such short-term response measures. Measuring the response to certain ad and IBP activities is faster and easier in the digital environment. For example, PetCo can easily count the number of downloads (and subsequent grooming appointments) that occur in response to the ads it places within Apple's App Store.[26] Digital response measures will be discussed in more detail in Chapter 14.

7-4c Method: Estimating Sales Derived from Advertising

Other advertisers really want to see evidence that the new ads will actually get people to do something: generally, to buy their product. It is, to some, the gold standard. But for reasons explained earlier, there are so many things that can affect sales that the use of actual sales as a measure of advertising effectiveness is considered inherently flawed, but not flawed enough not to be used. Here is a place where advertising and

promotion are really different. In the case of the more easily and precisely tracked effects of promotions, some IBPs, and some sales data collected via the Internet, sales are the gold standard. That's because you can better isolate the effect of the promotion. In the case of media advertising, statistical models are employed to try to isolate the effect of advertising on sales. Research shows that in some industries, very sophisticated and fairly time-intensive mathematical modeling can isolate advertising effects over time, but these powerful models are underused in practice and require more time, data, and expertise than many companies have at their disposal.[27] Results generally indicate that advertising has its greatest impact on sales early in the product life cycle, or when a new version or model or other innovation is made. After that, advertising loses steam. Sometimes a host of other variables that might also affect sales, from the weather to competing advertising, are factored into these mathematical models.

Another downside is that these models are constructed long after the ad campaign to be assessed has been in place and sales data have come in. But if the model is strong enough, it will be applicable to many situations. Behavioral data are sometimes derived from test markets, situations in which the advertising is tested in a few select geographic areas before its wider application. Although expensive, these tests can be telling. Ideally, measures of actual behavior would come from tightly controlled field experiments. Unfortunately, meaningfully controlled field experiments are incredibly difficult and expensive and thus very rare in real advertising and IBP practice. Now online advertisers, along with search engine providers and social media sites, are running field experiments continuously. In particular, online advertisers are interested in researching the effect of their campaigns on consumer buying behavior.[28]

> " We believe that advertising is more art than science; it wraps culture around goods and services in order to give brands meaning. Many current research methods are simply at odds with that reality. Others, particularly the more culturally and socially based methods, are much more fitting in this respect. "

7-4d Method: All-in-One Single-Source Data

Research firms are now able to engage in *single-source research* to document the behavior of individuals and households by tracking their behavior from the television screen to the checkout counter. **Single-source data** provide information from individual households about brand purchases, coupon use, and television advertising exposure by combining grocery store scanner data with TV-viewing data (and, increasingly, online search data). Single-source data helps agencies and advertisers assess the real impact of advertising and promotion on consumers' actual purchases and the competitive environment in which consumers make choices. This is not an inexpensive method of assessment, and it still remains difficult (if not impossible) to know exactly what specific aspects of advertising had what effects on consumers. One well-known supplier of this type of testing is IRI.[29]

7-4e Account Planning versus Advertising Research

Account planning assigns a specific planner who is knowledgeable about consumer research and consumer behavior on the agency team working to create advertising and choose media on behalf of clients.[30] Account planning differs from advertising research in three ways. First, rather than depending on a separate research department's occasional involvement, the agency appoints an account planner to a single client (just like an advertising executive) to stay with the projects on a continuous basis. In the more traditional system, the research department would tend to get involved from time to time as needed, and members of the research department would work on several different clients' advertising simultaneously.

Second, this organizational structure puts research in a different, more prominent role. In this system, researchers (or "planners") seem to be more actively involved throughout the entire advertising process and seem to have a bigger impact on it as well, especially in the area of developmental research. Third, agencies that incorporate account planning tend to do more qualitative research than their more traditional counterparts.

Media agencies also have account planners working on client projects with the purpose of integrating consumer insights into the process. For example, when Boone County National Bank in Missouri wanted an advertising campaign to introduce its new name, the bank's advertising agency worked closely with the bank's media agency. The account planner at the media agency understood that changing a brand after one hundred years required the target audience of 40,000 customers to be exposed to the message repeatedly and over an extended period of time. She also was aware of the need to plan the message and media based on how the bank's customers actually consume media, including television, print, social media, and so on. Once the new company name (Central Bank of Boone County) replaced the old one, the bank continued to monitor customer reaction for more than a year.[31]

7-4f Future of Advertising Research

None of the advertising research methods mentioned in this chapter is perfect, not even close. Advertisers sometimes think that consumers watch new television commercials the way they watch new, eagerly awaited feature films (or have other unrealistic ideas about the role of advertising in a consumer's life). Actually, most people multi-task, or do two or more things at once.[32] In reality, we watch TV while we work, talk, eat, and study; we use it as a night-light or for background noise. We often switch our attention between screens from moment to moment, searching on a tablet computer while a TV program is on and simultaneously receiving a text message on the phone. This can make it hard to get and keep customers attention.

In today's fast-paced and competitive business environment, in an age of content sharing and crowdsourcing of 24/7 media and brand communication, advertising and IBP research could benefit from some changes. The way we think about ads and advertising is certainly evolving. The move to an increasingly visual advertising style has also put into question the appropriateness of a set of tests that focus on the acceptance of message claims, as well as verbatim memory of words (copy). Also, the rapid acceptance of digital media and audience interactivity has significantly challenged and changed the whole concept of audience, response, and associated measures for more discussion.

Account planning brings research to the heart of creative and media planning, but more change is needed to provide accountability and input for better decisions. Better measures are needed to understand the influence of mobile advertising, for example.[33] And with so many advertisers active in global markets, more research is needed to determine which creative approaches and media choices are appropriate to reach and engage audiences in different cultures.[34] Clutter is an ever-larger problem, and ad blockers are increasingly popular—all of which points to the need for new and valid measures of what advertising can actually accomplish.[35] Sometimes statistics can be telling, and seeing statistics can lead to changing attitudes or even consumer behaviors. Related, even when there is a consumer behavior to research, just as buying an online daily deal, researchers cannot necessarily know if the deal was redeemed. In fact, nonredemption of vouchers or promotions is a concern for customers because it entails a loss of money.[36]

Another issue is that advertising is often more art than science; it wraps culture around goods and services in order to give brands meaning. Some current research methods are at odds with that reality. Therefore, advertisers and agencies need more culturally and socially based methods combined with more traditional experimental research to capture the nuances of brand meaning, communication, and consumer reaction.

Summary

1. Explain the purposes served by and methods used in developmental advertising research.

Developmental research through design thinking, concept testing, and audience profiling provides consumer insights and allows for trendspotting early in the process of planning advertising and integrated brand promotions. In the developmental phase, advertisers use diverse methods for gathering information, including focus groups, projective techniques, fieldwork and long interviews with consumers in the target market, and ethnographic research.

2. Identify sources of secondary data that can aid the IBP planning effort.

Because information is such a critical resource in the decision-making process, several sources of data are widely used. Advertisers can use netnography to analyze comments from users of online community sites and social media sites, and conduct online and/or mobile surveys of key groups. In this era of Big Data, internal company sources such as strategic marketing plans, research reports, customer service records, and sales data provide a wealth of information on consumer tastes and preferences. Government sources generate a wide range of details about trends in population, consumer spending, employment, and environmental issues. Commercial, industry, and nonprofit data sources can provide advertisers with information on consumers, industry trends, and market changes.

3. Discuss the purposes served by and methods used in copy research.

Copy research (evaluative research) aims to judge the effectiveness of actual ads. Advertisers and clients try to determine if audiences "get" the joke of an ad or retain key knowledge concerning the brand. Tracking changes in audience attitudes, feelings and emotions, behavior, and physiological response is important in gauging the overall success of an ad, and various methods are employed before and after the launch of a campaign to assess the impact on audiences. Communication tests, recall and recognition testing, and the thought-listing technique are a few of the methods that try to measure the persuasiveness of a message. Other copy research relies on implicit memory measures, brand knowledge tests, brand attitude studies, emotion and resonance tests, frame-by-frame tests, neuroscience techniques, eye-tracking systems, and behavioral intent studies.

4. Discuss the research methods used after ads are in the marketplace.

Once an ad campaign has reached the marketplace, agencies and firms turn to results-oriented research to try to determine whether the ad has succeeded—whether, quite simply, the ad prompted consumers to buy the product or service. One of the most commonly employed methods of results-oriented research is the use of tracking studies to measure the apparent effect of advertising over time. Another long-standing method is to measure the direct responses of consumers to a particular campaign. Ideally, advertisers want to be able to estimate sales derived from advertising and IBP. Advertisers can, in some instances, track household consumption patterns from the television to the checkout using single-source data. Researchers are also evaluating sophisticated models to more accurately track estimated sales from advertising, what has been a painstaking and expensive endeavor.

Key Terms

account planning
advertising effectiveness
attitude study
behavioral intent

big data
brand knowledge
communication test
concept test

consumer insights
dialogue balloons
direct response
embedded

ethnographic research	netnography	resonance test
evaluative research	normative test scores	secondary research
eye-tracking system	physiological assessment	single-source data
fieldwork	primary research	story construction
focus group	projective techniques	thought listing (cognitive response
frame-by-frame tests	qualitative research	analysis)
implicit memory measures	quantitative research	tracking studies
inquiry/direct response measures	recall tests	trendspotting
lifestyle (AIO) research	recognition	Zaltman Metaphor Elicitation Technique
long interview	recognition tests	(ZMET)

Endnotes

1. "The Future 100: 2021," *The Innovation Group JWT Intelligence,* January 19, 2021, https://www.wundermanthompson.com/insight/the-future-100-2021; and "The Future 100: Trends and Change in 2017," *The Innovation Group JWT Intelligence,* December 1, 2016, https://www.jwtintelligence.com/2016/12/future-100-trends-change-2017/; and Garett Sloane, "Facebook Is Developing Animated Selfie Masks for Brands," *Advertising Age*, January 30, 2017, http://adage.com/article/digital/facebook-teams-hollywood-selfie-masks-ad-execs/307712/.

2. Ben Davis, "Why Is Design Thinking Suddenly So Important?" *Econsultancy,* November 21, 2016, https://econsultancy.com/blog/68509-why-is-design-thinking-suddenly-so-important/.

3. Federico De Gregorio and Kasey Windels, "Are Advertising Agency Creatives More Creative Than Anyone Else? An Exploratory Test of Competing Predictions," *Journal of Advertising* 50, no. 2 (2020), 207–216.

4. Sharon Terlep, "Focus Groups Fall Out of Favor," *Wall Street Journal,* September 18, 2016, http://www.wsj.com/articles/focus-groups-fall-out-of-favor-1474250702.

5. Jack Neff, "How Butterfinger Used a Safety Net for 'Bolder Than Bold' Ad," *Advertising Age*, February 9, 2016, http://adage.com/article/cmo-interviews/nestle-s-butterfinger-safety-net-bolder-bold/302573/.

6. Christine Whitehawk, "IKEA's Data-Driven Campaign Reintroduces the Brand to U.S. Consumers," *DMNews*, November 1, 2016, http://www.dmnews.com/multichannel-marketing/ikeas-data-driven-campaign-reintroduces-the-brand-to-us-consumers/article/569660/; and Adrianne Pasquarelli, "See the Spot: IKEA Dreams Up New U.S. Campaign," *Advertising Age*, September 26, 2016, http://adage.com/article/cmo-strategy/spot-ikea-dreams-campaign/305991/.

7. Michael Essany, "How to Leverage the Power of Mobile Surveys for More Effective Marketing," *Mobile Marketingwatch*, May 17, 2016, http://mobilemarketingwatch.com/how-to-leverage-the-power-of-mobile-surveys-for-more-effective-marketing-66935/.

8. Michel Wedel and P. K. Kannan, "Marketing Analytics for Data-Rich Environments," *Journal of Marketing* 80, no. 6 (2016), 97–121.

9. "Unilever Seeks to Reinvent Research," *WARC,* July 25, 2016, https://www.warc.com/LatestNews/News/Unilever_seeks_to_reinvent_research.news?ID=37130; E. J. Schultz, "Need for Speed Puts Copy Testing to the Test," *Advertising Age*, September 15, 2015, http://adage.com/article/cmo-strategy/speed-digital-putting-copy-testing-test/300338/; and Kitty Dann and Matthew Jenkin, "Back from the Brink: Five Successful Rebrands and Why They Worked," *The Guardian (UK)*, July 23, 2015, https://www.theguardian.com/small-business-network/2015/jul/23/five-successful-rebrands-why-worked.

10. E. J. Schultz, "Need for Speed Puts Copy Testing to the Test," *Advertising Age,* September 15, 2015, http://adage.com/article/cmo-strategy/speed-digital-putting-copy-testing-test/300338/.

11. For more about testing for wear-in and wear-out, see Jiemiao Chen, Xiaojing Yang, and Robert E. Smith, "The Effects of Creativity on Advertising Wear-In and Wear-Out," *Journal of the Academy of Marketing Science* 4, no. 3 (2016), 334–349.

12. Yongdan Liu and Matthew Tingchi Liu, "Big Star Undercover: The Reinforcing Effect of Attenuated Celebrity Endorsers' Faces on Consumers' Brand Memory," *Journal of Advertising* 49, no. 2 (2020), 185–194.

13. Kathryn A. Braun, "Postexperience Advertising Effects on Consumer Memory," *Journal of Consumer Research* 25 (March 1999), 319–334.

14. Rodrigo Uribe, "Separate and Joint Effects of Advertising and Placement," *Journal of Business Research* 69, no. 2 (2016), 459–465.

15. Rajeev Batra, John G. Myers, and David A. Aaker, *Advertising Management,* 5th ed. (Upper Saddle River, NJ: Prentice Hall, 1996), 469.

16. For more about the challenges and the potential benefits, see Ayelet Gneezy, "Field Experimentation in Marketing Research," *Journal of Marketing Research* 54, no. 1 (February 2017), 140–143.

17. Michel Tuan Pham, Joel B. Cohen, John W. Pracejus, and G. David Hughes, "Affect Monitoring and the Primacy of Feelings in Judgment," *Journal of Consumer Research* 28 (September 2001), 167–188.

18. Brad Fay, Ed Keller, and Rick Larkin, "How Measuring Consumer Conversations Can Reveal Advertising Performance," *Journal of Advertising Research* 59, no. 4 (2019), 433–439.

19. Charles Young, Brian Gillespie, and Christian Otto, "The Impact of Rational, Emotional, and Physiological Advertising Images on Purchase Intention: How TV Ads Influence Brand Memory," *Journal of Advertising Research,* 59, no. 3 (2019), 329–341.

20. Moran Cerf and Sam Barnett, "Can Neuroscience Build a Better Ad?" *Kellogg Insights,* June 2, 2015, http://insight.kellogg.northwestern.edu/article/can-neuroscience-build-a-better-ad.

21. Jack Neff, "Neuromarketing Exits 'Hype Cycle,' Begins to Shape TV Commercials," *Advertising Age,* April 19, 2016, http://adage.com/article/cmo-strategy/neuromarketing-exits-hype-cycle-begins-shape-tv-ads/303582/.

22. Uma R. Karmarkar, Carolyn Yoon, and Hilke Plassmann, "Marketers Should Pay Attention to fMRI," Harvard Business Review blog,

November 3, 2015, https://hbr.org/2015/11/marketers-should-pay-attention-to-fmri; and Thomas Reynolds and Joan Phillips, "The Strata Model Predicting Advertising Effectiveness: A Neural-Network Approach Enhances Predictability of Consumer Decision Making," *Journal of Advertising Research* 59, no. 3 (2019), 268–280.

23. Jennifer Faull, "Online Ads Need to Be on Screen for at Least 14 Seconds to Be Seen, Finds Eye-tracking Study," The Drum, September 30, 2016, http://www.thedrum.com/news/2016/09/30/online-ads-need-be-screen-least-14-seconds-be-seen-finds-eye-tracking-study; and Emma Beuckels, et al., "Keeping Up with Media Multitasking: An Eye-Tracking Study among Children and Adults to Investigate the Impact of Media Multitasking Behavior on Switching Frequency, Advertising Attention, and Advertising Effectiveness," *Journal of Advertising* 50, no. 2 (2021), 197–206.

24. Natalie Mortimer, "Baileys Aims to Turn Around 'Lack of Inconsistent Messaging' in Brand Repositioning to Trigger Year-Round Success," *The Drum,* November 29, 2016, http://www.thedrum.com/news/2016/11/29/baileys-aims-turn-around-lack-inconsistent-messaging-brand-repositioning-trigger.

25. See German Zenetti and Daniel Klapper, "Advertising Effects Under Consumer Heterogeneity—the Moderating Role of Brand Experience, Advertising Recall and Attitude," *Journal of Retailing* 92, no. 3 (September 2016), 352–372.

26. Lauren Johnson, "Big Brands Are Already Targeting Their Competitors With Apple Search Ads," *Adweek*, November 4, 2016, http://www.adweek.com/news/technology/big-brands-are-already-targeting-their-competitors-apple-search-ads-174432.

27. Dominique M. Hanssens, P. Leeflang, and D. R. Wittink, "Market Response Models and Marketing Practice," *Applied Stochastic Models in Business and Industry* 21, nos. 4–5 (July–October 2005), 437–438.

28. Joel Barajas, et al., "Experimental Designs and Estimation for Online Display Advertising Attribution in Marketplaces," *Marketing Science* 35, no. 3 (2016), 465–483.

29. Harlan E. Spotts, Marc G. Weinberger, and Michelle F. Weinberger, "Advertising and Promotional Effects on Consumer Service Firm Sales," *Journal of Advertising Research* 60, no. 1 (2020), 104–116.

30. John Parker, et al., "How Does Consumer Insight Support the Leap to a Creative Idea?" *Journal of Advertising Research* 61, no. 1 (2021), pp. 30–43.

31. Beth Bramstedt, "What's in a Name?" *Columbia Business Times (Missouri)*, December 28, 2015, http://columbiabusinesstimes.com/2015/12/28/whats-in-a-name/.

32. Helen R. Robinson and Stavros P. Kalafatis, "Why Do People Choose to Multitask with Media?" *Journal of Advertising Research* 60, no. 3 (2020), 251–270.

33. Dhruv Grewal, et al., "Mobile Advertising: A Framework and Research Agenda," *Journal of Interactive Marketing* 34 (2016), 3–14.

34. See, for example, Jae-Eun Kim, Stephen Lloyd, and Marie-Cécile Cervellon, "Narrative-Transportation Storylines in Luxury Brand Advertising: Motivating Consumer Engagement," *Journal of Business Research* 69, no. 1 (2016), 304–313.

35. Arch G. Woodside, "Predicting Advertising Execution Effectiveness: Scale Development and Validation," *European Journal of Marketing* 50, no. 1/2 (2016), 306–311.

36. Angeline Close Scheinbaum, et al., "Regret and Nonredemption of Daily Deals: Individual Differences and Contextual Elements," *Psychology & Marketing* 37, no. 4, 535–555.

Chapter 8

Planning Advertising and Integrated Brand Promotion

Learning Objectives

After reading and thinking about this chapter, you will be able to do the following:

1 Identify the seven components of an advertising plan.

2 Explain the role of the introduction of an advertising plan and what it entails.

3 Know what a situation analysis is and how it entails a cultural context, historical context, industry analysis, market analysis, and competitor analysis.

4 Identify common advertising objectives and the differences between communications and sales objectives.

5 Know the importance of budgeting for advertising and explain four methods for setting advertising budgets.

6 Discuss the role of strategy in advertising planning.

7 Identify the components of executing the advertising plan.

8 Define the evaluation component of an advertising plan and identify why it is important.

9 Discuss the role of the agency in planning advertising and IBP.

There is great complexity involved in preparing and executing a comprehensive advertising and integrated brand promotion (IBP) effort. As you will see in this chapter, the marketing team and participating agencies follow a detailed process of building an advertising effort based on several key features of the advertising plan. An advertising plan is the culmination of all the analyses used to understand consumer behavior, segment the market and position the brand, and conduct advertising research to support the delivery of creative, effective advertising and IBP campaigns (see Exhibit 8.1).

Exhibit 8.1 ▶ The advertising plan results from a thorough analysis of the environment, as shown in this framework diagram.

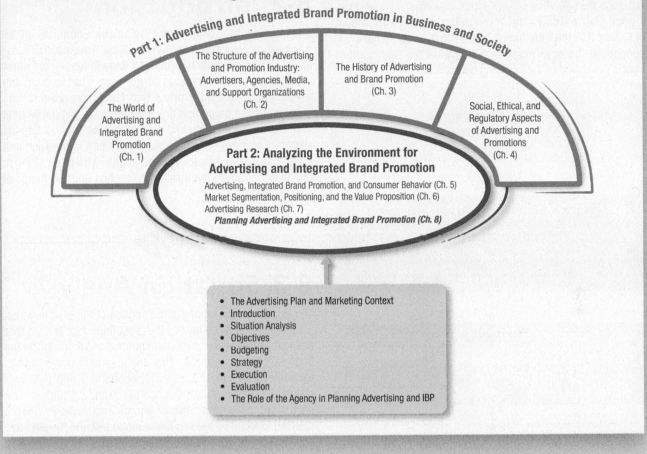

LO 1

8-1 The Advertising Plan and Marketing Context

An ad plan should be a direct extension of a firm's marketing plan. As suggested in the closing section of Chapter 6, one device that can be used to explicitly connect the marketing plan with the advertising plan is the statement of a brand's value proposition. A statement of what the brand is supposed to stand for in the eyes of the target segment stems from the firm's marketing strategy and will guide all ad-planning activities. The advertising plan, including all IBP activities, is a subset of the larger marketing plan. The IBP component must be integrated within the plan in a seamless and synergistic way. Everything has to work synergistically, whether the plan is for a global advertiser like Apple or for a small business with far fewer resources. At Apple, Steve Jobs knew that there is no substitute for good teamwork between agency and client in the development of compelling marketing and advertising plans.

An **advertising plan** outlines the thinking, tasks, and timetable needed to develop and implement an effective advertising effort. Apple is a good example of a company that uses advertising planning, because it activates the wide array of options that can be deployed in creating interest and communicating the value proposition for brands like the iPhone. When launching a new product, Apple and its multiple agencies choreograph a detailed plan of public relations activities, promotions and events, cooperative advertising, broadcast advertising, product placements, billboard advertising, digital media, and more to build anticipation and increase demand. The company and its agencies also plan for corporate advertising and IBP featuring the version of the logo of the apple with a bite removed in order to maintain overall brand preference and positive brand reactions.

As emphasized throughout this book, it's critical to think beyond traditional broadcast media and digital media when considering the best way to break through the clutter of the modern marketplace and get a message out to your customer. Apple does this by understanding consumer and business buying and media consumption behavior, harnessing the viral power of digital media, and using creativity to attract and engage targeted audiences. When you adopt the philosophy that *everything* is media, it's much easier to surround the consumer with a message and make a deep connection on behalf of the brand.[1]

Exhibit 8.2 shows the components of an advertising plan. Although the specifics will vary from advertiser to advertiser, a good plan will have the seven major components shown in Exhibit 8.2: the introduction, situation analysis, objectives, budgeting, strategy, execution, and evaluation. Each component is discussed in the following sections.

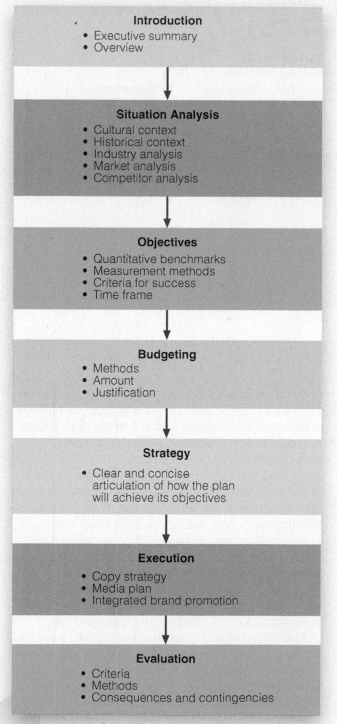

Introduction
- Executive summary
- Overview

Situation Analysis
- Cultural context
- Historical context
- Industry analysis
- Market analysis
- Competitor analysis

Objectives
- Quantitative benchmarks
- Measurement methods
- Criteria for success
- Time frame

Budgeting
- Methods
- Amount
- Justification

Strategy
- Clear and concise articulation of how the plan will achieve its objectives

Execution
- Copy strategy
- Media plan
- Integrated brand promotion

Evaluation
- Criteria
- Methods
- Consequences and contingencies

Exhibit 8.2 ▶ The advertising plan.

LO 2

8-2 Introduction

The introduction of an advertising plan consists of an **executive summary** and an overview. An executive summary, typically two paragraphs to a page in length, previews the most important aspects of the plan. That is what the reader should remember about the plan. An overview ranges in length from a paragraph to a few pages, setting out what is to be covered in the plan and highlighting the context. Use the summary and overview to make a good first impression and succinctly communicate with the people who must approve this plan, including the strategic direction and the financial considerations.

LO 3

8-3 Situation Analysis

The **situation analysis** is the section of the plan in which the client and agency lay out the most important factors that define the market and consumer situation and then explain the importance of each factor. This might include demographic, technology, social and cultural, economic, and political/regulatory factors that influence the brand's situation. The idea is not to be exhaustive or encyclopedic when writing a plan but to focus on the key factors that describe the situation and how they relate to the advertising and IBP decisions in the plan. For example, market segmentation and consumer research provide valuable insights that can be used for a situation analysis, as you saw in Chapters 6 and 7.[2]

Both demographic and psychographic trends are often important situational factors in advertising plans. Whether it's baby boomers, millennials, or members of generation Z, who or where the people are is usually where the sales are. As the population age distribution changes with time, new markets are created and eliminated. Knowing which generation(s) and what other elements to include in your targeting decisions is critical in your situation analysis.

For example, the fashion luxury brand Louis Vuitton recognizes that millennials and baby boomers alike have an interest in travel, and many of them prefer to travel with a purpose or to visit classic large cities in the world such as Paris, New York, Rome, and Tokyo. Therefore, the fashion company includes these important demographic segment in the situation analysis for its advertising plans. As shown in Exhibit 8.3, Louis Vuitton uses unique content marketing in a digital "magazine" microsite to inform and inspire the travel-seeking high-end customer, encouraging use of Louis Vuitton trunks and luggage (which are some of their most expensive products for sale on the brand e-commerce site). In addition, Louis Vuitton publishes city guides for many of these big cities that attract

Source: Louis Vuitton

Exhibit 8.3 ▶ The luxury brand Louis Vuitton helps sell the travel-oriented lifestyle as a way to subtly market their travel trunks and luggage as well as to help situate the brand as one that is compatible with high-end travel.

tourists as well as a photo book called *Cities on Earth*. Louis Vuitton's branding plans also provide for endorsers from pop culture, such as hiring actress HoYeon Jung from the Netflix series *Squid Game* as a brand ambassador (what they call a "global house ambassador").[3]

> "
> *When firms take the time to carefully research international markets, they can adapt their brands and avoid the serious pitfalls of ethnocentrism and self-reference criteria.*
> "

8-3a Cultural Context

International advertising is advertising that reaches across national and cultural boundaries. Adopting an international

perspective is often difficult for marketers and represents a major challenge in developing ad plans. The reason is that experience gained throughout a career and a lifetime creates a cultural "comfort zone." That is, one's own cultural values, experiences, and knowledge serve as subconscious guides for decision-making and behavior, which can introduce inadvertent bias.

Managers must overcome two related biases to be successful in international markets. **Ethnocentrism** is the tendency to view and value things from the perspective of one's own culture. Additionally, **self-reference criterion (SRC)** is the unconscious reference to one's own cultural values, experiences, and knowledge as a basis for decisions. These two closely related biases are the primary obstacles to success when conducting marketing and advertising planning that demands a cross-cultural perspective.

A decision maker's SRC and ethnocentrism can inhibit his/her/their ability to sense important cultural distinctions among markets. This in turn can blind advertisers to their own culture's "fingerprints" on the ads they've created. Sometimes these are offensive or, at a minimum, markers of "outsider" influence. Even the savviest of marketers can overlook cultural nuances in the development of their advertising plans.

Toyota's launch of the Prado Land Cruiser in China provides a nice example of the challenges a firm must overcome in developing advertising to reach across national and cultural boundaries. To launch its SUV in China, Toyota's ad agency Saatchi & Saatchi created a print campaign showing a Prado driving past two large stone lions, which were saluting and bowing to the Prado. This seems to make sense, as the stone lion is a traditional sign of power in the Chinese culture. As one Saatchi executive put it, "These ads were intended to reflect Prado's imposing presence when driving in the city: You cannot but respect the Prado."[4]

But Chinese consumers saw it differently. Chinese words often have multiple meanings, and "Prado" can be translated into Chinese as *badao*, which means "rule by force" or "overbearing." In addition, the use of the stone lions prompted scathing online comments about a contentious time in China's relationship with Japan.[5] These of course are not the kind of reactions that an advertiser is looking for when launching a new product. The automaker quickly pulled 30 magazine and newspaper ads and issued a formal apology. This controversy shows that no one, not even highly experienced global marketers and agencies, is immune to the subtle but powerful influences of culture.

To really understand cultural context, it's important to spend time researching consumers in any geographic market you are targeting. In doing so, several firms have cleverly and successfully adapted their brands to big foreign markets like India and China. PepsiCo learned that Indian consumers might find the firm's Frito-Lay chips somewhat bland, so they reformulated the product as a spicier snack called Kurkure. Similarly, Oreo's parent company altered the sandwich cookie for the Chinese market by using less sugar and adding green tea as a flavoring.[6] KitKat is a global brand that keeps innovating both products and promotions to fit each market (see Exhibit 8.4). When firms take the time to carefully research international markets, they can adapt their brands and avoid the serious pitfalls of ethnocentrism and self-reference criteria.[7]

8-3b Historical Context

No situation is entirely new, but all situations are unique. Just how a firm arrived at the current situation is very important. An advertising agency and the brand's management should be familiar with the history of the industry and the competitive dynamics, the brand, the corporate culture, critical moments in the company's past, its big mistakes, and its big successes. The fact is that no matter what advertising decisions are made in the present, the past has a significant impact. At the very least, you should know why previous ad campaigns were particularly effective or why they flopped, so you can apply the lessons learned when planning new and better campaigns. Also remember that what worked in the past may not work today, given changes in business and society or other factors in the overall advertising environment.[8] Use this section of the advertising plan to explain not only the historical context, but also the significance of this background as a foundation for IBP decisions to be implemented today and tomorrow.

8-3c Industry Analysis

An **industry analysis** is just that; it focuses on developments and trends within an entire industry and on any other factors that may make a difference in how an advertiser proceeds with an advertising plan. An industry analysis should enumerate and discuss the most important aspects of a given industry, including the supply side of the supply–demand equation. Most market analyses focus almost exclusively on a demand-side analysis—how much **market share** can we get and how many units can we sell? Market share is the percentage or portion of the market that a company or brand has in sales. But when great advertising overstimulates demand that can't be matched by supply, one can end up with lots of unhappy customers and a harmed brand position.

No industry faces more dramatic trends and swings in consumers' tastes than the food business. In recent years, the gluten-free trend has challenged industry giants—from Unilever to Kellogg's—to develop new products and reformulate old ones to satisfy consumers' growing concerns about healthy eating. With sales of gluten-free foods growing more than 10 percent a year, this is a sizable segment being targeted by many advertisers, both large and small (see Exhibit 8.5).[9] If your brand competes in the food industry, you'll be looking at this and other trends when you analyze the industry and the dynamics shaping its size and direction.

Source: Nestle

Exhibit 8.4 ▶ Integrated brand promotion in action: KitKat.
KitKat adapts its products and communications for each country's culture (South Africa at left, Japan at right). *Do you think KitKat's advertising plans should include translating the brand name into local languages?*

Source: Udi's Healthy Foods

Udi's Gluten Free @udisglutenfree · Dec 4

What's better with your daily latte than some Udi's #glutenfree cookies? Possibly nothing. #NationalCookieDay

Shop: bit.ly/2gK58pX

Exhibit 8.5 ▶ Udi's Gluten Free Tweet.

8-3d Market Analysis

A **market analysis** complements the industry analysis, emphasizing the demand side of the equation. In a market analysis, an advertiser examines the factors that drive and determine the overall market for a product or service category within which the advertiser offers a brand (or brands). First, the advertiser needs to decide what the market is for a product category. Don't look at current users alone, because that approach ignores consumers who might otherwise be entering the market category through lifestyle, demographic, technological, cultural, or attitudinal changes.

Instead, begin by identifying the current **user base** for your product category, which broadly refers to the current customers who are using (or who have recently used/purchased your product or service). Determine the size of this current customer base and the reason these people are current users. Consumers' motivations for using one product or service category but not another may give you insight regarding the future of that category. If there are forces signaling that demand for a product category may grow, then the firm's slice of that market has an opportunity to grow as well. The advertiser's job in a market analysis is to determine the most important market factors and understand how they may affect overall market demand. If cultural factors such as changing technology or fashion are affecting demand, for example, this should be explained in the market analysis.

8-3e Competitor Analysis

Once you've analyzed the industry and market, you need to conduct a **competitor analysis**. Here you identify the competitors to your firm's brand(s) and discuss their strengths and weaknesses and the opportunities and threats each may pose. Don't limit yourself to current competitors. You should also consider potential and indirect competition from different industries or from startups and the possible appeal these emerging brands could have among your targeted audiences. This enables you to build a flexible, realistic, and dynamic ad plan for competing in an ever-changing market.

When archrivals go head-to-head trying to win customers' loyalty, it is common to see their ads feature a competitive positioning strategy, as discussed in Chapter 6. Sometimes advertisers notice that an ad or IBP campaign is working so well for a competitor that they want to try a very similar approach. Case in point: Apple's ad campaigns that focus on "Privacy. That's iPhone," which run on websites and in other media. These feature aspects of the iPhone such as app tracking transparency and has made privacy front and center, as can be seen in Exhibit 8.6 by the privacy statement on the brand's website under "core values." It is smart for a company to align their ads and branding to their core values. In a similar fashion, Samsung (a main competitor) is also focusing more on privacy and it has confirmed that it will be removing ads from the apps that the new smart phones come with and its new Galaxy phone will be priced similarly to the iPhone.[10] Note however that analytics are still important in determining what advertising approach to use to best drive sales for any brand.[11]

8-4 Objectives

Advertising objectives lay the framework for the subsequent tasks in an advertising plan and take many different forms. Objectives identify the goals of the advertiser in concrete terms. The advertiser, more often than not, has more than one objective for an ad campaign. An advertiser's objective may be:

1. to increase consumer awareness of and curiosity about its brand,
2. to change consumers' beliefs or attitudes about its brand,
3. to influence the purchase intent of customers and potential customers,
4. to stimulate trial use of the brand,
5. to convert one-time brand users into repeat purchasers,
6. to switch consumers from a competing brand to its brand, or
7. to increase sales (which is not, strictly speaking, an appropriate objective for advertising alone to achieve).

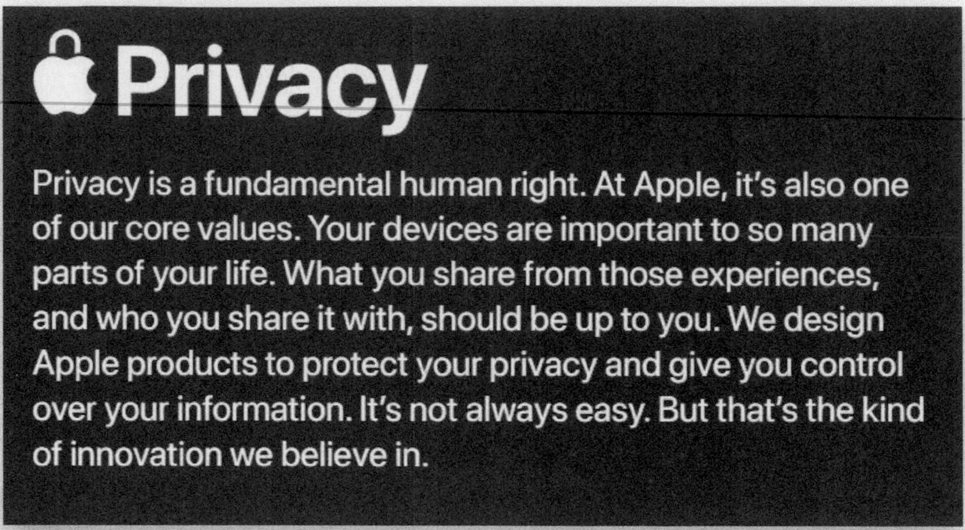

Privacy
Privacy is a fundamental human right. At Apple, it's also one of our core values. Your devices are important to so many parts of your life. What you share from those experiences, and who you share it with, should be up to you. We design Apple products to protect your privacy and give you control over your information. It's not always easy. But that's the kind of innovation we believe in.

Source: Apple Inc

Exhibit 8.6 ▶ Apple has shifted their campaign focus largely from camera quality to how they focus on privacy, which is stated as one of the company's core values.

Let's consider each of these objectives separately. Creating or maintaining brand awareness is a fundamental advertising objective. **Brand awareness** is an indicator of consumer knowledge about the existence of the brand and how easily that knowledge can be retrieved from memory. For example, a market researcher might ask a consumer to name "top-of-mind" companies. **Top-of-mind awareness** is represented by the brand listed first. Ease of retrieval from memory is important, because for many goods or services, ease of retrieval is predictive of market share.

This proved to be the case for Aflac (American Family Life Assurance Co.), the insurance company that uses a determined duck quacking *aaa-flack* in its ad campaigns to build brand awareness and positive associations. That duck, which is still an integral part of the company's advertising plans, helped Aflac become a household name, and a major player in the U.S. insurance market (see Exhibit 8.7). Targeting millennials with humorous messages, Aflac uses the duck to get the audience's attention and communicate important points about insurance.[12]

Social media offer tremendous opportunities for brand strategists to engage consumers and create brand awareness. Social media is great for measurable digital engagement, as we can see how many clicks, likes, comments, shares, or other online consumer behaviors resulted directly from the ad. For instance, some ads on social media even look like the

CRAZY LEGZ
LIL' CHUTE
KEEP YOUR LIFESTYLE HEALTHY
Aflac
aflac.com/lifestyle
0:26 / 0:30

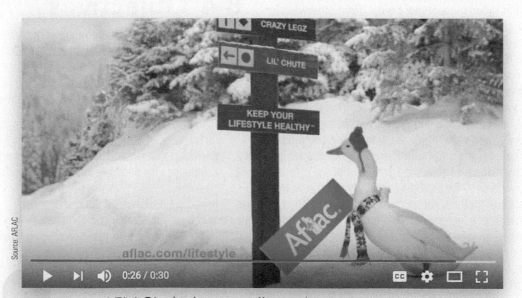

Source: AFLAC

Exhibit 8.7 ▶ AFLAC's duck gets millennial attention.

posts or consumer photos in a social media feed. This is a subtle way to keep top-of-mind awareness high when you are searching for a related good.[13]

Creating, changing, or reinforcing attitudes is another important function of advertising and thus makes for a common advertising objective. As we saw in Chapter 5, one way to go about changing people's attitudes is to give them information designed to alter their beliefs. There are many ways to approach this task. One way is to give some information and then suggest that the consumer go somewhere specific for more details, such as their doctor. The prescription drug ad in Exhibit 8.8 cannot possibly communicate much detailed medical information in its limited space, which is why it is crucial to get information from physicians more so than from advertisers. Conversely, one can let a picture tell the entire story of the brand and its image, as the iconic brand Chanel does in Exhibit 8.9. Notice how few words are in the ad and the prominence of the product. Think about how recent lipstick or makeup ads feature celebrities more prominently than the product; it is important to take a step back and make sure your advertising puts the product front and center in many cases. Whether through direct, logical arguments, or thought-provoking visual imagery, advertisements are frequently designed to deliver their objective of belief formation and attitude change.

Purchase intent is another objective often set by advertisers. Purchase intent is determined by asking consumers whether they intend to buy a product or service in the near future. The appeal of influencing purchase intent is that intent is closer to actual behavior, and thus closer to the desired sale, than attitudes are. Simply stated, using advertising and IBP to affect purchase intent is a matter of elevating the brand's esteem in the minds of consumers so that *next time* they make a purchase, the firm's brand is just that much closer to being the one chosen.

Trial usage reflects actual behavior and is commonly used as an advertising objective. Many times, the best that we can ask of advertising is to encourage the consumer to try our

Exhibit 8.8 ▶ When advertising prescription drugs, information is much more important than image to consumers. Consumers should always heed the call in such advertising that carefully says "ask your doctor about" the drug, as advertising in certain forms can't always give all the information that is truly needed when it comes to health.

Exhibit 8.9 ▶ Established advertisers such as Chanel do not need to give consumers a lot of information when the product takes front and center stage in advertising.

brand. At that point, the product or service must live up to the expectations created by our advertising.[14] In the case of new products, stimulating trial usage is critically important. In the marketing realm, the angels sing when the initial purchase rate of a new product or service is high. Of course, trial usage is facilitated by a variety of IBP tools—coupons, rebates, free samples, and premium offers (buy one item and get another item attached for free).

The **repeat purchase**, or conversion, objective is aimed at the percentage of consumers who try a new product and then purchase it a second time. A second purchase is also a reason for great rejoicing. The odds of long-term product success go way up when this percentage is high. In-package coupons and rebates on the initial purchases are IBP tools ideally suited to this objective.

Brand switching is the most competitively aggressive objective. In some product categories, switching is commonplace, even the norm—as in garbage bags or paper towels. In others, it is rare—as in toothpaste. When setting a brand-switching objective, the advertiser must neither expect too much nor rejoice too much over a temporary gain. Persuading consumers to switch brands can be a long and expensive task, needing careful budgeting to balance the return on investment.[15] For instance, brand switching and changes in the way consumers shop has been changed by the global COVID-19 pandemic, and one of the areas of new emphasis is for consumers to switch not just specific brands (say from Apple to Samsung or vice versa) but to new ways of doing things in the marketplace. Consider the example of Everlywell, a brand that does at home lab testing in healthcare and provides digital results quickly; this is a major switch for customers who previously went to the doctor's office or medical labs for such testing.[16]

What about setting an objective for "increasing sales" through advertising and IBP? This is actually a marketing plan objective, not an advertising plan objective. Why? First, only the right product, strategically priced, with proper distribution, and then supported by effective advertising and promotion, has the potential to increase sales. Second, to state that the objective is "to increase sales" is completely devoid of any strategic process or purpose. The next section delves into this discussion in more detail.

8-4a Communications versus Sales Objectives

Some advertising analysts argue that communications objectives are the *only* legitimate objectives for advertising, because advertising is but one variable in the marketing mix and cannot be held solely responsible for sales. Rather, advertising should be held responsible for creating awareness of a brand, communicating information about product features or availability, or developing a favorable attitude that can lead to consumer preference for a brand. All of these outcomes are long term and based on communications impact.

There are some major benefits to maintaining a strict communications perspective in setting advertising objectives. First, by viewing advertising as primarily a communication effort, marketers can consider a broader range of advertising strategies. Second, they can gain a greater appreciation for the complexity of the overall communications process. Designing an integrated communications program with sales as the sole objective neglects aspects of message design, media choice, public relations, or sales force deployment that should be effectively integrated across all phases of a firm's communication efforts. Using advertising messages to support the efforts of the sales force and/or drive people to your website is an example of integrating diverse communication tools to build synergy that then may ultimately produce a sale.

Yet there is always a voice somewhere in the organization forcibly offering the perspective that there is one leading rule: *Advertising must sell.*[17] Nowhere is the tension between communication and sales objectives better exemplified than in the annual debate about what advertisers really get for the tremendous sums of money they invest on Super Bowl ads. Every year, great fanfare accompanies the ads that appear during the Super Bowl, and numerous polls are taken after the game to assess the year's most memorable ads. But more often than not, these polls turn out to be nothing more than popularity contests, with the usual suspects—like Budweiser, for example—having all the fun. The question remains: Does likability translate to sales?

Although there is a natural tension between those who advocate sales objectives and those who push communications objectives, nothing precludes a marketer from using both types when developing an overall plan for a brand. Indeed, combining marketing plan sales objectives such as market share and **household penetration** (the number of homes that an ad or marketing effort gets to) with advertising plan communications objectives such as awareness and attitude change can be an excellent means of motivating and evaluating the planning effort. Unilever, the Anglo-Dutch consumer goods conglomerate, seeks to strike just the right balance between communications and sales objectives with the strategy the chief marketing officer (CMO) calls "magic along with logic." Unilever had a history of winning creative advertising awards (Cannes) but watching market share shrink. The CMO rebalanced the creative communications and sales emphasis and started producing sales growth in the 7 percent range—near the top of the firm's competitive set.[18] Looking ahead, Unilever is more fully integrating its marketing, digital advertising, and sales promotion activities to not just stimulate but actually facilitate consumer purchasing in stores and online.[19]

Objectives that enable a firm to make intelligent decisions about resource allocation must be stated in an advertising plan in terms specific to the organization. Articulating such well-stated objectives is easier when advertising planners do the following:

1. *Establish a quantitative benchmark.* Objectives for advertising are measurable only in the context of quantifiable variables. Advertising planners should begin with quantified measures of the current status of market share, awareness, attitude, or other factors that advertising is expected to influence. The measurement of effectiveness in quantitative terms requires a knowledge of the level of variables of interest before an advertising effort and also afterward. For example, a statement of objectives in quantified and measurable terms might be, "Increase the market share of heavy users of the product category using our brand from 22 to 25 percent."

2. *Specify measurement methods and criteria for success.* It is important that the factors being measured be directly related to the objectives being pursued. If changes in sales are expected, then measure sales. If increased awareness is the goal, then change in consumer awareness is the true measure of success. This may seem obvious, but in a classic study of advertising objectives, it was found that claims of success for advertising were unrelated to the original statements of objective in 69 percent of the cases.[20] In this research, firms cited increases in sales as proof of success of advertising when the original objectives were related to factors such as awareness, conviction to a brand, or product-use information.

3. *Specify a time frame.* Objectives for advertising should include a statement of the period of time allowed for the desired results to occur. For communications-based objectives, the measurement of response may occur frequently during the campaign (such as by measuring the number of branded hashtag retweets), but the final results will not be determined until the end of an entire multiweek campaign. The point is that the time period for accomplishment of an objective and the related measurement period must be stated in advance in the ad plan.

These criteria for setting objectives help ensure that the planning process is organized and well directed. By relying on quantitative benchmarks, an advertiser has guidelines for making future decisions. Linking measurement criteria to objectives provides a basis for the equitable evaluation of the success or failure of advertising. Finally, the specification of a time frame for judging results keeps the planning process moving forward. As in all things, however, moderation is a healthy thing. A single-minded obsession with watching the numbers can be dangerous in that it minimizes or entirely misses the importance of qualitative and intuitive factors.

8-5 Budgeting

Advertising is an investment, not an expense. One of the most challenging and important tasks is budgeting the funds for an advertising and IBP effort. **Budgeting** is the act of planning how much will be spent each period (month, quarter, year) and in what areas. Within a firm, budget recommendations come up through the ranks; for example, from a brand manager to a category manager and ultimately to the executive in charge of marketing. The sequence then reverses itself for the allocation and spending of funds. In a small firm, such as an independent retailer, the sequence just described may include only one individual who plays all the roles. In large firms, CMOs generally pay attention to the bigger picture and delegate budgetary responsibility to the vice president of communications or to managers at the brand strategy level.[21]

In some cases, a firm will rely on its advertising agency to make recommendations regarding the size of the advertising budget. When this is done, it is typically the account executive at the agency in charge of the brand who will analyze the firm's objectives and its creative and media needs and then make a recommendation to the company. The account exec's budget planning will likely include working closely with the brand and product-group managers to determine an appropriate spending level.

To be as judicious and accountable as possible in spending money on advertising and IBP, marketers rely on various methods for setting an advertising budget. Each of these methods has both advantages and disadvantages, as you will see.

8-5a Percentage of Sales

A **percentage-of-sales approach** to budgeting calculates the budget based on a percentage of the prior year's sales or the projected year's sales. This technique is easy to understand and implement. The budget decision makers merely specify that a particular percentage of either last year's sales or the current year's estimated sales will be allocated to the advertising process. It is common to spend between 2 and 12 percent of sales on advertising and IBP depending on the product category.

Even though simplicity is certainly an advantage in decision-making, the percentage-of-sales approach has drawbacks. First, when a firm's sales are decreasing, the advertising budget will automatically decline. Periods of decreasing sales may be precisely the time when a firm needs to increase spending on advertising; if a percentage-of-sales budgeting method is being used, this won't happen. Second, this budgeting method can easily result in overspending on advertising. Once funds have been earmarked, the tendency is to find ways to spend the budgeted amount. Third, and the most serious drawback from a strategic standpoint, is that the percentage-of-sales approach does not relate advertising and IBP dollars to objectives. Basing spending on past or future sales implicitly presumes a cause-and-effect relationship between advertising and sales, with sales appearing to "cause" advertising. That's backward.

A variation on the percentage-of-sales approach is to base current spending on "historical spending levels"—whatever that is. The only reason we raise this perspective here is that when managers are asked how they allocate their advertising budgets, nearly 70 percent have responded to surveys with the answer "based on historical levels."[22] We suspect they are referring to percentage-of-sales or an even less defensible "whatever we can get" approach to spending, but we want to alert you to the prospect of hearing language like this in budget discussions.

8-5b Share of Market/Share of Voice

"With this method, a firm monitors the amount spent by various significant competitors on advertising and allocates an amount equal to the amount of money spent by competitors or an amount proportional to (or slightly greater than) the firm's market share relative to the competition."[23] This will provide the advertiser with a **share of voice**, or an advertising presence in the market, that is equal to or greater than the competitors' share of advertising voice.

This method is often used for advertising-budget allocations when a new product is introduced. Conventional wisdom suggests that some multiple of the desired first-year market share, often 2.5 to 4 times, should be spent in terms of share-of-voice advertising expenditures. For example, if an advertiser wants a 2 percent first-year share, it would need to spend up to 8 percent of the total dollar amount spent in the industry (for an 8 percent share of voice). The logic is that a new product will need a significant share of voice to gain notice among a group of existing, well-established brands.[24]

Although the share-of-voice approach is sound in its emphasis on competitors' activities, there are important challenges to consider. First, it may be difficult to gain access to precise information on competitors' spending. Second, there is no reason to believe that competitors are spending their money wisely. Third, the flaw in logic with this method is the assumption that every advertising/IBP effort is of the same quality and will have the same effect from a creative-execution standpoint. Such an assumption is especially shaky when one tries to compare expenditure levels across today's diverse advertising forms.[25] Take Dove's experience with Super Bowl advertising versus its short films placed on YouTube. These films include topics of *#BeautyBias*, *My Beauty, My Say*, and *Feeling Good: Celebrating Black Natural Hair*. While the brand offers a variety of films designed to empower people, their short film, *Dove Evolution*, was an especially compelling example of a dichotomy in advertising investments. The short film generated a major traffic spike at CampaignForRealBeauty.com, three times more than Dove's Super Bowl ad.[26] The YouTube video aired for $0, versus $2 million or so for the Super Bowl ad. No doubt that *Dove Evolution* was a huge contributor to Dove's share of voice at the time, but predicting the effects of innovative executions such as this one will always challenge conventional models.

8-5c Response Models

Using response models to aid the budgeting process has been a widespread practice among larger firms for many years.[27] The belief is that greater objectivity can be maintained with such models. Although this may or may not be the case, response models do provide useful information on what a given company's advertising response function looks like. An **advertising response function** is a mathematical relationship that associates dollars spent on advertising and sales generated. To the extent that past advertising predicts future sales, this method is valuable. Using marginal analysis, an advertiser would continue spending on advertising as long as its marginal spending was exceeded by marginal sales. Margin analysis answers the advertiser's question, "How much more will sales increase if we spend an additional dollar on advertising?" As the rate of return on advertising expenditures declines, the wisdom of additional spending is challenged.

Theoretically, this method leads to a point at which an optimal advertising expenditure results in an optimal sales level and, in turn, an optimal profit. The relationship between sales, profit, and advertising spending is shown in the marginal analysis graph in Exhibit 8.10. Data on sales, prior advertising expenditures, and consumer awareness are typical of the numerical input to such quantitative models.

Unfortunately, the advertising-to-sales relationship assumes simple causality, even though many other factors in addition to advertising affect sales directly. Still, some feel that the use of response models is a better budgeting method than guessing, applying the percentage-of-sales, or using the other budgeting methods discussed thus far.

8-5d Objective and Task

The methods we just discussed for establishing an advertising budget all suffer from the same fundamental deficiency: a lack of specification of how expenditures are related to advertising objectives. The only method of budget setting that focuses on the relationship between spending and advertising/IBP objectives is the **objective-and-task approach**. This method begins with the stated objectives for a campaign. Goals related to production costs, target audience reach, message effects, behavioral effects, media placement, duration of the effort, and the like are then specified. Next, the specific

Sales ($)

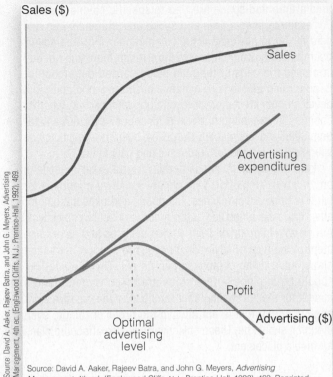

Source: David A. Aaker, Rajeev Batra, and John G. Meyers, Advertising Management, 4th ed. (Englewood Cliffs, N.J.: Prentice-Hall, 1992), 469.

Source: David A. Aaker, Rajeev Batra, and John G. Meyers, *Advertising Management*, 4th ed. (Englewood Cliffs, N.J.: Prentice-Hall, 1992), 469. Reprinted by permission of the authors.

Exhibit 8.10 ▶ Sales, profit, and advertising curves used in marginal analysis.

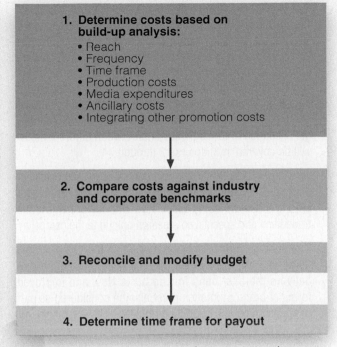

Exhibit 8.11 ▶ Steps in implementing the objective-and-task budgeting approach.

tasks necessary to achieve different aspects of the objectives are outlined, and the associated budget is determined.

There are many reasons to recommend this method for budgeting. A firm identifies any and all tasks it believes are related to achieving its objectives. Should the total dollar figure for the necessary tasks be beyond the firm's financial capability, a solution must be developed. But even if a compromise with a smaller budget is agreed upon, the firm has at least identified what *should* have been budgeted to pursue its objectives.

The objective-and-task approach is the most logical and defensible method for calculating and then allocating an advertising and IBP budget. It is the only budgeting method that specifically relates spending to the objectives being pursued. It is widely used among major advertisers. For these reasons, we will consider the specific procedures for implementing the objective-and-task budgeting method.

8-5e Implementing the Objective-and-Task Budgeting Method

Proper implementation of the objective-and-task approach requires a data-based, systematic procedure. Because the

approach ties spending levels to specific advertising goals, the process depends on proper execution of the objective-setting process described earlier. Once a firm and its agency are satisfied with the specificity and direction of stated objectives, a series of well-defined steps can be taken to implement the objective-and-task method. These steps are shown in Exhibit 8.11 and summarized in the following sections.

Determine Costs Based on Build-Up Analysis

Having identified specific objectives, an advertiser can now begin determining what tasks are necessary for the accomplishment of those objectives. In using a **build-up analysis**—building up the expenditure levels for tasks—the following factors must be considered in terms of costs:

- *Reach:* The geographic and demographic exposure the advertising is to achieve

- *Frequency:* The number of exposures required to accomplish the desired objectives

- *Time frame:* The estimate of when communications will occur and during what time period

- *Production costs:* The estimated costs associated with the planned execution of advertisements

- *Media expenditures:* Given the preceding factors, the advertiser can now define the appropriate media, media mix, and frequency of insertions that will directly address the objectives that have been set. Further, differences in geographic allocation, with special attention to regional or local media strategies, and digital and mobile strategies are considered at this point. For example, advertisers that want to encourage viral sharing of content need to budget for targeting influential social media users who will initiate the sharing phenomenon.[28] The complete discussion of strategic allocation of funds across and between different media will be covered in Chapters 12 through 14.

- *Ancillary costs:* There will be a variety of related costs not directly accounted for in the preceding factors. Prominent among these are costs associated with advertising to the trade itself and specialized research unique to the campaign.

- *Integrating other promotional costs:* In this era of advertising and IBP, sometimes it is the novel promotion that delivers the best bang for the buck. New and improved forms of brand promotion must also be considered as part of the planning and budgeting process.

Compare Costs against Industry and Corporate Benchmarks

After compiling all the costs through a build-up analysis, an advertiser will want to make a quick reality check. This is accomplished by checking the percentage of sales that the estimated set of costs represents relative to industry standards for percentage of sales allocated to advertising. If most competitors are spending 4 to 6 percent of gross sales on advertising, how does the current budget compare to this percentage? Another recommended technique is to identify the share of industry advertising that the firm's budget represents. Another relevant reference point is to compare the current budget with prior budgets. If the total dollar amount is extraordinarily high or low compared to previous years, this variance should be justified based on the objectives being pursued. The use of percentage of sales on both an industry and internal corporate basis provides a reference point only, to judge whether a budgeted amount is so unusual that it might need re-evaluation.

Reconcile and Modify the Budget

The objective-and-task approach is designed to identify what a firm will realistically need to spend in order to achieve the desired impact. To avoid major modifications to the ad budget, it's important to be familiar with corporate policy and financial resources at the outset while setting objectives and planning tasks. Modifications to a proposed budget are common, but having to make radical cuts in proposed spending can be disruptive.

Determine a Time Frame for Payout

When budgeting, know when the funding for tasks should be made available. Travel expenses, production expenses, and media time and space are tied to specific calendar dates. For example, media time and space are often acquired and paid for far in advance of the completion of finished advertisements. Knowing when and how much money is needed improves the odds of the plan being carried out smoothly. Bear in mind that today's dynamic business world and rapid developments in media will require budget flexibility, whether changes in expenditure levels or changes in payout allocation. Still, for accountability purposes, budgets should include specific time frames for purchases and payments.

Like any other business activity, a marketer must take on an advertising effort with clearly specified intentions for what is to be accomplished. Intentions and expectations for advertising are embodied in the process of setting objectives. Armed with information from market planning and an assessment of the type of advertising needed to support marketing plans, advertising objectives can be set. These objectives should be in place before steps are taken to determine a budget for the advertising effort and before the creative work begins. Again, this is not always the order of things, even though it should be. These objectives will also affect the plans for media placement.

— LO **6** —

8-6 Strategy

Look back at Exhibit 8.2, which shows that after budgeting, strategy is the next major component of the advertising plan. Strategy represents the mechanism by which something is to be done, the means to the end (accomplishing the objectives). Every plan should state clearly and concisely what strategy will be implemented to achieve the desired results. There are numerous possibilities for advertising strategies.

The Olympic Games are often the backdrop for advertising and IBP campaigns based on a variation of the strategy of associating a brand with sports excellence. For example, Athleta spotlighted Simone Biles and Allyson Felix during the recent Summer Olympics, part of the strategy to highlight the brand's commitment to showcasing women's limitless potential. Athleta wasn't an official Olympics sponsor and therefore couldn't include the word "Olympics" or show the famous interlocking rings in its campaign. Instead, the reinvigorated "Power of She" campaign focused on the physical and mental challenges of preparing to compete at the highest athletic level.[29]

More sophisticated goals call for more sophisticated strategies. You are limited only by your resources: financial, organizational, and creative. Ultimately, strategy formulation is a creative endeavor with input from diverse sources. Many ad agencies assign an account planner to synthesize all relevant consumer research about the brand and draw inferences that will help the agency and the advertiser develop an appropriate and effective strategy. You will learn a great deal more about the connection between ad objectives and creative strategy options in Chapter 10.

LO 7

8-7 Execution

The actual "doing" is the execution of the plan, making and placing ads across all media as well as coordinating IBP activities to achieve synergistic results. There are two elements to the execution of an advertising plan: determining the copy strategy and devising a media plan.

8-7a Copy Strategy

A copy strategy consists of copy objectives and methods, or tactics. The objectives state what the advertiser intends to accomplish in headlines, subheads, and text, while the methods describe how the objectives will be achieved. Chapter 11 will deal extensively with these executional issues.

8-7b Media Plan

The media plan specifies exactly where ads will be placed and what strategy is behind their placement. In an integrated communications environment, this is much more complicated than it might first appear. Back when there were just three broadcast television networks, there were already more than a million different combinations of placements that could be made. With the ubiquity of media and promotion options today, the permutations are almost infinite.

It is at this point—devising a media plan—where all the money is spent and so much could be saved. This is where the profitability of many agencies is really determined. Media placement strategy can make a huge difference in profits or losses and is considered in depth in Part 4 of the text. In addition, the dynamic influence on media planning of digital devices is another point of emphasis in Part 4, as advertisers plan for more precisely targeted messages delivered at precisely the right time, ideally with efficiency that keeps media costs in check.[30]

8-7c Integrated Brand Promotion

Many different forms of brand promotion may accompany the advertising effort in launching or maintaining a brand; these should be spelled out as part of the overall plan. There should be a complete integration of all communication tools in developing and activating the plan (see more about this in Part 5). For example, Mondelez International's advertising plans for the Oreo brand include commercials, print ads, social media messages, and other IBP activities to reinforce brand preference and to introduce new flavors and brand extensions (see Exhibit 8.12). Mondelez's situation analysis indicated the challenges of achieving revenue growth in a

Source: Oreo

Exhibit 8.12 ▶ Oreo is social media savvy and uses a humor appeal for hipsters; better yet, the message is measurable via digital engagement metrics such as likes or shares. Oreo is more than 100 years old, yet the brand has more than 42 million Facebook fans.

tepid global economy and highly competitive marketplace. But the historical context also indicated widespread brand awareness for Oreo. Market analysis showed significant opportunity for launching new Oreo-branded products in markets where chocolate consumption is high. Further, cultural context was a key element in the decision to develop product variations for different countries, including China and Japan.

The ad plans for Oreo have detailed budgets and schedules for integrated activities keyed to specific products and seasonal events (such as Halloween and Thanksgiving). They also have objectives and specific tasks for successfully introducing ongoing products like Oreo candy bars, Oreo Double Enjoyment cookies in China, and limited-edition tins of holiday Oreo cookies. Mondelez has been increasing its use of digital media not only to stretch its ad budget but also to encourage interactivity through messages on the Oreo Twitter account, the Oreo Facebook page, and other platforms. The company carefully measures results and then adjusts its plans or takes plans in a different direction as it sees what works and what doesn't work. If a particular message or creative approach is especially effective, Oreo looks for opportunities to apply lessons learned to other parts of its ad plan.[31]

8-8 Evaluation

The final, yet important, stage in the ad plan is the evaluation component. This is where an advertiser determines how it will measure the results of the plan's advertising and IBP activities. Metrics for evaluating advertising and IBP activities vary, depending on the objectives set and the creative and media choices made. If an outside agency is involved, this part of the plan also explains the criteria that will be applied to agency performance and how long the agency will have to achieve the agreed-upon objectives. In a world where the pressures on companies to deliver short-term profitability continue to intensify, advertising agencies find themselves under increasing pressure to demonstrate agreed-upon, quantifiable outcomes from all advertising and IBP activities. For example, digital analytics can show some results of digital advertising or social media marketing in real time, such as number of exposures, clicks, or shares. Many large advertisers are also seeking to pare the number of agencies they use, not just to save money but also to streamline and speed up the planning and implementation process.[32] Agency performance is therefore subject to formal evaluations.

Even when agencies perform well in helping their clients with effective advertising and IBP, a company that changes its advertising and IBP strategy may choose a new agency for a fresh take on the situation. For instance, the travel industry has become more mature and competitive, especially as a pandemic slowed down and changed the way in which people choose to travel. As a way to make some changes to the travel brand, Travelocity has changed their creative account from Proof Advertising to an ad agency named Doner (see Exhibit 8.13 for an example of a creative approach for Travelocity in their "Romantic Cabana" 30 second spot).[33]

8-9 The Role of the Agency in Planning Advertising and IBP

Now that we have covered key aspects of the advertising planning process, one other issue should be considered. Because most marketers rely heavily on the expertise of an advertising agency (or specialized agencies for specific creative or media assignments), understanding the role an agency plays in the advertising planning process is important. Various agencies will approach their craft with different points of emphasis. Even though not everyone does it the same way, it is still important to ask: What contribution to the planning effort can and should an advertiser expect from its agency?

The advertiser should be able to clearly identify, in the external environment, the opportunities and threats that can be addressed with advertising. It should also bring to the planning effort a well-articulated statement of a brand's value proposition and the marketing mix elements designed to gain and sustain competitive advantage. In some cases, the ad agency may take an active role in helping the client

What's stopping you from Seizing Your Someday? Travelocity is here to help.

Source: Travelocity

Exhibit 8.13 ▶ Travelocity is an example of a client who had an ad agency switch, which may have likely corresponded to a big change in how people perceive travel during and after a global pandemic and thus may benefit from a fresh creative strategy.

formulate the marketing plan. Indeed, when things are going right, it can be hard to say exactly where the client's work ended and the agency's work began. The agency's crucial role is to translate the current market and marketing status of a firm and its advertising objectives into advertising strategy and, ultimately, finished advertisements and IBP materials. Here, message strategies and tactics for the advertising effort and for the efficient and effective placement of ads in media need to be hammered out with the approval of the advertiser so the agency can use design and creative execution to bring marketing strategies to life.

Advertisers generally need help from agencies in two key areas. The first involves integration. Given the dynamic media environment, clients want and expect the agency to be an expert on a wide array of options for getting the message out to the target consumer. They need the various divisions and departments in an agency to be working as a team, coming up with *integrated brand promotion* solutions that build synergy between and among multiple channels. Second, clients need agencies to provide new ideas and fresh approaches to break through the ever-increasing clutter. In a survey that posed the question, "What do clients want?" the top four priorities are timeless: creativity (92.7 percent), data and analytics (92.0 percent), efficient business processes (91.4 percent), and effective money managers (89.4 percent).[34]

As discussed throughout this book, clients expect real results from their investments in advertising. The best way for

agencies to successfully manage this key issue is to invest time and attention in the client's business during the ad planning process so that everyone is clear on the goals for a campaign and the metrics that will be used in determining success or failure. Most clients don't expect magic, and they can live with an occasional failure if the agency can apply the lessons learned to improve. If a campaign didn't work as planned, the client should be told why and be given solid ideas for achieving better results the next time around.

From the agency's perspective, it wants to be treated as a partner, not a vendor. Partners entail more of a relationship, while vendors are more transaction oriented. The agency also needs the time and resources so that it can do its best work. But of course, there is never enough time, and the budget is never large enough. There are two things clients must do to help everyone cope with resource issues. First, the agency should be included in the planning process as soon as possible, so that they are well informed about dates and deadlines. Second, the agency needs honest, upfront assessments regarding budget to avoid last-minute disruptions that can hamper advertising and IBP implementation.

Finally, because agencies know that clients are going to be results oriented, they are looking for clients that will set them up for success. Agencies love clients who can clearly articulate the outcomes they seek, provide both constructive and timely feedback, respect and value their expertise, and who trust them as a partner.

Summary

1. Identify the seven components of an advertising plan.

An advertising plan entails: (1) an introduction, (2) situation analysis, (3) objectives, (4) budgeting, (5) strategy, (6) execution, and (7) evaluation. The ad plan is driven by the marketing planning process and provides the direction that ensures proper implementation of an advertising campaign. An advertising plan starts with an executive summary and introduction, then presents a situation analysis. It also explains the communications and/or sales objectives, the amounts budgeted for the campaign, the strategy and execution to be employed, and the measures that will be applied to evaluate the campaign's results.

2. Explain the role of the introduction of an advertising plan and what it entails.

An introduction is a brief yet important section because it summarizes the entire ad plan for someone quickly yet concisely. It entails an executive summary and an introduction of the entire ad plan. It is important because it is the only component of the plan that some executives who are not necessarily involved on the project may read.

3. Know what a situation analysis is and how it entails a cultural context, historical context, industry analysis, market analysis, and competitor analysis.

A situation analysis (including cultural context, historical context, industry analysis, market analysis, and competitor analysis) is the section of the advertising plan in which the client and agency lay out the most important factors that define the market and consumer situation—explaining the importance of each factor.

4. Identify common advertising objectives and the differences between communications and sales objectives.

Some common areas of advertising objectives relate with brand awareness, top-of-the-mind awareness, purchase intent, trial usage, repeat purchase, and brand switching. Ad objectives can be communication objectives or sales objectives, and most strong brands use both. Communication objectives focus on increased communication related outputs such as increasing brand awareness and changing or reinforcing brand beliefs or attitudes. Sales objectives are targets for using advertising to increase a brand's sales. However, advertising and IBP alone cannot actually increase sales; any objective aimed at increasing sales belongs in a marketing plan, not in an advertising plan. An integrated advertising and IBP program will effectively support the efforts of the sales force or attract consumers to a store or website, where the sales are ultimately made.

5. Know the importance of budgeting for advertising and explain four methods for setting advertising budgets.

Perhaps the most challenging aspect of any advertising campaign is arriving at a proper budget allocation. Budgeting is crucial to do before strategy or execution of advertising or branding in order to make sure that the plan is doable with the amount of money or resources. Four types of budgeting approaches used in the advertising industry entail: (1) percentage-of-sales, (2) share of market/share of voice, (3) response models, and (4) objective-and-task. A percentage-of-sales approach is a simple but naïve way to deal with this issue. In the share-of-voice approach, the activities of key competitors are factored into the budget-setting process. A variety of quantitative models may also be used for budget determination. Sometimes budgeting is informed by the use of an advertising response function, a mathematical relationship that associates dollars spent on advertising and sales generated. The objective-and-task approach is difficult to implement, but with practice, it is likely to yield the best value for a client's advertising dollars. Because it begins with the objectives set and identifies specific tasks and the associated costs necessary to achieve the objectives, this budget approach is widely used.

6. Discuss the role of strategy in advertising planning.

The role of strategy in advertising planning shows the importance of clear and concise articulation of how the plan will achieve its objectives. The strategy component is the one that entails planned tactics and how the ad or campaign will be implemented.

7. Identify the components of executing the advertising plan.

The execution of the advertising plan entails the copy strategy (words and verbal messaging), the media plan (a flowchart or spreadsheet of the specific media types and vehicles to be used), and the plan for integrating various components of integrated brand promotion. The evaluation component is done after the execution or implementation is complete, and the evaluation entails specific criteria, the methods of evaluation, and the consequences and contingencies.

8. Define the evaluation component of an advertising plan and identify why it is important.

The evaluation component is defined as the stage where an advertiser determines how it will measure the results of the plan's advertising and IBP activities. Metrics or analytics for evaluating advertising and IBP activities vary, depending on the objectives set and the creative and media choices made. If an outside agency is involved, this part of the plan also explains the criteria that will be applied to agency performance and how long the agency will have to achieve the agreed-upon objectives. The reason evaluation is important because brands and companies have pressure to show results and short-term profits in order to justify advertising and marketing investments or expenses. If the ads or IBP tactics are not working, brands may reconsider their strategies and adjust them. Both advertising strategies and agencies are subject to evaluation. Post agency evaluations, some clients may select a different agency as a result of ineffective campaigns or simply for a fresh perspective.

9. Discuss the role of the agency in planning advertising and IBP.

Ad agencies generally are involved in the planning of advertising and IBP, especially in integration and how to reduce clutter with expertise on an array of options for getting the message effectively to the target consumer. They need the various divisions and departments in an agency to be working as a team, coming up with integrated brand promotion solutions that build synergy between and among multiple channels. Second, clients need agencies to provide ideas and approaches to break through clutter. An advertising plan will be an especially powerful tool when firms partner with their advertising agencies in its development. The firm can lead this process by doing its homework with respect to marketing strategy development and objective setting. The agency can then play a key role in managing the preparation and placement phases of campaign execution—particularly with respect to integration of advertising and all brand promotion activities.

Key Terms

advertising plan	budgeting	executive summary
advertising response function	build-up analysis	household penetration
brand awareness	competitor analysis	industry analysis
brand switching	ethnocentrism	market analysis

market share
objective-and-task approach
percentage-of-sales approach
purchase intent

repeat purchase
self-reference criterion (SRC)
share of voice
situation analysis

top-of-the-mind awareness
trial usage
user base

Endnotes

1. Harlan E. Spotts, et al., "Advertising and Promotional Effects on Consumer Service Firm Sales," *Journal of Advertising Research* 60, no. 1, (2019), 104–116.

2. Deborah J. MacInnis, et al., "Creating Boundary-Breaking Marketing-Relevant Consumer Research," *Journal of Marketing* 84, no. 2, (2019), 1–23.

3. Ad Age Datacenter Weekly, "A 'Squid Game' Star's Phenomenal Instagram Engagement Boosts Adidas and Louis Vuitton: Datacenter Weekly," *Ad Age*, October 15, 2021, https://adage.com/article/datacenter/squid-game-stars-instagram-boosts-adidas-and-louis-vuitton/2373921.

4. Norihiko Shirouzu, "In Chinese Market, Toyota's Strategy Is Made in USA," *The Wall Street Journal*, May 26, 2006, A1, A8.

5. Laurel Wentz, "China's Ad World: A New Crisis Every Day," *Advertising Age*, December 11, 2006, 6.

6. A. Schumpeter, "The Emerging-World Consumer Is King," *The Economist*, January 5, 2013, 53.

7. Wei-Na Lee, "Exploring the Role of Culture in Advertising: Resolving Persistent Issues and Responding to Changes," *Journal of Advertising* 48, no. 1, (2019), 115–125.

8. Frank Findley, et al., "Effectiveness and Efficiency of TV's Brand-Building Power: A Historical Review," *Journal of Advertising Research* 60, no. 4, (June 2020), 361–369.

9. Deena Shanker, "You Can Eat Gluten Again, America," *Bloomberg News*, October 14, 2016, https://www.bloomberg.com/news/articles/2016-10-14/you-can-eat-gluten-again-america.

10. Clare Duffy, "Samsung's New Ad for its S21 Ultra Phone Is…A Series on Hulu", CNN Business, April 24, 2021, https://www.cnn.com/2021/04/24/tech/samsung-hulu-photography-series/index.html.

11. Ceren Kolsarici, et al., "The Anatomy of the Advertising Budget Decision: How Analytics and Heuristics Drive Sales Performance," *Journal of Marketing Research* 57, no. 3 (2020), 468–488.

12. Tanya Gazdik, "Aflac Targets Millennials with Humor," *MediaPost*, December 1, 2016, http://www.mediapost.com/publications/article/290052/aflac-targets-millennials-with-humor.html.

13. Yoori Hwang and Se-Hoon Jeong, "Consumers' Response to Format Characteristics in Native Advertising," *Journal of Advertising Research* 61, no. 2, (2020), 212–224.

14. Samuel Stäbler, "Why Cheap, Low-Quality Giveaways Are Bad for Brands: Quality of Freebies Drives Consumer Attitudes, But Personalization Can Help," *Journal of Advertising Research* 61, no. 2, (2021), 164–177.

15. Rosa-Branca Esteves and Joana Resende, "Competitive Targeted Advertising with Price Discrimination," *Marketing Science* (2016), 576–587; and Consiglio Irene and Stijn M. J. van Osselaer, "The Devil You Know: Self-Esteem and Switching Responses to Poor Service," *Journal of Consumer Research* 46, no. 3, (2019), 590–605.

16. Darrell Etherington, "Everlywell Acquires Two Healthcare Companies and Forms Parent Everly Health," Tech Crunch, March 25, 2021, https://techcrunch.com/2021/03/25/everlywell-acquires-two-healthcare-companies-and-forms-parent-everly-health/

17. Jack Neff, "How Unilever Found the Balance between Creativity and Sales," *Advertising Age*, September 10, 2012, 58.

18. Martinne Geller, "Unilever Ends 2016 with Sales Growth Below Estimates on India, Brazil," *Reuters*, January 26, 2017, http://www.reuters.com/article/us-unilever-nv-results-idUSKBN15A16M; and Jack Neff, "Why the Wall Is Crumbling Between Sales, Marketing," *Advertising Age*, April 7, 2016, http://adage.com/article/cmo-strategy/wall-crumbling-sales/303381/ and Harlan E. Sprotts et al., "Advertising and Promotional Effects on Consumer Service Firm Sales," *Journal of Advertising Research* 60, no. 1 (2019), 104–116.

19. Stewart Henderson Britt, "Are So-Called Successful Advertising Campaigns Really Successful?" *Journal of Advertising Research* 9 (1969), 5–15.

20. Brian Steinberg, "Meet the Marketing Execs Who Dole Out the Money," *Advertising Age*, September 9, 2012, www.adage.com; accessed September 10, 2012.

21. Jack Neff, "Marketers Don't Practice ROI They *Preach." Advertising Age*, March 12, 2012, 1, 19.

22. The classic treatment of this method was first offered by James O. Peckham, "Can We Relate Advertising Dollars to Market-Share Objectives?" in Malcolm A. McGiven (Ed.), *How Much to Spend for Advertising* (New York: Association of National Advertisers, 1969), 24.

23. James C. Shroer, "Ad Spending: Growing Market Share," *Harvard Business Review* (January–February 1990), 44–50.

24. Nicholas De Canha, et al., "The Impact of Advertising on Market Share," *Journal of Advertising Research* 60, no. 1 (2019), 87–103.

25. Jack Neff, "A Real Beauty: Dove's Viral Makes a Big Splash for No Cash," *Advertising Age*, October 10, 2006, 1, 45.

26. James E. Lynch and Graham J. Hooley, "Increasing Sophistication in Advertising Budget Setting," *Journal of Advertising Research*, (February–March 1990), 72.

27. Bo-Lei Zhang, et al., "Budget Allocation for Maximizing Viral Advertising in Social Networks," *Journal of Computer Science and Technology* 31, no. 4 (2016), 759–775; see also Lane Wakefield, et al. "Are Brands Wasting Money on Sport Sponsorships?" *Journal of Advertising Research* 61, no. 2 (2020), 192–211.

28. Niraj Chokshi, "Apple's iPad Advertising Aspirations," *theatlantic.com/business*, March 29, 2010.

29. Angela Doland, "How Advertisers Are Tapping Into China's Crazy Live-Streaming Culture," *Advertising Age*, August 26, 2016, http://adage.com/article/digital/advertisers-tapping-china-s-crazy-livestreaming-culture/305599/; Eric Shroeder, "Mondelez Debuts Chocolate Bar Featuring Oreos," *Food Business News*, November 14, 2016, http://www.foodbusinessnews.net/articles/news_home/New-Product-Launches/2016/11/Mondelez_debuts_chocolate_bar.aspx?ID=%7B38C13953-D43C-451F-9926-1946E09ABDFB%7D&cck=1; Peter Frost, "Mondelez Has a New Plan to Boost Sales, and It Includes Oreo," *Crain's Chicago Business*, November 12, 2016, http://www.chicagobusiness.com/article/20161112/ISSUE01/311129991/mondelez-has-a-new-plan-to-boost-sales

-and-it-includes-oreo; Douglas Yu, "Mondelez Debuts Holiday Gift Tins via E-commerce Pilot," *Confectionery News,* December 6, 2016, http://www.confectionerynews.com/Manufacturers /Mondelez-debuts-Oreo-holiday-gift-tins-via-e-commerce-pilot; and Karlene Lukovitz, "Oreo Taps Shaq, Aguilera, Neymar Jr. For Global 'Dunk Challenge,'" *MediaPost,* February 8, 2017, http://www .mediapost.com/publications/article/294612/oreo-taps-shaq -aguilera-neymar-jr-for-global-d.html.

30. Nathalie Tadena and Serena Ng, "Big Companies Put the Squeeze on Ad Agencies," *Wall Street Journal,* April 27, 2015, http://www.wsj .com/articles/p-g-joins-movement-to-cut-ad-costs-1430093596.

31. Quoted in Patrick Coffee, "Nationwide Drops McKinney as Its Agency of Record After a 7-Year Relationship," *Advertising Age,* February 3, 2016, http://www.adweek.com/news/advertising -branding/nationwide-drops-mckinney-its-agency-record

-169395; Maureen Morrison, "Nationwide Is on Ogilvy's Side, Names Shop Lead Agency," *Advertising Age,* March 16, 2016, http://adage.com/article/agency-news/nationwide-confirms -ogilvy-lead-agency/303147/; and Adrianne Pasquarelli, "Nationwide Switches Up Jingle to Show Its Many Sides," *Advertising Age,* August 4, 2016, http://adage.com/article/cmo-strategy /nationwide-taps-musicians-show-sides/305226/.

32. Kartik Kalaignanam, et al., "Marketing Agility: The Concept, Antecedents, and a Research Agenda," *Journal of Marketing* 85, no. 1 (2020), 35–58.

33. Erik Oster, "Travelocity Sends Creative Account to Doner," Adweek Agency Spy, May 11, 2021, https://www.adweek.com/agencyspy /travelocity-sends-creative-account-to-doner/172276/.

34. Julie Liesse, "What Clients Want," *Advertising Age*, July 12, 2012, C4–C5.

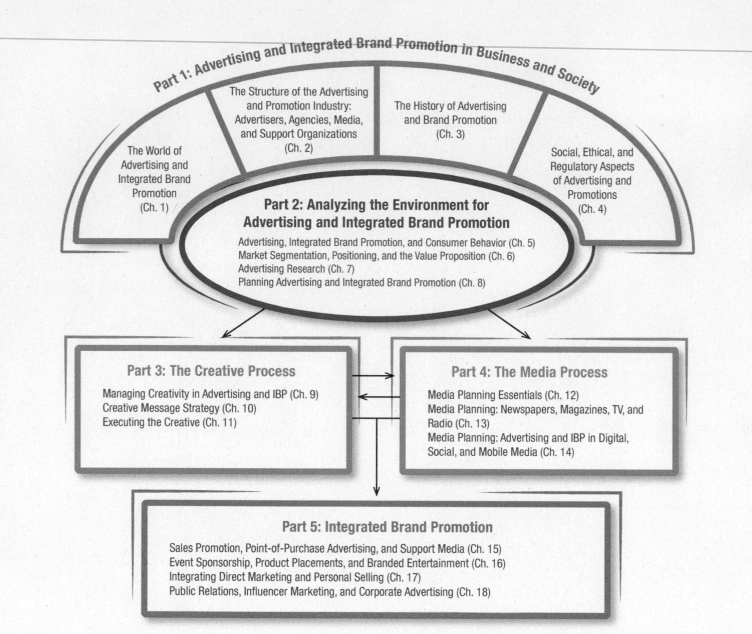

Part 1: Advertising and Integrated Brand Promotion in Business and Society

The World of Advertising and Integrated Brand Promotion (Ch. 1)

The Structure of the Advertising and Promotion Industry: Advertisers, Agencies, Media, and Support Organizations (Ch. 2)

The History of Advertising and Brand Promotion (Ch. 3)

Social, Ethical, and Regulatory Aspects of Advertising and Promotions (Ch. 4)

Part 2: Analyzing the Environment for Advertising and Integrated Brand Promotion

Advertising, Integrated Brand Promotion, and Consumer Behavior (Ch. 5)
Market Segmentation, Positioning, and the Value Proposition (Ch. 6)
Advertising Research (Ch. 7)
Planning Advertising and Integrated Brand Promotion (Ch. 8)

Part 3: The Creative Process

Managing Creativity in Advertising and IBP (Ch. 9)
Creative Message Strategy (Ch. 10)
Executing the Creative (Ch. 11)

Part 4: The Media Process

Media Planning Essentials (Ch. 12)
Media Planning: Newspapers, Magazines, TV, and Radio (Ch. 13)
Media Planning: Advertising and IBP in Digital, Social, and Mobile Media (Ch. 14)

Part 5: Integrated Brand Promotion

Sales Promotion, Point-of-Purchase Advertising, and Support Media (Ch. 15)
Event Sponsorship, Product Placements, and Branded Entertainment (Ch. 16)
Integrating Direct Marketing and Personal Selling (Ch. 17)
Public Relations, Influencer Marketing, and Corporate Advertising (Ch. 18)

This section of the text marks an important transition. In Part 1, you learned about the business and societal context of advertising and integrated brand promotion, key trends that are shaping advertising and the industry, and the broad impact of these factors. In Part 2, you were introduced to aspects of the environment that are vital for effective advertising and integrated brand promotion, including analysis of consumer behavior, segmentation and positioning, advertising research, and detailed planning. Now, as shown in the framework exhibit, Part 3 focuses on the creative process.

Part

3

The Creative Process

9 Managing Creativity in Advertising and IBP *186*

10 Creative Message Strategy *204*

11 Executing the Creative *228*

*C*reative, ***consumer-based strategy*** *is truly the soul of advertising and IBP.* Consumer-based strategy is a way of doing business and developing advertising that starts with consumer psychology; first, we understand consumers with respect to the product or brand and how they use it and then use the consumer insights to help build or shape the **creative strategy**, or the strategic approach that a company takes to develop and implement a blueprint for the creative work and the creative team management. Without creative strategy and execution that actually resonates with consumers, no one would pay attention to messages, and marketers could not inform, entertain, or engage targeted audiences in any media. We first consider the idea of creativity itself (Chapter 9). What is it, what distinguishes it, what is its beauty, and what makes creative people creative? Then we examine message creativity from the lens of goals and objectives and the role of multiple creative strategies (Chapter 10). Finally, we describe how creative concepts are brought to life through message copywriting, art direction, and production, as well as the involvement of account planning and media planning (Chapter 11).

Managing Creativity in Advertising and IBP

9-1 Why Does Advertising Thrive on Creativity?

Why is creativity such a big deal in the advertising business? Let's start with clutter, the enemy of effective advertising. Great creative content can defeat clutter. Everyone hates ad clutter. But to try to overcome it, advertisers generate more ads, so clutter begets clutter in a cycle that no one seems to be able to curb.[1] If you want your message to be heard and seen, you'll need to distinguish yourself from the crowd, and that will require good—or preferably great—creativity. This also holds true for messages targeting business buyers.[2] Research shows that one of the primary benefits of award-winning,

creative ads is that they break through the clutter and are remembered.[3] To get the message across, even the most creative ads are often repeated again and again.[4] But creativity in advertising is much more than getting attention; it makes the ads or other branding efforts make sense to consumers, sets the agenda, and gives meaning to the brand. And since brands are packages of popular meaning,[5] there is no sustainable branding without message creativity. The strategic process should start with understanding consumer psychology and making the consumer psyche (the business consumer or the household consumer) the driver of the brand strategy (see the framework in Exhibit 9.1).

Great brands make meaningful, often emotional connections with consumers. Think about some fantastic brands that you love or couldn't live without. Many consumers feel loyalty to brands they connect emotionally with—such as

Exhibit 9.1 ▶ As shown in this framework, analysis of the advertising and IBP environment sets the stage for managing creativity within the creative process.

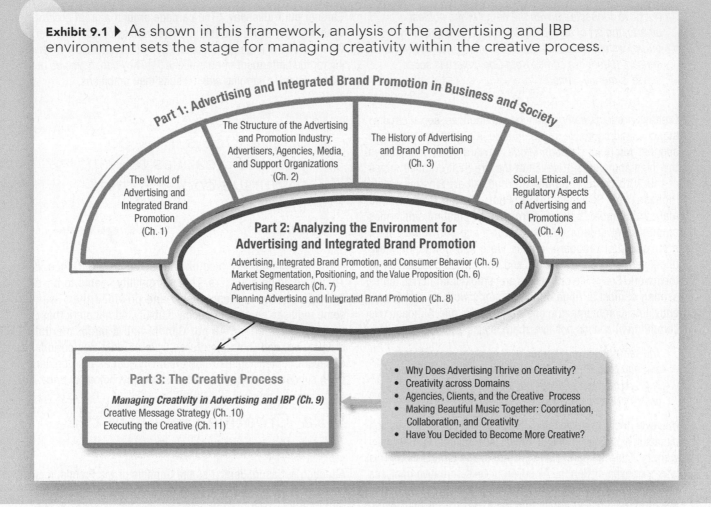

Apple, Starbucks, the New York Yankees, the Atlanta Braves, or others. When consumer-based IBP strategy is done well, brands make emotional connections by engaging consumers through sensory experiences and emotional episodes.[6] Advertising and IBP in their many forms help create these experiences, but great creative execution brings it all to life.[7]

LO 1

9-2 Creativity across Domains

You can't use up creativity. The more you use, the more you have.

—Maya Angelou

Before examining how the creative function plays out in the world of advertising and IBP, let's consider creativity in other domains. Creativity in its essence is the same no matter what the context. People who create simply create, whether they write novels, take photographs, ponder the particle physics that drives the universe, craft poetry, write songs, play a musical instrument,

dance, make films, design buildings, paint, or make ads. Great ads can be truly great creative accomplishments.

Creativity is the ability to consider and hold together seemingly inconsistent elements and forces, making a new connection. This ability to step outside of everyday logic, to free oneself of thinking in terms of "the way things are" or "the way things have to be," apparently allows creative people to develop things in a way that, once we see it, makes sense, is interesting, and is thus creative. To see love and hate as the same entity, to see "round squares," or to imagine a new feminine standard of style, as Coco Chanel did, is to have this ability. Ideas born of creativity reveal their own logic, and then we all say, "Oh, I see."

You have probably heard the term "creative genius." Creativity is usually seen as a gift—a special way of seeing the world. Throughout the ages, creative people have been seen as special, revered, and reviled. There is also a dark side to creativity. Creative geniuses have served as powerful political instruments (for good and evil), and they have been ostracized, imprisoned, and killed for their art. Creativity has been associated with various forms of madness, even from the time of Socrates:

Madness, provided it comes as the gift of heaven, is the channel by which we receive the greatest blessings... [T]he men of old who gave their names saw no disgrace or reproach in madness; otherwise they would not have connected it with the name of the noblest of all arts, the art of discerning the future, and called by our ancestors, madness is a nobler thing than sober sense... [M]adness comes from God, whereas sober sense is merely human.

—Socrates[9]

Creativity reflects early childhood experiences, social circumstances, and cognitive styles. In a book on creativity that we suggest you read, *Creating Minds*, Howard Gardner examines the lives and works of seven of the greatest creative minds of the 20th century: Sigmund Freud, Albert Einstein, Pablo Picasso, Igor Stravinsky, T. S. Eliot, Martha Graham, and Mahatma Gandhi.[10] His work reveals fascinating similarities among great creators. All seven of these individuals, from a physicist to a modern dancer, were self-confident, alert, unconventional, hardworking, and committed obsessively to their work. Social life or hobbies are almost immaterial, representing at most a fringe on the creator's work time.[11] Apparently, total commitment to one's craft is the rule. Although this commitment sounds positive, there is also a darker reflection:

The self-confidence merges with egotism, egocentrism, and narcissism: highly absorbed, not only wholly involved in his or her own projects, but likely to pursue them at costs of other individuals.[12]

However, these creative minds had troubled personal lives and did not seem to make time for others. According to Gardner, they were typically not particularly good to others around them. This was true even of Gandhi. All seven of these creative geniuses were also great self-promoters. Well-recognized creative people are not typically shy about seeking exposure for their work. Apparently, fame in the creative realm rarely comes to the self-effacing and timid.

All seven of these great creators were, very significantly, childlike in a critical way. All of them had the ability to see things as a child does. Einstein spent much of his career revolutionizing physics by pursuing in no small way an idea he produced as a child: What would it be like to move along a strand of pure light? Picasso commented that it ultimately was his ability to paint like a child (along with superior technical skills) that explained much of his greatness. Freud's obsession with and interpretation of his childhood dreams had a significant role in what is one of his most significant works, *The Interpretation of Dreams*.[13] T. S. Eliot's poetry demonstrated imaginative abilities that typically fade after childhood. The same is true of Martha Graham's modern dance. Even Gandhi's particular form of social action was formulated with a very simple and childlike logic at its base. These artists and creative thinkers never lost the ability to see the ordinary as extraordinary, to not have their particular form of imagination beaten out of them by the process of "growing up."

Of course, the problem with childlike thinking is that these individuals also behaved like children throughout their lives. Their social behavior was often selfish. They expected those around them to be willing to sacrifice at the altar of their gift.

Gardner put it this way: "The carnage around a great creator is not a pretty sight, and this destructiveness occurs whether the individual is engaged in solitary pursuit or ostensibly working for the betterment of humankind."[14] They can, however, be extraordinarily charming when it suits their ambitions.

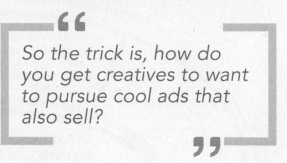

> *So the trick is, how do you get creatives to want to pursue cool ads that also sell?*

Creative minds are also ok with being on the fringes.[15] They love being outsiders. This marginality seems to have been necessary to these people and provided them with some requisite energy. Emotional stability did not mark these creative lives, either. All but Gandhi had a major mental breakdown, and Gandhi suffered from at least two periods of severe depression. Extreme creativity, just as the popular myth suggests, seems to come at some psychological price.

9-2a Creative Genius in the Advertising Business

Although not as influential as the Gandhis or the Freuds, it is common to see individuals from the ad business praised for remarkable careers of creative genius. One example is Lee Clow, the main creative force with TBWA/Chiat/Day. His work includes the Energizer Bunny, billboards for Nike, and the classic "1984" spot that launched Apple's Mac. For example, Google thinks outside the box and has Cookie Monster do an online tutorial for Google Play. This is a simple example of changing the mold from boring tutorials led by executives; Cookie Monster is much cooler, and we will probably remember the tutorial because it is a novel approach that stands out from the expected, mundane online tutorials. For synergy, the Google logo can even be creatively adapted to feature Sesame Street characters such as Cookie Monster. Exhibit 9.2 shows some examples of creative adaptations of the Google logo. Google is great at displaying creativity with its logo; you may have noticed how it changes to fit holidays or special occasions.

Lee Clow is one of the great creative maestros of the modern advertising business. He is perhaps most noted for his work on Absolut vodka; the art direction, especially for the brand's print and outdoor ads, is iconic. The copywriting is also legendary yet simple; see Exhibit 9.3 for an example of simple art direction with creative copywriting (i.e., the words in the ad). Lee Clow is one of the creatives who was behind some of the most recognizable ad and brand campaigns in the last decades, and besides Absolut, he was involved with famous campaigns such as Apple "Think Different" and Adidas

Source: Google

Exhibit 9.2 ▶ Google is known for having creative adaptations for it's logo; here are a few examples of how the Google logo can feature children's characters that can synergize with the creative idea to have Cookie Monster do the Google Play tutorial.

"Impossible is Nothing" as well as helping create the Energizer Bunny and Taco Bell's chihuahua.[16]

But those who have worked with the creative Lee Clow say his real gift is being "the synthesizer." To have synergy in branding, a creative must pull various elements of the creative strategy together within ads and among all forms of integrated brand promotion. Sorting through a wall full of creative ideas in the form of rough sketches, Clow is the guy who knows how to pick a winner: the one—often the simplest—idea that is most likely to resonate with consumers, as in Mac vs. PC or "Think Different" for Apple or "Shift" for Nissan. In his retirement, he "penned a love letter to advertising" which began:

The years I spent doing this thing called advertising have been fun, challenging, rewarding, maddening, sometimes painful, but mostly joyful.

And I wouldn't trade a day of it for anything else.

Every day to come to "work" with the smartest, freest, most passionate people in business; all of us with the goal of creating messages to put out into the world that will be noticed, that people will talk about, even become famous.

They make people laugh, or cry, or think. Discover something new, see the world differently, maybe even buy something?

To be Media Artists.[17]

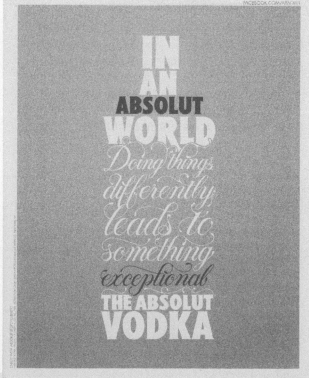

Source: ABSOLUT SPIRITS CO., NEW YORK, NY.

Exhibit 9.3 ▶ Absolut ad.

9-2b Creativity in the Business World

The difficulty of determining who is creative and who is not or what is creative and what is not in the artistic world is paralleled in the business world. Certainly, no matter how this trait is defined, creativity is viewed in the business world as a strength. It has been said that creative individuals assume almost mythical status in the corporate world. Everybody needs them, but no one is sure who or what they are. Furthermore, working with creative people is not always easy, but it can be rewarding and stimulating. It takes the right mix of organizational culture alignment and mutual respect to set the stage for supporting creative talent in an agency or client situation.[18] It also takes a management team that is willing to approve the implementation of truly creative ideas rather than sticking to safe or routine solutions as well as being mindful that great creative ideas sometimes tend to get rejected.[19] As an example of thinking outside the box for a consumer-based creative strategy, note what Priceline, a website for helping consumers find deals on hotels and travel, is doing. It brings in a celebrity (Kaley Cuoco) to serve as "the Negotiator" for consumers in the hotel deals, and this strategy has worked well for the brand for many years, helping it remain viable in the very competitive travel market.

The availability of more and better data about customers, purchases, and results is a key trend transforming the application of creativity to business problems. In the words of ad agency executive Melanie Johnston, CEO and Global Board Member of Forsman & Bodenfors Canada:[20]

> … every message needs to be framed in a way that makes the consumer pay attention and feel motivated enough to take action. This is where creativity plays a huge role. Creative ideas are needed to stir feelings and propel the consumer along the journey to purchase. It's this beautiful partnership of data and creativity that transforms generic needs into specific brand purchases.

Certainly, creativity is an essential ingredient in developing and implementing effective advertising and IBP messages that serve the business needs of organizations worldwide. Take a look at Exhibit 9.4 to see how Hotels.com relies on creativity to stand out in the crowded market for travel services.

9-2c Can You Become Creative?

The genius of a Picasso or an Einstein is a very high standard, one that most of us will not be able to achieve. But the question of whether we can *become* creative really depends on the meaning of *creativity.* Is a person creative because they can produce a creative result? Or is a person creative because of the way they think? Although some people may be more creative than others, you can find ways to unleash latent creative abilities. Further, who gets to determine what is creative and what is not? To us, creativity is a form of intelligence—maybe the best form of intelligence. Computers can do amazing math; only humans can be creative and there are some challenges with artificial intelligence and advertising creativity, such as the use of sarcasm.[21]

9-2d Notes of Caution

In concluding our discussion about the traits of extraordinarily creative people, a couple of notes of caution are in order. First, just because you are in a "creative" job, it doesn't mean that you are actually creative. Second, just because you are on the account or business side (a.k.a., "a suit"), it does not mean you are uninspired. Sometimes the client has creative ideas! Listen to the clients and take their ideas seriously, because even though they are paying you for the campaign, they tend to know their brand inside and out.[22] Many times, big, disruptive ideas are an iterative and team-based process stemming from many people, including consumers, advertisers, and the client. Tension and conflict (e.g., suits versus the

Exhibit 9.4 ▶ Integrated brand promotion in action: Hotels.com

Hotels.com's messages feature creative twists on the familiar. On the left, a testimonial from a "spokesperson." On the right, clicking on "skip ad" starts the characters skipping in the video. *How does the creativity of these messages attract and engage audiences?*

creatives) can be important drivers of great creative content development. But one needs to anticipate and manage this conflict in positive ways to get good outcomes. Don't shut other people's ideas down; think about them, try to see their perspective, and help shape the idea if possible.

Consider some unusual ideas that may have seemed a bit weird at first but actually have become legendary examples of creative work; Taco Bell used a talking Chihuahua that said "Yo Quiero Taco Bell!" as one example (Exhibit 9.5). Another is Apple's iconic iPod campaign that changed the music business. When the Apple iPod hit the market, the simple and colorful ads showed silhouettes of people dancing with their iPod and ionic Apple earbuds in their ears (Exhibit 9.6). With minimal copy and bold visuals, these old-school Apple ads said in very small print, "Welcome to the digital music revolution." They were right. It is interesting to think about how these ads were developed and how the agencies or in-house teams collaborated with clients and contributed to the creative process.

We now discuss the importance of agencies and clients working together to engage in an effective and inspiring creative process.

Exhibit 9.5 ▶ Taco Bell ad.

Exhibit 9.6 ▶ Apple iPod ad.

9-3 Agencies, Clients, and the Creative Process

As an employee in an agency creative department, you will spend most of your time with your feet up on a desk working on an ad. Across the desk, also with her feet up, will be your partner—in my case, an art director. And she will want to talk about movies.

In fact, if the truth be known, you will spend fully one-fourth of your career with your feet up talking about movies. The ad is due in two days. The media space has been bought and paid for. The pressure is building. And your muse is sleeping off a drunk behind a dumpster somewhere. Your pen lies useless. So you talk movies.

That's when the traffic person comes by. Traffic people stay on top of a job as it moves through the agency; which means they also stay on top of you. They'll come by to remind you of the horrid things that happen to snail-assed creative people who don't come through with the goods on time...

So you try to get your pen moving. And you begin to work; and working in this business means staring at your partner's shoes.

That's what I've been doing from 9 to 5 for almost 20 years. Staring at the bottom of the disgusting tennis shoes on the feet of my partner, parked on the desk across from my disgusting tennis shoes. This is the sum and substance of life at an agency.

—Luke Sullivan, copywriter and author[23]

While many things have changed in the agency business, such as a move toward digital, one thing remains the same—good ideas often take time and require multiple perspectives. Ample time is spent trying to spark an idea, or the hone in on the right one. As Chad Rea, who taught in the creative sequence at The University of Texas at Austin, told his advertising students, "Think first. Execute later." This is sage advice. You turn things over and over in your head, trying to see the light. You try to find that one way of seeing it that makes everything fall into place. Or it just comes to you, easily, just like that. Magic. Every creative pursuit involves this sort of thing.

However, advertising and IBP, like all creative pursuits, are unique in some respects. Advertising and branding professionals try to solve a problem—often under demanding time constraints. Commonly the problem is poorly defined, or there are politics to navigate. They work for people who seem not to be creative at all and who seem to be doing their best not to let them be creative. They are housed in the "creative department," which makes it seem as if it's some sort of warehouse where the executives keep all the creativity contained so that they can find it when they need it and so that it won't get away. We think that creativity should not be limited to one department; creativity should permeate all aspects of the business.

9-3a Oil and Water: Conflicts and Tensions in the Creative/Management Interface

Sometimes the conflict between creatives and the more business or client/account side of advertising is due to a view that creatives are interested in the ad as a form of art or something that wins creative awards more than thinking about the ad as a strategic form of brand communication that will help sell products. As you can see in this parody by Team One Advertising, many joke that creatives in advertising are motivated, namely, by awards and food (Exhibit 9.7).

We challenge you, as future professionals, to think bigger and to get the fact that creatives and the account planners and clients are on the same team! Old ways of thinking are antiquated on this topic because they focus on differences rather than on what the various players have in common. Here are some thoughts on management and creativity by two advertising greats:

The majority of businessmen are incapable of original thinking, because they are unable to escape from the tyranny of reason. Their imaginations are blocked.

—William Bernbach[24]

If you're not a bad boy, if you're not a big pain in the ass, then you are in some mush in this business.

—George Lois[25]

As you can see, this topic rarely yields tepid, diplomatic comments. Advertising is produced through a social process. As a social process, however, it's marked by the struggles for control and power that exist within departments, among departments, and between the agency and its clients on a daily basis.[26]

Most research concerning the contentious environment in advertising agencies places the creative department in a central position within these conflicts. One explanation hinges on reactions to the uncertain nature of the product of the creative department. What do they do? From the outside, it sometimes appears that "the creatives" (e.g., art directors, copywriters) are having fun and screwing around while everyone else has to wear a suit to the office and interface with the client and/or other stakeholders. This perception of who is really putting in the work can create tension between the creative department and the account services team. We need to note that there are different types of works, all that is critical to the process; and it is vital that we respect the various kinds of roles and contributions that go into developing creative and strategic brands via advertising and IBP.

In addition, these two departments do not always share the same ultimate goals for advertising and integrated brand promotion. Creatives greatly value awards and recognition for their work; account executives, serving as liaisons between client and agency, see the goal as achieving some predetermined objective in the marketplace, like growing market share for the client's brand.

Another source of tension is attributed to conflicting perspectives due to differing background knowledge of members

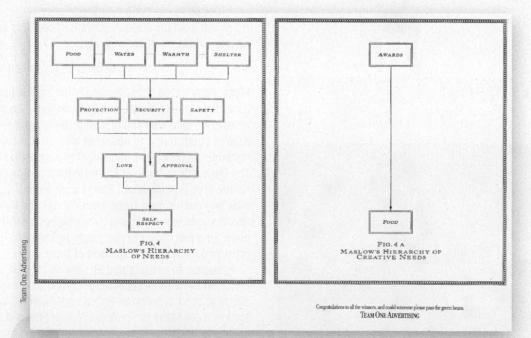

Exhibit 9.7 ▶ Team One Advertising has an interesting spin on what motivates agency creatives; here, it parodies Maslow's hierarchy to make its point.

of creative groups versus account services teams. Account managers must be generalists with broad knowledge of the agency and all of its functions, whereas creatives are specialists who must possess great expertise in a single area. Creatives, above all, must be tuned in to the contemporary culture.

Regardless of its role as a participant in conflict, the creative department is recognized as an essential part of any agency's success. It is a key quality for potential clients when they select advertising agencies. Creativity has been found to be crucial to a positive client–advertiser relationship.

However, many clients don't recognize their role in killing the very same breakthrough ideas that they claim to be seeking.[27] Anyone who has worked in the creative department of an advertising agency for any length of time has a full quiver of client stories—like the one about the client who wanted to produce a single 30-second spot for his ice cream novelty company. The creative team who went to work and brought in a single spot that everyone agreed delivered the strategy perfectly, set up further possible spots in the same campaign, and, in the words of the copywriter, was really funny. It was the kind of commercial that you actually look forward to seeing on television. During the storyboard presentation, the client laughed in all the right places and admitted the spot was on strategy. He then decided to move his money to a national coupon drop and not use ads at all.

It's easy and sometimes fun to blame clients for all of the anxieties and frustrations of the creatives, especially if you've worked in a creative department. You can criticize the clients all you want; and, since they aren't in the office next to you, they can't hear you. But, despite the obvious stake that creative departments have in generating superior advertising, it should be mentioned that no creative ever put $10 million of their own money into a campaign.

Indeed, you can't always blame the client. Sometimes the conflicts and problems that preclude wonderful creative work occur within the walls of the advertising agency itself. Here's why. When a client is unhappy, it fires the agency. Billings and revenue drop. Budgets are cut and layoffs begin. It's no wonder that conflict occurs; agency–client relationships can become strained, and international client relationships can be especially important and challenging due to cultural differences in how business is done.[28] With jobs at stake, it's tough not to get involved in struggles over control of the creative product.

Account executives (AEs) are the liaison between the agency and the client. For AEs to rise in their careers, they must excel in the care and nurturing of clients (see Exhibit 9.8).

For some 25 years, I was an advertising agency "AE," eventually rising through the crabgrass to become a founder, president, chairman, and now chairman emeritus of Borders, Perrin and Norrander, Inc.

During all those years, I pondered the eternal question: Why do some advertising agencies consistently turn out a superior creative product while others merely perpetuate mediocrity? Is the answer simply to hire great writers and art directors? Well, certainly that has a lot to do with it, but I would suggest that there is another vital component in the equation for creative success.

Outstanding creative work in an ad agency requires a ferocious commitment from all staffers, but especially from the account service person. The job title is irrelevant—account executive, account manager, account supervisor—but the job function is critical, particularly when it comes to client approvals. Yes, I am speaking of the oft-maligned AE, the "suit" who so frequently is the bane of the Creative Department.

So how in the wide world does one identify this rare species, this unusual human being who is sensitive to the creative process and defends the agency recommendations with conviction and vigor? As you might expect, it is not easy. But there are some signals, some semihypothetical tests that can be used as diagnostic tools.

To begin with, look for unflappability, a splendid trait to possess in the heat of battle. In Australia last year, I heard a chap tell about arriving home to "find a bit of a problem" under his bed. An eight-foot python had slithered in and coiled around the man's small dog. Hearing its cries, he yanked the snake out from under the mattress, pried it loose from the mutt, tossed it out the door, and "dispatched it with a garden hoe." Was he particularly frightened or distressed? Not at all. "I've seen bigger snakes," he said, helping himself to another Foster's Lager. Now, that's the kind of disposition that wears well in account service land.

Wes Perrin, "How to Identify a Good AE," *Communication Arts Advertising Annual 1988* (Palo Alto, CA: Coyne and Blanchard, Inc., 1988), 210.

Exhibit 9.8 ▶ How to identify a good AE.

It's a job of negotiation, gentle prodding, and ambassadorship. For creatives to rise, their work must challenge. It must arrest attention, provoke, and, at times, shock. It must do all the things a wonderful piece of art must do. Yet as we indicated earlier, this is all the stuff that makes for nervous clients and an account executive's nightmare.

This nightmare situation for the AEs produces the kind of ads that win awards for the creatives. People who win awards are recognized: Their work gets published in *Advertising Age* magazine and websites or appears on the Clios. They are in demand, and they are sought after by rival agencies. They become famous and, yes, rich by advertising standards.

So the trick is, how do you get creatives to want to pursue cool ads that *also* sell? The ideal AE finds a way to keep both clients and creatives happy—not an easy thing to do but an essential dynamic to achieve. Given the critical role of AEs in bridging the gap between clients and creatives, emphasizing the vital role the account executive (AE) plays is one way to help mitigate any potential friction between agencies and clients; it has been suggested to not cut account executives when budgets get tight because of the crucial role that AEs play in the advertising process.[29]

Even though consumer insights often generate empirical bases for a leap to a creative idea, determining advertisement

One of the advantages of being a practitioner-turned-educator is the opportunity to interact with a large number of agencies. Much like Switzerland, an academic is viewed as a neutral in current affairs and not subject to the suspicions of a potential competitor.

The result of my neutral status has been the opportunity to watch different agencies produce both great and poor work. And, as a former associate creative director, I'd like to share the trends I've seen in the development of bad creative. The revelation: Bad work is more a matter of structure than talent. Here are 12 pieces of advice if you want to institutionalize bad creative work in your agency:

1. Treat your target audience like a statistic.

Substituting numbers for getting a feel for living, breathing people is a great way to make bad work inevitable. It allows you to use your gut instinct about "women 55 to 64" rather than the instinct that evolves from really understanding a group of folks. The beauty with staying on the statistical level is that you get to claim you did your homework when the creative turns out dreadful. After all, there were 47 pages of stats on the target.

2. Make your strategy a hodgepodge.

Good ads have one dominant message, just one. Most strategies that result in lousy work have lots more than one. They are political junkyards that defy a creative wunderkind to produce anything but mediocrity. So make everybody happy with the strategy and then tell your creatives to find a way to make it all work. You'll get bad work, for sure.

3. Have no philosophy.

William Bernbach believed in a certain kind of work. His people emulated his philosophy and produced a consistent kind of advertising that built a great agency. Now, to be controversial, I'll say the exact same thing about Rosser Reeves. Both men knew what they wanted, got it, and prospered.

The agency leaders who do hard sell one day, then new wave the next, create only confusion. More important, the work does not flow from a consistent vision of advertising and a code of behavior to achieve that advertising. Instead, there is the wild embrace of the latest fashion or the currently faddish bromide making the rounds at conventions. So beware of those who have a philosophy and really are true to it. They are historically at odds with lousy work.

4. Analyze your creative as you do a research report.

The cold, analytical mind does a wonderful job destroying uncomfortable, unexpected work. Demand that every detail be present in every piece of creative and say it is a matter of thoroughness. The creative work that survives your ice storm will be timid and compromised and will make no one proud.

5. Make the creative process professional.

"Creative types collect a paycheck every two weeks. They'd better produce and do it now. This is, after all, a business." The corporate performance approach is a highly recommended way of developing drab print and TV. Treating the unashamedly artistic process of making ads as if it were an offshoot of the local oil filter assembly plant promises to destroy risk taking and morale. Your work will become every bit as distinctive as a gray suit. More important, it will be on schedule. And both are fine qualities in business and we are a business, aren't we?

Continued

6. Say one thing and do another.

Every bad agency says all the right things about risk taking, loving great creative, and admiring strong creative people. It is mandatory to talk a good game and then do all the things that destroy great work. This will help keep spirits low and turnover high in the creatives who are actually talented. And then you'll feel better when they leave after a few months because you really do like strong creative people—if they just weren't so damn defensive.

7. Give your client a candy store.

To prove how hard you work, insist on showing numerous half-thought-out ideas to your client. The approved campaign will have lots of problems nobody thought about and that will make the final work a mess.

Campaigns with strong ideas are rare birds, and they need a great deal of thinking to make sure they're right. So insist on numerous campaigns and guarantee yourself a series of sparrows rather than a pair of eagles.

8. Mix and match your campaigns.

Bring three campaigns to your client, and then mix them up. Take a little bit of one and stick it on another. Even better, do it internally. It's like mixing blue, red, and green. All are fine colors, but red lacks the coolness of blue. Can't we add a little? The result of the mix will be a thick muddy clump. Just like so many commercials currently on the air.

9. Fix it in production.

Now that your procedure has created a half-baked campaign that is being mixed up with another, tell the creative to make it work by excellent production values. Then you can fire the incompetent hack when the jingle with 11 sales points is dull.

10. Blame the creative for bad creative.

After all, you told them what they should do. ("Make it totally unexpected, but use the company president and the old jingle.") The fault lies in the fact that you just can't find good talent anymore. Never mind that some creative departments have low turnover and pay smaller salaries than you do.

11. Let your people imitate.

"Chiat/Day won awards and sales for the Apple *1984* commercial, so let's do something like that for our stereo store account." This approach works wonders because your imitation appears lacking the original surprise that came from a totally expected piece of work. You can even avoid the controversy that surrounded Chiat/Day when half the industry said the ad was rotten. Your imitation can blend right in with all the other imitations and, even better, will have no strategic rationale for your bizarre execution.

12. Believe posttesting when you get a good score.

That way you can be slaughtered by your client when your sensitive, different commercial gets a score 20 points below norm. The nice things you said about posttesting when you got an excellent score with your "singing mop" commercial cannot be taken back. If you want to do good work, clients must somehow be made to use research as a tool. If you want to do bad creative, go ahead, and believe that posttesting rewards excellent work.

Naturally, a lot of bad creative results from egomania, laziness, incompetence, and client intractability—but a lot less than most believe. I have found that bad work usually comes from structures that make talented people ineffective and that demand hard work, human dedication, and tremendous financial investment to produce work that can be topped by your average high school senior.

John Sweeney, a former associate creative director at Foot, Cone & Belding, Chicago, teaches advertising at the University of North Carolina—Chapel Hill.

Exhibit 9.9 ▶ Assuring poor creativity.

success can also create conflict and attempts for control between the creative department and other departments, such as the research department. [30] One authority states that the tumultuous social environment between creative departments and ad testers represents the "historical conflict between art and science . . . these polarities have been argued philosophically as the conflict between Idealism and Materialism or Rationalism and Empiricism." [31] In the world of advertising, people in research departments are put in the unenviable position of judging the creatives. So, again, "science" judges art. Creatives don't like this, particularly when it's bad science or not science at all. Of course, researchers are sometimes creative themselves, and they don't typically enjoy being an additional constraint on those in the creative department.

So is there any way around all the tension and conflict inherent in the very people-intensive business of creating advertising and IBP? As detailed in Exhibit 9.9, the insights of John Sweeney—an expert on advertising creativity—make it clear what *not* to do if creativity is the goal. He notes that bad work is more a matter of structure than of talent. So given a pool of talented people, we have to provide some structure that allows them to produce their best work. Creative types, AEs, marketing managers, and ad researchers have to find a way to make beautiful music together. Here's how they can.

9-4 Making Beautiful Music Together: Coordination, Collaboration, and Creativity

Metaphors help us understand. Let's use a metaphor to appreciate the challenge of executing sophisticated advertising and IBP campaigns. Executing an IBP campaign is very much like the performance of a symphony orchestra. To produce glorious music, many individuals must make their unique contributions to the performance, but it sounds right only if the maestro brings it all together at the critical moment.

If you can attend a symphony, get there early so you can hear each musician warming up with their instrument. Each musician has put in many years of dedicated practice to master that instrument and many hours of rehearsal to learn their specific part for this performance. As you listen to the warm-up, notice how the random collection of sounds becomes increasingly painful to the ears. With each musician doing their own thing, the sound is a collection of hoots and clangs that grows louder as the performance approaches. Mercifully, the maestro finally steps to the podium to quell the cacophony. All is quiet for a moment. The musicians focus on their sheet music for reassurance, even though by now they could play their individual parts in their sleep. Finally, the maestro calls the orchestra into action. As a group, as a team, with each person executing a specific assignment as defined by the composer, under the direction of the maestro, they make beautiful music together.

Consider Nike's IBP; the firm literally uses the team metaphor of a soccer team going to the soccer field as a battlefield. In its creative work, the team metaphor illuminates in a powerful way that fits well with Nike's image.

So it goes in the world of advertising. Preparing and executing breakthrough IBP campaigns is a people-intensive business. Many different kinds of expertise will be needed to pull it off, and this means many different people must be enlisted to play a variety of roles. But some order must be imposed on the collection of players. Frequently, a maestro will need to step in to give the various players a common theme or direction for their work. Lee Clow of TBWA Worldwide quite naturally received a conductor's baton as a gift; this symbolizes how coordinating creativity is just as important as being a creative individual in the field of advertising and marketing.

Coordination and collaboration will be required for executing any kind of advertising, which simply means that advertising is a team sport. Moreover, the creative essence of the campaign can be aided and elevated by the skillful use of teams. Teams can generate a synergy that allows them to rise above the talents of their individual members on many kinds of tasks. So even without a creative genius in our midst, a group of diverse and motivated people can be expected to not only generate big ideas but also put them into action.

Great advertising and great teamwork go hand in hand, which of course means that we don't just want to hope for a good team; we need to make it happen. Great teamwork can't be left to chance. It must be planned for and facilitated if it is to occur with regularity. So next we will introduce several concepts and insights about teams to make you better at teamwork. In addition, you will come to appreciate how important teams can be in producing that one elusive thing that everyone wants: *creativity*.

9-4a What We Know about Teams

No doubt you have taken a class in which part of your grade was determined by teamwork. Teamwork in educational settings reflects the business reality that interpersonal skills are highly valued in the real world of work. In fact, an impressive body of research indicates that teams have become essential to the effectiveness of modern organizations. In their book *The Wisdom of Teams*, consultants Jon Katzenbach and Douglas Smith review many valuable insights about the importance of teams. Here, we summarize several of their key conclusions, along with other comments about the role of teams.[31]

Teams Rule

There is little doubt that in a variety of organizations, teams have become the primary means for getting things done. The growing number of performance challenges faced by most businesses—as a result of factors such as more demanding customers, technological changes, government regulation, and intensifying competition—demand speed and quality that are simply beyond the scope of what an individual can offer. The complexity of today's business problems can only be solved through collaboration.[32] In most instances, teams are the only valid option for getting things done. This is certainly the case in advertising.

It's All about Performance

Research shows that teams are effective in organizations where the leadership makes it perfectly clear that teams will be held accountable for performance. Teams are expected to produce results that satisfy the client and yield financial gains for the organization.

Synergy through Teams

Modern organizations require many kinds of expertise to get the work done. The only reliable way to mix people with different areas of expertise to generate solutions in which the whole is greater than the sum of the parts is through team discipline. Research shows that blending expertise from diverse areas often produces the most innovative solutions to many different types of business problems.[33] The "blending" must be done through teams.

The Demise of Individualism?

Rugged individualism is the American way. Are we suggesting that a growing reliance on teams in the workplace must mean a devaluation of the individual and a greater emphasis on conforming to what the group thinks? Not at all. In fact, teams are not incompatible with individual excellence. Effective teams find ways to let each person on the business team bring their unique contributions to the forefront. When an individual on a team does not have their own contribution to make, then one can question that person's value to the team. As the old saying goes, "If you and I think alike, then one of us is unnecessary."

Teams Promote Personal Growth

An added benefit of teamwork is that it promotes learning for each individual team member. In a team, people learn about their own work styles and observe the work styles of others. This learning makes them more effective team players in their next assignment. Once team principles take hold in an organization, momentum builds. Many ad agencies promote teamwork in the office by providing opportunities for teamwork outside the office. As an example, Peppercomm, a New York agency, sponsors kickball games and other team events after work hours.[34]

Leadership in Teams

A critical element in the equation for successful teams is leadership. Leaders do many things for their teams to help them succeed.[35] Teams ultimately must reach a goal to justify their standing, and here is where the leader's job starts. The leader's first job is to help the team build consensus about the goals they hope to achieve and the approach they will take to reach those goals. Without a clear sense of purpose, the team is doomed. Once the goals and purpose are agreed upon, the leader plays a critical role in ensuring that the work of the

team is consistent with the organization's strategy or plan. This is a particularly important role in the context of creating IBP campaigns.

Finally, team leaders must facilitate the real work of the team, meaning that they must be careful to contribute without dominating. There are two other key things that team leaders should never do: *They should not blame or allow specific individuals to fail, and they should never excuse away shortfalls in team performance.*[36] Mutual accountability must be emphasized over individual performance.

Direct Applications to the Account Team

Think of an agency's **account team** as a bicycle wheel, with the team leader as the hub. The spokes of the wheel reach out to the diverse disciplinary expertise needed in today's world of advertising and IBP. The spokes will represent team members from direct marketing, public relations, broadcast media, graphic design, interactive, creative, accounting, etc. The hub connects the spokes and ensures that everyone works in tandem and in a way that makes the wheel roll smoothly. To illustrate the multilayered nature of the team approach to IBP, each account team member can also be thought of as a hub in their very own wheel. For example, the direct marketing member on the account team is the team leader for their own set of specialists charged with preparing direct marketing materials. Through this type of multilevel "hub-and-spokes" design, the coordination and collaboration essential for effective IBP campaigns can be achieved.

Fostering Collaboration through the Creative Brief

The **creative brief** is a little document with a huge role in promoting good teamwork and fostering the creative process. It establishes the goal for any advertising effort in a way that gets everyone moving in the same direction but should never force or mandate a particular solution. It provides basic guidelines with plenty of room for the creatives to be creative. Preparation of the creative brief is a joint activity involving the client lead and the AE. When the creative brief is done right, a host of potential conflicts are prevented. An efficient template for the creative brief is featured in Exhibit 9.10.

Teams Liberate Decision-Making

With the right combination of expertise assembled on the account team, a carefully crafted creative brief, and a leader who has the team working well as a unit, what appears to be casual or spur-of-the-moment decision-making can turn out to be breakthrough collaborations. This is one of the huge benefits of healthy teamwork. As they say at Crispin Porter + Bogusky (CP+B), a good idea can come from anywhere. Teams composed of members who trust one another are liberated to

CLIENT: **DATE:**   **JOB NO.:**
Prepared by:

WHAT IS THE PRODUCT OR SERVICE?
Simple description or name of product or service.

WHO/WHAT IS THE COMPETITION?
Provide a snapshot of the brand situation, including current position in the category, brand challenges, competitive threats, and future goals.

WHO ARE WE TALKING TO?
Clear definition of who the target is both demographically and psychographically. Be as specific as possible in defining the target so that the creative can connect target and brand in the most compelling way.

WHAT CONSUMER NEED OR PROBLEM DO WE ADDRESS?
Describe the unmet consumer need that this product or service fills or how this product addresses a need in a way that's unique.

WHAT DOES THE CONSUMER CURRENTLY THINK ABOUT US?
Uncover target insights to get at attitudes and behaviors related to broader context as well as specific category and brand. Determine whether insights currently exist or whether new research needs to be conducted.

WHAT ONE THING DO WE WANT THEM TO BELIEVE?
Be as single-minded as possible. Write in benefit (functional, emotional, or self-expressive) language. Should differentiate us... no other brand in the category can or is currently saying it.

WHAT CAN WE TELL THEM THAT WILL MAKE THEM BELIEVE THIS?
Not a laundry list of available support but the few things that clearly support the "one thing we want them to believe."

WHAT IS THE TONALITY OF THE ADVERTISING?
A few adjectives or phrase that captures the tonality and personality of the advertising.

Of particular note:
Write it in the consumer's language; not business-speak.

Make every word count; be simple and concise.

Make as evocative as possible. Think of the brief as the first "ad." The brief should make creatives jump up and down in their excitement to start executing it!

Exhibit 9.10 ▶ Template for a creative brief.

be more creative because no one is worried about having their best ideas stolen or trying to look good for the boss. It's the team that counts. This type of "safe" team environment allows everyone to contribute and lets the whole be greater than the sum of the parts.

9-4b When Sparks Fly: Igniting Creativity through Teams

Whether account teams, subspecialist teams, creative teams, or hybrid teams involving persons from both the client and agency side, all will play critical roles in preparing and executing integrated advertising campaigns. Moreover, impressive evidence shows that when managed in a proactive way, teams develop better ideas, that is, ideas that are both creative and useful in the process of building brands.[37] One can get pretty serious about the subject of managing creativity, and good teamwork may be serious stuff. But it doesn't have to be complicated, and it certainly will get rowdy at times. The primary goals are to build teams with the right expertise and diversity of thought, to encourage individuals on those teams to challenge and build on each other's ideas, and to create just the right amount of tension to get the sparks flying.

Cognitive Styles

It has been suggested that there is a division in marketing thinking where business types favor left-brain thinking and advertising types (especially the creatives) favor right-brain thinking; Business types like to talk about testing and data and return on investment, whereas advertising types like to talk about movies and the Cannes Film Festival.[38] Although such stereotypes misrepresent individual differences, they remind us that people approach problem solving differently.

Each person's unique preferences for thinking about and solving a problem are a reflection of their **cognitive style**. For instance, some people prefer logical and analytical thinking; others prefer intuitive and nonlinear thinking. Numerous categorization schemes have been developed for classifying people based on their cognitive styles. Psychologist Carl Jung was an early pioneer among cognitive stylists. He proposed essential differences among individuals along three dimensions of cognitive style: sensing versus intuiting, thinking versus feeling, and extraverted versus introverted. The important point for teams and creativity is that the more homogeneous a team is in terms of cognitive style, the more limited the range of their solutions to a problem will be. Simply stated, diversity of thought nourishes creativity and enables agencies to better understand and address the target audience. And Creatives have the opportunity to embrace that diverse communities are shaping consumer culture. Shavone Charles, the head of global music and youth culture at Instagram stated,

"It's time to stop looking at these communities as niche. They are controlling culture and purchasing your products."[39]

Creative Abrasion

Teamwork is not a picnic in the park. That's why it's called team *work*. Moreover, when teams bring together people with diverse cognitive styles and they truly get engaged in the task, there will be friction. Friction can be both good and bad.[40] On the one hand, we can have **creative abrasion**, which is the clash of ideas, and from which new ideas and breakthrough solutions can emerge. That's the good thing. On the other hand, we can have **interpersonal abrasion**, which is the clash of people, from which communication shuts down and new ideas get slaughtered. That's obviously the bad thing. So, as we pointed out earlier, teams must have leadership that creates a safe environment allowing creative abrasion to flourish while always looking to defuse interpersonal abrasion. It's a fine line, but getting it right means the difference between creativity and chaos.

Using Brainstorming and External Perspectives

Many of us have participated in a team meeting and, when it was all over, decided we'd just wasted another hour. Groups can waste a lot of time if not proactively managed, and one of the key means for getting groups or teams to generate novel solutions is through the use of a process called brainstorming. **Brainstorming** is an organized approach to idea generation in groups, as discussed in Exhibit 9.11.

Adding more diversity to the group is always a way to foster creative abrasion and help make progress. **Diversity** refers here to including a variety of people from different backgrounds, ages, cultures, genders, sexual orientations, abilities, and experiences on the business team. Moreover, well-established teams can get stale and stuck in a rut. Ramping up the creative abrasion may require insights from an external perspective. They can be from elsewhere in your organization or from outside the organization entirely. Perhaps the team will need to take a field trip together to observe or meet with others external to the team. Group creativity is crucial, even if it does bring some "creative abrasion."[41] Tranquility and sameness can be enemies of creativity. As Andy Stefanovich, a thought leader on innovation and growth, says, the key to cultivating creativity is looking at more stuff and thinking about it harder.

9-4c Final Thoughts on Teams and Creativity

Creativity in the preparation of an IBP campaign can be fostered by the trust and open communication that are hallmarks of effective teams. But it is also true that the creativity required

#1—Define the question. Ask the right question for your creative situation—a question that actually can be answered, even if you don't yet know the answer.

#2—Build off each other. One proven path to creativity entails building on existing ideas; don't just generate ideas, build on each others'.

#3—Fear drives out creativity. If people believe they will be teased, demoted, or otherwise humiliated in the group, no need to even consider brainstorming. It won't work.

#4—Prime individuals before and after. Encourage individuals to learn about the problem before and after the group session; teams always benefit when individuals apply their unique expertise.

#5—Make it happen. Great organizations develop a brainstorming culture where everyone knows the rules and honors them; to achieve such a culture, it is essential that ideas developed in brainstorm sessions lead to actions. We can't just talk big ideas; we must also put them to work.

#6—It's a skill. Leading a productive brainstorming session is not a job for amateurs; facilitating a brainstorming session is a skill that takes months or years to master. Don't pretend to brainstorm without a skilled facilitator.

#7—Embrace a bit of creative abrasion. If your team has been formed appropriately, it will contain people with conflicting cognitive styles. Celebrate that diversity, welcome everybody into the group, and then let the sparks fly!

#8—Listen and learn. Good brainstorming sessions foster learning among people who have diverse expertise and divergent cognitive styles. Trust builds and suspicion fades.

#9—Allow time. Don't rush the process. Set aside quality time to think about the creative question you want to answer.

#10—Follow the rules, or you're not brainstorming (and pretending just wastes everybody's time).

Based on Robert I. Sutton, "The Truth about Brainstorming," *Inside BusinessWeek*, September 25, 2006, 17–21.

Exhibit 9.11 ▶ Ten rules for effective brainstorming.

for breakthrough campaigns will evolve as personal work products generated by individuals laboring on their own. Both personal and team creativity are critical in the preparation of advertising ad campaigns. The daunting task of facilitating both often falls in the lap of an agency's creative director.

The position of creative director in any ad agency is very special because, much like the maestro of the symphony orchestra, the creative director must encourage personal excellence and demand team accountability at the same time. We interviewed veteran creative directors to get more insights about the challenge of channeling the creative energies of their teams. All acknowledge that creativity has an intensely personal element, often motivated by the desire to satisfy one's own ego or sense of self. But despite this, team unity must also be a priority.

In orchestrating creative teams, these are some good principles to follow:

■ Take great care in assigning individuals to a team in the first place. Be sensitive to their existing workloads and the proper mix of expertise required to do the job for the client.

■ Get to know the cognitive style of each individual. Listen carefully. Because creativity can be an intensely personal matter, one has to know when it is best to leave people alone versus when one needs to support them in working through the inevitable rejection.

■ Make teams responsible to the client. Individuals and teams are empowered when they have sole responsibility for performance outcomes. Beware of adversarial and competitive relationships between individuals and between teams. They can quickly lead to mistrust that destroys camaraderie and synergy.

■ In situations where the same set of individuals will work on multiple teams over time, rotate team assignments to foster fresh thinking, or bring in some fresh, external perspectives.

Here, we see once again that the fundamentals of effective teams—communication, trust, complementary expertise, and leadership—produce the desired performance outcome. There's simply no alternative. Advertising is a team sport. Subaru understands the role of teams, and it seems that it has brilliantly bridged some creative strategy with some smart social media strategy; for example, Subaru has developed a Facebook app through which consumers can chat with dogs. It works for this brand because their ads often feature dogs and the concept aligns with the target psychographic of outdoor-loving dog owners.

9-5 Have You Decided to Become More Creative?

A great way to summarize the factors that foster creativity, which entails both uniqueness and consistency, is via the **3Ps creativity framework**.[42] People is the first P, and as we emphasized at the beginning of this chapter, the field of advertising has always embraced the concept of great creative minds. But we also know that the Process used in developing creative work and the Place or environment wherein the work is done are also big factors in generating creative outcomes. As one agency leader put it, "We sell ideas, and if your employees are unhappy, you are not going to get a lot of good ideas."[43] All that makes sense, but now, as promised, it's time to circle back to YOU.

Most of us are not going to model our lives after those of creative geniuses like Pablo Picasso or Martha Graham. Even though it's great to have role models to inspire us, we don't think it's realistic to aspire to be the next Gandhi or Einstein. But we all can take stock of our own special skills and abilities and should candidly assess our own strengths and weaknesses. For example, referring to some of the terminology used earlier in this chapter, we all can complete assessments that reveal our own cognitive styles and then compare ourselves to others. And if you want to measure your level of creativity, just search the Internet for "creativity tests" or "creativity assessments," and a host of options will present themselves. It is a good thing to get to know yourself better

and to start thinking about your unique skills and abilities. In addition, if you have any interest in a career in advertising, it would be good to decide right now that you are going to make yourself more creative. Although we all may start in different places, it is a worthy goal to develop your creative capacity. Yale psychologist Robert Sternberg, who has devoted his professional career to the study of intelligence and creativity, advises his students as follows:

> To make yourself more creative, decide now to:
> Redefine problems to see them differently from other people;
> Be the first to analyze and critique your own ideas, since we all have good ones and bad ones;
> Be prepared for opposition whenever you have a really creative idea;
> Recognize that it is impossible to be creative without adequate knowledge;
> Recognize that too much knowledge can stifle creativity;
> Find the standard, safe solution and then decide when you want to take a risk by defying it;
> Keep growing and experiencing, and challenging your own comfort zone;
> Believe in yourself, especially when surrounded by doubters;
> Learn to cherish ambiguity, because from it comes the new ideas.
> Remember that research has shown that people are most likely to be creative when doing something they love.[44]

It's good advice; especially if you are interested in careers in creative aspects of advertising such as art direction, copywriting, and/or in managing those aspects of advertising in an account executive or other business role.

Summary

1. Describe the core characteristics of great creative minds.

A look at the shared sensibilities of great creative minds provides a constructive starting point for assessing the role of creativity in the production of great advertising. What Picasso had in common with Gandhi, Freud, Eliot, Stravinsky, Graham, and Einstein—including a strikingly exuberant self-confidence, (childlike) alertness, unconventionality, and an obsessive commitment to the work—both charms and alarms us. Self-confidence, at some point, becomes crass self-promotion; an unconstrained childlike ability to see the world as forever new devolves, somewhere along the line, into childish self-indulgence. Without creativity, there can be no advertising. How we recognize and define creativity in advertising rests on our understanding of

the achievements of acknowledged creative geniuses from the worlds of art, literature, music, science, and politics.

2. Contrast the role of an agency's creative department with that of business managers/account executives and explain the tensions between them.

What it takes to get the right idea (a lot of hard work) and the ease with which a client may dismiss that idea underlies the contentiousness between an agency's creative staff and its AEs and clients. Creatives provoke. Managers restrain. Ads that win awards for creative excellence don't necessarily fulfill a client's business goals. All organizations deal with the competing agendas of one department versus another, but in advertising agencies, this competition plays out at an amplified level. The difficulty of assessing the effectiveness of any form of advertisement only adds to the problem. Advertising researchers are put in the unenviable position of judging the creatives, pitting "science" against "art." None of these tensions changes the fact that creativity is essential to the vitality of brands. Creativity makes a brand, and it is creativity that reinvents established brands in new and desired ways.

3. **Assess the role of teams in managing tensions and promoting creativity in advertising and IBP applications.**

There are many sources of conflict and tension in the business of creating great advertising. It's the nature of the beast. One way that many organizations attempt to address this challenging issue is through systematic utilization of teams. Teams, when effectively managed, will produce outputs that are greater than the sum of their individual parts. Teams need to be managed proactively to promote creative abrasion but limit interpersonal abrasion if they are to produce "beautiful music together." Guidance from a maestro (like a Lee Clow or an Alex Bogusky) will be required. Another important tool to get teams headed in the right direction and to preempt many forms of conflict in the advertising arena is the creative brief. It's a little document with a very big function.

4. **Examine yourself and your own passion for creativity.**

Self-assessment is an important part of learning and growing, and now is the perfect time to be thinking about yourself and your passion for creativity. If advertising is a profession that interests you, then improving your own creative abilities should be a lifelong quest. Now is the time to decide to become more creative.

Key Terms

3Ps creativity framework
account executive (AE)
account team
brainstorming

cognitive style
consumer-based strategy
creative abrasion
creative brief

creative strategy
creativity
diversity
interpersonal abrasion

Endnotes

1. Matthew Creamer, "Caught in the Clutter Crossfire: Your Brand," *Advertising Age,* April 2, 2007, 1, 35.
2. Daniel W. Baack et al., "Advertising to Businesses: Does Creativity Matter?" *Industrial Marketing Management* 55 (2016), 169–177.
3. Federico De Gregorio and Kasey Windels, "Are Advertising Agency Creatives More Creative Than Anyone Else? An Exploratory Test of Competing Predictions," *Journal of Advertising* 50, no. 2 (August 2020), 207–216; and Brian Till and Daniel Baack, "Recall and Persuasion: Does Creative Advertising Matter?" *Journal of Advertising* (Fall 2005), 47–57; and Daniel Baack, Pack Wilson, and Brian Till, "Creativity and Memory Effects," *Journal of Advertising* (Winter 2008), 85–94.
4. Chen Jiemiao, Xiaojing Yang, and Robert E. Smith, "The Effects of Creativity on Advertising Wear-in and Wear-out," *Journal of the Academy of Marketing Science* 4, no. 3 (2016), 334–349.
5. Thomas C. O'Guinn and Albert Muniz, Jr., "The Social Brand: Towards a Sociological Model of Brands," in Barbara Loken, Rohini Ahluwalia, and Michael J. Houston (Eds.), *Brands and Brand Management: Contemporary Research Perspectives* (New York and London: Routledge, 2010), 133–159.
6. Marc Gobe, *Emotional Branding: The New Paradigm for Connecting Brands to People* (New York: Allworth, 2011).

7. John Parker et al., "How Does Consumer Insight Support the Leap to a Creative Idea?" *Journal of Advertising Research* 61, no. 1 (June 2020), 30–43.
8. Carl G. Jung, cited in Astrid Fitzgerald, *An Artist's Book of Inspiration: A Collection of Thoughts on Art, Artists, and Creativity* (New York: Lindisfarne, 1996), 58.
9. Socrates, quoted in Plato, *Phaedrus and the Seventh and Eighth Letters,* Walter Hamilton, trans (Middlesex, England: Penguin, 1970), 46–47; cited in Kay Redfield Jamison, *Touched with Fire: Manic-Depressive Illness and the Artistic Temperament* (New York: Free Press, 1993), 51.
10. Howard Gardner, *Creating Minds: An Anatomy of Creativity Seen through the Lives of Freud, Einstein, Picasso, Stravinsky, Eliot, Graham, and Gandhi* (New York: Basic Books, 1993).
11. Ibid., 364.
12. Ibid., 145.
13. Sigmund Freud, *The Interpretation of Dreams,* in A. A. Brill (Ed.), *The Basic Writings of Sigmund Freud* (New York: Modern Library, 1900/1938).
14. Gardner, *Creating Minds,* 369.
15. Ibid.

16. Jeff Beer, "Apple Advertising Legend Lee Clow, One of the Last Larger-than-Life Creative Titans, Is Retiring," *Fast Company*, February 14, 2019, https://www.fastcompany.com/90307081/apple-advertising-legend-lee-clow-one-of-the-last-larger-than-life-creative-titans-is-retiring.

17. Ibid.

18. Frederic Godard and David Dubois, "Creative Types Need a Balance of Searching and Selling," *INSEAD Knowledge,* October 13, 2016, http://knowledge.insead.edu/leadership-organisations/creative-types-need-a-balance-of-searching-and-selling-4983.

19. Jennifer Deal, "Leaders Say They Want More Creativity. But They Really Don't," *Wall Street Journal,* September 18, 2016, http://blogs.wsj.com/experts/2016/09/18/leaders-say-they-want-more-creativity-but-they-really-dont/; and Mark Kilgour et al., "Why Do Great Creative Ideas Get Rejected?" *Journal of Advertising Research* 60, no. 1 (July 29, 2019), 12–27.

20. Quoted in Jonathan Nelson, "Is Data Killing Creativity?" *Campaign,* June 16, 2016, http://www.campaignlive.com/article/data-killing-creativity/1399071.

21. Vakratsas, Demetrios, and Xin (Shane) Wang, "Artificial Intelligence in Advertising Creativity," *Journal of Advertising* 50, no. 1, (December 21, 2020), 39–51.

22. Mahsa Ghaffari, Chris Hackley, and Zoe Lee, "Control, Knowledge, and Persuasive Power In Advertising Creativity: An Ethnographic Practice Theory Approach," *Journal of Advertising* 48, no. 2 (March 18, 2019), 242–249.

23. Luke Sullivan, "Staring at Your Partner's Shoes," in *Hey Whipple, Squeeze This: A Guide to Creating Great Ads* (New York: Wiley, 1998), 20–22.

24. William Bernbach, quoted in Thomas Frank, *The Conquest of Cool: Business Culture, Consumer Culture, and the Rise of Hip Consumerism* (Chicago, IL: University of Chicago Press, 1997).

25. George Lois, quoted in Randall Rothenberg, *Where the Suckers Moon* (New York: Knopf, 1994), 135–172.

26. Christy Ashley and Jason Oliver, "Creative Leaders," *Journal of Advertising,* Spring 2010, 115–130.

27. Sheila Sasser and Scott Koslow, "Desperately Seeking Advertising Creativity," *Journal of Advertising* (Winter 2008), 5–19.

28. Shu-Chuan Chu et al., "Understanding Advertising Client–Agency Relationships in China: A Multimethod Approach to Investigate Guanxi Dimensions and Agency Performance," *Journal of Advertising* 48, no. 5 (August 2019), 473–494. For more on Guanxi in business, see Scheinbaum, Angeline Close, and Stephen W. Wang, "Customer Centricity and Guanxi Prevalence as Social Capital: A Study of International Business Relationships," *Journal of Business & Industrial Marketing* 33, no. 8 (2018), 1209–1220.

29. Jeremy Mullman, "Think Twice before Axing Account Management," *Advertising Age,* April 26, 2010, 8; and A. J. Kover and S. M. Goldberg, "The Games Copywriters Play: Conflict, Quasi-Control,

a New Proposal," *Journal of Advertising Research* 25, no. 4 (1995), 52–62.

30. R. L. Vaughn, "Point of View. Creatives versus Researchers—Must They Be Adversaries?" *Journal of Advertising Research* 22, no. 6 (1983), 45–48; and John Parker, Scott Koslow, Lawrence Ang, and Alexander Tevi, "How Does Consumer Insight Support the Leap to a Creative Idea?: Inside the Creative Process: Shifting the Advertising Appeal from Functional to Emotional," *Journal of Advertising Research* 61, no. 1 (2021), 30-43.

31. Jon R. Katzenbach and Douglas K. Smith, *The Wisdom of Teams: Creating the High-Performance Organization* (Boston, MA: Harvard Business School Press, 1993).

32. Roger Martin, *The Opposable Mind* (Boston, MA: Harvard Business School Press, 2009).

33. Dorothy Leonard and Susan Straus, "Putting Your Company's Whole Brain to Work," *Harvard Business Review* (July–August 1997), 111–121.

34. Ed Frauenheim and Kim Peters, "Here's the Secret to How the Best Employers Inspire Workers," *Fortune,* August 22, 2016, http://fortune.com/2016/08/22/advertising-best-workplaces/.

35. Katzenbach Smith, *The Wisdom of Teams,* Ch. 7.

36. Ibid., 144.

37. Jacob Goldenberg, Amnon Levav, David Mazursky and Sorin Solomon, *Cracking the Ad Code* (Cambridge, UK: Cambridge University Press, 2009); Douglas West et al., "Future Directions for Advertising Creativity Research," *Journal of Advertising* 50, no. 1 (September 2018), 102–114.

38. Dale Buss, "Bridging the Great Divide in Marketing Thinking," *Advertising Age,* March 26, 2007, 18, 19.

39. Krystle M. Davis, "12 Quotes to Motivate CMOs to Make Diversity a Priority," *Forbes,* June 5, 2018, https://www.forbes.com/sites/forbescontentmarketing/2018/06/05/12-quotes-to-motivate-cmos-to-make-diversity-a-priority/?sh=75a4bbaf4392.

40. Dorothy Leonard and Walter Swap, *When Sparks Fly: Igniting Creativity in Groups* (Boston, MA: Harvard Business School Press, 1999).

41. Ibid, p. 19.

42. Sasser, Sheila L., and Scott Koslow. "Desperately seeking advertising creativity: Engaging an imaginative "3Ps" research agenda." *Journal of Advertising* 37, no. 4 (2008), 5–20; and Mafael, Alexander, Sascha Raithel, Charles R. Taylor, and David W. Stewart. "Measuring the Role of Uniqueness and Consistency to Develop Effective Advertising." *Journal of Advertising* 50, no. 4 (2021), 494–504.

43. Brooke Capps, "Playtime, Events, Perks Go Long Way in Team Building," *Advertising Age,* January 15, 2007, 30.

44. Robert J. Sternberg, "Creativity as a Decision," *American Psychologist,* May 2002, 376; and Robert J. Sternberg, "Identifying and Developing Creative Giftedness," *Roeper Review* 23, no. 2 (2000), 60–65.

Creative Message Strategy

LO **1**

10-1 Creative Message Strategy

As shown in the framework in Exhibit 10.1, this chapter focuses on the actual development of messages. It offers you a framework to consider when developing messages as you think about what you want to accomplish with your advertising and other brand messaging and how you will use advertising and IBP to achieve marketing goals and give the brand meaning. Also bear in mind that creative messages are just as important for business-to-business advertising as they are for consumer advertising.[1]

Creative message strategy refers to the set of objectives and methods or tactics used to create and disseminate a relevant and resonating message (such as about a product, service, experience, or brand) to customers and potential customers. Creative message strategy is where the advertising and branding battle is usually won or lost. It's where real creativity exists. It's where the agency has to be smart and determine just how to turn the wishes of the client into effective advertising. It is where the creatives have to get into the minds of consumers, realizing that the message will be received by different people in different ways. It is where advertisers merge culture, mind, and brand. Great messages are developed by people who can put themselves into the minds (and culture) of their audience members and anticipate their response, leading to the best outcome: selling the advertised brand.

Exhibit 10.1 ▶ This is the framework and context for Chapter 10, with the focus on creative message strategy.

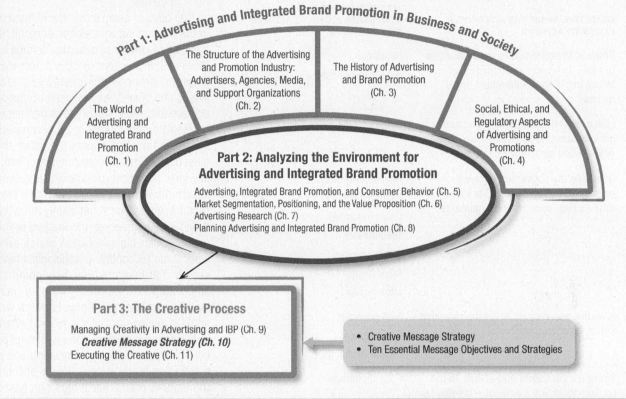

Part 1: Advertising and Integrated Brand Promotion in Business and Society

The World of Advertising and Integrated Brand Promotion (Ch. 1)

The Structure of the Advertising and Promotion Industry: Advertisers, Agencies, Media, and Support Organizations (Ch. 2)

The History of Advertising and Brand Promotion (Ch. 3)

Social, Ethical, and Regulatory Aspects of Advertising and Promotions (Ch. 4)

Part 2: Analyzing the Environment for Advertising and Integrated Brand Promotion

Advertising, Integrated Brand Promotion, and Consumer Behavior (Ch. 5)
Market Segmentation, Positioning, and the Value Proposition (Ch. 6)
Advertising Research (Ch. 7)
Planning Advertising and Integrated Brand Promotion (Ch. 8)

Part 3: The Creative Process

Managing Creativity in Advertising and IBP (Ch. 9)
Creative Message Strategy (Ch. 10)
Executing the Creative (Ch. 11)

- Creative Message Strategy
- Ten Essential Message Objectives and Strategies

The message strategy outlines the advertiser's goals. This chapter offers 10 essential message objectives and then discusses and illustrates the methods most commonly used to achieve them. Exhibit 10.2 summarizes the 10 message strategy objectives and methods presented here. Some of the ads in this chapter, as with some that you encounter in life, will use a combination of strategies. When you see an ad, you should ask: What is this ad trying to do, and how is it trying to accomplish that?

LO 2

10-2 Ten Essential Message Objectives and Strategies

The 10 message objectives are presented from simplest to most sophisticated, social and cultural branding through advertising, and IBP. Through each lens, we will discuss the logic behind the strategy, the basic mechanisms involved, how it works, how success or failure is typically determined, and a strategic summary and assessment of those methods.

10-2a Objective #1: Promote Brand Recall

Since modern advertising's earliest days, getting consumers to remember the advertised brand's name has been an important goal. The very obvious idea is that if consumers remember the brand name and can easily recall it, they are more likely to buy it. And while it is true that remembering a brand doesn't automatically mean the consumer will ultimately purchase it, all else being equal, remembering the brand name raises the odds that they will.

Although memory is a very complex topic, the relationship between repetition and recall has been pretty well understood for a long time. We know that repetition generally increases the odds of recall. So by repeating a brand name over and over, the advertiser increases the odds of consumers recalling that brand name.

But advertisers typically don't just want consumers to remember their name; they want their name to be the *first* brand consumers remember, or what advertisers call *top of mind*. At a minimum, they want to be in the **evoked set**, a small list of brand names (typically five or fewer) that comes to mind when a product or service category (e.g., soft drinks [Coke, Pepsi] or toothpaste [Crest, Colgate]) is mentioned. So if someone says "soft drink," the folks in Atlanta (the Coca-Cola Company headquarters) want you to say

Exhibit 10.2 ▶ Message strategy objectives and methods.

OBJECTIVE: WHAT THE ADVERTISER HOPES TO ACHIEVE	METHOD: HOW THE ADVERTISER PLANS TO ACHIEVE THE OBJECTIVE
Promote brand recall: To get consumers to recall its brand name(s) first; that is, before any of the competitors' brand names	Repetition Slogans and jingles
Link a key attribute to the brand name: To get consumers to associate a key attribute with a brand name and vice versa	Unique selling proposition (USP)
Persuade the consumer: To convince consumers to buy a product or service through high-engagement arguments	Reason-why ads Hard-sell ads Comparison ads Testimonials Demonstration Advertorials Infomercials
Affective association: To get the consumer to feel good about the brand	Feel-good ads Humor ads Sexual-appeal ads
Scare the consumer into action: To get consumers to buy a product or service by instilling fear	Fear-appeal ads
Change behavior by inducing anxiety: To get consumers to make a purchase decision by playing to their anxieties; often, the anxieties are social in nature	Anxiety ads Social anxiety ads
Define the brand image: To create an image for a brand by relying predominantly on visuals rather than words and argument	Image ads
Leverage social disruption and cultural contradictions: To leverage disruption and cultural contradictions in society to the brand's advantage. Get consumers to see the brand as a way to resolve these tensions and contradictions.	Tie brand to social/cultural movement as a way to resolve cultural contradictions
Situate the brand in a social context: To give the brand the desired social meaning	Slice-of-life ads Product placement/short Internet films Light-fantasy ads
Transform consumption experiences: To create a feeling, image, or mood about a brand that is activated when the consumer uses the product or service	Transformational ads

"Coke," preferably before any other brand name but certainly in the first group mentioned before you pause to think of others.

The odds of being either top of mind or in the evoked set increase with recall. In the case of **parity products** (defined as those with few major objective differences between brands—for example, paper towels and other "low-involvement" goods and services—the first brand remembered is often the most likely to be purchased. First-remembered brands are often the most popular. In fact, consumers may actually infer popularity, desirability, and even superiority from the ease with which they recall brands. The most easily recalled brand may be seen as the leading brand (most popular, highest market share), even when it isn't. Cognitive psychologists have shown that humans infer how common something is (frequency) by how easily they remember it. So consumers will actually believe brand X's market share to be higher because it comes to mind so quickly. If people think a particular brand is the leading brand, it can actually become the leading brand. For things purchased routinely, you can't expect consumers to deliberate and engage in extensive consideration of product attributes. Instead, in the real world of advertising and brand promotion, you rely on recall of the brand name or of a previously made judgment (e.g., *I like Bounty*) to get the advertised brand in the shopping cart. Sometimes the simplest strategy is the best one. This is what we termed mindshare advertising in Chapter 5.

Clearly, there is a large advantage in simple brand recall with routinely purchased product categories, like consumer packaged goods. So how do advertisers promote easy recall? There are two popular methods: repetition and memory aids—slogans, jingles, and point-of-purchase branding.

Method A: Repetition

Repetition is a tried-and-true way of facilitating the retrieval of brand names from a consumer's memory. Advertisers do this by buying a lot of ads and/or by frequently repeating the brand name within the ad itself. This is typically done with television and radio, but it can be accomplished visually with promotional placement in television shows and movies as well as online and in social media. The idea is that things said (or shown) more often will be remembered more easily than things said (or shown) less frequently. So the advertiser repeats the brand name over and over again. Then, when the consumer stands in front of, say, a shelf of laundry detergents, the advertised brand name is recalled from memory.

The more accessible (easier-to-remember) brand names are retrieved first and fastest from memory, making them (all else being equal) more likely to end up in the shopping cart. Getting into the consumer's evoked set gets you close to the actual purchase, and achieving the top of mind gets you even closer. But does repetition always work? Not always. There are plenty of times when consumers remember one brand but then buy another. They may actually dislike the most easily remembered brand and never buy it. This type of advertising plays a pure probability game—being easily recalled tilts the odds of being purchased in favor of the advertisers willing to pay for the recall that repetition buys.

Repetition strategies are fundamental to many IBP efforts. Also, think visuals, including logos such as an apple with a bite out of it from Apple. Seeing a name over and over (and having it in a TV shot or featured in live streaming), for brand awareness and recall through repetition, is certainly one of the ideas behind named arenas such as FedEx Field and Minute Maid Park. So repetition in hearing the brand name—if applicable to the media type (e.g., event sponsorship announcements, television, radio) is important.

Visual repetition is also important. The very frequent image of the Geico Gecko, paired with frequent use of the word, makes this ongoing campaign successful. It has repetition, verbal–visual pairing, and no doubt owns a big piece of the mindshare of American consumers. Although psychologists are less sure about how repeated images function in recall than they are about recalling words, there is a general belief that they are related. In the case of Geico–Gecko pairing, the image is linked to words, and we know that helps. See how Geico uses this pairing on its website (Exhibit 10.3).

Method B: Slogans and Jingles

Slogans are one small step up from raw repetition in the degree of complexity. Here, slogans and jingles are used to enhance the odds of recalling the brand name. The basic mechanism at work here is still memory, and the goal is still brand-name recall. Slogans are linguistic devices that link a brand name to something memorable by means of the slogan's simplicity, meter, rhyme, or some other factors. Jingles do the same thing, just set to a melody. Examples are numerous: "Ba-da-ba-ba-baaa…I'm Lovin' It" (McDonald's); "Give Me a Break" (Kit Kat); "They're Magically Delicious" (Lucky Charms), and "I'm a Big Kid Now" (Huggies). Some slogans can even imply a good deal, such as Subway's "Five Dollar Foot Long." Or they could simply be the brand name itself, such as "Riiiiiiiicolaaaaaaaaa" for Ricola cough drops. Slogans and jingles provide rehearsal—that is, encourage repetition because they are catchy, or people are prone to repeat them—and the inherent properties of the slogan or jingle provide a retrieval cue for the brand name.

Brands sometimes update their jingles for new target audiences or new associations. As shown in Exhibit 10.4, the Procter & Gamble brand Mr. Clean recently released commercials with a more modern version of the household cleaning brand's traditional jingle. Targeting a diverse audience throughout North America, the jingle was also translated into Spanish and French for use in new commercials.[2]

Also consider a practical application of the consumer behavior tendency to complete or "close" a verse: For example, when you say, "Snap! Crackle! Pop!," you pretty much are compelled to complete the phrase with "Rice Krispies!" As you know, slogans and jingles are hard to get out of your head. And that's the idea.

Method C: Point-of-Purchase Branding

Part of remembering is being reminded. In the contemporary advertising IBP world, marketers often use point-of-purchase displays that help trigger, or cue, the brand name (and maybe an ad) from memory. That is the main idea behind point-of-purchase advertising—to provide a memory trigger. The in-store visual triggers retrieval of the brand name, and maybe memories of the actual ad itself, importantly, at the point-of-purchase decision—when it goes in the cart or stays on the shelf.

Source: GEICO

Exhibit 10.3 ▶ This screenshot of Geico's insurance website prominently features wordplay on the brand name with the Gecko lizard, which has been a crux of the firm's integrated branding/IBP strategy.

Source: Mr. Clean

Exhibit 10.4 ▶ Mr. Clean (a household cleaning brand) uses a jingle to help update its branding; jingles, when done well, can be integrated seamlessly into other forms of IBP for maximum efficacy.

The aisle itself (its look, smell, etc.) or the packaging may cue the category. That is, on the shopper's often-repeated and highly routinized path down this aisle, the aisle itself and the packaging may prompt recollections about the category (say, paper towels) and may make the heavily advertised brand (say, Bounty) come right to mind.

Evaluation of repetition, slogans, and jingles is typically done through **day-after-recall (DAR)** tests (where ad elements are tested for recall the day after exposure) and other tracking studies emphasizing recall (for instance, "name three paper towel brands"). In other words, these ads are evaluated with the traditional ad copy research of simple recall measures.

Strategic Implications of Repetition, Slogans, and Jingles

- *Extremely resistant to forgetting.* These methods make it difficult to forget the brand. Once established, the residual amount of impact from the campaign can be significant. If some advertisers stopped advertising today, you would remember their slogans, jingles, and names for a long, long time.

- *Efficient for consumers.* For routinely purchased items, consumers rely on a simple and easy decision rule: Buy what you remember. So this kind of advertising works well for repeat-purchase and low-involvement items.

- *Long-term commitment/expense.* To achieve an adequate level of recall, advertisers have to sign on for a lot of adver-

tising. It takes lots and lots of repetition, particularly early on, or a very memorable slogan or jingle. Once advertisers have achieved a high recall level, they can fine-tune their spending so that they are spending just enough to maintain their desired position. But they have to get there first, and it can be a very expensive journey.

- *Competitive interference.* This is less of a problem with repetition, but consumers may learn a slogan or jingle only to associate it with the wrong brand. For example, "… is on your side" It's State Farm, right? Wait, actually is it Nationwide? Not absolutely sure? This is not good for the brand. This is why it is absolutely vital to firmly link the brand name with the slogan. You don't want to pay for your competitor's success.

- *Creative resistance.* Creatives generally hate this type of advertising. Can you imagine why? These ads are rarely called creative and don't usually win a lot of creative awards. So experienced creatives are less likely to enjoy working on them, and clients may wind up with more junior creative teams.

10-2b Objective #2: Link Key Attribute(s) to the Brand Name

Sometimes advertisers want consumers or business customers to remember the brand and associate it with one or at most two attributes.[3] This type of advertising is most closely identified with the **unique selling proposition (USP)** style, a type of ad that strongly emphasizes a supposedly unique quality (or qualities) of the advertised brand. It is more complicated than simple brand recall and a bit more challenging. It is one step up from Objective #1 in complexity, requiring slightly more thought and learning. So it requires more from those planning and developing the ads. The ads provide a reason to buy; but they don't require the audience to think too much about that reason, just to associate it with the brand name. The primary mechanisms are memory and learning. The appeal may be through words (copy) and/or visuals (art direction). Head & Shoulders shampoo does a good job communicating why their shampoo has a unique feature to it that will benefit users; the fact that it has clinically proven dandruff protection is prominent in the ad and made relevant by the use of celebrity athlete endorsers Patrick Mahomes and Troy Polamalu, as seen in the ad in Exhibit 10.5.

Method

USP stands for unique selling proposition. The idea of emphasizing a single brand attribute is a very good one—but sometimes two are used if they are complementary, such as "strong but gentle." Ads that try to link several attributes to a brand while working to establish recall often fail—they are too confusing and give too much information. Evaluation of the USP method is typically done through recall tests, communication tests, and tracking studies. Did the consumer remember the USP?

Sometimes the price is the USP, but as you might imagine, many advertisers make that claim, so it tends to be a pretty crowded space—and therefore not very unique.

Strategic Implications of the USP Method

- *Big carryover.* USP advertising is very efficient. Once this link has been firmly established, it can last a long time. An investment in this kind of advertising can carry you through some lean times.

- *Very resistant.* This type of advertising can be incredibly resistant to competitive challenges. Being the first to claim an attribute can result in a meaningful and sustainable advantage. Professionals will often say "Brand X owns that space" (meaning that attribute). For example, "Google owns the search engine space."

- *Long-term commitment and expense.* If advertisers are going to use the USP method, they have to be in it for the long haul. You can't keep switching strategies and expect good results. Pick an attribute and stay with it.

- *Some creative resistance.* Creatives tend not to hate this quite as much as simple repetition, but it does seem to get old with them pretty fast. Don't expect the best or most experienced creative teams when pursuing this method.

Exhibit 10.5 ▶ This ad from Head & Shoulders shows a USP—in that it has a strong dandruff protection and also it is good enough for some of the top football stars.

10-2c Objective #3: Persuade the Consumer

This style of advertising is about arguments. Here, we move up from linking one or possibly two attributes to a brand name using soft logic and simple learning to actually posing one or more (usually more) logical arguments to an engaged consumer. This is high-engagement advertising. That is, it assumes an actively engaged consumer, one who is paying attention and considering the arguments. Its goal is to convince the consumer through arguments that the advertised brand is the right choice. The advertiser says, in effect, you should buy my brand because of x, y, and z reasons. These arguments have typically been verbal (copy) but in the past few decades have employed more visual elements as well. As detailed in what follows, this type of advertising takes several shapes.

For this type of advertising to work as planned, the consumer has to think about what the advertiser is saying, understand the argument, and generally agree with it. In a pure persuasion ad, there is an assumed dialogue between the ad and the consumer, and some of the dialogue contains the consumer disagreeing and counterarguing with a message. As mentioned in Chapter 7, some research has found counterarguments to be the single most common consumer response to these types of ads. Actually, the most common response is no response at all; consumers just ignore them. Further, the inherent wordiness, the antiquated style, and that it is now speaking to the most distracted population in history are the reasons such advertising has become less popular.

Method A: Reason-Why Ads

In a reason-why ad, the advertiser reasons with the potential consumer. The ad emphasizes that there are good reasons why this brand will be satisfying and beneficial. Advertisers are usually relentless in their attempt to reason with consumers when using this method. They begin with some claim, like "Seven great reasons to buy Brand X," and then proceed to list all seven, finishing with the conclusion (implicit or explicit) that it would make no sense, after such compelling evidence, to do anything other than purchase Brand X. Other times, the reason or reasons to use a product can be presented deftly.

Psychologists have shown that humans value conclusions they have reached on their own more than those made for them. So really great reason-why ads will often outline why that brand is best but will let the consumer actually make the (obvious by then) conclusion that the advertised brand is the winner. The biggest success factor when using this method is ensuring that the reasons outlined in the ad make sense and that consumers actually care about them, which is why sometimes the reason-why ads include the reason why the choice actually matters.

Price advertising can be a reason why. There is a great deal of price advertising, and for that reason, it is hard to make that claim unique or ownable. Wise advertisers have argued that value is a superior claim to price; someone may beat you on the objectively lower price, but you can always claim that your brand is a better value. Note how Geico, in Exhibit 10.6,

Exhibit 10.6 ▶ Geico insurance has an ad that shows reasons why a consumer should choose its brand of insurance. The ad encourages consumers to read a few statistics on other brands and then says: "The choice is yours, and it's simple."

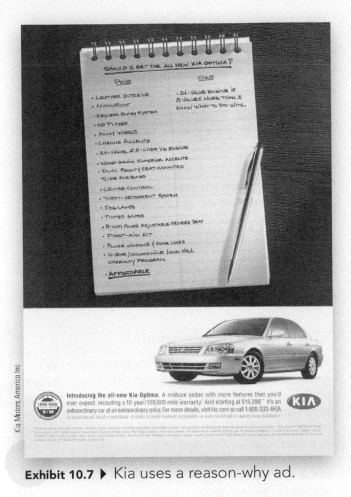

Kia Motors America Inc

Exhibit 10.7 ▶ Kia uses a reason-why ad.

offers a few reasons why its insurance brand is a good consumer choice. Similarly, Kia also uses a reasons-why approach that features a consumer's pros and cons for buying a Kia. As seen in Exhibit 10.7, it works by visually showing one con juxtaposed to a page full of pros, or "reasons why" consumers should buy a Kia (Exhibit 10.7).

Strategic Implications of Reason-Why Ads

■ *Permission to buy.* Gives consumers reasons for purchasing the advertised brand.

■ *Socially acceptable defense.* Sometimes we have to defend our purchase decisions to friends and family. These types of ads are chock-full of reasons why the purchase was a smart idea.

■ *High level of involvement.* Consumers have to be paying attention for these ads to work. They have to engage with these ads. How much of the time do you think that actually happens? Sometimes consumers get swamped with too much information and just do something simple like buy what they did last time or what a friend or *Consumer Reports* recommended.

■ *Potential for counterarguments.* This type of advertising might actually convince consumers why *not* to buy the advertised brand. Remember, consumers like to argue with ads.

■ *Legal/regulatory challenges/exposure.* The makers of these ads tend to get dragged into court or summoned by a regulatory body quite a bit. Be sure all your reason-why ads can stand up in court. Some haven't.

■ *Some creative resistance.* Creatives are often ho-hum on these types of ads.

Method B: Hard-Sell Ads

Hard-sell ads are a subcategory of reason-why ads: the reason why with urgency. They are characteristically high pressure and urgent and thus "hard." Phrases such as "act now," "limited-time offer," "your last chance to save," and "one-time-only sale" are all representatives of this method. The idea is to create a sense of urgency so that consumers will act quickly. Sometimes these are done as IBP and include "call or click *now.*" Of course, many consumers have learned to ignore or otherwise discount these messages. We've all seen "Going Out of Business Sale" signs that remained up and the store open for months and even years.

Strategic Implications of Hard-Sell Approaches

■ *"Permission to buy now."* The sale was about to end.

■ *Socially acceptable defense.* "I had to act." "It was on sale that day only." "It was such a good deal."

■ *Low credibility.* A lot of consumers know this is just a scam, and that "last chance" almost never means last chance.

■ *Legal/regulatory challenges/exposure.* The makers of these ads tend to face the same legal and regulatory problems as the reason-why ads.

■ *Some creative resistance.* Again, these are not the kind of ads creatives beg to work on.

Method C: Comparison Ads

Comparison advertisements are another form of advertising designed to persuade the consumer. Comparison ads try to demonstrate a brand's ability to satisfy consumers by comparing a product's features to those of competing brands. Comparisons can be an effective and efficient means of communicating a large amount of information in a clear, interesting, and convincing way; or they can be extremely confusing and create a situation of information overload where the market leader usually wins. Comparison advertising as a technique has traditionally been used by marketers of convenience goods in mature categories such as pain relievers, laundry detergents, and household cleaners.

Advertisers in a wide range of product lines have tried comparison advertising from time to time. Exhibit 10.8 shows Microsoft's humorous comparison ad pitting its Surface Pro computer against Apple's MacBook Air.

Evaluation of comparison ads is typically done through tracking studies that measure attitudes, beliefs, and preferences over time. Using comparison as a strategy can be direct and name competitors' brands, or it can be indirect and refer only to the "leading brand" or "Brand X." Here are a few rules gleaned from consumer research:

- Direct comparison by a low-share brand to a high-share brand increases receivers' attention and increases their intent to purchase the low-share brand.

- Direct comparison by a high-share brand to a low-share brand does not attract additional attention to the high-share brand but actually helps the low-share brand.

- Direct comparison is more effective if members of the target audience have not demonstrated clear brand preferences in their product choices.[4]

For these reasons, established market leaders use comparison ads less frequently than underdog brands, which wish to be seen in the company of the market leaders. For instance, if Apple is a category exemplar or market leader, a smart strategy for its competitors such as Microsoft is to compare their products or brand to Apple.

Strategic Implications of Comparison Ads

- *Can help a low-share brand.*
- *Provides social justification (to others) for purchase of the less popular brand.*

- *Gives permission to buy.* Enables the consumer to consider the advertising claim and then come to their own conclusion that it really is the best brand. (Consumer-generated conclusions are more powerful than those made on behalf of the advertiser.)

- *Significant legal/regulatory exposure.* Companies can and do raise objections to comparisons, resulting in legal and regulatory reviews. Factor in legal costs.

- *Not done much outside the United States.* In much of the world, comparison advertising is either outlawed, not done by mutual agreement, or considered to be in such poor taste as to be never done.

- *Not for established market leaders.*

- *These ads are sometimes evaluated as more offensive and less interesting than noncomparative ads.* They have a tendency to turn some consumers off.

Method D: Testimonials

Testimonials are another type of persuade-the-consumer ads. A frequently used message tactic is to have a spokesperson who champions the brand in an advertisement rather than simply providing information. When an advocacy position is taken by a spokesperson in an advertisement, it is known as a **testimonial**. The value of the testimonial lies in the authoritative presentation of a brand's attributes and benefits by the spokesperson. There are three basic versions of the testimonial message tactic.

The most conspicuous version is the *celebrity testimonial*. Professional athletes, actors, and supermodels are widely used as spokespeople, who also can be termed as endorsers or influencers (more detail on social media influencers in the media chapters). The belief is that a celebrity testimonial will attract attention and ignite a desire in the receivers to emulate or imitate the celebrities they admire. For example, Cheetos incorporates implicit celebrity testimonials from Mila Kunis, Ashton Kutcher, and Shaggy; Exhibit 10.9 shows a screenshot of a Cheetos Super Bowl television ad featuring these celebrities because they are recognizable and a fit with the brand's target audience and lifestyle. It can seem relatable in the ad that a husband and wife could quarrel a bit over snack foods in the house, such as when someone eats the last of the snack and then denies it. The ad also does a good job of IBP because it has synergy with social media marketing, which can be seen in the #ItWasntMe. So when this storyline is depicted in advertising, it is effective because the storyline is relatable. Celebrity

Source: Microsoft Corporation

Exhibit 10.8 ▶ Consider this example of comparison advertising from Microsoft showing its Surface Pro compared with an Apple MacBook.

Source: Cheetos

Exhibit 10.9 ▶ A Super Bowl ad for Cheetos used a relatable situation where a couple fusses over who ate the last of the snack.

testimonials should be authentic and fitting with the target market as well as integrated through the brand's IBP such as at events, with sponsorships, and in digital advertising.

Note that this persuasion principle can be used not just for branding but also to persuade more prosocial consumer behavior, such as promoting healthy foods in general. Exhibit 10.10 shows a mock celebrity testimonial that uses "star power" to promote nutritious food. This is part of a multimedia IBP campaign targeting children and teenagers, launched by the Partnership for a Healthier America for the FNV (fruits 'n veggies) brand. The campaign features real-life celebrities and sports stars such as Jessica Alba, Cam Newton, Stephen Curry, and Ashanti promoting their favorite fruits and vegetables for healthy eating.[5]

Expert spokespeople for a brand are viewed by the target audience as having expert product knowledge. A spokesperson portrayed as a doctor, lawyer, scientist, gardener, or any other expert relevant to a brand is intended to increase the credibility of the message being transmitted. There are also real experts. Advertising for the Club, a steering-wheel locking device that deters auto theft, uses police officers to demonstrate the effectiveness of the product. And celebrities can also be experts. Retired NBA superstar Michael Jordan's sports achievements have earned him a lifetime deal to advertise Nike basketball sneakers and apparel. Basketball's LeBron James and soccer's Ronaldo are also expert spokespeople signed to lifetime deals with Nike that will continue long after they retire from sports.[6] Another example is Nationwide Insurance hiring celebrity actress Julia Roberts for their marketing.

Source: People Magazine

Exhibit 10.10 ▶ Blending humor appeal with the notion of celebrity power, this image plays on People Magazine's "sexiest man of the year" idea. The sexiest yam of the year is part of a multimedia IBP campaign targeting children and teenagers, launched by the Partnership for a Healthier America for the FNV (fruits 'n veggies) brand with testimonials from celebrities.

There is also the *average-user testimonial*. Here, the spokesperson is not a celebrity or portrayed as an expert but rather as an average user speaking for the brand. The philosophy here is that the target market can relate to this person. An interpretation of reference-group theory in this context suggests that consumers may rely on opinions or testimonials from people they consider similar to themselves rather than on objective product information. Simply put, the consumer's logic in this situation is, "That person is similar to me and likes that brand; therefore, I will also like that brand." In theory, this sort of logic frees the receiver from having to scrutinize detailed product information by simply substituting the reference-group information. Of course, in practice, the execution of this strategy is rarely that easy. Consumers are very adept at detecting this attempt at persuasion. Evaluation is usually done through tracking studies and communications tests. Importantly, testimonials can also be prosocial and help scare consumers into thinking about the consequences of unhealthy choices. Note how powerful the campaign featured in Exhibit 10.11 is because it is a sad testimonial from real smokers discussing their morbid health conditions.

Strategic Implications of Testimonial Advertising

- *Very popular people can generate popularity for the brand.*

- *People perceived to be very similar to the consumer or as experts can be powerful advocates for the brand.*

Exhibit 10.11 ▶ Real smokers share their stories.

- *Consumers often forget who likes what, particularly when stars promote multiple goods and services.*

- *Can generate more popularity for the star than for the brand.*

Celebrities, because they are human, are not as easy to manage as cartoon characters: think Tony the Tiger versus Tiger Woods. There is the ever-present risk that a celebrity will fall from grace, as several have in recent years, and in doing so potentially damage the reputation of the brand for which they were once the ambassador. A notable example is Michelob Ultra, which at one time featured Lance Armstrong—a professional cyclist notorious for doping allegations who turned out *not* to be an authentic model for beer drinkers who lead active lifestyles, and as a result, the brand and other affiliated brands needed to unaffiliate.

Method E: Demonstration

How sparkling a detergent gets dishes, how clear a facewash gets your skin, and how simple a blender is to use are all product benefits that can be showcased by using a method known simply as a demonstration. "Seeing is believing" is the motto of this school of advertising. When it's done well, the results are striking. Contrast the two demonstrations by Blendtec shown in Exhibit 10.12, created to highlight the product's capabilities in very different ways. Blendtec has posted hundreds of demonstration videos on social media sites and attracted the attention of millions of viewers over the years.[7] Evaluation of demonstration ads is typically done through tracking studies that measure attitudes, beliefs, and brand preferences over time. Blendtec assesses the results of its ads by tracking video views and—equally as important—analyzing sales trends.

Strategic Implications of Demonstration Ads

- *Inherent credibility of "seeing is believing."*

- *Can be used as social justification.* Helps the consumer defend the decision to buy.

- *Provides clear permission to buy.* "I saw a test; it was the best."

- *Fairly heavy regulatory/legal exposure.*

Method F: Infomercials

With an **infomercial**, an advertiser typically buys from 5 to 60 minutes of television time and runs an information/entertainment program that is really an extended advertisement. Real estate investment programs, weight-loss and fitness products, motivational programs, and cookware have traditionally dominated the infomercial format. The infomercial usually has a host who provides product information and features guests who give testimonials about how successful they have been

Blendtec @Blendtec · 2 Dec 2016
What's the most dangerous thing Tom has ever blended? Watch this clip from @KUTV2News to find out!

Inside the Story: 'Will it Blend?' is still a YouTube sensation after 10 ye...
(KUTV) A simple kitchen appliance has become a YouTube sensation. Blendtec's blenders have been showcased for 10 years on its Will it Blen...
kutv.com

Blendtec
December 15, 2016 · 🌐

Best Blender Hot Chocolate

3 cups milk of your choice
1 1/2 cups chocolate chips (milk, semi-sweet, dark, white)
1 tsp vanilla extract... See More

Exhibit 10.12 ▶ Integrated brand promotion in action: Blendtec

Blendtec uses a mix of outrageous product demonstrations and practical demonstrations to show off the power and versatility of its blenders. *What are the pros and cons of featuring clearly unrealistic demonstrations, compared with demonstrations that customers can replicate at home?*

using the advertised product. Most infomercials run on cable or satellite channels, although networks have sold early-morning and late-night time as well. Now the infomercial is being

updated for the digital age, running several minutes long and posted online only for cost efficiency as well as reach. Some of these newer infomercials rely heavily on humor to increase the entertainment value while selling.[8]

Strategic Implications of Infomercials

- *Long format gives advertisers plenty of time to make their case.*

- *As network ratings fall, day-parts (e.g., Sunday mornings 9–11) that were previously unaffordable have now opened, making infomercials better deals for advertisers.*

- *Has the advantage of looking like an entertainment show when it's really an ad.*

- *These ads have a somewhat negative public image, which doesn't help build credibility or trust in the advertised brand.*

- *Some infomercials are posted online in addition to airing on television, and some run online only.*

There are other persuade-the-consumer formats, including ads posing as newspaper or magazine articles (advertorials), but all of them have the same basic mechanism at their core—here's why you should buy this—providing supportive arguments to encourage purchase.

10-2d Objective #4: Affective Association: Get the Consumer to Feel Good about the Brand

Advertisers want consumers to like their brand, because they believe that this will lead to purchase. But rather than providing the consumer with hard reasons to like the brand, these ads more frequently use an emotional appeal—a more complex approach than the ones discussed earlier.

There are several well-known methods to getting the consumer to like one's brand. Let's look at some of the general approaches; the most specific examples are merely finer distinctions within these more general categories.

Method A: Feel-Good Ads

The basic idea is that by creating ads with positive feelings, advertisers will lead consumers to associate those positive feelings with the advertised brand, leading to a higher probability of purchase. They try to either link the good feeling elicited by the ad with the brand (affective association) or leverage the propensity for humans to distort information in favor of liked brands without knowing they are doing so (predecision distortion).

Of course, getting from liking the ad to liking the brand can be a big leap. Studies by Stanford researcher Baba Shiv[9] and others have demonstrated an enrichment effect that occurs when the consumer thinks of a brand with associated positive emotions. The consumer will actually, prior to conscious consideration, bias information in the direction of the emotionally enriched brand. The consumer doesn't even know they are doing this. So if you can get a brand to be liked, even just a little and not even consciously, you can theoretically get more purchases. The evidence on effectiveness is mixed. It may be that positive feelings are transferred to the brand, or it could be that they actually interfere with remembering the message or the brand name.

From an advertising and IBP perspective, how do you get good results from this method? The key is not to make the ad liked but to make the *brand* liked. Liking the ad doesn't necessarily mean liking the brand. But liking the ad may lead to a higher probability of purchase. We believe you must clearly associate the brand name and/or image with the feeling. Lots of ads don't do this—not even close. You may love ads for Budweiser but be a Coors fan. You may think, "Nice ads—wish they made a better beer."

Some feel-good advertising campaigns do work. Sometimes, feel-good ads try to get the consumer *not* to think about certain things. United Airlines could show how often its planes depart and arrive on schedule. Instead, it has shown successful business meetings and the happy reunion of family members, which create a much richer message, a wider field of shared meanings. As an Olympics sponsor, the airline has also aired commercials featuring top U.S. athletes like gymnast Simone Biles. Gold medalist Biles has starred in other feel-good ads, appearing for Procter & Gamble's Tide detergent pods and for Kellogg's Special K cereal.[10] The emotions become the product attribute linked to the brand.

Underlying the mechanics behind feel-good advertising, it is becoming clearer that thought and feelings are, at some basic level, separate systems.[11] Feelings are believed to emanate from a part of the brain that responds quickly to stimuli in the environment. The classic example is that a loud noise frightens us (feeling) even before we know what we are frightened of (thought). So emotions are faster than thought and sometimes even stronger. There is also evidence that as the media environment gets more cluttered, the affective (or feeling) ads may actually do better than thought-based ads that require a great deal of processing. Feeling ads may have a leg up in the contemporary media environment. Evaluation of feel-good ads is typically done by measuring attitude change via **pre- and post-exposure tests**, tracking studies, theater dial-turning tests, and communication tests.

Strategic Implications of Feel-Good Advertising

- *Eager creatives.* Creatives win awards and advance their careers with this style of advertising.

- *May perform better in the cluttered media environment.*

- *May generate competing thoughts and connections.*

OUR KIDS ARE FULL OF SURPRISES. FROM **TOWELS** TO TOYBOXES, THEY **TREAT** EVERYTHING LIKE AN ADVENTURE. SAME WITH **YOU** AND YOUR KIDS, **RIGHT**?

MARTEX
BATH & BEDDING | IN TOUCH WITH YOU.

WestPoint Stevens, Inc. and Chillingworth/Redding, Inc.

Exhibit 10.13 ▶ A touching ad for Martex Bath & Bedding that is an example of feel-good advertising.

An emotional ad about family and business travel may get viewers to think about their lives and their time on the road—but not really make any enduring connections to the brand. Your expensive emotional ad may make consumers better (or guilty) parents but not make them customers. For instance, a bath and bedding brand, Martex, uses a feel-good appeal showing the love between a father and his son (along with the Martex towels).[12] Consider how this approach may work as compared to one that lists the features or benefits of the towels (Exhibit 10.13). Another brand that has been great at developing feel-good ads is Volkswagen (VW); in its teaser ad for one Super Bowl, VW showed the brand's "sunny side."

Method B: Humor Ads

The goal of a humor ad is to create a pleasant and memorable association with the brand. But research suggests that the positive impact of humor is not as strong as the intuitive appeal of the approach. Quite simply, humorous versions of advertisements often do not prove to be more persuasive than nonhumorous versions of the same ad. Funny ads are usually great entertainment but may be poor business investments. Moreover, men and women react differently to ads containing comedic aggression, which is why audience research is vital when developing effective message strategies.[13]

How many times have you been talking to friends about your favorite ads, and you say something like, "Remember the one where the guy knocks over the drink, and then says ..." Everybody laughs, and then maybe someone says something like, "I can't remember who it's for, but what a great ad." If you remember the gag but not the brand, it's *not* a good ad. Why do you recall the brand in some funny ads and not in others? The difference may be that in the ads you recall, the payoff for the humor is an integral part of the message strategy. Thus, it better ensures the memory link between humor and brand. If the ad doesn't link the joke (or the punch line) to the brand name, then the advertiser may have bought some very expensive laughs without a business result. Evaluation of humorous ads is typically done through pre- and postexposure tests, dial-turning attitude tests, and tracking studies that measure attitudes, beliefs, and preferences over time.

Strategic Implications of Humor Advertising

- *If the joke is integral to the copy platform, humor can be very effective.* If it is not, it is just expensive entertainment.

- *Very eager creatives.* Creatives love to develop funny ads because they win awards and advance careers.

- *Humorous messages may adversely affect comprehension.* Humor can actually interfere with memory processes. The consumer doesn't remember what brand the ad was for; it happens all the time.

- *Very funny messages can wear out very quickly, leaving no one laughing, especially the advertiser.*[14] It's like hearing the same joke over and over. Advertisers who use this technique have to keep changing the gag, which gets expensive.

Method C: Sex-Appeal Ads

Sex-appeal ads are a type of feelings-based advertising. Not a big surprise: Humans tend to think about sex from time to time. Sex appeal ads tend not to require much thought, relying instead on arousal and affect (feelings). But, the question remains: Does sex sell?

In a literal sense, the answer is no, because nothing, not even sex, *makes* someone buy something. However, sex appeals are attention getting and occasionally arousing, which may affect how consumers feel about a brand. When using sex appeal, the advertiser is trying to get attention and link some degree of sexual arousal and positive feelings with the brand. Sometimes this works, but the commonly held notion

that "sex sells" is more myth than reality. Another consideration is that women's attitudes are changing. Today, even women with feminist views tend to have positive attitudes toward ads with sexual imagery.[15] Ads with sexual appeals do not reduce a woman's preference for products related to romance, and ads with romantic imagery do not reduce a man's preference for products related to sex.[16]

Fashion brand Gucci and many other advertisers have used sexual imagery to mold brand image. But these ads are for products such as clothes and perfumes, which emphasize how people look, feel, and smell. The context for the sex appeal is congruent; it fits, it makes sense. Does the same appeal work as well for cars and file cabinets? In general, no. As noted by Professor Tom Reichert at the University of Georgia,[17] traditional wisdom in the ad business was that the use of sex is "amateurish and sophomoric, and a desperate—not to mention ineffective—attempt to rescue plummeting sales." Research generally confirms that sex-appeal ads can be effective when the context is appropriate but a distraction or worse when it is not. The lingerie brand, Fleur Du Mal, wants to get you to associate its brand with sex, and it has been very successful doing just that. On the other hand, some condom ads emphasize security or effectiveness, while others emphasize the obvious link between buying some and getting some.

Evaluation of sex-appeal ads is typically done through communication tests, focus groups, pre- and postexposure tests, and tracking studies that measure attitudes, beliefs, and preferences over time. When using sex appeal, clients sometimes order more focus groups and communication tests to make sure that they are not going overboard or offending the target audience. For instance, Guess uses sex appeal in the advertising in Exhibit 10.14.

Exhibit 10.14 ▶ Why does/doesn't sex help sell Guess clothing and fashion? Explain the role of sex appeal in advertising in terms of the Guess brand.

Strategic Implications of Sex-Appeal Advertising

- *Higher attention levels.*

- *Higher arousal and affect (feeling).* This can be good if it can be tied to brand meaning, bad if it can't.

- *Possible poor brand memorability due to interference at the time of exposure.* In other words, the viewer is thinking about something else.

- *Product–theme continuity excludes many goods and services.*

- *Legal, political, and regulatory exposure, as well as ethical issues raised by stereotyping or targeting.*

10-2e Objective #5: Scare the Consumer into Action

Advertisers use fear to scare the consumer into acting. Fear appeals are typically designed to elicit a specific feeling (fear) as well as a specific thought (buy x to prevent y). Fear is an extraordinarily powerful emotion and may be used to motivate consumers to take some very important action. But this fear must be coupled with some degree of thought in order for it to work. That's why we place this strategy a bit higher up the ladder in terms of its degree of complexity. It is generally considered hard to use effectively and is fairly limited in application. It is only used in a few product and service categories.

Method: Fear-Appeal Ads

A fear appeal highlights the risk of harm or some other negative consequence of not using the advertised brand or not taking some recommended action.[18] Usually it's a little bit of fear designed to induce a little bit of thought and then to inspire action. Getting the balance right is the tricky part. The intuitive belief about fear as a message tactic is that fear will motivate the receiver to buy a product that will reduce or eliminate the portrayed threat.

The contemporary social environment has provided advertisers with an ideal context for using fear appeals. In an era punctuated by drive-by shootings, carjackings, public health concerns, and terrorism, many Americans fear for their personal safety. Manufacturers of security products such as home alarms, webcams, and safety apps leverage this fearful environment. Other advertisers have tried fear appeals as well. A long-running and effective campaign from the U.S. Centers for Disease Control and Prevention has portrayed the health consequences of smoking with very graphic images of diseased or damaged bodies. Coupled with other marketing efforts, this campaign has helped to reduce the number of smokers over time.[19]

Traditional wisdom holds that intense fear appeals actually short-circuit persuasion and result in a negative attitude toward the advertised brand.[20] Other researchers argue that the tactic is generally beneficial to the advertiser.[21] The latest neuroscience confirms that even abstract threats can be made more concrete and induce fear if properly presented in advertising.[22] We believe that to be successful, a fear-appeal ad must have a very clear benefit from doing something specific, at any fear level. Fear ads must offer a "way out" of harm's way. The ideal fear-appeal ad would thus be one that is entirely believable[23] and offers a clear and easy way to avoid the bad thing threatened in the ad. Thus, to avoid the threat of having a hole in your throat from cancer, don't start smoking or stop smoking now. Evaluation of fear-appeal ads is typically done through tracking studies that measure attitudes, beliefs, and preferences over time; pre- and post-exposure tests; and communication tests.

Strategic Implications of Fear-Appeal Advertising

- *You must have a plausible threat to motivate consumers.*

- *You must have a completely clear and easy-to-discern link between the alleviation of the threat and the use of the advertised brand (or, in the case of public health, the link between avoiding the threat and changing behavior).*

- *If a fear-appeal ad is not believable nor relatable, it will have a low impact.*

10-2f Objective #6: Change Behavior by Inducing Anxiety

Anxiety is not quite outright fear, but it is uncomfortable and can last longer. Although it's hard to keep people in a state of outright fear, people can feel anxious for an extended period of time. People try to avoid feeling anxious. They try to minimize, moderate, and alleviate anxiety. They use all sorts of mechanisms to avoid anxiety and will often buy or consume things to help them manage it. They might listen to a podcast or watch videos on TikTok, drink, exercise, eat, or take medication. They might also buy toothpaste, napkins, coffee, a "family car," orthodontics, sports season tickets, or a financial investing account, and advertisers know this. Advertisers pursue a change-behavior-by-inducing-anxiety objective by playing on consumer anxieties through both thought and feelings.

Such ads are also used to play on anxieties about product scarcity, as in messages that urge immediate action because of a product's high demand or limited availability. Scarcity ads are most effective when the audience expects to encounter scarcity in the marketplace and less effective when the audience is less concerned about being able to access the product.[24]

Method A: Anxiety Ads

Advertisers use many levers to demonstrate why you should be anxious and what you can do to alleviate the anxiety. Social, medical, and personal-care products frequently use anxiety ads. The message conveyed in anxiety ads is that (1) there is a clear and present problem and (2) the way to avoid this problem is to buy the advertised brand. Anxiety ads tout the likelihood of being stricken by athlete's foot, calcium deficiency, body odor, heart disease, and on and on. The idea is that these anxiety-producing conditions are out there, and they may affect you unless you take the appropriate action. For instance, a company selling personal security devices like Body Alarm instills some anxiety with their copy about "how to scream for help while being strangled" and relates it to how their alarm-like product can help reduce that anxiety (Exhibit 10.15).

Method B: Social Anxiety Ads

This is a subcategory of anxiety ads in which the danger is negative social judgment, as opposed to a physical threat. Procter & Gamble (P&G) has long relied on such presentations for its household and personal-care brands. Most personal-care products have used this type of appeal.

Anxiety ads are often used in the context of important social roles and the consumer's perceived inadequacy in that role. Billions of dollars have been made selling products by first making mothers feel a little more inadequate about their mothering skills or fathers about their ability to adequately provide for the family or one's desirability, then offering a solution by the advertiser.

This type of ad works by pointing to anxieties that reside right on the surface of consumers in these roles or are just slightly latent or beneath the surface. We tend to worry about the things we care most about and the things where the standards of adequacy and excellence are unknown. What makes a great husband, father, mother, worker, and so on? We are not quite sure. So advertisers target that anxiety, provoke it, and then offer the consumers a solution. Evaluation of anxiety ads is typically done by measuring attitudes and beliefs through tracking studies and communication tests.

Strategic Implications of Anxiety Advertising

- *Anxiety appeals can generate the perception of widespread (and thus personal) threat and motivate action (buying and using the advertised product).* These ads have a pretty good track record of working.

- *The brand can become the solution to the ever-present problem, and this results in long-term commitment to the brand.* Once a solution (brand) is found, the consumer doesn't have to think about it again.

- *Be efficient.* A little anxiety goes a long way.

- *If the anxiety-producing threat is not linked tightly enough to your brand, you may increase category demand and provide business for your competitors, particularly the market leader.* If total category share goes up, market leaders get most of it. Still, if the creative is good and the link to the specific brand is strong, it is a good method for any size player.

- *Consider ethical issues.* There is more than enough to feel anxious about without advertisers adding more.

- *These ads have historically been disproportionately targeted at women.* Critics correctly note the inherent unfairness and sexism.

10-2g Objective #7: Define the Brand Image

The term "brand image" suggests the meaning of a brand, but at the level of impression, it refers to the quick takeaway of what the brand is all about. It is expressed in visual terms (image) because brand images typically rely on the visual impression a brand makes with only a glance. Truly iconic

Susan Van Etten

Exhibit 10.15 ▶ Body Alarm instills some anxiety with ad copy about "how to scream for help while being strangled" and relates this anxiety to how the product can help reduce that anxiety.

brands have the ability to convey their essential meaning with just the black and white Cow (Chic-Fil-A), the lower case black a with the yellow curved arrow (Amazon), or a small green tree (Dollar Tree). Not surprisingly, defining brand image is typically achieved visually. Brand images are important for several reasons. For one, they allow for an enormously efficient form of communication in a crowded media environment. The Instagram logo delivers a meaning with just a glance because it represents a camera icon from a smart phone, so it can make one think about photo sharing. Second, once established (and properly maintained), they create clear differentiation for the brand. Finally, they are not very dependent on any one language and are thus perfect for the transnational company.

Method: Image Ads

Image advertising attempts to distill the brand's essential meaning with a very sparse use of words and a heavy reliance on visuals. Image ads in any medium, including digital, social, and mobile media, don't tend to contain much hard product information. They instead use visuals to point to a

Exhibit 10.16 ▶ This image-based ad from Calvin Klein for the fragrance "Defy" is an example of how in some cases, the image of the product and the setting around it (in this case a clean, industrial design feel) can be enough where copy or words are not needed in an ad.

brand quality or attribute or evoke a certain set of feelings. But whether provoking feelings or thoughts or both, the idea is to define brand meaning in an efficient visual manner. Notice the image advertising done by Calvin Klein in Exhibit 10.16; there is no copy in the ad, as the only words are the brand name "Calvin Klein Defy" on the fragrance bottle. This Calvin Klein ad is an image ad due to how it "sells the brand image" rather than specific product attributes about the fragrance. The ad, which only features the fragrance bottle, is also a good example of the modern evolution of a very simple or minimalist design with little to no copy (words).

Evaluation of image ads is typically done through qualitative methods, and sometimes associative tests are used, along with longitudinal attribute-related attitude tracking studies. As we've said before, the evaluation of visual communication is still not where it should be. Further, these ads are often figurative rather than literal and require evaluation methods like the Zaltman (ZMET) metaphor-based techniques (discussed in Chapter 7). They are also heavily dependent upon the maker of the ad being completely in touch with the contemporary culture so that the audience "gets" the ad. It is the skillful use of this social and cultural knowledge that develops brand equity and can elevate the brand into an icon.[25]

Brand managers must work closely with advertising professionals to make sure that (1) the desired brand identity is really understood by all parties and (2) that typical verbal description is translated into a visual. Think about the most successful brands in the world. They are almost all "iconic," meaning that their essential meaning is captured and efficiently transmitted visually. Apple, Nike, McDonald's, and Coke come to mind. To get and retain that iconic status requires an enduring and culturally connected creative effort.

Strategic Implications of Image Advertising

- *Generally fewer counterarguments are generated by consumers.*

- *Relatively little or no legal/regulatory exposure.* Hard to litigate the truth or falsity of a picture.

- *Try to maximize the iconic potential that your image advertising can have on society or pop culture.*

- *Very common in some categories (e.g., fashion, fragrance).* Your image can get lost in the competitive cloud.

- *Can be quickly rejected if the advertised image rings untrue or poorly matches what the consumer currently thinks of the brand, particularly through direct experience.*

- *Don't tend to copy-test well, because traditional copy-test procedures are designed predominately for words not images.*

- *Be prepared for managerial resistance.* Client often argues for more words.

- *Creatives tend to love this type of advertising.*

10-2h Objective #8: Give the Brand the Desired Social Meaning

Billions of dollars are spent annually in efforts to achieve specific social meanings for advertised brands. The point is to shape the meaning of branded goods (and branded services like FedEx) beyond their everyday function. Advertisers do this by placing the brand in the right social setting. In an ad, a branded promotion in a real environment or a product placement in a television, show, movie, or video game, the brand takes on some of the characteristics of its surroundings.

Most watches keep good time. But a Shinola is different than a Tag Heuer, a Rolex, and so on. A branded watch is not just a watch. A watch is a way of communicating social status, wealth, fashion, and a sense of self. For men, it is one of the most accepted statements of social identity. In the watch category, these kinds of ads are common because the brands rely so heavily on desired social meaning. Think of fashion ads—same thing. Effective social meaning advertising lets the advertiser shape that connotation. If done well, these can be very successful.

> " *Getting to that iconic status requires an enduring and very culturally connected creative effort. It requires management wise enough to either help in this effort or trust the creatives.* "

Method A: Slice-of-Life Ads

Slice-of-life advertisements depict an ideal usage situation for the brand. The social context surrounding the brand rubs off and gives the brand a social meaning. Consumers may, of course, reject or significantly alter that meaning, but often they accept it. The candy company Mars applied this method with its U.K. commercials for Maltesers chocolates (see Exhibit 10.17), featuring consumers with disabilities telling light-hearted stories of everyday life while snacking on the branded candy. These candid and original slice-of-life ads not only won awards but also won Mars free air time from the British television channel airing the Paralympics—and importantly, they increased Maltesers sales.[26]

Evaluation of slice-of-life ads is typically done through tracking studies that measure attitudes, beliefs, and preferences over time; pre- and postexposure tests; and communication tests.

Strategic Implications of Slice-of-Life Ads

- *Generally, fewer counterarguments made by consumers.*

- *Legal/regulatory advantages.* Advertisers' attorneys like pictures more than words because determining the truth or falsity of a picture is much tougher than words. Have you ever noticed how heavily regulated industries tend to use lots of pictures and little copy (other than mandated warning labels)?

- *Authenticity.* To make their brands another Coca-Cola or Apple is the dream of many advertisers. Socially embedding your brand in everyday life gives you this chance.

- *Creation of brand–social realities.* You may be able to create the perfect social world for the brand and its space in it.

- *Be unique.* Unless the creative is outstanding (particularly visually) and you are generally willing to spend a reasonable amount for repetition, these ads can get lost in the clutter. In certain categories, such as fashion, a lot of ads are of this type.

- *Be prepared that these ads don't tend to copy-test well.* This is because so much of copy-testing is still designed around remembering words and verbal claims. **Copy-testing** is where the effectiveness of the words in the ad (copy) is tested for effectiveness. This technique has simply not caught up with the new reality of the prominence of visual forms of advertising and brand promotion.

- *Creatives tend to love these ads (at least, art directors do).* You will get some top-flight creative folks on the job.

Exhibit 10.17 ▶ Maltesers "Look on the Light Side" slice-of-life based campaign brings diversity to advertising, as consumers in wheelchairs are underrepresented in advertising.

Source: Maltesers

Method B: Branded Entertainment: Product Placement

In the age of new media, we have gone well beyond a few product placements in movies and TV shows to an increasingly broad and integrated set of methods that bring brand messages to consumers. These techniques are often gathered under one umbrella called Madison & Vine. It began as a conference to bring together Hollywood (the famous intersection of "Hollywood and Vine") and the advertising industry (traditionally based along New York's Madison Avenue, although agencies are now all over the place): thus "Madison & Vine." Madison & Vine then became a book and an *Ad Age* column and now encompasses a wide array of nontraditional IBPs. Recording, gaming, and cell phone industries are involved as well now. The most important recent development is how many major advertisers are now involved in producing movies, television series, cell phone content—and more—that are all really just branded promotions. We will dig deeper into this topic in Chapter 16, but for now, we'll focus on a common application of this concept and one that is in this strategic set: product placement and integration.

One way to integrate the product or brand into a desired setting is to place it in a television show, film, online entertainment, or sporting event. An actor picks up a can of Mt. Dew, not just any soda, and hopefully the correct image association is made. A growing number of firms are developing branded entertainment as the setting for their goods and services. For branded entertainment, it must be valuable and consumers must want to watch it for consumers to engage with the content.[27]

Advertisers want their brands to become integral parts of a desired social reality, a media-created world in which the brand is absolutely normal, expected, and almost invisible. Some contemporary theories of memory suggest that this would indeed be best over time, as the source of the brand image becomes disassociated from the brand memory. Recent research has, however, suggested that the effects of placement are strongest with so-called low-involvement goods and services that are lower priced and purchased as the result of fairly quick decision-making. When consumers have to take time to consider a major purchase, like a car, the effects of brand promotion appear to be much weaker and may even backfire.

Strategic Implications of Branded Entertainment

- *Low counterargument if the placement is not too obvious.*
- *May reduce defensive measures by consumers, such as source discounting.*
- *May actually increase consumers' estimates about how many other people use the brand, thus making it appear more prevalent and popular than it actually is.*
- *A perceived cost advantage over very expensive network TV.*
- *Nonstandardized rate structure; hard to price these; deals done in private.*
- *May not be very effective for high-involvement categories.*
- *Science is unclear as to how well branded entertainment works.*

10-2i Objective #9: Leverage Social Disruption and Cultural Contradictions

We have now risen to the top of the sophistication scale. As mentioned in Chapter 3, some really great brands have used advertising to successfully leverage social disruption. The idea is to identify a point at which the social fabric is frayed (usually gender, race, age, politics, labor, economy, or other opportunity inequities) and suggest that your brand gets it and is the unofficially sanctioned brand of the counterculture. Brands like Mountain Dew (disaffected Gen-X slackers) and Apple (creative thinkers)—among others—have attempted this.[28]

Most advertisers tend to ignore or even deny the existence of major social disruptions. So while this strategy has succeeded with a few amazingly successful brands, most advertisers appear to not use it. The concern seems to be that the brand becomes associated with an unpleasant event.

Method: Tie Brand to Social/Cultural Movement

Sometimes this is done very explicitly, other times very implicitly. This is a very sophisticated and typically difficult method. The reason it is difficult is not in the execution but being culturally attuned enough to know in the present what various target marketers are conflicted about and how to offer a brand as a solution, even a partial one. This is different than merely chasing trends; it is seeing the cultural land beneath your feet shifting in significant ways and understanding that different generations respond to social issues and advertising in different ways.[29] What would you say are the ones going on these days: addressing/ending systemic racism, widening income inequality, gender identity issues, or another topic addressing social justice? Think about how you could authentically leverage those (or others) to a societal benefit and a brand's advantage.

Beauty brands, for example, are connecting with consumers by leveraging the diversity movement in their advertising and IBP activities. Cover Girl and Maybelline were among the very first beauty brands to enlist young men as a brand ambassadors on social media, building on their YouTube popularity to promote products and introduce new looks.[30] Cover Girl also has a Cover Boy appearing in some cosmetics ads. The beauty brand broke new ground when it featured a Muslim-American mother—also a YouTube star—wearing a hijab as a brand ambassador in advertising and on social media (see Exhibit 10.18).[31] Victoria's Secret is boldly championing women's empowerment by changing their brand position from "what men want" to "what women want." These "firsts" help the brands by increasing awareness and associations with the cultural importance of the diversity movement.[32]

10-2j Objective #10: Transform Consumption Experiences

We view this as the most sophisticated strategy going. But it is also very hard to do well.

You know how it's sometimes difficult to explain to someone else just exactly why a certain experience was so special, why it was so good? It wasn't just this or that; the entire experience was somehow better than the sum of the individual parts. Sometimes that feeling is at least partly due to your expectations of what something will be like, your positive memories of previous experiences, or both.

Sometimes advertisers try to provide that anticipation and/or familiarity bundled in a positive memory of an advertisement or other brand communication, to be activated during the consumption experience itself and recalled positively after the experience. That's right: The advertiser is trying to help create positive memories of brand usage even before the consumer has used the brand and (more commonly) weave those memories of actual use together with advertiser-supplied "memories" in a way that the advertising can effectively shape consumer memories of brand usage. The advertising or promotional experience is thus said to have *transformed* the actual consumption experience, both at the time of consumption and in the consumer's memory.

Method: Transformational Ads

The idea behind transformational advertising is that it can actually make the consumption experience better. Transformational advertising attempts to create a brand feeling, expectation, and mood that are activated when the consumer uses the product or service. Actual usage is thus transformed—made better. Transformational ads that are effective are said to connect the experience of the advertisement so closely with the brand experience that consumers cannot help but think of material from the ads (or, in a more general sense, the memory of many elements from many ads) when they think of the brand.

Under Armour has employed transformational advertising to compete more effectively with Nike and Adidas, long the market leaders in sports shoes and clothing. With visually engaging commercials and IBP content featuring sports champions, Under Armour delves below the surface of the athletic experience to connect with consumers who appreciate and understand how much hard work, commitment, and determination are required to succeed in sports. Under Armour's message is about more than winning a medal—it builds a bridge between the brand and the authentic athletic experience; this authenticity may be why their ad with Olympian Michael Phelps is one of the most shared ads relating to the Olympics.[33] In their

Exhibit 10.18 ▶ Cover Girl is bringing more diversity into its creative message strategy. The brand broke new ground by featuring a Muslim-American woman wearing a hijab as brand ambassador in advertising and on social media.

Source: Under Armour

Exhibit 10.19 ▶ Under Armour at times uses transformational appeals in its branding or messaging to imply that using their sports attire, you also can transform through hard work.

advertisement with the copy "You Give it All. We Give it Back", it shows an athlete (Jonathan Taylor) transforming himself through hard work and playing in the cold. Exhibit 10.19 shows two images from this Under Armour campaign. In these images advertising Under Armour's UA Rush line, Jonathan Taylor powers through to push his limits in a workout to prepare for championship football. The implication of the ad is that his Under Armour clothing helps in cold weather and protects so that professional athletes and weekend warriors alike can have the power to push their limits during workouts.

What if you sign up for a trip to go to a theme park, take a cruise, or reserve a hotel room? Prior to engaging in the actual experience, you saw an ad or video portraying the ideal trip to that location, an idyllic preview. What is seen becomes part of memory. Then, maybe after going, you have a similar memory of your own and maybe this time it includes photos or video of your trip there—great moments. Those also become part of long-term memory. If, as researchers have shown, it is possible to create false memories of brands that don't even exist, isn't it possible that over time, commercial content and actual experience begin to merge in memory, and the consumers remember things as they and the advertisers want them to? In this way, when you remember your time at the park, the hotel, the cruise, or the store, you remember a blend of things: some from your actual experience, some from what was provided by the marketer. This has benefits for

your feelings toward the brand and your recommendations to others, increases the likelihood to repurchase, and actually may shape or transform actual future consumption experiences. Product placements in movies and television shows and other forms of branded entertainment as well as social media can accomplish the same thing. Traditional ads can do this as well. How much of this is manipulation, and how ethical is a deliberate effort to use advertising and IBP to manipulate memories and feelings? Evaluation of transformational ads and other forms of IBP is typically done through field studies, tracking studies, ethnographic (on-site, qualitative) methods, and communication tests. Sometimes small-scale experiments are conducted.

Strategic Implications of Transformational Advertising

- *Can be extremely powerful due to a merging of ad and brand experience.*

- *Fosters long-term commitment.*

- *If not done well, can ring false and hurt the brand.*

- *Ethical issues.* Some believe that certain types of transformational ads are designed to actually manipulate experience and are therefore unethical.

Summary

1. Identify what creative message strategy is, and why it is important for advertisers and brands.

Creative message strategy refers to the set of objectives and methods or tactics used to create and disseminate a relevant and resonating message (such as about a product, service, experience, or brand) to customers and/or potential customers. The objective refers to what the advertiser hopes to achieve. Methods refer to how the advertiser plans to achieve the objective. Creative message strategy is important because it is where the advertising and branding battle is usually won or lost, and it helps make for effective advertising that is both relevant to consumers and their needs and resonating, in that the message works or gets through to consumers.

2. Examine how the 10 objectives of creative message strategy are achieved and the implications of various methods used to execute each message strategy objective.

Advertisers can choose from a wide array of message strategy objectives as well as methods for implementing these objectives. Three fundamental message objectives are promoting brand recall, linking key attributes to the brand name, and persuading the customer. The advertiser may also wish to create an affective association in consumers' minds by linking good feelings, humor, and sex appeal with the brand itself. Such positive feelings associated with the advertised brand can lead consumers to a higher probability of purchase. The advertiser may try to scare the consumer into action or change behavior by inducing anxiety, using negative emotional states as the means to motivate purchases. Transformational advertising aims to transform the nature of the consumption experience so that a consumer's experience of a brand becomes connected to the glorified experiences portrayed in ads. A message may also situate the brand in an important social context to heighten the brand's appeal. Finally, advertisers seek to define a brand's image by linking certain attributes to the brand, mostly using visual cues.

Advertisers use any number of methods to achieve their objectives. To get consumers to recall a brand name, advertisers use repetition, slogans, and jingles. When the advertiser's objective is to link a key attribute to a brand, USP ads emphasizing unique brand qualities are employed. If the goal is to persuade a consumer to make a purchase, reason-why ads, hard-sell ads, comparison ads, testimonials, demonstrations, and infomercials are all viable options. Feel-good ads, humorous ads, and sex-appeal ads can raise a consumer's preferences for one brand over another through affective association. Fear-appeal ads, judiciously used, can motivate purchases, as can ads that play on other anxieties. Transformational ads attempt to enrich the consumption experience. With slice-of-life ads, product placement, and short digital films, the goal is to situate a brand in a desirable social context. Finally, ads that primarily use visuals work to define the brand image.

Each method used to execute a message strategy objective has pros and cons. Methods that promote brand recall or link key attributes to a brand name can be extremely successful in training consumers to remember a brand name or its specific, beneficial attributes. However, these methods require long-term commitment and repetition to work properly, and advertisers can pay high costs while generating disdain from creatives. Methods used to persuade consumers generally aim to provide rhetorical arguments and demonstrations for why consumers should prefer a brand, resulting in strong, cognitive loyalty. However, these methods assume a high level of involvement and are vulnerable to counterarguments that neutralize their effectiveness—more-sophisticated audiences tune them out altogether, rejecting them as misleading, insipid, or dishonest. Methods used in creating affective association have short-term results and please creatives; however, the effect on audiences wears out quickly, and high expense dissuades some advertisers from taking the risk. Methods designed to play on fear or anxiety are compelling, but legal and ethical issues arise, and most advertisers wish to avoid instigating consumer panic. Finally, methods that transform consumption experiences, situate the brand socially, or define brand image have powerful enduring qualities but often get lost in the clutter or can ring false to audiences.

Key Terms

comparison advertisements
copy-test
creative message strategy
day-after recall (DAR)

evoked set
infomercial
parity products
pre- and postexposure tests

testimonial
unique selling proposition (USP)

Endnotes

1. Daniel W. Baack, Rick T. Wilson, Maria M. van Dessel, and Charles H. Patti, "Advertising to Businesses: Does Creativity Matter?" *Industrial Marketing Management* 55 (2016), 169–177.

2. Jack Neff, "See the Spot: Mr. Clean Jingle Returns, Rocking a New World in Three Languages," *Advertising Age,* July 1, 2016, http://adage.com/article/see-the-spot/spot-mr-clean-jingle-returns-languages/304792/.

3. For more about B2B advertising in this regard, see Maarten J. Gijsenberg, "Riding the Waves: Revealing the Impact of Intra-year Category Demand Cycles on Advertising and Pricing Effectiveness," *Journal of Marketing Research* 54, no. 2 (2016), 171–186.

4. Conclusions in this list are drawn from William R. Swinyard, "The Interaction between Comparative Advertising and Copy Claim Variation," *Journal of Marketing Research* 18 (May 1981), 175–186; Cornelia Pechmann and David Stewart, "The Effects of Comparative Advertising on Attention, Memory, and Purchase Intentions," *Journal of Consumer Research* 17 (September 1990), 180–191; and Sanjay Petruvu and Kenneth R. Lord, "Comparative and Noncomparative Advertising: Attitudinal Effects under Cognitive and Affective Involvement Conditions," *Journal of Advertising* 23 (June 1994), 77–90. For a consideration of online involvement, see H.-C. (Angel) Hwang, Jeeyun Oh, and Angeline Close Scheinbaum, "Interactive Music for Multisensory e-commerce: The Moderating Role of Online Consumer Involvement in Experiential Value, Cognitive Value, and Purchase Intention," *Psychology & Marketing* 37, no. 8, 1031–1056.

5. Liz Webber, "Farm Fresh Reports on FNV Produce Marketing Partnership," *Supermarket News,* December 14, 2016, http://www.supermarketnews.com/retail-financial/farm-fresh-reports-fnv-produce-marketing-partnership.

6. Ahiza Garcia, "Cristiano Ronaldo Is the Third Athlete to Sign Nike 'Lifetime' Deal," *CNN Money,* November 6, 2016, http://money.cnn.com/2016/11/09/news/companies/cristiano-ronaldo-nike-lifetime-contract/.

7. Dan Rascon, "Inside the Story: 'Will It Blend?' Is Still a YouTube Sensation After 10 Years," *KUTV.com (Salt Lake City),* December 1, 2016, http://kutv.com/features/inside-the-story/inside-the-story-will-it-blend-is-still-a-youtube-sensation-after-10-years.

8. T. L. Stanley, "How Brands Like Squatty Potty Are Making the Infomercial Fun Again," *Adweek,* December 5, 2016, http://www.adweek.com/news/advertising-branding/how-brands-squatty-potty-are-making-infomercial-fun-again-174875.

9. Baba Shiv and Antoine Bechara, "Revisiting the Customer Value Proposition," in Barbara Loken, Rohini Ahluwalia, and Michael J. Houston (Eds.), *Brands and Brand Management: Contemporary Research Perspectives* (New York and London: Routledge, 2010), 189–206.

10. Tanya Dua, "'The Quintessential American Dream,' Simone Biles Can Expect a Post-Rio Brand Windfall," *Digiday,* August 17, 2016, http://digiday.com/brands/already-brand-favorite-simone-biles-can-expect-post-rio-windfall-worth-millions/.

11. See Michel Tuan Pham, Joel B. Cohen, John W. Pracejus, and G. David Hughes, "Affect Monitoring and the Primacy of Feelings in Judgment," *Journal of Consumer Research,* 28 (September 2001), 167–188.

12. Kelly O. CowartSc Violence and Its Impact on Brand Responses," *Journal of Advertising Research* 60, no. 1 (2019), 202–212.

13. Michelle G. Weinberger et al., "Understanding Responses to Comedic Advertising Aggression: The Role of Vividness and Gender Identity," *International Journal of Advertising* 36 , no. 4 (2017), 562–587; Malgorzata Karpinska-Krakowiak, "Gotcha! Realism of Comedic Violence and Its Impact on Brand Responses," *Journal of Advertising Research* 60, no. 1 (2019), 38–53.

14. This claim is made by Video Storyboards Tests, based on its extensive research of humor ads, and cited in Kevin Goldman, "Ever Hear the One about the Funny Ad?" *The Wall Street Journal,* November 2, 1993, B11.

15. Hojoon Choi, Kyunga Yoo, Tom Reichert, and Michael S. LaTour, "Do Feminists Still Respond Negatively to Female Nudity in Advertising? Investigating the Influence of Feminist Attitudes on Reactions to Sexual Appeals," *International Journal of Advertising* (2016), 1–23.

16. Jingjing Ma and David Gal, "When Sex and Romance Conflict: The Effect of Sexual Imagery in Advertising on Preference for Romantically Linked Products and Services," *Journal of Marketing Research* 53, no. 4 (August 2016), 479–496.

17. Tom Reichert, *The Erotic History of Advertising* (Amherst, NY: Prometheus, 2004).

18. Yanwen Wang et al., "Investigating the Effects of Excise Taxes, Public Usage Restrictions, and Antismoking Ads Across Cigarette Brands," *Journal of Marketing* 85, no. 3 (April 2021), 150–167.

19. "Can Neuroscience Make Your Message Stickier?" *Kellogg Insight* (Kellogg School of Management at Northwestern University), July 7, 2016, https://insight.kellogg.northwestern.edu/article/can-neuroscience-make-your-message-stickier.

20. Irving L. Janis and Seymour Feshbach, "Effects of Fear Arousing Communication," *Journal of Abnormal Social Psychology* 48 (1953), 78–92.

21. Michael Ray and William Wilkie, "Fear: The Potential of an Appeal Neglected by Marketing," *Journal of Marketing* 34, no. 1 (January 1970), 54–62.

22. Moran Cerf, Eric Greenleaf, Tom Meyvis, and Vicki G. Morwitz, "Using Single-Neuron Recording in Marketing: Opportunities, Challenges, and an Application to Fear Enhancement in Communications," *Journal of Marketing Research* 52, no. 4 (August 2015), 530–545.

23. E. H. H. J. Das, J.B.F. de Wit, and W. Strobe, "Fear Appeals Motivate Acceptance of Action Recommendations: Evidence for a Positive Bias in the Processing of Persuasive Messages," *Personality and Social Psychology Bulletin* 29 (2003), 650–664.

24. Ashesh Mukherjee and Seung Yun Lee, "Scarcity Appeals in Advertising: The Moderating Role of Expectation of Scarcity," *Journal of Advertising* 45, no. 2 (2016), 256–268.

25. Douglas B. Holt, "What Becomes an Icon Most?" *Harvard Business Review,* March 2003. https://hbr.org/2003/03/what-becomes-an-icon-most.

26. Patrick Kulp, "Mars Candy's Latest Ad Campaign Brings a Refreshing Take on Life with Disabilities," *Mashable,* September 9, 2016, http://mashable.com/2016/09/09/portrayals-of-people-with-disabilities/#_eRJf4yAeaqm.

27. Chantal Tode, "How Marriott Is Rewriting the Script for Branded Content," *Marketing Dive,* November 3, 2016, http://www.marketingdive.com/news/how-marriott-is-rewriting-the-script-for-branded-content/429631/.

28. For a good discussion, see Thomas C. O'Guinn and Albert Muniz, Jr., "The Social Brand: Towards a Sociological Model of Brands,"

in Barbara Loken, Rohini Ahluwalia, and Michael J. Houston (Eds.), *Brands and Brand Management: Contemporary Research Perspectives* (New York and London: Routledge, 2010), 133–159.

29. Yoon-Joo Lee and Eric Haley, "How Do Generational Differences Drive Response to Social-Issue Ads?" *Journal of Advertising Research* 60, no. 3 (April 2019), 271–289.

30. Kristina Rodulfo, "Maybelline Debuts Its First-Ever Male Ambassador, Manny Gutierrez," *Elle,* January 5, 2017, http://www.elle .com/beauty/news/a41853/maybelline-manny-gutierrez-first -male-ambassador/.

31. Rheana Murray, "Meet Nura Afia, Cover Girl's First Hijab-Wearing Ambassador," *Today,* January 23, 2017, http://www.today.com /style/nura-afia-covergirl-s-first-muslim-ambassador-t104674.

32. Yashoda Bhagwat et al., "Corporate Sociopolitical Activism and Firm Value," *Journal of Marketing* 84, no. 5 (June 2020), 1–21.

33. Katie Richards, "Why Under Armour's Michael Phelps Ad Is One of the Most Shared Olympics Spots Ever," *Advertising Age,* August 11, 2016, http://www.adweek.com/news/advertising-branding/why -under-armours-michael-phelps-ad-one-most-shared-olympics -spots-ever-172931.

Executing the Creative

The heart and soul of advertising is the creative, which shapes the meaning of the brand and brings it to life. Chapter 9 ("Managing Creativity in Advertising and IBP") and Chapter 10 ("Creative Message Strategy") examined the creative process and how firms try to stimulate and energize the creative effort in advertising and integrated brand promotion (IBP). These chapters also highlighted specific message objectives and strategies and detailed the methods associated with each, as shown in Exhibit 11.1. Now, in this chapter, you'll see how all of these efforts come together to bring the creative to life.

Exhibit 11.1 ▶ This is the framework diagram for executing the creative strategy in integrated brand promotion.

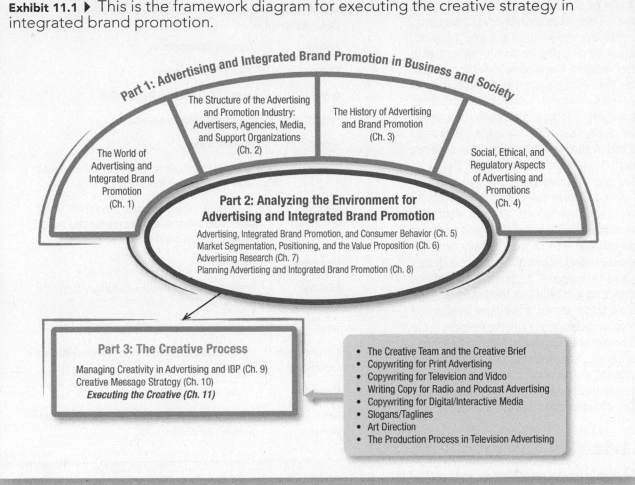

11-1 The Creative Team and the Creative Brief

11-1a The Creative Team

The entire **creative team** generally consists of copywriters, art directors, media planners, and account planners. In an advertising agency, the creative team working on advertising and IBP materials often includes a **media planner** and/or an *account planner*. Media are evolving quickly and are now more important than ever to both message strategy and creative execution, particularly with the proliferation of streaming media content, social media networks, and mobile marketing options. Account planners on the team act as the voice of the consumer within the creative planning process and execution.

During this process, copywriters, in addition to their role in creating the "language" of the messages, also might suggest

the idea for the visuals. Likewise, art directors may come up with the headline or tagline. Media planners convey what is possible through the various media choices. Account planners check the research and ensure the profile of the target consumer remains in mind during the planning for creative strategy and the execution.

11-1b Copywriters and Art Directors

Two of the key creative team members are copywriters and art directors. **Copywriting** is the process of crafting the meaning of a brand through words. As such, copywriters are the advertising professionals who specialize in this. Copywriting requires far more than the ability to string product descriptions together in coherent sentences. One apt description of copywriting is that it is a never-ending exploration of ideas integrated with a constant search for divergent ways to express them. Copywriting has to be tailored to its medium or media, and in today's explosion of media, that could be anything from a fully stylized, copy-laden magazine ad to dialogue in a branded entertainment film or even a brand "shout out" in social media. Even if you don't plan to be a copywriter, understanding the craft is essential to understanding advertising.

Effective copywriters are well informed, astute advertising decision makers with creative talent. Copywriters are able to assess and then incorporate the complexities of marketing, consumer behavior, and advertising strategies into powerful communications that clearly convey the message.[1] They must do this in such a way that the copy does not interfere with but rather enhances the visual aspects of the message.

An astute advertiser will go to great lengths to provide copywriters with as much information as possible about the objectives for a particular advertising effort. The responsibility for keeping copywriters informed lies with the client's **brand managers,** the team responsible for developing and adapting the brand strategy for the target market. It is filtered through the account executives and creative directors in the ad agency or brand communication firm. Without this information, copywriters are left without guidance and direction; and they must rely on intuition about what sorts of information are relevant and meaningful to a target audience.

Exhibit 11.2 ▶ A sample creative brief.

CREATIVE BRIEF

Agency	Creative Stupor, Austin
Client	Jake's Fried Chicken
Brand	Jake's Fried Chicken Restaurants
Project	Best Fried Chicken Anywhere.
Author	Blake N. Milton
Purpose	To remind fried chicken lovers of Jake's chicken's USP: *High Fat and Proud of It.*
Creative opportunity	To leverage the underserved segment of "don't care about my arteries; give me the real thing"... Unapologetic comfort food.
Media mix	Open
Message objective	Brand recall USP: *Real fried chicken; forget the guilt.*
Tone	In your face, dripping down your chin.
Key consumer opportunity	Give consumer permission to indulge with Jake's Fried Chicken.
Message	*You want it; go for it.*
Reason to believe	You already know it; know you have permission. Besides: Jake told you so.

11-1c The Creative Brief

The creative team is guided by the creative brief in executing the creative strategy. The **creative brief** is the document that outlines and channels an essential creative idea and objective guiding the creative team. It can be thought of as the unique creative thinking that serves as the foundation of a campaign, has been described as the "ignition" for the creative team.[2] As said earlier, which can't be understated, is that effective brand communication relies on a good creative brief.

The creative brief serves as the guide used in the copywriting process to specify the message elements that must be coordinated during the preparation of copy. The key word is brief, as it is a common mishap in developing a creative brief when they are too long or complex; they should illuminate the big creative leap. These elements include main brand claims, creative devices, media that will be used, special creative needs a brand might have, and what we want the receivers to think or feel once they receive the message.[3] Part of the typical copywriting challenge is creating excitement around what can otherwise be a static and boring list of product features.

Some of the key elements that should be considered when developing a creative brief include the following:

1. The single most important thought you want a member of the target market to take away from the advertisement
2. The product features to be emphasized
3. The benefits a user receives from these features

4. The media chosen for transmitting the information and the length of time the advertisement will run
5. The suggested mood or tone for the ad or promotion
6. The production budget for the ad or brand promotion[4]

There are times, however, when these considerations can be modified or even disregarded. For example, sometimes a brilliant creative execution demands a different medium, or a creative thought may require a completely different mood than the one specified in the creative brief. A creative brief should be considered a starting point and big picture for planning the creative execution. Copywriting should be strategic in its execution of the creative brief's objectives. A sample creative brief is shown in Exhibit 11.2.

11-2 Copywriting for Print Advertising

In preparing copy for a print ad, the first step in the copy development process is deciding how to use (or not use) the three separate components of print copy: the headline, the subhead, and the body copy. (Slogans and taglines are also part of the copywriting process, but we consider that effort separately later in the chapter.) Be aware that the full range of components applies most directly to print ads that appear in magazines, newspapers, or direct mail pieces. These guidelines also apply to other "print" media such as billboards, transit advertising, specialty advertising, websites, digital and social media, and mobile marketing.

11-2a The Headline

The **headline** in an advertisement is the leading sentence(s), usually at the top or bottom of the ad, that attracts attention, communicates a key selling point, or achieves brand identification. Many headlines fail to attract attention, and the ad itself then becomes another piece of clutter battling for mindshare with their target audience. Lifeless headlines do not compel the reader to examine other parts of the ad. Simply stated, a headline can either motivate a reader to move on to the rest of an ad or can lose the reader for good. In fact, there are certain ads where the creative execution depends completely on the headline, and the entire piece is carried by it. Many print ads, such as this one from BMW (Exhibit 11.3), do not have a classic headline and subhead and rely instead on strong visuals. Ads like this may be aesthetically pleasing, but the risk with such a bold, clean layout is that the small print and heavy copy at the bottom can be dominated by the visuals and may be ignored.

Source: BMW

Exhibit 11.3 ▶ BMW, in this print ad, challenges some traditional advertising formatting that features a prominent headline and subhead.

11-2b The Subhead

A **subhead** consists of a phrase or a short sentence and usually appears above or below the headline. It offers the opportunity for the advertiser to share important brand information that is not included in the headline. A subhead serves basically the same purpose as a headline—to communicate key selling points or brand information quickly. A subhead is normally in smaller print than the headline but larger than the body copy. In most cases, the subhead is lengthier than the headline and can be used to communicate more complex selling points. The subhead should reinforce the headline and stimulate a more complete reading of the entire ad.

11-2c The Body Copy

Body copy is the textual component of an advertisement and tells a more complete story of a brand. Effective body copy is written in a fashion that takes advantage of and reinforces the headline and subhead, is compatible with and gains strength from the visuals, and is interesting to the reader. Whether body copy is interesting is a function of how accurately the copywriter and other decision makers have assessed various components of message development and how good the copywriter is. Even the most elaborate body copy will be useless if it is "off creative strategy." It will not matter if it's very clever but has little to do in advancing the strategy. And to be effective, it will have to overcome the biggest challenge facing body copy—few people ever read it.

There are several standard techniques for preparing body copy. The **straight-line copy** approach explains in a direct way why a reader will benefit from the use of a brand. This technique is used many times in conjunction with a benefits message strategy. Body copy that uses **dialogue** delivers the selling points of a message to the audience through a character or group of characters in the ad. Dialogue can also depict two people in the ad having a conversation, a technique frequently used in slice-of-life messages. A *testimonial* uses dialogue as if the spokesperson is having a one-sided conversation with the reader through the body copy.

Narrative is a method for preparing body copy that simply displays a series of statements about a brand. A person may or may not be portrayed as delivering the copy. It is difficult to make this technique lively for the reader, so when using this technique, it is important to acknowledge the sizeable risk of developing an ad that falls flat for the receiver. For instance, MasterCard is known for having developed some excellent narrative-style copywriting ads with their "Priceless" campaign (Exhibit 11.4).

Direct response copy is, in many ways, the least complex of the copy techniques. In writing direct response copy, the copywriter is trying to highlight the need to act immediately. Hence, the range of possibilities for direct response copy is more limited. In addition, many direct response advertisements rely on sales promotion devices, such as coupons, contests, and rebates, as a means of stimulating action. Giving deadlines to the reader is also a common approach in direct response

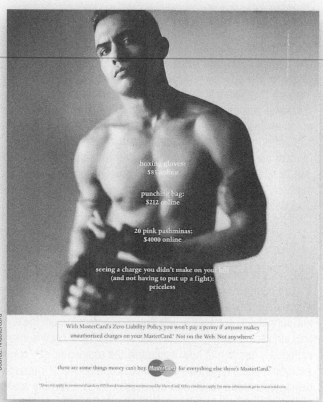

Source: Mastercard

boxing gloves:
$85 online

punching bag:
$212 online

20 pink pashminas:
$4000 online

seeing a charge you didn't make on your bill
(and not having to put up a fight):
priceless

With MasterCard's Zero Liability Policy, you won't pay a penny if anyone makes
unauthorized charges on your MasterCard. Not on the Web. Not anywhere.

there are some things money can't buy. MasterCard for everything else there's MasterCard.

*Does not apply to commercial cards or PIN-based transactions not processed by MasterCard. Other conditions apply. For more information, go to mastercard.com

Exhibit 11.4 ▶ MasterCard is known for some excellent narrative-style copywriting with the "Priceless" campaign.

advertising. As an example, Proactiv, a skin care brand, uses direct response copy and television-based sales to become a successful product to help people clear their skin.

These techniques for copywriting establish a general set of styles that can be used as the format for body copy. Again, be aware that any message objective can be employed within any particular copy technique. There are an almost infinite number of compatible combinations. Direct response copy is great for products that are being sold via e-commerce, such as Rhianna's (the musician/celebrity and beauty brand founder) diverse makeup line Fenty Beauty. In Exhibit 11.5, check out the copywriting in their post and how it ties to direct response to entice customers, and their ads often show the exact products featured on the model with a link to their e-commerce site to buy the featured products.

11-3 Copywriting for Television and Video

Relative to print media, television presents totally different set of challenges for a copywriter. It is obvious that the audio and visual capabilities of television and video offer different

opportunities for a copywriter. Compared to print media, however, video media have inherent constraints. In print media, a copywriter can write longer and more involved copy to more thoroughly communicate complex brand features. For consumer goods, such as automobiles or home entertainment systems, a brand's basis for competitive differentiation and positioning may lie with complex, unique functional features. In this case, print media provide a copywriter the time and space to communicate these details, along with helpful illustrations. In addition, the printed page allows the reader to dwell on the copy and process the information at a personalized, comfortable pace. These advantages do not exist in most video media, including broadcast television.

11-3a Writing Copy for Television (Video)

Great print can make you famous. Great TV can make you rich.

—Anonymous[5]

Television has always been a vastly creative forum for the copywriter and art director. In the current era of social media, the addition of online video offers the same opportunities as television. The comments in this section apply to ads placed on social media sites and/or on mobile devices. The ability to create a mood or demonstrate a brand's value is an important capability of both television and video. Obviously, copy for television must be highly sensitive to the ad's visual aspects. Television is a visual medium, and it is important to try and not let the words get in the way when using it.[6]

The opportunities inherent to television as an advertising medium represent challenges for the copywriter as well. Certainly, television's inherent capabilities do much to bring a copywriter's words to life. But the action qualities can create problems. First, the copywriter must remember that words do not stand alone. Visuals, special effects, and sound techniques may ultimately convey a message far better than the cleverest phrase. Second, television commercials present a difficult timing challenge for the copywriter. It is necessary for the copy to be precisely coordinated with the visuals. If the visual portion was one continuous illustration, the task would be difficult enough. Contemporary television ads, however, tend to be heavily edited (i.e., lots of cuts), and the copywriting task can become exponentially more challenging. The copywriter not only makes sure all of the critical details are included (based on creative platform and strategy decisions) but also has to carefully arrange all of the information within, between, and around the display.

To make sure this coordination is precise, the copywriter, producer, and director assigned to a television advertisement work closely together to make sure the copy supports and enhances the video element. The roadmap for this coordination effort is known as a **storyboard,** and these are commonly digital in modern times. A storyboard

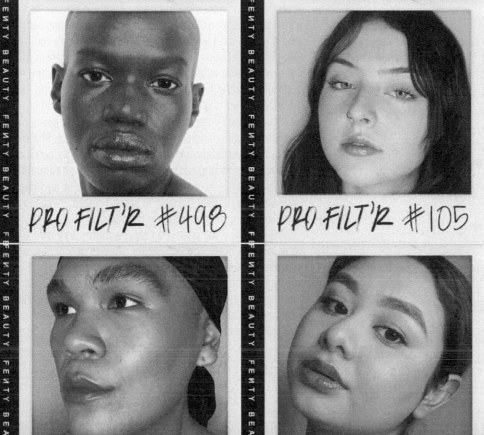

fentybeauty tagged products from their **shop**.
September 24 at 7:17 PM · 🌐

Beauty for all since day 1! 🟤🟤🟤🟤 That's why we created
#PROFILTRSOFTMATTEFOUNDATION in 50 shades to deliver REAL skin in your perfect match! ✨ Get Pro Filt'r Foundation and all of your **#FENTYBEAUTY** faves for 25% OFF only on fentybeauty.com! No code needed! Sale ends 9/27.

PRO FILT'R #498   *PRO FILT'R #105*

Source: Facebook.com

Exhibit 11.5 ▶ The beauty brand Fenty shows an example of smart copywriting for social media and e-commerce integration, as well as being excellent at embracing diversity of beauty in its models.

is an important-shot-by-important-shot sketch depicting in sequence the visual scenes and copy that will be used in the advertisement. The procedures for coordinating audio and visual elements through the use of storyboards will be presented later in the chapter when television production is discussed in more detail.

11-3b Guidelines for Writing Television Copy

Writing copy for television advertising has its own set of unique opportunities and challenges. The following are some general guidelines:

- **Use the video.** Allow the video portion of the commercial to enhance and embellish the audio portion. Given the strength and power of the visual presentation in television advertising, leverage its impact with copy.[7]

- **Support the video.** Make sure that the copy doesn't simply ride the coattails of the video. If all the copy does is verbally describe what the audience is watching, an opportunity to either communicate additional information or strengthen the video communication has been lost.

- **Coordinate the audio with the video.** In addition to strategically using the video, it is essential that the audio and video complement each other in a way that achieves the goals of the ad.

- **Sell the brand as well as entertain the audience.** Television ads can sometimes be more entertaining than television programming. A temptation for the copywriter and art director is to get caught up in the excitement of a good video presentation and forget that the main purpose is to deliver persuasive communication. How many times have you seen a great, entertaining ad and then have no idea what brand the ad was promoting?

- **Be flexible.** Due to media-scheduling strategies, commercials are produced to run as 10-, 15-, 20-, 30-, or 60-second spots. The copywriter may need to ensure that the audio portion of an ad is complete and comprehensive within varying time frames. Also, consider how the ad would play in the small formats of mobile devices. Amazon has produced dozens of 10-second television, online, and social media spots to showcase the funny questions people ask its Alexa artificial intelligence system via Amazon's Echo speaker. The brief format underscores the speed of Alexa's responses and lets the humor shine through; this parlays nicely with the informative and entertainment-related reasons that consumers seek from media.[8]

- *Use copy judiciously.* If a television ad is too wordy, it can create information overload and interfere with the visual impact. Ensure that every word is contributing to the impact of the message.

- *Reflect the brand personality and image.* All aspects of an ad, copy and visuals, should be consistent with the personality and image the advertiser wants to build or maintain for the brand.

- *Build campaigns.* When copy for a particular advertisement is being written, evaluate its potential as a sustainable idea. Can the basic appeal in the advertisement be developed into multiple versions placed in other media to form a campaign?[9]

11-4 Writing Copy for Radio and Podcast Advertising

Some writers consider radio the ultimate forum for copywriting creativity. Because radio is restricted to an audio-only presentation, a copywriter is freed from some of the more complex elements of visual presentations. Yet it has been said that radio *is* actually visual. The copywriter must (inevitably) create images in the minds of listeners. The creative potential of radio rests in its ability to stimulate a "theater of the mind," which allows a copywriter to create images and moods for audiences that transcend those created in any other medium.

Despite these creative opportunities, the drawbacks of this medium should not be underestimated. Few radio listeners actively listen to radio programming (talk radio is an exception), much less the commercial interruptions. Radio may be viewed by some as the theater of the mind, but others have labeled it audio wallpaper—wallpaper in the sense that radio is used as a filler or unobtrusive accompaniment to reading, driving, household chores, or homework.

These days, podcasts are reinventing audio entertainment. New media offers additional opportunities for creative and engaging audio advertising that reaches listeners who download or stream content. Podcast popularity is on the upswing, attracting 117.8 million listeners monthly and encouraging mainstream advertisers like Sephora (a beauty retailer) and Blue Apron (a meal delivery service) to target this growing

audience.[10] Many podcast ads or branded content podcasts are simple brand announcements or rely on improvised comments about products by podcast hosts, although some are more tightly scripted and produced. For instance, the podcast with Blue Apron is entitled "why we eat what we eat," and takes an informative tone.

A copywriter should recognize the unique character of audio advertising and galvanize the opportunities it offers. First, radio adds the dimension of sound to the basic copywriting effort, and sound (other than voices) can become a primary tool in creating copy. Second, radio can conjure images in the mind of the receiver that extend beyond the starkness of brand "information" actually being provided. Audio copywriting should, therefore, strive to stimulate each receiver's imagination. As an example, Disney+ used smart copy in their radio spots to help promote the steaming service. For food examples, McDonald's (the fast-food restaurant) and Little Caesars (the pizza chain) are known for strong radio copy. McDonald's often uses radio copy as a way to evoke emotions namely joy or surprise, and Little Caesars repeats the simple phrase "Pizza, Pizza" to make an auditory connection with the brand.

Writing copy for radio begins the same way that writing copy for print does. The copywriter reviews components of the creative brief to take advantage of and follow through on the marketing and advertising strategies integral to the brand's market potential. Let's consider several formats for radio ads and guidelines for copy preparation that the copywriter can turn to for direction.

11-4a Guidelines for Writing Radio Copy

Due to the unique mix of opportunities and challenges associated with the radio medium, copywriters can benefit from the use of a set of guidelines as they work to enhance the probability of effective communication. The following are a few suggestions for writing strong radio copy:

- *Capture attention and get to the point early.* The first 5 seconds of an ad can capture or lose the radio listener. Grab their attention, then get to the main point, and stick with it.

- *Use common, familiar language.* The use of words and language easily understood and recognized by the receiver is even more important in radio than in print copy preparation. Esoteric language or phrases will confuse and ultimately alienate the listener.

- *Use short words and sentences.* The probability of communicating verbally increases if short, easily processed words and sentences are used. Long, involved, elaborate verbal descriptions make it difficult for the listener to follow the copy.

- *Stimulate the imagination.* Copy that can conjure up concrete and stimulating images in the receiver's mind can have a powerful impact on recall.

- *Repeat the brand name.* Because the impression made by a radio ad is fleeting, it may be necessary to repeat the brand name several times for it to register. The same is true for location if the ad is being used to promote a retail operation.

- *Stress the unique selling proposition.* The premise of the ad should always revolve around the creative brief. If the main selling points of a brand are mentioned only in passing, there is little reason for the listener to believe or remember them.

- *Use sound and music with care.* A copywriter should take advantage of all the creative audio capabilities afforded by the radio medium, including the use of sound effects and music. Although these devices can contribute greatly to attracting and holding a listener's attention, care must be taken to ensure that they do not overwhelm the copy and ultimately the persuasive impact of the commercial.

- *Tailor the copy to the time, place, and specific audience.* Take advantage of any unique aspect of the advertising context. If the ad is created for a particular geographic region, use colloquialisms unique to that region as a way to tailor the message. The same is true with time-of-day factors or unique aspects of the audience.[11]

LO 5

11-5 Copywriting for Digital/ Interactive Media

In digital and interactive media, *audience* has a significantly different meaning than it does in traditional one-way (noninteractive) media. Here, audience members often seek out the ads or other online IBP material rather than the other way around, and they are doing it in much smaller formats like a laptop, tablet, or smartphone. In digital settings, ads may be direct response oriented as they may link with e-commerce or enticing other online consumer behaviors. In addition, digital ads can pop up as one moves across Web pages (more on this in Chapter 14). The media—computers and mobile devices—are fundamentally more user directed than print, television, or radio. This means that consumers approach (and read) digital ads differently than other types of ads. Furthermore, digital and interactive media copy is often (but not always) direct response, which dictates copy style. Digital and interactive media copywriters are trying to meet the demands of vastly different audiences and often real-time media creation (as in tweets).[12] The basic principles of good print and broadcast copywriting generally apply. But the copy should assume a more active and engaged audience and the creative brief objectives must be adapted to accommodate the smaller format and potentially real-time challenges of the reception environment. Still, remember that odds are that receivers are not there for your ads.

11-5a Copywriting Approaches to Digital/Interactive Advertising

In this time of screaming technological advances, I find that what is considered old and near death is also what will never be replaced by technology. Mainly, that is good old-fashioned creativity.

—Tracy Wong[13]

Digital/interactive ads can be considered as hybrids between print and broadcasting advertisements. On the one hand, the receiver encounters the message in a print format (such as a website, email, blog, or social media platform). On the other hand, the message is delivered electronically—similar to television or radio. And, as the quote highlights, creativity is vital, regardless of technology. The common approaches to copywriting are as follows:[14]

- At a **long-copy landing page,** a website designed to sell a product directly, the copy might be the equivalent of a four- to eight-page letter to a potential customer. The brand and its benefits are described in great detail, with visuals included throughout.

- A **short-copy landing page** is simply a brand offer that may be accessed by a consumer through a key word search and has the length and look of a magazine ad. Its components will resemble a magazine ad as well with headline, subhead, and body copy.

- A **long-copy email** is designed to offer the receiver all sorts of incentives to buy the product and usually offers a link to a short-copy landing page.

- A **teaser email** is a short message designed to drive readers to a long-copy landing page where they can order the brand directly.

- A **pop-up/pop-under ad,** discussed in Chapter 14, refers to those sometimes annoying little ads that involuntarily show up while you are Web browsing. The **pop-up/pop-under copy** in this sort of ad resembles a series of headlines and subheads without much—or any—body copy. Such an ad usually makes a special offer or drives the receiver to a specific website.

- **Social media copy** rarely has headlines or subheads and instead functions more like pure copywriting. Something to consider when writing for social media is that in some formats, such as on Twitter, a # (termed a **hashtag**) is often used to help aggregate or organize information on that topic or brand as well as to help measure digital engagement. "Tweets" about a brand or brand "callouts" in a blog are subtle references to the brand and can build awareness and positive affinity. The reality is that in many cases the advertiser is not in total control of the copy here.

Even when a tweet emanates from the firm, the author is offering a free-form discussion of the brand—the same with a blog entry. Furthermore, many times the copy may be **ephemeral,** or short-lived as a "disappearing message." Social media platforms such as Instagram stories are such an example where copy is fleeting.

LO 6

11-6 Slogans/Taglines

Regardless of the media type, copywriters are often asked to develop a good slogan or tagline for a product or service. A **slogan** or **tagline** is a short phrase that is used, in part, to help establish an image, identity, or position for a brand or organization but is most often leveraged to increase the memorability a brand's key benefit.[15] A slogan is established by repeating the phrase in a firm's advertising and other public communications as well as through salespeople and event promotions. Slogans are often

Exhibit 11.6 ▶ Classic and memorable slogans used for brands and organizations.

BRAND/COMPANY	SLOGAN
Allstate Insurance	You're in Good Hands with Allstate.
Apple	Think Different.
Beef Industry Council	Real Food for Real People.
BMW	The Ultimate Driving Machine.
Budweiser	The King of Beers.
Chevrolet Trucks	Like a Rock.
De Beers	Diamonds Are Forever.
Ford Trucks	Built Ford Tough.
Gillette	The Best a Man Can Get.
Harley-Davidson	The Legend Rolls On.
Lay's	Betcha Can't Eat Just One.
L'Oréal	Because I'm Worth It.
Maybelline	Maybe She's Born with It. Maybe It's Maybelline.
Red Bull	Red Bull Gives You Wings.
Skittles	Taste the Rainbow.
Taco Bell	Think Outside the Bun.
Verizon	Can You Hear Me Now?
Visa	It's Everywhere You Want to Be.

used as a headline or subhead in print advertisements or as the tagline at the conclusion of radio and television advertisements. Slogans typically appear directly below the brand or company name, on the brand website, or spoken in broadcast commercials, just as "Bet ya can't eat just one," as Lay's (a potato chip brand) does in most of their ads or digital applications. Some classic and memorable ad slogans and taglines are listed in Exhibit 11.6.

A good slogan or tagline can serve several positive and important purposes for a brand or a firm. First, a slogan can be an integral part of a brand's image and personality. Sephora's (the makeup retail brand) recent Pride campaign tagline, "Identify As We," expresses the experience of supporting the LGBTQ+ community and developing a culture where "diversity is expected, self expression is honored, all are welcomed, and all are included." The tagline is supported by the hashtag #belong, which reflects the brand personality of inclusivity in every IBP execution (see Exhibit 11.7).[16] The ad in Exhibit 11.7 shows a powerful representation of identity by depicting an image of a confident woman, which aligns well with the tagline "We Belong to Something Beautiful." It is important that her image aligns with the tagline. It is important that her image aligns with the tagline for message consistency. When an image and the tagline are congruent, it reinforces the message. In this case, the image and tagline are consistent in reinforcing a message of inclusive beauty and confidence.

Second, if a slogan is carefully and consistently developed over time, it can act as shorthand identification for the brand and convey important brand benefits. The "Built Ford Tough" slogan has communicated the ruggedness and reliability of Ford's pickup trucks for more than 35 years (see Exhibit 11.8). In this image, Ford shows their classic blue and white logo around the words "Built Tough", which are in all capitals as to represent the strength of the truck. Again, the tagline and the image are consistent and reinforce each other.

Finally, a good slogan also provides continuity across different media and among advertising campaigns. Dunkin' (a fast-food brand) "America runs on the Dunkin' slogan gives the firm an underlying theme for a wide range of campaigns and other promotions. The reason that it is a good slogan is because it is now more broad than the limiting older brand name (Dunkin' Donuts) and it implies that Americans, who are often on the go, are fueled by the food and beverages that Dunkin' serves. In this sense, a slogan is a useful tool in helping to bring about thematic IBP for a firm.

11-6a The Copy Approval Process

"The client has some issues and concerns about your ads." This is how account executives announce the death of your labors: "issues and concerns." To understand the portent of this phrase, picture the men lying on the floor of that Chicago garage on St. Valentine's Day. Al Capone had issues and concerns with these men.

I've had account executives beat around the bush for 15 minutes before they could tell me the bad news.

Exhibit 11.7 ▶ In this ad from Sephora, a retailer specializing in makeup and skincare, it shows how inclusion, diversity, and representation is important in this industry by showing multiple pronouns along with the tagline "We Belong to Something Beautiful."

As the story above illustrates, getting the client to approve or "sign off" on the copywriting may require the copywriter to address client or legal "issues and concerns." The final step in copywriting is getting the copy approved. During the approval process, the proposed copy is likely to pass through the hands of a wide range of client and agency representatives, many of whom are not equipped to judge the quality of the copy. And there are those who argue convincingly that the approval process stifles creativity, as the creative team strives for approval rather than creative excellence.[18] The challenge at this stage is to preserve the creative potency of the copy while simultaneously making sure the client is comfortable with and confident in the work. As David Ogilvy suggests in his commandments for advertising, "Committees can criticize advertisements, but they can't write them."[19]

The copy approval process usually begins within the creative department at the advertising agency. A copywriter submits a draft copy to either a senior writer or creative director or both. From there, the redrafted copy is forwarded to the account management team. The main concern at this level is to evaluate the copy on legal grounds. After the account management team has made recommendations, a meeting is likely held to present the copy, along with proposed visuals, to the client's product category manager, brand manager, and/or marketing staff. Inevitably, the client representatives feel compelled to make recommendations for altering the copy. In some cases, these suggestions realign the copy in accordance with important marketing strategy objectives. In other cases, the recommendations are amateurish and problematic. From the copywriter's point of view, they are rarely welcome, although the copywriter usually has to act as if they are.

Depending on the assignment, the client, and the traditions of the agency, the creative team may also decide to turn to various forms of copy research to resolve any differences of opinion. Typically, copy research is either developmental or evaluative. *Developmental copy research* (see Chapter 7) can actually help copywriters at the early stages of copy development by providing audience interpretations and reactions to the proposed copy. *Evaluative copy research* (see Chapter 7) is used to judge the copy after it has been produced. Here, the audience expresses its approval or disapproval of the copy used in an ad. Copywriters are usually not fond of these evaluative report cards. In our view, they are completely justified in their suspicion; for many reasons, state-of-the-art evaluative copy research just isn't very good.

Finally, the copy should always be submitted for final approval to the advertiser's senior executives. Many times, these executives have little interest in evaluating advertising plans, and they leave this responsibility to middle managers. In some firms, however, top executives get very involved in

Exhibit 11.8 ▶ Ford does a good job in copywriting by pulling the theme "Built Ford Tough" through much of the ad copy or voice-over.

"Well, we had a good meeting."

"Yes," you say, "but are the ads dead?"

"We learned a lot?"

"But are they dead?"

"Wellll... They're really not dead. They are just in a new and better place."

—Luke Sullivan[17]

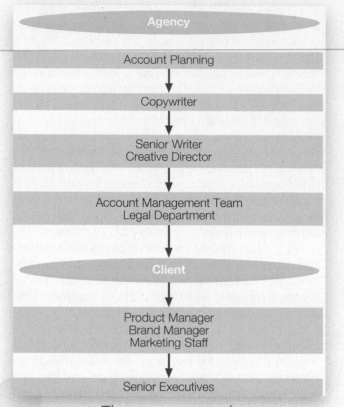

Exhibit 11.9 ▶ The copy approval process.

the approval process. The various levels of approval for the copy are summarized in Exhibit 11.9. For the advertiser, it is best to recognize that copywriters, like other creative talent in an agency, should be allowed to exercise their creative expertise with guidance but not overbearing interference. Copywriters typically provide energy, originality, and distinctiveness to an often dry marketing strategy.

11-7 Art Direction

At this point, we can turn our attention to the process of art direction. In the above discussion on copywriting, the issue of coordinating the copy with visuals was raised several times. Now, we will focus on the process of how both the visual elements of an advertisement and the associated IBP materials are developed.

A hundred years ago, advertisers largely relied on words to persuade consumers. Now, advertising has become mostly visual. There are several reasons for this trend. Among them are (1) improved technologies, which facilitate better and more affordable illustration and the opportunity to rotate visuals nearly instantaneously in digital media; (2) the inherent advantage of pictures to quickly demonstrate the value of a brand; (3) the ability to build brand "images" through visuals; (4) the legal advantage of pictures over words in that the truth or falsity of a picture is almost impossible to determine; (5) the widely held

belief that pictures, although culturally equivalent to words, permit a certain type of global portability that words do not; and (6) pictures allow advertisers to place brands in desired social contexts, thus transferring important social meaning to them.

11-7a Illustration, Design, and Layout

The three primary visual elements of a print or digital ad are illustration, design, and layout. As a print or digital/interactive ad is being prepared, certain aspects of each should be specified, or at least considered. An advertiser must appreciate the technical aspects of coordinating the visual elements in an ad with the mechanics of the layout and ultimately with the procedures for print production or Web placement. Today, art directors and their designers use specialized software to quickly and effectively design and refine illustration, layout, and design that spans digital, mobile, and social media.

Initially, the creative team decides on the general purpose and content of an advertising visual. Then the art director, usually in conjunction with a graphic designer, takes this raw idea for the visual and develops it further. Art directors, with their specialized skills and training, coordinate the ad's various design and illustration elements. The creative director oversees the entire process. The copywriter is still in the loop to ensure word/visual coordination.

Illustration

Illustration, in the context of print and digital advertising, is the actual drawing, painting, photography, or computer-generated art that creates the picture in an advertisement. Simply stated, illustration is the look of the ad. For example, consider how developing the desired social context for a brand advances the slice-of-life method of socially situating. Consider how a unique selling proposition (USP) strategy would be advanced by communicating a certain brand feature visually. One of the primary roles of illustration, along with the headline, is to attract and hold attention, as discussed earlier. With all of the advertising clutter in the ecosystem, this is no easy task. In some advertising situations (e.g., the very early stages of a new product launch or for very-low-involvement repeat-purchase items), just being noticed by consumers may be enough. In most cases, however, being noticed is a necessary but not sufficient goal. An illustration is made to communicate with a particular target audience and, generally, must support other components of the ad to achieve the intended communication impact, especially when exposure to the ad (in any medium) may be quite brief.

One of the traditional roles of art direction is to make the brand "heroic." Visual techniques such as backlighting, low-angle shots, and dramatic use of color can communicate heroic proportions and qualities. Professionals call this the "hero" or "beauty shot."

Perhaps the most straightforward illustration is one that simply displays brand features, benefits, or both. Even though a print ad is static, the product can be shown in use through an "action" scene or even through a series of illustrations. The benefits of the product use technique can be demonstrated with before-and-after shots or by demonstrating the result of having used the product.

Brand image is projected through illustration and is supported by the packaging, associated brand imagery (e.g., the brand logo), and evoked feelings. The "mood" of an ad can facilitate this—created by color tones and highlighting. Whether these goals are achieved with an ad depends on the technical execution of the illustration. The lighting, color, tone, and texture of the illustration can have a noticeable impact. Even the way the logo is framed and its position as part of the visual design can affect perceptions of risk and influence purchase intent.[20]

Just as a headline can stimulate examination of the illustration, the illustration can stimulate reading of the body copy. Because body copy generally carries essential selling messages, any tactic that encourages reading is helpful. Normally, an illustration and headline need to be fully coordinated and play off each other for this level of interest to occur. One caution is to avoid making the illustration too clever a stimulus to motivate copy reading. Prioritizing cleverness over clarity in choosing an illustration can confuse the receiver and cause the body copy to be ignored. As one expert puts it, such ads win awards but can camouflage the benefit offered by the product.[21]

As described earlier, advertisers often try to situate their brands within a type of social setting, thereby linking it with certain "types" of people and certain lifestyles. Establishing desired social contexts is a highly prized function of modern art direction.

Design

Design is "the structure itself and the plan behind that structure" for the aesthetic and stylistic aspects of a print advertisement.[22] Design represents the effort on the part of the creative team to physically arrange all the components of a printed or digital/interactive advertisement in such a way that order and beauty are achieved—order in the sense that the illustration, headline, body copy, and special features of the ad are easy to read; beauty in the sense that the ad is visually pleasing to a reader. Even digital ads (which we will consider specifically in a few pages) need visual appeal to complement the interactive options they present. Examples of ads in Exhibits 11.10 (Polo) and 11.11 (Beck's) illustrate brands that emphasized art direction and design.

There are aspects of design that directly relate to the potential for an ad to communicate effectively based on its artistic form. As such, design factors are highly relevant to creating effective print advertising, and we will consider those now.

Principles of Design

Principles of design govern how a print advertisement should be prepared. Remember that, just as language has rules of grammar and syntax, visual presentation has rules of design. The **principles of design** relate to each element within an advertisement and to the arrangement of and relationship to the elements as a whole.[23] Principles of design suggest the following:

- A design should be in balance.

- The proportion within an advertisement should be pleasing to the viewer.

- The components within an advertisement should have an ordered and directional pattern.

- There should be a unifying force within the ad.

- One element of the ad should be emphasized above all others.

We will consider each of these principles of design and how they relate to the development of an effective advertisement. Of course, as surely as there are rules, there are occasions when the rules should be broken. An experienced designer knows the rules and follows them but is also prepared to break the rules to achieve the desired creative outcome. For an example of focus on one element of the ad, see Exhibit 11.12 where McDonald's focuses on the product to put the main attention on the McRib sandwich.

© Thomas C. O'Guinn

Exhibit 11.10 ▶ The art direction for this Polo ad tries to make the brand "heroic."

Exhibit 11.11 ▶ The Beck's ad tries to get you to read the body copy because of some unusual art direction. Does the art direction work to entice you to read the copy?

Exhibit 11.12 ▶ While the art and image dominate this McDonald's brand post, imagine all of the possibilities for creative and effective copywriting. How would you caption this image to best reflect the brand image and help sales?

Balance

Balance in an ad is an orderliness and compatibility of presentation. Balance can be either formal or informal. **Formal balance** emphasizes symmetrical presentation—components on one side of an imaginary vertical line through the ad are repeated in approximate size and shape on the other side. Formal balance creates a mood of seriousness and directness and offers the viewer an orderly, easy-to-follow visual presentation.

Informal balance emphasizes asymmetry—the optical weighing of nonsimilar sizes and shapes. Informal balance in an ad should not be interpreted as imbalance. Rather, components of different sizes, shapes, and colors are arranged in a more complex relationship, providing asymmetrical balance to an ad and a visually intriguing presentation to the viewer. For instance, the Harley-Davidson motorcycle ad in Exhibit 11.13 uses informal balance for creative effect. As another example, Kenzo (a fashion brand) uses informal balance and beauty of nature in the ad, which is a not perfectly symmetrical yet very pretty and pleasing to the eye (Exhibit 11.14).

Source: First Base Imaging, London

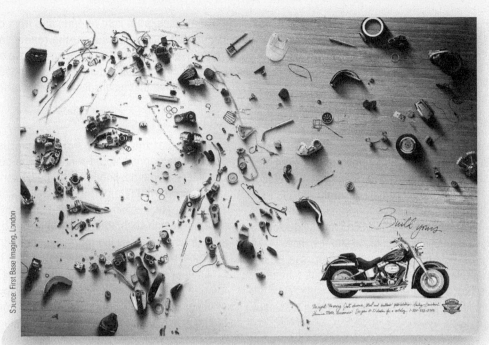

Exhibit 11.13 ▸ This Harley-Davidson motorcycle ad uses informal balance for creative effect.

Source: Kenzo/Facebook.com

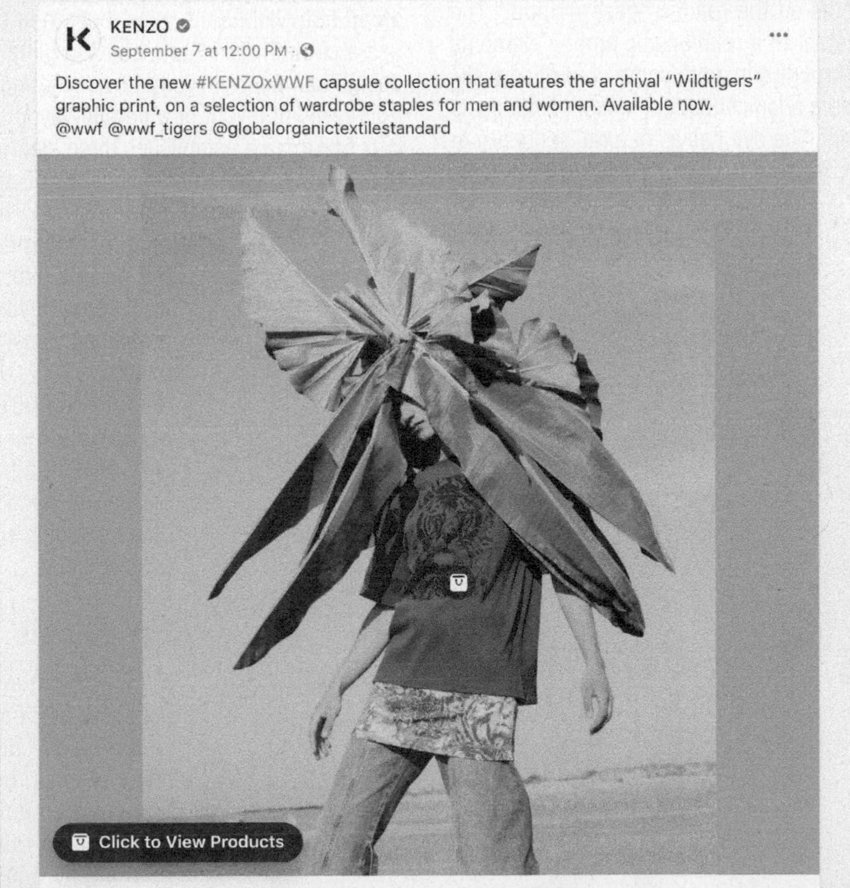

Exhibit 11.14 ▸ This ad for Kenzo, a fashion brand, shows how an image or ad can use creativity in balance and symmetry while still keeping a reference to the brand.

Proportion

Proportion has to do with the size and tonal relationships among different elements in an advertisement. Whenever two elements are placed in proximity, proportion results. Proportional considerations include the relationship of the width of an ad to its depth, the width of each element to the depth of each element, the size of one element relative to the size of every other, the space between two elements and the relationship of that space to a third element, and the amount of light area as opposed to the amount of dark area. Ideally, factors of proportion vary so as to avoid monotony in an ad. Further, the designer should pursue pleasing proportions, which means the viewer will not detect mathematical relationships among elements. In general, unequal dimensions and distances make for some of the liveliest designs in advertising. See Exhibit 11.15 for an example of proportion; Parmalat milk features a huge dog and a tiny product placement. The contrast of big and small is compelling and can even call attention to the tiny product in the corner.

Order

Order in an advertisement is also referred to as a sequence or, in terms of its effects on the reader, "gaze motion." The designer's goal is to establish a relationship among elements that leads the reader through the ad in some controlled fashion. A designer can create a logical path of visual components to control eye movement. The eye has a "natural" tendency to move from left to right, from up to down, from large elements to small ones, from light to dark, and from color to noncolor. Order also includes inducing the reader to jump from one space in the ad to another, creating a sense of movement. The essential contribution of this design component is to establish a visual format that results in a focus or several focuses.

Unity

Ensuring that the elements of an advertisement are tied together and appear to be related is the purpose of **unity.** Considered the most important of the design principles, unity results in harmony among the diverse components of an advertisement: headline, subhead, body copy, and illustration. Several design techniques contribute to unity. The border surrounding an ad keeps the ad elements from spilling over into other ads or into the printed matter next to the ad.

Another construct of unity is the axis. In every advertisement, an axis will naturally emerge. The **axis** is a line, real or imagined, that runs through an ad and from which the elements in the advertisement flare out. A single ad may have one, two, or even three axes running vertically and horizontally. An axis can be created by blocks of copy, by the placement of illustrations, or by the items within an illustration, such as the position and direction of a model's arm or leg. Elements in an ad may violate the axes, but when two or more elements use a common axis as a starting point, unity is enhanced. A design can be more forceful in creating unity by using either a three-point layout or a parallel layout. A **three-point layout structure** establishes three elements in the ad as dominant forces. The uneven number of prominent elements is critical for creating a gaze motion in the viewer. Notice the difference between the layout structure of the ad in Exhibit 11.16 (which has a three-point layout structure via three prominent visual layouts) and the ad in Exhibit 11.17, which has a parallel layout structure. **Parallel layout structure** has art on the right-hand side of the page and repeats the art on the left-hand side. This is an obvious and highly structured technique to achieve unity.

Emphasis

At some point in the decision-making process, someone needs to decide which major component—the headline, subhead, body copy, or illustration—will be emphasized. The key to good design relative to emphasis is that one item is the primary focus in an ad. If one element is emphasized to the exclusion of the others, then a poor design has emerged, and ultimately a poor communication will result.

Parmalat
Fortified Milk.
It gives you
more energy.

Source: Parmalat

Exhibit 11.15 ▶ This ad for Parmalat milk shows that proportion can result in an inspired display of the oversized versus the undersized.

Source: Hidesign

FOR ONCE,
SKIN THAT'LL
ACTUALLY LOOK BETTER
WITH AGE.

MAKES YOU HATE IT,
DOESN'T IT.

Exhibit 11.16 ▶ In this example, there is a three-point layout structure; note the three prominent visual elements in the ad. What are they?

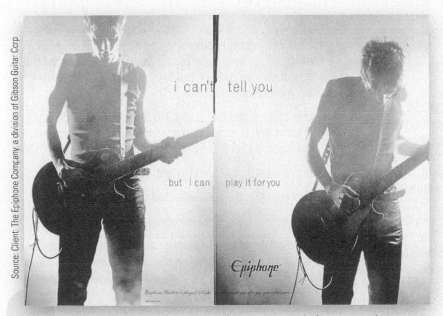

Source: Client: The Epiphone Company a division of Gibson Guitar Corp

i can't tell you

but i can   play it for you

Epiphone

Exhibit 11.17 ▶ This example shows an ad that employs a parallel layout structure.

Balance, proportion, order, unity, and emphasis are the basic principles of design. As you can see, the designer's objectives extend beyond the strategic and message-development elements associated with an ad. Design principles relate to the aesthetic impression an ad produces. Once a designer has been informed of the components that will make up the headline, subhead, body copy, and illustration, it's the designer's job to arrange those components according to the principles of creative design.

Layout

In contrast to design, which emphasizes the structural concept behind a print ad, layout is the mechanical aspect of design—the physical manifestation of design concepts. A **layout** is a drawing or digital rendering of a proposed print advertisement (digital interactive ads are digitized from the start, of course) showing where all the elements in the ad are positioned. An art director uses a layout to work through various alternatives for visual presentation and sequentially develop the print ad to its final stages. It is part and parcel of the design process and inextricably linked to the development of an effective design.

An art director typically proceeds through various stages in the construction of a final design for an ad. The following are the different stages of layout development, in order of detail and completeness, which an art director typically uses.

Thumbnails

Thumbnails are the first drafts of an advertising layout. The art director will produce several thumbnail sketches to work out the general presentation of the ad. Although the creative team refines the creative concept, thumbnails represent the placement of elements—headline, images, body copy, and tagline. Headlines are often represented with zigzag lines and body copy with straight, parallel lines. Typically, thumbnails are drawn at one-quarter the size of the finished ad.

Rough Layout

The next step in the layout process is the **rough layout.** Unlike a thumbnail sketch, a rough layout is done in the actual size of the proposed ad and is usually developed using a program such as InDesign. This allows the art director to experiment with different headline fonts and easily manipulate the placement and size of images to be used in the ad.

Comprehensive

The comprehensive layout, or **comp,** is a polished draft of the ad—but it is not the final version. Most frequently, comps are computer-generated and are a representation of what the final ad will look like. At this stage, the final headline font is determined, the images that will be incorporated—photographs or illustrations—are digitized and placed in the ad, and the actual body copy is often included. Comps are generally printed in full color if the final ad is to be in color. Comps produced in this way make it very easy for the client to imagine (and approve) what the ad will look like when it is published. The client will make one last approval of the digital file before it is finalized. Changes that a client requests, prior to the ad being sent to the printer, are still easily and quickly made. The stages of layout development discussed here provide the artistic blueprint for a print advertisement.

We now turn our attention to the matter of typography in print production.

Typography in Print Production

The issues associated with typography have to do with the typeface chosen for headlines, subheads, and body copy, as well as the various size components of the type (height, width, and running length). Designers think critically about typography because those decisions affect both the readability and the mood of the overall visual impression. For our purposes, some knowledge of the basic considerations of typography is useful when developing an appreciation of the choices that must be made.[24]

Categories of Type

Typefaces have distinct personalities, and each can communicate a different mood and image. A **type font** is a basic set of typeface letters. For those of us who create documents in Word or Google Docs, the choice of type font is generally a quick and easy one. In choosing type for an advertisement, however, the consequences are far reaching, and the art director has thousands of choices based on typeface alone.

There are six basic typeface groups: blackletter, roman, script, serif, sans serif, and miscellaneous. The families are divided by characteristics that reflect the personality and tone of the font. **Blackletter,** also called *gothic,* is characterized by the ornate design of the letters. This style is patterned after hand-drawn letters in monasteries where illuminated manuscripts were created. You can see blackletter fonts used today in very formal documents, such as college diplomas. **Roman** is the most common group of fonts used for body copy because of its legibility. This family is characterized by the use of thick and thin strokes in the creation of the letterforms. Script is easy to distinguish by the linkage of the letters in the way that cursive handwriting is connected. Script is often found on wedding invitations and documents that are intended to look elegant or of high quality. **Serif** refers to the strokes or "feet" at the ends of the letterforms. Notice the serifs that are present in these letters you read now. Their presence helps move your eye across the page, allowing you to read for a long time without losing your place or tiring your eyes. **Sans serif** fonts, as the name suggests, do not have serifs; hence the use

of the French word *sans,* meaning "without." Sans serif fonts are typically used for headlines and not for body copy. Miscellaneous types are typefaces that do not fit easily into the other categories. Novelty display, garage, and deconstructed fonts all fall into this group. These fonts were designed specifically to draw attention to them and not necessarily for their legibility. The following example displays serif and sans serif type:

This line is set in serif type.

This line is set in sans serif type.

Type Measurement

There are two elements of type size. **Point** refers to the size of type in height, traditionally running from 6 to 120 points. But in today's electronic environment, point could range anywhere between 2 and 720 points. **Picas** measure the width of lines. A pica is 12 points wide, and each pica measures about one-sixth of an inch. Layout software makes it very easy for the art director to fit copy into a designated space by reducing or enlarging a font with a few keystrokes.

Readability

Readability is critical. Type should facilitate the communication process. The following are some traditional recommendations when deciding what type to use (however, remember that these are only guidelines and should not necessarily be followed in every instance):

- Use capitals and lowercase, NOT ALL CAPITALS. (It makes it seem one is screaming according to some consumer's perceptions.)

- Arrange letters from left to right, not up and down.

- Run lines of type horizontally, not vertically.

- Use even spacing between letters and words.

Different typefaces and styles also affect the mood conveyed by an ad. Depending on the choices made, typefaces can connote grace, power, beauty, modernity, simplicity, or any number of other qualities.

11-7b Art Direction and Production in Digital/Interactive/Mobile Media

We've referenced art direction and production in digital/interactive media in the previous sections. In general, ads produced for television or radio can certainly be made available online. In that case, the considerations for radio and television production hold. But when an ad is prepared primarily with the characteristics of headline, body copy, and illustration—like an email, banner, pop-up, website, or app—digital/interactive ads are closer to print than to anything else. Even though the basic principles of art direction (design and concept) apply, digital, interactive, and mobile media are fundamentally different in the way the audience approaches them, navigates them, and responds to them. This difference presents one of the real challenges of electronic advertising.

In most respects, cyber production does not differ significantly from print production, but it does differ from print in how the various aspects of production are combined with programming languages, such as HTML, and with each other. Advances in streaming audio and digital video make art direction a dynamic and fast-moving target. All media have to find their own way, their own voice. This is not just an aesthetic matter. It's figuring out what works, which is related to design. How the information is laid out matters. In the early years of television advertising, the ads went on forever and seemed to be written for radio. In fact, many of the early TV writers were radio writers. Similarly, online and mobile ads can't simply be translated to print. They should invite interaction and be adaptable to different size screens, as well as make the best use of visuals, sound, motion, and even augmented or virtual reality.[25] And, crucially, mobile ads should load quickly to avoid being skipped by impatient viewers, a challenge because of the increasingly sophisticated and complex ads being produced today.[26]

As noted in Chapter 3, some brands have engaged the public and energized the creative process by inviting *consumer-generated content (CGC):* people making their own ads for their favorite brands. YouTube and other venues have allowed consumers to say "Hey it's my brand too…I get it more than you do…here's my ad." For a decade, Doritos aired consumer-generated commercials during Super Bowl games, adding an air of excitement with contests and online voting, and garnering extra publicity at the same time.[27] The retailer Target has employed a variation of CGC by inviting children to submit storyboards, create backdrops, direct, and act in some back-to-school ads. The project was supervised by Adolescent, an ad agency specializing in content by and for children, teens, and twenty-something adults. A short online video provided background about this creative initiative (note the brand logo in Exhibit 11.18).[28]

Exhibit 11.18 ▶ Target's back-to-school campaign is an example of user-generated content that was created and directed by kids.

11-7c Art Direction and Production in Television Advertising

In many ways, television was simply made for advertising. It is everywhere, serving as a background to daily life. But as a background, it tends to be ignored or only partially paid attention to. If you consider the 10 message strategies detailed in Chapter 10, use of the TV medium would dictate very different strategies. In some cases, you need high attention levels, which are difficult to get; in other strategies, you might actually prefer lower levels of attention and the counterarguing that comes with it. Sometimes, it's just about leaving impressions or setting moods or getting you to notice; sometimes it tells stories. But in all of these cases, the visual is important—whether it's the main feature or it plays a key supportive role.

The Creative Team in Television Advertising

Due to its complexity, television production involves a lot of people. These people have different but often overlapping expertise, responsibility, and authority. This requires expert organizational skills. At some point, individuals who actually shoot the film or the tape are brought in to execute the copywriter's and art director's concepts. Usually they are in contact with a media planner and/or account planner, making sure that what is being done for TV is consistent with, compatible with, or can do double duty with other media choices. The account planner is there to make sure that the consumer's values and interests continue to be represented.

At this point, the creative process becomes intensely collaborative: The film director applies their craft and is responsible for the actual production. The creative team (i.e., the art director, copywriter, media director, and account planner) rarely relinquishes control of the project, even though the film director may prefer that. Getting the various players to perform their particular specialties at just the right time, while avoiding conflict with other team members, is an ongoing challenge in TV ad production. Someone has to be in charge on the set, and that is usually the chief creative on site.[29]

Creative Guidelines for Television Advertising

Just as with print advertising, there are general creative principles for television advertising.[30] These principles are not foolproof or definitive, but they certainly represent best practices and offer organizational structure. Again, truly great creative work has at one time or another violated some or all of these conventions, but the decision to venture off guidelines was no doubt guided by the creative brief—so all is well.

■ *Use an attention-getting and relevant opening.* The first few seconds of a television commercial are crucial, because receivers can make split-second assessments of the message's relevance and interest.[31] The opening can either turn a receiver off or grab attention for the balance of the commercial. It is incredibly easy to avoid commercials, so advertisers must have a good hook to suck viewers in and maintain their attention. Ads just don't get much time to develop. There is the belief that "slower" ads (ads that take time to develop) don't wear out as quickly as the hit-and-run ads.[32] So, if you have a lot of money in the budget, an ad that "builds" might be best. If you don't, go for the quick hook.

■ *Emphasize the visual.* The video capabilities of television should be highlighted in every production effort. To some degree, this emphasis is dependent upon the creative concept, but the visual should carry the selling message even if the audio portion is ignored by the receiver. Visuals are often quite vivid to capture audience attention.[33]

■ *Coordinate the audio with the visual.* The images and copy of a television commercial must reinforce each other. Divergence between the audio and visual portions of an ad only serves to confuse and distract the viewer.

■ *Persuade as well as entertain.* It is tempting to produce a beautifully creative television advertisement rather than a beautifully effective television advertisement. Creating an entertaining commercial is an inherently praiseworthy goal except when the entertainment value of the commercial completely overwhelms its persuasive impact.

■ *Show the brand.* Unless a commercial is using intrigue and mystery to surround the brand, the brand should be highlighted in the ad. Close-ups and shots of the brand in action help receivers recall the brand and its appearance. The client often greatly appreciates this.

LO 8

11-8 The Production Process in Television Advertising

The television production process can best be understood by identifying the activities that take place before, during, and after the actual production of an ad. These stages are referred to as preproduction, production, and postproduction, respectively. By breaking the process down into this sequence, we can appreciate both the technical and the strategic aspects of each stage.

11-8a Preproduction

The **preproduction** stage is that part of the television production process in which the advertiser and the advertising agency carefully work out the precise details of how the creative planning behind an ad can best be brought to life with the opportunities offered by television. Exhibit 11.19 shows the sequence of six events in the preproduction stage.

Storyboard and Script Approval

The preproduction stage begins with storyboard and script approval. A storyboard is a shot-by-shot sketch depicting, in sequence, the visual scenes and copy that will be used in an advertisement. A **script** is the written version of an ad; it specifies the coordination of the copy elements with the accompanying video scenes. The script is used by the producer and director to set the location and content of scenes, by the casting department to choose actors and actresses, and by the producer in budgeting and scheduling the shoot. Exhibit 11.20 is a classic storyboard from the Miller Lite "Can Your Beer Do This?" campaign. This particular spot was entitled "Ski Jump" and involved rigging a dummy to a recliner and launching the chair and the dummy from a 60-meter ski jump. The storyboard gives the creative team and the client an overall idea of the look and feel of the ad. While these were once drawn by hand, storyboards are now developed digitally with software and apps.

The art director and copywriter are significantly involved at this stage of production. It is important that the producer discusses the storyboard and script with the creative team and fully understands the creative concept and objectives for the advertisement before production begins. Because it is the producer's responsibility to solicit bids for the project from production houses, the producer must be able to fully explain to bidders the requirements of the job so that cost estimates are as accurate as possible.

Budget Approval

Once there is agreement on the scope and intent of the production as depicted in the storyboard and script, the advertiser must give budget approval. The producer needs to work carefully with the creative team and the advertiser to estimate the approximate cost of the shoot, including production staging, location costs, actors, technical requirements, staffing, and a multitude of other considerations. It is essential that these discussions be as detailed and comprehensive as possible, because it is from this budget discussion that the producer will evaluate candidates for the directing role and will solicit bids from production houses to handle the job.

Assessment of Directors, Editorial Houses, and Music Suppliers

A producer has dozens (if not hundreds) of directors, postproduction editorial houses, and music suppliers from which to

Exhibit 11.19 ▶ This figure shows the sequence of six events in the preproduction stage of television advertising, which may be, but are not always, linear stages.

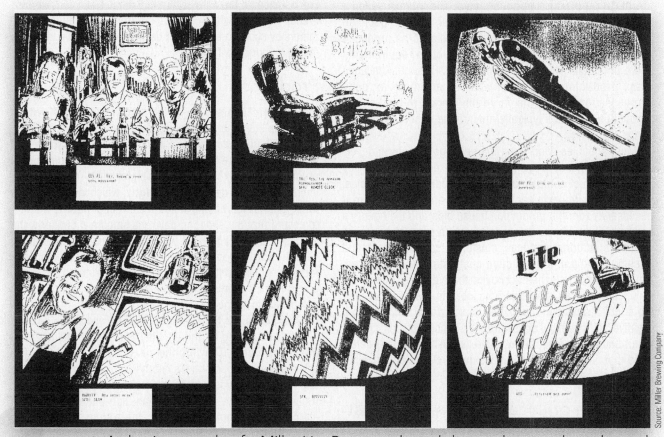

Source: Miller Brewing Company

Exhibit 11.20 ▶ A classic example of a Miller Lite Beer storyboard shows what storyboards used to look like before they became more digitized with modern software and storyboard apps.

choose. An assessment of those well suited to the task takes place early in the preproduction process. The combination of the creative talents of ad agencies and production houses can produce creative, eye-catching ads. Directors of television commercials, like directors of feature films, develop specializations and reputations. Some directors are known for their work with action or special effects. Others are more highly skilled in working with children, animals, outdoor settings, or food.

The director of an advertisement is responsible for interpreting the storyboard and script and managing the talent to bring the creative concept to life. A director specifies the precise nature of a scene, how it is lit, and how it is filmed. Choosing the proper director is crucial to the execution of a commercial. Aside from the fact that a good director commands a hefty fee,

the director can have a tremendous effect on the quality and impact of the presentation. An excellent creative concept can be undermined by poor direction. Among the now-famous feature film directors who have made television commercials and branded short films for online audiences are Ridley Scott (Apple), Martin Scorsese (Dolce and Gabbana), Spike Jonze (IKEA), Spike Lee (Nike), Sergio Leone (Renault 18 Diesel), as well as Wes Anderson and Roman Coppola (Prada Candy L'Eau).[34]

Similarly, editorial houses and music suppliers (and musicians) have particular expertise and reputations. The producer, the director, and the agency creative team actively review the work of suppliers that are particularly well suited to the production. In some cases, geographic proximity to the agency facilities is important, as members of the agency team try to maintain a tight schedule.

Review of Bids from Production Houses and Other Suppliers

Production houses and other suppliers, such as lighting specialists, represent a collection of specialized talent and also provide needed equipment for ad preparation. The expertise in production houses relates to the technical aspects of filming a commercial. Producers, production managers, sound and stage specialists, camera operators, and others are part of a production house team. The agency sends a bid package to several production houses. The package contains all the details of the commercial to be produced and includes a description of the production requirements and a timetable. An accurate timetable is essential because many production personnel work on an hourly or daily compensation rate. Costs vary from market to market, but production expenses typically run into the hundreds of thousands of dollars.

Most agencies send out a bid package on a form developed by the agency. By using a standardized form, an agency can make direct comparisons among production house bids. The producer reviews each of the bids and revises them if necessary. From the production house bids *and* the agency's estimate of its own costs associated with production (travel, expenses, editorial services, music, on-camera talent, and agency markups), a production cost estimate is prepared. Once the advertiser has approved the estimate, one of the production houses is awarded the job. The lowest production bid is not always the one chosen. Aside from cost, there are creative and technical considerations. A popular director may command higher fees, for example, or the agency may determine that one production house is more reliable than another bidding for the job.

Selection of Location, Sets, and Cast

Once a bid has been approved and accepted, both the production house and the agency production team begin to search for appropriate, affordable locations if the commercial is to be shot outside a studio setting.

A delicate stage in preproduction is casting. Although not every ad uses actors and actresses, when an ad calls for individuals to perform roles, casting is crucial. Every individual appearing in an ad is, in a very real sense, a representative of the advertiser and the brand (e.g., actress Jennifer Aniston represents Smartwater). This is another reason why the agency creative team stays involved. Actors and actresses help set the mood and tone for an ad and affect the image of the brand. The successful execution of various message strategies depends on proper casting. For instance, a slice-of-life message requires actors and actresses with whom the target audience can readily identify. Testimonial message tactics require a search for particular types of people, either celebrities or representatives of the target audience, who will attract attention and be credible. The point to remember is that successfully casting a television commercial depends on much more than simply picking people who are good actors. Individuals must be matched to the brand, the nature of the audience, and the scene depicted in the ad. For video-based ads, we are often seeing consumers featured or cast in the ad showing how they use the product, along with some copy or quotes of what they think about the product advertised. For instance, in the ad by Chirp in Exhibit 11.21 (an exercise brand), notice how the copywriting attempts to engage customers by showing a customer using their product and asking "What is your chirp face?"

Production

The **production stage** of the process, or the **shoot,** is where the storyboard and script come to life and are filmed. The actual production of the spot may also include some final preparations before the shoot begins. The most common final preparation activities are lighting checks and rehearsals. An entire day may be devoted to **prelight**, which involves setting up lighting or identifying times for the best natural lighting to ensure that the shooting day runs smoothly. Similarly, the director may want to work with the on-camera talent along with the camera operators to practice the positioning and movement planned for the ad. This work, known as **blocking**, can save a lot of time on a shoot day, when many more costly personnel are on the set.

Shoot days are the culmination of an enormous amount of effort beginning all the way back at the development of the creative brief. They are the culmination of the advertiser's and agency personnel's extensive planning efforts. The set on a shoot day is a world all its own. For the uninformed, it can appear to be little more than high-energy chaos or a lot of nothing going on between camera setups. For the professionals involved, however, a shoot has its own tempo and direction.

A successful shoot depends on the effective management of a large number of diverse individuals—creative performers, highly trained technicians, and skilled laborers. Logistical and technical problems always arise, not to mention the ever-present threat of a random event (a thunderstorm or intrusive noise) that disrupts filming and tries everyone's patience. There is a degree of tension and spontaneity on the set that is a necessary part of the creative process but that must be kept at a manageable level. Much of the tension that can arise stems from trying to execute the various tasks of production correctly and at the proper time.

Another contributing factor to this tension has to do with expense. As pointed out earlier, most directors, technicians, and talent are paid a daily rate plus overtime after 10 hours. Daily shooting expenses, including director's fees, can run into

Chirp
June 22 · 🌐

You know that moment when you've just pushed up onto your 10" wheel, arms at your side and your head tilts back in relaxation? Well, take a moment and think about what your face is doing . . . Because your #ChirpFace says a lot about you.

This is Marlie's
#ChirpFace

Exhibit 11.21 ▶ Copywriting for brands on social media often features user reviews or regular customers using the product to show its effectiveness. In this example, the customers rave about this exercise product and how it has helped them obtain their fitness goals.

six figures; so the agency and the advertiser, understandably, want the shoot to run as smoothly and quickly as possible.

There is the real problem of not rushing creativity, however, and advertisers often have to learn to accept the pace of production. For example, a well-known director made a Honda commercial in South Florida, where he shot film for only one hour per day—a half-hour in the morning and a half-hour at twilight. His explanation? "From experience you learn that cars look flat and unattractive in direct light, so you have to catch the shot when the angle [of the sun] is just right."[35] Despite the fact that the cameras were rolling only an hour a day, the $9,000-per-hour cost for the production crew was charged all day for each day of shooting. Advertisers have to accept, on occasion, that the television advertising production process is not like an assembly-line production process.

Summary

1. **Identify the main members of a creative team and how the creative brief guides their efforts.**

Effective creative execution depends on the input of the creative team; traditionally this consists of an art director, copywriter, account planner, and media planner. The creative team will have access to a wide variety of inputs, including the client's, and information sources, such as market research. A creative brief is used as a device to assist the creative team overall and the copywriter in particular in dealing with this challenge. Key elements in the creative brief include brand features and benefits that must be communicated to the audience, the mood or tone appropriate for the audience, and the intended media for the ad.

2. **Detail the elements of copywriting for print media, including the headline, subhead, and body copy.**

The three unique components of print copy are the headline, subhead, and body copy. Headlines should motivate additional processing of the ad. Good headlines communicate information about the brand or make a promise about the benefits the consumer can expect from the brand. If the brand name is not featured in the headline, then that headline must entice the reader to examine the body copy or visual material. Subheads can also be valuable in helping lead the reader to and through the body copy. A subhead appears above or below the main headline and carries additional information beyond the headline. In the body copy, the brand's complete story can be told. Effective body copy must be crafted carefully to engage the reader, furnish supportive evidence for claims made about the brand, and avoid clichés and exaggeration that the consumer will dismiss as hype.

3. **Detail the elements of copywriting for television and video.**

Several formats can be considered in preparing television ad copy. These are demonstration, problem and solution, music and song, spokesperson, dialogue, vignette, and narrative. For television, coordinate the copy with the visual presentation and seek a synergistic effect between audio and video. Don't let the brand name or selling points get lost, and develop copy consistent with the heritage and image of the brand. Finally, try to create copy that can be adapted to various time lengths and modified to sustain audience interest over the life of a campaign.

4. **Detail the elements of copywriting for radio and podcast advertising.**

Four basic formats used to create radio copy and for podcast advertising are: music format, dialogue format, announcement format, and celebrity announcer format. In general, audio advertising employs simple sentence construction and language familiar to the intended audience. When using music, humor, or imaginative language to attract and hold the listener's attention, the copywriter should not short-change the brand name or key selling points for the sake of entertainment.

5. **Describe the copywriting approaches for digital, interactive, and mobile ads.**

Digital/interactive ads are hybrids between print and broadcasting advertisements. The receiver encounters a message in a print format either at a website, in an email, at a blog, or from social media and mobile communication. But the message is delivered electronically, similar to television or radio. Common approaches to copywriting include long-copy landing page, short-copy landing page, long-copy email, teaser email copy, pop-up/pop-under ad copy, and social media copy. Copywriting in each of these digital/interactive formats may or may not employ the elements of headline and subhead or even body copy (in the case of pop-ups and pop-unders). In digital settings, ads may be direct response oriented as they may link with e-commerce or driving other online consumer behaviors. But there are copy elements in each case that communicate brand information.

6. **Identify the role of slogans/taglines in copywriting.**

A slogan/tagline is a short phrase that helps establish an image, identity, or position for a brand or organization. It is generally used by advertisers, especially the creative team including the copywriter, to enhance or increase memorability of the main benefit of the brand/branded product or service. Slogans/taglines are often used as a headline or subhead in print ads, and also for digital ads. Regardless of media type (print, TV, radio, digital), slogans have an important role in reinforcing a brand's image, personality, identification, and continuity.

7. **Identify the components of art direction that are essential in creative execution of print ads.**

In print ad design, all the verbal and visual components of an ad are arranged for maximum impact and appeal. Several principles can be followed as a basis for a compelling design. These principles feature issues such as balance, proportion, order, unity, and emphasis. The first component of an effective design is focus—drawing the reader's attention to specific areas of the ad. The second component is movement and direction—directing the reader's eye movement through the ad. The third component is clarity and simplicity—avoiding a complex and chaotic look.

The layout is the physical manifestation of all design planning for print ads. An art director uses various forms of layouts to bring a print ad to life. There are several stages in the evolution of a layout. The art director starts with a hand-drawn thumbnail, proceeds to the digitized rough layout, and continues with a tight comprehensive layout that represents the look of the final ad. With each stage, the layout becomes more concrete and more like the final form of the advertisement. In the last stage, the digitized ad is sent out for placement in print media.

8. Describe the production process in creating a television commercial.

The intricate process of TV ad production can be divided into three major stages: preproduction, production, and postproduction. In the preproduction stage, scripts and storyboards are prepared, budgets are set, production houses are engaged, and a timetable is formulated. Production includes all those activities involved in the actual filming of the ad. The shoot is a high-stress activity that usually carries a high price tag. The raw materials from the shoot are mixed and refined in the postproduction stage. Today's editors use digital tools almost exclusively to create the final product—a finished television ad.

Key Terms

axis	informal balance	roman
balance	layout	rough layout
blackletter	long-copy email	sans serif
blocking	long-copy landing page	script
brand manager	media planner	serif
comp	narrative	short-copy landing page
copywriting	order	slogan/tagline
creative brief	parallel layout structure	social media copy
creative team	pica	storyboard
design	point	straight-line copy
dialogue	pop-up/pop-under ad	subhead
direct response copy	pop-up/pop-under copy	teaser email
ephemeral	prelight	three-point layout structure
formal balance	preproduction	thumbnails
hashtag	principles of design	type font
headline	production stage/shoot	unity
illustration	proportion	

Endnotes

1. Paul Edwin Ketelaar, Jonathan van't Riet, Helge Thorbjornsen, and Moniek Buijzen, "Positive Uncertainty: The Benefit of the Doubt in Advertising," *International Journal of Advertising* (2016), 1–14.
2. Mario Pricken, *Creative Advertising* (London: Thames & Hudson, Ltd., 2008), 8.
3. Tom Altsteil and Jean Grow, *Advertising Creative: Strategy, Copy and Design,* 2nd ed. (Los Angeles: Sage Publications, 2010), 53.
4. The last two points in this list were adapted from the classic perspectives of A. Jerome Jewler, *Creative Strategy in Advertising,* 3rd ed. (Belmont, CA: Wadsworth, 1989), 196.
5. Cited in Luke Sullivan, *Hey Whipple, Squeeze This: A Guide to Creating Great Ads* (Hoboken, NJ: John Wiley and Sons, 2012), 103.
6. Ivan A. Guitart and Stefan Stremersch, "The Impact of Informational and Emotional Television Ad Content on Online Search and Sales," *Journal of Marketing Research* 58, no. 2 (2020), 299–320.
7. Norris I. Bruce et al., "Communicating Brands in Television Advertising," *Journal of Marketing Research* 57, no. 2 (2020), 236–256.
8. Patrick Barwise et al., "Why Do People Watch So Much Television and Video?" *Journal of Advertising Research* 60, no. 2 (2019), 121–134; and Tim Nudd, "Amazon Made More Than a Hundred 10-Second Ads Asking Alexa the Funniest Things," *Adweek,* October 5, 2016, http://www.adweek.com/creativity/amazon-made-more -hundred-10-second-ads-asking-echo-funniest-things-173901/.
9. The last three points in this list were adapted from Kennett Roman and Jane Maas, *The New How to Advertise,* 6. Michael Learmonth, "Lowered Expectations: Web Redefines 'Quality,'" *Advertising Age,* February 22, 2010, 8.
10. I-Hsien Sherwood, "Want to Reach Those Unreachable Ad-Blockers? Try Podcast Ads," *Campaign (US),* March 15, 2017,

http://www.campaignlive.com/article/want-reach-unreachable-ad-blockers-try-podcast-ads/1427408 and "Podcast Industry Report: Market Growth and Advertising Statistics in 2021," *Insider Intelligence,* July 29, 2021, https://www.insiderintelligence.com/insights/the-podcast-industry-report-statistics/.

11. Tom Alsteil and Jean Grow, *Advertising Creative: Strategy, Copy and Design,* 2nd ed. (Los Angeles: Sage Publications, 2010), 218–219.

12. Michael Learmonth, "Lowered Expectations: Web Redefines 'Quality'" *Advertising Age,* February 22, 2010, 8.

13. Quoted in Christy Ashley and Jason D. Oliver, "Creative Leaders: Thirty Years of Big Ideas," *Journal of Advertising,* no. 1 (Spring 2010), 126.

14. Content in this section is drawn from Robert W. Bly, *The Copywriter's Handbook,* 3rd ed. (New York: Henry Holt and Company, 2006), 263–264.

15. John R. Rossiter, "Defining the Necessary Components of Creative, Effective Ads," *Journal of Advertising* 37, no. 4 (Winter 2008), 141.

16. Leah Prinzivalli, "Sephora's Pride 2019 Campaign Was Made By and For the LGBTQ+ Community," *Allure,* June 4, 2019, https://www.allure.com/story/sephora-pride-2019-identify-as-we-campaign.

17. Luke Sullivan, *Hey Whipple, Squeeze This: A Guide to Creating Great Ads,* 182.

18. Jean Halliday, "How GM Stifled 'Passion and Creativity' in Its Marketing Ranks," *Advertising Age,* June 12, 2009, 13.

19. David Ogilvy, *On Advertising* (New York: Vintage Books, 1985).

20. Tatiana M. Fajardo, Jiao Zhang, and Michael Tsiros, "The Contingent Nature of the Symbolic Associations of Visual Design Elements: The Case of Brand Logo Frames," *Journal of Consumer Research* 43, no. 4 (December 2016).

21. Tony Antin, *Great Print Advertising* (New York: Wiley, 1993), 38.

22. This discussion is based on Roy Paul Nelson, *The Design of Advertising,* 7th ed. (Boston: McGraw-Hill, 1996), 136.

23. Ibid., 149.

24. Ryan S. Paquin et al., "Superimposed Text Size and Contrast Effects in DTC TV Advertising," *Journal of Advertising Research* 61, no. 2 (2020), 178–191.

25. For more about virtual and augmented reality advertising, see Katie Richards, "Why More Brands Aren't Making Quality Virtual Reality and Augmented Reality Experiences," *Adweek,* January 6, 2017, http://www.adweek.com/digital/why-more-brands-arent-making-quality-virtual-reality-and-augmented-reality-experiences-175392/.

26. Mike Shields, "MRC Says Mobile Ads Take Too Long to Load," *Wall Street Journal,* June 29, 2016, https://www.wsj.com/articles/mrc-says-mobile-ads-take-too-long-to-load-1467214153.

27. Dale Buss, "Super Bowl Watch: Prepare for a Different Ad Mix in Next Big Game," *Brand Channel,* December 16, 2016, http://www.brandchannel.com/2016/12/16/super-bowl-watch-ad-mix-121616/.

28. Roo Ciambriello, "From Writers to Directors to Musicians, Kids Made Target's Back-to-School Ads," *Adweek,* July 25, 2016, http://www.adweek.com/creativity/writers-directors-musicians-kids-made-targets-back-school-ads-172628/.

29. Reto Hofstetter et al., "Constraining Ideas: How Seeing Ideas of Others Harms Creativity in Open Innovation," *Journal of Marketing Research* 58, no. 1 (2020), 95–114.

30. Tom Altsteil and Jean Grow, *Advertising Creative: Strategy, Copy and Design,* 2nd ed. (Los Angeles: Sage Publications, 2010), 228–229.

31. Millie Elsen, Rik Pieters, and Michel Wedel, "Thin Slice Impressions: How Advertising Evaluation Depends on Exposure Duration," *Journal of Marketing Research* 53, no. 4 (August 2016), 563–579.

32. For more about ad wear-in and wear-out, see Jiemiao Chen, Xiaojing Yang, and Robert E. Smith. "The Effects of Creativity on Advertising Wear-in and Wear-out," *Journal of the Academy of Marketing Science* 44, no. 3 (2016), 334–349.

33. See, for example, Marc G. Weinberger et al., "Understanding Responses to Comedic Advertising Aggression: The Role of Vividness and Gender Identity," *International Journal of Advertising* (2016), 1–26.

34. Bronwyn Cosgrave, "A Fragrance Debut? First, It's Lights, Camera, Action," *New York Times,* October 2, 2016, https://www.nytimes.com/2016/10/03/fashion/fragrance-film-kenzo-world.html?_r=0.

35. Jeffrey A. Trachtenberg, "Where the Money Goes," *Forbes,* September 21, 1987.

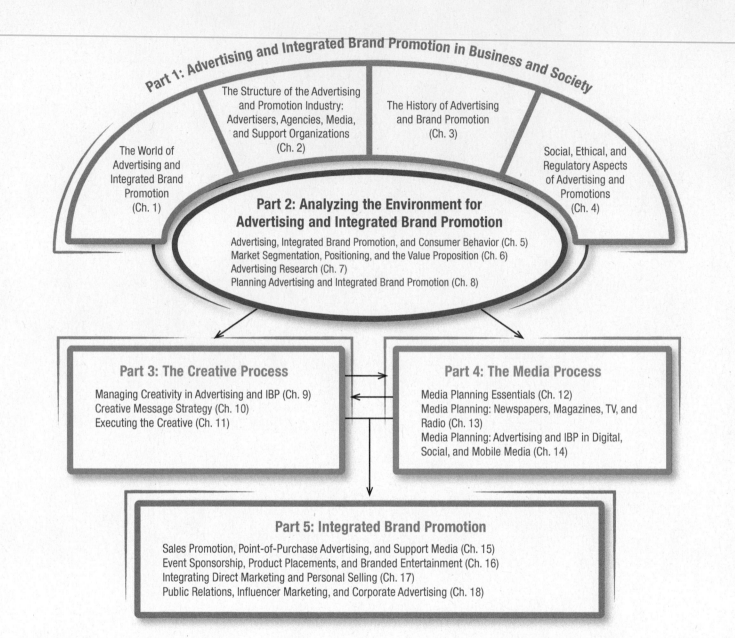

Part 1: Advertising and Integrated Brand Promotion in Business and Society

The World of Advertising and Integrated Brand Promotion (Ch. 1)

The Structure of the Advertising and Promotion Industry: Advertisers, Agencies, Media, and Support Organizations (Ch. 2)

The History of Advertising and Brand Promotion (Ch. 3)

Social, Ethical, and Regulatory Aspects of Advertising and Promotions (Ch. 4)

Part 2: Analyzing the Environment for Advertising and Integrated Brand Promotion

Advertising, Integrated Brand Promotion, and Consumer Behavior (Ch. 5)
Market Segmentation, Positioning, and the Value Proposition (Ch. 6)
Advertising Research (Ch. 7)
Planning Advertising and Integrated Brand Promotion (Ch. 8)

Part 3: The Creative Process

Managing Creativity in Advertising and IBP (Ch. 9)
Creative Message Strategy (Ch. 10)
Executing the Creative (Ch. 11)

Part 4: The Media Process

Media Planning Essentials (Ch. 12)
Media Planning: Newspapers, Magazines, TV, and Radio (Ch. 13)
Media Planning: Advertising and IBP in Digital, Social, and Mobile Media (Ch. 14)

Part 5: Integrated Brand Promotion

Sales Promotion, Point-of-Purchase Advertising, and Support Media (Ch. 15)
Event Sponsorship, Product Placements, and Branded Entertainment (Ch. 16)
Integrating Direct Marketing and Personal Selling (Ch. 17)
Public Relations, Influencer Marketing, and Corporate Advertising (Ch. 18)

The chapters in Part 4 explore both the fundamentals and the modern trends influencing media decisions today. The media landscape has changed with the proliferation of technology; yet the fundamentals of media planning still apply, especially in the context of integrated brand promotion (Chapter 12). A great deal of creative effort—and money—is invested in traditional media such as newspapers, magazines, television, and radio (Chapter 13). Advertisers are also taking advantage of digital, social, and mobile media to develop and execute truly integrated advertising and IBP campaigns for maximum audience impact (Chapter 14).

The Media Process

12 Media Planning Essentials *256*

13 Media Planning: Newspapers, Magazines, TV, and Radio *276*

14 Media Planning: Advertising and IBP in Digital, Social, & Mobile Media *298*

After learning about the creative process for advertising and IBP in Part 3, we move to the media process in Part 4, where reaching the target audience and shaping consumer behavior are key concerns. The framework diagram shows how creative and media must work in tandem to achieve the synergy and integration needed by effective advertisers. This challenge has been made more complex by the widespread use of digital, social, and mobile media, which has added to consumer control and media fragmentation. In the modern media environment, the most effective way to communicate with audiences is by integrating the creative process and the media process for all brand promotion activities.

Chapter 12 | Media Planning Essentials

Learning Objectives

After reading and thinking about this chapter, you will be able to do the following:

1 Describe measured versus unmeasured media and estimate how much each represents of total advertising and IBP dollars.

2 Describe the basic ideas and essential terms used in media planning.

3 Understand the meaning of competitive media assessment and share of voice.

4 Discuss media efficiency.

5 Discuss what makes social media different.

6 Discuss the basics of branded entertainment.

7 Discuss the benefits and the realities of media planning models.

8 Discuss making the media buy and programmatic media buying.

The media process works in tandem with the creative process in the drive to communicate effectively with target audiences and to influence consumer behavior. As with the creative side, technology is changing both the actual media channels and the planning for media placement. The trend toward programming media buys with software and automated bidding for keyword-related advertising on search result pages is one very important example.[1] Even as media and advertising are evolving, consumers are more heavily involved with social and mobile media for self-expression and interaction, adding nuance and complication to the planning process.[2] However, the media process must be carefully coordinated with planning and budgeting for all integrated brand promotion efforts to achieve the desired results through synergy.[3]

In this chapter, we explain the essential ideas and concepts that form the foundation of the media process (see Exhibit 12.1). As you think about advertising and media, remember that for some advertisers, traditional media remain the most efficient and effective way to reach a target audience.[4] For instance, Darden Restaurants, which owns restaurant brands like Olive Garden, relies on television advertising as a big part of their media investments. Even though the company has added social media and other IBP activities, it has learned over the years that when it runs more television ads, Olive Garden's sales go up.[5]

This shows the bottom-line importance of effective media planning and buying, getting the right message in front of the right audience at the right time, whether in traditional or new media—or both. Spending on nontraditional media is rising steadily year after year as customers evolve their media habits and advertisers adjust their mix of media accordingly. Another factor is that many advertisers are moving away from the traditional way of paying agencies based on media billings, as noted in Chapter 2. A byproduct of changing the compensation model is that advertisers often free up more money to invest in additional media investments.[6]

256

Exhibit 12.1 ▶ This diagram depicts the framework for chapter 12 of this text—media planning essentials.

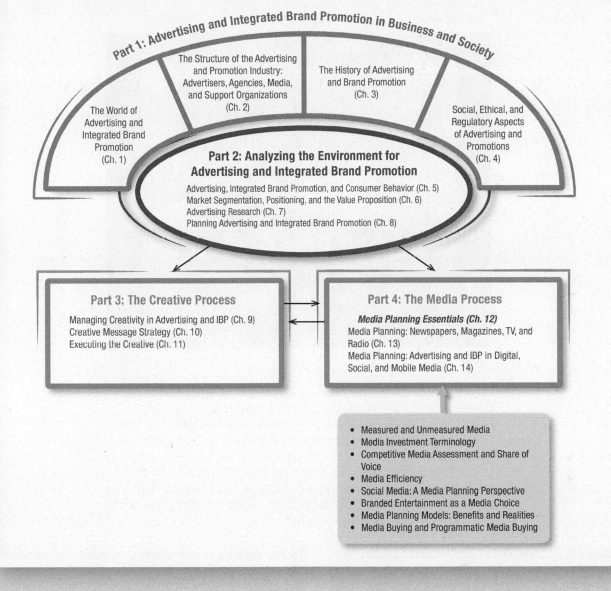

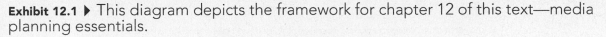

12-1 Measured and Unmeasured Media

Most advertisers of goods and services invest a considerable amount of money to compete at the national or international level. Management and stockholders demand accountability for these media investments to ensure that advertising and IBP expenditures are helping achieve the company's goals.[7]

While most well-known brands do heavy media investments, some big brands do relatively little mass advertising. Starbucks,

for example, avoided television advertising for more than 26 years, relying instead on public relations and other IBP activities. Even today, Starbucks spends less than $300 million yearly on advertising, less than the company rings up in global revenues during a typical week.[8] Chipotle's ad budget is only about $160 million annually, which includes some television advertising and a growing amount of digital, social, and mobile advertising.[9] In general, big businesses tend to have correspondingly big advertising budgets. McDonald's is a good example: it spends nearly $650 million every year on advertising as it reaches out to hungry consumers in competition with Taco Bell, Dunkin, Popeye's, and other casual restaurant chains.[10]

Another sector that allocates hundreds of millions in media investments and advertising is the pharmaceutical industry. A lot of this is with measured media, by way of social media

Abbott ✓
September 9 at 2:00 PM · 🌐

FreeStyle Libre 2 integrates glucose management so life doesn't take a backseat to levels:
https://abbo.tt/3CVHGjj

Important safety info: https://abbo.tt/3Cgi1kP

PADDLE BOARDING

Sensor is water-resistant in up to 1 meter (3 feet) of water and should not be immersed longer than 30 minutes.

👍❤️ 98   35 Comments 8 Shares

Source: Abbott Pharmaceuticals

Exhibit 12.2 ▶ Even the healthcare industry and specifically pharmaceutical products are now being successfully advertised on social media. Here is an example of a social media ad or sponsored post by Abbott to showcase its glucose management product (FreeStyle Libre 2), and how consumers who need to manage their glucose can enjoy their best life while wearing it. Notice how the ad features a young woman paddle boarding while wearing the small circular medical product on her arm.

marketing. For example, Abbott (a pharmaceutical company) advertises its products on a variety of media platforms, such as on television and through sponsored posts on social media. While we may think about social media ads being prominent in consumer package goods, fashion, or other low involvement goods, the healthcare industry and specifically pharmaceutical products are also investing in and measuring their social media marketing. In Exhibit 12.2, see an example of a social media ad (also referred to as a sponsored post) by the healthcare brand Abbott to showcase its glucose management product (FreeStyle Libre 2). The art direction in the ad shows a young woman paddle boarding while wearing the small circular medical product on her arm in order to show that she can continue an active lifestyle while monitoring her health. The target market is for consumers who need to manage their glucose for health reasons such as due to diabetes. Thus, a broad media investment such as network TV is not the best choice compared to social media, which is highly targeted.

A smart question is how should companies such as Abbott allocate potentially hundreds of millions of dollars for the most impactful and effective media investments? Thus, it is crucial to consider media investment allocations.

12-1a Media Investment Allocations

Think of a brand's media investment allocations, or how much a brand is going to invest or spend on media, as a big pie that is sliced into separate activities like mass media advertising, direct mail, point-of-purchase promotion, coupons, promotional emails, buzz marketing, product placement, and special events. These can be classified as (1) **above-the-line promotion,** meaning traditional **measured media** advertising, and (2) **below-the-line promotion,** which is everything else. For consumer package goods companies, below-the-line promotion might be desirable retail shelving, in-store promotions, coupons, and events; for durable goods (say cars), it might be for dealer incentives and financing incentives. Below-the-line promotion is also referred to as **unmeasured media.** It's not really unmeasured, but it is just called "unmeasured" because it is hard to measure it with traditional means.

Measured media include network TV, cable TV, spot TV, syndicated TV, network Spanish TV, the Internet (some aspects), streaming radio, spot radio, local radio (500 stations, top-28 markets), magazines (Sunday, consumer, business-to-business, and 30 local magazines), 250 local newspapers, Spanish newspapers, national newspapers (*The Wall Street Journal, USA Today, The New York Times*), and outdoor. Unmeasured media is everything else: paid Internet search, coupons, product placement, mobile advertising, social media, special events, and so on.

The slices of the big pie change in size from year to year as advertisers increase or decrease media spending and shift dollars among media investments. For years, measured media

constituted more than half of the media investment allocations. These days, the ratio of measured and unmeasured media is in flux as more advertisers put more money into digital, social, and mobile media to reach consumers who use their mobile devices at home, at work, at school, and everywhere in between.

We want to stress the importance of investing in a variety of media to be effective in integrated brand promotions. To show what types of media brands are investing in, refer to Exhibit 12.3, which is showing spending by media type. Note that advertising investments in the United States were estimated at $71.4 billion in television, $12.5 billion in magazine advertising, and $7 billion in newspaper advertising. The exhibit also shows the prominent investment in many forms of digital media. Furthermore, growth in event sponsorship is worth watching closely. Expenditures per media vary from year to year, so consider this a snapshot of media spending during one point in time.

U.S. measured-media spending by medium in 2019
From Kantar for all advertisers and Ad Age Leading National Advertisers' top 200. Dollars in billions.
The 200 Leading National Advertisers in 2019 accounted for 62 percent of measured-media TV spending.

Medium	Measured-media spending		
	All advertisers (including 200 LNA)	200 Leading National Advertisers	200 LNA's share
TV	$74.1	$46.0	62%
Magazine	12.5	5.5	44
Newspaper	7.0	1.1	16
Radio	7.1	2.9	41
Outdoor	5.6	1.5	27
Subtotal	106.3	56.9	54
Desktop search	24.4	8.3	34
Desktop internet display	11.7	3.0	26
Subtotal including search and display	142.4	68.1	48
Other digital	26.8	NA	NA
Free-standing inserts	NA	0.6	NA
Cinema	0.6	NA	NA
Total	$169.9	$68.7	NA

Source: Ad Age Datacenter. Numbers rounded. Measured-media spending from Kantar. More info: kantar.com/media. About LNA 2020: AdAge.com/aboutlna2020.

Exhibit 12.3 ▶ U.S. ad investments entail a variety of media types, and it is important to look at the allocations of media investments by type to keep up with optimal media investment strategy. This table overviews measured-media spending by all advertisers and the 200 leading national advertisers in the United States based on latest available data.

12-2 Media Investment Terminology

Media planning and media investment determines where and when the advertiser's money is spent. It requires creativity and strategic thinking to understand what the advertiser is trying to accomplish through media and why. It then requires the ability to evaluate the various tools in the integrated brand promotion area to determine the best fit.

A **media plan** specifies the media in which advertising messages will be placed to reach the desired target audience. A **media class** is a broad category of media, such as television, radio, or newspapers. A **media vehicle** is a particular option for placement within a media class. For example, *Vogue* is a media vehicle within the magazine-media class. The **media mix** is the blend of different media that will be used to effectively reach the target audience.

A media plan includes strategy, objectives, media choices, and a media schedule for placing a message. And remember: Everything must work together with synergy. The advertising plan (Chapter 7) developed during the planning stage of the advertising effort is the driving force behind a media plan. Market and advertising research determine which media options hold the highest potential for shaping the consumer behavior (Chapter 5) of the target audience. And the message strategy (Chapter 10) has enormous implications for media decisions. More than ever before, media planning and creative planning work hand in hand so that the message is prepared for the appropriate media to reach and influence the target market.

12-2a Media Strategies, Objectives, and Data

The true strength of a media plan lies in the media strategy. What are you trying to do with your media: build brand awareness, counter a competitor's claims, reposition your brand, react to good or bad media publicity, or establish an image and good feelings for your brand? You need to match message objectives with media choices. It is not simply about advertising via the latest or trendiest media platform.

This strategy is then tactically executed in media terms of message weight, reach, frequency, continuity, audience duplication, and newer terms associated with branded entertainment and digital advertising. But don't miss the big picture; you should always know and pay close attention to the fundamental qualities of each medium and specific vehicle in terms of what your brand is trying to accomplish. Then take a step back and examine the media buys in the larger, strategic context of brand communication and consumer behavior goals.

A crucial media objective is that the vehicle chosen *reaches the target audience.* Recall that a target audience can be defined by demographics, psychographics, geography, lifestyle, attitude dimensions, or usage category. Some advertisers encourage loyalty by targeting current users who prefer their products, while other advertisers target current users of a competing product to encourage switching and increase market share.[11]

As you saw in Chapters 2 and 7, marketing and advertising research firms provide all kinds of specialized input to inform decision making. In the media process, a media research organization can increase the precision and usefulness of traditional media buys. An example of the type of information supplied is shown in Exhibit 12.4, where market statistics for four brands of men's aftershave and cologne are compared: Eternity for Men, Jovan Musk, Lagerfeld, and Obsession for Men. The most revealing data are contained in columns C and D. Column C shows each brand's strength relative to a demographic variable, such as age or income. Column D provides an index indicating that particular segments of the population are heavier users of a particular brand. Specifically, the number expresses each brand's share of volume as a percentage of its share of users. An index number above 100 shows particular strength for a brand. The strength of Eternity for Men as well as Obsession for Men is apparent in both the 18–24 and the 25–34 age cohorts.

Suppliers of single-source data, such as IRI, offer information not only on demographics but also on brands, purchase size, purchase frequency, prices paid, and media exposure. With demographic, behavioral, and media-exposure correlations provided by research services like these, advertising and media planners can address issues such as the following:

- How many members of the target audience have tried the advertiser's brand, and how many are repeat purchasers?

- What appears to affect brand sales more—increased amounts of advertising or changes in advertising copy?

- What other products do buyers of the advertiser's brand purchase regularly?

- What television programs, magazines, and newspapers reach the largest number of the advertiser's audience?

Another critical element in setting advertising objectives is determining the **geographic scope** of media placement. Media planners need to identify media that cover the same geographic area as the advertiser's distribution system and avoid media that reach consumers outside this geographic area. Some analysts suggest that when certain geographic markets demonstrate unusually high purchasing tendencies by product category or by brand, then geo-targeting should be the basis for the media placement decision. **Geo-targeting** is the placement of ads in geographic regions where higher purchase tendencies for a brand are evident. See Exhibit 12.5 for an example of a

Exhibit 12.4 ▶ Commercial research firms can provide advertisers with an evaluation of a brand's relative strength within demographic segments. This data table from Mediamark Research shows how various men's aftershave and cologne brands perform in different demographic segments.

Aftershave Lotion & Cologne for Men

BASE: MEN	TOTAL U.S. '000	Eternity for Men A '000	B % DOWN	C % ACROSS	D INDEX	Jovan Musk A '000	B % DOWN	C % ACROSS	D INDEX	Lagerfeld A '000	B % DOWN	C % ACROSS	D INDEX	Obsession for Men A '000	B % DOWN	C % ACROSS	D INDEX
All Men	92674	2466	100.0	2.7	100	3194	100.0	3.4	100	1269	100.0	1.4	100	3925	100.0	4.2	100
Men	92674	2466	100.0	2.7	100	3194	100.0	3.4	100	1269	100.0	1.4	100	3925	100.0	4.2	100
Women	—	—	—	—	—	—	—	—	—	—	—	—	—	—	—	—	—
Household Heads	77421	1936	78.5	2.5	94	2567	80.4	3.3	96	1172	92.4	1.5	111	2856	72.7	3.7	87
Homemakers	31541	967	39.2	3.1	115	1158	36.3	3.7	107	451	35.5	1.4	104	1443	36.8	4.6	108
Graduated College	21727	583	23.7	2.7	101	503	15.8	2.3	67	348	27.4	1.6	117	901	23.0	4.1	98
Attended College	23842	814	33.0	3.4	128	933	29.2	3.9	113	*270	21.3	1.1	83	1283	32.7	5.4	127
Graduated High School	29730	688	27.9	2.3	87	1043	32.7	3.5	102	*460	36.3	1.5	113	1266	32.2	4.3	101
Did Not Graduate H.S.	17374	*380	15.4	2.2	82	*715	22.4	4.1	119	*191	15.0	1.1	80	*475	12.1	2.7	65
18–24	12276	754	30.6	6.1	231	*391	12.2	3.2	92	*7	0.5	0.1	4	747	19.0	6.1	144
25–34	20924	775	31.4	3.7	139	705	22.1	3.4	98	*234	18.5	1.1	82	1440	36.7	6.9	162
35–44	21237	586	23.8	2.8	104	1031	32.3	4.9	141	*311	24.5	1.5	107	838	21.3	3.9	93
45–54	14964	*202	8.2	1.4	51	*510	16.0	3.4	99	*305	24.0	2.0	149	481	12.3	3.2	76
55–64	10104	*112	4.6	1.1	42	*215	6.7	2.1	62	*214	16.9	2.1	155	*245	6.2	2.4	57
65 or over	13168	*37	1.5	0.3	10	*342	10.7	2.6	75	*198	15.6	1.5	110	*175	4.4	1.3	31
18–34	33200	1529	62.0	4.6	173	1096	34.3	3.3	96	*241	19.0	0.7	53	2187	55.7	6.6	156
18–49	62950	2228	90.4	3.5	133	2460	77.0	3.9	113	683	53.9	1.1	79	3315	84.5	5.3	124
25–54	57125	1563	63.4	2.7	103	2246	70.3	3.9	114	850	67.0	1.5	109	2758	70.3	4.8	114
Employed Full Time	62271	1955	79.3	3.1	118	2141	67.0	3.4	100	977	77.0	1.6	115	2981	76.0	4.8	113
Employed Part-time	5250	*227	9.2	4.3	163	*141	4.4	2.7	78	*10	0.8	0.2	14	*300	7.7	5.7	135
Sole Wage Earner	21027	554	22.5	2.6	99	794	24.9	3.8	110	332	26.2	1.6	115	894	22.8	4.3	100
Not Employed	25153	*284	11.5	1.1	42	912	28.6	3.6	105	*281	22.2	1.1	82	643	16.4	2.6	60
Professional	9010	*232	9.4	2.6	97	*168	5.3	1.9	54	*143	11.3	1.6	116	504	12.8	5.6	132
Executive/Admin./Mgr.	10114	*259	10.5	2.6	96	*305	9.6	3.0	88	*185	14.6	1.8	134	353	9.0	3.5	82
Clerical/Sales/Technical	13212	436	17.7	3.3	124	*420	13.2	3.2	92	*231	18.2	1.7	128	741	18.9	5.6	132
Precision/Crafts/Repair	12162	624	25.3	5.1	193	*317	9.9	2.6	76	*168	13.2	1.4	101	511	13.0	4.2	99
Other Employed	23022	631	25.6	2.7	103	1071	33.5	4.7	135	*261	20.6	1.1	83	1173	29.9	5.1	120
H/D Income																	
$75,000 or More	17969	481	19.5	2.7	101	*320	10.0	1.8	52	413	32.5	2.3	168	912	23.2	5.1	120
$60,000–74,999	10346	*368	14.9	3.6	134	*309	9.7	3.0	87	*142	11.2	1.4	100	495	12.6	4.8	113
$50,000–59,999	9175	*250	10.2	2.7	103	*424	13.3	4.6	134	*153	12.1	1.7	122	*371	9.4	4.0	95
$40,000–49,999	11384	*308	12.5	2.7	102	*387	12.1	3.4	99	*134	10.6	1.2	86	580	14.8	5.1	120
$30,000–39,999	12981	*360	14.6	2.8	104	542	17.0	4.2	121	*126	10.0	1.0	71	*416	10.6	3.2	76
$20,000–29,999	13422	*266	10.8	2.0	75	*528	16.5	3.9	114	*164	12.9	1.2	89	*475	12.1	3.5	84
$10,000–19,999	11867	*401	16.3	3.4	127	*394	12.3	3.3	96	*67	5.3	0.6	41	*481	12.3	4.1	96
Less than $10,000	5528	*31	1.3	0.6	21	*291	9.1	5.3	153	*69	5.4	1.2	91	*194	4.9	3.5	83

Source: Mediamark Research Inc., Mediamark Research Men's, Women's Personal Care Products Report (Mediamark Research Inc., Spring 1997), 16.

Source: Based on "GfK MRI, GfK MRI Men's Women's Personal Care Products Report," GfK MRI, Spring 1997, 16.

brand doing geo-targeting via social media because the social media ad is targeted to people who are around the Columbus, Ohio area as that is the location of the ice cream shop that is advertising.

Media planning is increasingly sophisticated and targeted, thanks to Big Data. Social networking sites and search engines can track online behavior, and stores can even track in-store movement through your cell phone's signals using **geofencing,** or a way to determine or where someone is using their mobile technology. The mobile app for directions, Waze, shows an example of geofencing when it shows locations and icons of brands, such as Shell, McDonald's, Adidas, and AT&T. In short, so much data are available that advertisers can then **micro-target** you with appropriate messages when and where you would be most receptive.

Reach refers to the number of people or households in a target audience that will be exposed to a media vehicle or schedule at least once during a given period of time. It is often expressed as a percentage. If an advertisement placed on a TV network program is watched at least once by 10 percent of the advertiser's target audience, then the reach is said to be 10 percent. Media vehicles with broad reach make sense for consumer convenience goods, such as toothpaste and cold remedies. These are products that are frequently purchased by consumers across the market. Broadcast television, cable television, and national magazines have the largest and broadest

Source: Graeter's Ice Cream

Exhibit 12.5 ▶ Integrated Brand Promotion in Action: Graeter's
Cincinnati-based Graeter's operates 40 ice cream shops in the Midwest and wholesales ice cream in containers to retailers in 46 states. *Why would the company identify some social media content according to geographic scope?*

reach of any of the media, due to their national and even global coverage, even though their audiences have been shrinking (with some exceptions in live sports programming).

Frequency is the average number of times an individual or household within a target audience is exposed to a media vehicle in a given period of time (typically a week or a month). For example, say an advertiser places an ad on a weekly television show with a 20 rating (20 percent of households) four weeks in a row. The show has an (unduplicated) reach of 43 (percent) during the four-week period. So, frequency is then equal to 20 × 4/43, or 1.9. This means that an audience member had the opportunity to see the ad an average of 1.9 times.

Advertisers often struggle with the dilemma of increasing reach at the expense of frequency, or vice versa. At the core of this struggle are the concepts of effective frequency and effective reach. **Effective frequency** is the number of times a target audience needs to be exposed to a message before the objectives of the advertiser are met—either communications objectives or sales impact. Many factors affect the level of effective frequency. New brands and brands laden with features may demand high frequency. Simple messages for well-known products may require less frequent exposure for consumers to be affected.[12] Although

most analysts agree that one exposure will typically not be enough, there is debate about how many exposures are enough. A common industry practice is to place effective frequency at three exposures, but analysts argue that as few as two or as many as nine exposures are needed to achieve effective frequency.[13]

Effective reach is the number or percentage of consumers in the target audience that are exposed to an ad a specified, minimum number of times. The minimum-number estimate for effective reach is based on a determination of effective frequency. If effective reach is set at four exposures, then a media schedule must be devised that achieves at least four exposures over a specified time period within the target audience. With all the advertising clutter (too many ads) that exists today, effective reach is likely to be a much higher number; some experts have estimated six as a minimum.

Message weight is another media measure; it is the total mass of advertising delivered. Message weight is the gross number of advertising messages or exposure opportunities delivered by the vehicles in a schedule. Media planners are interested in the message weight of a media plan because it provides a simple indication of the size of the advertising effort being placed against a specific market.

Message weight (at least in traditional media) is typically expressed in terms of gross impressions. **Gross impressions** represent the sum of exposures to the entire media placement in a media plan. Planners often distinguish between two types of exposure. *Potential ad impressions,* or *opportunities* to be exposed to ads, are the most common and refer to exposures by the media vehicle carrying advertisements (e.g., a program or publication). *Message impressions,* on the other hand, refer to exposures to the ads themselves. Information on ad exposure probabilities can be obtained from a number of companies. This information can pertain to particular advertisements, campaigns, media vehicles, product categories, ad characteristics, and target groups.

For example, consider a media plan that, in a one-week period, places ads on three television programs and in two national magazines. The sum of the exposures to the media placement might be as follows:

Exhibit 12.6 ▶ This table shows examples of gross impressions and media weight.

MEDIA CLASS/VEHICLE	RATING (REACH)	NUMBER OF AD INSERTIONS (FREQUENCY)	GRP
Television			
Program A	25	4	100
Program B	20	4	80
Program C	12	4	48
Program D	7	2	14
Magazines			
Popular Magazine A	22	2	44
Specialized Magazine B	11	2	22
News Magazine C	9	6	54
Total			**362**

The total gross impressions figure is the media weight.

Of course, this does not mean that 30,450,000 separate people were exposed to the programs and magazines or that 9,176,300 separate people were exposed to the advertisements. Some people who watched TV program A also saw program B and read magazine 1, as well as all other possible combinations. This is called **between-vehicle duplication** (remember, "vehicles" are shows, newspapers, magazines—things that carry ads). It is also possible that someone who saw the ad in magazine 1 on Monday saw it again in magazine 1 on Tuesday. This is **within-vehicle duplication**. That's why we say that the total *gross* impressions number contains audience duplication. Data available

from outside services report both types of duplication so that they may be removed from the gross impressions to produce the *unduplicated* estimate of audience, or *reach,* as discussed above.

Exhibit 12.6 shows an example of media classes (television and magazines) and vehicles (specific programs or magazines) along with the ratings (reach), number of advertising insertions (frequency), and gross rating points (GRP). This represents the importance of not just gross or total impressions, but also the media weight.

Another way of expressing media weight is in terms of gross rating points (GRP). GRP is the product of reach times frequency $(GRP = r \times f)$. When media planners calculate the GRP for a media plan, they multiply the rating (reach) of each vehicle in a plan times the number of times an ad will be inserted in the media vehicle and sum these figures across all vehicles in the plan. Exhibit 12.7 shows the GRP for a hypothetical combined magazine and television schedule. The GRP number is used as a relative measure of the intensity of one media plan versus another. Whether a media plan is appropriate is ultimately based on the judgment of the media planner.[14]

The message weight objective provides only a broad perspective for a media planner. What does it mean when we say that a media plan for a week produced more than 30 million gross impressions? It means only that a fairly large number of people were potentially exposed to the advertiser's message as a general point of reference. And for marketing priorities such as new product introductions, message weight is important because advertisers want to

Exhibit 12.7 ▶ This table shows gross rating points (GRPs) for a media plan.

	GROSS IMPRESSIONS	
	MEDIA VEHICLE	ADVERTISEMENT
Television		
Program A audience	16,250,000	5,037,500
Program B audience	4,500,000	1,395,000
Program C audience	7,350,000	2,278,500
Sum of TV exposures	28,100,000	8,711,000
Magazines		
Magazine 1	1,900,000	376,200
Magazine 2	450,000	89,100
Sum of magazine exposures	2,350,000	465,300
Total gross impressions	**30,450,000**	**9,176,300**

Richard Baker/In Pictures/Getty Images

Exhibit 12.8 ▶ Alfa Romeo planned a smart media buy when introducing a new car via Super Bowl advertising.

increase awareness and interest from the targeted audience during the campaign. Think about the message weight Fiat Chrysler achieved by airing not one but three Super Bowl commercials to introduce its luxury Alfa Romeo sedan to an enormous game-day audience (see Exhibit 12.8). Three different ads enabled the automaker to highlight the car's design, performance, and Italian heritage.[15] Viewers got interested and checked out the car on the Edmunds.com car shopping site. Edmunds reported that traffic on the Alfa Romeo's pages rose by 802 percent during the Super Bowl compared with a typical Sunday—indicating that the commercials did their job.[16]

Continuity is the pattern advertisers use to place ads in a media schedule. There are three strategic scheduling alternatives: continuous, flighting, and pulsing. **Continuous scheduling** is a pattern of placing ads at a steady rate over a period of time. Running one ad each day for four weeks during the TV show *Grey's Anatomy* would be a continuous pattern. Similarly, an ad that appeared in every issue of *Southern Living* magazine for a year would also be continuous. **Flighting** is another media-scheduling strategy. Flighting is achieved by scheduling heavy advertising for a period of time, usually two weeks, then stopping advertising altogether for a period, only to come back with another heavy schedule.

Flighting is often used to support special seasonal merchandising efforts, new product introductions or as a response to competitors' activities. The financial advantages of flighting are that discounts might be gained by concentrating media buys in larger blocks. Communication effectiveness may be enhanced because a heavy schedule can achieve the repeat exposures necessary to achieve consumer awareness. For example, the ad for Reddi-wip® in Exhibit 12.9 was run

ConAgra Foods, Inc.

Exhibit 12.9 ▶ An example of a print ad that was flighted during December—a month in which whipped-cream dessert toppings sell prominently due to holiday baking and consumption.

heavily in December issues of magazines to take advantage of seasonal dessert-consumption patterns.

Finally, **pulsing** is a media-scheduling strategy that combines elements from continuous and flighting techniques. Advertisements are scheduled continuously in media over a window of time, but with periods of much heavier scheduling (the flight). Pulsing is most appropriate for products that are sold fairly regularly all year long but have certain seasonal requirements, such as candy because it tends to spike in sales for Halloween and other holidays such as Valentine's Day.

12-2b Continuity and the Forgetting Function

Industry media continuity practices were strongly influenced by academic research in the area of human memory. When people first started trying to understand how and when to place ads, the idea of forgetting soon came into play. It turns out that people's tendency to forget is fairly predictable; that is, all else being equal, we know at about what interval things fade from people's memory. It seems to follow a mathematical function pretty well; thus it is often called the **forgetting function.** The original work for this was done more than a century ago by psychologist Hermann Ebbinghaus in the late 19th century and most notably in the advertising world by Hubert Zielske in 1958.

In his notable study, Zielske sent food ads to two randomly selected groups of women. One received the ad every 4 weeks for 52 weeks (13 total exposures); the other received the ad once every week for 13 straight weeks (13 total exposures). Exhibit 12.10 shows what happened in "The 1858 Repetition Study." The group that received all 13 ads in the first 13 weeks (called a flighting schedule) scored much higher in terms of peak unaided recall, but the level of recall fell off very fast and, by halfway through the year, was very low. The group that got the ads at an evenly spaced schedule (called a continuous schedule) never attained as high a level of recall as the other group but had an overall higher average recall at the end of the year.

This research has been very influential in terms of guiding industry media planners for several decades. The real-world implications are pretty clear. If you need rapid and very high levels of recall—say for the introduction of a new product, a strategic move to block the message of a competitor, or a political ad campaign, where there is only one day of actual shopping (election day)—use a flighting (sometimes called "heavy-up") schedule. A continuous schedule would be more broadly effective and would be used for established brands with an established message.

However, recall and its measurement have received criticism from both industry managers and academic researchers because remembering a brand is often not enough. Simple memory measures are inadequate on their own in most advertising situations. As discussed earlier, they are most

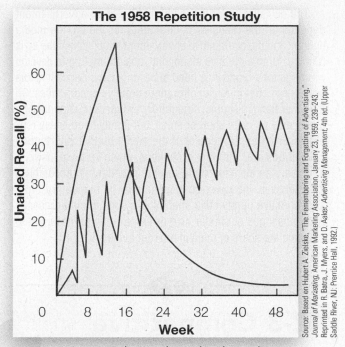

Exhibit 12.10 ▶ Take a close look at this graph of a very influential piece of media research. It links what we know about the manner in which humans forget things with the frequency of advertising.

appropriate when a simple outcome like brand name recall is sought. If the brand's goal is enhancing name recall, then forgetting (or not forgetting) is an especially important factor in advertising success or failure.

12-2c Length or Size of Advertisements

Beyond whom to reach, how often to reach them, and in what pattern, media planners must make strategic decisions regarding the length of an ad in electronic media or the size of an ad in print media. Certainly, the advertiser, creative director, art director, and copywriter have made determinations in this regard as well. Television advertisements (excluding infomercials) can range from 10 to 60 seconds and sometimes run several minutes in length.

Sizes of ads and images determines recognition rates in advertising. Some research shows an increase in recognition scores of print advertising with increasing image size. Some call this the **square root law;** that is, "the recognition of print ads increases with the square of the illustration."[17] So a full-page ad should be twice as memorable as a quarter-page ad. Such "laws" should not be considered laws but rather general guidelines; they show a general relationship but are not completely precise. Still, advertisers use full-page newspaper ads when a product claim, brand image, or market situation warrants it.

The decision about the length or size of an advertisement depends on the creative requirements for the ad, the media budget, and the competitive environment within which the ad is running. From a creative standpoint, ads attempting to develop an image for a brand may need to be longer in broadcast media or larger in print media to offer more creative opportunities. On the other hand, a simple, straightforward message announcing a sale may be quite short or small, but it may need heavy repetition. From the standpoint of the media budget, shorter and smaller ads are, with few exceptions, much less expensive. If a media plan includes some level of repetition to accomplish its objectives, the lower-cost option may be mandatory. From a competitive perspective, matching a competitor's presence with messages of similar size or length may be essential to maintain the share of mind in a target audience.

LO 3

12-3 Competitive Media Assessment and Share of Voice

Even though media planners normally do not base an overall media plan on how much competitors are investing or where competitors are placing their ads, a competitive media assessment can provide a useful perspective. A competitive media assessment is particularly important for product categories where all the competitors are focused on a narrowly defined target audience. This condition exists in several product categories in which heavy-user segments dominate consumption—for example, snack foods, soft drinks, beer and wine, and chewing gum. Brands of luxury cars and financial services also compete for common-buyer segments.

When a target audience is narrow and attracts the attention of several major competitors, an advertiser must assess its competitors' IBP investing and the relative share of voice its brand is getting. **Share of voice** is a calculation of any one advertiser's brand expenditures relative to the overall spending in a category:

$$\text{Share of voice} = \frac{\text{one brand's advertising expenditures in a medium}}{\text{total product category advertising expenditures in a medium}}$$

This calculation can be done for all advertising by a brand in relation to all advertising in a product category, or it can be done to determine a brand's share of product category spending on a particular advertising medium, such as network television or magazines.[18] For a hypothetical example, assume that athletic-footwear marketers invest $310 million per year in measured advertising media for their new shoe line each year. Now assume that every year, Nike and Reebok invest

approximately $160 million and $55 million, respectively, in measured advertising media for the new shoe lines. The share-of-voice calculations for both brands follow:

$$\text{Share of voice, Nike} = \frac{\$160 \text{ million} \times 100}{\$310 \text{ million}} = 51.6\%$$

$$\text{Share of voice, Reebok} = \frac{\$55 \text{ million} \times 100}{\$310 \text{ million}} = 17.7\%$$

In this hypothetical example, the two brands dominate the product category advertising with a nearly 70 percent combined share of voice. Yet Nike's share of voice is nearly three times that of Reebok in this example.

Research data can provide an assessment of share of voice in various media categories. A detailed report will show how much a brand was advertised in a particular media category versus the combined media category total for all other brands in the same product category. Knowing what competitors are investing in a medium and how dominant they might be allows an advertiser to strategically schedule within a medium. Some strategists believe that scheduling in and around a competitor's schedule can create a bigger presence for a small advertiser.[19]

LO 4

12-4 Media Efficiency

The advertiser and the agency team determine which media class is appropriate for the current effort. These criteria give a general orientation to major media and the inherent capabilities of each media class.

Each medium under consideration in a media plan must be evaluated for the efficiency with which it performs. In other words, which media deliver the largest target audiences at the lowest cost? A common measure of media efficiency is **cost per thousand (CPM),** which is the dollar cost of reaching 1,000 (the M in CPM comes from the Roman numeral for 1,000) members of an audience using a particular medium. The CPM calculation can be used to compare the relative efficiency of two media choices within a media class (magazine vs. magazine) or between media classes (magazine vs. radio). The basic measure of CPM is straightforward; the dollar cost for placement of an ad in a medium is divided by the total audience and multiplied by 1,000. Let's do a hypothetical calculation to see the CPM for a full-page black-and-white ad in a Friday edition of *USA Today:*

$$\text{CPM} = \frac{\text{cost of media buy} \times 1,000}{\text{total audience}}$$

$$\text{CPM for } USA\ Today = \frac{\$72,000 \times 1,000}{5,206,000} = \$13.83$$

In this sample calculation, *USA Today* has a CPM of $13.83 for a full-page black-and-white ad. But this calculation shows the cost of reaching the entire readership of *USA Today.*

12-4a Digital/ Internet Media

Although Internet media is covered in more detail in Chapter 14, the most important thing to remember now is that with a few exceptions, Internet or digital media are pull media. With **pull media,** consumers go looking for the advertiser or advertising and thus "pull" the advertised brand toward them (the way so many consumers seek out Super Bowl commercials posted by popular brands even before game day). This is just the opposite of most traditional media, which is usually **push media** (e.g., a 30-second television ad) in which the brand is "pushed" at the consumer (rather than the consumer seeking it out). The consumer has more control with pull media, deciding if and when to access the advertising. In contrast, consumers may choose to be exposed to push media or may use technology to skip or avoid such ads.

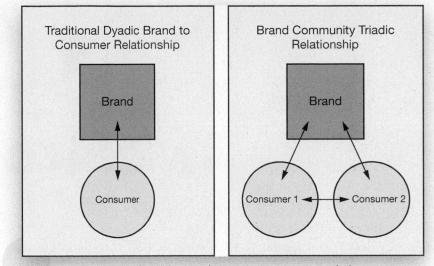

Exhibit 12.11 ▶ Online brand communities and the brand–consumer relationship.

─────── LO **5** ───────

12-5 Social Media: A Media Planning Perspective

12-5a Social Networks and Integrated Brand Promotions

Facebook, Twitter, and others have revolutionized the way we think about mediated communication. From the earliest work on brand communities, Muniz and O'Guinn noted that this paradigm is represented by three nodes rather than the traditional two: marketer–consumer–consumer (see Exhibit 12.11). Consumers talk to other consumers and like to talk about stuff—consumer stuff. Now, through social media, they can do this in brand communities, at almost no cost, instantaneously, and with the power of huge audiences. And, as noted throughout this book, marketers are well aware of the cost-efficient brand promotion opportunities represented by social media.

We know social media are used to discuss brands, and we know that marketers use these media to create buzz and eventual sales for their brands. But how social media impressions or exposures are counted and priced is still evolving. An emerging research discipline known as **social listening** specializes in tracking conversations about brands on the Web,

Exhibit 12.12 ▶ Advertisers calculate the level of brand conversations for digital and social media; here is a hypothetical output that focuses on the KPI (key performance indicator) of conversion, such as converting exposures into sales.

RANK	BRAND	CONVERSATION VOLUME	POSITIVE CONVERSATIONS
1	Apple	921,267	74.6%
2	Microsoft	574,004	78.9%
3	Fox	496,865	61.4%
9	AT&T	476,450	62.1%
24	Dannon	415,751	65.2%
4	Disney	334,655	86.5%
6	Sony	306,763	85.9%
5	Nintendo	303,326	84.3%
7	Tiffany & Co.	264,768	86.9%
8	Ford	237,433	87.6%
15	ABC	220,226	71.7%
19	ESPN	178,039	68.0%
21	Glade	165,085	82.6%
16	UPS	160,202	69.3%
13	Canon	144,291	89.7%

Source: Avocados from Mexico

Exhibit 12.13 ▶ Avocados From Mexico uses flighting media strategy and social media because it is a seasonal produce product.

analyzing the data, and reporting various metrics, including numbers of people discussing a brand, sentiments expressed, and volume (how much conversation about a brand occurs in a given period), and so on. Exhibit 12.12 shows brand-chat volume for a one-week period.

Smart brands focus on the synergy of traditional media advertising and social media interactions. Avocados From Mexico does this with its Super Bowl advertising, a media strategy specifically designed to generate social media conversations, starting with influencers. Avocados From Mexico encouraged sharing and discussion before, during, and after the Super Bowl with the hashtag #AvoSecrets, achieving far more reach and engagement on social media than through its TV ad alone. By one estimate, Avocados From Mexico achieved 2 billion impressions with its IBP campaign tied to the Super Bowl. Cinco de Mayo is another occasion for Avocados From Mexico to promote their brand, and they use advertising flights along with social media engagement tactics to reach and influence consumers who love guacamole and other foods made from fresh avocados (see Exhibit 12.13).[20]

LO 6

12-6 Branded Entertainment as a Media Choice

As more companies adopt integrated brand promotions, options such as event sponsorship, direct marketing, branded entertainment, sales promotion, and public relations are drawing many firms away from traditional mass media advertising. But even these newer approaches still require coordination with any advertising that reaches a mass audience, as you just saw in the Avocados From Mexico example.

12-6a Branded Entertainment

Branded entertainment, as discussed in Chapters 3 and 10, originated with simple product placements in movies, radio, and then television shows. Today, the trend is to merge media through branded entertainment on television, in games, in retail settings called brandscapes (think of stores such as NikeTown), on mobile phones—all across the board. We discussed the basic mechanism in Chapter 10, but it also is important to consider branded entertainment from the media perspective.[21]

For clients seeking branded entertainment opportunities, there typically are various approaches including product placement (such as on television or movies) and sport marketing. The most straightforward and least expensive is product placement.[22] A character on television might be seen drinking Sprite, driving a Subaru, or shopping for a Gucci belt. A sophisticated approach involves storyline integration, such as having a scene in *Modern Family* where a character talks about being a licensed realtor (an actual deal arranged by the National Association of Realtors).[23]

Original content, such as when BMW produced short online film clips featuring its vehicles, is an expensive (compared to product placement) but potentially compelling form of branded entertainment. In fact, PepsiCo is betting big on branded entertainment with a business unit to handle such projects. For example, there is a feature film starring Uncle Drew, a character who at times appears in Pepsi's online videos (see Exhibit 12.14). How did the company measure the results of such media exposure? "There are different ways to do it through impressions, though ROI—meaning on your 'return on investment' in the content—but also ROI on the

Rodrigo Varela/Stringer/Getty Images Entertainment/Getty Images

Exhibit 12.14 ▶ PepsiCo uses branded entertainment as part of its media strategy.

executions, each reinforces the brand image. In the Facebook (Meta) approach, Pepsi uses #PepsiHalftime as a way to inform and remind consumers that it sponsors the Super Bowl halftime show; it is also a way to help the brand and it's agency measure some of the social media conversations about it. In the official Pepsi Instagram page, also featured in Exhibit 12.15, the brand integrates music, quizzes, and games with some stunning visual posts and Instagram stories to its 1.7 million followers. In the image depicting Pepsi's official Twitter page, the social media copy is also entertaining as it says "Turns out today's weather is cooler than us"—along with an ice cube emoji and an image of a winter coat on a Pepsi can. Last, the brand's YouTube page/channel reinforces the branded entertainment investment of the Super Bowl halftime show to its almost 900,000 subscribers.

products," notes PepsiCo's senior vice president of global brand development.[24]

Another common way of branded entertainment is tied into sport marketing and entertainment marketing, which Pepsi tends to invest heavily in. In fact, Pepsi has recently sponsored the Super Bowl halftime show, which is one of the most prolific examples of branded entertainment in sports in America. More examples of how Pepsi integrates entertainment in four different social media platforms are in Exhibit 12.15. It is important to leverage branded entertainment investments through social media. Pepsi does so on Facebook (Meta), Instagram, Twitter, and YouTube. As can be seen in these four social media

LO 7

12-7 Media Planning Models: Benefits and Realities

The explosion of available data on markets and consumers means media planners have access to electronic databases and software systems to assist with the various parts of the media planning effort, as well as the evaluation of the results.[25]

Source: Pepsi Co.

Exhibit 12.15 ▶ Pepsi has done a good job targeting consumers in various media platforms including social media and branded entertainment. In these four different images, notice how they are asking consumers to "stay on the pulse, follow Pepsi" on four different social media platforms: Facebook, Twitter, Instagram, and YouTube so that they can encourage top of mind awareness. This is an example of social media integration, where a message and image is reinforced on multiple, synergistic channels. The Facebook post showcases their Super Bowl marketing, the official Pepsi Twitter page is showing the art direction of a winter coat over a can of Pepsi, the Instagram page shows visuals from the various creative ads in their respective campaigns, and the YouTube channel shows a variety of video content such as ads and short films.

All of the major syndicated research services offer electronic data to their subscribers, including advertisers, agencies, and media organizations. These databases contain information helpful in identifying target markets and audiences, estimating or projecting media vehicle audiences and costs, analyzing competitive advertising activity, and much more. Such software often produces summary reports, tabulations, rankings, reach-frequency analysis, optimization, simulation, scheduling, buying, flowcharts, and a variety of graphical presentations.

Many media measurement firms and software companies offer specialized and standardized products to help advertisers, agencies, and media organizations develop and evaluate markets, audiences, and multimedia plans. Exhibit 12.16 shows an example of media results for a brand (Disney World) from one such advertising media data supplier; the first column in the table is reach and cost data for spot TV ads, and the second column in the table is the combined reach and cost data for spot TV and newspaper ads.

Exhibit 12.16 ▶ Traditionally, advertisers relied on computerized media planning tools, such as those by ADPlus. These tables show Walt Disney World's Spot TV and Daily Newspaper results for the Jacksonville, FL DMA along with the vehicle lists, Gross Rating Points (GRPs), Cost-per-Thousand (CPMs), and Cost-per-Rating Points (CPPs). In modern times, advertisers use programmatic advertising and rely on analytics such as from Google AdWords or other digital analytics on ads and campaigns.

ADplus(TM) RESULTS: SPOT TV (30S)
Walt Disney World
Off-Season Promotion
Monthly
Target: 973,900
Jacksonville DMA Adults

Message/vehicle = 32.0%

Frequency (f) Distributions

f	VEHICLE % f+	VEHICLE % f+	MESSAGE % f	MESSAGE % f+
0	5.1	-	9.1	-
1	2.0	94.9	7.5	90.9
2	2.2	92.9	8.1	83.4
3	2.3	90.7	8.1	75.2
4	2.4	88.3	7.8	67.1
5	2.4	85.9	7.2	59.3
6	2.5	83.5	6.6	52.1
7	2.5	81.0	6.0	45.5
8	2.5	78.5	5.3	39.5
9	2.5	76.0	4.7	34.2
10+	73.5	73.5	29.5	29.5
20+	49.8	49.8	6.1	6.1

Summary Evaluation

Reach 1+ (%)	94.9%	90.9%
Reach 1+ (000s)	923.9	885.3
Reach 3+ (%)	90.7%	75.2%
Reach 3+ (000s)	882.9	732.8
Gross rating points (GRPs)	2,340.0	748.8
Average frequency (f)	24.7	8.2
Gross impressions (000s)	22,789.3	7,292.6
Cost-per-thousand (CPM)	6.10	19.06
Cost-per-rating point (CPP)	59	186

Vehicle List	RATING	AD COST	CPM-MSG	ADS	TOTAL COST	MIX %
WJKS-ABC-AM	6.00	234	12.51	30	7,020	5.1
WJXT-CBS-AM	6.00	234	12.51	30	7,020	5.1
WTLV-NBC-AM	6.00	234	12.51	30	7,020	5.1
WJKS-ABC-DAY	5.00	230	14.76	60	13,800	9.9
WJXT-CBS-DAY	5.00	230	14.76	60	13,800	9.9
WTLV-NBC-DAY	5.00	230	14.76	60	13,800	9.9
WJKS-ABC-PRIM	10.00	850	27.27	30	25,500	18.4
WJXT-CBS-PRIM	10.00	850	27.27	30	25,500	18.4
WTLV-NBC-PRIM	10.00	850	27.27	30	25,500	18.4
Totals:			19.06	360	138,960	100.0

ADplus(TM) RESULTS: DAILY NEWSPAPERS (1/2 PAGE), SPOT TV (30S)
Walt Disney World
Off-Season Promotion
Monthly
Target: 973,900
Jacksonville DMA Adults

Message/vehicle = 28.1%

Frequency (f) Distributions

f	VEHICLE % f+	VEHICLE % f+	MESSAGE % f	MESSAGE % f+
0	1.2	-	4.0	-
1	0.8	98.8	4.9	96.0
2	0.9	98.0	5.9	91.1
3	0.9	97.2	6.5	85.2
4	1.0	96.2	6.7	78.7
5	1.1	95.2	6.8	72.0
6	1.1	94.2	6.6	65.2
7	1.2	93.0	6.3	58.6
8	1.3	91.8	5.9	52.4
9	1.3	90.6	5.5	46.5
10+	89.3	89.3	41.0	41.0
20+	73.3	73.3	9.6	9.6

Summary Evaluation

Reach 1+ (%)	98.8%	96.0%
Reach 1+ (000s)	962.6	934.6
Reach 3+ (%)	97.2%	85.2%
Reach 3+ (000s)	946.5	829.7
Gross rating points (GRPs)	3,372.0	948.0
Average frequency (f)	34.1	9.9
Gross impressions (000s)	32,839.9	9,232.3
Cost-per-thousand (CPM)	10.96	38.99
Cost-per-rating point (CPP)	107	380

Vehicle List	RATING	AD COST	CPM-MSG	ADS	TOTAL COST	MIX %
1 Daily Newspapers		Totals:	114.00	80	221,040	61.4
Times-Union	42.00	8,284	104.93	20	165,680	46.0
Record	4.00	866	115.18	20	17,320	4.8
News	3.20	926	153.95	20	18,520	5.1
Reporter	2.40	976	216.35	20	19,520	5.4
2 Spot TV (30s)		Totals:	19.00	360	138,960	38.6
WJKS-ABC-AM	6.00	234	12.51	30	7,020	2.0
WJXT-CBS-AM	6.00	234	12.51	30	7,020	2.0
WTLV-NBC-AM	6.00	234	12.51	30	7,020	2.0
WJKS-ABC-DAY	5.00	230	14.76	60	13,800	3.8
WJXT-CBS-DAY	5.00	230	14.76	60	13,800	3.8
WTLV-NBC-DAY	5.00	230	14.76	60	13,800	3.8
WJKS-ABC-PRIM	10.00	850	27.27	30	25,500	7.1
WJXT-CBS-PRIM	10.00	850	27.27	30	25,500	7.1
WTLV-NBC-PRIM	10.00	850	27.27	30	25,500	7.1
		Totals:	38.99	440	360,000	100.0

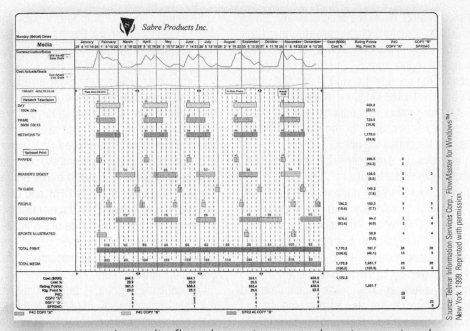

Exhibit 12.17 ▶ A media flowchart gives an advertiser a visual representation of the overall media plan. While the media types invested in change for companies, the concept of an organized media flowchart remains important.

Automation (including programmed buys and automated bidding for advertising) and modeling can never substitute for planning and judgment by media strategists. Computer modeling does, however, allow for the assessment of a wide range of possibilities before making costly media buys to uncover different ways that advertisers can save money.

One of the most important aspects of the media-scheduling phase involves creating a visual representation of the media schedule. Exhibit 12.17 shows a media schedule flowchart that includes both print and electronic media placement. With this visual representation of the schedule, the advertiser has tangible documentation of the overall media plan, helpful in both planning and execution.

12-8 Media Buying and Programmatic Media Buying

Once an overall media plan and a schedule are in place, the focus turns to **media buying,** securing the electronic media time and print media space specified in the schedule.

Today, much of media buying occurs through **programmatic media buying,** which refers to automatic buying of ads based on data such as online consumer behavior. Oftentimes this data comes from third parties that sell the data as a B2B service. Programmatic media buying, which generally occurs in digital media but is spreading to other forms of media buying such as television, typically relies on technologies that track a consumer's online behavior, such as where the person clicks or the key terms in that person's social media messages. Programmatic media buying has the potential for further improving effective target marketing and customized advertising in ways driven by artificial intelligence. Thanks to Big Data, advertisers are able to make media buys based on information such as which consumers have demonstrated an interest, via online consumer behavior, in the product category, or in a particular brand.

Consider some statistics about programmatic (digital) media from Zenith's Programmatic Marketing Forecasts, a report that includes top media markets. While the following statistics from the report refer to programmatic media buying for digital media, it is reiterated that the process of programmatic media exchange (i.e., media sales and media buying) is taking over the media buying process for traditional media, such as TV, radio, and digital outdoor. Their most recent available report on programmatic media forecasts (for 2021) that 72 percent of all investments on digital media advertising will be traded programmatically and the amount is forecasted to reach $147 billion for 2021. Note, their classification of digital media entails paid advertising in online settings such as social media, online video, and banners but does not include classified ads or paid search. While the programmatic advertising industry is prolific, it entails challenges due to privacy laws (namely the GDPR law in the EU and the California Consumer Privacy Act). The report finds 64 percent of the global programmatic advertising spending coming from the United States, with China and the United Kingdom in second and third place, respectively. Programmatic media buying for digital display advertising already accounts for the majority of such media buys and is now becoming the norm.[26]

Exhibit 12.18 displays the prominent role that programmatic media buying has in digital media.

Despite the dramatic rise in programmatic media buying, you still need to know how media buying traditionally works in advertising. Not all media investments need be automated. An important part of the media-buying process is the decision to handle media buying in-house or to use an agency of record for media. The **agency of record** is the advertising agency chosen by the advertiser to purchase media time and space; the agency may or may not also do the creative. The agency of record coordinates media discounts and negotiates all contracts for time and space. Any other agencies involved in the advertising effort submit insertion orders for time and space within those contracts.

Each spring, television programming and ad executives participate in the "**upfronts.**" This is a period where the television networks reveal their fall lineups and presell advertising to air during the programs. About 75 percent of prime-time television advertising is bought this way, in advance. Only the remaining 25 percent is really "in play" for the season. Networks attract buyers on the basis of program content and scheduling and with proprietary data and opportunities to extend reach and impact. Disney, for example, has highlighted new programs and new audience measurement tools during upfront presentations.[27]

Rather than using an agency of record, some advertisers use a **media-buying service**, which is an independent organization that specializes in buying large blocks of media time and space and reselling it to advertisers. Some agencies and companies have developed their own media-buying units to control both the planning and the buying processes. Regardless of the structure used to make the buys, media buyers evaluate the audience reach, CPM, and timing of each buy. The organization responsible for the buy also monitors the ads and estimates the actual audience reach delivered. If they are not successful in their efforts, then media organizations have to *make good* by repeating ad placements or offering a refund or price reduction on future ads.

A final case in point, is that media investment trends are dynamic, and change over time. For instance, see the bar charts in Exhibit 12.19, which show an unusual spike in cinema based advertising (an anomaly due to closing of theaters during the COVID-19 pandemic), out-of-home media, Internet-based advertising, and direct mail. It is also important to examine which forms of media may be on the decline in any given year, such as directories and newspapers according to these data. Of course, media investments are not one size fits all and should be unique to the goals and needs of the client or brand, so while media type trends are relevant and interesting, make sure to invest in the right type of media that suits their needs rather than what is simply trending or falling out of favor.

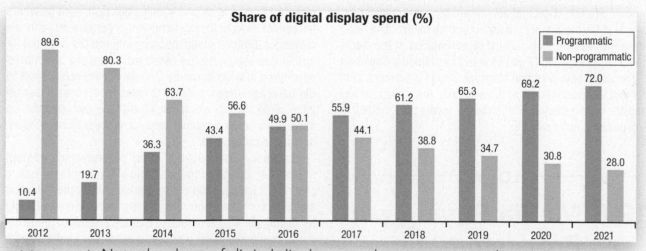

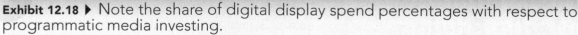

Exhibit 12.18 ▶ Note the share of digital display spend percentages with respect to programmatic media investing.

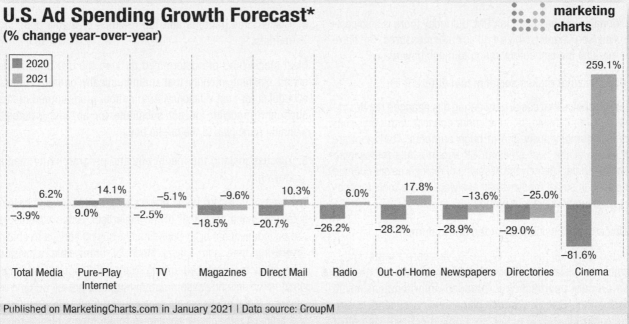

U.S. Ad Spending Growth Forecast*
(% change year-over-year)

marketing charts

Legend: 2020, 2021

Category	2020	2021
Total Media	−3.9%	6.2%
Pure-Play Internet	9.0%	14.1%
TV	−2.5%	−5.1%
Magazines	−18.5%	−9.6%
Direct Mail	−20.7%	10.3%
Radio	−26.2%	6.0%
Out-of-Home	−28.2%	17.8%
Newspapers	−28.9%	−13.6%
Directories	−29.0%	−25.0%
Cinema	−81.6%	259.1%

Published on MarketingCharts.com in January 2021 | Data source: GroupM

*Includes digital extensions with traditional media, and also includes political advertising

Exhibit 12.19 ▶ This table shows the U.S. Advertising Spending Growth Forecast as a percentage change over years 2020–2021. What really sticks out in terms of growth is in branded entertainment—specifically in cinema (which is an anomaly because in 2020 when movies/cinema had a hard time during the pandemic closings), and out-of-home media. Both Internet-based media and direct mail are also growing.

Summary

1. Describe measured versus unmeasured media and estimate how much each represents of total advertising and IBP dollars.

Measured media include network TV, cable TV, spot TV, syndicated TV, network Spanish TV, the Internet (some aspects), streaming radio, spot radio, local radio (500 stations, top 28 markets), magazines (Sunday, consumer, business-to-business, and 30 local magazines), 250 local newspapers, Spanish newspapers, national newspapers (*The Wall Street Journal, USA Today, The New York Times*), and outdoor (200-plus markets). Unmeasured media are everything else: coupons, product placement, special events, social media, mobile marketing, and the like. The ratio of money invested in measured and unmeasured media is currently in flux as more advertisers increase their use of digital, social, and mobile media to reach consumers.

2. Describe the basic ideas and essential terms used in media planning.

A media plan specifies the media and vehicles that will be used to deliver the advertiser's message. Developing a media plan involves setting objectives such as effective reach and frequency

and developing strategies to achieve those objectives. Media planners use several quantitative indicators, such as CPM, to help them judge the efficiency of prospective media choices. The media planning process culminates in the scheduling and purchase of a mix of media vehicles expected to deliver the advertiser's message to specific target audiences at precisely the right time to affect their consumption decisions. Although media planning is a methodical process, human judgment is also needed, even when computer decision-making models and statistical measurements are used.

3. Understand the meaning of competitive media assessment and share of voice.

Competitive media assessment means determining how much your brand is spending on IBP relative to the category as a whole. Share of voice is a calculation of any one advertiser's brand expenditures relative to the overall spending in a category.

4. Discuss media efficiency.

Media efficiency is traditionally evaluated in terms of the cost of reaching a certain number of prospective consumers.

Traditionally, this has been in CPM, but today there is also cost-per-click (see Chapter 14) as well as other measures. The basic idea remains the same: how much to reach how many?

5. Discuss what makes social media different.

Research shows that social networking has changed the brand–consumer relationship as consumers connect with other consumers instantaneously and in huge numbers. Marketers are well aware of the cost-efficient IBP opportunities represented by social media. The way impressions or exposures are counted and priced in social media is still evolving, as are tools for analyzing conversations about brands.

6. Discuss the basics of branded entertainment.

Branded entertainment is where advertisers create entertainment vehicles for promoting their brands. There are three primary approaches to branded entertainment media opportunities. One is product placement, a second is storyline integration, and a third is original content (the most expensive but potentially most compelling).

7. Discuss the benefits and the realities of media planning models.

Most media buys are determined through the use of computerized planning models that mathematically optimize media schedules for cost efficiency. Automation, programmed media buys, and modeling do not substitute for applying strategic planning principles to the media buy.

8. Discuss making the media buy and programmatic media buying.

The agency of record is the agency responsible for purchasing time and space on behalf of the advertiser. Some advertisers use an independent or in-house media-buying service to obtain advertising time and space. Much of prime-time television advertising is purchased during "upfronts," spring meetings when networks showcase programming and presell ad time in advance. Much media buying is now automated, with algorithms and artificial intelligence helping to make media buying more effective, based on real-time consumer behavior.

Key Terms

above-the-line promotion	geofencing	micro-target
agency of record	geo-targeting	programmatic media buying
below-the-line promotion	geographic scope	pull media
between-vehicle duplication	gross impressions	push media
continuity	measured media	pulsing
continuous scheduling	media-buying service	reach
cost per thousand (CPM)	media buying	share of voice
effective frequency	media class	social listening
effective reach	media mix	square root law
flighting	media plan	unmeasured media
forgetting function	media vehicle	upfronts
frequency	message weight	within-vehicle duplication

Endnotes

1. Thomas H. Davenport and Judah Phillips, "The Future of Marketing Automation," *Applied Marketing Analytics* 2, no. 3 (2016), 213–224.
2. Mark Deuze, "Living in Media and the Future of Advertising," *Journal of Advertising* 45, no. 3 (2016), 326–333.
3. See, for example, Rodrigo Uribe, "Separate and Joint Effects of Advertising and Placement," *Journal of Business Research* 69, no. 2 (2016), 459–465.
4. Artie Bulgrin, "Why Knowledge Gaps in Measurement Threaten the Value of Television Advertising," *Journal of Advertising Research* 59, no. 3 (2019), 9–13.
5. Bradley Johnson, "How Nation's Top 200 Marketers Are Honing Digital Strategies," *Advertising Age,* June 27, 2016, http://adage.com/article/advertising/top-200-u-s-advertisers-spend-smarter/304625.
6. Ibid.
7. Dominique M. Hanssens and Koen H. Pauwels, "Demonstrating the Value of Marketing," *Journal of Marketing* 80, no. 6 (November 2016), 173–190.
8. A. Guttman, "Starbucks Advertising Spending Worldwide in the Fiscal Years 2011 to 2020," *Statista,* March 4, 2021,

https://www.statista.com/statistics/289363/starbucks-advertising-spending-worldwide; Al Ries, "Forget Your Ps; Mind the Four Ms of Marketing," *Advertising Age,* September 5, 2016, http://adage.com/article/al-ries/forget-ps-mind-ms-marketing/305712/.

9. S. Lock, "Chipotle Mexican Grill's Ad & Marketing Cost Worldwide," *Statista*, February 17, 2021, https://www.statista.com/statistics/504077/chipotle-ad-marketing-spend/.

10. S. Lock, "McDonald's Ad Spend 2014-2020," *Statista*, April 26, 2021, https://www.statista.com/statistics/286541/mcdonald-s-advertising-spending-worldwide/.

11. The financial results depend, in part, on advertising costs and whether users who prefer competing products are an attractive target market. See Rosa-Branca Esteves and Joana Resende, "Competitive Targeted Advertising with Price Discrimination," *Marketing Science* (2016), 576–587.

12. Frank Findley et al., "Effectiveness and Efficiency of TV's Brand-Building Power: A Historical Review," *Journal of Advertising Research* 60, no. 4 (June 2020), 361–369.

13. Navdeep Sahni et al., "An Experimental Investigation of the Effects of Retargeted Advertising: The Role of Frequency and Timing," *Journal of Marketing Research* 56, no. 3 (March 2019), 401–418.

14. Frank Findley et al., "Effectiveness and Efficiency of TV's Brand-Building Power: A Historical Review," *Journal of Advertising Research* 60, no. 4 (June 2020), 361–369.

15. Ian Thibodeau, "Sleek Alfa Romeo Giulia the Star of FCA Super Bowl Ads," *Detroit News,* February 5, 2017, http://www.detroitnews.com/story/business/autos/chrysler/2017/02/05/alfa-romeo-giulia-focus-first-fca-super-bowl-ad/97526216/.

16. Tanya Gazdik, "Lexus, Kia, Alfa Romeo Big Auto Winners in Super Bowl," *MediaPost,* February 6, 2017, http://www.mediapost.com/publications/article/294398/lexus-kia-alfa-romeo-big-auto-winners-in-super-b.html.

17. John R. Rossiter, "Visual Imagery: Applications to Advertising," in *Advances in Consumer Research* (Provo, UT: Association for Consumer Research, 1982), 101–106.

18. Daniel McDuff, and Jonah Berger, "Why Do Some Advertisements Get Shared More than Others?" *Journal of Advertising Research* 60, 4 (July 2020), 370–380.

19. Andrea Rothman, "Timing Techniques Can Make Small Ad Budgets Seem Bigger," *The Wall Street Journal,* February 3, 1989, B4; see also Robert J. Kent and Chris T. Allen, "Competitive Interference Effects In Consumer Memory for Advertising: The Role of Brand Familiarity," *Journal of Marketing* (July 1994) 97–105.

20. Jill Schiefelbein, "Secrets From a Super Bowl Campaign That's Had 2 Billion Impressions," *Entrepreneur,* February 5, 2017, https://www.entrepreneur.com/article/288734; Jennifer Rooney, "Super Bowl 2017 Advertisers That Garnered the Most Social Conversation," *Forbes,* February 6, 2017, https://www.forbes.com/sites/jenniferrooney/2017/02/06/super-bowl-2017-advertisers-that-garnered-the-most-social-conversation/#3fa27fa37bd3; Jessica Wohl, "Avocados from Mexico Ready for Second Biggest Celebration," *Advertising Age,* May 3, 2016, http://adage.com/article/cmo-strategy/avocados-mexico-ready-biggest-celebration/303837/.

21. Chingching Chang, "How Branded Videos Can Inspire Consumers and Benefit Brands: Implications for Consumers' Subjective Well-Being," *Journal of Advertising* 49, no. 5 (September 2020), 613–632.

22. Cristel Antonia Russell, "Expanding the Agenda of Research on Product Placement: A Commercial Intertext," *Journal of Advertising* 48, no. 1 (November 2018), 38–48.

23. Jenna Susko and Amy Coral, "Interactive: Can You Spot the Newest Advertising Tricks?" *NBC Los Angeles I-Team,* February 21, 2017, http://www.nbclosangeles.com/investigations/Can-You-Spot-the-Newest-Advertising-Tricks--414393203.html.

24. E. J. Schultz, "Pepsi Wants to Be a Movie Mogul," *Advertising Age,* February 21, 2017, http://adage.com/article/cmo-strategy/pepsi-a-movie-mogul/308035/.

25. German Zenetti and Daniel Klapper, "Advertising Effects Under Consumer Heterogeneity—The Moderating Role of Brand Experience, Advertising Recall and Attitude," *Journal of Retailing* 92, no. 3 (September 2016), 352–372.

26. Zenith's Programmatic Marketing Forecasts, 2019, https://s3.amazonaws.com/media.mediapost.com/uploads/Programmatic-MarketingForecasts2019.pdf.

27. Jason Lynch, "Disney-ABC's New Ad Sales Chief Is Pushing for New Partnerships at Kids Upfronts," *Adweek,* February 28, 2017, http://www.adweek.com/tv-video/disney-abcs-new-ad-sales-chief-is-pushing-for-new-partnerships-at-kids-upfronts/.

Media Planning: Newspapers, Magazines, TV, and Radio

Learning Objectives

After reading and thinking about this chapter, you will be able to do the following:

1 Explain some considerations of the present and future of traditional mass media.

2 Identify the advantages and disadvantages of newspapers/digital newspapers, identify newspaper advertising categories, and consider the future of newspapers as a medium.

3 Explain the advantages and disadvantages of magazines as a media class, identify magazine advertising categories, and consider the future of magazines as a medium.

4 Identify the advantages and disadvantages of television as a media class, identify television advertising categories, describe audience measurement for television, and consider the future of television as a medium.

5 Explain the advantages and disadvantages of radio as a media class, identify radio advertising categories, and consider the future of radio as a medium.

If the consumer does not see the message, no matter how new or modern the media placement is, it is not an effective message. That is why the media process is so important to advertising and integrated brand promotion. In Chapter 12, "Media Planning Essentials," you gained an overall perspective of media. As shown in the framework diagram, this chapter focuses on key aspects of integrating brands' communication via print, TV, and radio to reach target markets, which form the foundation of many advertising campaigns. We suggest that media plans involving traditional media should synergize with digital marketing approaches, which are the focus of the next chapter (Chapter 14).

There are certain objectives advertising can achieve—particularly creative goals—only with traditional mass media because digital, social, and mobile media cannot match them in their effectiveness. Despite changes in technology and media consumption, these traditional media represent robust and attractive communication alternatives for many advertisers—especially as the traditional media increase their presence in the digital, social, and mobile platforms for reach and synergy. Another factor to bear in mind is the

Exhibit 13.1 ▶ This figure depicts a framework overview for newspapers, magazines, TV, and radio for integrated brand promotion (IBP).

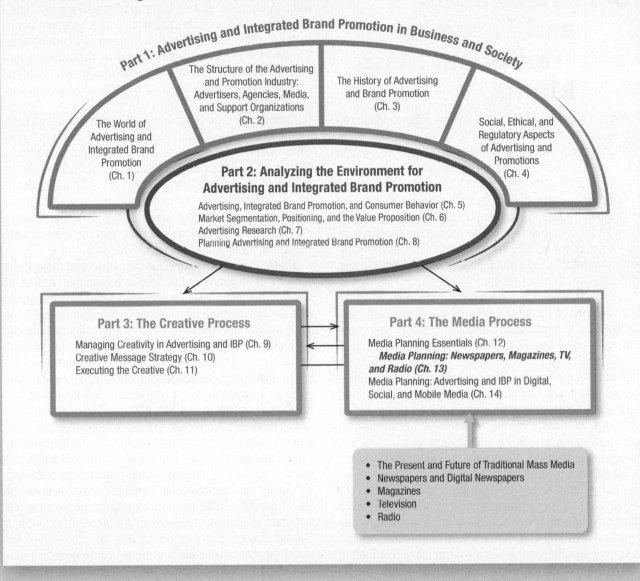

trend toward programmatic buying, especially as artificial intelligence (AI) technology advances and advertisers gain the ability to identify and analyze multiple media for pinpoint targeting.[1] Human judgment is necessary throughout the media process for considerations like the reputation and authoritativeness of traditional media categories and vehicles.[2] You were introduced to programmatic media buying in the last chapter. Here, we again discuss programmatic media buying for television.[3]

A framework for this chapter is shown in Exhibit 13.1. With respect to print media—newspapers and magazines—we'll first examine the advantages and disadvantages of the media themselves. Next, we'll look at the types of newspapers and magazines from which advertisers can choose and identify buying procedures and audience measurement techniques. Finally, we consider TV and radio in the same way, examining the various options available, discussing their advantages and disadvantages, and reviewing both how to measure the audience and how to buy these media. Much of media buying in these areas will most likely be more automated or programmatic in the future.

13-1 The Present and Future of Traditional Mass Media

In Chapters 1 and 2, we said that the advertising industry as a whole continues to evolve and change in significant ways. Traditional mass media—newspapers, magazines, TV, and radio—have reinvented themselves and are often very convergent and synergistic with digital. Consumers have turned to multiple new sources of information and entertainment and are more active in their media choices and exert more control over content exposure. User-generated content from viral videos, social media sites, and other sources offer non-commercial information about brands and brand experiences, a trend that is only accelerating.

As a result, advertisers are turning more often to digital, social, and mobile media that offer new, different, and cost-effective ways to reach target markets—including when those consumers could benefit from select ads based on mobile device use and their physical location. In addition, such media allow advertisers to make rapid changes in campaigns—changes that might take months to execute with traditional media. Planning and executing a global IBP campaign can be a challenge with traditional media alone. Yet it becomes both possible and practical with the availability of digital, social, and mobile media options and today's sophisticated media analysis and programmatic buying tools.[4]

These changes in media options are affecting not only advertisers' perceptions of how to develop effective campaigns but also the way they are investing their money on media. For example, advertisers seeking to reach consumers in very specific local areas have traditionally turned to newspapers, TV, and radio. They are still using those media, just not investing as much as in the past. Instead, advertisers are boosting media investments on digital, social, and mobile media because of more precise targeting capabilities and the opportunity to communicate when and where consumers are making brand decisions. In fact, with an eye on consumer behavior, investing on mobile media is surpassing spending on digital ads accessed by desktop computers.[5]

The media environment does not have a predictable structure, and media companies are using analytics to properly position themselves for the new ways consumers seek out brand information. Media organizations like the New York Times Company (publisher of *The New York Times*) and Tribune Publishing Company (publisher of the *Los Angeles Times*) are investing in technology and expertise to give advertisers more and better data and service throughout the media process.[6]

Despite the shift to include digital, social, and mobile media (detailed in Chapter 14), traditional media command a significant portion of many advertising budgets, and while their format may be changing, they will not be replaced nor eliminated. For example, top advertisers seeking to reach parents buying for their children continue to invest heavily in TV advertising.[7] *The future of effective advertising and IBP campaigns means synergizing digital, social, and mobile media with the use of traditional mass media, such as TV, radio, outdoor, and print advertising.*

Consider the case of one of the most successful print campaigns in history—Absolut Vodka, who now integrates print advertising with digital platforms. At one point in its history, Absolut was on the verge of extinction. The Swedish brand was selling just 12,000 cases a year in the United States—not enough to register a percentage point of market share. The name Absolut was seen as gimmicky; bartenders thought the bottle was ugly and hard to pour from; consumers gave little credibility to vodka produced in Sweden.

TBWA ad agency in New York aimed to overcome these liabilities of the brand and decided to rely on print ads *alone*. TBWA developed magazine and newspaper ads that would build awareness, communicate quality, achieve credibility, and avoid the Swedish clichés etched in the minds of American consumers. The firm developed one of the most famous and successful print campaigns of all time. The concept was to feature the strange-shaped Absolut bottle as the hero of each ad, and the only copy was a two-word tagline beginning with *Absolut* and usually ending with a "quality" word such as *perfection* or *clarity*. The two-word description evolved from the original quality concept to a variety of creative combinations. For classic examples, "Absolut Perfection" showed the bottle with an angel halo over it, "Absolut Security" features the bottle with a chain and lock around it, and "Absolut Squeeze" features the Absolut Mandarin bottle over an orange juicer. They also had ads that featured prominent cities, such as "Absolut Boston" and "Absolut Chicago" with depictions of aspects of those cities. For recent examples, the brand is integrating drinking responsibly messages integrating print ads with social media with headlines that say "Drink Responsibly" in place of the usual headline and end with hashtags such as "#SexResponsibly." The vodka with little credibility and the difficult-to-pour-from bottle became sophisticated and fashionable with well-conceived and well-placed print heavy campaigns.[8]

Overall, the Absolut campaign is not only a creative masterpiece but also a market success. Using print media alone in the early stages and now integration with social media has helped Absolut to become a leading import vodka in the United States. To this day, the Absolut brand still relies heavily on magazine advertising in the IBP mix with continued success by integrating the images with social media. Exhibit 13.2 is an example of the type of ad Absolut has been running in magazines over these many years. Exhibit 13.3 shows some of Absolut's IBP in social media.

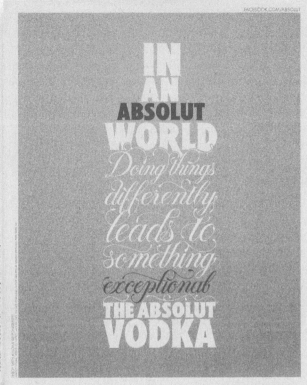

Exhibit 13.2 ▶ Absolut vodka has relied for many years on magazines to effectively reach its target audience with high quality and carefully targeted print ads; recently the print campaigns are integrated with social media and aspects of social responsibility, such as awareness of consent in sexual encounters.

---LO 2---

13-2 Newspapers and Digital Newspapers

Almost all newspapers now offer a digital version, with accompanying digital ads. Newspaper is a medium accessible to a wide range of advertisers; digital newspapers and apps complement the traditional paper for more synergy, flexibility, and reach. They can be categorized by target audience, geographic coverage, and frequency of publication. Newspapers, with the exception of national newspapers, are ideally suited to reach a geographic area—precisely the type of audience local retailers, for instance, want to reach. Note the examples of top newspapers by circulation and you notice they often have a major U.S. city in the title. Some top newspapers in the United States are *The Wall Street Journal*, *The New York Times*, *USA Today*, *The Washington Post*, and *The Los Angeles Times*. Meanwhile, the Huffington Post is an example of an exclusively digital newspaper.

However, as print circulation and ad revenues decline in the digital age, newspapers have reinvented themselves and revamped their business models to remain competitive. Newspapers are now updating their content in real time, and the future of some newspapers may be limiting the print options that are available, such as Sunday print editions only. This is because fewer people are subscribing to printed

Absolut ✔ @absolutvodka · Feb 14
Love is in the share! Happy Valentine's Night to all. #ValentinesDay #AbsolutNights

 Save

absolut.com

Exhibit 13.3 ▶ Integrated brand promotion in action: Absolut
Absolut vodka posts images and videos on multiple social media outlets in addition to continuing its long-running print campaign. *How do the social media content and placement contribute to synergy in reinforcing the brand's image?*

newspapers while paid digital subscriptions are growing. Another issue is the high number of people who search online for a news item but don't read further on the newspaper's site after they locate the specific information they sought. So newspapers can have high digital *readership* that doesn't translate into digital *subscriptions*. The way that consumers seek information, news, and branded content has changed to become more search oriented. Given today's financial realities for publishers to make and deliver print editions, fewer daily newspapers are in print than even a decade ago, as some choose to exist in digital-only format.[9] Note that newspapers should offer consumers a choice of delivery methods with respect to digital content; *The Wall Street Journal* does a good job with offering choice with a WSJ.com e-reader, a WSJ print edition, and even a WSJ magazine.

Another important consideration is that the percentage of adults reading daily newspapers is declining. Research demonstrates that these consumers are now getting their news from TV, news websites, news apps, and radio more frequently than they do from traditional newspapers.[10] Although TV shows such as *Fox & Friends* and *Anderson Cooper 360* cannot provide the breadth of coverage that newspapers can, they do offer news in a synthesized, lively and multisensory format. Viewers can get additional details from the online, mobile, and social components of such shows, making them both popular and convenient alternatives to printed news.

13-2a Advantages of Newspapers

Printed newspapers may have lost some of their luster during the past four decades, but they still do reach about 75 million of U.S. households earning more than $100,000 per year, representing about 124 million adults who read the newspaper each week.[11] And, as mentioned earlier, the newspaper is still an excellent medium for retailers or other local businesses targeting local geographic markets. But broad reach isn't the only attractive feature of newspapers as a medium. Newspapers offer other advantages to advertisers, in addition to being very synergistic with digital and social media.

Geographic Selectivity

Daily newspapers in cities and towns across the United States offer advertisers the opportunity to reach a geographically well-defined target audience—particularly with densely populated urban markets. Some newspapers run zoned editions, which target even more narrowly defined geographic areas within a metropolitan market. Zoned editions are typically used by merchants doing business in the local area. Especially in rural areas, daily or weekly newspapers are prime sources of local news, without the intense competition of media that cover a wider region. These newspapers provide solid advertising opportunities for reaching rural audiences.[12]

Timeliness

The newspaper is timely even in its printed form. Because of the short time needed for producing a typical newspaper ad and the regularity of daily or weekly publication, the newspaper allows advertisers to reach audiences in a timely way. Brands can create and place ads in newspapers quickly, in response to or anticipation of an event or a news development, a plus when **lead time**—or the time to develop and place the ad—is limited.

Creative Opportunities

Even though the newspaper page does not offer the breadth of creative options available in the broadcast media, there are some opportunities for imaginative messaging. Since the newspaper page offers a large and relatively inexpensive format, advertisers can provide a lot of information to the target audience at a relatively low cost. This is important for products or services with extensive or complex features that need lengthy and detailed copy. Most newspapers have color capabilities and offer exposure for visual or video ads via their digital or mobile elements.

Credibility

Newspapers have long benefited from the perception that "if it's in the paper, it must be true." Even as newspapers battle recent accusations of "fake news," many also hold an important position as the "paper of record" in their communities, publishing the most in-depth coverage of current events available to consumers.

Audience Interest and Demographics

Regular newspaper readers, either digitally or via print, are truly interested in the information they are reading and staying current with local and or world happenings. Even though overall print readership may be down in the United States, apps are growing in popularity, and many readers remain interested and digitally engaged. Newspaper readers are relatively upscale; newspapers reach a higher percentage of highly educated and affluent consumers (in both the print and digital versions) than do broadcast or cable TV. In addition, many readers buy a newspaper specifically to see what's on sale or for coupons at stores in the local area, making this an ideal environment for local merchants.

Cost

In terms of both production and space, newspapers offer a low-cost alternative to advertisers. The cost per contact may be higher than with TV and radio options, but the **absolute cost**—also referred to as the unit cost or vehicle cost—for placing a black-and-white ad is still within reach of even a small advertising budget.

13-2b Disadvantages of Newspapers

Newspapers have some significant disadvantages, as detailed next.

Limited Segmentation

Although newspapers can achieve good geographic selectivity and reach upscale consumers, the ability to target a specific audience with any precision is limited. Newspapers cut across too broad of an economic, social, and demographic audience to allow for the isolation of specific targets. Some newspapers are developing special sections to enhance their segmentation capabilities—food sections, personal health sections, and the like. Many papers have regular or special sections such as entertainment and personal finance to target specific audiences. In addition, more newspapers are linked with digital and social media content distributions.

Creative Constraints

The opportunities for creative executions in printed newspapers are certainly outweighed by the creative constraints. First, newspapers have comparatively poor reproduction quality. For advertisers whose brand images depend on accurate, high-quality reproduction (color or not), newspapers are more limited compared to other media options. Second, printed newspapers are static, lacking sound and motion. For brands that demand a broad creative execution, this medium is often not the best choice.

Cluttered Environment

The average printed newspaper is filled with headlines, subheads, photos, and announcements—not to mention news stories. This presents a terribly cluttered environment for an advertisement, especially when multiple advertisers in a product category try to use the same sections to target audiences. For example, home equity loan and financial services ads are often presented in the business section.

Short Life

In most U.S. households, newspapers are read quickly and set aside. The way advertisers can overcome this limitation is by buying several insertions in each daily issue, buying space several times during the week, or both. This way, even if a reader doesn't spend much time with the newspaper, multiple exposures are possible.

13-2c Categories of Newspaper Advertising

Advertisers have several options when it comes to the types of ads that can be placed in newspapers: display advertising, inserts, and classified advertising.

Display Advertising

Advertisers of goods and services rely most on display advertising.

Display advertising in newspapers includes the standard components of a print ad—headline, body copy, and often an illustration—to distinguish it from the news content of the paper. An important form of display advertising is co-op advertising sponsored by manufacturers. In *co-op advertising* (introduced in Chapter 1), a manufacturer pays part of the media bill when a local merchant features the manufacturer's brand in advertising. Co-op advertising can be done on a national scale as well. Intel invests heavily in co-op advertising with computer manufacturers who feature the "Intel Inside" logo in their print ads. However, billions of dollars in co-op money offered by brands go unused by eligible retailers and other partners because of the complexities of arranging for payments and submitting proof that advertising was placed as planned.[13]

Inserts

Inserts do not appear on the printed newspaper page but rather are folded into the newspaper before distribution. There are two types of insert advertisements. The first is a **preprinted insert**, which is an advertisement delivered to the newspaper fully printed and ready for insertion into the newspaper.

The second type of insert ad is a **free-standing insert (FSI)**, which contains cents-off coupons for a variety of products and is typically delivered with Sunday newspapers. Kroger (a national grocer) is a heavy user of free-standing inserts to offer consumers coupons. Kroger's free-standing insert ads stand out to the newspaper reader for two reasons. First, it is a separate large-format page which helps attract attention. Second, free-standing inserts are often printed on higher-quality paper than the newspaper itself and can use bright, attractive colors to highlight Kroger's grocery products.

Classified Advertising

Classified advertising is newspaper advertising that appears as all-copy messages under categories such as sporting goods, employment, and automobiles. Many classified ads are taken out by individuals; but real estate firms, automobile dealers, and construction firms also buy classified advertising. In the past 10 years, billions of dollars in classified advertising has shifted from traditional newspaper posting to digital placement on free or specialized sites like craigslist.

13-2d The Future of Newspapers

There will likely be more digital newspapers while traditional newspapers also become more digitized. Earlier in the chapter, we talked about the fact that newspaper circulation has been declining—even as digital subscriptions and online readership are growing.[14] To survive as a viable advertising medium, newspapers will have to evolve with the demands of both audiences and advertisers, who provide them with the majority of their revenue. Primarily, newspapers will have to leverage their role as the source for local news—which some newer media can't always do as authoritatively. Some analysts refer to this opportunity for newspapers as **hyper-localism**, where people will get their global and national news online but turn to local newspapers to find sales on paint at the local hardware store.[15]

Some analysts suggest that newspapers consider adopting a pay-for-inquiry advertising model.[16] A **pay-for-inquiry advertising model** is a payment model in which the medium, in this case newspapers, gets paid by advertisers based solely on the inquiries an advertiser receives in response to an ad. Radio, TV, and the Internet (pay-per-click) have been using pay-for-inquiry models of various types for several years. In general, to remain a viable advertising medium, newspapers will have to do the following:

- Continue to provide in-depth coverage of issues that focus on the local community.

- Continue to provide some coverage of national and international news for readers who want both global and local news.

- Borrow from the Internet's approach to advertisers—be accountable to advertisers and offer local advertisers a pay-per-inquiry model for ad costs.

- Maintain and expand their role as the best local source for consumers to find specific information on advertised product features, availability, and prices (hyper-localism).

- Provide consumers/buyers the option of shopping through an online newspaper computer service, similar to eBay or craigslist.

- Take advantage of social media for local coverage of events, user-generated content, and dialogues with readers.

- Become more mainstream in IBPs relating to newer media.

----- LO 3 -----

13-3 Magazines

Like newspapers, magazines have also been struggling in a changing media world. Even as some magazines fold, others are enjoying increases in circulation and readership. Magazines like *Golf Digest* and *US Weekly* have growing audiences for specialized content, targeted audiences that advertisers want to reach both via print and digital versions of the magazines.[17] In fact, many advertisers find that magazines "work hard" to reach target customers effectively and efficiently. A Nielsen study revealed that for consumer package goods, the return on advertising investments from magazine ads is higher than the return on investment (ROI) from traditional TV ads, display ads, mobile ads, and others.[18] An Australian survey of food-magazine readers found that 82 percent were influenced by magazine content, and 58 percent were influenced specifically by the ads. Moreover, readers who saw ads in food magazines had higher awareness of and higher trust in advertised brands.[19]

Note once again that as with newspapers, investing in magazines by several top advertisers is down, reflecting the general decline in advertising placement in traditional media. Like newspapers, magazines have advantages and disadvantages, offer various ad costs and buying procedures, and measure their audiences in specific ways.

13-3a Advantages of Magazines

In addition to being synergistic with digital media, magazines have some advantages over newspapers and even broadcast media: audience selectivity, audience interest, creative opportunity, and long life.

Audience Selectivity

The key advantage of magazines relative to other media is their ability to target a highly selective audience. This selectivity can be based on demographics (for instance, *AARP The Magazine* targets Americans over 50 and is the top-circulation magazine in the United States with almost 23 million subscriptions), lifestyle (*Better Homes and Gardens*, *Good Housekeeping*), or special interests. *Tennis* magazine, published by Sinclair Broadcast Group, reaches a selective audience for advertising by offering special interest content to a select readership who is interested in the sport of tennis, its gear, and its athletes. The audience segment can be narrowly defined, as is the one that reads *Shape* or it may cut broadly across a variety of interests, like *People* does. *People*, in fact, attracts a great deal of advertising investment because of its broad reach. Still, many (but not all) of the advertising page leaders in the magazine industry are specialized publications that enjoy loyal readership, such as *Fortune*, *Vogue*, *Rolling Stone*, and *Sports Illustrated*.[20] Magazines also offer geographic selectivity on a regional basis, such as *Southern Living*, or city magazines, like *Atlanta*, which highlight happenings in major metropolitan areas. Celebrity-oriented tabloid magazines like *US Weekly*, *Hollywood Life, and OK! Magazine* are also popular. Another magazine trend deals with food and cooking, such as *Food Network Magazine*, *Eating Well*, and *All Recipes*.

Audience Interest

Perhaps more than any other medium, magazines attract an audience because of content. Although TV programming can attract audiences through content interest as well, magazines have the additional advantage of voluntary exposure to the advertising. Parents seek out publications that address the joys and challenges of parenting in a wide range of strong-circulation magazines like *Parents*. When a magazine attracts a highly interested readership, advertisers, in turn, find a highly receptive audience for their brand messages. The Escort radar detector ad in Exhibit 13.4 appeared in *Car and Driver* magazine. This specialized product can reach its specialized target market because reader interest in *Car and Driver* magazine content attracts them to the magazine and results in exposure for the Escort radar detector brand.

Creative Opportunities

Magazines offer a wide range of creative opportunities. Because of the ability to vary the size of an ad, use color, use white space, and play off the special interests of the audience, magazines offer a favorable creative environment. The paper quality of most magazines is high, so color reproduction can be outstanding—another creative opportunity. Magazines also

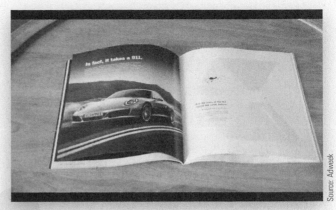

Exhibit 13.5 ▶ Porsche 911's ad in *Fast Company* magazine included a tear-out acetate prism for viewing the product in 3D video via tablet computer.

have the ability to include engaging physical elements like scent strips or pop-up models.

These factors are precisely why brands like Porsche invest in magazine advertising. Not long ago, Porsche placed a multipage ad in *Fast Company* to reach affluent car buyers (see Exhibit 13.5). Readers were invited to remove and assemble a plastic prism "viewer," place it atop a tablet computer, and view a 3D video of the Porsche 911 in action. Magazine advertising was the perfect medium for this IBP campaign, which also included social media and direct mail. The uniqueness of the ad generated a lot of publicity and won the agency an award.[21]

Long Life

Many magazine subscribers hold onto various issues. This means that, unlike newspapers, a magazine can be re-examined over a week or a month. And some magazines, such as *Architectural Digest*, *National Geographic*, and *Travel & Leisure,* are saved for even longer periods for future reference. In addition to multiple-subscriber exposure, this long life increases the chance of **pass-along readership** as people share copies with friends or families or browse through issues in professional offices.

It is important to note that social media can help preserve a long-lasting digital footprint for magazines as well. *Food Network Magazine*, for example, has 12.1 million readers and over 47 million social media followers according to their media kit, making it an attractive vehicle for food brands seeking a large and interested audience.[22] And magazines are very synergistic with other forms of IBP. An example of an iconographic from the Food Network is in Exhibit 13.6. A **media kit** is defined as a resource of information provided by a publisher to assist ad buyers, reporters, and media professionals who are seeking information on circulation, readership, subscribers, and prices to evaluate advertising opportunities. While most magazines offer advertisers/potential

Exhibit 13.4 ▶ An advantage of magazines: Specialized magazine content attracts audiences with special interests, and those audiences attract advertisers. This ad by Escort Radar appeared in *Car and Driver* magazine.

Food Network Magazine Media Kit

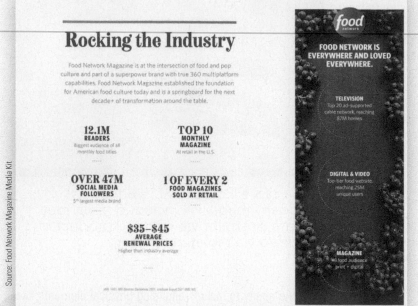

Rocking the Industry

Food Network Magazine is at the intersection of food and pop culture and part of a superpower brand with true 360 multiplatform capabilities. Food Network Magazine established the foundation for American food culture today and is a springboard for the next decade+ of transformation around the table.

12.1M
READERS
Biggest audience of all monthly food titles

TOP 10
MONTHLY MAGAZINE
At retail in the U.S.

OVER 47M
SOCIAL MEDIA FOLLOWERS
5th largest media brand

1 OF EVERY 2
FOOD MAGAZINES SOLD AT RETAIL

$35–$45
AVERAGE RENEWAL PRICES
Higher than industry average

food network

FOOD NETWORK IS EVERYWHERE AND LOVED EVERYWHERE.

TELEVISION
Top 20 ad-supported cable network, reaching 87M homes

DIGITAL & VIDEO
Top-tier food website, reaching 25M unique users

MAGAZINE
#1 food audience print + digital

Exhibit 13.6 ▶ Media kits often provide a packet of information that is especially of interest to advertisers and potential advertisers who are seeking a good fit with their target markets. Here is an iconographic on some magazine readership statistics and social media followings for the Food Network. Note how magazine and social media readership can often overlap, which stresses the importance of synergy for IBP.

advertisers a media kit, often the media kit gives statistics and information on other channels as well, such as social media followers.

13-3b Disadvantages of Magazines

Although having selectivity is a strength, magazines that are too selective in their reach can be problematic and actually attract too many advertisers. Other disadvantages include long lead time and relative cost.

Limited Reach and Frequency

The tremendous advantage of selectivity actually creates a limitation for magazines. The more narrowly defined the interest group, the less overall reach a magazine will have. Since most magazines are published monthly or weekly, there is little chance for an advertiser to achieve frequent exposure using a single magazine. To overcome this limitation, advertisers often use several magazines targeted at the same audience. For example, many readers of *Vogue* may also be readers of *Harper's Bazaar*. By placing ads in both

publications, an advertiser can increase both reach and frequency within a targeted audience.

Clutter

Magazines are not quite as cluttered as newspapers, but they still represent a fairly difficult context for message delivery. The average magazine is about half **editorial and entertainment content—** content intended to inform or entertain— and half advertising material, but some highly specialized magazines, like *Golf Digest*, can have as much as 80 percent of their pages devoted to advertising. And given the narrowly defined audiences, this advertising tends to be for brands directly competing with one other. An additional complication for magazine advertisers is the specific sort of clutter that can plague some magazine categories. As soon as a new market segment is recognized, there is a flood of "me too" magazines competing for readers and advertisers. The food magazine category is an example, with significant expansion two decades ago followed by a period of consolidation in the last decade. Now more narrowly targeted food magazines are again emerging, targeting readers interested in particular types of foods (such as *Clean Eating*) and foods of specific regions (such as *Louisiana Cookin'*).[22] Note that some magazines are more narrowly targeted to consumer lifestyles or demographics (e.g., *Wine Enthusiast, Elle Man*). Overall, the collage of magazine covers in Exhibit 13.7 shows some of the

Exhibit 13.7 ▶ This image shows a collage of some specialty magazines that are lifestyle oriented, such as *Elle, Elle Man, Rolling Stone, Harper's Bazaar, W, Vanity Fair,* and *Out.*

creative opportunities and ability to cater to audience selectivity and audience interest.

Long Lead Times

Advertisers are required to submit magazine ads as much as 90 days in advance of the date of publication. If the submission date is missed, there can be as much as a full month's delay in placing the next ad. And once an ad is submitted, it cannot be changed during that 90-day period, even if some significant event alters the communications environment.

Cost

While the cost per contact in magazines is not nearly as high as in some media (direct mail in particular), it is more expensive than most newspaper space and many times the cost per contact in broadcast media. The absolute cost for a single insertion can be prohibitive. For magazines with circulations that run into the millions of readers, such as *AARP*, magazine advertising entails sizable investments. According to their media kit, the cost for a one-time, full-page, four-color ad for the age fifty plus full run costs $782,150 based on a national base rate of 22.5 million readers. Buying the back cover or inside cover costs even more—up to just over $1 million.

13-3c The Future of Magazines

Two important factors need to be considered as influences on magazines as an advertising medium in the future. First, magazines are, like other traditional media, adapting to digital, social, and mobile media opportunities. Many are already formatting their content and ads specifically for access on mobile devices, tablets as well as phones. Magazine publishers have to worry about cannibalizing their print circulation, which would lower advertising revenue possibilities from that format, so many are generating revenues from separate print and digital subscription offers.

The second factor affecting the future of magazines is that publishers are exploring other ways to take advantage of the interactive environment beyond just digital version publications. In an effort to generate additional revenue, some magazines are starting to make the products advertised in the publication available for sale online—in order to earn a margin on the sales. Magazines are also leveraging content in other media, such as TV and social media, to engage consumers beyond the printed page, building audiences and encouraging buzz about the magazine brand. Editors at Hearst Media, which publishes such popular magazines as *Cosmopolitan* and *Men's Health*, plan and deliver content for each publication's social media presence. As a result, Hearst's magazines have attracted 239 million followers across social media like Facebook and YouTube.[24]

─────── LO **4** ───────

13-4 Television

With the benefit of sight and sound, color and music, action and special effects, TV advertising can be the most powerful advertising of all because it has advantages over all other media.[25] In many parts of the world, particularly in the United States, TV is the medium most widely used by consumers for entertainment and information.[26] Television presents two valuable opportunities to advertisers. First, the diversity of communication possibilities allows for outstanding creative expression of a brand's value. Dramatic color, sweeping action, and spectacular sound effects can cast a brand in an exciting and unique light—especially with today's TV technology. Second, once this expressive presentation of a brand is prepared, it can be disseminated to millions of consumers through multiple channels—broadcast, cable, satellite, and interactive means—often at a fraction of a penny per contact despite a relatively higher up-front investment.[27] Suppose a 30-second Super Bowl spot costs $5.6 million. Divide that by the reach and the fact that it is a time when consumers look forward to watching ads rather than skipping them, and the impact of the investment begins to grow exponentially. Plus, TV is easily integrated with digital, not just social media but also brand and network websites for maximum synergistic effect.

On average, each U.S. household has more than two TV sets—although the number of households without a TV set is increasing as more consumers choose to view content on digital devices.[28] Whether viewing occurs on a set or another device, the opportunities to reach mass audiences have not been lost on advertisers. To fully appreciate all that TV means to advertisers, we need to understand much more about this complex medium that is growing digital legs.

13-4a Television Categories

It is a common mistake to classify TV as a single type of broadcast medium. The reality is that during the past 25 years, several distinct versions of TV have evolved, from which consumers can choose news and entertainment programming and advertisers can choose programming best suited to reach those consumers. There are four categories of basic TV: network, cable, syndicated, and local TV (we'll get to Web and interactive TV shortly).

Network Television

Network TV broadcasts programming over airwaves to affiliate stations across the United States under a contract agreement. "Broadcast" is a bit of a misnomer since programming from these networks can be delivered on air, over cable, through satellite transmission, or by mobile apps to smartphones and tablets. The method of delivery does not change the fact that advertisers can buy time within these "broadcast" programs to reach audiences in hundreds of markets. Estimates are that network TV reaches more than 90 percent of U.S. households.

Despite all the competition faced by network TV, the broadcast networks still continue to flourish—mostly due to innovative programming. For example, the Super Bowl now draws 92 million viewers on TVs and nearly 4.6 million viewers per minute on live streaming.[29] A 30-second commercial during this event costs in excess of $5.5 million.[30] Regular programming costs are somewhat more reasonable. No other TV option gives advertisers the breadth of reach of network TV, delivering huge audiences and generating solid advertising revenues.

Cable Television

From its modest beginnings as community antenna TV (CATV) in the 1940s, cable TV has grown into a worldwide communications force. **Cable TV** transmits a wide range of programming to subscribers through wires rather than over airwaves. Even in the streaming era, cable TV still has the dominant share of

the TV market according to Nielsen Media. In the United States, about 75 million households are wired for cable reception and receive dozens of channels of sports, entertainment, news, music video, and home-shopping programming.[31] Cable's power as an ad option has grown enormously as its share of the prime-time viewing audience has increased. Aside from offering more channels and hence more programming, cable networks are also investing in the development of original programming to continue to attract well-defined audiences. Popular programs like ABC's *The Bachelorette* attract specific and very large target audiences.[32] And some cable networks, like ESPN, have programming designed to appeal to large audiences defined by interest (in this case, sports), a good advertising context for many brands.[33]

Video on Demand

One of the fastest-growing TV options is **video on demand (VOD).** Cable TV and network TV organizations alike are offering VOD programming, with some advertising opportunities, but they're not alone. Netflix and Amazon both have subscription-based VOD programming, and others are testing advertising-supported VOD programming. Hulu, owned by a Disney and Comcast, offers a choice of monthly subscriptions: pay more for no-ad viewing or pay less and see the ads. It also offers live streaming of network programming, not just VOD entertainment, giving consumers more control over what they view and when.[34]

As more consumers turn to VOD for entertainment on *their* schedule and to avoid the heavy ad loads on broadcast and cable TV, media organizations are testing viewer-friendly promotional messages for VOD environments. Hulu, which has ad-targeting capabilities appreciated by brands, caters to binge-watchers by allowing advertisers to run different spots in between episodes or, as with Bank of America, run spots that together tell a story, to retain viewer interest.[35] It is important however to note that even with all of the buzz around VOD and streaming, cable TV and broadcast TV still have a stronghold among TV consumption with 39 percent and 25 percent respectively according to Nielsen (a leading media company), as can be seen in Exhibit 13.8. Streaming consists of 26 percent of U.S. National TV Panel Data plus Streaming Video Ratings and specifically is dominated by Netflix, YouTube/YouTubeTV, Hulu, Prime Video, and Disney+ ().[36] This image in Exhibit 13.8 shows a pie chart of Nielsen's Total TV and Streaming breakdown, which includes the above listed streaming brands in the order of popularity at the time of when Nielsen measured the

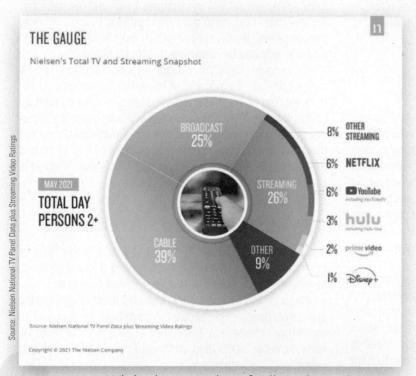

Exhibit 13.8 ▶ While there is a lot of talk in the industry about streaming and VOD, note that for TV, Cable and Broadcast still have an ample if not dominant share of the TV market. Streaming in its first years have been dominated by Netflix, YouTube/YouTube TV, Hulu, Prime Video, and Disney +. This image from Neilsen (a media company) shows the overall pie chart of TV consumption in the United States by type of TV viewership (cable, broadcast, steaming, and other).

streaming market share. While our focus here is on streaming, which consists of the brands just listed, it is of note that cable, broadcast, and other are again major media investments even in the streaming era.

Syndicated Television

Television syndication is either original programming or programming that initially appeared on network TV. It is then rebroadcast on either network or cable stations with pending distribution on the Internet. Syndicated programs provide advertisers with proven programming that typically attracts a well-defined, if not enormous, audience. There are several types of TV syndication. **Off-network syndication** refers to programs or episodes of programs that were previously run during network prime time, such as *Young Sheldon* and *Seinfeld*. **First-run syndication** refers to programs developed specifically for sale to individual stations. The most famous first-run syndication show is *Star Trek: The Next Generation.* **Barter syndication** takes both off-network and first-run syndication shows and offers them free or at a reduced rate to local TV stations, with some national advertising presold within the programs. Local stations can then sell the remainder of the time to generate revenues. This option allows national advertisers to participate in the national syndication market conveniently. Two of the most widely recognized barter syndication shows are *Jeopardy!* and *Judge Judy.*

Local Television

Local TV is the programming, other than the network broadcast, that independent stations and network affiliates offer local audiences. Completely independent stations air old movies, sitcoms, or children's programming. Network affiliates get about 90 hours of programming a week from the major networks, but they are free to air other programming beyond what is provided. News, movies, syndicated programs, and community-interest programs typically round out the local TV fare. Local TV commands significant advertising dollars.

Satellite

Programming transmitted to audiences via **satellite** transmission is another popular option for consumers. The most widely accessed satellite programming is available from DirecTV (merged with AT&T) and DISH Network. Another version of satellite transmission is direct transmission or **closed circuit.** The distinction is the technology for delivery. The best known of the closed-circuit programming comes from the CNN Airport Network, which transmits news and weather programming directly to airport terminals around the world (and is available via digital devices as well). The popularity of satellite transmission among consumers is the result of extensive programming, VOD options, and high-quality video transmission.

Streaming Services and Digital Downloads

Of course, the next evolution of TV transmission is underway with programs being accessed by consumers over the Web, with tablet and smartphone streaming or downloads, or via smartphones. "TV everywhere" capability is making its mark among today's connected audiences, and the potential for reaching audiences has advertisers excited. Given the dynamic nature of these TV distribution models and the fast pace of technological advances, what you're reading about here may already have changed.

First, let's consider online distribution. Tracking data indicate that hundreds of billions of video streams of TV programming occur each year, with Hulu adding another billion or so streams through its video-sharing site. Major media players like Disney/ESPN, CBS, and NBC all have platforms to stream programming online. The extent of the programming varies, often with an option to view ad-free entertainment. *CBS All Access*, for example, offers streaming with ads at one monthly subscription price and streaming without ads at a higher monthly price. YouTube TV has deals with CBS and other entertainment providers for a subscription-based, live-streaming service that includes YouTube's own program content. And Amazon's Prime Video and Disney + represent emerging streaming platforms. With these alternatives to traditional cable TV, more consumers are likely to "cut the cord."[37] Manufacturers like Apple and Samsung have sold tens of millions of smartphones with the capability of streaming or downloading TV programming, enabling advertisers to reach these viewers ubiquitously.

13-4b Advantages of Television

There are some very good reasons why advertisers such as Amazon, Comcast, AT&T, and Procter & Gamble invest hundreds of millions of dollars annually in TV advertising.[38] The specific advantages of this medium are discussed below.

Creative Opportunities

The overriding advantage of TV compared to other media is the ability to communicate using both sight and sound, with brilliantly sharp visuals and advanced sound capabilities. Although 3D TV and curved-screen sets didn't catch on with consumers, ultra-high-definition TV presents all sorts of new creative opportunities.[39]

Coverage, Reach, and Repetition

Television, in one form or another, reaches approximately 126 million households in the United States—an estimated

287 million people.[40] These households represent every demographic segment in the United States, which allows advertisers to achieve broad coverage. We have also seen that the cable and satellite options enhance TV's coverage and reach capabilities even more. Further, no other medium allows an advertiser to repeat a message as frequently as TV. Yet with programmatic buying, advertisers can select and target audiences by market rather than making a national buy. That's how Bank of America reaches affluent consumers—by programmatic buying of TV time in the top 15 markets for its target audience, as identified by sophisticated analyses.

Cost per Contact

For advertisers that sell to broadly defined mass markets, TV offers a cost-effective way to reach millions of members of a target audience. The average prime-time TV program generally reaches 11 million households, and according to Statista, there are about 121 million households using TV during the 2020-2021 season. This brings an advertiser's cost-per-contact figure down to an amount unmatched by any other media option—literally fractions of a penny per contact.

Audience Selectivity

Television programmers are doing a better job of developing shows that attract well-defined target audiences. **Narrowcasting** is the development and delivery of specialized programming to well-defined audiences. Cable and satellite TV are the most selective TV options. They provide not only well-defined programming but also entire networks—such as ESPN—developed around the concept of attracting selective audiences. "TV everywhere" delivered via streaming online or on mobile devices can be even more selective, using advanced targeting made possible by Big Data analytics; due in part to audience selectivity, TV is the second-ranked advertising medium based on revenues (after digital) as it entails about 25 percent of all media advertising revenue in the United States—amounting to $60 billion.[41]

13-4c Disadvantages of Television

Television has great capabilities as an advertising medium, but it is not without limitations. Some of these limitations are serious enough to significantly detract from the power of TV advertising.

Fleeting Message

One problem with the sight and sound of a TV advertisement is that it is gone in an instant. The fleeting nature of a TV message, as opposed to a print ad (which a receiver can contemplate), makes message impact difficult. Some advertisers

invest huge amounts of money in the production of TV ads to overcome this disadvantage.

High Absolute Cost

Although the cost per contact of TV advertising is the best of all traditional media, the absolute cost may be the worst. The average cost of airtime for a single 30-second TV spot during prime time is about $285,000, with the most popular shows, like first-run episodes of *This is Us*, commanding as much as $476,000 for a 30-second spot.[42] Remember this is prime-time pricing. Off-prime-time slots go for a more modest $100,000-$115,000 for 30 seconds.[43] In addition, the average cost of producing a quality 30-second TV spot is around $300,000 to $400,000, or even higher. These costs make TV advertising prohibitively expensive for many advertisers. Of course, large national consumer products companies—for which TV advertising is best suited anyway—find the absolute cost acceptable for the coverage, reach, and repetition advantages discussed earlier.

Poor Geographic Selectivity

Although programming can be developed to attract specific audiences, program transmission cannot target small geographic areas nearly as well. For a national advertiser that wants to target a city market, the reach of a TV broadcast is often too broad. Similarly, for a local retailer that wants to use TV to reach local segments, the TV transmission is likely to reach a several-hundred-mile radius—which will increase the advertiser's cost with little likelihood of drawing patrons. But there is good news on the horizon for TV advertisers seeking to improve targeting; newer and more sophisticated tools are being developed and are improving TV's overall geographic selectivity.

Poor Audience Attitude and Attentiveness

Since the inception of TV advertising, consumers have bemoaned the intrusive nature of commercials. Just when a movie is reaching its thrilling conclusion, on come the ads. The involuntary and frequent intrusion of advertisements on TV has made TV advertising the most distrusted form of advertising among consumers. In one of the few surveys tracking consumer sentiment, only 17 percent of consumers surveyed felt that TV advertising affected them in their purchase of a new car, compared with 48 percent who claimed that direct mail advertising was a factor in their decision.[44] But be aware that it is not fundamentally the job of TV advertising to motivate an immediate purchase. Image and awareness building are also key objectives of TV ads.

Because of this generally negative attitude toward TV ads, consumers have developed ways to avoid watching them. Making a trip to the refrigerator or chatting with fellow viewers are the preferred low-tech ways to avoid exposure. On the low-tech side, **channel grazing**, or using a remote control to monitor programming on other channels while an advertisement is being broadcast, is one way to avoid commercials. It will come as no surprise that these and other avoidance behaviors increase when, among other things, audiences are repeatedly exposed to the same ad.[45]

One first way that consumers avoided TV advertising is with **digital video recorders (DVRs)** that stored hundreds of hours of TV programming for viewing at the user's convenience. Consumers frequently used these devices to skip commercials and watch only the programming. As a result, more brand placement within programming and those little "runners" at the bottom of the screen during programs are ways for brands to reach users who aim to skip or minimize exposure to TV advertising. Today, one of the ways consumers avoid or minimize ads while watching TV shows is to watch the shows via a subscription-based streaming service, such as Netflix. While the technology has evolved, the concept that consumers may eagerly avoid advertising while TV content consumption is constant and important for advertising professionals to consider.

Clutter

All the advantages of TV as an advertising medium have created one significant disadvantage: clutter, with many minutes per hour of programming devoted to advertising. No wonder 65 percent of a surveyed group of consumers felt that they were "constantly bombarded with too much" advertising.[46] By one estimate, viewers who watch ad-free streaming programs on Apple TV+ are avoiding 25 minutes of commercials per day—over the course of a year, more than one full day.[47] Critics of TV advertising have also raised an issue beyond clutter. There are those who feel that TV advertising has a unique power over its viewers. As such, there is occasionally a call for banning certain types of advertising all together.

13-4d Measuring Television Audiences

Television audience measurements identify the size and composition of audiences for different TV programming. Advertisers choose where to buy TV time based on these factors. These measures also determine the cost for TV time. The larger the audience or the more attractive the composition, the more costly the time will be.

The following are brief summaries of the information used to measure TV audiences.

TV Households

TV households is an estimate of the number of households that are in a market and own a TV. Since more than 98 percent of all households in the United States own a TV, the number of total households and the number of TV households are virtually the same, more than 120 million.

Households Using TV

Households using TV (HUT), also referred to as sets in use, is a measure of the number of households tuned to a TV program during a particular time period.

Program Rating

A **program rating** is the percentage of TV households that are in a market and are tuned to a specific program during a specific time period. Expressed as a formula, program rating is:

$$\text{Program rating} = \frac{\text{TV households tuned to a program}}{\text{Total TV households in the market}}$$

A **ratings point** indicates that 1 percent of all the TV households in an area were tuned to the program measured. If an episode of a popular program like *The Bachelorette* is watched by 19.5 million households, then the program rating would be calculated as follows:

$$\frac{The\ Bachelorette}{\text{rating}} = \frac{19,500,000}{95,900,000} = 20\ \text{rating}$$

The program rating is the best-known measure of TV audience, and it is the basis for the rates TV stations charge for advertising on different programs. Recall that it is also the way advertisers develop their media plans from the standpoint of calculating reach and frequency estimates, such as gross rating points.

Share of Audience

Share of audience provides a measure of the proportion of households that are using TV during a specific time period and are tuned to a particular program. If 65 million households are using their TVs during *The Bachelorette*'s time slot, and that program attracts 19.5 million viewers, then the share of audience is:

$$\frac{The\ Bachelorette}{\text{share}} = \frac{\text{TV households tuned to a program}}{\text{Total TV households using TV}}$$

$$= \frac{19,500,000}{65,000,000} = 30\ \text{share}$$

Last, a more basic but useful way to measure program viewing via streaming, is simply the cumulative hours spent by consumers on each show. Netflix, for example, is now measuring the amount of time spent in hours on the streaming platform as a newer way for program measurement. This way, it is possible to say which shows or movies are the most popular at any given time.

13-4e The Future of Television

Streaming is likely a big part of the future of television. The prospects for TV's future include greater viewer participation in programming, as is the case with Fox's *The Masked Singer*. Equally important is the "TV everywhere" concept raised earlier in the chapter. But remember: A significant percentage of households are also "cutting the cord" by using entertainment-streaming sites to substitute for cable TV, which affects the size and composition of cable TV audiences and again this streaming media consumption can be measured with a simple total viewing hours accumulated.[48]

Another issue in understanding today's TV advertising environment relates to "ad loads" that consumers are willing to tolerate while watching on their TVs versus the much lighter ad load of online viewership. For more than a decade, the ad load in broadcast TV has hovered between 10 and 12 minutes, compared with the ad load in cable TV, which is between 11 and 13 minutes. Some networks are testing lighter ad loads to see whether viewership will be affected by having fewer or briefer commercial periods or commercials interspersed with content related to programming.[49] This lighter ad load is seen as unsustainable in order for online TV to achieve profitability. But the question remains—will heavier loads reduce online viewership? Or can online TV devise more engaging and interactive experiences to retain viewers for brand messaging? And it is important to keep in mind that consumers especially dislike ads that interrupt their online/mobile experience.[50] At the same time, the industry is experimenting with shorter TV ads.

The "partnership" between TV and social media has many possibilities. Analysts say that TV can benefit the most by virtue of advertisers using social media as a "megaphone" for brands—engaging consumers in social media driven by TV advertising.[51] The pioneering effort in social TV was Fox Network's *Glee*.[52] Now many TV commercials carry a hashtag or other social elements encouraging interactivity and generating word of mouth.[53] Even not showing an ad can spark interactivity. Think of the brands that have invited consumers to go online to view commercials that they weren't allowed to air during the Super Bowl.

Although it is hard to predict what the future will bring, TV is very likely to hold its own as an entertainment and information medium. The convenience, low cost, and diversity of programming make TV an ideal medium for consumers. As a result, TV, despite its limitations, will continue to be an important part of the IBP mix for many advertisers.

LO 5

13-5 Radio

Radio plays an integral role in the media plans of some of the most astute advertisers. Radio advertising also has key advantages. The ability to reach consumers in multiple locations and the creative power of radio rank as important communications opportunities. Because of the unique features of radio, advertisers invest about $17.8 billion annually in radio advertising to reach national and local audiences in the US and Canada.[54] There are good reasons why advertisers of all sorts use radio to reach target audiences. Let's turn our attention to the different radio options.

13-5a Radio Categories

Radio offers an advertiser several possibilities for reaching target audiences. The basic split of national and local radio broadcasts presents an obvious geographic choice. More specifically, though, advertisers can choose among the following categories, each with specific characteristics: networks, syndication, AM versus FM, satellite, and streaming.

Networks

Radio networks operate much like TV networks in that they deliver programming via satellite to affiliate stations across the United States. Network radio programming concentrates on news, sports, business reports, and short features. Some of the more successful radio networks that draw large audiences are ABC, CNN, and AP News Network.

Syndication

Radio syndication provides complete programs to stations on a contract basis. Large syndicators offer stations complete 24-hour-a-day programming packages that totally relieve a station of any programming effort. In addition to full-day programming options, they also supply individual programs, such as talk shows. Large syndication organizations such as Westwood One place advertising within programming, making syndication a good outlet for advertisers.

AM and FM Radio

AM radio stations send signals that use amplitude modulation (AM) and operate on the AM radio dial at signal designations 540 to 1600. AM was the foundation of radio until the 1970s. Today, AM radio broadcasts, even the new stereo AM transmissions, cannot match the sound quality of FM. Thus, most AM stations focus on local community broadcasting or news and talk formats that do not require high-quality audio. Talk radio has, in many ways, been the salvation of AM radio. FM radio stations transmit using frequency modulation (FM). FM radio transmission is of a much higher quality. Because of this, FM radio has attracted the wide range of music formats that most listeners prefer. AM/FM broadcast is now available online and through smartphones, providing mobile advertising opportunities to advertisers. Note how radio's primetime is daytime (10:00 a.m. to 7:00 p.m.), and the Radio Advertising Bureau notes this fact on its webpage (Exhibit 13.9).

Exhibit 13.9 ▶ The Radio Advertising Bureau, www.rab.com gives information on radio advertising and notes some key facts for radio.

Satellite Radio

Now more than 15 years old, satellite radio features a variety of programming, more crisp and clear sound reproduction, access to radio in places where broadcast does not reach, and limited or no advertising, depending on the station. Sirius/XM satellite radio has more than 34 million monthly subscribers and provides hundreds of channels of news, sports, music, and entertainment programming in the United States and Canada.[55] Satellite radio is primarily installed in consumers' vehicles, although there is some in-home installation as well.

Internet/Mobile Radio

Internet radio has a wide and enthusiastic following. Examples include Spotify, iHeart Media, and Pandora. Sites like Pandora allow listeners to access radio stations or build their own "stations" that play listeners' preferred music genres and playlists and Pandora's pricing starts at $1500 per month for advertisers.[56] Traditional radio stations often stream their content free online, including the ads. Some digital radio is offered on a subscription basis, some is free; and the mix is constantly changing in line with consumer preferences and media company strategies. Mobile access once again provides advertisers the opportunity to reach target audiences while they are at the gym, on the train, jogging, or taking a walk in the park.

13-5b Types of Radio Advertising

Advertisers have three basic choices in radio advertising: local spot radio advertising, network radio advertising, or national spot radio advertising. Very few dollars are invested in advertising time on radio websites, aside from streamed radio station content, at this time. Local spot radio advertising attracts 80 percent of all radio advertising dollars in a year. In **local spot radio advertising,** an advertiser places advertisements directly with individual stations rather than

with a network or syndicate. Local spot radio dominates the three classes of radio advertising because there are more than 10,000 individual radio stations in the United States, giving advertisers a wide range of choices. And local spot radio reaches well-defined geographic audiences, making it the ideal choice for local retailers.

Network radio advertising is advertising placed within national network programs. Since there are only a few network radio programs being broadcast, only about $600 million a year is invested by advertisers in this format.

The last option, **national spot radio advertising**, offers an advertiser the opportunity to place advertising in nationally syndicated radio programming. An advertiser can reach millions of listeners nationwide on more than 5,500 radio stations by contracting with Premiere Networks, for example.

13-5c Advantages of Radio

Radio has some distinct advantages over newspapers, magazines, and TV.

Cost

On both a per-contact and absolute basis, radio is often the most cost-effective medium available to an advertiser. A 30-second network radio spot often varies by city, frequency (how many spots are purchased), time of day aired, demand, and most importantly by the number of active listeners. While these factors make it difficult to generalize an "average radio ad" price, it is clear that radio is a bargain compared with the other media we've discussed. In addition, production costs for preparing radio ads are quite low; an ad often costs nothing to prepare if the spot is read live during a local broadcast.

Reach and Frequency

Radio offers extremely wide exposure, with more than 90 percent of the population over the age of 12 (243 million people in the United States) listening to radio in some form on a weekly basis.[57]

It reaches consumers in their homes, cars, offices, and backyards, even while they exercise. The low cost of radio time gives advertisers the opportunity to frequently repeat messages at a low absolute cost and cost per contact.

Target Audience Selectivity

Radio can selectively target audiences on a geographic, demographic, and psychographic/lifestyle basis. The narrow transmission of local radio stations gives advertisers the best opportunity to reach well-defined geographic audiences. For a local merchant with one store, this is an ideal opportunity. Radio programming formats and different **dayparts** (i.e., times during the day) also allow target audience selectivity. In addition, various radio formats such as hard rock, oldies, new age, easy listening, country, classical, news, and talk radio formats all attract different audiences.

Flexibility and Timeliness

Radio is the most flexible medium because of short closing periods for submitting an ad. This means an advertiser can wait until close to the air date before submitting. With this flexibility, advertisers can take advantage of special events or unique competitive opportunities in a timely fashion. Also, on-air personalities can read altered copy on the day of a scheduled ad.

Creative Opportunities

Even though radio may be unidimensional in sensory stimulation, it can still have powerful creative impact. Radio has been described as the "theater of the mind." Additionally, the musical formats that attract audiences to radio stations can also attract attention to radio ads. Research has revealed that audiences who favor certain music may be more prone to listen to an ad that uses songs they recognize and like.

13-5d Disadvantages of Radio

As good as radio can be, it also suffers from some severe limitations as an advertising medium. Advertising strategists must recognize these disadvantages when deciding what role radio should play in an integrated brand promotion program.

Poor Audience Attentiveness

Just because radio reaches audiences almost everywhere doesn't mean that everyone is paying attention. Radio is often described as "verbal wallpaper." It provides a comfortable background distraction while a consumer does something else—hardly an ideal level of attentiveness for advertising communication. Consumers who are listening and traveling in a car often switch stations when an ad comes on and divide their attention between the radio and the road.

Creative Limitations

Although the theater of the mind may be a wonderful creative opportunity, taking advantage of that opportunity can be difficult. The audio-only nature of radio communication is a tremendous creative compromise. An advertiser whose product depends on demonstration or visual impact is at a loss when it comes to radio. And like its TV counterpart, a radio message creates a fleeting impression that is often gone in an instant.

Fragmented Audiences

The large number of stations that try to attract the same audience in a market has created tremendous fragmentation. Think about your own local radio market. There are probably four or five different stations that play the kind of music you like. Or consider that in the past few years, more than 1,000 radio stations in the United States have adopted the talk-radio format. This fragmentation means that the percentage of listeners tuned to any one station is likely very small.

Chaotic Buying Procedures

For an advertiser who wants to include radio as part of a national advertising program, the buying process can be sheer chaos. Since national networks and syndicated broadcasts do not reach every geographic market, an advertiser has to buy time in individual markets on a station-by-station basis. This could involve dozens of negotiations and individual contracts.

13-5e The Future of Radio

Satellite radio generally minimizes advertising clutter and offers listeners multiple, detailed choices to match their listening preferences. This is a huge advantage along with the increased audio quality, which is also a factor in HD (high-definition) radio. Also, there has been a large degree of consolidation in the traditional radio market. Opportunities for consumers lie in the consistency of radio programming quality, and advertisers have an easier time buying and placing radio spots. In addition, access to radio via digital devices is changing where and when consumers listen and how actively they listen. At the same time, advertisers are looking at the impact on reach and exposure as subscription-based streaming radio gains ground.

In summary, there are many reasons while the more traditional mass media types such as radio, TV, newspapers, and magazines are important for brands to blend in their media portfolios along with digital and social media. As long as there is a solid "fit" for both the media channel/media vehicle and the brand, there should be positive outcomes for media companies and advertised brands alike.[58]

Summary

1. Explain some considerations of the present and future of traditional mass media.

The changes in the advertising industry are tangible and dramatic with respect to advertisers' use of traditional media—newspapers, magazines, TV, and radio. Consumers have turned to multiple new sources of information and entertainment and are more active in their media choices and exert more control over content exposure. Streaming is one example of this, which is important because consumers can more easily avoid or reduce TV ad exposures. Advertisers are therefore turning more often to digital, social, and mobile media that offer new, different, and cost-effective ways to reach target markets—including when those target markets are on the move with their mobile devices. In addition, digital media allow advertisers to rapidly make changes in campaigns that might take months to accomplish with traditional media. Also, if the advertiser chooses, an Internet campaign can easily be a global campaign—a monumental task in traditional media. Although advertisers are shifting billions of dollars out of traditional media and into digital media, traditional media still command a significant portion of advertising budgets.

2. Identify the advantages and disadvantages of newspapers/digital newspapers, identify newspaper advertising categories, and consider the future of newspapers as a medium.

Newspapers can be categorized by target audience, geographic coverage, and frequency of publication. As a media class, newspapers provide an excellent means for reaching large and local audiences with informative advertising messages. Precise timing of message delivery can be achieved at modest expenditure levels. But for products that demand creative and colorful executions, this medium simply cannot deliver. Newspaper costs are typically transmitted via rate cards and are primarily a function of a paper's readership levels. Traditional newspapers are offering digital editions and focusing on hyper-localism as a competitive advantage.

3. Explain the advantages and disadvantages of magazines as a media class, identify magazine advertising categories, and consider the future of magazines as a medium.

Because of their specific editorial content, magazines can be effective in attracting distinctive groups of readers with common interests. Thus, magazines can be effective tools for reaching specific market segments. Also, magazines facilitate a wide range of creative executions and excellent color reproduction. Of course, the selectivity advantage turns into a disadvantage for advertisers trying to achieve high-reach levels. Clutter is an issue, along with long lead times for advertising. Costs of magazine ad space can vary dramatically because of the wide range of circulation levels associated with different types of magazines. Like newspapers, magazines are adapting to the digital/interactive era, offering both editorial content and advertising content formatted for digital devices and generating revenues from print and digital subscriptions.

4. Identify the advantages and disadvantages of television as a media class, identify television advertising categories, describe audience measurement for television, and consider the future of television as a medium.

The four basic forms of TV are network, cable, syndicated, and local TV. Television's principal advantage is the potential for almost limitless possibilities in creative execution, an extraordinary tool for affecting consumers' perceptions of a brand. Also, it can be an efficient device for reaching huge audiences; however, the absolute costs for reaching these audiences can be high. Lack of audience interest and involvement can limit the effectiveness of commercials in this medium, and technology like DVRs and ad-free streaming make TV advertising nonexistent for many viewers. As with any medium, advertising rates will vary as a function of the size and composition of the audience that is watching. Advertisers look at households using TV (HUT), program rating, ratings points, and share of audience. With "TV everywhere," including streaming (e.g., Hulu, Netflix, Disney +) and VOD options, advertisers can reach target markets in numerous ways and encourage interactivity, although ad load remains a consideration affecting viewership. Netflix, for example, is now measuring the amount of time spent in minutes on the streaming platform as a newer way for program measurement.

5. Explain the advantages and disadvantages of radio as a media class, identify radio advertising categories, and consider the future of radio as a medium.

Radio categories include networks, syndication, AM and FM, satellite radio, and digital radio. Advertisers can choose from three basic types of radio advertising: local spot, network radio, or national spot advertising. Radio can be a cost-effective medium, and because of the wide diversity in radio programming, it can be an excellent tool for reaching well-defined audiences. Poor listener attentiveness is a drawback to radio, as are fragmented audiences. The audio-only format places constraints on creative execution. Radio ad rates are driven by the average number of listeners tuned to a station at specific times throughout the day. Buying and placing ads for radio is becoming easier due to programmatic media buying and increasing consolidation in the industry. Access to streaming radio and other developments are changing where and when consumers listen and how actively they listen, which in turn is impacting advertisers' decisions about this medium.

Key Terms

absolute cost	households using TV (HUT)	pay-for-inquiry advertising model
barter syndication	hyper-localism	preprinted insert
cable TV	lead time	program rating
channel grazing	local spot radio advertising	radio networks
classified advertising	local TV	radio syndication
closed circuit	media kit	ratings point
dayparts	narrowcasting	satellite
digital video recorder (DVR)	national spot radio advertising	share of audience
display advertising	network radio advertising	television syndication
editorial and entertainment content	network TV	TV households
first-run syndication	off-network syndication	video on demand (VOD)
free-standing insert (FSI)	pass-along readership	

Endnotes

1. Edward Craig, "When Programmatic Meets Artificial Intelligence ... The Future Begins," *Campaign US,* March 2, 2017, http://www.campaignlive.com/article/when-programmatic-meets-artificial-intelligence-future-begins/1426070.

2. Tony Silber, "Magazine Media's Half-Full Glass," *Folio,* February 17, 2017, http://www.foliomag.com/magazine-medias-half-full-glass.

3. Gian M. Fulgoni and Andrew Lipsman, "Measuring Television in the Programmatic Age," *Journal of Advertising Research* 57, no. 1 (2017), 10–14.

4. Thomas H. Davenport and Judah Phillips, "The Future of Marketing Automation," *Applied Marketing Analytics* 2, no. 3 (2016), 213–224.

5. Suman Bhattacharyya, "Digital Ads to Overtake Traditional Ads in U.S. Local Markets by 2018," *Advertising Age,* October 26, 2016, http://adage.com/article/cmo-strategy/local-ads-digital-2018-bia-kelsey/306468/; George Slefo, "Desktop Search Ads Fall for First Time, IAB Says, as Digital Ad Revenue Sets Another Record," *Advertising Age,* November 1, 2016, http://adage.com/article/digital/iab-digital-ad-revenue-breaks-record/306557/#.

6. George Slefo, "Time Inc. Moves to Acquire Programmatic Advertising Platform Adelphic," *Advertising Age,* January 23, 2017, http://adage.com/article/digital/time-moves-acquire-adelphic/307657.

7. Kacy K. Kim, Jerome D. Williams, and Gary B. Wilcox, "'Kid Tested, Mother Approved': The Relationship Between Advertising Expenditures and 'Most-Loved' Brands," *International Journal of Advertising* 35, no. 1 (2016), 42–60.

8. Historical information about the Absolut Vodka campaign was adapted from information in Nicholas Ind, "Absolut Vodka in the U.S.," in *Great Advertising Campaigns* (Lincolnwood, IL: NTC Business Books, 1993), 15–32; and Ethan Craft, "Absolut Debuts New 'Sex Responsibly' Campaign to Highlight Importance of Consent," *Ad Age,* February 14, 2020, https://adage.com/article/news/absolut-debuts-new-sex-responsibly-campaign-highlight-importance-consent/2237241

9. Michael Barthel, "State of the News Media 2016—Newspapers: Fact Sheet," *Pew Research Center,* June 15, 2016, http://www.journalism.org/2016/06/15/newspapers-fact-sheet.

10. Ibid.

11. "The Power of Newspapers, Print and Digital" *Mansi Media,* 2019 https://mansimedia.com/expertise/newspaper-data/.

12. Damian Radcliffe and Christopher Ali, "If Small Newspapers Are Going to Survive, They'll Have to Be More Than Passive Observers to the News," *Nieman Lab,* February 2, 2017, http://www.niemanlab.org/2017/02/if-small-newspapers-are-going-to-survive-theyll-have-to-be-more-than-passive-observers-to-the-news.

13. Laurie Sullivan, "Up To $35B of Co-Op Ad Funds Go Unclaimed Annually," *MediaPost,* November 7, 2016, http://www.mediapost.com/publications/article/288514/up-to-35b-of-co-op-ad-funds-go-unclaimed-annually.html.

14. Tien Tzuo, "Why Newspaper Subscriptions Are on the Rise," *TechCrunch,* March 4, 2017, https://techcrunch.com/2017/03/04/why-newspaper-subscriptions-are-on-the-rise.

15. Michael Kinsley, "The World in 2010," *The Economist,* January 2010, 50.

16. Nat Ives, "Pay-for-Inquiry Ad Model Gains Modest Traction at Newspapers," *Advertising Age,* February 8, 2010, 2, 21; Rance Crain, "Newspapers Ought to Embrace the Pay-per-Inquiry Ad Model," *Advertising Age,* February 12, 2010, 12.

17. "Ad Age's Magazines of the Year 2016: See All the Winners," *Advertising Age,* December 19, 2016, http://adage.com/article/media/ad-age-s-magazines-year-20016/307205.

18. Jack Neff, "Sweeping CPG Study Finds Magazines Deliver Biggest Bang for Buck, Digital Video Lags," *Advertising Age,* June 14, 2016, http://adage.com/article/media/sweeping-cpg-study-finds-magazines-digital-video-worst/304491.

19. Hannah Edensohr, "Study: 82% of Food Magazine Readers Are Influenced by the Content (Ads Included!)," *B&T (Australia),* November 22, 2016, http://www.bandt.com.au/media/study-82-of-food-magazine-readers-are-influenced-by-the-content-ads-included.

20. See, for example, "Magazine Ad Page Leaders, January–September 2014," *Advertising Age,* October 22, 2014, http://adage.com/article/datacenter/pib-index-page/106442.

21. David Gianatasio, "Ad of the Day: This Porsche Magazine Ad Brings the 911 to Life as a Floating Hologram," *Adweek,* March 30, 2016, http://www.adweek.com/brand-marketing/ad-day-porsche-magazine-ad-brings-911-life-floating-hologram-170495.

22. Alex Witchel, "Ground Beef, Yes; Sumac, No. This Editor Knows What Food Magazine Readers Want," *Washington Post,* July 5, 2016, https://www.washingtonpost.com/lifestyle/food/ground-beef-yes-sumac-no-this-editor-knows-what-food-magazine-readers-want/2016/07/01/b5e8a884-3d6e-11e6-80bc-d06711fd2125_story.html?utm_term=.24ee18428f78.

23. Charlotte Druckman, "The Art of Preservation, in a New Food Magazine," *New York Times,* August 10, 2016, https://www.nytimes.com/2016/08/10/t-magazine/food/cured-magazine-preservation-darra-goldstein.html?_r=0; Suzanna Caldwell, "New Magazine Hopes to Capitalize on the Alaska Food Movement," *Alaska Dispatch News,* June 21, 2016, https://www.adn.com/culture/food-drink/2016/06/21/new-magazine-hopes-to-capitalize-on-the-alaska-food-movement.

24. Data drawn from *"Hearst Media Solutions"* Hearst, 2021, https://www.hearst.com/hearst-media-solutions.

25. Andrea Ciceri, et al., "A Neuroscientific Method for Assessing Effectiveness of Digital vs. Print Ads," *Journal of Advertising Research* 60, no. 1 (2019), 71–86.

26. Patrick Barwise, et al., "Why Do People Watch So Much Television and Video?" *Journal of Advertising Research* 60, no. 2 (2019), 121–134.

27. Ivan A. Guitart, and Stefan Stremersch, "The Impact of Informational and Emotional Television Ad Content on Online Search and Sales," *Journal of Marketing Research* 58, no. 2 (2020), 299–320.

28. Andrew Gebhart, "You Probably Don't Have as Many TVs as You Used To," *CDNet,* February 28, 2017, https://www.cnet.com/news/you-probably-dont-have-as-many-tvs-as-you-used-to.

29. Mocia Marie Zorrilla, "TV Ratings: CBS' Super Bowl LV Telecast Down From Last Year, Draws About 92 Million TV Viewers," *Variety,* February 9, 2021 https://variety.com/2021/tv/news/tv-ratings-cbs-super-bowl-lv-game-1234903247/.

30. Kelly Main, "Everything You Need to Know About TV Advertising Costs," *Fit Small Business,* January 21, 2021, https://fitsmallbusiness.com/tv-advertising//.

31. Alex Sherman, "Media Executives Are Finally Accepting the Decline of Cable TV as They Plot a New Path Forward," *CNBC News,* October 24, 2020 https://www.cnbc.com/2020/10/24/big-media-companies-reorganize-for-world-of-50-million-tv-subscribers.html.

32. Jeanine Poggi, "Why Cable Has Become More Like Broadcast TV," *Advertising Age,* May 14, 2012, 16.

33. Gerry Smith, "Home Is Where the Heart (of Cable) Is," *Business Week,* January 9, 2017, 18–19.

34. Tim Baysinger, "For Ad VOD Players, Success Is Blend of Linear, Digital Models," *Broadcasting & Cable,* August 15, 2016, http://www.broadcastingcable.com/news/currency/ad-vod-players-success-blend-linear-digital-models/158816.

35. Ibid; and Shalini Ramachandran, "Hulu Reaches Deal With CBS for Live-Streaming Content," *Wall Street Journal,* January 4, 2017, https://www.wsj.com/articles/cbs-nearing-a-deal-with-hulu-for-live-streaming-service-1483549218.

36. Jeanine Poggi, "Mondelez Strikes Deal With Fox to Innovate Ad Model," *Advertising Age,* July 25, 2016, http://adage.com/article/media/mondelez-strikes-deal-fox-innovate-ad-model/305105.

37. Sarah Perez, "YouTube Unveils YouTube TV, Its Live TV Streaming Service," *TechCrunch,* February 28, 2017, https://techcrunch.com/2017/02/28/youtube-launches-youtube-tv-its-live-tv-streaming-service.

38. Norris I. Bruce, et al., "Communicating Brands in Television Advertising." *Journal of Marketing Research* 57, no. 2 (2020), 236–256.

39. Ashley Rodriguez, "The Curved and 3D TV Revolution Is Already Dead," *Quartz Media,* January 5, 2017, https://qz.com/878798/should-you-buy-a-curved-or-3d-tv-nope-the-revolution-is-already-dead.

40. Julia Stoll, "Number of TV households worldwide from 2010 to 2019," *Statista* January 13, 2021, https://www.statista.com/statistics/268695/number-of-tv-households-worldwide/; and Toni Fitzgerald, "For The First Time In Almost 10 Years, Time Watching TV Is Up," *Forbes,* April 28, 2020, https://www.forbes.com/sites/tonifitzgerald/2020/04/28/for-the-first-time-in-almost-10-years-time-watching-tv-is-up/?sh=7ae79fce20a8.

41. Mike Shields, "Advertising on Streaming TV Devices Is About to Get More Targeted," *Wall Street Journal,* February 27, 2017, https://www.wsj.com/articles/advertising-on-streaming-tv-devices-is-about-to-get-more-targeted-1488193202; and A. Guttman, "TV Advertising in the U.S.," *Statista,* April 14, 2021, https://www.statista.com/topics/5052/television-advertising-in-the-us/#dossierKeyfigures.

42. Kelly Main, "Everything You Need to Know About TV Advertising Costs" *Fit Small Business,* January 21, 2021, https://fitsmallbusiness.com/tv-advertising/; and Julia Stoll, "Cost of a 30-second TV spot during This Is Us in the United States from 2016/17 to 2020/21 TV season" *Statista,* January 13, 2021 https://www.statista.com/statistics/756867/this-is-us-ad-price-usa/.

43. A. Guttman "Average cost of a 30-second commercial on TV in the United States from 2014 to 2019," *Statista,* November 15, 2019 https://www.statista.com/statistics/302200/primetime-tv-cost-commercial-usa.

44. Jean Halliday, "Study Claims TV Advertising Doesn't Work on Car Buyers," *Advertising Age,* October 13, 2003, 8.

45. Kenneth C. Wilbur, "Advertising Content and Television Advertising Avoidance," *Journal of Media Economics* 29, no. 2 (2016), 51–72.

46. 2004. Yankelovich Partners poll, cited in Gary Ruskin, "A 'Deal Spiral of Disrespect,'" *Advertising Age,* April 26, 2004, 18.

47. Travis M. Andrews, "Six Days' Worth of Commercials: That's How Much Watching Netflix Instead of Cable Saves the Average TV Viewer Annually, *Washington Post,* May 11, 2016, https://www.washingtonpost.com/news/morning-mix/wp/2016/05/11/six-days-worth-of-commercials-thats-how-much-watching-netflix-instead-of-cable-saves-the-average-tv-viewer-annually/?utm_term=.982847133f91.

48. Oriana Schwindt, "Cord Cutting Accelerates: Study Finds 25% of U.S. Homes Don't Have Pay TV Service," *Variety,* July 15, 2016, http://variety.com/2016/biz/news/cord-cutting-accelerates-americans-cable-pay-report-1201814276; and John Glenday, "Netflix Pulls Back Its Ratings Curtain in Transparency Drive," *The Drum,* Nov. 17, 2021, https://www.thedrum.com/news/2021/11/17/netflix-pulls-back-its-ratings-curtain-transparency-drive

49. Jeanine Poggi, "How Ad Tech Just Might Save TV," *Advertising Age,* February 21, 2017, http://adage.com/article/media/ad-tech-save-tv/307995.

50. John McDermott, "Mobile Ads More Disruptive Than TV Spots: Consumers Especially Dislike Ads That Interrupt the App Experience," *Advertising Age,* December 12, 2012, www.adage.com.

51. Mike Mikho, "Why Social Media Needs TV and TV Needs Social Media," *Advertising Age,* October 15, 2012, www.adage.com.

52. Simon Dumenco, "Believe the Hype? Four Things Social TV Can Actually Do," *Advertising Age,* April 16, 2012, 4.

53. For more about this topic, see Beth L. Fossen and David A. Schweidel, "Television Advertising and Online Word-of-Mouth:

An Empirical Investigation of Social TV Activity," *Marketing Science* (2016), 105–123.

54. "US Online and Traditional Media Advertising Outlook, 2020–2024" *Marketing Charts*, September 28, 2020, https://www.marketingcharts.com/advertising-trends-114887; and Aaron Michelon, et al., "A New Benchmark for Mechanical Avoidance of Radio Advertising," *Journal of Advertising Research* 60, no. 4 (2020), 407–416.

55. "Number of Sirius XM subscribers in the United States from 1st quarter 2011 to 1st quarter 2021," *Statista*, June 30, 2021, https://www.statista.com/statistics/252812/number-of-sirius-xms-subscribers/.

56. Aaron Michelon, et al. "A New Benchmark for Mechanical Avoidance of Radio Advertising." *Journal of Advertising Research* 60, no. 4 (2020), 407–416; and Lindsay Haskell, "How Much does Radio Advertising Cost?", Fast Capital 360, October 13, 2021, https://www.fastcapital360.com/blog/radio-advertising-costs/.

57. "How America Listens: The American Audio Landscape," *Insights*, April 5, 2018, https://www.nielsen.com/us/en/insights/article/2018/how-america-listens-the-american-audio-landscape/.

58. Scheinbaum, Angeline Close, Russell Lacey, and Minnette Drumwright, "Social Responsibility and Event-Sponsor Portfolio Fit: Positive Outcomes for Events and Brand Sponsors," *European Journal of Marketing* 53, no. 2 (2019), 138–163.

Media Planning: Advertising and IBP in Digital, Social, and Mobile Media

Learning Objectives

After reading and thinking about this chapter, you will be able to do the following:

1 Describe the synergistic role of digital, social, and mobile media in advertising and IBP along with the options available to brands in these media.

2 See the importance in virtual identity for consumers and brands online.

3 Discuss the basics of digital advertising and search.

4 Understand the basics of e-commerce as related to IBP and how it can stem from online advertising, social media, mobile, and search.

5 Identify the advantages of digital, social, and mobile media for implementing advertising and IBP campaigns, along with the dark side of social media, such as security and privacy concerns.

6 Understand how to synergize with different IBP tools.

LO 1

14-1 The Role of Digital, Social, and Mobile Media for IBP Synergy

The role of digital, social, and mobile media in advertising is substantial. These media are bringing a new vernacular to consumers. Friend me. Upload it to TikTok. Have a client Zoom meeting. Tweet that. Saw it on Insta. Facetime tonight? Got a Skype interview. These online terms and brands have changed online consumer behavior, advertising, and branding—as well as the way you search for and obtain a career in advertising.[1]

It is crucial to understand how consumers think, feel, and respond to social media, online advertising, mobile marketing, and e-commerce. Online advertisers want to know where and why consumers go online and how that relates to where they spend or shop offline. Marketers for nonprofit organizations also seek to understand online consumer behavior so they can raise awareness and make online donating easy. The framework diagram in Exhibit 14.1 shows how planning for digital/social/mobile media fits within the overall media process for advertising and IBP.

Online advertisers understand the importance of embracing channels like consumer blogs, Snapchat, Pinterest, Facebook, Instagram, Twitter, LinkedIn, YouTube, TikTok, and other social media platforms to enhance their online presence. Some of the world's leading brand visionaries, as well as new brands, align their corporate websites and digital/social/mobile media objectives based on consumer behavior to enhance their return on

Exhibit 14.1 ▶ Consider this framework diagram for digital, social, and mobile advertising and the overall importance of integrating these digital platforms with traditional media for strong brands.

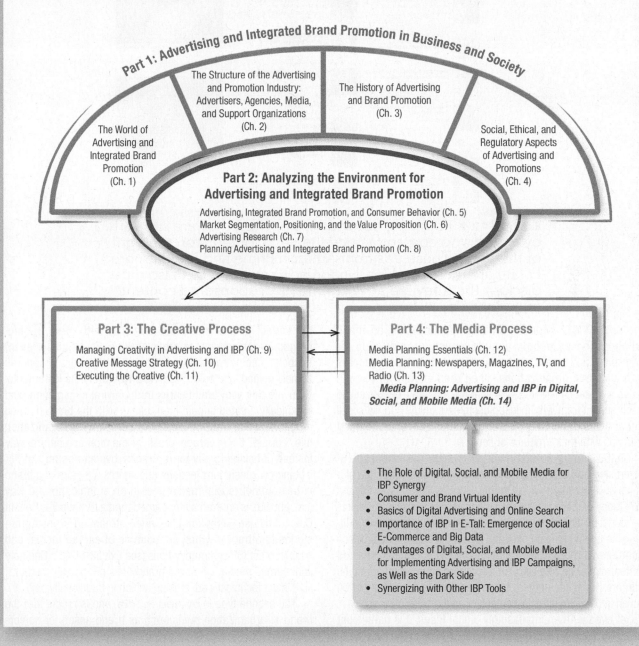

Part 1: Advertising and Integrated Brand Promotion in Business and Society

The World of Advertising and Integrated Brand Promotion (Ch. 1)

The Structure of the Advertising and Promotion Industry: Advertisers, Agencies, Media, and Support Organizations (Ch. 2)

The History of Advertising and Brand Promotion (Ch. 3)

Social, Ethical, and Regulatory Aspects of Advertising and Promotions (Ch. 4)

Part 2: Analyzing the Environment for Advertising and Integrated Brand Promotion

Advertising, Integrated Brand Promotion, and Consumer Behavior (Ch. 5)
Market Segmentation, Positioning, and the Value Proposition (Ch. 6)
Advertising Research (Ch. 7)
Planning Advertising and Integrated Brand Promotion (Ch. 8)

Part 3: The Creative Process

Managing Creativity in Advertising and IBP (Ch. 9)
Creative Message Strategy (Ch. 10)
Executing the Creative (Ch. 11)

Part 4: The Media Process

Media Planning Essentials (Ch. 12)
Media Planning: Newspapers, Magazines, TV, and Radio (Ch. 13)
Media Planning: Advertising and IBP in Digital, Social, and Mobile Media (Ch. 14)

- The Role of Digital, Social, and Mobile Media for IBP Synergy
- Consumer and Brand Virtual Identity
- Basics of Digital Advertising and Online Search
- Importance of IBP In E-Tail: Emergence of Social E-Commerce and Big Data
- Advantages of Digital, Social, and Mobile Media for Implementing Advertising and IBP Campaigns, as Well as the Dark Side
- Synergizing with Other IBP Tools

investment for advertising and IBP.[2] Also note that more and more media buys are being made programmatically, a trend that is increasing even as digital, social, and mobile media are evolving.[3]

14-1a Social Media and Web 3.0

Whereas **Web 2.0** refers to the progression of the Internet from static one-way information to include interactive online communication, participation, engagement, and dynamic content.[4] The next stage is the transition to **Web 3.0**, which entails sites and e-services that use **machine learning** and **artificial intelligence**, to interpret a web full of data. Examples of what Web. 3.0 synergizes with includes smart speakers (e.g., Google Home), virtual assistants (e.g., Alexa), and other technologies that connect to a network; Thus, virtual assistants, smart speakers, and network-connected home appliances are some examples of what Web 3.0 involves.[5] As noted in Chapter 3, consumers create information and post comments while adding value to socially embedded websites. This is *user-generated content (UGC)* or *consumer-generated*

Source: USA TODAY (NEWSPAPER)

Exhibit 14.2 ▶ For many newspaper websites, they are supported by advertising content; notice the "Ad Content" on the right of the page. These ads from Amazon Prime and the Biltmore Estate are meant to blend in the news content, but also must disclose that they are advertisements or sponsored content.

content (CGC).[6] Modern web usage depends on mass collaboration as people simultaneously create value for themselves and others.[7] In a marketing context, there is a focus on brands and organizations "liked" and mentioned through network effects, including viral sharing. Similarly, organizations reach and interact with existing customers online and via social media while becoming part of customer conversations and solutions with their products or services.[8]

Digital marketing continues to change the landscape of advertising and branding. See Exhibit 14.2 for an example of a digital advertisement for the Biltmore House that is shown on the USA Today website. In this digital advertising example, it depicts the tourist destination as it is decorated for the holidays along with a tagline about blending past and present. It hopes that audience members who read USA Today online will see this sponsored content/digital ad and click on it for more information about the Biltmore House. As seen in the image, the digital ads are often woven in between editorial content, or on the sides of websites.

Yet even with an increasingly digital focus, it is paramount for advertisers to use digital, social, and/or mobile media in a synergistic way that supports other forms of IBP, such as outdoor, print, public relations, or events.[9] Subaru is an example of a company that does a good job with this integrative approach (see Exhibit 14.3), as the brand uses digital media to link its car brand to an event.

14-1b Media Types in Social Media

Social media refer to platforms like TikTok, Twitter, YouTube, Facebook, Snapchat, LinkedIn, and Pinterest that are designed to connect people and their networks with other people, brands, organizations, or other entities. Especially relevant to social media are the three categories of media in general: earned, owned, and paid.[10] **Earned media** is the incremental exposure that your brand earns through viral engagement and organically created unpaid interactions with the brand. Earned media is called that, because the company or organization has "earned" the coverage, press, or mention in a natural way instead of having to pay for it. Brands love earned media! For instance, a consumer mentions and shares a picture of a brand in use on their social media post in an organic, natural way (i.e., unpaid), is an example of earned media. Brands like Benefit Cosmetics use Facebook Live video streaming or Instagram stories to attract viewers, an example of earned media, and support other IBP communications (see Exhibit 14.4).[11] One note with earned media is that the brand does not pay for the buzz; so it is not technically advertising, which is traditionally paid.

The second type is **owned media**, and is media that the brand or organization owns such as brand assets or objects created within social networks by your organization, Owned media can be online, such as a Facebook page, website, app, and official social media pages/channels. Owned media can also be offline as well, but usually it is referred to in digital contexts. Owned media may cost some money to generate (such as paying to build an app or a branded website), but it does not necessarily entail payments to place messages in the media or social media.

Paid media are advertisements that can be purchased on a social network or on other digital platforms, as well as any form of traditional advertising. Any advertisement by the traditional definition is "paid" per se. This is not to be confused with paid traditional advertising that leverages a

Exhibit 14.3 ▶ Subaru uses digital advertising to link their car brand to an event—the Wagathon Walkathon in Austin, a locale that fits well with their target market of eco-friendly yet urban consumers.

Exhibit 14.4 ▶ Benefit Cosmetics promotes products and cross-promotes its other social media accounts on Twitter to engage customers through multiple conversations.

call to action to like the brand on Twitter, TikTok, Snapchat, Instagram, Pinterest, Facebook, or other social media sites. Here, in the context of social media, note that some brand integration can be officially paid to the site such as Facebook, while others are not paid; for example, earned media is when your Facebook friend raves about Southwest Airlines after flying them, viewing a Live video, or seeing Twitter posts. There is a big difference when we think about the inherent bias; thus, we tend to find earned media in social networks particularly compelling. For many brands, including beauty brands, the focus is on getting the right ad in front of the right influencers on social media to accelerate viral sharing and extend reach.[12]

It is important for brands to embrace social media because it can garner digital engagement in a measurable way with likes, clicks, shares, and so on.[13] An earlier tool that offered advertisers a way to measure some aspects of engagement was the QR code, which looks like a small black-and-white square such as in the DKNY ad in Exhibit 14.5. While QR codes did not originally catch on as a marketing tool, they did become very widely adopted and used for sharing information in a touchless manner during the COVID-19 pandemic. The bigger idea of measuring responses with technology has become increasingly important for IBP and brand integration.

Source: DKNY

Exhibit 14.5 ▶ DKNY uses digital and social media in the Be Delicious campaign. They use a QR code for consumers to scan to view how to join their core club.

14-1c Options via Digital or Social Media: Definitions and Categories

Definitions of Social Media

You were introduced to social media in Chapter 2. *Social media* are "media designed to facilitate dissemination of content through social interaction among individuals, groups and organizations using Internet and web-based technologies to enable the transformation of broadcast monologues (one to many) into social dialogues (many to many)."[14] A second definition of social media is a set of web-based applications or platforms that allows for individuals, companies, and organizations to create, and exchange user-generated content (which may entail brand-related content too).[15]

Social media are accessible in that they are simple to find and use for a broad audience and they are scalable, as network effects play a key role.[16] The core of social media is information sharing, individual empowerment and democratization of knowledge. This is because consumers are content producers—sometimes even creating Super Bowl ads for brands, as done in the past with crowdsourced campaigns for Pizza Hut, Lincoln, Pepsi, and Doritos. Of these, Frito Lay's Doritos was the most buzzed about, because it was the first brand to rely on consumers to generate a Super Bowl ad, and they kept the contest going for a decade.

Social Media Categories

Here are some brief descriptions of social media categories, along with their use for integrated brand promotion (IBP) and digital advertising or messaging, including social networking websites/mobile applications (often news, photo/video, or professional oriented) and blogs and microblogs.[17]

Social Networking Websites and Mobile Applications

In this section, we overview some leading social media websites and **mobile applications** (i.e., the applications or apps on a smartphone for the social media platform). The most popular social networking sites with a general social orientation are Facebook (whose corporate name is Meta), Twitter, and Pinterest. Meanwhile, YouTube, TikTok, and Instagram are distinguished by their video and photo sharing orientations.

Snapchat is known as the ephemeral video social media platform, as the video content disappears after a brief amount of time. **Ephemeral** means that the content lasts for just a short time. Others, such as LinkedIn, are positioned around professional and business networking. Social networking sites and mobile applications (informally called apps) are services on which users can create an individual profile page, find and add friends and contacts, send messages, and update their personal profiles to notify friends, contacts, or colleagues about themselves. Social networking websites now combine several features into one platform; for example, Facebook gives users the opportunity to post status updates (i.e., microblogs), notes (i.e., blogs), pictures, and live-stream videos. Often, users are able to tag other users in their networks in such posts, creating additional links among users, content, and physical location. For example, checking in at a restaurant or store is based on mobile **location-based technologies**. Location-based technologies, often associated with mobile, use geographical coordinates to determine where the person is and can synergize with digital advertising for nearby businesses.

Video and Photo Sharing via Social Media

A favorite of many consumers for showing their Starbucks cups with misspelled names, new purchases, family, friends, pets and more, are social media sites and mobile applications that focus on consumers' ability to watch, upload, and share videos. Typically, unregistered users can watch videos already posted to the site, while registered users are permitted to upload videos and comment on other users' videos (note however that TikTok made a change to where one has to register to view content).[18] While TikTok has become a sensation especially for younger consumers, YouTube remains the largest and most well-known of the video sharing sites due to its general nature and wide scope from videos of statistics tutorials to music videos to videos of people playing video games. Instagram has traditionally been very popular for photo sharing and has transformed to become a video-sharing platform as well as having success with its Instagram Stories. *There is a fine line between social media video and photo sharing sites because these platforms are constantly evolving, repositioning, and rolling out new features.*

Other social media sites/apps—such as Instagram—are oriented around picture and video sharing. A picture is worth a thousand words, an old adage says. Starbucks uses Instagram to encourage photo sharing of its seasonal products, complete with appropriate hashtags. For example, #PSL and #pumpkin are the identifiers for Pumpkin Spice Latté; and every fall—or even late summer—Starbucks kicks off an Instagram sharing campaign tied to the drink's menu launch. Hundreds of thousands of images and posts that consumers tagged to these drinks or hashtags resulted in substantial earned media for Starbucks. The beverage is so popular that Starbucks set up a separate Instagram account just for it, called "The Real Pumpkin Spice Latté" (see Exhibit 14.6).[19]

Social media websites and mobile applications are positioned in the consumer's mind based on how they personally use(s) the site and or its features (e.g., posts, groups, reactions, etc.). The trending news stories and posting and sharing of news and media articles is an important and timely aspect of social media. In fact, there are many people who exclusively get their news content and information from social media. This can be problematic when some things that are perceived as credible news with legitimate sources are shared. Some have attributed social media with contributing to **fake news**, which could range from incorrect information (misinformation) that is inaccurate, attention-getting and unsubstantiated, to completely fabricated stories in general. Furthermore, if we tend to have social media friends and connections exclusively with people who are similar to us, there are some psychological biases to consider.

Comments on news stories and associated links can offer insight into the consumer mindset on some news issues. These comments can be especially heated when it comes to controversial topics and/or subjects that advertisers and marketers have integrated into their images. For instance, websites and mobile applications such as Reddit are wonderful for increasing reach and can even help get the right story or video to viral status. Social and news-oriented websites/mobile applications are most valuable to advertisers when they maintain a stable community where links can be added and voting can occur.

Blogs

As defined in Chapter 2, blogs are sites written and maintained by individuals but hosted and technically owned by an organization that provides access to Web space and a content-management system. Bloggers develop regular posts that may include text, graphics, videos, or links to other blogs and Web pages. These are usually posted in chronological order. Blogs often focus on news and views about particular topics—such as fashion, art, culture, celebrity, and business, and so on. Key characteristics of the blog are its journal format and its informal style. Because of their more personal nature and credibility, blogs can be helpful environments for advertising messages.[20] **Microblogs** are social networking services that enable users to post and read short messages. Posters are restricted by the number of characters in the message. The best known is Twitter, where users can send tweets—text-based posts of up to 140 characters, plus optional images, displayed on the author's profile page and delivered to the author's followers. Senders can restrict delivery to those in their circle of friends or, by default, allow open access to any site visitors. Users can send and receive tweets via the Twitter website or mobile app and also through text messaging on cell phones and external applications that can access the site. Twitter has gained much prominence in the Super Bowl, not just for the game (which can generate upwards of 27 million tweets) but for comments about brands, including commercials and sponsored half-time entertainment.[21]

Exhibit 14.6 ▶ Starbucks has a special Pumpkin Spice Latté Instagram account just for this popular drink to encourage photo sharing and drive earned media.

——————— LO2 ▶ ———————

14-2 Consumer and Brand Virtual Identity

14-2a Consumer Virtual Identity

Virtual identity is how the consumer or brand uses images and text online to construct or showcase its identity. This concept is crucial to understand as it relates to IBP, social media, and digital advertising. Online identity, in the virtual world and in the on-ground world, is increasingly becoming an important pseudo-image for today's connected consumer. Avatars are consumer-generated images that an online user portrays, which may or may not accurately coincide with the consumers' "real identity." Interestingly, there is startling evidence that consumers' online identity is often more a reflection of their desired identity and in some extreme cases is highly exaggerated from their "real identity."[22] Consumers may embellish to enhance their sense of self-concept (perhaps even lying to themselves) or—more drastically—to lure an unknowing potential dating partner.[23] Findings of incongruity are also found in the context of avatars, or cartoon-based pictorial representations of the image an online consumer wishes to portray. In some cases, such avatars are brands, designers, sports teams, or other nonhuman images. While they are depersonalized compared to an avatar that is purported to look like the consumer, these nonhuman avatars or mascots, like The University of Georgia Bulldog or The University of Texas Longhorn, or the Clemson Tiger, are attractive and represent an image transfer from the brand to the person adopting that image.

To fully understand online identity, one must consider the notion that more than one world exists in the modern consumer's mind. There is the "real world," which, for many, consists of work, family, social activities, and shopping at brick-and-mortar stores and service providers. Some of this is difficult, if not impossible, to do online. Until someone

invents an application that can put gas in one's car or bring one's child to day care, such interactions in the real world are necessary. Consumers have their "real-world" image. The twist is that this image is not necessarily congruent with their image in the virtual world. Behind the screen, a consumer may create a new identity, a new attitude, and in a sense become a different person online. We must understand that virtual identities are indeed real to consumers. Understanding this concept can help consumer-minded businesses and organizations cater better to customer wants. A consumer's aspirational identity, for instance, may correlate with some luxury brands and as such, consumers may discuss and post images of desirable or exclusive brands such as Gucci (Exhibit 14.7). In the Gucci ad in Exhibit 14.8, note how the focus is on the luxury brand name, with only a very small and subtle call in fine print directing consumers to the digital flagship store of Gucci.com.

14-2b Social Media as a Brand Management Tool: Brand Image and Visibility

We will discuss social media definitions and issues primarily from a consumer (user) context, because as a digital advertiser, you need to have knowledge of online consumer

Source: Gucci

Exhibit 14.7 ▶ Gucci employs stunning art direction and photography in their ad showing their new styles. On the second page of this two-page spread, there is a call to action for consumers to visit their digital flagship store at Gucci.com.

behavior to create an effective advertising strategy. Social media are important tools for brand managers who are interested in establishing and maintaining a brand image, reputation, or position. Especially during times of crisis, companies are expected to communicate directly with the impacted consumers and their communities. Brands should leverage social media as a digital advertising opportunity that can target consumers by lifestyle factors. Managers too should use social media as a way to monitor and build a brand image, reputation, and position and communicate with customers and their networks. As shown in Integrated Brand Promotion in Action, the retailer Zappos is actively engaging customers in social media while projecting a brand image that supports a particular identity and differentiates the e-tailer from competitors (see Exhibit 14.8).

From a brand manager perspective, key questions posed by Botha and Mills (2012) remain:[24] How do we find out what is being said about a brand via social media? What is being said about competing brands? How is that different from our brand? Is our brand more or less visible in some social media than others, and how does that differ from our competitors? Are we "liked," and what does that mean for advertising and marketing effectiveness? Brand managers must track what consumers say about the brand or service on social media, interpret consumer-generated information, and respond to social media posts and comments. This entails spending time Snapchatting, scrolling Instagram, following Twitter feeds, looking at Pinterest boards, and reading comments on YouTube.[25]

International House of Pancakes (IHOP), for example, sets up a "social media war room" inside its ad agency's headquarters to post content and monitor comments on National Pancake Day. The restaurant chain offers a free short stack of pancakes that day, requesting that, in exchange, customers donate money to one of its charity partners (see Exhibit 14.9). In addition to measuring the amount of money donated, IHOP aims to engage customers via social media. In the war room, agency and brand personnel watch social networks to track and respond to what social media users post or repost, including both IHOP–generated and consumer-generated content. To prepare, IHOP has Snapchat filters, hashtag identifiers (#NatlPancakeDay), and other conversation starters ready. The restaurant and its agency respond to every post by every consumer, personalizing the interaction and strengthening the relationship. This one-day campaign results in thousands of new social media followers for IHOP, tens of thousands of positive messages, viral sharing—and millions of dollars raised for charity.[26]

In addition to monitoring electronic word of mouth, managers are keenly interested in metrics from any social media and social media ads. There are questions around social media measurement. For instance, even though digital measurement helps place media accurately, why does such precise targeting bring consumer resistance? What is digital engagement? And then, once finding the count of how many consumers like a brand on Facebook, you may wonder, "what is a 'like' really worth?" Some metrics from Internet advertising do apply to social media. For instance, **site stickiness**, or how long someone spends on a site, is a relevant metric. **Bounce rate**, or the percentage of people who come from or go to another site after clicking on your site, is also relevant. Another metric more specific to social media is engagement with the social media site—although digital overengagement can be a negative for consumers and advertisers.[27]

Let's not forget the omnichannel nature of shopping these days, with consumers choosing how they wish to browse and buy. Nearly 70 percent of all Americans have shopped online, and half of all Americans have bought via mobile device—yet 46 percent say they still prefer traditional stores.[28] So another important metric for advertisers and brand marketers is sales in bricks-and-mortar stores as well as online sales from websites

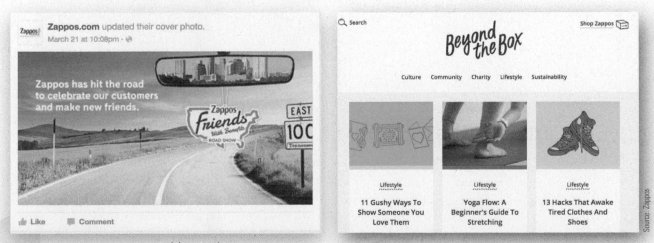

Exhibit 14.8 ▶ Integrated brand promotion in action: Zappos
E-retailer Zappos uses social media like Facebook and its blog, "Beyond the Box," for brand image and to support special promotional events. *What elements of brand image does Zappos appear to be emphasizing with these posts, and why?*

Source: IHOP

Exhibit 14.9 ▶ IHOP founded National Pancake Day as a fundraiser for children's charities. The restaurant chain uses its website and social media accounts to spread the word and to engage brand fans for a more personal connection.

or mobile apps. Amazon, for instance, is opening physical stores to complement its online retail presence and allowing customers to browse products in person. This has implications for its advertising and IBP strategy, including the need to attract shoppers by communicating locations and building excitement about the products and the shopping experience.[29] Again, it is not a question of traditional *or* digital; it is how to seamlessly integrate both. For instance, Amazon does the IBP integration well, as its print ads are often designed to bring consumers to its websites (Exhibit 14.10).

Source: Amazon.com

Exhibit 14.10 ▶ Amazon.com/Fashion is a new initiative from the top e-tailer. E-search is a big part of Amazon's business. Here, their ad notes their new free return policy and how consumers can e-search hundreds of top fashion brands.

14-3 Basics of Digital Advertising and Online Search

14-3a Digital Advertising Investments

As you learned in the earlier media chapters, the way media is bought and sold is changing drastically and becoming increasingly automated; this fact is especially true and relevant in digital, social media, and mobile advertising. This bid-based (often automated) model of advertising payment works via bidding for specific ad words in search engines and social media such as Facebook. It is a good idea, if possible, to bid higher than the site's (e.g., Google, Facebook) suggested bid amount to reach your target audience, who, in turn, will engage with your ads at a faster pace (low frequency). As with traditional media, it is smart to keep reach and frequency in check so as not to spark consumer resistance. The goal is to get a high effective exposure rate and digital engagement rate, not to annoy consumers.

For social media advertising to be effective, the brand page must have a fan base. That is, consumers must be motivated to find your page and "like it." A smart way to do this is to give an incentive—a chance to win something, a first look at new products, or a special offer. This online consumer base can be served by an IBP campaign that is more interactive in nature, another advantage of social media. Develop a strong portfolio of assets upon which you can build your campaigns and drive interaction within Facebook. In order to capitalize on social ads and sponsored stories, you must have a scalable fan base. With a larger network, there is a higher exposure rate, which can in turn enhance engagement with both the ad and the brand. Once you have a fan base, you can engage in interactive conversations and reinforce brand preference and loyalty.

Not all digital or mobile advertisers use key-word bidding or automated media buying. One of the primary reasons behind this is that some advertisers worry about the lack of control they would have over what websites would feature their digital or mobile ad.[30] In the past, and still the case for some digital advertisers, digital advertising has had revenue models based on cost-per-thousand exposures (CRM) or **cost-per-click (CPC)**. If they had to be compared via a cost-per-thousand (CPM) basis, the cost of digital ads compares favorably with traditional media. Digital media investments have changed away from CPM and CPC. In the early 2000s, about 90 percent of agencies priced banner ads on a CPM basis.[31] Today, it is much less common.

CPC is an advertising revenue model where the advertiser is charged by the number of people who click on, or tap, the ad to pull it up for more information or to see the ad in its entirety. Thus, when you see an online ad and click on it, the advertiser is charged. An advantage is that the advertiser can pay for a pulled exposure rather than a message pushed to all watching that TV channel or reading that magazine. A disadvantage is in click fraud, where this process could be exploited in unethical or even illegal ways. Now, as discussed in the other media chapters, much of digital advertising is now programmatic and search or display advertising based. The real attraction of digital is not found in raw numbers and CPMs but rather in terms of highly synergistic and segmentable media. Digital advertising investments are ideally suited for niche marketing—finding consumers most likely interested in a very specific product or service.

Types of Digital Ads

There are several types of digital ads, including social media ads, display/banner ads, and pop-up and pop-under ads.

Social Media Ads

Note that even within one social media site, such as Facebook, there are different types of ads. **Post ads** are ads embedded in a post. These types of ads tend to have higher relative response rates because they are within a consumer's post to his/her/their network. They are sponsored content seen in consumers' news feeds on Facebook, for example. They tend to be a form of **native advertising**, because the ad seemingly is in its natural environment and a part of the content, such as the news feed.[32]

App ads, meanwhile, are ads associated with a third-party application or game (such as Pokémon); these tend to generate consumer loyalty and can provide consumer data for more accurate key-word targeting. Some key words are very expensive, but slight variations of those words can be much more affordable and still reach the type of consumer the brand is targeting. Like traditional media, digital, social, and mobile media need to both be in line with the brand/IBP or campaign objectives and designed to attract psychographic target markets. In particular, advertising on social media sites is most effective in influencing consumer behavior when the message is congruent with the content in which it is placed.[33]

Display Ads

Display ads are paid placements of advertising on sites that contain copy or images. One feature of a display ad is that consumers can click on the ad (this is the "click-through" defined earlier). Thus, the challenge of creating and placing display/banner ads is not only to catch people's attention but also to entice them to visit the marketer's home page and stay for a while.[34] The ability to create curiosity and provide the viewer resolution to that curiosity can have an important impact on learning and brand attitude.[35] In fact, depending on how recently a consumer has visited the website, banner advertising is well suited to generating awareness for new products and for brand building.[36] The downside to display ads is the clutter.

Frequency can be a factor: Low-frequency web advertising on a search site, for example, may result in a spillover effect that benefits competitors, whereas high-frequency advertising favors the brand being advertised.[37]

A more targeted option is to place these ads on sites that attract specific market niches. Specialized firms assess the costs of display ads on a variety of sites and provide an estimate to advertisers of the audience reached. For example, there are sites that speak to consumers with an interest in events related to culture, art, theater, and symphony in their areas. These events have to be promoted within a specific time frame; thus, it is crucial that event ads be placed in specific outlets such as cultural calendars, event sites, local happenings sections of local media, and in related outlets that reach the specific psychographic or lifestyle segments.

Interstitial Ads

Another type of ad is the **interstitial**, which loads while you browse; it appears on a site after a page has been requested but before it has loaded and stays onscreen long enough for the message to be registered. Sometimes these ads are called "pre-rolls," as they roll out the ad before the consumer sees his/her/their desired content. However, research shows that mobile users may view interstitial ads for only 800 milliseconds—that's not even one full second. They view mobile banner ads for barely 200 milliseconds, a tiny fraction of a second. In other words, consumers are practiced at ignoring such ads.[38] In fact, there is resistance to digital ads even if the messages are somewhat accurate. See an example of a digital

ad by Grammarly that is shown between YouTube videos in Exhibit 14.11. In this ad, which depicts women discussing the product, notice how there is a "Skip Ad" icon that appears on the screen. One important point about these types of digital ads, and other digital ads, is that people tend to skip ads if possible (unless they are interested or unable to skip the ad). This means that digital ads do not always have the desired exposure.

14-3b Search

Other digital ads are more search oriented and are a function of search engine optimization. Online awareness and social media tactics are means to enhance online advertising effectiveness and consumer search. **Search** refers to how consumers look for ideas, brands, and information online for purchases or entertainment. To show its power, consider election years and online political advertising: some say elections were won in part by how some candidates used online and social media advertising to speak to younger voters.

Paid Search and Search Engine Optimization

Paid search is the process by which advertisers pay websites and portals to place ads in or near relevant search results based on key words. For example, if you Google "tennis shoes," you will find links to Wilson, and Prince next to the search results as sources for purchasing tennis shoes. A related paid search concept is **search engine optimization (SEO)**. SEO is a

Exhibit 14.11 ▶ In this ad by grammarly, note how consumers can skip the ad by clicking in the small box on the right.

Internet advertising in United States

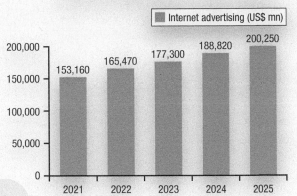

Exhibit 14.12 ▶ IAB and PwC show a chart that depicts a strong and steady growth of Internet advertising revenue to 2025 projections.

process by which the volume and quality of traffic to a website from search engines are improved based on browsers' profiles. Basically, the goal is that the higher a site is presented in search results, the more likely consumers are to visit that site.

Consider these facts about paid search and SEO: (1) The first three paid advertising spots receive most of the clicks on the page; (2) Google searches for cost-per-click (CPC) on Google have decreased significantly since June 2004; and (3) search volume on AdWords Google Trends has risen.[39] Thus, as suggested prior in this chapter, the older models of CPC are declining, while paid search has grown astronomically. This is not surprising, as the Interactive Advertising Bureau reports that U.S. advertisers invested $34.28 billion in digital advertising in 2020, which represents a dramatic increase over previous years (see the growth of digital advertising in Exhibit 14.12); Interactive Advertising Bureau and PwC forecasts U.S. Internet advertising will total $165 billion in 2022, and by 2025, Internet ad spending is projected to hit $200 billion.[40]

One catalyst for growth in digital advertising and specifically paid search is the success of Google, which

Exhibit 14.13 ▶ Google has been a leader of revolutionizing digital advertising and paid search with its Ad Words platform.

pushed the concept from its beginning, although all sites can accommodate paid search. Paid search advertising is valued by firms as they try to improve the efficiency of the Internet as an IBP tool and convert clicks to sales.[41] One study found that Amazon is a leader in paid search through Google on desktop computers, generating more than 470 million clicks per year to bring customers to its e-commerce pages.[42] Google is especially important for digital advertising, as Google's Ad Words has revolutionized paid search (Exhibit 14.13).

14-4 Importance of IBP in E-Tail: Emergence of Social E-Commerce and Big Data

Big Data is all the rage, with advertisers analyzing consumers' digital, social media, and mobile behavior. The goal is to deliver more relevant, useful and appreciated ads or to offer reminders that are specific to consumer wants and needs. Assume you're searching for a SUV, and you visit the BMW website. You might then appreciate being presented with ads by this brand because you are interested in learning about the new models and their features such as those seen in the BMW X5 SUV ad in Exhibit 14.14. You then may see a digital ad for a BMW X5 as a function of **retargeting**, which means serving consumers digital ads that are directly based on previous clicks. Retargeting is also known as *behavioral retargeting*. In a way, advertisers are trying to help make push advertising more like pull advertising in that they provide messages based on the consumer's online behavior that implies an interest in the brand or product category.

Digital advertising or social media plugs may spark consumers to browse various shopping sites, place items or service tickets into virtual shopping carts, and hopefully convert cart placements into sales and longer-term relationships.[43] Here we provide some statistics on e-commerce's projected growth. The e-commerce and online shopping landscape has grown substantially in size and scope over the last decade. Hundreds of millions of online buyers bring e-commerce revenues in excess of U.S. $791 billion a year.[44] The increase in the number of online shoppers, increasing revenues, and the development of new forms of online shopping highlight the need to understand the online shopping process. An understanding of the online shopping process is important to online both advertisers and for online retailers. Further, knowing the conditions in which trust makes a consumer click on an ad, watch an online ad, or patronize an online retailer is important.[45]

Source: BMW

Exhibit 14.14 ▶ BMW is a leader in digital media. In their ads for the BMW X5 with xDrive, the ads show the dealer site, but the true focus, as it should be in product marketing for luxury goods, is on the product. Note the four distinct views of their SUV.

LO 5

14-5 Advantages of Digital, Social, and Mobile Media for Implementing Advertising and IBP Campaigns, as Well as the Dark Side

Social media have many challenges and opportunities.[46] Here, we start with the pros, then turn to the cons and consumer privacy concerns—and even discuss "the dark side of social media."[47]

14-5a Advantages of Digital, Social, and Mobile Media

Advantages of digital, social, and mobile media include interactivity, target market selectivity, integration, and ease of use. These media offer a way to engage and integrate brands with consumers' lifestyles as revealed by their **digital footprint**, the trail of social media posts, videos, photos, status updates, and online information on a person, organization, or brand. A plus for digital, social, and mobile media is their popularity and the frequency with which consumers use these media. Another plus is the sheer breadth of social media sites. Consumers have accounts in various types of social media. In the United States, 72 percent of all adults use one or more social networking sites; while slightly more women (78 percent) versus men (65 percent) use social media, there are no significant differences among races. Younger consumers ages 18 to 29 are the highest social media consumers (71 percent), and 30- to 49-year-olds are next highest (62 percent).

And 51 percent of consumers aged 65 and over use social media, although this group is adopting social media over time.[48] For marketers, analyzing digital footprints and using qualitative research to examine consumer behavior can yield a deeper understanding of how and why consumers use these media, perceive advertising, and make decisions.[49]

Interactivity

Interactivity, or two-way communications that can feed off one another, is an advantage of digital media. A consumer can go to a site or click through from a display/banner ad and get an understanding of a brand's features and values. A **click-through** is a measure of the number of page elements (hyperlinks) that have actually been requested (i.e., "clicked through" from the display/banner ad to the link). If advertisers can attract browsers to the brand website, there is the opportunity to convert that person to a buyer if the site is set up for e-commerce. Design components of various digital or mobile or tablet ad formats can have an important effect on click-through and sales potential.[50] Social media provide opportunities for advertisers with respect to interactivity.

Integration

Digital, social, and mobile advertising are most easily integrated and coordinated with other forms of promotion. The integration of digital, social, and/or mobile with other components of the marketing mix is one of the easiest integration tasks in the IBP process. This is due to the flexibility and deliverability of online advertising discussed earlier. Digital media specifically provide a seamless interface with the most traditional of IBP tools—television. Television ratings for live events, such as the Grammys and the Oscars, have spiked in recent years as viewers tweet and post on Facebook to alert friends to the awards and comment on the proceedings.[51] With IBP, advertising on TV can have a positive effect on brand and program word-of-mouth mentions on digital and social media, delivering more results for the budget.[52]

Engagement via a Digital Footprint

Companies, nonprofits, and human brands alike can engage others via their online presence. With social media, you can be an open book if you so choose and consciously or unconsciously share the brands you use or like. By tagging a location, branded places become part of your Web 2.0 storyline. Posting photos of you in your Honda in a Falcons hat with a Red Bull in hand is another way brands are benefitting in an organic way from social media. We all have a story, or our personal book, and when documented online, it leaves a digital footprint. The question is, how much of your book do you choose to share in social media? What aspects of your identity do you share with your social media world, and how are those shaped by brands? Or do you choose to avoid social media and keep a closed book when it comes to your digital footprint?

Your personal information is readily available online if you choose to make it so in social media. You may have your resume on LinkedIn and have your fraternity formal photos on Facebook. You may have selected to publicly "like" brands like Victoria's Secret, Birkenstock, ZARA, Jeep, and Disney. The combination of these self-confessions, evolving technology, and Web 2.0 tools make it simple to share your life story—your open book. It is your choice to share your life information in social media or not.[53] In this way, you are reaching out to your network to help you cope through tough times and congratulate you on your milestones.

There is something to be said for maintaining a strong network of friends, family, and professionals, and social media is a tool to make this easier to manage in large numbers. Brands can use this to integrate themselves into your life story. The information that you share creates a "digital footprint," defined as your profile of personal information, accessible online to a spectrum of people.[54] Note that this spectrum of audience in social media is based on your privacy settings. You may choose to post to all of your social media connections, friends of friends, or close friends. In some cases, future employers, spouses, and parents follow your digital footprint, so it is important to keep your online presence congruent with your true and aspirational self. It is also important to consider privacy aspects of social media.[55]

14-5b Privacy Issues and the Dark Side of Digital, Social, and Mobile Media

One cannot have a responsible conversation about digital, social, and mobile media without discussing the role of authenticity, privacy, security, and related fears about one's personal and financial information.

The Dark Side

The book, "The Dark Side of Social Media: A Consumer Psychology Perspective" highlighted some of the dark side issues for consumers and brands that social media brings or intensifies. Since then, many of these issues have come out as being legitimized, as we have seen in Congressional Hearings with some of the social media giants and multiple calls for reform. One of the issues is inauthenticity—which could even entail fraud. It is harder to judge authenticity behind a screen.[56] The thought of having one's identity stolen by online or digital means, or **cyber-identity theft**,[57] is enough to inhibit some consumers from shopping and banking online or via an app. It is critical to explore consumer perception of both privacy and security, because security refers to how safe the site or app is, and privacy is more about how the host maintains consumer data and online consumer behavior. Many Internet, social media, and mobile media users don't know all the ways to protect themselves from cyber-identity theft.[58] Establishing the highest standards for privacy and security is vital for online brand managers. Today's brand managers have a wealth of resources at their fingertips to help establish their brand's identity and to connect with their customers. TikTok, Facebook, Twitter, LinkedIn, and other social networking sites are not just tools for consumers to connect with each other (C2C). Instead, we must look at social networks as brand management tools. Just as touch points with the brand are key at live events (e.g., sponsor signage at a sporting event), virtual touch points are helpful in leveraging those on-the-ground consumer relationships. While social networking can never replace the authenticity of a handshake and personalized service, these virtual touch points can reinforce extant relationships or spark a new interest or an unrealized need.

Online Resistance

We suspect that there is some **online resistance**, which is an attitude or behavior against the digital movement at times. For some consumers, and for the authors as well, social networks are designed to be a vehicle that connects us with people who have crossed our paths. Be it our marketing and advertising students, high school pals, current colleagues, or yes, parents, it is this constant connection with people that draws consumers to log on for hours on end to social networking sites. In fact, Facebook is the third most visited social media site in the United States, after Google and YouTube, respectively. Make these vehicles another way to market to us and sell to us, and we may resist. There could be the perception that marketers and advertisers are stomping on consumers' sacred territory. That said, if done correctly, there can be some subtle synergies from online advertisers that can actually enhance one's social networking experience. For example, after one of the authors changed her Facebook status from "in a relationship" to "engaged," a sidebar on the social media site appeared from a wedding dress vendor, then honeymoon destinations, jewelers, and florists galore. This is life stage marketing at its finest—the dress is one of the first things on the newly engaged woman's mind, and Facebook and their advertisers were right there to assist in the search. But do consumers resent and resist such highly targeted messages?

Privacy and Information in Social Media

Marketplace exchanges embedded with social media may be publicly visible. For instance, when you order photos from the drugstore CVS via a Facebook app, you may choose to have this visible on your Facebook page. This makes a usually more private purchase more socially embedded. The e-environment lends itself to casual information sharing.

Privacy involves the control of information disclosure and the prevention of unwanted intrusions into a consumer's environment.[59] In this era, privacy now encompasses control over personal exchanges that use information technology to enhance autonomy or minimize vulnerability, which can diminish covert marketing practices online.[60] Often, online consumers do not use the privacy tools available to them by regularly clearing needless cookies, reading privacy policies, or paying attention to logos that show the site has been endorsed or is a member of a third-party privacy endorser, known as a **privacy seal**.[61] Such consumer apathy toward online privacy protection can lead to unwanted intrusions or being contacted by someone out of your networks. The landscape changes so quickly that you may not be as aware of your digital footprint as you should. In fact, many consumers don't bother to read the terms and conditions on various websites or apps, even when doing so might lead to ways of saving money on a digital purchase.[62]

Do you remember each of your digital footprints? If not, you are not alone. Few people remember not only self-posted information but also details posted by others to their online profiles. Especially as online users gain additional social networking accounts (e.g., Twitter, Facebook, LinkedIn, Pinterest, TikTok), they might forget various elements found within their comprehensive digital footprint. Although it may seem unlikely that a reputable business would use or sell private information that identifies customers, a minimal compilation of anonymous information (e.g., zip code, date of birth) could generate enough information to identify someone. Thus, it is important to take note of which companies respect consumer privacy and to be aware of your opt-in or opt-out settings.

Main Social Media Platforms and Disclosure

Disclosure on each of these main platforms (e.g., Facebook, Instagram, LinkedIn, Pinterest, TikTok) helps you build and maintain relationships and conduct business. Yet, it is important for you to stay smart—and safe—with what you post, to whom, and when. "We are on vacation for a week" is not designed to say "Come rob us this week!" Common use of social networking brings disclosure issues to different audiences. There are some vulnerabilities to be aware of: consumers' loss of information control, privacy intrusions due to friends' behaviors, and digital vigilance. Unauthorized viewers, employers, and third-party applications can gain access to social media profiles.[63] Most U.S. employers review candidates' social media profiles—most often without their consent—before making hiring decisions. Is your social media digital footprint ready for employers to view? Realizing that future employers do not want to see spring break trips, fraternity parties, and your brother's new dog, you may want to keep your settings private. Graduates often need to conceal their social networking profiles during job searches to avoid misunderstandings as they navigate the transition from student to professional.[64]

Now there are different social media platforms that you may use for different images in different contexts. For one, the LinkedIn platform is more appropriate for sharing your resume, your skills, your employment history, and any professional accolades. The group setting in LinkedIn can help you find, make, and maintain connections in your industry. With LinkedIn, it is simple and convenient to share relevant content with specific groups who would be interested, positioning yourself as a **subject matter expert (SME)** in the process. A second social media platform that crosses professional and personal boundaries is Pinterest. Pinterest is reminiscent of the days when consumers would tear out ads or articles of interest to pin to their corkboard. You can post articles relevant to business or pleasure. Pinterest is also a wonderful shopping tool. Love that iPad case? Pin it up to your Pinterest page for your friends to check out. Social media brings the social element back to online shopping. Then again, there's Snapchat, highly popular among teens and twenty-somethings for mobile-based sharing of images and videos—which makes it a vehicle of interest to advertisers, as well.[65]

Negative Effects for Advertisers

As discussed in Chapter 4, billions of dollars in advertising funds are being lost to **click fraud**.[66] Another concern is that social media conversations initiated by consumers will harm brand perceptions.[67] This is why advertisers must constantly monitor social media to understand what is being said, who's saying it, and how to respond. Brands can be caught up in rumors or fake news stories and have their reputations harmed in a matter of hours if they're not vigilant and proactive in responding with corrections and detailed explanations.[68]

A third concern for advertisers is what kind of content will be adjacent to digital, social, and mobile ads. Social media platform such as YouTube have at times lost an exodus of advertising dollars when major brands withdrew ads because ads had appeared next to videos containing offensive themes or language. Many such ads are placed through programmatic buying, so it's difficult to know in advance exactly where every ad will appear. Google responded to advertisers' concerns by tightening controls and guidelines to keep branded advertising away from inappropriate content.[69]

14-6 Synergizing with Other IBP Tools

It is critical to synergize a brand's digital presence with the other marketing tools in your toolkit. Not every communication or sales objective needs a hammer (national advertising); some objectives are much better suited to a precise, small

screwdriver (a local event sponsorship). And many times, you will need both tools, at least, to get the job done. Consider synergizing digital media with other tools in your toolkit, such as advergaming, sales promotions, coupons, contests, and other price deals.

14-6a Video Games and Advergaming

You may be surprised to learn that the "gamer" stereotype may not be accurate. The average game player is around 30 years old, and the most frequent game buyer is around 35. Almost half of the players are women. This is an attractive demographic and psychographic, as gamers are relatively young, digital, on social media, and have peer influence. Social media and gaming are synergizing (just as marketing, advertising, and PR seem to be blurring definitional lines). Gaming has become increasingly social; more than 60 percent play with others virtually or in person, and a growing number are playing on mobile devices.[68]

Different than an ad shown during a game, advertising and brand placement within video games is called **advergaming**. It is important to note the following points and differences of types of advergames.[69] Advergames are designed with the intent of promoting and marketing a brand; the game content centers around the brand, and that's why players have better brand recall and more positive brand attitudes after playing.[70] Note that there are levels of brand promotion within an advergame. Advergaming brand integration can occur at an associative (lowest), illustrative (medium), or demonstrative (highest) level.[71] An associative advergame brand integration merely makes a brand association during the game; for example, consider a Honda billboard in the scenery of an auto-racing game. Advergaming is often at the associative level; it is done primarily via embedded billboards and posters in video games. For example, some auto-racing games from Electronic Arts are full of ads on billboards, storefronts, and the racing cars themselves.

An illustrative advergame brand integration incorporates a brand spokesperson or personality as a main character within the game; for example, the Jolly Green Giant would be a character in an advergame at the illustrative level. A demonstrative advergaming brand integration features the brand, service, or product as a key part of the game. In some demonstrative advergames, the game has consumers learn about and virtually use the products within the game to advance to higher levels of the game. Pepsi, a Frito-Lay brand, featured a branded game, in which one of the characters was Pepsiman. Unilever's Axe also used a game on its website to launch one of its products.

A question for advertisers to examine is the effectiveness of in-game placement at each level. Although there is some evidence of a positive effect on brand recall, there is also evidence that repeated playing of the game can have a negative effect on players' attitudes toward embedded brands,[72] which could be due to a wear-out effect, also seen in some traditional advertising research.

Advergames are under ethical scrutiny, especially when geared toward children.[73] Often, as many as one in three advergames ask the player, presumably a child, to pass the game along to a friend. Hence, when considering this emerging and plausibly fun tool, think about the appropriateness of targeting children with the content, how they may not be able to yet process the content as more than a video game, and if it is appropriate to ask children to pass along the brand message to their friends. Perhaps this tool is best used for prosocial messages toward adolescents (e.g., anti–cyber bullying, peer pressure, the role of sports, and a healthy lifestyle). There is a difference in the way advergames' tools may be put to use by for-profit and nonprofit marketers,[74] as the nonprofit marketers may seek to create awareness of a social cause or to prompt a positive change in consumer behavior.

14-6b Sales Promotion

The digital and interactive options on the Internet are ideally suited to executing various aspects of sales promotion as part of the IBP effort. Coupon distribution and contests are the leading tools that are well suited to digital/interactive implementation, but sampling and trial offers can be promoted as well. The newer online sales promotion ideas are flash sales, more accurately sales events. Such emerging forms of sales promotion enhance trial use and give consumers opportunities to check out new products from favorite as well as new brands, without the pressure of a salesperson.

Coupons

Companies such as Retail-Me-Not, and individual influencers share online coupon codes with the world for e-commerce. Other **social couponing** sites, or sites that give or sell price discounts under the condition that a set number of other consumers buy or download the deal, distribute coupons via the sites of other commercial online services. Some social couponing sites allow users to print coupons on their home printers and then take them to the store for redemption. The company charges clients a set rate per thousand coupons distributed. However, only a small portion of those coupons are even clipped (2 to 3 percent redemption rate), whereas with online coupons, the manufacturer is paying only per thousand clipped, or in this case printed, by consumers. This makes digital distribution more effective in getting the coupons into the hands of consumers.

Contests and Sweepstakes

A contest often entails showing a skill, rather than a sweepstakes which is more of a game of chance. While we will detail these as forms of promotion in the next chapter, here we aim to show how they often manifest by way of digital, social, or mobile media. Many times, contests and sweepstakes are run via social media; for instance TikTok has various unofficial consumer challenges and contests. However, here we refer to official branded contests or sweepstakes that brands or companies launch or sponsor. A notable example is Goldfish's #GoForTheHandful, where consumers tried to put more goldfish in their hand than the record (which has held by an NBA player) in order to become a spokesperson and receive a year's supply of goldfish. It was a very successful brand contest as it earned over 11 billion impressions via TikTok. There are other, offline examples of such contests, where Pepsi had an under-the-bottle-cap contest that allowed users to earn points or discounts from under-the-cap awards on bottles of brands across the Pepsi product line. The contest was also launched on network TV and local spot radio. Drinkers of Pepsi brands were able to redeem points online and accumulate enough points to purchase goods or get discounts from various retailers.

Sampling, Trial Offers, Price-Off Deals

Firms can use their websites or email communications to offer consumers a wide range of sales promotion special deals. Samples, trial offers, and price-offs (discounts) can be offered via mobile or digital with email campaigns, pop-up or banner ads, or directly on the company website. Consumers merely need to click on an interactive ad, respond to an email, or visit the website to explore and take advantage of the offer. One advantage of using the Internet for these sales promotion techniques is that the firm acquires the consumer's email information and achieves a de facto opt-in contact.

14-6c Public Relations and Publicity

Companies can use the Web to disseminate information about the firm in a classic public relations sense. Web organizations like Business Wire (www.businesswire.com) and PR Newswire (www.prnewswire.com) offer services through which firms can request the dissemination of a press release over the Internet. These are often highly targeted press releases. Cost of the service varies by topic category—business, entertainment, news, or sports. These press releases can be picked up by major news services and online news sites like the *Huffington Post*.

14-6d Direct Marketing and E-Commerce

Digital is well suited to implementing a direct marketing IBP effort. Aside from the direct contact through email, mobile marketing, or virtual mail, direct marketing efforts can be coordinated with traditional media advertising campaigns by directing consumers to either company websites or e-commerce sites. One of the major shifts in the industry is in consumer empowerment with information on pricing and values. For instance, sites such as Zillow.com share real-time real estate estimate valuation. In the automobile industry, auto brands such as Chevrolet and Ford drive consumers to their dealer websites or to the brand sites. On the site of Ford, a digital leader, consumers can design their own vehicles with their choice of color, interior, sport package, rims, audio, and other features. This is a way to use e-commerce to have customers place orders for new vehicles, engage consumers prior to (or even instead of) the dealer visit and promote interactivity.

Email

The strength of email marketing stems from its inherent low cost and media advantages. Email is one of the least expensive marketing tools and provides the highest return on investment relative to other forms of online marketing.[75] Second, email marketing is fast, flexible, and up to date.[76] Third, email's further edge over other communication media is the wide variety of scopes for design (e.g., pictures, sounds, Flash animations, or videos).[77] Fourth, and perhaps the most important, is its ability to offer enhanced campaign effectiveness measurement (e.g., via tracking click-through rates).[78] In consideration of these advantages, advertisers are recognizing email marketing as an important digital tool.

Despite these benefits, there are some disadvantages associated with email marketing. First, spammers have compromised privacy and tainted the general attitude toward email marketing messages. The second veritable challenge confronting marketers is information overload and consumers' desire to cut through online clutter. The thousands of emails and embedded information that reach consumers daily exceed the limited processing capacity of the human memory.[79] To overcome this limitation, advertisers can combat information overload with eye-catching and attention-getting advertising design. Combining style with the interactive nature of email videos, embedding a video in email can be an effective marketing tool—that is, if there are no technical inhibitors preventing the video from downloading promptly and easily, which is the third limitation. A fourth limitation to email, specific to email with video, is that it may reach the recipient in a place where the video could disturb others with the sound. Despite these limitations, video has proven itself to be favorable to consumers and a preferred form of media—especially if it goes viral.

Viral Video

While it sounds like a disease, going viral is a good thing in industry lingo. The top viral brand messages have over 100 million views. Consumers or advertisers can encourage viral marketing. **Viral marketing** is when consumers market to other consumers over the Internet through electronic or in-person word of mouth. YouTube is often the host of video-based viral marketing, as is TikTok. A venue for viral campaigns is online videos of either television ads or follow-ons to television ads; Super Bowl ads are often leaked or posted officially in a viral manner before the game to generate buzz. Most viral videos have a humor appeal. Viral content is good in marketing. Use it or lose out on the viral movement and its inherent role in generating earned media.

14-6e Mobile Marketing and M-Commerce

Mobile marketing, as discussed in Chapter 1, is the process of optimizing digital content for reaching consumers on Internet-enabled mobile devices like smartphones and tablets. Consider these statistics about mobile marketing: (1) More than half (53 percent) of paid-search clicks are from mobile devices, (2) almost seventy percent of mobile searchers call the business found on the search directly from Google Search, and (3) almost 40 percent of Google searches are associated with location.[80]

These statistics point to a big opportunity in mobile. We stress the need for cross-device measurement, or measuring advertising effectiveness on various forms of digital advertising, because online consumer experiences are typically occurring on multiple screens. Consider how you watch TV, for instance, if at all. It may be with a laptop on and with a smartphone in your hand. This reflects the need for the integration and synergy among advertising and IBP that we have made a key emphasis for this book.

With the importance of cross-device advertising in mind, we now focus on mobile advertising from both a business and ethics lens due to the privacy issues therein with location-based marketing. We are in the midst of an exciting mobile marketing movement. Even though mobile marketing is really a phenomenon brought about by mobile, wireless access through smartphones, laptops, and tablet devices, it represents a form of direct marketing as well by virtue of wireless technology. Use of mobile devices is very high worldwide, and is increasing yearly, with more than 6 billion smartphones in use already.[81] Because most people in the world are mobile subscribers, marketers can initiate direct marketing campaigns if consumers have opted in—which in theory means the communication is invited by the consumer. For example, it can be helpful to get a text from the fast food restaurant Wendy's on a Saturday for a free small frosty desert with a burger order that weekend—if you were going to order burgers anyway. That said, it can be annoying and intrusive—even costing consumers if they don't have unlimited texts.

It is not only that email campaigns, text messaging, or sales promotions will reach mobile users directly on their devices, firms can also sponsor mobile videos that are downloaded on video handsets. IBP communications delivered through mobile devices achieve surprisingly high recall and effectiveness if the consumer prefers to enable his/her/their location. This way, any messages you get can be from local businesses. But again, this elevates a new privacy issue. Most consumers with smartphones get messages, albeit some unwanted, to their phones, so it is important to be aware of changes associated with geocaching, opt-in laws, and other pending mobile guidelines. The industry review board Interactive Advertising Bureau is working on mobile measurement guidelines, and industry reports based on big data with Facebook are creating new exposure rate metrics for social media. The next frontier involves advertising and measurement across devices—meaning how to plan, place, execute, and measure message exposure and engagement on digital, social, *and* mobile media.[82]

Summary

1. **Understand the synergistic role of digital, social, and mobile media in advertising and IBP along with the options available to brands in these media.**

The role of digital, social, and mobile in advertising and IBP is a crucial one. The shift towards Web 3.0 distinguishes the progression of the Internet to interactive networks leveraging artificial intelligence and machine learning, to transcend the already established role of interactivity, consumer-generated content, and digital engagement seen in Web 2.0. There is an array of creative and strategic options to brands available through digital or social media.

2. **See the importance in virtual identity for consumers and brands online.**

To best execute in digital platforms, it is key to understand online consumer behavior, namely the importance of virtual identity for consumers and brands online. Brands can and should manage their brand identity and online reputation.

3. **Understand the basics of digital advertising and search.**

Digital advertising and search have progressed to automated media placement and key-word bidding, SEO, and platforms such as Google Ad Words. A change has come from looking at digital media investments as a function of CRM or CPC to advertising that largely hinges on display advertising, search advertising, or a combination of the two. Therefore, it is important to know the basics of them and the digital media investment models such as CPC.

4. **Understand the basics of e-commerce as related to IBP and how it can stem from online advertising, social media, mobile, and search.**

E-commerce can be leveraged by understanding search and online advertising; digital advertisers should look for ways to enhance click-through and conversions to sales. As noted in the chapter, many mobile searches relate in a direct call to the business.

5. **Note the advantages of digital, social, and mobile media for implementing advertising and IBP campaigns, along with the dark side of social media, such as security and privacy concerns.**

The advantages of digital, social, and mobile media for implementing advertising and IBP campaigns include target market selectivity and flexibility, interactivity, consumer engagement, ease of use, and the ability to leverage a consumer's digital footprint with a brand relationship, among other pros. The main dark-side issues are privacy, security, and authenticity concerns. For advertisers, negative effects include click fraud, negative social media conversations harming brand perceptions, and content adjacent to messages.

6. **Understand how to synergize with different IBP tools.**

Digital and social media have many advantages for implementing advertising and IBP campaigns and synergize with various IBP tools such as advergaming, sponsorship, events, viral video, mobile marketing, email, sampling, POP, and traditional media. The next frontier is advertising and measurement across devices—meaning how to plan, place, execute, and measure message exposure and engagement on digital, social, *and* mobile media.

Key Terms

advergaming
app ads
bounce rate
click-through
click fraud
cost-per-click (CPC)
cyber-identity theft
digital footprint
display ads
earned media
ephemeral
fake news

interactivity
interstitial
location-based technologies
microblogs
mobile applications
native advertising
online resistance
owned media
paid media
paid search
post ads
privacy seal

retargeting
search
search engine optimization (SEO)
site stickiness
social couponing
subject matter expert
viral marketing
virtual identity
Web 2.0
Web 3.0

Endnotes

1. Angeline G. Close, (Ed.), *Online Consumer Behavior: Theory and Research in Social Media, Advertising, and E-tail* (New York/London: Routledge/Taylor & Francis Group, 2012).
2. See: Kelly Hewett, William Rand, Roland T. Rust, and Harald J. van Heerde, "Brand Buzz in the Echoverse," *Journal of Marketing* 80, no. 3 (2016), 1–24; and Rajeev Batra and Kevin Lane Keller, "Integrating Marketing Communications: New Findings, New Lessons, and New Ideas," *Journal of Marketing* 80, no. 6 (2016), 122–145.
3. Roland T. Rust et al., "Real-Time Brand Reputation Tracking Using Social Media," *Journal of Marketing* 85, no. 4 (2021), 21–43.
4. Elsamari Botha and Adam J. Mills, "Managing New Media: Tools for Brand Management in Social Media," in Angeline G. Close (Ed.), *Online Consumer Behavior: Theory and Research in Social Media, Advertising, and E-tail* (New York/London: Routledge/Taylor & Francis Group, 2012), 83–100.
5. Priye Rai, "What is Web 3.0?". *Fossbytes*, November 15, 2021. https://fossbytes.com/what-is-web-3/.
6. Pierre Berthon, Leyland Pitt, D. Cyr, and Colin Campbell, "E-readiness and Trust: Macro and Micro Dualities for e-Commerce in a Global Environment," *International Marketing Review* 25, no. 6 (2008), 700–714.
7. Don Tapscott and Anthony D. Williams, *Wikinomics: How Mass Collaboration Changes Everything* (New York: Penguin, 2007).
8. Ya You, and Amit M. Joshi, "The Impact of User-Generated Content and Traditional Media on Customer Acquisition and Retention," *Journal of Advertising* 49, no. 3 (2020), 213–233.
9. Sungjun (Steven) Park and Byungho Park, "Advertising on Mobile Apps versus the Mobile Web," *Journal of Advertising Research* 60, no. 4 (2019), 381–393.
10. Angeline G. Close, *Online Consumer Behavior: Theory and Research in Social Media, Advertising, and E-tail,* Routledge/Psychology Press.
11. Tanya Dua, "Marketers Are Still into Facebook Live," *Digiday*, March 1, 2017, https://digiday.com/marketing/despite-waning-publisher-interest-marketers-still-eyeing-facebook-live.
12. Bo-Lei Zhang, Zhu-Zhong Qian, Wen-Zhong Li, Bin Tang, Sang-Lu Lu, and Xiaoming Fu, "Budget Allocation for Maximizing Viral Advertising in Social Networks," *Journal of Computer Science and Technology* 31, no. 4 (2016), 759–775.
13. Angeline Close Scheinbaum, "Digital Engagement: Opportunities and Risks for Sponsors," *Journal of Advertising Research* 56, no. 4 (2016), 341–345.
14. Ibid.
15. Andreas M. Kaplan and Michael Haenlein, "Users of the World, Unite! The Challenges and Opportunities of Social Media," *Business Horizons* 53, no. 1 (2010), 59–68.
16. Dan Zarella, *The Social Media Marketing Book* (North Sebastopol, CA: O'Reilly Media, 2010).
17. Elsamari Botha and Adam J. Mills, "Managing New Media: Tools for Brand Management in Social Media," in Angeline G. Close (Ed.), *Online Consumer Behavior: Theory and Research in Social Media, Advertising, and E-tail* (New York/London: Routledge/Taylor & Francis Group, 2012)," 83–100.
18. Ibid.
19. Lauren Johnson, "Starbucks' Pumpkin Spice Lattes Are Killing It on Instagram," *Adweek*, September 8, 2016, http://www.adweek.com/digital/starbucks-pumpkin-spice-lattes-are-killing-it-instagram-173351.
20. Rodrigo Uribe, Cristian Buzeta, and Milenka Velásquez, "Sidedness, Commercial Intent and Expertise in Blog Advertising," *Journal of Business Research* 69, no. 10 (2016), 4403–4410.
21. Alfred Ng, "Super Bowl 51 Bowls Over Social Media," *CNET*, February 6, 2017, https://www.cnet.com/news/super-bowl-51-twitter-facebook-social-media-tom-brady-lady-gaga-patriots-social-cues.
22. Angeline Close, *E-Dating and Information Technology*, Doctoral Dissertation, Athens: The University of Georgia Press, 2006.
23. Ibid.
24. Elsamari Botha, Mana Farshid, and Leyland Pitt, "How Sociable? An Exploratory Study of University Brand Visibility in Social Media," *South African Journal of Business Management* 42, no. 2 (2011), 15–23.
25. Ibid.
26. Katie Richards, "An Inside Look at IHOP's Social Media War Room on National Pancake Day," *Adweek*, March 9, 2016, http://www.adweek.com/brand-marketing/these-tech-savvy-cmos-embody-all-the-talents-the-modern-marketer-needs.

27. Angeline Close Scheinbaum, "Digital Engagement: Opportunities and Risks for Sponsors," *Journal of Advertising Research* 56, no. 4 (2016): 341–345.

28. Coral Ouellette, "Online Shopping Statistics You Need to Know in 2021" *OptinMonster*, January 6, 2021, https://optinmonster.com /online-shopping-statistics/ and Marian Zboraj "Consumers Still Prefer In-Store Shopping" Progressive Grocer, January 5, 2021, https://progressivegrocer.com/consumers-still-prefer-store-shopping.

29. Nick Wingfield, "Unboxing Amazon's Ambitions," *New York Times*, March 26, 2017, BU1, BU7.

30. George Slefo, "YouTube to Offer Third-Party Brand Safety Tools Following Revolt by Marketers," *Ad Age*, April 3, 2017, http://adage.com/article/digital/youtube-offer-party-brand-safety -tools/308525.

31. Fuyuan Shen, "Banner Advertisement Pricing, Measurement, and Pretesting Practices: Perspectives from Interactive Agencies," *Journal of Advertising* 31, no. 3 (2002), 59–68.

32. Yoori Hwang, and Se-Hoon Jeong, "Consumers' Response to Format Characteristics in Native Advertising," *Journal of Advertising Research* 61, no. 2 (2020), 212–224.

33. Jing Zhang and En Mao, "From Online Motivations to Ad Clicks and to Behavioral Intentions: An Empirical Study of Consumer Response to Social Media Advertising," *Psychology & Marketing* 33, no. 3 (2016), 155–164.

34. As they do in traditional advertising, brands are using copy testing to improve paid search ads. See Oliver J. Rutz, Garrett P. Sonnier, and Michael Trusov, "A New Method to Aid Copy Testing of Paid Search Text Advertisements," *Journal of Marketing Research* (2017, in press).

35. Satya Menon and Dilip Soman, "Managing the Power of Curiosity for Effective Web Advertising Strategies," *Journal of Advertising* 31, no. 3 (2002), 1–14.

36. Lara Lobschat, Ernst C. Osinga, and Werner J. Reinartz, "What Happens Online Stays Online?—Segment-Specific Online and Offline Effects of Banner Advertisements," *Journal of Marketing Research* (2017), in press. doi: http://dx.doi.org/10.1509/jmr.14.0625

37. Navdeep S. Sahni, "Advertising Spillovers: Evidence from Online Field-Experiments and Implications for Returns on Advertising," *Journal of Marketing Research* 53, no. 4 (2016), 459–478.

38. Marty Swant, "Mobile Ad Study Finds Interstitials Only Slightly Better Than Banners for Being Seen," *Adweek*, July 1, 2016, http://www.adweek.com/digital/mobile-ad-study-finds-interstitials-only-slightly -better-banners-being-seen-171980.

39. *PPC Trends and Statistics*, http://www.powertraffick.com/ppc -trends-and-statistics, accessed April 7, 2017.

40. Data drawn from *Statista*, August 6, 2021 https://www.statista.com /statistics/455840/digital-advertising-revenue-; and http://www .insideradio.com/free/digital-ad-spending-forecast-to-rise-8-next -year-but-iab-says-consumers-are-changing/article_27f4649a -3c6a-11ec-a565-e3d76edb7449.html.

41. Chris K. Anderson and Ming Cheng, "Multi-Click Attribution in Sponsored Search Advertising: An Empirical Study in Hospitality Industry," *Cornell Hospitality Quarterly* (2017). First published online: DOI: https://doi.org/10.1177/1938965516686112.

42. Ilyse Liffreing, "Amazon Had the Most US Desktop Search Clicks in 2016, Study Finds," *Campaign (US)*, March 13, 2017, http://www.campaignlive.com/article/amazon-us-desktop -search-clicks-2016-study-finds/1427076.

43. For more about shopping carts and consumer behavior, see Angeline G. Close and Monika Kukar-Kinney, "Beyond Buying: Motivations Behind Consumers' Online Shopping Cart Use," *Journal of Business Research* 63, no. 9 (2010), 986–992.

44. Data drawn from *The United Nations Conference on Trade and Development Report*, May 3, 2021. https://unctad.org/news /global-e-commerce-jumps-267-trillion-covid-19-boosts-online -sales

45. Pierre Berthon, Leyland Pitt, D. Cyr, and Colin Campbell, "E-readiness and Trust."

46. Andreas M. Kaplan and Michael Haenlein, "Users of the World, Unite! The Challenges and Opportunities of Social Media," *Business Horizons*, vol. 53, no. 1 (2010), 59–68."

47. Angeline Close Scheinbaum, (Ed.), *The Dark Side of Social Media: A Consumer Psychology Perspective* (New York /London: Routledge /Taylor & Francis Group, 2018).

48. "Social Media Fact Sheet" Pew Research Center, April 7, 2021 https://www.pewresearch.org/internet/fact-sheet/social-media/

49. Russell W. Belk, "Qualitative Research in Advertising," *Journal of Advrtising* 46, no. 1 (2017), 1–12.

50. Chongyu Lu and Rex Yuxing Du, "Click-through Behavior across Devices in Paid Search Advertising," *Journal of Advertising Research* 60, no. 4 (2020), 394–406.

51. Andrew Hampp, "Live TV's Alive as Ever, Boosted by Social Media," *Advertising Age*, February 15, 2010, 1–2.

52. Beth L. Fossen and David A. Schweidel, "Television Advertising and Online Word-of-Mouth: An Empirical Investigation of Social TV Activity," *Marketing Science* 36, no. 1 (2016), 105–123.

53. Ereni Marcos, Lauren L. Labrecque, and George R. Milne, "Web 2.0 and Consumers' Digital Footprint: Managing Privacy Disclosure Choices in Social Media," in Angeline G. Close (Ed.), *Online Consumer Behavior: Theory and Research in Social Media, Advertising, and E-tail* (New York/ London: Routledge/Taylor & Francis Group, 2012), 157–184

54. Ereni Marcos, Lauren L. Labrecque, and George R. Milne, "Web 2.0 and Consumers' Digital Footprint: Managing Privacy Disclosure Choices in Social Media," in Angeline G. Close (Ed.), *Online Consumer Behavior: Theory and Research in Social Media, Advertising, and E-tail* (New York/ London: Routledge/Taylor & Francis Group, 2012), 157–184; George R. Milne and Shalini Bahl, "Are There Differences between Consumers' and Marketers' Privacy Expectations? A Segment- and Technology-Level Analysis," *Journal of Public Policy & Marketing* 29, no. 1 (2010), 138–149; Amit Poddar, Jill Mostellar, and Pam Scholder-Ellen, "Consumers' Rules of Engagement in Online Information Exchanges," *Journal of Consumer Affairs* 43, no. 3 (2009), 419–448.

55. Mary Madden, Susannah Fox, Aaron Smith, and Jessica Vitak, "Digital Footprints: Online Identity Management and Search in the Age of Transparency," 2007, http://pewresearch.org/pubs/663 /digital-footprints.

56. See, for example, A-Reum Jung, "The Influence of Perceived Ad Relevance on Social Media Advertising: An Empirical Examination of a Mediating Role of Privacy Concern," *Computers in Human Behavior* (2017, forthcoming).

57. Lauren I. Labrecque, Shabnam H. A. Zanjani, and George R. Milne, "Authenticity in Online Communications: Examining Antecedents and Consequences," in Angeline G. Close (Ed.), *Online Consumer Behavior: Theory and Research in Social Media, Advertising, and E-tail* (New York /London: Routledge/Taylor & Francis Group, 2012), 133–156.

58. Angeline G. Close, G. M. Zinkhan, and R. Z. Finney, *Cyber Identity Theft* (Chicago: American Marketing Association, 2007).

59. Kenneth Olmstead and Aaron Smith, "What the Public Knows About Cybersecurity," *Pew Research Center*, March 22, 2017, http://www.pewinternet.org/2017/03/22/what-the-public -knows-about-cybersecurity.

60. Ereni Marcos, Lauren L. Labrecque, and George R. Milne et al., "Web 2.0 and Consumers' Digital Footprint"; Goodwin, Cathy, "Privacy: Recognition of a Consumer Right," *Journal of Public Policy & Marketing* 10, no. 1 (1991), 149–166.

61. George R. Milne, Andrew Rohm, and Shalini Bahl, "Consumers' Protection of Online Privacy and Identity," *Journal of Consumer Affairs* 38, no. 2 (2004), 217–232; Marcos et al., Lauren L. Labrecque, and George R. Milne, "Web 2.0 and Consumers' Digital Footprint."

62. George R. Milne, Shalini Bahl, and Andrew Rohm, "Toward a Framework for Assessing Covert Marketing Practices," *Journal of Public Policy and Marketing* 27, no. 1 (2008), 57–62; Anthony D. Miyazaki "Online Privacy and the Disclosure of Cookie Use: Effects on Consumer Trust and Anticipated Patronage," *Journal of Public Policy and Marketing* 27, no. 1 (2008), 19-33; Anthony D. Miyazaki and Sandeep Krishnamurthy, "Internet Seals of Approval: Effects on Online Privacy Policies and Consumer Perceptions," *Journal of Consumer Affairs* 36, no. 1 (2002), 28–49.

63. Yefim Roth, Michaela Wänke, and Ido Erev, "Click or Skip: The Role of Experience in Easy-Click Checking Decisions," *Journal of Consumer Research* (2017), forthcoming.

64. Ereni Marcos, Lauren L. Labrecque, and George R. Milne et al., "Web 2.0 and Consumers' Digital Footprint: Managing Privacy Disclosure Choices in Social Media," in Angeline G. Close (Ed.), *Online Consumer Behavior: Theory and Research in Social Media, Advertising, and E-tail* (New York/London: Routledge/Taylor & Francis Group, 2012), 157–184.

65. Ibid.

66. Danielle Gibson, "Snapchat to Become More Popular among Advertisers than Twitter and AOL by 2020 Says Study," *The Drum*, March 27, 2017, http://www.thedrum.com/news/2017/03/27/snapchat-become-more-popular-among-advertisers-twitter-and-aol-2020-says-study.

67. Gian M. Fulgoni, "Fraud in Digital Advertising: A Multibillion-Dollar Black Hole," *Journal of Advertising Research* 56, no. 2 (2016), 122–125.

68. Andrea Kähr, Bettina Nyffenegger, Harley Krohmer, and Wayne D. Hoyer, "When Hostile Consumers Wreak Havoc on Your Brand: The Phenomenon of Consumer Brand Sabotage," *Journal of Marketing* 80, no. 3 (2016), 25–41.

69. Ilyse Liffreing, "So Your Brand Is the Victim of Fake News. Now What?" *Campaign (US)*, November 21, 2016, http://www.campaignlive.com/article/so-brand-victim-fake-news-what/1416180.

70. Daisuke Wakabayashi and Sapna Maheshwari, "YouTube Advertiser Exodus Highlights Perils of Online Ads," *New York Times*, March 23, 2017, https://www.nytimes.com/2017/03/23/business/media/youtube-advertisers-offensive-content.html?_r=0.

71. Industry Facts, Entertainment Software Association, 2013, www.theesa.com/facts, accessed March 2013.

72. Vincent Cicchirillo and J. Lin, "Stop Playing with Your Food: A Comparison of For-Profit and Non-Profit Food Related Advergames," *Journal of Advertising Research* 51, no. 3 (2011), 484–498.

73. Zeph M. Van Berlo et al., "The Gamification of Branded Content: A Meta-Analysis of Advergame Effects," *Journal of Advertising* 50, no. 2 (2021), 179–196.

74. Cicchirillo and J. Lin, "Stop Playing with Your Food."

75. Zeph M. Van Berlo et al., "The Gamification of Branded Content: A Meta-Analysis of Advergame Effects," *Journal of Advertising* 50, no. 2 (2021), 179–196.

76. Cicchirillo and Lin, "Stop Playing with Your Food." and Van Zeph M. Berlo et al. "The Gamification of Branded Content: A Meta-Analysis of Advergame Effects," *Journal of Advertising* 50, no. 2, 26 (2021), 179–196.

77. Ibid.

78. Oleg Pavlov, Nigel Melville, and Robert Plice, "Toward a Sustainable Email Marketing Infrastructure," *Journal of Business Research* 61, no. 11 (2008), 1191–1199.

79. Debbie Du Frene, Brian Engelland, Carol Lehman, and Rodney Pearson, "Changes in Consumer Attitudes Resulting from Participation in a Permission E-Mail-Campaign," *Journal of Current Issues and Research in Advertising* 27, no. 1 (2005), 65–77.

80. Cicchirillo and Lin, "Stop Playing with Your Food."

81. Nigel Melville, Aaron Stevens, Robert Plice, and Oleg Pavlov, "Unsolicited Commercial E-Mail: Empirical Analysis of a Digital Commons," *International Journal of Electronic Commerce* 10, no. 4 (2006), 143-168.

82. Jacob Jacoby, "Information Load and Decision Quality: Some Contested Issues," *Journal of Marketing Research* 14, no. 4 (1997), 569–573.

83. "Surprising Statistics on Pay Per Click Management Trends in 2016 and 2017," *Powertraffic*, Jan. 1, 2017, http://www.powertraffick.com/ppc-trends-and-statistics.

84. S. O'Dea, "How Many Smartphones are Active Worldwide?", August 6, 2021, https://www.statista.com/statistics/330695/number-of-smartphone-users-worldwide/.

85. Ray Schultz, "Users and Devices: The New Ecommerce," *Media Post*, March 6, 2017, http://www.mediapost.com/publications/article/296416/users-and-devices-the-new-ecommerce.html.

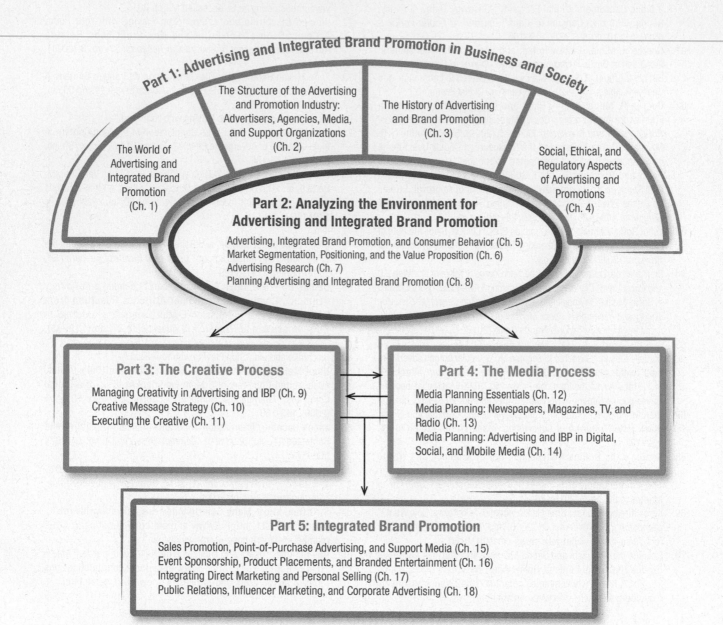

Part 1: Advertising and Integrated Brand Promotion in Business and Society

The World of Advertising and Integrated Brand Promotion (Ch. 1)

The Structure of the Advertising and Promotion Industry: Advertisers, Agencies, Media, and Support Organizations (Ch. 2)

The History of Advertising and Brand Promotion (Ch. 3)

Social, Ethical, and Regulatory Aspects of Advertising and Promotions (Ch. 4)

Part 2: Analyzing the Environment for Advertising and Integrated Brand Promotion

Advertising, Integrated Brand Promotion, and Consumer Behavior (Ch. 5)
Market Segmentation, Positioning, and the Value Proposition (Ch. 6)
Advertising Research (Ch. 7)
Planning Advertising and Integrated Brand Promotion (Ch. 8)

Part 3: The Creative Process

Managing Creativity in Advertising and IBP (Ch. 9)
Creative Message Strategy (Ch. 10)
Executing the Creative (Ch. 11)

Part 4: The Media Process

Media Planning Essentials (Ch. 12)
Media Planning: Newspapers, Magazines, TV, and Radio (Ch. 13)
Media Planning: Advertising and IBP in Digital, Social, and Mobile Media (Ch. 14)

Part 5: Integrated Brand Promotion

Sales Promotion, Point-of-Purchase Advertising, and Support Media (Ch. 15)
Event Sponsorship, Product Placements, and Branded Entertainment (Ch. 16)
Integrating Direct Marketing and Personal Selling (Ch. 17)
Public Relations, Influencer Marketing, and Corporate Advertising (Ch. 18)

As shown in the framework diagram for this section, advertisers can enrich their campaigns with a full range of consumer and trade sales promotion techniques, along with support media like outdoor signage and out-of-home media (Chapter 15). With the convergence of advertising, branding, and entertainment, IBP campaigns often include event sponsorships, product placements, and branded entertainment (Chapter 16). Advertisers can use direct marketing to communicate with a target audience and seek an immediate response, and many also rely on the power of personal selling (Chapter 17). Finally, advertisers need to plan for the use of public relations, influencer marketing, and corporate advertising to create brand buzz and enhance a firm's image and reputation (Chapter 18).

Part

5

Integrated Brand Promotion

15 Sales Promotion, Point-of-Purchase Advertising, and Support Media *322*

16 Event Sponsorship, Product Placements, and Branded Entertainment *350*

17 Integrating Direct Marketing and Personal Selling *370*

18 Public Relations, Influencer Marketing, and Corporate Advertising *394*

Part 5 highlights the full range of communication tools a firm can use in developing and supporting an integrated brand promotion campaign. The variety and breadth of communication options discussed here represent a tremendous opportunity for marketers to be creative and break through the clutter in today's crowded marketplace. Each of the tools discussed in Part 5 has the unique capability to influence the audience's perception of and desire to own a branded good or service while ensuring that consistency with advertising and other forms of marketing are maintained.

Sales Promotion, Point-of-Purchase Advertising, and Support Media

Learning Objectives

After reading and thinking about this chapter, you will be able to do the following:

1 Define sales promotion and the three broad audiences for sales promotion.

2 Explain the importance and growth of sales promotion.

3 Describe the sales promotion techniques used in the consumer market.

4 Describe the sales promotion techniques used in the trade channel and business markets.

5 Identify the risks of using sales promotion that brands may face.

6 Understand the role and techniques of point-of-purchase advertising.

7 Describe the role of support media in a comprehensive IBP strategy.

Introduction

Sales promotion, point-of-purchase (P-O-P) advertising, and support media (like billboards, transit advertising, and packaging) offer advertisers a wide range of opportunities to communicate to consumers that are vastly different from other forms of media. These IBP tools work in ways that traditional media and digital media don't (see Exhibit 15.1) because they are often used in IBP campaigns as support media—as media that often supplement more substantial or longer-term media investments.

Consider these ways of attracting you to brands. You unlock your hotel room with your phone; and immediately, a sensor sets the lights and the room temperature, switches on the TV to Netflix—the technology is set to know all of your set preferences. You're on your way home from work and you get a text that the grocery store has a special on vitaminwater, which you drink—the grocery store scanner knows this. Or you drive by a billboard, and it informs you that you need a tire rotation. Technology is in place for such sales promotions and point of purchase (P-O-P) IBP campaigns. The potential for knowing when and where consumers are is blurring the lines between advertising and promotions. While P-O-P plays an important role at the point of purchase in online shopping or in a store, it is not the leading tool in IBP as often times it is considered as a form of support media that helps strengthen IBP campaigns. The more complex and information-rich tools of IBP are really what create brand loyalty and competitive advantage.

This chapter will explore all the possibilities and opportunities that sales promotion, P-O-P advertising, and other support media offer the advertiser. These types of support media are being adapted quickly to new technologies available for forward-thinking IBP campaigns. See Exhibit 15.2 for an example of support media; it is a sales promotion by Subway, who is enticing customers to order sandwiches from their mobile app and giving limited time offers. In this image showing their sales promotion for free delivery

Exhibit 15.1 ▶ Framework diagram for Chapter 15.

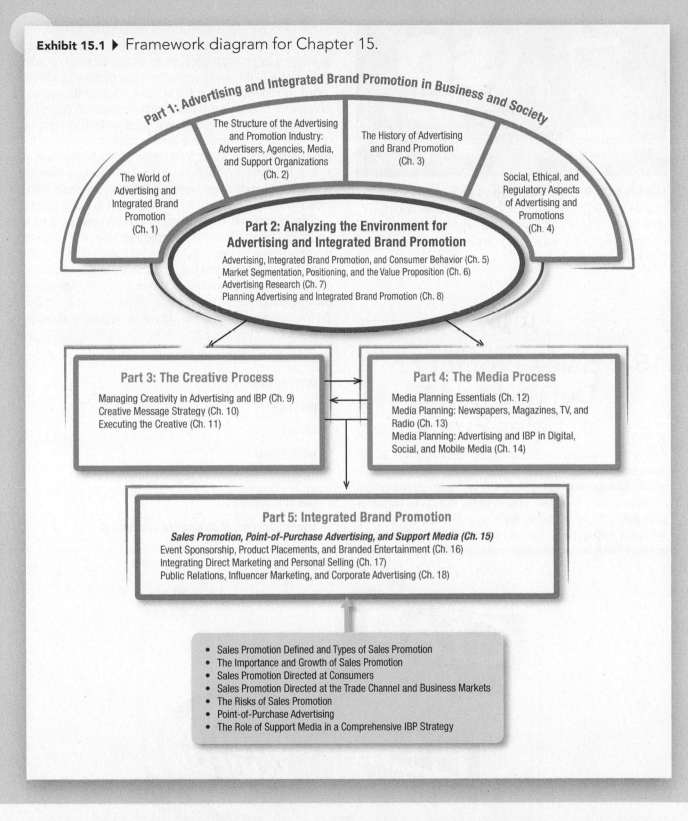

for a limited time for customers who order their food on their app (mobile application), it makes the price savings prominent.

In the image, showing a hand with a phone with the Subway app, it hints at the convenience factor as well.

Source: Subway IP Inc.

Exhibit 15.2 ▶ Subway uses sales promotion in their IBP mix and with this promotion, the brand encourages the use of their mobile app as a way to order food, with perks of free delivery.

LO 1

15-1 Sales Promotion Defined and Types of Sales Promotion

Sales promotion is often a key component within an IBP campaign—particularly campaigns seeking short-term sales effects. Sales promotions can work well with online and/or in store purchases. Some examples include: dealer incentives, consumer price discounts, and samples. Sales promotions attract attention to brands' social media and help with word-of-mouth buzz for brands. While mass media advertising is designed to build a brand image over time, sales promotion is designed to make things happen in the short run, particularly with mobile or location-based techniques as just described. When integrated properly with other forms of IBP, sales promotions are capable of almost instant demand stimulation. For instance, consider the demand increase for a brand that is linked with a compelling contest or sweepstakes. The "message" in a sales promotion features price reduction, free samples, a prize, or some other incentive for consumers to try a brand or for a retailer to feature the brand in a store. The Glad trash bag package in Exhibit 15.3 is an example of a sales promotion, a free sample in this case, that could entice consumers to try the product for the first time or to switch brands.

Sales promotion is the use of incentive techniques that create a perception of greater brand value among consumers, the trade, and business buyers. The intent is to generate a short-term increase in sales by motivating trial use, encouraging larger purchases, or stimulating repeat purchases. **Consumer-market sales promotion** can be either price promotions or not and includes the following ways to reach the end-user (individual or household consumer):

- coupons/e-coupons
- price-off deals
- premiums
- contests
- sweepstakes
- sampling
- trial offer rebates
- loyalty/frequency programs (for consumers)
- gift cards

GLAD® and ODOR SHIELD® are registered trademarks of The Glad Products Company. Used with Permission.

Exhibit 15.3 ▶ Sales promotion often creates the perception of greater value for the consumer. Here, the promise of a free sample inside the Glad Tall Kitchen Bag package is just such a sales promotion offer.

Exhibit 15.4 ▶ The fashion brand Kate Spade offers sales promotions that center around the major American shopping day of Black Friday.

All of these incentives are ways of encouraging household consumers to try or purchase a firm's brand rather than a competitor's brand (in the short run). Notice that some incentives reduce price or encourage consumer visits to the brand's website or app. For instance, the fashion brand Kate Spade at times offers promotions positioned around Black Friday; during this time the brand has offered customers as much as 50% off with their price promotions. See Exhibit 15.4 for an example from Kate Spade. In this example, the image depicts imagery associated with a party, such as an invitation, martini, and lipstick in an artistic design that captures attention and interest. Then any consumer desire to preview the Black Friday merchandise can do so via the "Go to Sale" icon. The Kate Spade website gives a further price incentive by sharing a code for shoppers to enter at the checkout phase of select purchases. Thus, the brand offers price incentives along with creative content.

Trade-market sales promotion uses the following ways of motivating distributors, wholesalers, and retailers to stock and feature a firm's brand in their store merchandising programs or online and mobile platforms:

- P-O-P displays
- salesperson incentives
- allowances
- cooperative advertising
- sales training

Business-market sales promotion is designed to cultivate buyers in organizations or corporations who are making purchase decisions about a wide range of products, including computers, office supplies, and consulting services.

Techniques used for business buyers are similar to the trade-market techniques and include the following:

- trade shows
- premiums
- incentives
- loyalty/frequency programs (for business buyers)

15-2 The Importance and Growth of Sales Promotion

Sales promotion is designed to impact demand differently than advertising does. Whereas most advertising is designed to have long-term brand awareness and image- and preference-building effects, sales promotion is used primarily to elicit an immediate purchase from a customer group.[1] Coupons, samples, rebates, contests, sweepstakes, and similar techniques offer household consumers, trade buyers, or business buyers an immediate incentive to choose one brand over another. As an example, Oreo offered a dunk challenge as a way to generate excitement and short-term sales for the cookie that consumers are known to dunk in milk, as exemplified in Exhibit 15.5.

Sales promotions tend to be price promotions or non-price related promotions. **Price promotions** typically

Source: Oreo

Exhibit 15.5 ▶ Oreo has done a creative promotion for consumers called the Oreo Dunk Challenge and has integrated celebrity and events into the promotion that plays on the consumer behavior of dunking the Oreo cookies into milk.

feature price reductions, such as coupons, and are effective in the convenience goods category (paper towels, soft drinks, etc.), where frequent purchases, brand switching, and a perceived homogeneity (similarity) among brands characterize consumer behavior.

Also, some brands, stores, or companies/organizations offer **loyalty programs**, which are designed to attract new customers and/or retain existing customers to offer rewards for being loyal to a brand, company, or store. The most common examples are airline frequent-flyer programs and grocery store frequent-shopper loyalty programs. These sales promotions also provide an affiliation value for a brand, which increases a consumer's ability and desire to identify with a particular brand. Loyalty programs are often designed to be longer-term in nature than many short sales promotions, and are technically not permanent as at times companies and brands can eliminate or revamp their loyalty programs.

Sales promotions are used across all consumer goods categories and in the trade and business markets as well. When a firm determines that a more immediate response than advertising can accomplish is needed—whether the target customer is a household, business buyer, distributor, or retailer—sales promotions are designed to provide that effect. The goals for sales promotion versus those of advertising are compared in Exhibit 15.6. Notice the key differences in the goals for these different forms of promotion.

Sales promotion encourages more immediate and short-term responses, whereas the purpose of advertising is to cultivate an image, loyalty, and repeat purchases over the long term.

As an example of sales promotion versus traditional advertising, consider the band Victoria's Secret, which sells underwear, pajamas, and fragrances. While they often air television commercials, they also at times offer sales promotions for certain types of products to spark short-term demand for those. For instance, Victoria's Secret has offered a sales promotion around the holidays for their pajamas. See Exhibit 15.7 for the example. In this image, it depicts four models of various ages wearing the brand's pajamas, and it offers a sales promotion. Specifically, the sales promotion is a limited time price incentive of 50% off of select styles with an e-commerce code. The call to action for their sales promotion is to drive consumers to the products online with the "Shop Now" icon on their web banner.

15-2a The Importance of Sales Promotion

When a firm determines that a more immediate response than advertising can accomplish is needed—whether the target customer is a household, business buyer, distributor, or retailer—sales promotions are designed to provide that effect.

The importance of sales promotion should not be underestimated. Sales promotion may not seem as stylish and sophisticated as mass media advertising or as exciting as new digital media opportunities, but expenditures on this tool are strategic and impressive. Big consumer-products

Exhibit 15.6 ▶ Sales promotion and advertising serve different purposes in IBP. What would you describe as the key differences between the two based on the features listed here?

PURPOSE OF SALES PROMOTION	PURPOSE OF ADVERTISING
Stimulate short-term demand	Cultivate long-term demand
Encourage brand switching	Encourage brand loyalty
Induce trial use	Encourage repeat purchases
Promote price orientation	Promote image/feature orientation
Obtain immediate, often measurable results	Obtain long-term effects, often difficult to measure

Exhibit 15.7 ▶ The brand Victoria's Secret uses the holidays as a platform for one of their sales promotions featuring pajamas, which are a popular holiday gift.

firms began shifting dollars out of media advertising and into promotions to encourage consumers to try and then buy (in store or online). "When you talk about increasing trial and sampling at point of market entry and point of market change with noticeably superior products, that moves markets over time," observes the CFO of Procter & Gamble, which owns billion-dollar brands like Downy, Pampers, Tide, Always, and Head & Shoulders.[2] The development and management of an effective sales promotion program requires a major commitment by a firm. During any given year, as much as 30 percent of brand management time might be devoted to designing, implementing, and overseeing sales promotions. As an example, Doritos partnered with EA Sports and its successful Madden video game, as seen in Exhibit 15.8.

15-2b Growth in the Use of Sales Promotion

Again, many marketers have shifted emphasis toward promotional investments. There are several reasons why many marketers have been moving funds from mass media advertising to sales promotions; the first reason is that promotions are often measurable, which is very important in today's IBP environment that demands accountability for IBP investments.

Demand for Greater Accountability

In an era of cost cutting and shareholder scrutiny, companies are demanding greater accountability across all functions, including

Exhibit 15.8 ▶ Doritos partnered with EA Sports and its successful Madden video game. Why does this partnership make sense for a consumer sales promotion?

marketing, advertising, and promotions. When activities are evaluated for their contribution to sales and profits, it is often difficult to draw specific conclusions regarding the effects of advertising. But the more immediate effects of sales promotions are typically easier to document. Various studies have shown that only 18 percent of TV advertising campaigns produced a short-term positive return on investment (ROI) on promotional dollars. Conversely, other studies have shown that P-O-P in-store displays have been shown to positively affect sales by as much as 35 percent in some product categories.[3]

Short-Term Orientation

Several factors have created a short-term orientation among managers. Pressures from stockholders to increase quarter-by-quarter revenue and profit per share are one factor. A bottom-line mentality is another. Many organizations are developing marketing plans—with rewards and punishments for manager performance—that are based on short-term revenue generation. This being the case, companies are seeking tactics that can have short-term effects. There is some sound reasoning behind the strategy, though. If a customer stops in for free fries, they might also buy a burger and drink—an immediate effect on sales. And a free product also presents

the chance to "convert the curious into loyalists." McDonald's, for example, claims that at least half the customers who come in for free coffee wind up buying something else.[4]

Consumer Response to Promotions

The precision shopper in the contemporary marketplace is demanding greater value across all purchase situations, and that trend is battering overpriced brands. These precision shoppers search for extra value in every product purchase. Coupons, premiums, price-off deals, and other sales promotions increase the value of a brand in these shoppers' minds. Be careful here—coupons, price reduction, and value seeking do not necessarily mean consumers are choosing the *lowest*-priced item. Sales promotion techniques act as an incentive to purchase the brand *featuring* a promotion, even if another brand has a lower basic price. For example, the comfortable footwear and accessories brand Ugg offers a sales promotion technique that offers free expedited shipping for a limited time. So if a customer was on the fence about buying some Ugg slippers, which are not necessarily a lowest-price item, they may be motivated to purchase in order to receive the free shipping because that promotion or offer could expire. See Exhibit 15.9 for an example of a sales promotion by Ugg.

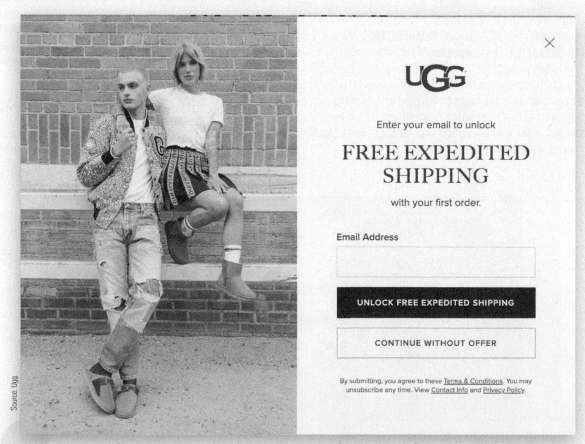

Exhibit 15.9 ▶ The brand Ugg, which is known for its comfortable shearling lined slippers, shoes, and boots does a promotion where they ask for consumers' email addresses to subscribe in order to unlock a deal for free expedited shipping.

Proliferation of Brands

Each year, thousands of new brands are introduced into the consumer market. The drive by marketers to design products for specific market segments to satisfy ever more narrowly defined needs has caused a proliferation of brands that creates a mind-dulling maze for consumers. Consider this case of brand proliferation—in one 12-month period, Coca-Cola's head of marketing launched 1,000 new drinks or new variations of existing brands worldwide.[5] At any point in time, consumers are typically able to choose from about 60 spaghetti sauces, 100 snack chips, 50 laundry detergents, 90 cold remedies, and 60 disposable diaper varieties. As you can see in Exhibit 15.10, gaining attention in this blizzard of brands is no easy task. Because of this proliferation and "clutter" of brands, marketers turn to sales promotions—contests, coupons, premiums, loyalty programs, P-O-P displays—to gain some attention for individual brands.

Increased Power of Retailers/E-Tailers

Big retailers (often with e-commerce capabilities) like Wal-Mart, Amazon, Kroger, Home Depot, Costco, Walgreens, Target, CVS, Lowe's, and Albertsons dominate retailing in the United States and they want to know how to allocate their digital and advertising budgets accordingly[6]. These powerful retailers have responded quickly to changing consumer behavior trends, with interest in more and better products and services at lower prices. In turn, retailers are demanding more deals from manufacturers. Many of the deals are delivered in terms of trade-oriented sales promotions: P-O-P displays, slotting fees (payment for shelf space), case allowances, and co-op advertising allowances. In the end, manufacturers use more and more sales promotions to gain and maintain good relationships with the powerful retailers—a critical link to the consumer. And retailers use the tools of sales promotion as a means of competing with one another.

Clutter

Many advertisers target the same customers because their research has led them to the same conclusion about which segment is the most attractive. The result is that advertising media are cluttered with ads all seeking the attention of the same people. When consumers encounter a barrage of ads, they tune out. One way to break through the clutter is to feature a novel sales promotion. In print ads, the featured deal is often a coupon. In television and radio advertising, sweepstakes, premium, and rebate offers can attract consumers' attention. Mobile coupons and offers are increasingly pushed or pulled to consumers' smartphones. The combination of mobile/digital marketing and creative sales promotions has proven to be a good way to break through the clutter, as exemplified by some brands' interest in joining Pokémon Go. With this trend of consumer sales promotions, consumers were rewarded with discounts or freebies by checking in with the augmented-reality mobile app (see Exhibit 15.11).

Exhibit 15.10 ▶ As you can see by this shelf of spaghetti sauces, getting the consumer to pay attention to any one brand is quite a challenge. Sales promotion techniques often provide the answer for gaining attention. Notice the P-O-P promotion attached to the shelves.

Source: Niantic, Inc.

Exhibit 15.11 ▶ Pokémon Go brought a trend of consumer sales promotions in which consumers were rewarded with discounts or freebies by checking in with the augmented-reality mobile app.

— LO 3 —

15-3 Sales Promotion Directed at Consumers

U.S. consumer-product firms have made a tremendous commitment to sales promotion in their overall marketing plans. During the 1970s, consumer-goods marketers allocated only about 30 percent of their budgets to sales promotion, with about 70 percent allocated to mass media advertising. Now we see that for many consumer-goods firms, more is being spent on various forms of promotion and P-O-P materials than on traditional advertising, with digital/social/mobile spending also increasing. Let's examine the objectives for sales promotion in the consumer market.

15-3a Objectives for Consumer-Market Sales Promotion

To help ensure the proper application of sales promotion, specific strategic objectives should be set. The following basic objectives can be pursued with sales promotion in the consumer market.

Stimulate Trial Purchase

When a brand wants to attract new customers, sales promotion tools can reduce the consumer's risk of trying something new. A reduced price, offer of a rebate, or a free sample may stimulate trial purchase. Note that for an established product category, sales promotion is geared toward stimulating trial of a particular brand, not the product category. Recall the discussions in Chapters 2 and 4 (primary vs. selective demand stimulation) highlighting that advertising and promotion cannot initiate product category use in mature product categories, like coffee, but can only affect brand choice among people who already use the product category. Starbucks, for instance, covers multiple IBP objectives with different promotions; Starbucks partnered with Pokémon Go (recall Exhibit 15.11) to cut the clutter and stimulate a trial purchase for a Frappuccino by offering a free beverage upon buying one with a different promotion (Exhibit 15.12).

Stimulate Repeat Purchases

In-package coupons designed for the next purchase or the accumulation of points with repeated purchase can help keep consumers loyal to a particular brand. Loyalty or frequent-purchase programs are the best techniques for pursuing this objective (more detail on these shortly). Firms try to retain their most loyal and lucrative customers by enrolling them in loyalty programs, as Chipotle does with burrito lovers. Adding a hashtag (for example, #chipotle royalty) is a great way to add measurability and digital engagement while stimulating repeat purchases. Another brand that uses promotions to stimulate repeat purchases is Domino's; they used a digital promotion with the hashtag (#FreeAdvicein-5Words) for customers to engage digitally with the brand in order to earn points to save money on repeat orders (see Exhibit 15.13).

Stimulate Larger Purchases

Encouraging consumers to buy larger purchase amounts or in larger quantities offers benefits to both the manufacturer and retailer. Both get increased dollar volume, and both realize the benefit of faster inventory turnover. Price reductions or two-for-one sales can motivate consumers to stock up on a brand, thus allowing firms to reduce inventory or increase cash flow. For examples, shampoo is often double-packaged with a bottle of conditioner to offer value added for consumers. Powerade and Gatorade at times offer discounts on multiple 6- or 12-packs purchased at the same time.

Source: Dominos pizza

Exhibit 15.13 ▶ Domino's promotes its buyer rewards program on social media such as Twitter, reminding customers of the value of repeat purchasing.

Introduce a New Brand, Service, or Product

Because sales promotion can attract attention and motivate trial purchase, it is commonly used for new brand, service, or product introductions. One of the most successful uses of sales promotions to introduce a new brand was when the maker of Curad bandages introduced its kid-size bandage by distributing 7.5 million sample packs in McDonald's Happy Meal sacks. The promotion, now a classic example, was a huge success, with initial sales exceeding estimates by 30 percent. Other times, large companies such as General Mills, will offer sales promotions for a variety of their new products or flavors—such as lime mojito or pina colada sorbet from their Häagen-Dazs brand, protein bars for their Fibre One brand, and Skittles flavored yogurt for their Yoplait brand. In a much more unique example, Axe introduced a new product line with a promotion called "Come back a hero," though which consumers could win a trip to space (Exhibit 15.14). This was a novel way to get consumers talking about their new products and going to the website that Axe made specifically for the promotion.

Combat or Disrupt Competitors' Strategies

Because sales promotions often motivate consumers to buy in larger quantities or try new brands, they can be used to disrupt

Source: Starbucks

Exhibit 15.12 ▶ One of the most common and successful forms of consumer sales promotions is a price discount or buy-one-get-one (BOGO) promotion, such as this one by Starbucks to honor Penang Heritage Day. Sharing a Starbuck's treat is much better than going alone, so BOGO promotions are great for such products prone for sharing and socialization.

Exhibit 15.14 ▶ Axe did one of the most unusual promotions by offering consumers a chance to go to space.

promotion can add yet another type of communication to the mix. Sales promotions suggest an additional value, with price reductions, premiums, or the chance to win a prize. This is a specific message designed to be used in the sales promotion mix and to fit within the overall communications strategy and IBP effort.

Petco, for instance, uses in store and P-O-P promotions that synergize with their other integrated brand promotions, such as price promotions for certain products. See Exhibit 15.15 for an example of how Petco's buy two get one free promotion can contribute to the retailer's IBP. In this image, it shows how Petco contributes to IBP by synergizing their in store marketing with a price promotion of "Buy 2 get 1 Free" for select holiday pet attire. The image creatively shows three dogs wearing holiday sweaters as a way to showcase that one of the three sweaters can be free.

competitors' marketing strategies. If a firm knows that one of its competitors is launching a new brand or initiating a new advertising campaign, a well-timed sales promotion offering deep discounts or extra quantity can disrupt the competitor's strategy. Add to the original discount an in-package coupon for future purchases, and a marketer can severely compromise competitors' efforts. A common industry that uses sales promotions to disrupt competitors strategies is the cell phone data industry; it is common to see sales promotions featured that directly encourage customers to switch providers in order to receive price or upgrade incentives.

Contribute to Integrated Brand Promotion

In conjunction with advertising, direct marketing, public relations, and other programs being carried out by a firm, sales

15-3b Consumer-Market Sales Promotion Techniques

Several sales promotion techniques are used to stimulate demand and attract attention in the consumer market. Some of these are coupons, price-off deals, premiums, contests and sweepstakes, samples and trial offers, gift cards, rebates, and loyalty programs.

Coupons

A **coupon** entitles a buyer to a designated reduction in price for a product or service. Coupons are the oldest and most widely used form of sales promotion. Annually, about 360 billion

Exhibit 15.15 ▶ Petco offers a "Merry Makings" sales promotion with a "buy 2 get one free" deal for holiday merchandise in their store or online. This is a way to enhance the classic "BOGO" or buy one get one promotion deal.

coupons are distributed to American consumers.[7] One counter-intuitive fact is that more affluent households dominate coupon usage, with 41 percent of heavy coupon-using households having incomes greater than $70,000.[8] Also, coupon users tend to redeem multiple coupons on each shopping occasion, indicating that these consumers are price sensitive.[9] A growing number of Millennials prefer online coupon sites and mobile coupon delivery, as well as app-based rebates (discussed later in the chapter), rather than traditional paper coupons; furthermore, there are trends towards buying "daily deals" or short term promotions on certain products or service vouchers sold online.[10] So online sites such as coupons.com offer the option of printing coupons, copying coupon codes for online use, or downloading a couponing app for digital coupons (see Exhibit 15.16).

There are five advantages to the coupon or coupon code as a sales promotion tool:

- The use of a coupon makes it possible to offer a discount to a price-sensitive consumer while still selling the product at full price to other consumers.

- The coupon-redeeming customer may be a competitive-brand user, so the coupon can induce brand switching.

- A manufacturer can control the timing and distribution of coupons. This way a retailer is not implementing price discounts in a way that can damage brand image.

- A coupon is an excellent method of stimulating repeat purchases. Once a consumer has been attracted to a brand, with or without a coupon, an in-package coupon can induce repeat purchase.

- Coupons can get regular users to trade up within a brand array. For example, users of low-priced disposable diapers may be willing to try the premium version of a brand with a coupon.

There are also challenges and risks with coupon use or coupon codes:

- Although coupon price incentives and the timing of distribution can be controlled by a marketer, the timing of

redemption cannot. Some consumers redeem coupons immediately; others hold onto them for months.

- Heavy redemption by regular brand buyers merely reduces a firm's profitability.

- Coupon programs require careful administration. They include much more than the cost of the face value of the coupon. There are costs for production and distribution and for retailer and manufacturer handling, which typically equate to about two-thirds of the face value of the coupon.[11]

- Fraud is a chronic and serious problem in the couponing process. The problem relates directly to misredemption practices. There are three types of misredemption that cost firms money: redemption of coupons by consumers who do not purchase the couponed brand; redemption of coupons by salesclerks and store managers without consumer purchases; and illegal collection or copying of coupons by individuals who sell them to unethical store merchants, who redeem the coupons without the accompanying consumer purchases. Digital couponing reduces the risk of fraud through illegal copying, in particular, which is a plus for brands that issue coupons.[12] Furthermore, when consumers get distracted during online or mobile checkouts to go to another website to find a coupon code, the consumer is more likely to abandon the electronic shopping cart and purchase.

Price-Off Deals

The price-off deal is another straightforward promotional technique. A **price-off deal** offers a consumer cents or even dollars off merchandise at the P-O-P through specially marked packages. The typical price-off deal is a 10 to 25 percent price reduction. The reduction is taken from the manufacturer's profit margin rather than the retailer's (another point of contention in the power struggle). Manufacturers like the price-off technique because it is controllable.[13] Plus, the price off, judged at the P-O-P, can create a positive price comparison relative to competitors. Consumers like a price-off deal

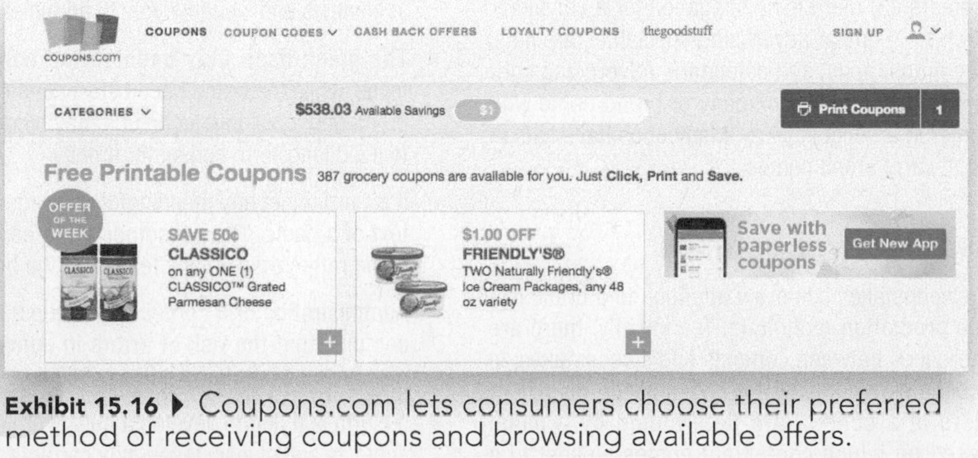

Source: Coupons.com

Exhibit 15.16 ▶ Coupons.com lets consumers choose their preferred method of receiving coupons and browsing available offers.

because it is straightforward and automatically increases the value of a known brand. Regular users tend to stock up during price-off deals. Retailers are less enthusiastic about this technique. Price-off promotions can create inventory and pricing problems for retailers. Also, most price-off deals are snapped up by regular customers, so the retailer often doesn't benefit from new business.

Premiums and Advertising Specialties

Premiums are items offered free or at a reduced price with the purchase of another item. Many firms offer a related product as a premium, such as a free granola bar packed inside a box of granola cereal. Service firms, such as a car wash or dry cleaner, may use a two-for-one offer to persuade consumers to try the service. There are two options available for the use of premiums. A **free premium** provides consumers with an item at no cost. The item can be included in the package of a purchased item, mailed to the consumer after proof of purchase is verified, or simply given away at the P-O-P or at an event. The most frequently used free premium is an additional package of the original item or a free related item placed in the package (e.g., free toothbrush with the purchase of toothpaste).

A **self-liquidating premium** requires a consumer to pay most of the cost of the item received as a premium. For example, Clinique might offer a "7-piece Clinique gift set" with a $50 dollar Clinique purchase at Nordstrom. Self-liquidating premiums are particularly effective with loyal customers. However, these types of premiums must be used cautiously. Unless the premium is related to a value-building strategy for a brand, it can serve to focus consumer attention on the premium rather than on the benefits of the brand. Focusing on the premium rather than the brand erodes brand equity. For example, if consumers buy a brand just to get a really great looking T-shirt at a very cheap price, then they won't purchase the brand again until there is another great premium available at a low price.

Advertising specialties have three key elements: (1) they are useful items that carry a key message, (2) they are given to consumers, (3) there is no obligation for a consumer to make a purchase. Popular advertising specialties are hats, T-shirts, coffee mugs, pens, and calendars. Advertising specialties allow a firm to tout its company or brand name with a target customer in an ongoing way. Many of us have hats or coffee mugs that carry brand names.

Contests and Sweepstakes

Contests and sweepstakes can draw attention to a brand like no other sales promotion technique. Technically, there are important differences between contests and sweepstakes. In a **contest**, consumers compete for prizes based on skill or ability. Winners in a contest are determined by a panel of judges, based on which contestant comes closest to a predetermined criterion for winning, or determined by consumer vote. Contests can be costly to administer because each entry must be judged against winning criteria.

M&M's has used contests to engage brand fans, invite submissions of consumer-generated content, and associate its chocolate candy products with pop culture. In the Bite-Sized Beats contest, consumers used tools on the contest website to create a short musical selection by mixing beats, voices, effects, and melodies. Contestants were encouraged to share on social media with the #bitesizebeat hashtag, and also to listen to beats created by other contestants. As an extension of this contest, M&M's made its debut at Austin's South by Southwest music festival, where it sponsored a studio for sampling M&M's candies, recording Bite-Sized Beats music, and taking selfies with branded social-media-ready props (see Exhibit 15.17).[14]

A **sweepstakes** is a promotion in which winners are determined purely by chance. Consumers need only to enter their names in the sweepstakes as a criterion for winning. Sweepstakes often use official entry forms as a way for consumers to enter the sweepstakes. Other popular types of sweepstakes use scratch-off cards. Instant-winner scratch-off cards tend to attract customers. Gasoline retailers, grocery stores, and fast-food chains commonly use scratch-off-card sweepstakes as a way of building and maintaining store traffic. Sweepstakes can also be designed so that repeated trips to the retail outlet are necessary to gather a set of winning cards. In order for contests and sweepstakes to be effective, advertisers must design them in such a way that consumers perceive value in the prizes and find playing the games intrinsically interesting.

Contests and sweepstakes often create excitement and generate interest for a brand, but the challenges associated with administering these promotions are substantial. Consider how these issues could impact the use of contests and sweepstakes in the IBP effort:

- There are strict regulations and restrictions on contests and sweepstakes. Advertisers must be sure that the design and administration of a contest or sweepstakes complies with both federal and state laws. Each state may have slightly different regulations. The legal problems are complex enough that most firms hire agencies that specialize in contests and sweepstakes to administer the programs.

- The game itself may become the consumer's primary focus, while the brand becomes secondary. Like other sales promotion tools, this technique may hinder a brand's ability to build long-term consumer affinity.

- It is hard to get any meaningful message across in the context of a game. The consumer's interest is focused on the game rather than on any feature of the brand.

- Administration of a contest or sweepstakes is sufficiently complex that the risk of errors in administration is fairly high and can create negative publicity.

- If a firm is trying to develop a quality or luxury brand image, contests and sweepstakes may detract from these efforts.

Source: M&M

Exhibit 15.17 ▶ Integrated brand promotion in action: M&M's

M&M's uses contests such as Bite-Size Beats to engage consumers and crowdsource IBP content. *Do you agree with M & M's decision not to include the brand name in the contest hashtag (#bitesizebeat) and website name (www.bitesizebeats.com)?*

Consider the fit for a sweepstakes done by Ford with the Professional Bull Riders; consumers can enter to win a Ford F-150 and two tickets to Las Vegas for the world finals (Exhibit 15.18).

Sampling and Trial Offers

Sampling is a sales promotion technique designed to provide a consumer with an opportunity to use a brand on a trial basis with little or no risk. To say that sampling is a popular technique is an understatement. Most consumer-product companies use sampling in some manner, and they invest approximately $2.2 billion a year in the technique. Surveys have shown that consumers are very responsive to sampling, with 43 percent indicating that they would consider switching brands if they liked a free sample that was being offered.[15]

Source: Ford.com

Exhibit 15.18 ▶ Ford did a successful sweepstakes with the Professional Bull Riders association, which is a good fit for the firm's F150 trucks.

Sampling is particularly useful for new products but should not be reserved for product introductions alone. This technique can be used successfully for established brands with weak market share in specific geographic areas. Five techniques are used in sampling:

- **In-store sampling** is popular for food products (Kroger or Costco) and cosmetics (Sephora). This is a preferred technique for many marketers because the consumer is at the P-O-P and may be swayed by a direct encounter with the brand. Increasingly, in-store demonstrators are handing out coupons as well as samples, as any trip to Costco or Kroger will verify.

- **Mail sampling** allows samples to be delivered through the postal service. Again, the value here is that certain zip-code markets can be targeted. A drawback is that the sample must be small enough for mail to be economically feasible. Specialty sampling firms provide targeted geodemographic door-to-door distribution as an alternative to the postal service. A newer iteration of mail sampling is the consumer "box" subscription (see Exhibit 15.19), where consumers order boxes of samples in a category of their interest (e.g., beauty, pets, babies).

- **On-package sampling**, a technique in which the sample item is attached to another product package, is useful for brands targeted to current customers. Attaching a small bottle of Pantene conditioner to a regular-sized container of Pantene shampoo is a logical sampling strategy.

- **Mobile sampling** is carried out by logo-emblazoned vehicles that dispense samples, coupons, and premiums to consumers at malls, shopping centers, fairgrounds, and recreational areas. Planters, the peanut brand owned by Kraft Heinz, has Nutmobiles traveling the country distributing free samples and encouraging sharing of selfies with Mr. Peanut on Instagram and other social media (see Exhibit 15.20).[16]

Sampling has its critics. Unless the brand has a clear value and benefit over the competition, a trial of the brand is unlikely to persuade a consumer to switch brands. This is especially true for convenience goods because consumers perceive a high degree of similarity among brands, even after trying them. The perception of benefit and superiority may have to be developed through advertising in combination with sampling. In addition, sampling is expensive. This is especially true when a sufficient quantity of a product, such as shampoo or laundry detergent, must be given away for a consumer to truly appreciate a brand's value. Finally, sampling can be a very imprecise process. Despite the emergence of special agencies to handle sampling programs, a firm can never completely ensure that the product is reaching the targeted audience and not just consumers in general.

Trial offers have the same goal as sampling—to encourage consumers to try a brand—but they are used for more expensive items. Exercise equipment, appliances, watches, hand tools, and consumer electronics are typical of items offered on a trial basis. Trial offers can be free for low-priced products. Or trials can be offered for as little as a day to as long as 90 days for more expensive or long-term items like streaming subscriptions, computer software, and even cars. The expense to the firm can be substantial, so segments chosen for this sales promotion technique must have high sales potential.

Gift Cards

Gift cards represent an increasingly popular form of sales promotion. Manufacturers or retailers offer either free or

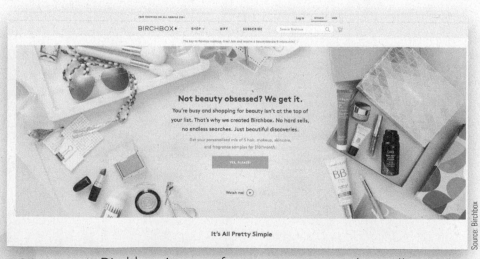

Exhibit 15.19 ▶ Birchbox is one of many companies that sell samples of products to consumers by mail via monthly subscription.

Source: Nutmobile

Exhibit 15.20 ▶ Planters takes its NUTmobile around America, giving away samples and posting Instagram photos along the way.

for-purchase debit cards that provide the holder with a pre-set spending limit. The cards are designed to be colorful and memorable. A wide range of marketers, including luxury car manufacturers like Mercedes and retailers like Target, have made effective use of gift cards. The good news about gift cards is that gift card holders tend to use them freely to pay the full retail price for items, which means retailers and brand marketers earn higher profit margins from gift card purchases. Exhibit 15.21 shows a Starbucks gift card as a promotional tool. Once a consumer visits a Starbucks and uses the card, the extra benefit can be that repeat visits will occur and brand loyalty is achieved. Firms like Starbucks often find that loyal shoppers use a gift card as a way to introduce friends and family to a brand they like, and one of the hottest trends for shoppers in this mobile world is to visit a website, purchase a card, and then have it delivered via email—instant gratification.[17]

Rebates

A **rebate** is a money-back offer requiring a buyer to mail in a form (although many are redeemed instantly at checkout) requesting the money back from the manufacturer rather than from the retailer (as in couponing). The rebate technique has been refined throughout the years and is now used by a wide variety of marketers for products as diverse as paint (Behr) to teeth whiteners (Crest). Rebates are particularly well suited for increasing the quantity purchased by consumers, so rebates are commonly tied to multiple purchases.

Another reason for the popularity of rebates is that relatively few consumers actually take advantage of the rebate offer after buying a brand. The best estimate of consumer redemption of rebate offers is that only 40 percent of buyers ever bother to fill out and then submit the rebate request—resulting

Susan Van Etten

Exhibit 15.21 ▶ Firms use gift cards as a way to draw attention to the brand and as a way for loyal customers to introduce their friends to the brand's offerings.

in more than $2 billion in extra revenue for the manufacturers and retailers who offer rebates.[18]

Millennials prefer the convenience of paperless rebates, which is fueling innovation in rebate apps. The mobile app Ibotta, for example, allows users to browse available rebates, buy at any participating retailer, scan their receipts, and receive cash back in an online account. Brands such as Horizon Organic milk have used Ibotta to encourage trial and repurchasing.[19]

Loyalty (Frequency/Continuity) Programs

In recent years, one of the most popular sales promotion techniques among consumers has been loyalty programs. **Loyalty programs**, also referred to as continuity programs or frequency programs, offer consumers discounts or free product rewards for repeat purchase or patronage of the same brand, company, or retailer. These programs were pioneered by airline companies. Frequent-flyer programs such as JetBlue's True Blue, frequent-stay programs such as Hilton's Honors, and frequent-diner programs such as Panera's MyPanera are examples of such loyalty-building strategies. Research shows that loyalty programs tend to benefit larger firms more than smaller firms in highly competitive markets.[20] So if you run a small coffee shop or flower store, launching a frequent buyer program might not have the big effect on loyalty you would hope for. Online retailers are also launching loyalty programs. Zappos, for example, rewards customers not just for buying but also for writing online product reviews. Thus, loyalty programs can encourage closer ties with customers in multiple ways rather than one size fits all.[21]

15-4 Sales Promotion Directed at the Trade Channel and Business Markets

Sales promotions, like advertising, can also be directed to members of the trade—wholesalers, distributors, and retailers—as well as to business markets.[22] For example, Apple designs sales promotion programs for its retailers, like Target, in order to ensure that the iPhone line gets proper attention and display. But Apple will also have sales promotion campaigns aimed at business buyers like Conde Nast. The purpose of sales promotion as a tool does not change from the consumer market to the trade or business markets. It is still intended to stimulate demand in the short term and help *push* the product through the distribution channel or cause business buyers to act more immediately and positively toward the marketer's brand. Firms spend big money to attract businesses to their brands with sales promotions.

15-4a Objectives for Promotions in the Trade Channel

As in the consumer market, trade-market sales promotions should be undertaken with specific objectives in mind. Generally speaking, when marketers offer incentives for the trade market, they are executing a **push strategy**; that is, sales promotions directed at the trade help push a brand into the distribution channel until it ultimately reaches the consumer. Four primary objectives can be identified for promotions in the trade channel.

Obtain Initial Distribution

Because of the proliferation of brands in the consumer market, there is fierce competition for shelf space. Sales promotion incentives can help a firm gain initial distribution and shelf placement. Like consumers, members of the trade need a reason to choose one brand over another when it comes to allocating shelf space. A well-designed promotion incentive may sway them.

Increase Order Size

One of the struggles in the channel of distribution is over who holds the inventory. Manufacturers prefer that members of the trade maintain large inventories so that the manufacturer can reduce inventory-carrying costs. Conversely, members of the trade would rather make frequent, small orders and carry little inventory. Sales promotion techniques can encourage wholesalers and retailers to order in larger quantities, thus shifting the inventory burden to the trade channel.

Encourage Cooperation with Consumer-Market Sales Promotions

It doesn't benefit the manufacturer to initiate a sales promotion in the consumer market if there is little cooperation in the channel. Wholesalers may need to maintain larger inventories, and retailers may need to provide special displays or handling during consumer-market sales promotions. To achieve synergy, marketers often run trade promotions alongside consumer promotions.

Increase Store Traffic

Retailers can increase store traffic through special promotions or events. Door-prize drawings, parking-lot sales, or live radio broadcasts from the store are common sales promotion traffic builders. Manufacturers, in addition to retailers, can also design sales promotions that increase store traffic. A promotion that generates a lot of interest within a target audience can drive consumers to retail outlets. For example, Craftsman could run a springtime promotion for its lawnmower line featuring corporate representatives at stores like Lowes and Home Depot and support its retailers with a special promotion.

15-4b Trade-Market Sales Promotion Techniques

The sales promotion techniques used within the trade market are incentives, allowances, trade shows, sales-training programs, and cooperative advertising.

Incentives

Incentives to members of the trade include a variety of tactics much like those used in the consumer market. Awards in the form of travel, gifts, or cash bonuses for reaching targeted sales levels can encourage retailers and wholesalers to give a firm's brand added attention. Consider this incentive ploy: The Volvo national sales manager put together an incentive program for dealerships where the leading dealership in the nation would win a trip to the Super Bowl, including dinner with a Hall of Fame football player. But the incentive does not have to be large or expensive to be effective. Weiser Lock offered its dealers a Swiss Army knife with every dozen cases of locks ordered. The program was a huge success. A follow-up promotion featuring a Swiss Army watch was an even bigger hit.

Another form of trade incentive is referred to as push money. **Push money** is carried out through a program in which retail salespeople are offered a monetary reward for featuring a marketer's brand with shoppers. The program is quite simple. If a salesperson sells a particular brand of, say, a refrigerator for a manufacturer as opposed to a competitor's brand, the salesperson will be paid an extra $50 or $75 "bonus" as part of the push money program.

One risk with incentive programs for the trade is that salespeople can be so motivated to win an award or extra push money that they may try to sell the brand to every customer, whether it fits that customer's needs or not. Also, a firm must carefully manage such programs to minimize ethical dilemmas. An incentive technique can look like a bribe unless it is carried out in a highly structured and open manner.

Allowances

Various forms of allowances are offered to retailers and wholesalers with the purpose of increasing the attention given to a firm's brands. Allowances are typically made available to wholesalers and retailers approximately every four weeks during a quarter. **Merchandise allowances**, in the form of free products packed with regular shipments, are payments to the trade for setting up and maintaining displays. The payments are typically far less than the amount manufacturers would have to spend to maintain the displays themselves.

Shelf space has become so competitive, especially in supermarkets, that manufacturers are making direct cash payments, known as **slotting fees**, to entice food chains to stock an item. The slotting fee for a new brand is sometimes called a "product introduction fee." The proliferation of new products has made shelf space such a precious commodity that these fees now run in the hundreds of thousands of dollars per product. And manufacturers pay these fees willingly. Research shows that shelf facings have a strong impact on consumer evaluation, particularly among frequent users of a brand and for brands with low market share.[23] However, not all retailers levy slotting fees, which can work against startup brands and small firms. Kroger's, for example, is moving away from this policy.[24]

Another form of allowance is called a bill-back allowance. **Bill-back allowances** provide retailers a monetary incentive for featuring a marketer's brand in either advertising or in-store displays. If a retailer chooses to participate in either an advertising campaign or a display bill-back program, the marketer requires the retailer to verify the services performed and provide a bill for the services. A similar program is the **off-invoice allowance**, in which advertisers allow wholesalers and retailers to deduct a set amount from the invoice they receive for merchandise. This program is really just a price reduction offered to the trade on a particular marketer's brand. The incentive for the trade with this program is that the price reduction increases the margin (and profits) a wholesaler or retailer realizes on the off-invoiced brand.

Sales-Training Programs

An increasingly popular trade promotion is to provide training for retail store personnel. This method is used for consumer durables and specialty goods, such as computers, mobile devices, home theatre systems, heating and cooling systems, security systems, and exercise equipment. The increased complexity of these products has made it important for manufacturers to ensure that the proper factual information and persuasive themes are reaching consumers at the P-O-P. For personnel at large retail stores, manufacturers can hold special classes that feature product information, demonstrations, and training about sales techniques.

Cooperative (Co-Op) Advertising

Cooperative advertising as a trade promotion technique is also referred to as vertical cooperative advertising and provides dollars directly to retailers for featuring a company's brand in local advertising. Such efforts are also called vendor co-op programs. Manufacturers try to control the content of co-op advertising in two ways. They may set strict specifications for the size and content of the ad and then ask for verification that such specifications have been met. Alternatively, manufacturers may send the template for an ad, into which retailers merely insert the names and locations of their stores. Such an ad is featured in Exhibit 15.22. Notice that the Hublot watch ad elements are national (even international), with the co-op

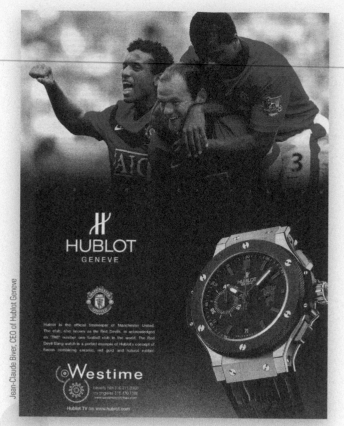

Exhibit 15.22 ▶ Here is a classic example of co-op advertising by a manufacturer in support of a retailer. Hublot is being featured by a California retailer in a magazine ad. Manufacturers will provide the ad template for the retailer to run, featuring the firm's brand.

sponsorship of the California retailer highlighted in the lower left. With this ad, Hublot controls the look and feel of the ad and ensures that the image of the brand is supported.

15-4c Business-Market Sales Promotion Techniques

Often the discussion of sales promotion focuses only on consumer and trade techniques. But it is a major oversight to leave the business market out of the discussion. The Promotional Product Association estimates that several billion dollars a year in sales promotion is targeted to business buyers. The following are the primary forms of sales promotion used in the business market.

Trade Shows

Trade shows are events where several related products from many manufacturers are displayed and demonstrated to members of a trade. Literally every industry has trade shows, from those featuring gourmet products to those showcasing building equipment. Advertisers are finding that a trade show is an efficient way to reach interested current and potential buyers, with the brand right at hand for discussion and actual use. The Promotional Products Association International reports that when trade show visitors receive a promotional item from a firm at a trade show booth, more than 70 percent of the visitors remember the name of the company that gave them the item.[25]

At a typical trade show, company representatives staff a booth that displays a company's products or service programs. The representatives are there to explain the products and services and perhaps make an important contact for the sales team. Trade shows can be critically important to a small firm that cannot afford advertising and has a sales staff too small to reach all its potential customers. Through the trade-show route, salespeople can make far more contacts than they could with direct sales calls.

Business Gifts

Estimates are that nearly half of corporate America gives business gifts. These gifts are given as part of building and maintaining a close working relationship with suppliers. Business gifts that are part of a promotional program may include small items like logo golf balls, jackets, or small items of jewelry. Extravagant gifts or expensive trips that might be construed as "buying business" are not included in this category of business-market sales promotion.

Premiums and Advertising Specialties

As mentioned earlier, the key chain, ball cap, T-shirt, or calendar that reminds a buyer of a brand name and slogan can be an inexpensive but useful form of sales promotion. Although business buyers are professionals, they are not immune to the value perceptions that an effective advertising specialty can create. In other words, getting something for nothing appeals to business buyers as much as it does to household consumers. Will a business buyer choose one consulting firm over another to get a small promotional gift? Probably not. But advertising specialties can create awareness and add to the satisfaction of a transaction nonetheless.

Trial Offers

Trial offers are particularly well suited to the business market. First, since many business products and services are costly and often result in a significant time commitment to a brand (i.e., many business products and services have long life), trial offers provide a way for buyers to lower the risk of making a commitment to one brand over another. Second, a trial offer is a good way to attract new customers who need a compelling reason to try something different. The chance to try a new product for a few weeks with no financial risk can be persuasive. General Tire used a 45-day trial to launch new tire products for the commercial light truck and van market.[26]

Loyalty Programs

The high degree of travel associated with many business professions makes loyalty programs an ideal form of sales promotion for the business market. Airline, hotel, and restaurant loyalty programs are dominated by the business-market traveler. But loyalty programs for the business market are not restricted to travel-related purchases. Costco, for example, offers Executive membership for business buyers. This is a fee-based program in which members receive cash rebates based on purchases made during the year plus discounts on business services. More than 11 million businesspeople are members of Costco's program.[27]

LO 5

15-5 The Risks of Sales Promotion

The discussion so far has demonstrated that sales promotion techniques can be used to pursue important sales objectives. As we have seen, there is a wide range of sales promotion options for the consumer, trade, and business markets. But there are also significant risks associated with sales promotion, and these risks must be carefully considered.

15-5a Creating a Price Orientation

Since most sales promotions rely on some sort of price incentive or giveaway, a firm runs the risk of having its brand perceived as cheap, with no real value or benefits beyond the low price. Creating this perception in the market contradicts the concept of IBP. If advertising messages highlight the value and benefit of a brand only to be contradicted by a price emphasis in sales promotions, then a confusing signal is being sent to the market. Brands are therefore reassessing their sales promotion activities. For example, Procter & Gamble is partnering with retailers to make the most of its sales promotion investments rather than relying heavily on pricing promotions. "Combining our efforts and resources on joint marketing programs can be more productive to drive additional shoppers into the store and to our categories than deep discounts," states P&G's chief financial officer.[28]

Over time, consumers may become immune to the constant sales promotions, resulting in lower response rates. Mondelez International, owner of brands like Ritz and Cadbury, is moving money from promotions to advertising, particularly digital/mobile/social advertising, because of disappointing promotional responses. "We did not see the kind of returns that we had hoped for and, in fact, it basically took our spending away from some of the other longer-term equity-building activities," the CEO explains.[29] Brands now recognize how competitive promotional spending can be and that higher spending may not lead to correspondingly higher sales and revenues.[30] In light of these concerns, brands need to carefully assess consumer behavior and marketplace realities to determine the proper balance of advertising, sales promotion, and other IBP.

15-5b Borrowing from Future Sales

Management must admit that sales promotions are typically short-term tactics designed to reduce inventories, increase cash flow, or show periodic boosts in market share. The downside is that a firm may simply be borrowing from future sales. Consumers or trade buyers who would have purchased the brand anyway may be motivated to stock up at the lower price. This results in reduced sales during the next few time periods of measurement. This can create difficulties for the measurement and evaluation of the effect of advertising campaigns or other image-building communications. If consumers are responding to sales promotions, it may be impossible to tease out the effects of advertising.

15-5c Alienating Customers

When a firm relies heavily on sweepstakes or loyalty programs to build loyalty among customers, particularly their best customers, there is the risk of alienating these customers with any change in the program. Airlines suffered just such a fate when they began adjusting the mileage levels needed for awards in their frequent-flyer programs. Ultimately, many of the airlines had to give concessions to their most frequent flyers as a conciliatory gesture.

15-5d Managerial Time and Expense

Sales promotions are both costly and time consuming. The process is time consuming for the marketer and the retailer in terms of handling promotional materials and protecting against fraud and waste in the process. As we have seen in recent years, funds allocated to sales promotions are taking dollars away from advertising. Advertising is a long-term, franchise-building process that should not be compromised for short-term gains.

15-5e Legal Considerations

With the increasing popularity of sales promotions, particularly contests and premiums, there has been an increase in legal scrutiny at both the federal and state levels. Legal experts recommend that before initiating promotions that use coupons, games, sweepstakes, and contests, a firm should check into lottery laws, copyright laws, state and federal trademark laws, prize notification laws, right-of-privacy laws, tax laws, and FTC and FCC regulations. The best advice for staying out of legal trouble with sales promotions is to carefully and clearly state the rules and conditions related to the program so that consumers are fully informed.

15-6 Point-of-Purchase Advertising

Annual expenditures on P-O-P advertising are estimated to be more than $23 billion per year.[31] Why this huge investment in in-store promotional materials? First, consider that P-O-P is the only medium that places advertising, brands, and a consumer together in the same place at the same time. Then think about these results. Research conducted by the trade association Point-of-Purchase Advertising International (www.popai.com) indicates that 76 percent of all product selections involve some final deliberation by consumers at the P-O-P.[32] No wonder P-O-P advertising receives a lot of attention in today's IBP campaigns.

15-6a Point-of-Purchase Advertising Defined

Point-of-purchase (P-O-P) advertising refers to materials used in the retail setting to attract shoppers' attention to a brand, convey primary brand benefits, or highlight pricing information. P-O-P displays may also feature price-off deals or other consumer sales promotions. A corrugated-cardboard bin and an attached header card featuring the brand logo or related brand information can be produced for pennies per unit. When the bin is filled with a brand and placed as a freestanding display at retail, sales gains may follow. Effective deployment of P-O-P advertising requires careful coordination with the marketer's sales force so that displays are in stores when advertising and other IBP activities launch. Having a sales force that can work with retailers to develop and deliver effective P-O-P programs is a critical element for achieving a successful IBP.

15-6b Objectives for Point-of-Purchase Advertising

The objectives of P-O-P advertising are similar to those for sales promotion in general. The goal is to create a short-term impact

on sales while preserving the long-term image of the brand being developed and maintained by advertising for the brand. Specifically, the objectives for P-O-P advertising are as follows:

- Draw consumers' attention to a brand in the retail setting.
- Maintain purchase loyalty among brand-loyal users.
- Stimulate increased or varied usage of the brand.
- Stimulate trial use by users of competitive brands.

These objectives are self-explanatory and follow closely on the objectives of sales promotion. Key to the effective use of P-O-P is to maintain the brand image being developed by advertising efforts. But remember from the discussions of consumer decision making in Chapter 5 (Advertising, Integrated Brand Promotion, and Consumer Behavior) that consumers bring to the point of purchase a wide range of experiences and prior knowledge that affects their choices.

15-6c Types of Point-of-Purchase Advertising and Displays

A myriad of displays and presentations are available to marketers. P-O-P materials generally fall into two categories: *short-term promotional displays*, which are used for six months or less, and *permanent long-term displays*, which are intended to provide P-O-P presentation for more than six months. Within these two categories, marketers have a wide range of choices:

- *Window and door signage:* Any sign that identifies or advertises a company or brand or gives directions to the consumer.
- *Counter/shelf unit:* A smaller display designed to fit on counters or shelves.
- *Floor stand:* Any P-O-P unit that stands independently on the floor.
- *Shelf talker:* A printed card or sign designed to mount on or under a shelf.
- *Mobile/banner:* An advertising sign suspended from the ceiling of a store or hung across a large wall area.
- *Checkout:* P-O-P signage or small display mounted near a cash register designed to sell impulse items such as gum, lip balm, or candy.
- *Full-line merchandiser:* A unit that provides the only selling area for a manufacturer's line; often located as an end-of-aisle display.
- *End-of-aisle display or gondola:* Usually a large display of products placed at the end of an aisle.
- *Dump bin:* A large bin with graphics or other signage attached.

- *Illuminated sign:* Lighted signage used outside or in-store to promote a brand or the store.

- *Motion display:* Any P-O-P unit that has moving elements to attract attention.

- *Interactive unit:* A computer-based kiosk where shoppers get information such as tips on recipes or how to use the brand. Can also be a unit that flashes and dispenses coupons.

- *Overhead merchandiser:* A display rack that stocks products and is placed above the cash register. The cashier can reach the product for the consumer. The front of an overhead merchandiser usually carries signage.

- *Cart advertising:* Any advertising message adhered to a shopping cart.

- *Aisle directory:* Used to delineate contents of a store aisle; also provides space for an advertising message.

- *Retail digital signage:* The newest P-O-P device available is retail digital signage. These are video displays that have typically been ceiling or wall mounted and are now being moved to end-of-aisle caps or given strategic shelf placement to relay special pricing or new product introductions.

This wide array of in-store options gives marketers the opportunity to attract shoppers' attention, encourage purchase, and provide reinforcement for key messages that are being conveyed through other components of the IBP plan. Retailers see P-O-P displays as ways to differentiate and provide ambience for their individual stores, which means that the kind of displays valued by Wal-Mart versus CVS versus Kroger versus Dollar General (to name just a few) will often vary considerably. Once again, it is the marketer's field sales force that will be critical in developing the right P-O-P alternative for each retailer stocking that marketer's products. Retailers usually need to cooperate or give permissions to brands to use P-O-P advertising. As another type of example, some brands offer pop-up retail locations.

15-6d P-O-P Advertising and Mobile or Location Marketing

In many ways, mobile advertising has similarities with P-O-P advertising as they are often on the go and out of home.[33] Mobile adds another dimension to the retailers' in-store or near-store marketing. What a billboard used to do—alert the consumer to a nearby location—a smartphone can now do. A single system coordinates advertising on double-decker tourist buses with electronic billboards and mobile messaging, helping advertisers like Cover Girl reach consumers with IBP activities at a given time and place.[34] When the consumer is in front of a store shelf, sensors can identify the location and let the marketer send one last message to try to convert browsing

into purchase. The full breadth of potential for location marketing and P-O-P is still being explored—particularly consumers' attitude and reaction toward the practice. In one test, Crate and Barrel invited shoppers to pick up an in-store tablet and scan product codes to use as a reminder list or a wish list or to facilitate checkout. The idea was to analyze in-store consumer behavior, while providing consumers with a more convenient checkout experience.[35]

15-6e P-O-P Advertising and the Trade and Business Markets

Although we have focused our discussion of the use of P-O-P advertising as a technique to attract consumers, this promotional tool is also strategically valuable to manufacturers as they try to secure the cooperation in the trade and business markets. Product displays and information sheets offered to retailers often encourage retailers to support one distributor's or manufacturer's brand over another. P-O-P promotions can help win precious shelf space and exposure in a retail setting. From a retailer's perspective, a P-O-P display can enhance the atmosphere of the store and make the shopping experience easier for customers. Brand manufacturers and distributors obviously share that interest. When a retailer is able to move a particular brand off the shelf, it in turn positively affects both the manufacturer's and distributor's sales.

LO 7

15-7 The Role of Support Media in a Comprehensive IBP Strategy

This section discusses traditional support media: outdoor signage and billboard advertising, transit and aerial advertising, cinema advertising, directory advertising, and packaging. We placed this section in this chapter because these supportive IBP tools are more similar to sales promotion and P-O-P devices than they are to the major media covered in Chapters 12 and 13.

Support media are used to reinforce or supplement a message being delivered via some other media vehicle; hence the name support media. Support media are especially productive when used to deliver a message near the time or place where consumers are actually contemplating product selections, like the billboards along a highway advertising gas stations, restaurants, or motels.[36] Since these media can be tailored to local markets, they can add value to any organization that wants to reach consumers in a particular venue, neighborhood, or metropolitan area.

15-7a Outdoor Signage and Billboard Advertising

Today, the creative challenge posed by outdoor advertising is the same as it has always been—to grab attention and communicate with minimal verbiage and striking imagery. Total spending on outdoor advertising in the United States has been increasing fairly steadily and now stands at about $8 billion per year.[37] Outdoor advertising offers several distinct advantages. This medium provides an excellent means to achieve wide exposure for a message and a brand in specific local markets. The size of the display makes this medium particularly attention-getting, especially when combined with special lighting and moving features. Billboards can be captivating when clever creative is developed for the board that highlights the brand or company name. Billboards created for a retail store in Minneapolis have even wafted a mint scent throughout the city as part of a candy promotion for Valentine's Day. Billboards also offer around-the-clock exposure for an advertiser's message and are well suited to showing off a brand's distinctive packaging or logo.

Billboards are especially effective when they reach viewers with a message that speaks to a need or desire that is immediately relevant. For instance, we all know that billboards are commonly deployed by fast-food restaurants along major freeways to help hungry travelers know where to exit to enjoy a Cracker Barrell meal or where to get Quick Trip gas. Exhibit 15.23 features a clever example of putting outdoor signage in the right place at the right time to maximize its appeal. The German eyeglass company that sponsored this billboard has created a clever, entertaining, and timely communication. The product categories that rely most heavily on outdoor advertising are local services (like gas stations), real estate and insurance companies, hotels, financial institutions, and automobile dealers and services.

Billboards have obvious drawbacks. Long and complex messages simply make no sense on billboards; some experts suggest that billboard copy should be limited to no more than six words. In addition, the impact of billboards can vary dramatically depending on their location, and assessing locations is tedious and time consuming. To assess locations, companies may have to send individuals to the site to see if the location is desirable. This activity, known in the industry as *riding the boards*, can be a major investment of time and money. Considering that billboards are constrained to short messages, often fade into the landscape, and are certainly not the primary focus of anyone's attention, their costs may be prohibitive for many advertisers.

Despite the cost issue and frequent criticism by environmentalists that billboards represent a form of visual pollution, there are advocates for this medium who contend that important technological advances will make outdoor advertising an increasingly attractive alternative in the future. The first of these advances offers the prospect of changing what has largely been a static medium to a dynamic medium. Digital and wireless technologies have created meaningful new opportunities for billboard marketers. As an example,

David Auerbach Opticians

Exhibit 15.23 ▶ Here is a clever and entertaining example of how a billboard can deliver the right message at the right time.

Coca-Cola has purchased 14-by-48-foot LED screens in 27 markets so that the company can run its own ads exclusively 24 hours a day.[38] Digital billboard displays let advertisers rotate their messages on a board at different times during the day.[39] This capability is especially appealing to local marketers—like television stations and food sellers—whose businesses are very time sensitive. Ultimately, billboard time may be sold in dayparts like radio or television, making them more appealing to time-sensitive advertisers.

15-7b Out-of-Home Media Advertising: Transit, Aerial, Cinema

A variety of support media are referred to as out-of-home media advertising. **Out-of-home media advertising** includes various advertising venues that reach primarily local audiences. **Transit advertising** is a close cousin to billboard advertising, and in many instances it is used in tandem with billboards. This is a popular advertising form around the world. Transit ads can appear in many venues, including on backs of buildings, in subway tunnels, throughout sports stadiums, and on taxis, buses, and trucks. Transit ads also appear as signage on terminal and station platforms or actually envelop mass transit vehicles. One of the latest innovations in out-of-home media is digital signage that can deliver customized messages by neighborhood. Such digital messages can be seen in retail settings (covered earlier in the chapter) or on taxi tops.

As exemplified in Exhibit 15.24, a company called Lamar Advertising showcase how their clients can use transit advertising to help promote their brand. In the example, the company refers to bus or transit advertising as "moving billboards" that offer brand exposure to not only bus commuters, but pedestrians or drivers as well. The company notes as well an advantage of transit advertising is that it can help give exposure in instances where other forms of out-of-home media advertising is prohibited.

Transit advertising is especially valuable when an advertiser wishes to target adults who live and work in major metropolitan areas. The medium reaches people as they commute to and from work, and because it taps into daily routines repeated week after week, transit advertising offers an excellent means for repetitive message exposure. In large metro areas such as New York City—with its 200 miles of subways and 3 million subway riders—transit ads can reach large numbers of individuals in a cost-efficient manner. Transit advertising can also be appealing to local merchants because their messages may reach passengers as they are traveling to a store to shop.

Transit advertising works best for building or maintaining brand awareness. But as with outdoor billboards, lengthy or complex messages don't fare well in this medium. Also, transit ads can easily go unnoticed in the hustle and bustle of daily life. People traveling to and from work via a mass transit system are certainly one of the hardest audiences to engage with an advertising message. They can be bored, exhausted, preoccupied with their own thoughts, or engaged with some other medium.

When advertisers can't break through on the ground or under the ground, they can always look to the sky. **Aerial advertising** can involve airplanes pulling signs or banners, skywriting, or those majestic **blimps** or ultralight aircrafts that go through the air with

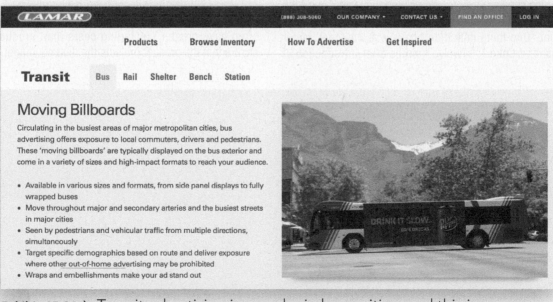

Exhibit 15.24 ▶ Transit advertising is popular in large cities, and this image shows an example of an advertising company (Lamar Advertising) that is known for selling outdoor and transit advertising, such as on busses.

its own power. For several decades, Goodyear dominated the blimp scene; now, they are relatively uncommon. Aerial billboards, pulled by small planes or jet helicopters equipped with loudspeakers, have also proliferated in recent years, as advertisers look for new ways to connect with consumers.

Cinema advertising includes those (sometimes annoying) ads that run in movie theaters before the film as well as other advertising messages appearing off-screen within a theater. Although consumers often claim that they are not particularly interested in watching advertising before a film they paid to see, research shows that 63 percent of movie goers surveyed actually don't mind the ads before the film, and firms continue to invest in this form of out-of-home advertising.[40] Today, cinema advertising is an $800 million business in the United States alone.[41] Cinema advertising is not just on-screen. Off-screen advertising and promotion include sampling, concession-based promotion (the ad on the side of your popcorn box), and lobby-based advertising. **Directory advertising** plays an important role in the media mix for many types of organizations, as evidenced by the $3.7 billion spent in this medium annually.[42]

15-7c   Packaging

Why consider the brand package as an element of support media? It is not a medium in the classic sense; but it carries important brand information nonetheless. In the simplest terms, **packaging** is the container or wrapping for a product. Classic quotes from consultants describe packaging as "the last five seconds of marketing" and "the first moment of truth."[43] Although the basic purpose of packaging seems fairly obvious, it can also make a strong positive contribution to the promotional effort. One of the best historical incidents of the power of packaging is when Dean Foods created the "Milk Chug," the first stylish, single-serving milk package. Dean Foods officials noted that "One thing milk didn't have was the 'cool' factor like Pepsi and Coke."[44] Twelve months after introduction of

the new package, sales of white milk increased 25 percent, and chocolate and strawberry flavors saw increases as much as 50 percent. In addition, the Point-of-Purchase Advertising Institute has research to show that more than 70 percent of supermarket purchases now result from in-store decisions.[45]

Promotional Benefits of Packaging to the Advertiser

Packaging provides several strategic benefits to the brand manufacturer. First, there is a general impact on IBP strategy. The package carries the brand name and logo and communicates the name and symbol to a consumer. In the myriad of products displayed at the retail level, a well-designed package can attract a buyer's attention and induce the shopper to more carefully examine the product. Also, packaging can reinforce the product's features and benefits. PRE Brands, which specializes in grass-fed beef, uses a clear vacuum-pack for each cut of meat, attached to a paperboard backer. The paper portion provides nutritional and promotional information, while the clear pack enables consumers to examine the beef from every angle, front and back, reassuring them of the quality.[46]

Another opportunity that packaging provides has to do with creating a perception of value for the product—remember that the "value" message is a key part of IBP communication. The formidable packaging surrounding computer software is made more substantial simply by adding tangibility to an intangible product. Similarly, when consumers are buying image, the package must reflect the appropriate image. The color, design, and shape of a package have been found to affect consumer perceptions of a brand's quality, value, and image— and their willingness to pay a premium price over other brands.[47] Perrier, one of the most expensive bottled waters on the market, has an aesthetically pleasing bottle compared to the rigid plastic packages of its competitors. Perfume manufacturers often have greater packaging costs than product costs to ensure that the product projects the desired image.

Summary

1. Define sales promotion and the three broad audiences for sales promotion.

Sales promotion is the use of incentive techniques that create a perception of greater brand value among consumers, the trade channel, and business buyer markets. The broad audiences for sales promotions are consumers (consumer-market sales promotions), trade/channel partners (trade-market sales promotions), and other business buyer-market sales promotions (business-market sales promotions). Sales promotions use incentives to motivate action on the part of consumers, members of the trade channel, and business buyers.

2. Explain the importance and growth of sales promotion.

Sales promotions serve different purposes than mass media advertising does; and for some companies, sales promotions receive just as much or more funding compared to other forms of advertising and IBP. The growing reliance on sales promotions are attributed to the heavy pressures placed on marketing managers to account for their spending and meet sales objectives in short time frames. Deal-prone shoppers, brand proliferation, the increasing power of large retailers, and media clutter also contribute to continued growth of sales promotion.

3. Describe the sales promotion techniques used in the consumer market.

Sales promotions directed at consumers serve various goals. For example, they can be employed as a means to stimulate trial, repeat, or large-quantity purchases. They are important tools for introducing new brands or for reacting to a competitor's advances. Coupons, price-off deals, gift cards, and premiums provide incentives for purchase, while contests and sweepstakes stimulate brand interest. A variety of sampling and trial-offer techniques can help get a product into the hands of the target audience with little or no risk to the consumer. Rebates and loyalty (frequency/continuity) programs provide rewards for repeat purchase. A newer method for product sampling is with consumer subscriptions to mailed boxes of samples.

4. Describe the sales promotion techniques used in the trade channel and business markets.

Sales promotions directed at the trade can also serve multiple objectives. They are a necessity in obtaining initial distribution of a new brand. For established brands, they can be a means to increase distributors' order quantities or obtain retailers' cooperation in implementing a consumer-directed promotion. Incentives and allowances can be offered to distributors to motivate support for a brand. Sales-training programs and cooperative advertising programs are additional devices for effecting retailer support. In the business market, professional buyers are attracted by various sales promotion techniques. Loyalty (frequency/continuity) programs are very valuable in the travel industry and have spread to business-product advertisers. Trade shows are an efficient way to reach a large number of highly targeted business buyers. Gifts to business buyers are a form of sales promotion that is unique to this market. Finally, premiums, advertising specialties, and trial offers have proven to be successful in the business market.

5. Identify the risks of using sales promotion that brands may face.

There are risks associated with heavy reliance on sales promotion. Offering constant deals for a brand can erode brand equity and reputation, and sales resulting from a promotion may simply be borrowing from future sales. Constant deals can also create a customer mindset that leads consumers to abandon a brand as soon as a deal is retracted. Sales promotions are expensive to administer and fraught with legal complications. Sales promotions yield their most positive results when carefully integrated with an overall advertising plan.

6. Understand the role and techniques of point-of-purchase advertising.

Point-of-purchase (P-O-P) advertising refers to materials used in the retail setting to attract shoppers' attention to a firm's brand, convey primary brand benefits, or highlight pricing information. The effect of P-O-P can be to reinforce a consumer's brand preference or change a consumer's brand choice in the retail setting. P-O-P displays may also feature price-off deals or other consumer and business sales promotions. A myriad of displays and presentations are available to marketers. P-O-P materials generally fall into two categories: short-term promotional displays, which are used for six months or less, and permanent long-term displays, which are intended to provide P-O-P presentation for more than six months. In trade and business markets, P-O-P displays encourage retailers to support one manufacturer's brand over another; they can also be used to gain preferred shelf space and exposure in a retail setting. Also, P-O-P can be deals and offers sent to consumers via mobile devices.

7. **Describe the role of support media in a comprehensive IBP strategy.**

The traditional support media include billboard, transit, aerial, cinema, and directory advertising. Billboards and transit advertising are excellent means for carrying simple messages into specific metropolitan markets. Street furniture is becoming increasingly popular as a placard for brand builders around the world. Aerial advertising can also be a great way to break through the clutter and target specific geographic markets in a timely manner.

Directory advertising can be a sound investment because it helps a committed customer locate an advertiser's brand. Again, new technologies have allowed for digitization of billboard, transit, and aerial ads. Cinema advertising is becoming more prevalent, and despite consumer protests, most consumers are not opposed to ads in theaters. Finally, packaging can be considered in the support media category because the brand's package carries important information for consumer choice at the P-O-P, including the brand logo and the "look and feel" of the brand.

Key Terms

advertising specialties
aerial advertising
bill-back allowances
blimps
business-market sales promotion
cinema advertising
consumer-market sales promotion
contest
coupon
directory advertising
free premium
in-store sampling

loyalty program (also known as
    frequency programs)
mail sampling
merchandise allowances
mobile sampling
off-invoice allowance
on-package sampling
out-of-home media advertising
packaging
point-of-purchase (P-O-P) advertising
premiums
price promotions
price-off deal

push strategy
rebate
sales promotion
sampling
self-liquidating premium
slotting fees
support media
sweepstakes
trade-market sales promotion
trade shows
transit advertising
trial offers

Endnotes

1. Leigh McAlister, Raji Srinivasan, Niket Jindal, and Albert A. Cannella, "Advertising Effectiveness: The Moderating Effect of Firm Strategy," *Journal of Marketing Research* 53, no. 2 (2016), 207–224.

2. Leonie Roderick, "Why Unilever and P&G Are Pulling Back from Discounting," *Marketing Week*, November 1, 2016, https://www.marketingweek.com/2016/11/01/why-unilever-and-pg-are-pulling-back-from-price-promotions.

3. Jack Neff, "TV Doesn't Sell Packaged Goods," *Advertising Age*, May 24, 2004, 1, 30; Cara Beardi, "Pop-Ups Sales Results," *Advertising Age*, July 23, 2001, 27.

4. Kate MacArthur, "Give It Away: Fast Feeders Favor Freebies," *Advertising Age*, June 18, 2007, 10.

5. Dean Foust, "Queen of Pop," *BusinessWeek*, August 7, 2006, https://www.bloomberg.com/news/articles/2006-08-06 /queen-of -pop.

6. Sandy Smith, "2021 Top 100 Retailers," National Retail Federation, July 6, 2021, https://nrf.com/blog/2021-top-100-retailers; and Marc Pritchard, "Commentary: 'Half My Digital Advertising Is Wasted….'" *Journal of Marketing* 85, no. 1 (2020), 26–29.

7. Hyejin Lee et al., "Price No Object!: The Impact of Power Distance Belief On Consumers' Price Sensitivity," *Journal of Marketing* 84, no. 6 (2020), 113–129.

8. Heather Barry Kappes et al., "Beliefs about Whether Spending Implies Wealth," *Journal of Consumer Research* 48, no. 1 (2020), 1–21.

9. Marianne Wilson, "Coupon Usage—Print and Digital—Rises," *Drug Store News*, August 30, 2016, http://www.drugstorenews.com /article/coupon-usage--print-and-digital—rises.

10. Polly Mosendz, "Penny-Pinching Millennials Are Keeping the Coupon Alive," *Bloomberg*, June 16, 2016, https://www.bloomberg.com /features/2016-millennials-coupons; and Angeline C. Scheinbaum, Pratik Shah, Monika Kukar-Kinney, and Jacob Copple. "Regret and nonredemption of daily deals: Individual differences and contextual influences." *Psychology & Marketing* 37, no. 4 (2020): 535–555.

11. Ashok Lalwani and Jessie Wang, "How Do Consumers' Cultural Backgrounds and Values Influence Their Coupon Proneness? A Multimethod Investigation," *Journal of Consumer Research* 45, no. 5 (2019), 1037–1050.

12. Josh Perlstein, "Power Lunch: How to Be Successful in the New Digital Coupon Era," *Food Processing*, March 22, 2017, http://www.foodprocessing.com/articles/2017/how-to-be-successful -in-the-new-digital-coupon-era; and Angeline G. Close and Monika Kukar-Kinney. "Beyond buying: Motivations behind consumers' online shopping cart use." Journal of Business Research 63, no. 9–10 (2010): 986-992

13. Wiebke Keller et al., "Price Promotions and Popular Events," *Journal of Marketing* 83, no. 1 (2018), 73-88.

14. Rakin Azfar, "M&M's Wields Mobile Tech to Show Off Fans' Musical Talent," *Mobile Marketer*, March 1, 2017, http://www.mobilemarketer .com/ex/mobilemarketer/cms/news/advertising/24568.html; Ally Fleming, "M&M'S Makes its Debut at SXSW with the Premiere of M&M'S® Studios," *SXSW News*, March 10, 2017, https://www.sxsw .com/news/2017/mms-makes-debut-sxsw-premiere-mms-studios.

15. Patricia O'Dell, "Steady Growth," *PromoMagazine.com*, December 1, 2009.

16. Ilyse Liffreing, "Inside Mr. Peanut's 'NUTmobile' Instagram Account," *Campaign (US)*, May 23, 2016, http://www.campaignlive.com /article/inside-mr-peanuts-nutmobile-instagram-account/1395737.

17. Patricia Odell, "2012 Trends Report: The Outlook for Marketing Growth in Key Promotional Categories," *Chief Marketer*, www .chiefmarketer.com, accessed September 1, 2012.

18. Jeannine Mancini, "How Much Money Goes Unclaimed For Mail-In Rebates?," *Pocket Sense*, December 12, 2019 https://pocketsense. com/much-money-goes-unclaimed-mailin-rebates-9935.html

19. Mary Ellen Shoup, "Milk Is a Top-Performing Rebate Offer for Mobile Reward Shopping App Ibotta," *Dairy Reporter*, January 13, 2017, http://www.dairyreporter.com/Retail-Shopper-Insights/Milk -is-a-top-performing-rebate-offer-for-mobile-shopping-app-Ibotta.

20. Liu, Jia and Ansari, Asim, "Understanding Consumer Dynamic Decision Making Under Competing Loyalty Programs," *Journal of Marketing Research* 57 no. 3 (2020), 422–444.

21. Elyse Dupre, "Zappos' Customers Are the 'Sole' of Its Loyalty Program," *DMN*, October 13, 2016, http://www.dmnews.com /loyalty/zappos-customers-are-the-sole-of-its-loyalty-program /article/547009.

22. See, for example, Maarten J. Gijsenberg, "Riding the Waves: Revealing the Impact of Intra-Year Category Demand Cycles on Advertising and Pricing Effectiveness," *Journal of Marketing Research* (2016), http://www.mercurynews.com/2016/07/29 /how-supermarkets-persuade-shoppers.

23. Pierre Chandon, J. Wesley Hutchinson, Eric T. Bradlow, and Scott H. Young, "Does In-Store Marketing Work? Effects of the Number and Position of Shelf Facings on Brand Attention and Evaluation at the Point of Purchase," *Journal of Marketing* 73 (November 2009), 1–17.

24. Candice Choi, "How Supermarkets Persuade Shoppers," *Mercury News*, July 29, 2016, http://www.mercurynews.com/2016/07/29 /how-supermarkets-persuade-shoppers.

25. Data available at Promotional Products Association International website, www.ppai.org.

26. Bruce Davis, "General Tire Intros UHP, Truck Tires," *Tire Business*, March 31, 2017, http://www.tirebusiness.com/article/20170331 /NEWS/170339993/general-tire-intros-uhp-truck-tires.

27. Data drawn from: https://www.statista.com/statistics/1095660 /costco-membership-by-type/

28. Leonie Roderick, "P&G on How It Cut Agencies by Almost 50% to Optimize Its Marketing Spend," *Marketing Week*, November 21, 2016, https://www.marketingweek.com/2016/11/21/pg-cut -agencies-optimise-marketing-spend.

29. Leonie Roderick, "Mondelez Pledges a 'More Disciplined' Marketing Approach as Sales Fall," *Marketing Week*, February 8, 2017, https://www.marketingweek.com/2017/02/08/mondelez-take -disciplined-marketing-approach-after-sales-fall.

30. Leonie Roderick, "FMCG Brands Move Away from Promotions in 'Complete Change of Direction,'" *Marketing Week*, November 29, 2016, https://www.marketingweek.com/2016/11/29/fmcg -brands-pull-promotions.

31. Richard Alan Nelson and Pack Ebel, "Super Charged," *pubs.ppai. org*, Table 4, www.pubs.ppai.org.

32. Patricia O'Dell, "P-O-P Vital as More Shoppers Decide in Store: Study," *Chiefmarketer.com*, May 11, 2012, www.chiefmarketer.com.

33. Kunur Patel, "Forget Foursquare: Why Location Marketing Is the New Point-of-Purchase," *Advertising Age*, March 22, 2010, 1, 19.

34. Christopher Heine, "Mobile Advertisers Are Successfully Targeting Tourists on Double-Decker Buses," *Adweek*, June 1, 2016, http://www.adweek.com/digital/mobile-advertisers-are -successfully-targeting-tourists-double-decker-buses-171770.

35. Elyse Dupre, "Crate and Barrel Furnishes Its In-Store Experience With Digital," *DMN*, October 11, 2016, http://www.dmnews.com /multichannel-marketing/crate-and-barrel-furnishes-its-in-store -experience-with-digital /article/526883.

36. John L. Fortenberry, and Peter J. McGoldrick, "Do Billboard Advertisements Drive Customer Retention?" *Journal of Advertising Research* 60, no. 2, (2019), 135–147.

37. IBIS World Staff: "Billboard & Outdoor Advertising Industry in the US - Market Research Report" IBIS World, June 20, 202, https: //www.ibisworld.com/united-states/market-research-reports /billboard-outdoor-advertising-industry/.

38. Natalie Zmuda, "Coca-Cola Gets Hands-on with Its Own Digital Billboards," *Advertising Age*, February 18, 2010, 12.

39. "Sexy Signage," *The Economist*, January 26, 2013, 62.

40. Jack Loechner, "After the Popcorn, Before the Show," Center for Media Research, www.mediapost.com, June 18, 2010.

41. A. Guttman "Cinema advertising revenue in the United States from 2002 to 2019," Statista, September 8, 2021, https://www.statista .com/statistics/243147/cinema-advertising-revenue-in-the-us/

42. A. Guttman "Directory advertising spending in the United States from 2016 to 2021," *Statista*, June 4, 2018, https://www.statista .com/statistics/242768/directory-advertising-spending-in-the-us/.

43. Don Hootstein, "Standing Out in the Aisles," *Marketing at Retail*, June 2007, 22–24.

44. Catherine Arnold, "Way Outside the Box," *Marketing News*, June 23, 2003, 13–14.

45. *An Integrated Look at Integrated Marketing: Uncovering P.O.P's Role as the Last Three Feet in the Marketing Mix* (Washington, DC: Point-of-Purchase Advertising Institute, 2000), 10.

46. Kate Bertrand Connolley, "Flip-up Vacuum Pack Lets Shoppers See Quality of Grass-fed Beef Products from All Sides," *Packaging Digest*, April 3, 2017, http://www.packagingdigest.com/packaging-design /flip-up-vacuum-pack-lets-shoppers-see-quality-of-grass-fed -beef-products-from-all-sides-2017-04-03.

47. Don Hootstein, "Standing Out in the Aisles," *Marketing at Retail*, June 2007, 22–24.

Event Sponsorship, Product Placements, and Branded Entertainment

After reading and elaborating on this chapter, you will be able to do the following:

1 Explain the role of event sponsorship, product placements, and branded entertainment in integrated brand promotion, and justify their growing popularity with respect to the convergence of advertising and entertainment for brand-building.

2 Identify what event sponsorship is, who uses it, how it is measured, its benefits, and how to leverage it.

3 Summarize the uses and appeal of product placements in venues like TV, movies, and video games.

4 Identify what branded entertainment is, and explain the benefits and challenges of connecting with event venues or entertainment properties in building a brand.

5 Discuss the coordination challenges presented by the variety of communication and branding tools for achieving integrated brand promotion via the consumer experience.

LO 1

16-1 The Role of Event Sponsorship, Product Placements, and Branded Entertainment in IBP: Experiential Marketing and the Convergence of Advertising and Entertainment

This chapter discusses a variety of tools and tactics that marketers use to create unique experiences with and for consumers. This chapter first assesses event sponsorship. Next, the IBP tactic of product placement is considered. This is the strategy in which brands are prominently featured in television shows, films, and even video games. Finally, we'll examine branded entertainment. Events, product placements, and branded entertainment offer the advertiser some of the most exciting opportunities for integrated brand promotion (IBP), as shown in Exhibit 16.1. For digital engagement, sponsorship mixes well with social media.[1]

Exhibit 16.1 ▶ The framework diagram for Chapter 16 highlights the importance of event sponsorships, product placements, and branded entertainment for integrated brand promotion.

Part 1: Advertising and Integrated Brand Promotion in Business and Society

The Structure of the Advertising and Promotion Industry: Advertisers, Agencies, Media, and Support Organizations (Ch. 2)

The History of Advertising and Brand Promotion (Ch. 3)

The World of Advertising and Integrated Brand Promotion (Ch. 1)

Social, Ethical, and Regulatory Aspects of Advertising and Promotions (Ch. 4)

Part 2: Analyzing the Environment for Advertising and Integrated Brand Promotion

Advertising, Integrated Brand Promotion, and Consumer Behavior (Ch. 5)
Market Segmentation, Positioning, and the Value Proposition (Ch. 6)
Advertising Research (Ch. 7)
Planning Advertising and Integrated Brand Promotion (Ch. 8)

Part 3: The Creative Process

Managing Creativity in Advertising and IBP (Ch. 9)
Creative Message Strategy (Ch. 10)
Executing the Creative (Ch. 11)

Part 4: The Media Process

Media Planning Essentials (Ch. 12)
Media Planning: Newspapers, Magazines, TV, and Radio (Ch. 13)
Media Planning: Advertising and IBP In Digital, Social, and Mobile Media (Ch. 14)

Part 5: Integrated Brand Promotion

Sales Promotion, Point-of-Purchase Advertising, and Support Media (Ch. 15)
Event Sponsorship, Product Placements, and Branded Entertainment (Ch. 16)
Integrating Direct Marketing and Personal Selling (Ch. 17)
Public Relations, Influencer Marketing, and Corporate Advertising (Ch. 18)

- The Role of Event Sponsorship, Product Placements, and Branded Entertainment in IBP: Experiential Marketing and the Convergence of Advertising and Entertainment
- Event Sponsorship: Who Uses It, Measurement, Benefits, and Leveraging
- Product Placements
- Branded Entertainment
- The Coordination Challenge

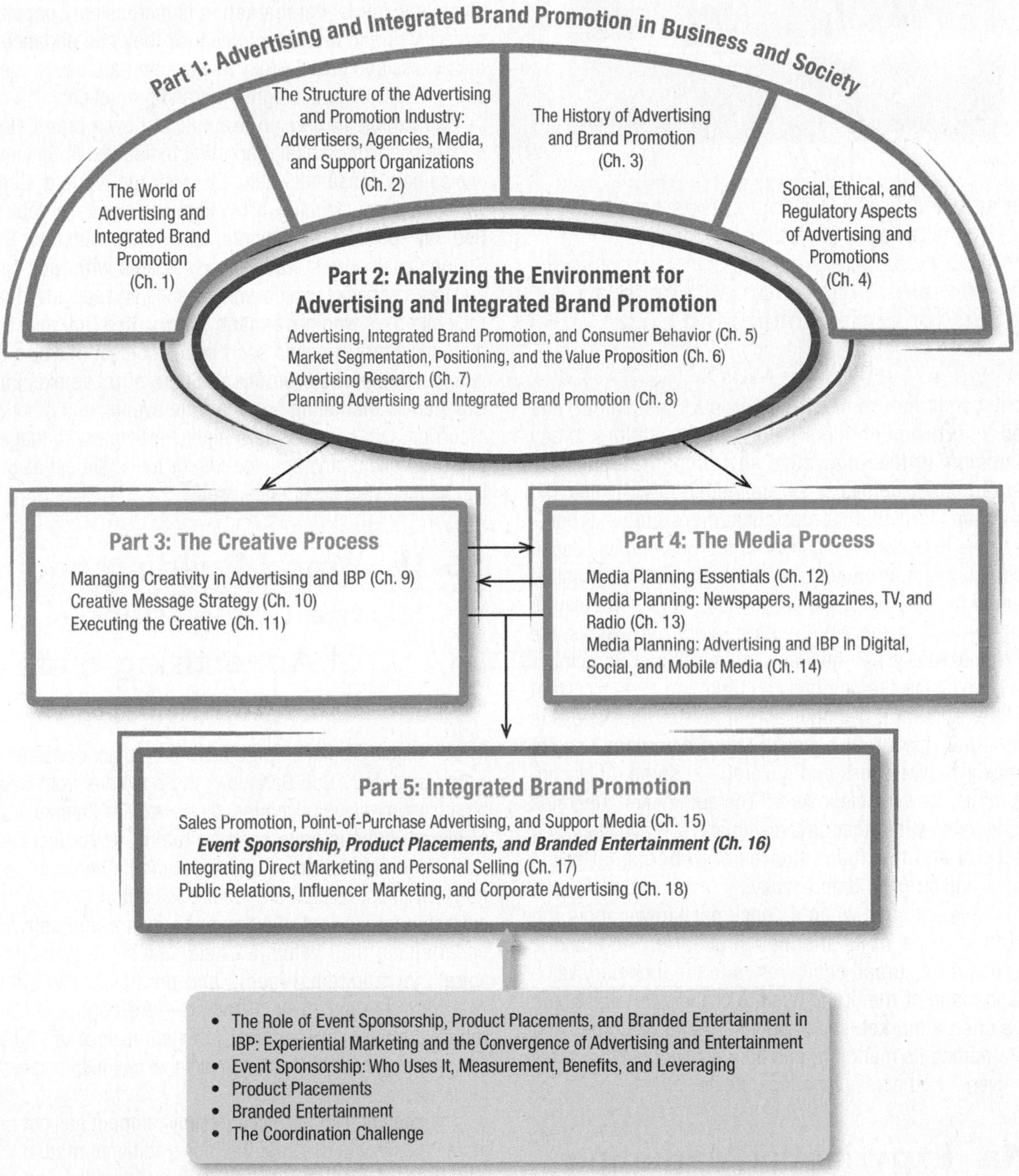

Source: Nissan Motor Corporation

Exhibit 16.2 ▶ Nissan Europe uses social media to leverage its sponsorship of Champions League soccer, combined with consumer sales promotion and hashtag identifiers for engagement and buzz.

The dynamic nature of events, product placement, and branded entertainment make them potent additions to any IBP campaign. In this innovative environment, brands are seeking out opportunities to be embedded in activities and entertainment that their target consumers enjoy. Japan's Nissan chose to become a sponsor of the Champions League European soccer tournament because of the highly visible opportunity to build its brand worldwide. "It is probably the only competition in the world where every two weeks, we have a rendezvous on TV between the months of September and May," explains the company's marketing vice president for Europe. Nissan is a global automotive brand, and this sponsorship is a good fit because "the Champions League has a massive awareness and coverage in some other core regions for us, for example in Asia." The automaker integrates this sponsorship with other advertising and IBP activities (see Exhibit 16.2) and has found the result to be higher brand awareness and stronger brand equity.[2]

Brand awareness is when a consumer knows about the brand and is aware of its offerings in general. The brand is merely "heard of." Brand equity refers to the monetary value of a brand name or the brand itself. A brand with high brand equity is often a market leader, powerful, and desirable; and therefore putting its mark or name on a product really creates value—even for otherwise mundane goods.

16-1a Experiential Marketing

When it comes to building brands, there are very few limits on what one can try with branded entertainment, and often quirky, edgy, or off-the-wall events will gain attention for a brand at a time when advertising and entertainment are converging. This convergence is seen with **experiential marketing** (marketing of and with the consumer experience) as a form of IBP, with events such as concerts or music

festivals marketed as experiences that are sponsored by brands. Collectively, event sponsorship, product placements, and branded entertainment are more experiential forms of marketing. Experiential marketing, or incorporating a brand with the consumer's lived experience is popular for consumers because they are unique, enjoyable, fit in with the consumer's lifestyle. Experiential marketing is increasingly popular with advertisers and marketers because they can enhance brand awareness and brand equity in ways that are easily integrated with advertising and integrated brand promotion.

See Exhibit 16.3 as an example of how a brand, Red Bull, engages in experiential marketing initiatives. In this image, it shows how consumers can "Discover the World of Red Bull," with images of climbing, art, and music events. It depicts how Red Bull sponsors a series of music events with their Red Bull Sound Crash series. Red Bull associates with rock climbing and has a series of videos with seasons and episodes featuring rock climbers who have made history. Red Bull also showed their adventure or action sport image contest (recall, a contest is an example of a promotion). Some of these executions of experiential marketing are one-time events, and other can be recurring. Often, consumers highly anticipate annual events, and this buildup and anticipation for fun is almost as compelling as the event experience itself.[3]

16-1b Brand-Building and the Convergence of Advertising and Entertainment

In the "Chaos Scenario" predicted more than a decade ago by *Advertising Age's* Bob Garfield, a mass exodus from traditional broadcast media was coming. As we saw in Chapter 13, some of his predictions have become reality. Advertisers' dollars have been diverted from traditional media because audience fragmentation, consumers' desire to control their information environment, and ad-avoidance hardware and software are undermining their value. Garfield saw an "inexorable death spiral" for traditional media and predicted a world where "marketing—and even branding—are conducted without reliance on the 30-second [television] spot or the glossy [magazine] spread."[4] Event sponsorship can help address these big issues.

The changing communication environment has not resulted in an "inexorable death spiral" for traditional media; instead, new technologies and in-person branded experiences have helped messages get to consumers in different ways. That is why we focus on *integration* of various media in this book. Traditional media still attract large audiences and major investments by advertisers. Billions of advertising dollars have been reallocated to other brand-building tools as advertising and entertainment continue to converge and give rise to new opportunities and ways to measure event sponsorship.

Discover the World of Red Bull

Reel Rock

The climbers who make history

7 Seasons · 55 episodes

CLIMBING

Photography lovers, drink in these winning shots from Red Bull Illume

Unveiling week for the world's greatest adventure and action sports imagery contest has revealed the 2021 overall and...

ART   5 min read

Red Bull SoundClash

2 Artists, 2 Stages, 1 Winner!

MUSIC   9 events in series

Source: Red Bull Company Limited

Exhibit 16.3 ▶ Red Bull is known for having an experiential marketing approach to their brand strategy. This figure shows examples of how the brand associates with entertainment or life experiences that are "on the edge" in three different areas: rock climbing (an extreme sport or hobby), photography of active or adventure, and rock music.

LO **2**

16-2 Event Sponsorship: Who Uses It, Measurement, Benefits, and Leveraging

One of the time-tested and effective means for reaching targeted groups of consumers on their terms—often while giving back to a community and incorporating corporate social responsibility—is event sponsorship. **Event sponsorship** involves a marketer providing financial support to help fund an event, such as a festival, concert, tennis tournament, or holiday event. In return, that marketer acquires the rights to display a brand name, logo, or advertising message on-site at the event. If the event is covered on TV or social media stream, the marketer's brand and logo will most likely receive exposure with the television and/or social media audience as well. Event sponsorship, product placements, and branded entertainment are popular with marketers because they can work in numerous ways to assist with a brand-building agenda beyond the capabilities of traditional media.[5] They are also great for building brand community.[6]

From a consumer psychology lens, events and sponsorship are an important context and industry to study because sponsorship and events involve consumer identity, passions, and sense of self as fitting with the event and/or its sponsors. Consumers who have been to an annual sponsored event many times often identify themselves as ambassadors for the event or sponsorship.[7] Attendees' sense of self may be influenced by the events they attend (as in a NFL game or a local team's sporting event), and brands associated with such venues may assist in embellishing and communicating that sense of self.[8] Being a fan or going to an event can also demonstrate group membership, or can reveal the attendee's social identity.

Recall the meaning-transfer process discussed in Chapter 5; it can change people's perceptions of the brand. That is, the fun and excitement of the Austin music festival South by Southwest can become part of your feelings about the brands that were there with you. No wonder big brands like Mazda, McDonald's, and Capital One have been involved in this annual event (see Exhibit 16.4) along with emerging sponsor brands such as White Claw Hard Seltzer. In fact, so many brands are at South by Southwest that a festival once known for "the magic of discovery, be it music or innovation" has turned into "a brand traffic jam," in the words of one ad agency exec.[9] Sponsorships change each year for some annual events, and the good news to the earlier sponsor is it still may get "credit" for being the sponsor in the consumer's memory—even when a new brand has replaced it. This additional benefit is referred to as **sponsor spillover**, which is great for the previous sponsor and bad for the incoming one.

As you might suspect, sports sponsorships draw the biggest share of advertising dollars when it comes to events.[10] The NFL and its 32 teams account for $1.62 billion in annual sponsorship investments by advertisers.[11] E-sports events (including videogame competitions) are also attracting advertiser interest; sponsorship and media rights revenue was $882.4 million and

Source: Mazda North American Operations

Exhibit 16.4 ▶ Mazda tweets about its SXSW sponsorship to engage brand fans and encourage attendees to view its new vehicles.

is forecasted to surpass $1 billion in the coming years.[12] Event spending has continued to grow at more than 4 percent a year and now exceeds $62 billion worldwide.[13]

Also note that **event social responsibility** provides an opportunity for sports sponsors to demonstrate good corporate citizenship, generate positive word of mouth, and boost both attendance and patronage intent.[14] When attendees are community minded, they will have a more positive view of the event sponsor as a result of the event experience, which in turn increases intentions to purchase the sponsor's products.[15] Event sponsorship, product placements, and branded entertainment are popular with marketers because they can work in numerous ways to assist with a brand-building agenda beyond the capabilities of traditional media. These forms of IBP are especially good for community involvement and some forms of corporate social responsibility.

Whether the economy is up or down, and even through a pandemic, automakers in the United States are typically large investors in event sponsorship. General Motors, one of the world's foremost advertising investors, typifies this commitment to events. GM and its brands have experimented with a number of ways to "get closer" to its prospective customers. Most entail sponsoring events that get consumers in direct contact with its vehicles or events that associate the GM name and brands with causes or activities that are of interest to its target customers. This is a documented way to improve consumer knowledge about a product.[16] For example, GM is the official motor sponsor of the Southwestern Athletic Conference (SWAC). GM's Chevrolet brand sponsors a youth sports initiative that focuses on empowering children through sports, among other sport-related initiatives in baseball and softball (Chevy Youth Baseball and Softball Program). GM's Chevrolet also sponsors the Authentic Voices of Pride Project to help support contributions and conversations around LGBTQ+ issues. Last, GM's Cadillac brand does not tend to sponsor

sports, instead sponsoring art exhibits and other cultural events that link the brand with luxury and good taste.[17] For instance, Cadillac sponsors the Ebony Power 100 Awards Ceremony and Gala, which is an annual event that recognizes leaders from the Black community.

16-2a Who Uses Event Sponsorship?

Event sponsorship can take a variety of forms. The events can be international in scope, as in the Formula 1 race series with big-name sponsors like DHL, Emirates, Heineken, Rolex, and Amazon Web Services. Or they may have a distinctive local flavor, like Ohios's Solheim Cup golf tournament, sponsored by BMW, Pepsi, and other brands.[18] Events provide a captive audience for a sponsor, may receive radio and television coverage, are often reported in print media and covered online, and are frequently included in social media posts by organizers, sponsors, and attendees. Hence, event sponsorship can yield face-to-face contact with real consumers and receive in the moment and follow-up publicity and buzz—all good things for a brand.

Amazon has used sport sponsorship as a form of IBP since 2012. Amazon is a sleeve sponsor of soccer team Serie A club Napoli, and is their official e-commerce partner. This sponsorship cost €2 million per season. It is also possible to have multiple brand or organization logos on a jersey sponsorship. Exhibit 16.5 depicts a jersey sponsorship. Especially when the event attendee is a visual processor and is high in their need for cognition, sponsorships in sports really work.[19]

The list of companies participating in various forms of event sponsorships seems to grow every year. Diet Coke, Apple Music, Truly Hard Seltzer, Nissan, Chase Bank, and a host of other

Catherine Ivill/Getty Images

Exhibit 16.5 ▶ Jersey sponsorships are one of the newer forms of sport sponsorship. As can be seen in this image of a jersey, having a sponsoring brand prominently displaying their logo and/or name is a way to have consumers associate the brand with the sport, city, league, team, or athlete.

companies have sponsored tours and special appearances for recording artists such as Taylor Swift, Drake, Dua Lipa, Beyoncé, and Blake Shelton. Soon after ESPN launched the X Games to attract younger viewers, a host of sponsors signed on, and today, sponsors include Monster Energy, Pacifico Beer, GEICO, and Wendy's. These brand builders are looking for benefits through unique associations with something different and hip by way of a process that anthropologist Grant McCracken has labeled "the movement of meaning."[20] The meaning can then be explained or articulated with traditional media or other forms of integrated brand promotion that explains the event sponsorship. This tactic is called **sponsorship articulation**. USA Cycling, for example, activates their sponsors on side (place activation) and online (digital activation), which includes featuring the sponsor brands on their race websites. Exhibit 16.6 helps demonstrate that event websites are an important way for sponsors to activate and also to tell consumers details and updates about the event.

Sometimes, brands or other entities have a formal way of considering potential sponsor partners. See Exhibit 16.7 for an example of how AT&T has a sponsorship portal for potential event or community sponsor partners. In this image, it shows how their website caters to other companies or brands or events who are interested in sponsorship partnerships with AT&T. As noted in the copy in the image, AT&T has partnerships with over 20 sport leagues or entertainment divisions. This portal is a smart strategy to centralize sponsorship inquiries to once central platform.

And the world is much engaged with football—no, not that kind of football. English professional soccer has become one of the darlings of the sports business because of the valuable marketing opportunities it supports. Heineken, PlayStation, and Lay's sponsor the Champions League to reach soccer fans worldwide. Adidas and other sponsors are eager to link their

Source: At&t

Exhibit 16.7 ▶ AT&T is heavily involved in sponsorship and event sponsorship. They have a sponsorship portal where they can accept proposals from potential partners.

brands with Manchester United of the English Premier Soccer League, a popular UK team that surpasses the New York Yankees in its ability to generate revenues while delighting its fans (see Exhibit 16.8).

Sports sponsorships truly come in all shapes and sizes, including with organizations like Professional Bull Riders and the Fishing League Worldwide. Advertisers thus have diverse opportunities to measure consumer behavior in sports contexts and study how sport event attendees associate their brands with the distinctive images of various participants, sports, and even nations.[21] Deloitte is a sponsor of the U.S. Tennis Association and its tennis matches because it wants to shine a spotlight on the many business services it offers beyond tax and financial consulting.

Source: USA Cycling National Championships

Exhibit 16.6 ▶ Event websites, such as this one by USA Cycling, are important for both sponsor activation and to give information about the event details.

SPONSORSHIP OPPORTUNITIES

GLOBAL PARTNERS

adidas
Official Kit Supplier of Manchester United

Aon
Principal Partner of Manchester United

Chevrolet
Principal Partner of Manchester United

20th Century Fox
Official Manchester United Feature Film Partner

Abengoa
Official Sustainable Technology Partner of Manchester United

Aeroflot
Official Carrier of Manchester United

AladdinStreet.com
Global Online Marketplace Partner of Manchester United

Aperol Spritz
Official Global Spirits Partner of Manchester United

Source: Manchester United

Exhibit 16.8 ▶ Manchester United has attracted many team sponsors, giving these brands high visibility in multiple media.

The firm is also a sponsor of the U.S. Olympic Committee, the WNBA, the U.S. Golf Association and other sporting and cultural events that attract national, regional, and local audiences.[22]

16-2b Finding the Sweet Spot for Event Sponsorship

Measurement used to be a downfall of events and other below-the-line forms of marketing investments. Now, **event sponsorship measurement** or measuring experiential marketing often with sponsors or partnering brands is sophisticated and analytical; for instance, event sponsorship measurement includes (but is not limited to) models and metrics on the following areas: event–sponsor fit, attitude, event social responsibility, sponsorship awareness, image transfer, affect transfer, brand meaning transfer, and sponsorship patronage (i.e., preference toward buying from the sponsoring brand).

You know enough about advertising and IBP at this point to recognize that the major sweet spot in event sponsorship comes when significant overlap is achieved between an event's participants and the marketer's target audience. If the event has big numbers of fans and/or participants, then that's even better. Moreover, marketers stand to gain the most in supporting an event as exclusive sponsors. However, exclusivity can be extremely pricey, if not cost prohibitive, except in those situations where one finds a small, neighborhood event with passionate supporters just waiting to be noticed.

Consider, for example, the World Bunco Association (WBA), which was chartered in 1996. Bunco is a dice game, usually played in groups of 8, 12, or 16. It's especially popular with middle-aged women. Bunco is a game of chance, so it leaves players with lots of time for eating, drinking, and intimate conversation about everything from a daughter's new baby to favorite recipes. Why is this a good sponsorship opportunity? Approximately 14 million women in the United States have played Bunco, and 4.6 million play regularly. Six out of 10 women say that recommendations from their Bunco group influence their buying decisions.[23] In addition, about a third of all regular Bunco players suffer from frequent heartburn, and it just so happens that 70 percent of frequent heartburn sufferers are women. Can you see where this is going now? The makers of Prilosec OTC, an over-the-counter heartburn medication, discovered Bunco and entered into a partnership with the World Bunco Association to sponsor the first Bunco World Championship. With a $50,000 first prize, associated fundraising for the National Breast Cancer Foundation, and lots of favorable word of mouth from regional Bunco tournaments, the event caught on fast. It wasn't long before cable TV caught Bunco fever and began covering the championship matches, where the Prilosec OTC purple tablecloths made it a **branded experience**. Branded experiences are the essence of experiential marketing. The difference is that the branded experience refers to the consumer experience itself, whereas experiential marketing, as introduced earlier in the chapter, is an IBP tactic/strategy to connect with consumers where they are.

16-2c Assessing the Benefits of Event Sponsorship

In the early days of event sponsorship, it often wasn't clear what an organization was receiving in return for its sponsor's fee. Traditionally, many critics contend that sponsorships, especially those of the sporting kind, can be ego driven and thus a waste of money.[24] Company executives like to associate with sports stars and celebrities. This is fine, but when sponsorship of a golf tournament, for example, is motivated mainly by a CEO's desire to play in the same foursome as famous golf professionals, the event sponsorship investment needs to be measured for efficacy.

One of the things fueling the growing interest in event sponsorship is that scholars and companies have found ways to make a case for the effectiveness of their sponsorship dollars. It is important that event sponsorship measurement is more than a simple advertising equivalency attempt, because impressions in events are so much better because they are experiential. In scholarship, advertising and marketing professors have published research papers that measure event sponsorship or sponsorship-linked marketing with consumer surveys during events, online surveys after attending events, experiments using scenarios of events and sponsors, qualitative interviews with event attendees, and even by looking at stock prices after sponsorship press releases or major sponsored events.

In industry, Boston-based financial services company John Hancock has been a pioneer in developing detailed estimates of the advertising equivalencies of its sponsorships. John Hancock began sponsoring a college football bowl game in 1986 and soon after had a means to judge the value of its sponsor's fee. Hancock employees scoured magazine and newspaper articles about the sponsored bowl game to determine name exposure in print media. Next they factored in the number of times the John Hancock name was mentioned in pregame promos and during the television broadcast. Early on, Hancock executives estimated that the firm received the equivalent of $5.1 million in advertising exposure for its $1.6 million sponsorship fee. However, as the television audience for the John Hancock bowl dwindled in subsequent years, Hancock's estimates of the bowl's value also plunged. Subsequently, Hancock moved its sports sponsorship dollars into other events, including the Boston Marathon, the Boston Red Sox baseball team, and Special Olympics Massachusetts.

Improving one's ability to gauge the effectiveness of dollars spent will generally drive more spending on any IBP tool.[25] No longer are TV ratings and event attendance the only measures of how many people were exposed to the sponsor's brand at, say, a championship game. Consider the experience of State Farm Insurance, a long-time sponsor of the NBA. When the Cleveland Cavaliers won against the Golden State Warriors in the NBA Finals, State Farm's red-and-white logo was clearly visible on the arm holding the basketball hoop. Throughout the game, the logo came into view again and again as players aimed for the basket and made dunks, giving State Farm an estimated air-time equivalent of as many as 96 30-second commercials. That exposure doesn't include the thousands of photos of the basket appearing in print and broadcast media and the more than 750,000 views of that game's key play on the NBA YouTube channel. Now add State Farm's own IBP activities during the game, including social media, and you can see the complexities of gauging audience size and engagement.[26]

The practice of judging sponsorship spending through media impressions is one approach to event sponsorship measurement, but remember that all media impressions are not equal and that experiential marketing impressions may be more impactful than some other forms of IBP. Establishing **media impressions** involves creating a metric that lets a marketer judge sponsorship spending in a direct comparison to spending in the traditional measured media. But gross impressions only tell part of the story. Sponsorships provide a unique opportunity to foster brand loyalty and a connection to local communities. When marketers connect their brand with the potent emotional experiences often found at rock concerts, in soccer stadiums, at the Bunco table, or on Fort Lauderdale beaches, positive feelings may be attached to the sponsor's brand that linger well beyond the duration of the event. Judging whether your brand is receiving this loyalty dividend is another important aspect of sponsorship assessment.

Evaluating the return from one's sponsorship dollars or event sponsorship measurement will require a mix of qualitative and quantitative approaches. Researchers have found that with respect to community-based events (like local marathons or music events), attendees who are more community minded come away from the event with a more positive opinion of the sponsor, which contributes to an increased intention to buy the sponsors' brands.[27] Since various types of events attract well-defined target audiences, marketers should also monitor event participants to ensure they are reaching a fitting target market.

Fit is important to measure in a few areas with event sponsorship measurement. When an event sponsor fits a consumer's image and sense of self, a **consumer–event congruity/fit** occurs where consumer participation in

the event enhances the persuasiveness of the event and, in turn, causes the participants to think more positively about the sponsor and increases the desire to patronize the sponsoring brand.[28] Another way to test for event sponsorship measurement success is with **sponsor–event congruity/fit**, or the degree to which consumers perceive the sponsor and sponsee as congruent in both image and function. Interestingly, this fit perception is more important for the sponsoring brands than for the event itself; that said, sponsors that fit are still desirable for events.[29] Both levels of fit (consumer–event and sponsor–event) are crucial because it is fit that connects brand sponsors with consumers' passions for sponsored events.[30] A checklist of guidelines for selecting the right events and maximizing their benefits for the brand is outlined in Exhibit 16.9. These guidelines revolve around: fit, target audience, message clarity, plot, exclusivity, relevance, digital articulation, and planning/integrating the event to the overall IBP strategy and brand image.

Exhibit 16.9 ▶ Guidelines for effectively using event sponsorship as an IBP tool

Guidelines for Event Sponsorship

1. **Match the brand to the event.** Be sure that the event matches the brand personality. Stihl stages competitions at Mountain Man events featuring its lumbering equipment. Would the Stihl brand fare as well sponsoring a boat race or a triathlon? Probably not.

2. **Tightly define the target audience.** Closely related to point number one is the fact that the best event in the world won't create impact for a brand if it's the wrong target audience. Too often the only barometer of success is the number of bodies in attendance. Far more important is the fact that the brand is getting exposure to the right audience. This is what JBL and TREK accomplished with the mountain bike tour sponsorship.

3. **Stick to a few key messages.** Most events try to accomplish too much. People are there to experience the event and can accommodate only a limited amount of persuasion. Don't overwhelm them. Stick to a few key messages and repeat them often.

4. **Develop a plot line.** An event is most effective when it is like great theater or a great novel. Try to develop a beginning, a middle, and an exciting ending. Sporting events are naturals in this regard, which explains much of their popularity. In nonsporting events, the plot line needs to be developed and delivered in small increments so that the attendees can digest both the event and the brand information.

5. **Deliver exclusivity.** If you are staging a special event, make it by invitation only. Or, if you are a featured sponsor, invite only the most important customers, clients, or suppliers. The target audience wants to know that this event is special. The exclusivity provides a positive aura for the brand.

6. **Deliver relevance.** Events should build reputation, awareness, and relationships. Trying to judge the success of an event in terms of sales is misleading and short-sighted. Don't make the event product centric; make it a brand-building experience for the attendees.

7. **Use the Internet.** The Internet is a great way to promote the event, maintain continuous communication with the target audience, and follow up with the audience after an event. Plus, it's a good way to reach all the people who can't attend the event in person. For golf fans, pga.com gets viewers involved with each event on the PGA tour and gives sponsors another chance to reach the target audience.

8. **Plan for the before and after.** Moving prospects from brand awareness to trial to brand loyalty doesn't happen overnight. The audience needs to see the event as part of a broad exposure to the brand. This is the synergy that needs to be part of the event-planning process. The event must be integrated with advertising, sales promotions, and advertising specialty items.

16-2d Leveraging Event Sponsorship

As noted, one way to justify event sponsorship is to calculate the number of viewers who will be exposed to a brand either at the event or through media coverage of the event and then assess whether the sponsorship provides a cost-effective way of reaching the target segment. This approach assesses sponsorship benefits in direct comparison with traditional advertising media. Some experts now maintain, however, that the benefits of sponsorship can be fundamentally different from anything that traditional media might provide. Finding ways to leverage the sponsorship is especially critical. Any collateral communication or activity reinforcing the link between a brand and an event is referred to as **leveraging** a brand or activating a sponsorship—known as **sponsorship activation.** As an example of activated sponsorship-linked marketing, Lexus activates their role of the official car of the professional tennis event The Davis Cup. Messages activating this sponsorship work well because Lexus provides the official transportation of the tennis players from 18 countries to and from the tennis village and the event and this helps in associating the luxury car brand with elite athletes in tennis.[31]

Events can be leveraged as ways to entertain important clients, recruit new customers, motivate the firm's salespeople, and generally enhance employee morale. Events provide unique opportunities for face-to-face contact with key customers. Marketers commonly use this point of contact to distribute specialty advertising items so that attendees will have a branded memento to remind them of the rock concert or their New York City holiday. Marketers may also use this opportunity to sell premiums such as T-shirts and hats, administer consumer surveys as part of their marketing research efforts, or distribute product samples.

As you will see again in Chapter 18, a firm's event participation may also be the basis for public relations activities that then generate additional media coverage. Consider Procter & Gamble's sponsorship and IBP campaign linked to the 2020 Summer Olympics held in Tokyo. P&G launched its "Lead with Love" integrated campaign with a highly emotional series of commercials that celebrates athletes who led with love through acts of good (see Exhibit 16.10. Not only did the commercials and P&G's associated commitment to do 2,021 "acts of good" in the year receive viral attention, the athletes involved made numerous media appearances to speak about their work. On a brand-specific basis, P&G linked its #leadwithlove campaign with Always and its Puberty & Confidence Education Program as well as with its Pampers brand. These integrated activities, plus the creative accolades for the various commercials, helped P&G and its brands to leverage the widespread positive publicity generated by broadcast, online, and print media.[32]

16-3 Product Placements

As noted early in this chapter, the fields of advertising, branding, and entertainment are converging and collapsing on one another. Brand builders aspire to be embedded in any form of entertainment that their target consumers enjoy. And even though event sponsorship has been around for decades, brand builders are also looking elsewhere to help put on the show. Indeed, in today's world of advertising and IBP, no show seems to be off limits. Brands can now be found whenever and wherever consumers are being entertained, whether at a sporting event, in a movie theatre, on the Internet, or in front of a TV set or video game console. If it entertains an audience, some brand will want to be there, on the inside.

Product placement is the practice of placing any branded product into the content and execution of an established entertainment vehicle. These placements are purposeful and paid for by the marketer to expose and/or promote a brand. Product placement has come a long way since E.T. nibbled on Reese's Pieces in the movie *E.T. the Extra-Terrestrial.* But that product (or brand) placement foreshadowed much that has followed.

In today's world, product-placement agencies work with marketers to build bridges to the entertainment industry. Working collaboratively, agents, marketers, producers, and writers find ways to incorporate the marketer's brand as part of the show. The show can be of almost any kind. Movies, short films on the Internet, reality TV, and video games are great

Source: Procter & Gamble Co.

Exhibit 16.10 ▶ Procter & Gamble's "Thank You, Mom" campaigns combine traditional media with social media such as this Facebook post to engage worldwide fans of the Olympic Games.

venues for product placements. There may be an opportunity for a brand to be involved anywhere and anytime people are being entertained. Worldwide, product placement investing is predicted to rise almost 14 percent, to $23.3 billion, in 2021 from a year earlier; compare this to a benchmark for overall marketing investment that is predicted to increase just 5.9 percent to $1.35 trillion based on data from researcher PQ Media.[33] More than ever before, product placement can give a brand visibility in a way that fits the consumer's lifestyle and media habits. "Consumers are much more difficult to find these days with the proliferation of digital," explains Monique Kumpis, senior group manager of advertising for Hyundai. "Not everybody is watching linear television, and even when they are, our competitors there are outspending us, so we always have to be on the lookout for smarter ways to reach these audiences." That's why Hyundai has used product placement to reach audiences of on-demand Netflix shows like *Daredevil* and *Jessica Jones* and in films like *Snake Eyes: G.I. Joe Origins*.[34] Streaming platforms such as Netflix or Hulu feature programs with product placement; in fact, product placement is being embraced which may be a response in part to market resistance against hyper-targeted advertising.

16-3a On Television

Television viewers have become accustomed, maybe even numb, to product placements. Soap operas and reality shows have helped make product placements seem the norm: Vietnam Airlines saves the day with transportation to Cambodia for contestants on *The Amazing Race*, and you can guess an answer to a sponsored question on *Jeopardy!* But the tactic has spread like wildfire, and now many TV shows include product placement. Comedy Central put its own twist on this idea, creating content that integrates branded products in a series of 2.5-minute mini-shows that entertain as well as convey brand attributes and benefits.[35]

There's even a school of thought contending that product placements can be television's savior as it is more conducive to consumer lifestyles.[36] Recall Bob Garfield's prediction discussed previously in this chapter, with its "inexorable death spiral" for the traditional media like TV. So, if consumers won't watch ads on TV, why not turn the programming itself into an ad vehicle? Brands that are integrated into entertainment are in effect receiving an implicit endorsement. Product placement isn't needed to save TV, but it certainly provides advertisers another reason to invest in this traditional medium. But remember: consumers are more likely to recall a product integrated into programming when it is supported by other promotional activities, such as commercials—because of the synergistic effects of advertising and IBP.[37]

Interestingly, a completely fictional ad campaign featured in episodes of *Mad Men* became a real campaign after the TV series ended, generating lots of publicity. Heinz was not involved in product placement on *Mad Men* when the Don Draper character proposed ads featuring foods under the headline "Pass the Heinz." The characters portraying Heinz

Source: Heinz

Exhibit 16.11 ▶ "Pass the Heinz" campaign finally gets Heinz's approval in this billboard version of an ad proposed by Don Draper on *Mad Men*.

managers rejected the campaign because the product wasn't visible in the ads. To celebrate the tenth anniversary of *Mad Men*'s premiere, Heinz's ad agency, David, worked with the show's production company, Lionsgate, to turn the fictional campaign into a real campaign. Painstakingly recreating the *Mad Men* drafts of the ads that had been pitched 50 years earlier (in the show's timeline), the agency produced versions for print, billboard, and social media, including hashtags for social sharing (see Exhibit 16.11). The head of the Heinz ketchup brand noted that Don Draper and his team were right to try to engage the audience in the ads: "What we loved about the campaign is that it doesn't require paragraphs of copy to explain it," she said. "It features mouth-watering food images, and all that's missing is the Heinz."[38]

16-3b At the Movies

The car chase is a classic component of many action/adventure movies and in recent years has been seized as a platform for launching new automotive brands.[39] If you'd like to immerse yourself in a superb example of branded entertainment, download *The Italian Job,* a movie starring the lovable Mini Cooper, like the one on display in Exhibit 16.12. BMW has been a pioneer in the product-placement genre, starting with its Z3 placement in the 1995 James Bond thriller *GoldenEye*. Audi has raised brand awareness and associated itself with technology through product placement in Marvel movies. For example, various Audi R8 models have been driven by *Iron Man* Tony Stark in multiple movies. Other Audi cars have appeared in *Captain America* and *Ant-Man*. Leveraging these placements, Audi creates movie posters for its dealers to display and develops TV spots and social media posts as well as other IBP tie-ins to make the most of its placement deals.[40]

BMW of North America LLC

Exhibit 16.12 ▶ The Mini Cooper (re-)launch campaign featured many innovative uses of IBP, including a starring role in the film *The Italian Job*.

It is not just automakers that have discovered product placements in movies and films. White Castle, American Express, Nokia, and the Weather Channel—to name just a few—have joined the party as well. All this activity is supported by research indicating that persons under 25 years old are most likely to notice product placements in films and are also willing to try products they see in movies and films.[41] As we have emphasized throughout, young consumers are increasingly difficult to reach via traditional broadcast media.

16-3c In Video Games

As you read in Chapter 14, product placements in video games is referred to as advergaming. There is good reason marketers are spending more than $24 billion a year on this venue to reach their target audiences. Brand placement in video games has wide reach and helps reach the unreachable.[42] Consider these numbers: According to Nielsen Research, 56 percent of U.S. households (about 60 million households) have at least one current-generation gaming console.[43] Moreover, most analysts conclude that around 40 percent of the hardcore players are in the 18-to-34 age cohort—highly sought after by advertisers because of their discretionary spending but expensive to reach via conventional media. Now factor in that video games are not only an attractive entertainment option but also a form of entertainment in which players rarely wander off during a commercial break. With all those focused eyeballs in play, is it any wonder that marketers want to be involved?

Billboard ads and virtual products have become standard fare in action games like Fortnite. The branded ad began simply. Epic integrated tie-ins with the NFL and for World Cup Soccer.

And it's not just with sports. Epic collaborated with Marvel for a Fortnite x Avengers crossover event where players could gather Infinity Stones and become the character Thanos. This event featured collaborations with major movies like Star Wars, John Wick and Avengers: Endgame.[44]

Nielsen research has established that the majority of players see brand placements as adding to the quality of play, and because of the repetitive brand exposures in games, they affect purchase intent more than old-style media do. Other research shows that winning players who are promotion focused view the brands and the game in a positive light.[45] Whether you call it "gamevertising" or "advergaming," you can expect to glimpse more of brands like these in the world of video games: Red Bull, Coca-Cola, BMW, Sony, Old Spice, Levi Strauss, Callaway Golf, Ritz Bits, Target, and the U.S. Army.

16-3d What We Know about Product Placement

The business of product placements has evolved at warp speed during the past decade. An activity that was once rare, haphazard, and opportunistic has become more systematic and, in many cases, even strategic. Even though product placement will never be as tidy as crafting and running a 30-second TV spot, numerous case studies make several things apparent about using this tool in terms of both challenges and opportunities.[46]

Integrate the Placement within the IBP Campaign

First, product placements can add the greatest value when they are integrated with other elements of an advertising plan. As with event sponsorship, the idea is to leverage the placement for synergy. One should avoid isolated product placement opportunities and should create connections to other elements of the advertising plan. For instance, a placement combined with a well-timed public relations campaign can yield synergy: novel product placements create great media buzz, and that often translates into consumers picking up the buzz and sharing it with their peer group. Research suggests that brands stand to gain the most from product placements when consumers are engaged enough to make it a part of their daily conversation.[47] So if you want to get people talking about your brand, give them something to talk about! Favorable word of mouth is always a great asset for a brand and helps in building momentum. This can make product placements just the right thing to complement other advertising initiatives that energize the launch of a new product such as a new car, pickup, or SUV.

Make the Placement Look Authentic

Another factor affecting the value of any placement has to do with the elusive concept of authenticity. **Authenticity** refers to the quality of being perceived as genuine and natural. Authenticity is emerging as a powerful influence on brand loyalty among consumers.[48] As advertisers and their agencies look for more and more chances to write their brands into the script of shows, it is to be expected that some of these placements will come off as phony. For example, when James Bond switched from drinking martinis to ordering Heinekens in *Skyfall*, it seemed forced and contrived. Why would he switch from his signature cocktail? For a $36 million sponsorship of course! Conversely, Eggo Waffles first make an appearance during season 1 of *Stranger Things*. The character Eleven enjoys the breakfast and even finds herself stealing a few boxes from a grocery store. This product placement feels natural while still giving Eggos a significant amount of airtime in the show, becoming the favorite snack of a main character.

Brands want to be embedded more naturally in the entertainment, not detract from it. Hyundai's senior group manager of advertising understands this, saying about the brand's placement in the Jessica Jones Netflix series: "We understand and appreciate that our role is not to interrupt the audience and their enjoyment. It always should feel organic."[49] Such authenticity is often a difficult goal to achieve, especially as the frequency of product placements increases and some viewers begin to resent the intent to sell.[50]

Develop the Right Industry Relationships

But like so many other things in the advertising business, success with product placements is fostered through developing deep relationships with the key players in this dynamic business. You need to have the right people looking for the right opportunities that fit with the strategic objectives that have been established for the brand. As was emphasized in Chapter 8, advertising is a team sport, and the best team wins most of its games. You want to be part of a team on which the various members understand each other's goals and are working to support one another. Good teams take time to develop. They also move product placement from an opportunistic and haphazard endeavor to one that supports IBP.

ROI

Product placements present marketers with major challenges in terms of measuring the success or ROI of the activity. Calculating media impressions for product placements (or sponsorships for that matter) does *not* tell the whole story regarding their value. Product placements can vary dramatically in the value they offer to the marketer.[51] Audi, for instance, measured brand awareness and attitudes during nearly a decade of product placement in Marvel movies. It found an almost 30 percent increase in brand awareness and positive opinion. Its dealers confirm that in the months following a movie release featuring Audi product placement, showroom traffic goes up. In short, Audi sees a definite return from its product placement investments.[52]

One key item many brands look for is the celebrity connection in the placement, which can increase awareness, attitude, and engagement.[53] Astute users of product placements are always looking for plot connections that could be interpreted by the audience as an implied brand endorsement from the star of the show. When Doritos are featured as a snack in the CW network's teen drama *Riverdale*, the implied endorsement can drive sales of the product. It's the same when Sara Jessica Parker puts on a pair of Manolo Blahniks in HBO Max's Sex and the City reboot *And Just Like That*. Viewers take notice.

16-4 Branded Entertainment

Branded entertainment can be seen as a natural extension and outgrowth of product placement. With product placement, the question is, "What shows are in development that might be a good platform for our brand?" With branded entertainment, one option for advertisers is to create their own shows, so they never have to worry about finding a place for their brand. This guarantees that the brand will be one of the stars of the show.

For a stock-car racing fan, there is nothing quite like being at the Charlotte Motor Speedway on the evening of the Coca-Cola 600. It's NASCAR's longest night. But being there live is a rare treat, and so the Monster Energy NASCAR Cup Series gets plenty of coverage on television. If you've never watched a NASCAR race, give it a try, because even though NASCAR is all about the drivers and the race, every race is also a colossal celebration of brands. There are the cars themselves carrying the logos large and small of hundreds of NASCAR sponsors. Cup series sponsor Monster brings a fan-friendly entertainment facility to each race so sponsored drivers and attendees have a place to mingle. Monster's vice president of sports marketing says, "For us, this is about giving NASCAR customers a lifestyle experience, not selling a product."[54] None of this comes as any surprise, because NASCAR openly and aggressively bills itself as the best marketing opportunity in sports. Said another way, a NASCAR race is a fantastic example of branded entertainment. See Integrated Brand Promotion in Action (Exhibit 16.13) for more about Monster's sports sponsorships.

It's not hard to understand why Monster or any brand would be willing to shell out millions of dollars to be involved with NASCAR. Huge television audiences and other media coverage will yield hundreds of thousands of media impressions, especially for those cars (and brands) leading the race, along with the branded facilities and logos visible around the track. A hundred thousand fans in the stands will make your brand a focal point, and many will visit a branded showcase before or after the race to meet the car and driver. Plus think of the many social media opportunities for conversations about your brand.

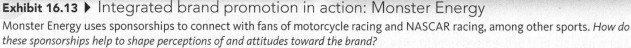

Exhibit 16.13 ▶ Integrated brand promotion in action: Monster Energy
Monster Energy uses sponsorships to connect with fans of motorcycle racing and NASCAR racing, among other sports. *How do these sponsorships help to shape perceptions of and attitudes toward the brand?*

In addition, general industry research indicates that NASCAR fans are unusually loyal to the brands that sponsor cars and have absolutely no problem with marketers plastering their logos all over their cars and their drivers. Indeed, many NASCAR fans often wear those logos proudly. Moreover, the data say that race fans are three times more likely to purchase a product promoted by their favorite NASCAR driver relative to the fans of all other sports.[55]

NASCAR is a unique brand-building "vehicle" with numerous marketing opportunities for brands large and small. But we use it here as an exemplar of something bigger, something more pervasive, and something that is growing in popularity as a way to support and build brands in the IBP program. Branded entertainment, as discussed throughout this book, entails the development and support of any entertainment property in which a primary objective is to feature a firm's brand or brands in an effort to impress and connect with consumers in a unique and compelling way.

What distinguishes branded entertainment from product placement is that in branded entertainment, the entertainment would not exist without the marketer's support, and in many instances, it is the marketers themselves who create the entertainment property. For example, Unilever helped produce two specials to promote its Axe body wash, which ran on MTV and SpikeTV. *The Fairway Gourmet*, featured on PBS, promoted images of the good life, courtesy of the Hawaii Visitors & Convention Bureau. Chipotle Mexican Grill captured the attention of the Grammys' TV audience (and attracted millions of YouTube views) with its animated film *Back to the Start*, focusing on the restaurant's practice of doing business only with farmers dedicated to humane practices.[56] Clorox's Brita brand worked with the digital studio Portal A to create a branded music video, *Best Roommate Ever*, starring Snapchat celebrity King Bach and NBA legend Stephen Curry and featuring Brita's water-filtering product. For synergy, this was followed up by a behind-the-scenes "making of"

viral video and shorter videos and images for multiple social media platforms (see Exhibit 16.14).[57] By creating shows themselves (often with their ad agencies), marketers seek to attract a specific target audience with a carefully tailored story that shows their brands at their best. This is something quite different from trying to find a special place for one's brand in an existing show. As others have suggested, "clients often enter the (general) realm of entertainment marketing via small product placements that eventually develop into larger promotional programs."[58]

On the path of brand building, it is natural to evolve from simple product placement to the more elaborate enterprise of branded entertainment. Taking branded entertainment to perhaps its ultimate manifestation, a Bollywood film titled *Zindagi Na Milegi Dobara* (roughly translated to mean "You Only Live Once") was essentially a feature-length tourism advertisement for the country of Spain. The three main characters embarked on an adventure-filled holiday across Spain. By the time the film was released in its final form, one

Exhibit 16.14 ▶ Brita's *Best Roommate Ever* YouTube video was followed up by a behind-the-scenes look at the making of this branded entertainment.

analyst remarked, "People talk about 'in-movie advertising.' In this case, the entire movie was 'in-movie advertising!'" Within a month after the movie's release, visa applications to visit Spain had doubled, and the number of Indian tourists to Spain jumped 65 percent the following year.[59]

16-4a Where Are Product Placement and Branded Entertainment Headed?

It is easy to understand the surging popularity of product placements and branded entertainment. Reaching the unreachable through a means that allows your brand to stand out and connect with the consumer can only mean more interest from marketers. But there are always complicating and countervailing forces. Although billions of dollars yearly are flowing to these two popular IBP activities, several forces could work to undermine that dollar flow.

One of the obvious countervailing forces is instant oversaturation. Like any other faddishly popular promotional tactic, if advertisers pile on too quickly, a jaded consumer and a cluttered environment will be the result.[60] Some will argue that creative collaboration can always yield new opportunities for branded entertainment, but at some point, yet another motion picture featuring another hot automobile will start to feel a little stale. Indeed, we may already be there.

A related problem involves the processes and systems that currently exist for matching brands with entertainment properties. Traditional media provide a well-established path for reaching consumers. Marketers like that predictability. Branded entertainment is an often unpredictable path. Yet in today's fragmented media environment, brands and their agencies must continue to explore fresh and unexpected ways to engage audiences, avoiding the well-worn approaches of the past that can cause audiences to shrug or turn away. This is both the challenge and opportunity of branded entertainment: Discovering what will attract and delight targeted customer groups while leveraging the synergy of IBP to support brand building in a positive way.

Finally, there is a concern about playing it straight with consumers. For example, some consumer advocacy groups charge that TV networks deceive the public by failing to disclose the details of product-placement deals. The argument seems to be that since many product placements are in fact "paid advertisements," consumers should be advised as such. It is conceivable that a federal agency could call for some form of disclosure when fees have been paid to place brands in U.S. TV shows. However, now that the practice has become so prevalent, consumers are likely to perceive that money is changing hands behind the scenes.

16-4b What's Old is New Again

It turns out that marketers, media moguls, ad agencies, and entertainers have much in common. They do what they do for business reasons. And they have and will continue to do business together. Smart advertisers have always recognized this and then go about their business of trying to reach consumers with a positive message on behalf of their brands. No firm has managed this collaboration better throughout the years than Procter & Gamble. To close this section, we take a then-and-now look at P&G initiatives to acknowledge that. Even though it is enjoying a huge surge of popularity recently, branded entertainment has been around for decades.

In 1923, P&G was on the cutting edge of branded entertainment in the then-new medium of radio. (Try if you dare to imagine a world without television or Facebook—how did people survive?) To promote their shortening product Crisco, they helped create a new radio program called *Crisco Cooking Talks*. This was a 15-minute program that featured recipes and advice to encourage cooks, like the one in Exhibit 16.15 who is taking notes about a new recipe being offered, to find more uses for Crisco. Although it was a good start, P&G's market

Procter & Gamble Company

Exhibit 16.15 ▶ P&G created its own Web-based documentary series, A Parent Is Born, as a way to feature the firm's brands—particularly the Pampers brand of disposable diapers.

research soon told them that listeners wanted something more entertaining than just a recipe show. So a new form of entertainment was created just for radio that would come to be known as the soap opera. These dramatic series used a storyline that encouraged listeners to tune in day after day. *Guiding Light*, P&G's most enduring "soap," was started on the radio in 1937. In 1952, *Guiding Light* made a successful transition to television, where it aired for nearly 60 years. One more thing—P&G has done all right selling soap (and today, many other products as well).

Fast-forward to the new millennium. P&G's consumer has changed, and new forms of IBP are necessary. Today P&G works with media partners to ensure that its brands are embedded in the entertainment venues preferred by its targeted consumers. On the other hand, P&G also sold the rights to the *People's Choice Awards*, which it owned for more than 30 years, saying "we are no longer focusing on producing entertainment as one of our core competencies."[61] Like many other marketers, P&G is also creating original online content. In January of 2020 P&G announced a partnership with Stone Village Television, the production company behind projects including NBC's "Las Vegas" and the HBO miniseries "Empire Falls," to develop a scripted series aimed at boosting themes of gender equality, diversity, and inclusion.

16-5 The Coordination Challenge

The choices for delivering messages to a target audience continue to evolve. As you have seen, marketers and advertisers are constantly searching for new, cost-effective ways to break through the clutter and connect with consumers. Today, everything from advertising in restrooms to sponsoring a marathon to advergaming to producing short online videos is part of the portfolio.

Here is a critical point about the explosion of advertising and IBP tools: Advertisers have a vast and ever-expanding array of options for delivering messages to current and potential customers. From cable TV and YouTube to national newspapers and bus shelter posters, from high-tech billboards to online contests and giveaways, the variety of options is staggering. The keys to success for any campaign are choosing the right set of options to engage a target segment and then coordinating the placement of messages to ensure coherent and timely communication.

From a practical standpoint, even in this era of a hyperfocus on integration, many factors make IBP coordination very challenging. As advertising and IBP have become more complex, organizations often become reliant on diverse functional specialists. For example, an organization might have separate managers for advertising, event sponsorship, branded entertainment, and digital development. Specialists, by definition, focus on their specialty and can lose sight of what others in the organization are doing. Specialists also want their own budgets and typically argue for more funding for their particular area. This competition for budget dollars often yields rivalries and animosities that work against coordination.

Coordination is further complicated by the fact that there can be an incredible lack of alignment around who is responsible for achieving the integration.[62] Should the client accept this responsibility? Or should integration be the responsibility of a "lead" agency? One vision of how things should work has the lead agency playing the role of an architect and general contractor. The campaign architect is charged with drawing up a plan that is media neutral and then hiring subcontractors to deliver those aspects of the project that the agency itself is ill suited to handle. The plan must also be profit neutral. That is, the budget must go to the subcontractors and specialty shops that actually create and execute the plan. If it is not clear who is accountable for delivering an integrated campaign, there is little chance that synergy or integration will be achieved.

Above all, the objective for coordination is to achieve a synergistic effect. Individual media can reach audiences, but advertisers get more for their dollars if various media and IBP tools build on one another and work together. Synergy from coordination, rather than pounding away endlessly with isolated messages in individual media, is the way to build brands over time. "We bombard consumers with thousands of ads a day, subject them to endless ad load times, interrupt their screens with popups, and overpopulate their screens and feeds," observes P&G's chief brand officer. "We're awfully busy, but all of this activity is not breaking through the clutter."[63] In fact, all the diverse messages and media contribute to clutter if not carefully coordinated.

The coordination challenge does not end here. Chapters that follow will add more layers of complexity to this challenge. Topics to come include direct marketing, personal selling, public relations, influencer marketing, and corporate advertising. These activities entail additional contacts with a target audience that *should* reinforce the messages being delivered through broadcast, print, digital/social/mobile, and support media. Integrating these efforts to speak with one voice represents a marketer's best hope for breaking through the clutter to engage with a target segment in today's crowded marketplace.

Summary

1. **Explain the role of event sponsorship, product placements, and branded entertainment as forms of integrated brand promotion, and justify their growing popularity with respect to the convergence of advertising and entertainment for brand-building.**

Collectively, event sponsorship, product placements, and branded entertainment are more experiential forms of marketing. Experiential marketing, or incorporating a brand with the consumer's lived experience is popular for consumers because they are unique, enjoyable, fit in with the consumer's lifestyle. Experiential marketing is increasingly popular with advertisers and marketers because they can enhance brand awareness and brand equity in ways that are easily integrated with advertising and integrated brand promotion.

2. **Identify what event sponsorship is, who uses it, how it is measured, its benefits, and how to leverage it.**

Event sponsorship entails a marketer providing financial support to help fund an event in exchange for a marketer acquiring the rights to display a brand name, logo, or advertising message on-site at the event. The list of companies sponsoring events grows with each passing year, and the events include a wide variety of activities. Of these sponsored events, sports by far attract the most sponsorship dollars. Sponsorship can help in building brand familiarity; it can promote brand loyalty by connecting a brand with powerful emotional experiences, and in most instances it allows a marketer to reach a well-defined target audience. Events can also facilitate face-to-face contacts with key customers and present opportunities to distribute product samples, sell premiums, and conduct consumer surveys.

3. **Summarize the uses and appeal of product placements in venues like TV, movies, and video games.**

Product placements have surged in popularity, and there are many reasons to believe that advertisers will continue to commit more resources to this activity. Like any other advertising tactic, product placements offer the most value when they are integrated with other elements of the advertising plan for synergy. One common use of the placement is to help create excitement for the launch of a new product. Implicit celebrity endorsements and authenticity are key issues to consider when judging placement opportunities. High-quality placements are most likely to result from great collaboration among marketers, agents, producers, and writers.

4. **Identify what branded entertainment is, and explain the benefits and challenges of connecting with event venues or entertainment properties in building a brand.**

Brand builders want to connect with consumers, and to do so, they are connecting with the entertainment business. What distinguishes branded entertainment from product placement is that in branded entertainment, the entertainment would not exist without the marketer's support, and in many instances, it is marketers themselves who create the entertainment property. Even though not everyone can afford a NASCAR sponsorship, in many ways NASCAR sets the standard for celebrating brands in an entertaining setting. However, the rush to participate in branded entertainment ventures raises the risk of oversaturation and consumer backlash, or at least consumer apathy. With the media environment so fragmented, brands and their agencies must continue to explore fresh and unexpected ways to engage audiences through traditional media and digital, social, and mobile marketing.

5. **Discuss the coordination challenges presented by the variety of communication and branding tools for achieving integrated brand promotion via the consumer experience.**

The tremendous variety of media options we have discussed thus far represents a monumental challenge for an advertiser that wishes to speak to consumers with a single voice. Achieving this single voice is critical for breaking through the clutter of the modern advertising environment and reinforcing key points of the campaign. However, it is a challenge to coordinate the work of functional specialists in order to achieve synergy through integration. We will return to this issue in subsequent chapters as we explore other options available to marketers in their quest to win customers.

Key Terms

authenticity	event sponsorship measurement	sponsor-event congruity/fit
branded experience	experiential marketing	sponsorship activation
consumer-event congruity/fit	leveraging	sponsorship articulation
event social responsibility	media impressions	sponsor spillover
event sponsorship	product placement	

Endnotes

1. Angeline Close Scheinbaum, "Digital Engagement: Opportunities and Risks for Sponsors," *Journal of Advertising Research* 56, no. 4 (2016), 341–345.

2. Bill Wilson, "Champions League: Why Nissan Uses Football for Its Sponsor Goals," *BBC News,* September 13, 2016, http://www.bbc.com/news/business-37324069.

3. Angeline G. Close and Russell Lacey, "How the Anticipation Can Be as Great as the Experience: Explaining Event Sponsorship Exhibit Outcomes via Affective Forecasting," *Journal of Current Issues & Research in Advertising* 35, no. 2 (2014), 209–224.

4. Bob Garfield, "The Post Advertising Age," *Advertising Age*, March 26, 2007, 1, 12–14.

5. Russell Lacey and Angeline G. Close, "How Fit Connects Service Brand Sponsors with Consumers' Passions for Sponsored Events," *International Journal of Sports Marketing and Sponsorship* 14, no. 3 (2013), 57–73.

6. James H. McAlexander, John W. Schouten, and Harold F. Koenig, "Building Brand Community," *Journal of Marketing* 66, no. 1 (2002), 38–54.

7. Russell Lacey, Julie Sneath, R. Zachary Finney, and Angeline G. Close, "The Impact of Repeat Attendance on Sponsorship Effects," *Journal of Marketing Communications* 13, no. 4 (2007), 243–255.

8. Chris Allen, Susan Fournier, and Felicia Miller, "Brands and Their Meaning Makers," in Curtis P Haugtvedt, Paul Herr, and Frank R. Kardes (Eds.), *Handbook of Consumer Psychology* (Hillsdale, NJ: LEA Publishing, 2008), Chapter 31.

9. Deborah Wilker and Abraham Hampp, "SXSW 2017: The Big Brands Are Pulling Back, and Maybe That's a Good Thing," *Billboard*, March 10, 2017, http://www.billboard.com/articles/news/7717945/sxsw-2017-brands-money-samsung-spotify-doritos.

10. Lane Wakefield et al., "Are Brands Wasting Money On Sport Sponsorships?" *Journal of Advertising Research* 61, no. 2 (2020), 192–211.

11. Christina Gough, "NFL League/Team Sponsorship Revenue 2010-2021," *Statista*, March 9, 2021, https://www.statista.com/statistics/456355/nfl-league-team-sponsorship-revenue-worldwide/.

12. E. J. Schultz, "Are You Game?" *Advertising Age*, April 3, 2017, http://adage.com/article/news/e-sports/308447.

13. Christina Gough, "eSports Sponsorship and Media Rights Revenue Worldwide," *Statista*, March 18, 2021, https://www.statista.com/statistics/672204/brand-esport-engagement-impact-consumer-opinion/.

14. Angeline Close Scheinbaum and Russell Lacey, "Event Social Responsibility: A Note to Improve Outcomes for Sponsors and Events," *Journal of Business Research* 68, no. 9 (2015), 1982–1986; also see Russell Lacey, Angeline G. Close, and R. Zachary Finney, "The Pivotal Roles of Product Knowledge and Corporate Social Responsibility in Event Sponsorship Effectiveness," *Journal of Business Research* 63, no. 11 (2010), 1222–1228.

15. Angeline G. Close, R. Zachary Finney, Russell Z. Lacey, and Julie Z. Sneath, "Engaging the Consumer through Event Marketing: Linking Attendees with the Sponsor, Community, and Brand," *Journal of Advertising Research* 46, no. 4 (2006), 420–433.

16. Russell Lacey, Angeline G. Close, and R. Zachary Finney, "The Pivotal Roles of Product Knowledge and Corporate Social Responsibility in Event Sponsorship Effectiveness," *Journal of Business Research* 63, no. 11 (2010), 1222–1228.

17. General Motors, "SWAC Announces General Motors as Exclusive Automotive Sponsor," October 26, 2021, https://swac.org/news/2021/10/22/southwestern-athletic-conference-announces-general-motors-as-its-exclusive-automotive-sponsor.aspx; Sam McEachern, Cadillac Sponsors 2021 Ebony Awards Ceremony, October 24, 2021, https://gmauthority.com/blog/2021/10/cadillac-sponsors-2021-ebony-100-awards-ceremony/.

18. Data drawn from https://www.solheimcupusa.com/2021-hospitality-opportunities/partners.

19. Ted Orme-Claye, "Amazon secures Napoli sleeve sponsorship," Insider Sport, August 24, 2021, https://insidersport.com/2021/08/24/amazon-secures-napoli-sleeve-sponsorship/; Angeline G. Close, Russell Lacey, and T. Bettina Cornwell, "Visual Processing and Need for Cognition Can Enhance Event-Sponsorship Outcomes," *Journal of Advertising Research* 55, no. 2 (2015), 206–215.

20. Grant McCracken, "Culture and Consumption: A Theoretical Account of the Structure and Movement of the Cultural Meaning of Consumer Goods," *Journal of Consumer Research* 13 (June 1986), 71–84.

21. Lynn R. Kahle and Angeline G. Close (eds.), *Consumer Behavior Knowledge for Effective Sports and Event Marketing* (New York: Routledge, 2011).

22. "How Deloitte Is Using Sponsorship to Showcase Digital Expertise," *Sponsorship.com*, January 30, 2017, www.sponsorship.com and https://www2.deloitte.com/us/en/pages/about-deloitte/articles/deloitte-sponsorships.html.

23. Ellen Byron, "An Old Dice Game Catches On Again, Pushed by P&G," *The Wall Street Journal,* January 30, 2007, A1, A13.

24. Amy Hernandez, "Research Studies Gauge Sponsorship ROI," *Marketing News*, May 12, 2003, 16; Ian Mount, "Exploding the Myths of Stadium Naming," *Business 2.0*, April 2004, 82, 83.

25. Kate Fitzgerald, "Events No Longer Immune to Marketer Demand for ROI," *Advertising Age*, March 19, 2007, S–3.

26. Jeff Katz, "Commentary: As Sports Consumption Changes, So Must the Measurement of Sponsorships," *MediaPost*, January 26, 2017, https://www.mediapost.com/publications/article/293769/as-sports-consumption-changes-so-must-the-measure.html.

27. Angeline Close, R. Zachary Finney, Russell Lacey, and Julie Sneath, "Engaging the Consumer through Event Marketing: Linking Attendees with the Sponsor, Community, and Brand," *Journal of Advertising Research* 46, no. 3 (2006), 420–433.

28. Angeline Close, Anjala Krishen, and Michael S. LaTour, "This Event Is Me!: How Consumer-Event Congruity Leverages Sponsorship," *Journal of Advertising Research* 49, no. 3 (2009), 271–284.

29. Angeline Close and Russell Lacey, "Fit Matters? Asymmetrical Impact of Effectiveness for Sponsors and Event Marketers," *Sport Marketing Quarterly* 22, no. 2 (2013), 71–82.

30. Russell Lacey and Angeline G. Close, "How Fit Connects Service Brand Sponsors with Consumers' Passions for Sponsored Events," *International Journal of Sports Marketing and Sponsorship* 14, no. 3 (2013), 57–73.

31. Bettina Cornwell, Clinton Weeks, and Donald Roy, "Sponsor-Linked Marketing: Opening the Black Box," *Journal of Advertising* 34 (Summer 2005), 21–42; Lexus Europe Newsroom, Lexus Announced as the Official Car of Davis Cup by Rakuten Finals 2021, September 9 2021, https://newsroom.lexus.eu/lexus-announced-as-the-official-car-of-davis-cup--by-rakuten-finals-2021/.

32. Jack Neff, "See the Spot: P&G Back in Games with New Olympics Work," *Advertising Age*, April 26, 2016, http://adage.com/article /special-report-the-olympics/p-g-back-games/303755/; Kelly Wallace, "Olympic Gymnast Simone Biles' Lessons from Mom," *CNN*, August 9, 2016, http://www.cnn.com/2016/04/27/health/simone -biles-olympics-mom-100-days-until-rio/; Barrett J. Brunsman, "P&G Declared Winner of Olympic Advertising," *Cincinnati Business Courier*, August 24, 2016, http://www.bizjournals.com/cincinnati /news/2016/08/24/p-g-declared-winner-of-olympic-advertising .html.

33. Kelly Gilbolm, "Product Placement, Now Starring in the Streaming Era," *Bloomberg Businessweek*, July 21, 2021, https://www.bloomberg.com/news/articles/2021-07-21 /marketers-embrace-product-placement-in-streaming-tv-shows.

34. Vince Bond Jr., "Supercar's Marvel Tie-in Helped Propel the Audi Brand. Now Hyundai Is Getting in on the Action," *Automotive News*, May 9, 2016, http://www.autonews.com/article/20160509 /RETAIL03/160509895/supercars-marvel-tie-in-helped-propel-the -audi-brand.-now-hyundai—is-.

35. Lucy Handley, "Goodbye Advertising, Hello Branded Content: Comedy Central Looks to New Ad Formats," *CNBC*, February 24, 2017, http://www.cnbc.com/2017/02/24/goodbye-ads-hello-branded -content-comedy-central-find-new-formats.html.

36. Marc Graser, "TV's Savior?" *Advertising Age*, February 6, 2006, S–1, S–2; Fu Guo et al., "Product Placement in Mass Media: A Review and Bibliometric Analysis," *Journal of Advertising* 48, no. 2 (2019), 215–231.

37. Davit Davtyan, Kristin Stewart, and Isabella Cunningham, "Comparing Brand Placements and Advertisements on Brand Recall and Recognition," *Journal of Advertising Research* 56, no. 3 (2016), 299–310.

38. Tim Nudd, "50 Years Later, Heinz Approves Don Draper's 'Pass the Heinz' Ads and Is Actually Running Them," *Adweek*, March 13, 2017, http://www.adweek.com/creativity/50-years-later -heinz-approves-don-drapers-pass-the-heinz-ads-and-is-actually -running-them/; Jessica Wohl, "Heinz Taps Sterling Cooper Draper Pryce for Campaign (Yes, Really)," *Advertising Age*, March 13, 2017, http://adage.com/article/cmo-strategy/heinz-taps-sterling -cooper-draper-pryce-campaign/308261.

39. Marc Graser, "Automakers: Every Car Needs a Movie," *Advertising Age*, December 11, 2006, 8.

40. Vince Bond Jr., "Supercar's Marvel Tie-in Helped Propel the Audi Brand. Now Hyundai Is Getting in on the Action," *Automotive News*, May 9, 2016, http://www.autonews.com/article/20160509 /RETAIL03/160509895/supercars-marvel-tie-in-helped-propel-the -audi-brand.-now-hyundai—is-.

41. Emma Hall, "Young Consumers Receptive to Movie Product Placements," *Advertising Age*, March 29, 2004, 8; Federico de Gregorio and Yongjun Sung, "Understanding Attitudes toward and Behaviors in Response to Product Placement," *Journal of Advertising* 39 (Spring 2010), 83–96.

42. Nielsen Newswire, "Trends in U.S. Video Gaming—the Rise of Cross-Platform," March 9, 2012, www.nielsen.com.

43. Zeph M. Van Berlo et al., "The Gamification of Branded Content: A Meta-Analysis of Advergame Effects," *Journal of Advertising* 50, no. 2 (2021), 179–196.

44. Matthew Leibl, "How Fortnite is Revolutionizing In-Game Advertising," *Fansided*, May 21, 2020, https://apptrigger.com/2020/05/23 /fortnite-advertising/

45. Tathagata Ghosh, "Winning versus Not Losing: Exploring the Effects of In-Game Advertising Outcome on Its Effectiveness," *Journal of Interactive Marketing* 36 (2016), 134–147.

46. Cristel Russell and Michael Belch, "A Managerial Investigation into the Product Placement Industry," *Journal of Advertising Research* 45 (March 2005), 73–92.

47. Federico de Gregorio and Yongjun Sung, "Understanding Attitudes toward and Behaviors in Response to Product Placement," *Journal of Advertising* 39 (Spring 2010), 83–96.

48. Rance Crain, "Want to Really Serve Consumers? Offer Them an Experience," *Advertising Age*, December 10, 2012, 26.

49. Vince Bond Jr., "Supercar's Marvel Tie-in Helped Propel the Audi Brand. Now Hyundai Is Getting in on the Action," *Automotive News*, May 9, 2016, http://www.autonews.com/article/20160509 /RETAIL03/160509895/supercars-marvel-tie-in-helped-propel-the -audi-brand.-now-hyundai—is-.

50. Laurent Muzellec, "James Bond, Dunder Mifflin, and the Future of Product Placement," *Harvard Business Review*, June 23, 2016, https://hbr.org/2016/06/james-bond-dunder-mifflin-and-the -future-of-product-placement.

51. Bond Jr., "Supercar's Marvel Tie-in Helped Propel the Audi Brand. Now Hyundai Is Getting in on the Action."

52. James Karrah, Kathy McKee, and Carol Pardun, "Practitioners' Evolving Views on Product Placement Effectiveness," *Journal of Advertising Research* 43 (June 2003), 138–149.

53. Jonathan A. Jensen et al., "Analyzing Price Premiums in International Sponsorship Exchange," *Journal of Advertising Research* 61, no. 1 (2020), 44–57.

54. Josh Jacquot, "The New NASCAR: Goodbye, Old and White; Hello, Piercings and Tattoos," *Car and Driver*, April 3, 2017, http://blog .caranddriver.com/the-new-nascar-goodbye-old-and-white-hello -piercings-and-tattoos.

55. Rich Thomaselli, "Nextel Link Takes NASCAR to New Level," *Advertising Age*, October 27, 2003, S–7.

56. Jack Neff and Natalie Zumba, "The Rise of Branded Experiences," *Advertising Age*, January 7, 2013, 13.

57. Abe Saur, "Not Watered Down: Q&A With Portal A on Brita's First Music Video," *Brand Channel*, March 10, 2017, http://www .brandchannel.com/2017/03/10/5-questions-brita-031017.

58. Cristel Russell and Michael Belch, "A Managerial Investigation into the Product Placement Industry," *Journal of Advertising Research* 45 (March 2005), 82, 83.

59. Neil Munshi, "Spain's Starring Role in Bollywood Movie a Boon to Tourism," *Advertising Age*, February 6, 2012, 6.

60. Larry Dobrow, "Is It Time to Put an End to Brand Integration?" *Advertising Age*, May 21, 2009, http://adage.com/article /madisonvine-news/tv-marketing-time-put-end-brand- integration /136797.

61. Barrett J. Brunsman, "Here's Why P&G Just Sold the People's Choice Awards Program," *Cincinnati Business Courier*, April 6, 2017, http://www.bizjournals.com/cincinnati/news/2017/04/06/heres -why-p-g-just-sold-the-people-s-choice.html.

62. Burt Helm, "Struggles of a Mad Man: Saatchi & Saatchi CEO Kevin Roberts," *BusinessWeek*, December 3, 2007, 44–50.

63. I-Hsien Sherwood, "Too Much 'Complexity' and 'Crap' Hinders Agency–Brand Relationships, says P&G CMO," *Campaign (US)*, April 4, 2017, http://www.campaignlive.com/article/complexity-crap -hinders-agency-brand-relationships-says-p-g-cmo/1429596.

Integrating Direct Marketing and Personal Selling

In this chapter, we overview direct marketing and database marketing and explain how they are used to synergize with other types of advertising and integrated brand promotion (IBP). We consider the privacy concerns as well as the inherent advantages. Further, we conclude this chapter with how direct marketing relates with personal selling and closing sales. Personal selling brings the human element into the marketing/advertising/IBP process and shares many important features with direct marketing. For instance, as with direct marketing, an organization's sales personnel are looking to develop a dialogue with customers that can result in product sales in the short run and repeat business over the long run. Trial purchases are desirable, but a satisfied customer who repurchases (and shares positive word-of-mouth for the brand) is a goal. Personal selling is ideally suited to encouraging brand loyalty. Exhibit 17.1 shows how direct marketing, database marketing, and personal selling fit into the overall framework of advertising and IBP.

Exhibit 17.1 ▶ Consider this framework for integrating direct marketing and personal selling.

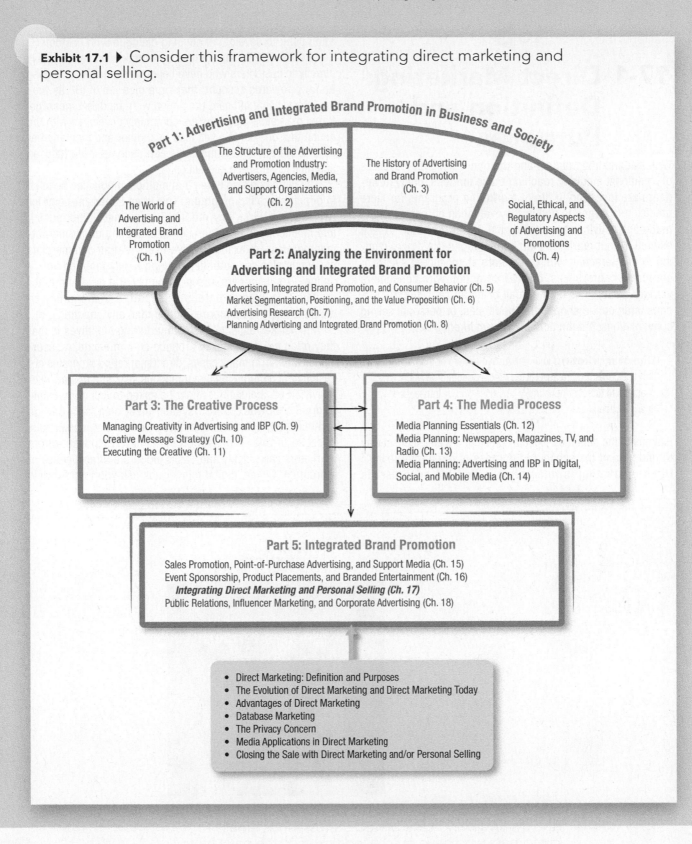

Part 1: Advertising and Integrated Brand Promotion in Business and Society

The Structure of the Advertising and Promotion Industry: Advertisers, Agencies, Media, and Support Organizations (Ch. 2)

The History of Advertising and Brand Promotion (Ch. 3)

The World of Advertising and Integrated Brand Promotion (Ch. 1)

Social, Ethical, and Regulatory Aspects of Advertising and Promotions (Ch. 4)

Part 2: Analyzing the Environment for Advertising and Integrated Brand Promotion

Advertising, Integrated Brand Promotion, and Consumer Behavior (Ch. 5)
Market Segmentation, Positioning, and the Value Proposition (Ch. 6)
Advertising Research (Ch. 7)
Planning Advertising and Integrated Brand Promotion (Ch. 8)

Part 3: The Creative Process

Managing Creativity in Advertising and IBP (Ch. 9)
Creative Message Strategy (Ch. 10)
Executing the Creative (Ch. 11)

Part 4: The Media Process

Media Planning Essentials (Ch. 12)
Media Planning: Newspapers, Magazines, TV, and Radio (Ch. 13)
Media Planning: Advertising and IBP in Digital, Social, and Mobile Media (Ch. 14)

Part 5: Integrated Brand Promotion

Sales Promotion, Point-of-Purchase Advertising, and Support Media (Ch. 15)
Event Sponsorship, Product Placements, and Branded Entertainment (Ch. 16)
Integrating Direct Marketing and Personal Selling (Ch. 17)
Public Relations, Influencer Marketing, and Corporate Advertising (Ch. 18)

- Direct Marketing: Definition and Purposes
- The Evolution of Direct Marketing and Direct Marketing Today
- Advantages of Direct Marketing
- Database Marketing
- The Privacy Concern
- Media Applications in Direct Marketing
- Closing the Sale with Direct Marketing and/or Personal Selling

17-1 Direct Marketing: Definition and Purposes

With fragmenting markets and the diminishing effectiveness of traditional media in reaching those markets, many advertisers are investing in direct marketing programs for more precision in targeting and in the evaluation of results. Direct marketing activities are often digital, but may be face-to-face as well. Direct marketing implementations are broad, ranging from interacting with consumers at sponsored events or corporate conferences, direct interaction with consumers via social media or online, mail or email sent directly to a consumer, online shopping experiences, or personal selling conversations. A definition of *direct marketing* is:

> **Direct marketing** is an interactive system of marketing that uses one or more advertising media or communication channels to affect a measurable response and/or transaction at any location.[1]

Examining the definition piece by piece offers an excellent way to understand the scope and purpose of direct marketing.[2] Direct marketing is *interactive* in that the advertiser is attempting to develop an ongoing dialogue with customers. See Exhibit 17.2 for an example by Amtrak, who sends emails directly to customers who have bought train tickets or signed up for a rewards account; they do a nice job of IBP as they are integrating a gift card promotion with the direct message. Direct marketing programs are commonly developed with the notion that one contact will lead to another and then another so that the marketer's message can become more focused and refined with each interaction.

The definition also notes that multiple media can be used in direct marketing programs. This is an important point for two reasons. First, any medium (including digital, social, and mobile media) can be used in executing direct marketingprograms. For example, advertisers that air commercials on TV can also see potential in airing highly targeted ads to online-TV subscribers based on behavioral data and other individual customer details.[3] Second, a combination of media is likely to be more effective than any one medium.

Another key aspect of direct marketing initiatives is that they often are designed to produce an immediate, measurable response. In many cases, direct marketing programs are designed to generate an instantaneous sale. In a magazine or television ad, a customer might be asked to call or go online to order a Bowflex, a Nutrisystem meal plan, or a George Foreman grill—products that have sold well via infomercials. Because of this emphasis on immediate response, direct marketers can quickly and easily judge the effectiveness of a program. Online, digital banner ads ask you to order now

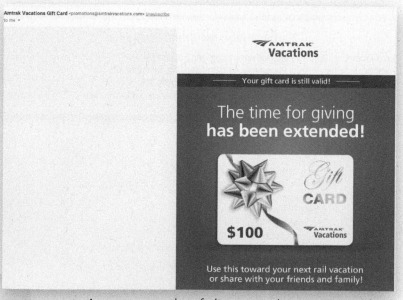

Source: Amtrak

Exhibit 17.2 ▶ As an example of direct marketing, Amtrak (the train/railway in the United States) sends emails to customers who have purchased tickets in the past. Note how they offer an opt-out or unsubscribe feature for their emails. It is a good example of IBP, as they integrate a direct message to a customer as well as integrating a promotion for a gift card with a ticket purchase.

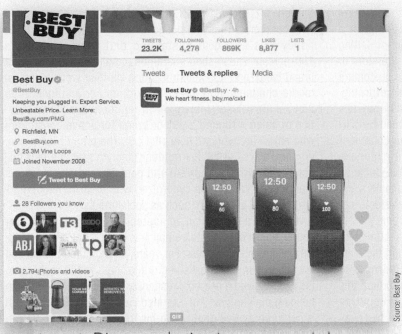

through an app or website.[4] And on your phone, a message or app may offer you an opportunity to place a mobile order.

The final phase of the definition notes that a direct marketing transaction can take place anywhere. Customers do not have to make a trip to a retail store for a direct marketing program to work. Follow-ups can be made by mail or email, social media, over the phone, on a mobile device, or online. With the rise of omnichannel marketing, it seems clear that consumers like the option of contacting companies and obtaining or evaluating the products in many ways. So smart retailers make themselves available in both the physical and virtual worlds. As the Best Buy homepage screenshot in Exhibit 17.3 shows, Best Buy uses social media (specifically Twitter in Exhibit 17.3) as a direct marketing tool as well as a communication channel. Note the product Best Buy is featuring in the Twitter post in Exhibit 17.3; it is a wearable device that can be used to monitor miles walked and heart rate, for instance. As such, Best Buy's Twitter post featuring the product is linked with copy that says "We heart fitness"; when the consumer clicks on the post, it takes the consumer to an online shopping page (Exhibit 17.4).

Exhibit 17.3 ▶ Direct marketing is very synergistic with social media; note how Best Buy's Twitter page directs interested consumers to a link to purchase the product promoted and how Best Buy uses video (via Vine loops) to further showcase their merchandise for e-commerce or in-store purchases.

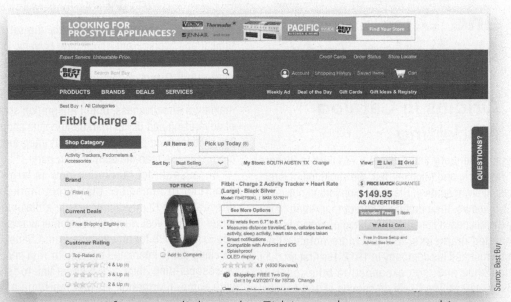

Exhibit 17.4 ▶ After you click on the Fitbit product promoted in Best Buy's Twitter feed (Exhibit 17.3), e-commerce and direct marketing takes over. Note how the e-commerce landing page is consumer friendly by giving product reviews, detailed information, the ability to compare products, and a choice of buying online with the price match guarantee OR picking it up at a Best Buy today.

A smart, consumer-based strategy is to let customers choose among online shopping, in-store shopping, or a hybrid of both. For instance, Target does a great job letting customers buy a product online and return it in the store or vice versa. As another example, Fitbit also allows customers flexibility in the channels for purchasing and returning. Notice in Exhibit 17.4 that the online shopper can buy this Fitbit online and pick it up that day in a store. Called **hybrid commerce** or an **omnichannel** strategy, the consumer can have the best of both digital and in-store channels. Specifically, an omnichannel approach has value because physical retail interaction can "revive" inactive customers and make them active again, while online options are effective in maintaining and developing the relationship over time.[5]

Furthermore, consumers should have the choice of returning an online purchase in the store or through the mail. The best strategy for consumer-friendly mail returns is to include a prepaid return shipping label with the product; this way, the customer is not inconvenienced. Zappos.com was one of the first online shopping sites to use free two-way shipping, and their consumer-friendly practice has now been adopted by other online retailers.

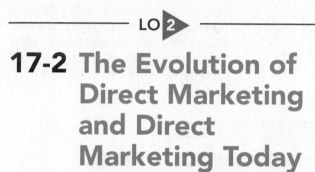

17-2 The Evolution of Direct Marketing and Direct Marketing Today

17-2a Origins in Catalog Marketing

From Johannes Gutenberg and Benjamin Franklin to Richard Sears, Alvah Roebuck, and Michael Dell, the evolution of direct marketing has involved some of the great pioneers in business. As Exhibit 17.5 shows, the practice of direct marketing today is shaped by the successes of notable catalog merchandisers.[6]

Among catalog marketers, few are more notable than L.L. Bean. Bean founded his company in 1912. His first product was a hunting shoe and then expanded to other outdoor clothing and equipment. The L.L.Bean catalog of 1917 shows the strategy underlying the direct marketing success. The catalog cover highlighted the brand's commitment to quality. It read: "Maine Hunting Shoe—guarantee. We guarantee this pair of shoes to give perfect satisfaction in every way. If the rubber breaks or the tops grow hard, return them together with this guarantee tag and we will replace them, free of charge.

Signed, L.L. Bean."[7] L.L.Bean realized that relationships with customers must be based on trust, and the guarantee policy was aimed at sustaining that trust. L.L.Bean's 100-percent-satisfaction guarantee remains as a pillar of the brand today, and it is communicated via their website, social media channels, and direct marketing. For instance, note how L.L.Bean uses Instagram to reinforce the brand position of being a rugged, outdoor brand for active consumers who enjoy the outdoors (Exhibit 17.6). The brand's Instagram in many ways "sells" the outdoor lifestyle that is a psychographic fit with their current and potential customers. Direct marketing is best when synergized with other forms of integrated brand promotion, such as social media.

L.L.Bean also showed an appreciation for database marketing, analytics, and mail/email lists to directly communicate with interested customers. For years, he promoted the catalog via ads in hunting and fishing magazines. Those replying to the ads received a personal response. The company's focus on building mailing lists (now termed **customer databases**) is captured by this quote from his friend John Gould: "If you drop in just to shake his hand, you get home to find his catalog in your mailbox."[9] Today, quality products, understated advertising, and customer-contact and distribution systems sustain the business. As you can see from Integrated Brand Promotion in Action (Exhibit 17.7), L.L.Bean builds the brand image via social media, which integrates well with direct marketing.

17-2b Direct Marketing Today

Direct marketing today is largely digital and should be ethical and transparent about data privacy. Direct marketing has grown to largely focus on online channels, such as Email marketing. Direct marketing today should be *integrated* with an organization's other advertising and IBP efforts. For maximum effectiveness, brand integration should be the goal of advertising and direct marketing/online shopping initiatives. The evidence supports the point that integrated programs are more effective than the sum of their parts.[10]

Because direct marketing now is largely digital, it is important to remember that direct marketing involves a direct attempt to interact or create a dialogue with the customer in an ethical way if the customer wants the information. See Exhibit 17.8 for an example from Chanel, who is directly reaching out to interested customers with information on their newest perfume; they give a direct link to "shop now" along with some information on their perfume and links to their other complementary products such as fashion, eyewear, and watches. They make it easy to unsubscribe for those who find it to be unwanted communication as well as giving clear information and transparency about the consumer data privacy rights and a link to their privacy policy. Chanel is a class-act in this example of sound direct marketing.

Exhibit 17.5 ▶ Select direct marketing milestones over the years.

c. 1450	Johannes Gutenberg invents movable type.
1667	The first gardening catalog is published by William Lucas, an English gardener.
1744	Benjamin Franklin publishes a catalog of books on science and industry and formulates the basic mail-order concept of customer satisfaction guaranteed.
1830s	A few mail-order companies began operating in New England, selling camping and fishing supplies.
1863	The introduction of penny postage facilitates direct mail.
1867	The invention of the typewriter gives a modern appearance to direct mail materials.
1872	Montgomery Ward publishes his first "catalog," selling 163 items on a single sheet of paper. By 1884 his catalog grows to 240 pages, with thousands of items and a money-back guarantee.
1886	Richard Sears enters the mail-order business by selling gold watches and makes $5,000 in his first six months. He partners with Alvah Roebuck in 1887, and by 1893 they are marketing a wide range of merchandise in a 196-page catalog.
1912	L.L.Bean founds one of today's most admired mail-order companies on the strength of his Maine Hunting Shoe and a guarantee of total satisfaction.
1917	The Direct Mail Advertising Association is founded. In 1973, it becomes the Direct Mail/Direct Marketing Association.
1928	Third-class bulk mail becomes a reality, offering economies for the direct mail industry.
1950	Credit cards first appear, led by the Diners' Club travel and entertainment card. American Express enters in 1958.
1951	Lillian Vernon places an ad for a monogrammed purse and belt and generates $16,000 in orders. She quickly recognizes that catalog shopping has great appeal to time-pressed consumers.
1951	First IKEA furniture catalog is distributed in Sweden.
1953	Publishers Clearing House is founded and soon becomes a major force in magazine subscriptions.
1955	Columbia Record Club is established, and eventually becomes Columbia House—a music-marketing giant.
1967	The term *telemarketing* first appears in print, and AT&T introduces the first toll-free 800 phone service.
1983	The Direct Mail/Direct Marketing Association drops Direct Mail from its name to become the DMA, as a reflection of the multiple media being used by direct marketers.
1992	The number of U.S. consumers who shop at home surpasses 100 million.
1998	The Direct Marketing Association merges with the Association for Interactive Media.
1999	U.S. Federal Deceptive Mail Prevention and Enforcement Act- places restrictions on direct mail marketing and lets the USPS protect consumers against deceptive advertising and mail in the form of contests, games, and sweepstakes. It can impose financial penalties and stop-mail orders.
2003	U.S. consumers register more than 10 million phone numbers in the first four days of the national Do Not Call Registry.
2003	CAN-SPAM legislation requires email marketers to be transparent about the purpose of their messages, avoid misleading subject lines, and provide opt-out methods for customers.
2009	JC Penney discontinues its "Big Book" catalog but continues mailing smaller, category-specific catalogs.
2016	The DMA changes its name to Data & Marketing Association, reflecting the full range of technical and communication functions and entities involved in direct marketing.
2018	California Privacy Notice is required, which is a part of the California Consumer Privacy Act for residents of that U.S. state to provide mandated disclosures about residents' online and offline information.
2018	European Union (EU) General Data Protection Regulation (GDPR) — Europe's data privacy and security law that has hundreds of pages of new requirements and laws for businesses and organizations around the globe.

Source: L.L.Bean Inc.

Exhibit 17.6 ▶ For L.L.Bean and other brands that had early direct marketing successes selling their products with catalogs, e-commerce and social media with e-commerce links may slowly replace catalogs due to higher convenience and less environmental waste.

Source: L.L.Bean Inc.

Exhibit 17.7 ▶ Integrated brand promotion in action: L.L.Bean.
L.L.Bean still distributes its catalog to millions of customers, while engaging brand fans through multiple social media. *How does promoting the printed catalog on Facebook and listing individual store Twitter accounts help L.L.Bean in direct marketing?*

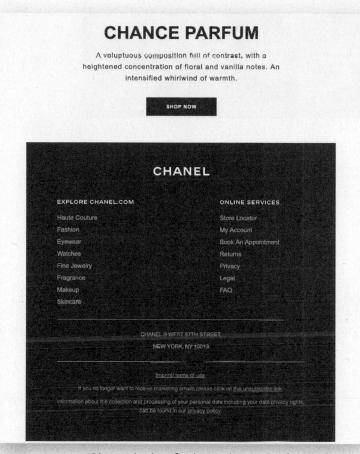

CHANCE PARFUM

A voluptuous composition full of contrast, with a heightened concentration of floral and vanilla notes. An intensified whirlwind of warmth.

SHOP NOW

CHANEL

EXPLORE CHANEL.COM

Haute Couture
Fashion
Eyewear
Watches
Fine Jewelry
Fragrance
Makeup
Skincare

ONLINE SERVICES

Store Locator
My Account
Book An Appointment
Returns
Privacy
Legal
FAQ

CHANEL 9 WEST 57TH STREET,
NEW YORK, NY 10013

Imprint/ terms of use

If you no longer want to receive marketing emails please click on this unsubscribe link.

Information about the collection and processing of your personal data including your data privacy rights, can be found in our privacy policy.

Source: Chanel.

Exhibit 17.8 ▶ Chanel, the fashion house, does direct marketing in a classy way with e-mail marketing to those who have expressed interest or purchased from them in the past. Key things to note in this image are the data privacy information, the link to their privacy policy, and the uncomplicated way for uninterested consumers to unsubscribe.

Multiple media are often employed in the direct marketing process, and direct marketing is characterized by the fact that a measurable response is often immediately available for assessing a program's impact. Direct marketing programs are commonly used for three primary purposes—closing a sale, prospecting future customers, and engaging customers. A first purpose of direct marketing is as a tool to close the sale with a customer. This can be done as a stand-alone program, or it can be coordinated with a firm's other advertising efforts. Telecommunications giants such as AT&T, T-Mobile, and Verizon make extensive use of the advertising/direct marketing combination. High-profile mass media campaigns build awareness for their latest offer, followed by systematic direct marketing follow-ups to close the sale. With online channels, a purchase is an example of making a sale.

A second purpose of direct marketing programs is to identify prospects for future contacts and, at the same time, provide in-depth information to selected customers. Any time you respond to an offer for more information or for a free sample, you've identified yourself as a prospect and can expect follow-up sales pitches from a direct marketer. Another example of prospecting via direct marketing is when a marketer directly interacts with a potential customer at a sponsored event and then follows up with an email. Some goals of a direct marketer relate to customer relationship management, building trust, trying to engage the prospective customer with the offer of a rebate, a coupon, a free starter kit, and/or the chance to interact with the company via a toll-free number, chat, or at their websites/social media pages. If the website or social media site does not have purchasing and/or online shopping capabilities, it is likely designed as a prospecting tool to encourage future purchases via a different channel or as a way to engage current and potential customers.

A third purpose of direct marketing programs is to initiate a goal of engaging customers (customer engagement). Direct communication from a brand to a consumer via social media is a common method of engaging with consumers. Direct marketing is a means to engage customers, seek their advice, furnish helpful information about using a product, reward customers for using a brand, and foster brand loyalty in general. The manufacturer of Valvoline motor oil ran one of the classic programs to build loyalty for its brand by encouraging young car owners to join the Valvoline Performance Team.[11] To join the team, young drivers filled out a questionnaire that entered them into the Valvoline database. "Team" members received posters, special offers on racing-team apparel, news about racing events that Valvoline sponsored, and promotional reminders at regular intervals that reinforced the virtues of Valvoline for the driver's next oil change. Today, Valvoline uses its website to engage customers, help them find the nearest service location, and offer promotions (see Exhibit 17.9).

Tobacco marketers are also using direct marketing, in part because they have relatively few options for communicating with customers. Cigarette advertising has been banned from TV since 1971, and public health advocates have raised concerns about other forms of tobacco or vaping advertising because of the possibility that young people may see the messages and be encouraged to try smoking or vaping. Therefore, some tobacco brands are using email marketing to communicate with adult smokers who opt in to receiving messages.[12] In the next chapter (18), we will discuss cigarette marketing in more detail from a corporate social responsibility lens. For now, we focus on some advantages of direct marketing.

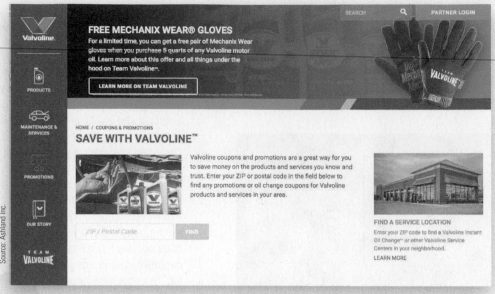

Source: Ashland Inc.

Exhibit 17.9 ▶ Valvoline's website helps build brand loyalty and encourages the use of its services at locations across the country.

LO 3

17-3 Advantages of Direct Marketing

In addition to being a marketing tool that some advertisers use when advertising is not allowed or feasible, there are other key advantages of direct marketing (which has progressed to include online channels). Namely, online shopping and informational websites are broad examples of "direct marketing" because the company communicates directly with consumers.

Other advantages of direct marketing have to do with changes in consumer lifestyles and technological developments that in effect create a climate more conducive to the practice of direct marketing. Sometimes, the consumer needs to buy something quickly and conveniently. In these instances, vending machines—another example of direct marketing—are a great option. Vending machines are making a big comeback as they are now selling products such as headphones, makeup, and consumer technology. Often, they are located in airports and other settings where the consumer may need something quickly. More traditionally, vending machines were associated with beverages and food or snack items. Coca-Cola was an early adopter of vending machine direct sales; and today the brand is modernizing vending machines to make them more innovative. See Exhibit 17.10 for an interesting example of innovations by Coca-Cola, where the customer can make their own drinks and mix and

match different coke products; it is a progression from their classic vending machines where customers buy a bottled beverage.

In addition, direct marketing programs offer advantages via mass media advertising, leading some organizations to budget for direct marketing activities. Recall that direct marketing includes activities such as: interacting with consumers at sponsored events or corporate conferences, direct interaction with consumers via social media or online channels, mail or Email sent directly to a consumer, a phone call, online shopping, online chats with consumers, or even in a face to face personal selling conversation. A final advantage is that direct marketing is measurable and easily integrated with synergistic forms of integrated brand promotion.

From the consumer's standpoint, direct marketing's advantage relates to *convenience*. Consider why online shopping is so popular, for instance. Dramatic growth in the number of dual-income and single-person households has reduced the time people have to visit retail stores. Direct marketers provide consumers access to a growing range of products and services in their homes, thus saving many households' time—their most precious resource. Further, in an era where a global pandemic is and has been prevalent, online or direct marketing via digital means is safer for customers who want to limit exposure in the marketplace.

Everyday access to credit and debit cards, as well as mobile payment options, has also contributed to the growth of direct marketing. Credit cards are the primary means of payment in most direct marketing transactions. The widespread availability of credit cards makes it ever more convenient to

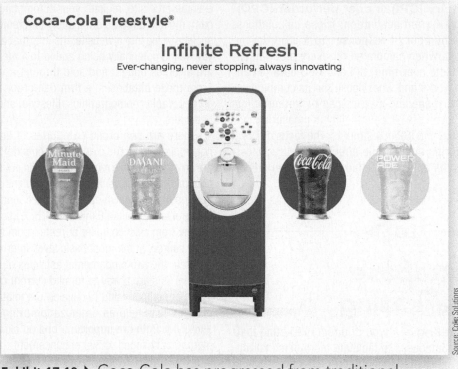

Coca-Cola Freestyle®

Infinite Refresh

Ever-changing, never stopping, always innovating

Source: Coke Solutions

Exhibit 17.10 ▶ Coca-Cola has progressed from traditional vending machines to freestyle machines, where consumers interact with various beverages and flavors so they can create unique and original beverages.

shop from the comfort of one's home. Third-party pay systems like PayPal and mobile payment options like ApplePay have also contributed to the ease of payment in direct marketing accessed via multiple media.[13]

Developments in telecommunications have also facilitated the direct marketing transaction. After getting off to a slow start in the late 1960s, toll-free telephone numbers have exploded in popularity to the point that there is no company website or a catalog that does not include an 800 number (or variations like 888) for interacting with the seller. The preferred mode of access for some consumers is online chat or the toll-free number when the consumer has questions or needs customer service, because these are real-time forms of communication. Research indicates that chat leads to higher customer satisfaction levels because the interaction is instantaneous. Warby Parker, for example, uses direct marketing to sell eyeglasses and sunglasses online and in its branded retail locations. The brand offers four customer-service options on its home page, including FAQs, Email, toll-free phone, and chat (see Exhibit 17.11).[14]

Advances in technology, including computers and mobile devices, and the introduction of 5G are impacting the growth of direct marketing. For companies and customers alike, technology facilitates convenient interactions, buying and selling, recordkeeping, analysis, and follow-up. The appeal of

direct marketing is enhanced further by the need for advertising and IBP to produce measurable effects.[15] For instance, in direct marketing, it is common to find calculations such

Need help buying glasses online?

FAQ   EMAIL   PHONE   CHAT

We're here Monday–Friday,
9 a.m.–9 p.m. ET.
888.492.7297 help@warbyparker.com

Join the world of Warby Parker

Source: Warby Parker

Exhibit 17.11 ▶ Warby Parker facilitates direct marketing of eyeglasses and sunglasses by offering four different options for contact with customers.

as **cost per inquiry (CPI)** or **cost per order (CPO)** being featured in program evaluation. These calculations simply divide the number of responses to a program by that program's cost. When calculated for every program an organization conducts over time, CPI and CPO data tell an organization what works and what doesn't in its competitive arena. These sorts of specific metrics can be gathered for many IBP tools, allowing for accountability in measuring the impact of advertising and IBP investments. The focus on producing and monitoring measurable effects is realized most effectively through an approach called database marketing, overviewed next.

17-4 Database Marketing

Database marketing is a type of direct marketing that relies on customer databases to facilitate more personalized communication or messages to market a product or service. key characteristic of direct marketing that distinguishes it from other tactics generally is its emphasis on database development. Knowing who the best customers are along with what and how often they buy is a direct marketer's secret weapon. This knowledge accumulates and manifests itself in the form of a marketing database.

Databases used as the centerpieces in direct marketing campaigns take many forms and can contain many different layers of information about customers. At one extreme is the simple mailing list that contains nothing more than the names and contact information of possible customers; at the other extreme is the customized marketing database that augments names and contact details with various additional information about customers' characteristics, past purchases, and product preferences. Understanding this distinction between mailing lists and marketing databases is important in appreciating the scope of database marketing.

17-4a Mailing Lists/Email Lists

A **mailing list/Email list** is a file of names and addresses that an organization might use for contacting prospective or prior customers. The lists are largely digital (for Emails); however postal mail lists are still relevant for many companies. Mailing lists are plentiful, easy to access, and inexpensive. The possibilities for targeting are enormous and include groupings like subscribers to certain media outlets, small business owners, new parents, or recent college graduates for example. Many times, when you subscribe to a magazine, order from an

e-commerce site, register your automobile, fill out a warranty card, redeem a rebate offer, apply for credit, join a professional society, or log into a website, the information you provide about yourself is potentially being added to a mailing list. These lists are at times bought and sold through a variety of channels. From these databases, a firm can order mailing lists based on geography, demographics, lifestyle, and specific purchase behaviors.

There are two broad categories of lists: the internal (or house) list versus the external (or outside) list. **Internal lists** are an organization's records of its own customers, subscribers, donors, and inquirers. Many organizations invite consumers to join the list to receive catalogs, promotional offers, and other communications (see Exhibit 17.12). **External lists** are purchased from a list compiler or rented from a list broker or some other source. At the most basic level, internal and external lists facilitate the two fundamental activities of the direct marketer. Internal lists are a way to remind current customers about the brand or company and to develop the relationship. Meanwhile, external lists help an organization bring in new customers and grow. Both are important, and as explained next, can be merged or changed via list enhancement.

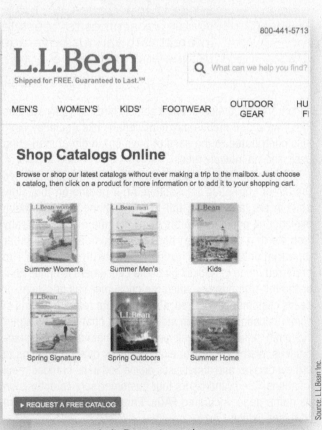

Exhibit 17.12 ▶ L.L.Bean's website invites consumers to browse or subscribe to its catalogs, building an internal list for direct marketing. Also note the toll-free number clearly visible to visitors.

17-4b List Enhancement

Email addresses, mobile device contacts, and/or addresses are a starting point for database marketing.[16] The next step in the evolution of a database is list enhancement. Often this involves augmenting an internal list by combining it with other externally supplied lists or databases. External lists can be appended or merged with a house list. One type of list enhancement involves adding names and addresses to an internal list. Proprietary name-and-address files may be bought from other companies who are not competitors. A second type of list enhancement involves merging information from external databases into an internal/house list. Here the organization ends up with a more complete description of who its customers are. Typically, this kind of enhancement includes any of four categories of information:

■ *Demographic data*—basic descriptors (such as gender and age) of individuals and households available from the Census Bureau.

■ *Geodemographic data*—information on the characteristics of the neighborhood in which a person resides.

■ *Psychographic data*—data on customer's general lifestyle, activities, interests, and opinions.

■ *Behavioral data*—information about other products and services a customer has purchased.

List enhancements that involve merging existing records with new information rely on software that allows the database manager to match records based on some piece of information the two lists share. For example, matches might be identified by sorting the zip codes and street addresses. Many suppliers gather and maintain databases that can be used for list enhancement. Often, advertisers work through agencies to identify suitable lists and databases and then arrange for enhancement and make sure that there are no duplications in the database. Mailing lists can become important sources of information about customers that advertisers can rely on to inform, remind, and persuade.

17-4c The Marketing Database

Although a marketing database is at times an extension of an internal mailing list, a **marketing database** is a more comprehensive set of data about a customer or household that includes information collected directly from individual customers as well as Email or contact information. Developing a marketing database involves pursuing dialogues with customers and learning about their individual preferences and behavioral patterns. This can be powerful information for developing marketing programs that are more effective. Relying on a database to identify distinct customer segments

can help provide for more effective advertising and IBP. For example, casinos maintain a database of visitors/customers that may contain demographic information, their zip code, and past purchase behaviors such as if they spend at certain types of gambling, the casino spa, or which restaurants at the casino they patronize. This information, in turn, helps the casino send more personalized promotions to the consumer (e.g., a spa promotion to incentivize customers who have shown an interest in the spa). In one study, writing different headlines for direct mail letters geared to specific target segments was shown to increase attention, positively influence attitude, and increase behavioral intention compared with more general headlines.[17]

Marketers would like to manage more relevant information about their consumers and potential buyers. A marketing database represents an organization's collective memory, which allows the organization to make the kind of personalized offer that once was characteristic of business. Database marketing can also yield important efficiencies that contribute to the marketer's bottom line. As seen in Exhibit 17.13, any multichannel retailer, like Cabela's, finds it useful to create

Exhibit 17.13 ▶ Firms are able to "slice and dice" their databases to create tailored communications with target customers. Here, rather than sending a 300- or 400-page master catalog to women, Cabela's produces a much shorter catalog for its current and potential female customers.

several targeted versions of their messaging, with seasonal, geographic, psychographic, or demographic distinctions for different target market segments. The gender- or age-specific versions run about 100 pages, versus more than 1,000 pages for some of Cabela's master catalogs. A customer or house-hold receives the targeted version of the catalog based on its profile in Cabela's database and the time of year. These streamlined catalogs are a way to make timely offerings to targeted households in a cost-effective manner, which is even more convenient for the consumer. In a nutshell, that's what database marketing is all about.

17-4d Marketing Database Applications

Diverse types of customer-communication programs are driven by marketing databases. One of the greatest benefits of a database is that it allows an organization to quantify how much business the organization is doing with its current best customers. An effective way to isolate the best customers is with a recency, frequency, and monetary (RFM) analysis. An **RFM analysis** asks how recently and how often a specific customer is buying from a company and how much money they are spending per order and over time. With this transaction data, it is simple to calculate the value of every customer to the organization and identify customers that have given the organization the most business in the past. Past behavior can be an excellent predictor of future behavior, so yesterday's best customers are likely to be any organization's primary source of future business.

Reinforcing and recognizing your best customers is an essential application of the marketing database. This application may be nothing more than a simple follow-up letter that thanks customers for their business or reminds them of the positive features of the brand to reassure them that they made the right choice. Since birthdate is a common piece of information in a marketing database, it is not uncommon for companies to contact customers via Email or direct mail on or near their birthday. The quick service restaurant chain Chopt has used a happy birthday Email campaign as a way to maintain a dialogue with its best customers. Of course, everyone likes a little birthday present, too, so along with the birthday greeting, Chopt includes a discount code good at any of their nationwide locations. Chopt executives maintain that this birthday promotion, targeted to current best customers identified from their marketing database, is one of its best investments of advertising/IBP dollars.

To recognize and reinforce the behaviors of preferred customers, marketers in many fields are offering loyalty programs (also known as frequency programs) that provide concrete rewards to frequent customers, as discussed in an earlier chapter as a separate IBP sales promotion technique. Loyalty programs have three basic elements: (1) a database, which is the collective memory for the program, (2) a benefit package, which is designed to attract and retain customers, (2) and a communication strategy, which emphasizes a regular dialogue with the organization's best customers.

The casino industry is renowned for its application of loyalty-marketing principles.[18] Caesars Entertainment's "Total Rewards" program started out as a way for 27 million members of Harrah's (now owned by Caesars) to accumulate points that could be cashed in for free meals and other casino amenities. Caesars now knows a great deal about its customers and uses that information for direct marketing and frequency rewards.[19] Whether you are a golfer, like down pillows, or prefer a room close to the elevator, your preferences are all in the marketer's database and get analyzed for Email marketing purposes. That is why companies need to know their best customers.

Another common application for the marketing database is **cross-selling**. Since most organizations today offer a variety of products or services, one of the best ways to build business is to identify customers who already purchase some of a firm's products and create marketing programs to sell additional products to these customers. If a customer has a checking account with a bank, the bank may cross-sell a savings account, for example. A marketing database can provide multiple opportunities for cross-selling.

A final application for the marketing database is a natural extension of cross-selling—pursuing new customers. Once an organization gets to know who its current customers are and what they like about various products and services, it is in a much stronger position to seek new customers. Knowledge about current customers is especially valuable when an organization is considering purchasing external mailing lists to append to its marketing database. If a firm knows the characteristics of current customers—knows what they like about products, knows where they live, and has information about their lifestyles and general interests—the selection of external lists will be much more efficient. The basic premise here is simply to try to find prospects who share many of the same characteristics and interests with current customers. And what's the best vehicle for coming to know the current, best customers? Marketing database development.

LO 5

17-5 The Privacy Concern

Many consumers are uneasy about the way their personal information is being gathered and exchanged by businesses and the government without their knowledge, participation, or consent. Of course, the Internet only amplifies these concerns, because the Internet makes it easier for all kinds of people and organizations to get access to personal information. In addition, some marketers are applying database development by merging offline data like credit rating, savings levels, and home value with individuals' online search activities. If you are online, some database or company is likely capturing your every click, especially if you accept cookies or give permissions. In addition to information gained for databases and mailing purposes, what about the ability of firms to track your mobile device via geotargeting? This can help brands offer discounts or promotions to shops nearby, to tell you where your friends are, or to help you save money or make you aware of a new promotion.

In response to public opinion, state and federal lawmakers have proposed and sometimes passed legislation to limit businesses' access to personal information. For instance, consumers' desire for privacy was clearly the motivation behind the launch of the Federal Trade Commission's Do Not Call Registry (recall the discussions on related topics in Chapter 4). It proved to be a popular idea with consumers because getting telemarketing calls can be annoying and invasive but has many opponents in business.[21] The Direct Marketing Association estimated that the list would cost telemarketers approximately $50 billion in lost sales. However, some marketers have found ways to circumvent the "do not call" list with tactics like the lead card.[22] The lead card asks unsuspecting consumers to send in a postcard to receive free information about a product or service, which may inadvertently give the company permission to reach out.

Companies can address customers' concerns about privacy if they remember two fundamental premises of database marketing. First, *a primary goal for developing a marketing database is to get to know customers in such a way that an organization can offer them products and services that better meet their needs.* The whole point of a marketing database is to keep junk mail and spam to a minimum by targeting only relevant programs to appropriate current and potential customers. If customers are offered something they value, they will welcome being in the database.

Second, developing a marketing database is about creating meaningful, long-term relationships with customers. *If you want people's trust and loyalty, it is important not to collect personal information and then sell it to a third party without consent.* When collecting information from customers, an organization must help them understand why it wants the information and how it will be used. If the organization is planning on selling this information to a third party, it must get customers' permission. If the organization pledges that the information will remain confidential, it must honor that commitment. Integrity is fundamental to all meaningful relationships, including those involving direct marketers and their customers. Recall that it was his integrity as much as anything else that enabled L.L. Bean to launch his career as a direct marketer. It will work for other advertisers, too. Also be aware of the role that the Federal Trade Commission plays in ensuring that businesses live up to their promises to protect and secure private consumer data (see Exhibit 17.14).

See Exhibit 17.15 for an example of direct marketing and information about privacy by Disney +/ESPN +/Hulu; via their website, they ask for the consumer's Email and collects information in a three-step process. They leave the default option to receive further updates and exclusive offers from the company checked, which from a consumer's perspective would be preferable to have it unchecked. From the company's perspective, they leave it checked so be sure to take note of this detail as both a consumer and a marketer. They do however have a clear communication and warning about their data personalization, privacy policy, and subscriber agreement. There is also a California Privacy Notice, which is a part of the California Consumer Privacy Act for residents of that U.S. state to provide mandated disclosures about residents' online and offline information. Thus, privacy laws vary by state as well as by country. The United States does not have one broad law spanning all kinds of data privacy; yet, it does have various specific laws about health care (HIPPA) and education/student data (FERPA). In a lot of states, companies can use and share sell data without notification (and those third parties can sell them again without notification) and there isn't a national law that says if or when a business has to notify consumers about a data breach.[20]

Source: FEDERAL TRADE COMMISSION

Exhibit 17.14 ▶ The Federal Trade Commission enforces regulatory compliance with rules concerning security of private consumer data.

Source: DisneyPlus

Exhibit 17.15 ▶ Disney+/ESPN+/Hulu uses their website as a form of direct marketing, and they comply with some of the privacy laws by providing subscriber terms and their privacy policy as well as disclosures for certain state privacy laws. Note however, they leave the default option checked for consumers to receive more information and offers from their companies so customers should be cautious to make sure they indeed want that communications before continuing. *Should there be rules on the default option of such boxes being unchecked vs. checked? Why or why not?*

Europe however does have one sweeping law addressing privacy. In fact, the European Union (EU) put out a massive **General Data Protection Regulation (GDPR)** in 2018. This is Europe's data privacy and security law that has hundreds of pages of new requirements and laws for businesses and organizations around the globe and even gives people in the jurisdictions the right to ask organizations to delete their personal information data, although the organizations do not always have to do so. Failure to comply with GDPR when needed and other laws can be very costly. (More information is available at GDPR.eu for those who are interested in the vast details and updates to this important European privacy law.)

It is important for companies to know and comply with the privacy laws that pertain to them and it is crucial for consumers to read these disclosures and know what they are signing up for and where their online and offline information is going. But unfortunately (yet understandably) many consumers do not due to the legal jargon and complexity of such. It is recommended that to address the very important and valid privacy concerns that consumers rightly have, to have consumers default to the opt-out setting, to be transparent, clear with more simple language, to let consumers know exactly what they are signing up for and what is being done with their personal information. Some companies, such as Apple are quite good about this, and even position their global brand around the paramount issue of consumer and data privacy. Other companies however have a lot of progress to make to gain and maintain consumer trust and address the crucial privacy concern that is one of the most crucial issues in the field of marketing today. The scrutiny that social media companies such as Facebook have gotten on this topic exemplify how important and at times troublesome it is when companies do not seem to take consumer data and privacy seriously.

LO 6

17-6 Media Applications in Direct Marketing

Because mailing lists and marketing databases are the focal point for originating most direct marketing programs, information and persuasive appeals need to be communicated to customers in implementing these programs. As we saw in the definition of direct marketing, multiple media can be deployed in program implementation, and some form of immediate, measurable response is typically a broad goal for the marketer. The immediate response desired may be an actual order for services or merchandise, a request for more information, social media engagement, or the acceptance of a free trial offer. Because advertising conducted in direct marketing campaigns is typified by this emphasis on immediate response, it is commonly referred to as *direct response advertising*.

As you probably suspect, **direct mail** and **telemarketing** are the direct marketer's traditional media. However, many forms of media, such as social media, magazines, radio, and television, can be used to deliver direct response advertising; more recently, companies and organizations use Email and text messages as a more economical means of interacting with customers. In addition, a transformation of the traditional television commercial—the infomercial—remains popular in direct marketing. Let us begin our examination of these media options by considering the advantages and disadvantages of direct mail and telemarketing.

17-6a Direct Mail

Direct mail has some notable faults as an advertising medium, not the least of which is cost. It can cost 15 to 20 times more to reach a person with a direct mail piece than it would to reach that person with a television commercial or newspaper advertisement because of the cost-per-contact advantages of mass media discussed in Chapter 13. In addition, in a society where people are constantly on the move, mailing lists are commonly plagued by bad addresses. Each bad address represents advertising dollars wasted. And direct mail delivery dates, especially for non–first-class mailings, can be unpredictable. When precise timing of an advertising message is critical to its success, direct mail can be the wrong choice.

But there will be times when direct mail is the right choice. The advantages of direct mail stem from the selectivity of the medium. When an advertiser begins with a database of prospects, direct mail can be the perfect vehicle for reaching those prospects with little waste. Also, direct mail is a flexible medium that allows message adaptations on literally a household-by-household basis—personal salutations and the like. Making direct mail personal (e.g., with the consumer's name on it) is more effective because it does not come across as a mass message. For instance, consider a direct mail piece received in the mail. Note in Exhibit 17.16 how this personalized direct mail piece from Southwest Airlines/Visa cut through the clutter, thanking the customer for 15 years of loyalty. It worked because it was personal and because they included a small gift of complementary cocktails for future Southwest flights. This is an example of how direct mail ties in with customer relationship management.

Now contrast this to a piece of direct mail you may have recently received and thrown away. It was perhaps not personal and came across more as an "advertisement" that was delivered in the mail. Even though it may mention a monthly promotion, making it more personal with your name—or, even better, customizing the promotions to services and products you bought in the past—the customer database is a way to improve direct mail effectiveness.

Direct mail also lends itself to testing and experimentation. With direct mail, it is common to test two or more different appeal letters using a modest budget and a small sample of households. The goal is to establish which version yields the largest response. When a winner is decided, that form of the message is backed by big-budget dollars in launching the organization's primary campaign.

In addition, the array of formats an organization can send to customers is substantial with direct mail. It can mail large, expensive brochures or include technology. Direct mail can be novel and unique to stand out and differentiate itself from **junk mail**—mail that is unwanted, and is useless to the consumer.

It is also worth considering the overall effectiveness of direct mail pieces. Many of us refer to direct mail as junk mail, and we have the impression that it cannot be effective. That is not necessarily true if it is done with a benefit to consumers, is personalized, and is done in a novel way that cuts clutter. There is about a 9 percent response rate to direct mail campaigns; however, engagement with direct mail was over 90 percent, and direct mail is actually *increasing* in effectiveness.[23] Advertisers invest an average of $167 per person for direct mail and nearly $38.5 billion annually in direct-mail programs; this is the largest percentage of *local* advertising investments in the United States.[24]

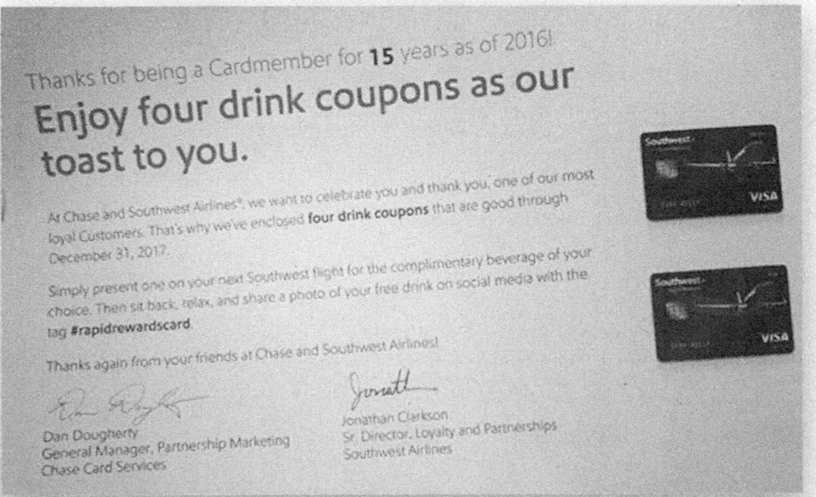

Exhibit 17.16 ▶ Southwest Air/Visa uses direct mail wisely by recognizing a five-year relationship and including a small token of appreciation (here, cocktails for an upcoming flight) that further develops the customer relationship.

17-6b Email

In digital form, **spam** is the new manifestation of junk mail. Perhaps the most controversial tool deployed by direct marketers has been unsolicited or bulk (also known as spam) Email. In a worst-case scenario, careless use of the Email tool can earn one's company the label of "spammer," which because of the community-oriented character of the Internet can then be a continuing source of negative buzz. Even the CAN-SPAM legislation passed in 2003 hasn't entirely stopped the deluge of unsolicited email. CAN-SPAM requires that marketers use an accurate and verifiable return Email address, be transparent about the nature of the Email content, provide opt-out options, and act on such requests or face stiff penalties.[25]

Consumers are not averse to receiving targeted and useful Email advertisements and that as the Internet continues to evolve as an increasingly commercial medium, those companies that observe proper **netiquette** (i.e., online etiquette) will be rewarded through customer loyalty. The key premise of netiquette is to get the consumer's permission to send information about specific products or services by requesting they opt in, where **Opt-in Marketing** is a type of permission marketing where the company gets a formal opt-in or positive action from a consumer to consent to receive further communication. This opt-in premise has spawned several online service providers who claim to have constructed Email lists of consumers who have "opted in" for all kinds of products and services. They contend that the future of direct marketing will be in reaching those people who have already said "Yes." But as cited earlier, the unsolicited email generates an extremely ineffective response rate. As many as one in five Emails either gets directed to the recipient's "spam" inbox or is screened out by one of the Internet service providers involved in the transmission.[26] **Opt-out** is just as important; it means that consumers should have the right to remove their permission marketing and no longer receive follow up communication or unwanted offers or contact from the company.

Our advice is to stay away from the low-cost temptations of bulk Email. A way to annoy consumers and damage your brand name is to start sending out bulk Emails to people who do not want to hear from you. As one analyst said, "Most consumers view their personal Email addresses and mobile phones as personal property. Violating that space ticks people off, no question."[27] Instead, through database development, ask your customers for permission to contact them via Email. *Honor their requests and follow the law on offering unsubscribe or "opt-out" options. Do not abuse the privilege by selling their Email addresses to other companies, and when you do contact them, have something important to say.* Seth Godin, whose 1999 book *Permission Marketing* launched the opt-in mindset, puts it this way: "The best way to make your [customer] list worthless is to sell it. The future is, this list is mine and it's a secret."[28] This isn't revolutionary—you can imagine L.L. Bean feeling the same way about his customer list a century ago.

B2B advertisers will not send Emails unless customers have volunteered their Email address or "opted in" to ongoing contact. The company uses outbound telemarketing to speak with small and mid-sized business customers, asking for an Email address and explaining the benefits of receiving periodic messages. It also works with its distributors to send Emails to customers who have given permission to receive messages.[29] See an example in Exhibit 17.17. Companies like Constant Contact and MailChimp can assist advertisers in

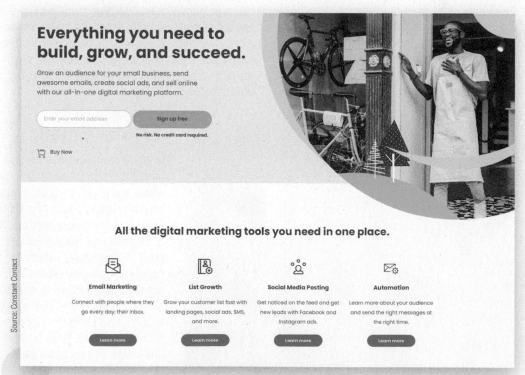

Source: Constant Contact

Exhibit 17.17 ▶ Companies such as Constant Contact, shown here, specialize in direct/e-mail marketing and help businesses by sending and managing Email communications and related forms of marketing communications in a digital manner. Companies can hire services like this, or do it in-house to save money if they have the expertise and time/ability to manage such communications.

managing Email lists, preparing and transmitting messages at specific intervals, and tracking results. And when using Email for direct marketing, don't overwhelm recipients with frequent messages or irrelevant content. Think about when and why consumers would be most receptive, time your messages and content accordingly, use subject lines to attract attention, and give recipients options for controlling the flow (such as convenient "subscribe" and "unsubscribe" links).

17-6c Telemarketing

Telemarketing is probably the direct marketer's most invasive tool. As with direct mail, contacts can be selectively targeted, the impact of programs is easy to track, and experimentation with different scripts and delivery formats is simple and practical. There are implicit privacy concerns, and fairness is a big issue with being reached by marketers especially those who rely on location-based services.[30] On the other hand, telemarketing is expensive on a cost-per-contact basis. Further, telemarketing does not share direct mail's flexibility in terms of delivery options. When you reach people in their home or workplace, you have a limited amount of time to convey information and request some form of response.

You already know the biggest concern with telemarketing. It is a powerful yet highly intrusive medium associated with privacy concerns and must be used with discretion. High-pressure telephone calls at inconvenient times can alienate customers. Telemarketing will give its best results over the long run if it is used to maintain constructive dialogues with existing customers and qualified prospects. Consumers have the option of signing up for the Do Not Call Registry, which blocks marketers from using this technique with those households. Companies that illegally call numbers on the Do Not Call list or that place an illegal robocall can be fined up to $43,792 per call.[31]

17-6d Direct Response Advertising in Other Media

Direct marketers have experimented with many methods in trying to convey their appeals for a customer response. In magazines, a popular device for executing a direct marketer's agenda is the bind-in insert card. Thumb through a copy of any magazine and you will see how effective these light-cardboard inserts are at stopping the reader and calling attention to themselves. Insert cards not only promote their product but also provide tempting discount and free sample offers.

When AT&T introduced the first 800 number in 1967, it simply could not have predicted how important this service would become to direct marketing. Newspaper ads from *The Wall Street Journal* provide toll-free numbers for requesting

everything from inexpensive online trading services to leasing a boat. Infomercials rely on toll-free numbers to sell.

As these diverse examples indicate, toll-free numbers make it possible to use nearly any medium for direct response purposes. The floral delivery firm 1-800-Flowers still uses its original toll-free phone number for its brand and for orders by phone, even when reaching out to customers via its social media accounts, its website, and its mobile apps (see Exhibit 17.18).

17-6e Infomercials

As defined in Chapter 2, an *infomercial* is a long direct-response television advertisement, ranging in length from 2 to 60 minutes. Although producing an infomercial is more like producing a television program than a 30-second commercial, infomercials are all about selling. There appear to be several keys to the successful use of this unique vehicle.[32] Infomercials typically appear during low-cost time periods (check out programming on Saturday and Sunday mornings).

A critical factor is testimonials from satisfied users. Celebrity testimonials can help catch a viewer as they are channel surfing past the program, but celebrities aren't

Source: 1-800-Flowers.com, Inc.

Exhibit 17.18 ▶ 1-800-Flowers has used the toll-free phone number for ordering as its brand for decades, continuing into the era of digital, social, and mobile media.

necessary; and, of course, they add to the production costs. Whether testimonials are from celebrities or from regular folks, they add to the appeal of infomercials.

Another key point to remember about infomercials is that viewers are not likely to stay tuned for the full 30 minutes. An infomercial is a 30-minute direct response sales pitch. The implication here is that the call to action should come not at the end of the infomercial only; most of the audience could be long gone by minute 28 into the show. A rule of thumb in a 30-minute infomercial is to divide the program into 10-minute increments and try to close a sale three times. Each closing should feature the toll-free number or the website where the viewer can order the product or request more information. And an organization should not offer information to the customer unless it can deliver speedy follow-up; same-day response should be the goal in pursuing leads generated by an infomercial.

Many different types of products and services have been marketed using infomercials. Brand marketers such as Beach Body, Nuwave, South Beach Diet, ShamWow, Disney, Hoover, even Mercedes-Benz have all used infomercials to help inform consumers about their offerings. Success in infomercials has even encouraged some advertisers to place products in brick-and-mortar retail distribution. For example, TeleBrands Inc. put products like Star Shower Motion and Pocket Hose into chain stores like Bed Bath & Beyond to take advantage of "As Seen on TV" awareness.[33]

─────────── LO 7 ───────────

17-7 Closing the Sale with Direct Marketing and/or Personal Selling

As noted throughout this book, the wide variety of options available for reaching customers poses a tremendous challenge with respect to coordination and integration. Organizations are looking to achieve synergy with a consistent and compelling message delivered through multiple advertising and IBP media. The evolution of direct marketing increases the challenge of raising integrated communication to new heights.

One classic approach to achieving integrated communication is the establishment of a marketing communications manager, or "marcom" manager for short. A **marcom manager** (some firms now fold these duties into the chief marketing officer role) plans an organization's overall communications program and oversees the various functional specialists inside and outside the organization. The goal is to ensure that everyone works together to deliver the desired message to the customer, which ultimately yields a product sale. Of course, the pivotal role for direct marketing programs in this process is to establish dialogue with customers and then close the sale.

17-7a Personal Selling

This brings us to the field of personal selling, yet another vital functional specialization in the business world. **Personal selling** is the use of one-to-one communication and persuasion for the purpose of selling; traditionally done via face-to-face communications, now personal selling has emerged to include personal chats, video sessions, calls, and other ways to communicate in a more personal manner with a consumer as it relates to a sale or service. Personal selling can be B2B (selling to a business representative) or B2C (selling to a consumer for personal or household use). Products that are higher priced, complicated to use, require demonstration, must be tailored to user needs, involve a trade-in, or are judged at the point of purchase are heavily dependent on personal selling. Household consumers and business buyers are frequently confronted with purchase decisions that are facilitated by interaction with a salesperson. In many decision contexts, only a qualified and well-trained salesperson can address the questions and concerns of a potential buyer. Fail to get the dialogue right at this critical stage of the purchase process, and other advertising efforts will end up being wasted.

For example, consider what makes a trip to an Apple store (Exhibit 17.19) a compelling experience. Employees are hired not for their technological expertise but for attitude and personality, so that every customer can expect to be greeted and assisted by a friendly employee well trained in customer service and with deep product knowledge. Apple employees know to listen carefully to customers' needs before demonstrating suitable products and services that will address these needs. By providing personalized service, Apple aims not for a one-time transaction but to develop a long-term customer relationship.[34]

There are many different types of sales jobs. The least complex type of personal selling is order taking. **Order taking** involves accepting orders for merchandise or scheduling services. Order takers deal with existing customers who are lucrative to a business due to the low cost of generating additional revenues from them. Order takers can also deal with new customers, which means that the order takers need to be trained well enough to answer the basic questions a new customer might have about a product or service. Order takers are responsible for communicating with buyers in such a way that a quality relationship is maintained. This type of selling rarely involves communicating large amounts of information; however, a careless approach to this function can be a real turn-off for the loyal consumer and can end up damaging the relationship.

Source: Apple Inc.

The Apple Store, Parc 66 Jinan

Exhibit 17.19 ▶ At the Apple stores, point of purchase is where the salesperson plays a critical role in determining the consumer's ultimate choice. Also, the salesperson can provide valuable information about product differences that can result in a sale and showcase services, such as their ability to help fix your personal technology devices.

Creative selling Is the type of selling in which customers rely heavily on the salesperson for technical information, advice, and service. Creative selling requires considerable effort and expertise. Situations in which creative selling takes place range from retail stores (like the Apple Store) to the selling of services to businesses and the sale of large industrial installations and component parts. Retail settings such as stores selling higher-priced items and specialty goods must have trained sales staffs and emphasize customer service and product knowledge. The services of an insurance agent, stockbroker, media representative, or real estate agent represent another type of creative selling. These salespeople provide services customized to the unique needs and circumstances of each buyer.

The most complex and demanding of the creative selling positions are in business-to-business markets. Many times, these salespeople have advanced degrees in technical areas like chemical engineering, computer science, or any of the medical professions. Technical salespeople who deal in large-dollar purchases and complex corporate decisions for specialized component parts, medical equipment, or raw materials have tremendous demands placed on them. They are often called on to analyze the customer's product and production needs and carry this information back to the firm so that product design and supply schedules can be tailored for each customer.

Another noteworthy form of creative selling that has emerged in recent years is system selling. **System selling** involves selling a set of interrelated components that fulfill all or most of a customer's needs in a particular area. System selling has emerged because of the desire on the

part of customers for "system solutions." Large industrial and government buyers have come to seek out one or a small number of suppliers that can provide a full range of products and services needed in an area. Rather than dealing with multiple suppliers, these buyers then "system buy" from a single source. This trend in both buying and selling emphasizes the customer-relationship-management aspects of selling.

Creative selling tasks call for high levels of preparation, expertise, and contact with the customer and are critical to the process of relationship building. Companies work hard to train their salespeople to address the needs of specific target markets and to provide good service that satisfies customers. General Motors, for example, has its dealers send salespeople to Disney Institute workshops to learn from Walt Disney's experts about how to deliver top-quality customer service.[35] BMW is taking a page from Apple's book by placing a highly trained BMW Genius in dealerships to demonstrate and explain the many features of its luxury vehicles (see Exhibit 17.20). A board member says BMW "is changing the entire retail experience, and the geniuses are the front line to make it more informative and friendly for our customers."[36]

Finally, when a sales force is deployed for the purpose of supportive communication, it is not charged with closing the sale. Rather, the objective is to provide information to customers, offer services, and generally to foster goodwill. The **missionary salesperson** calls on accounts with the express purpose of monitoring the satisfaction of buyers and updating buyers' needs but may also provide product information after a purchase. Many firms also use

Bayerische Motoren Werke AG

Exhibit 17.20 ▶ Customers can discuss BMW vehicles with a BMW Genius at the local dealership, via app, or via toll-free hotline.

direct marketing tools like telephone and Email reminders to complement the efforts of the missionary salesperson in maintaining a dialogue with key customers. Another direct marketing tool salespersons can rely on is event marketing, where customers evaluation of the event environment and perception of the branded event can lead to positive outcomes for brands.[37]

17-7b Customer Relationship Management

Salespeople can play a critical role as well in cultivating long-term relationships with customers—which often is referred to as a **customer relationship management (CRM)**

program. As an example, Merck spends 12 months training its sales representatives not only in knowledge of pharmaceutical products but also in trust-building techniques. Reps then are required to take regular refresher courses.

Salespeople no longer approach customers with the intention of making a sale. Rather, they are problem solvers who work in partnership with customers. The salesperson is in the best position to analyze customer needs and propose the right solution on a case-by-case basis. By accepting this role, the sales force helps determine ways in which a firm can provide total customer satisfaction through its entire market offering. The great thing about satisfied consumers is they come back and buy again and again, which ultimately is the mechanism that sustains any business.

Summary

1. Define direct marketing and identify its purposes.

Direct marketing is an interactive system of marketing that uses one or more advertising media or communication channels to affect a measurable response and/or transaction at any location. Many types of organizations invest in direct marketing for three primary purposes: direct marketing offers powerful, interactive tools for closing sales with customers, for identifying prospects for future contacts, and for offering information and incentives that can help produce a measurable response and foster loyalty. Direct marketing's popularity can be attributed to several factors. Direct marketers make consumption safer and convenient: credit cards, toll-free numbers, and digital/social/mobile access to stores take the hassle out of shopping. In addition, big data and database marketing have enhanced direct marketing's impact. The emphasis on producing and tracking measurable outcomes is well received by marketers in an era when everyone is trying to do more with less and management is focused on accountability for advertising and IBP investments.

2. Overview how direct marketing evolved and the purposes of direct marketing today.

Direct marketing evolved from catalogs. Catalogs began as a way for marketers to showcase their products, and often mailed to consumers for them to do direct orders. Direct marketing has also evolved from mailing lists, which are internal and external contact lists that companies use to market to consumers. Characteristics of direct marketing today are that it is broad in scope and largely digital. It has grown to include online channels, such as e-mail marketing. Direct marketing today should be *integrated* with an organization's other advertising and IBP efforts. A purpose of direct marketing is to help close sales. A second purpose of direct marketing is to identify prospects for future contacts and provide information to select customers. Another purpose of direct marketing is customer engagement.

3. Identify the advantages of direct marketing.

An advantage is that direct marketing and e-commerce align with changes in lifestyles and tech developments where consumers need a safe way to buy something quickly and conveniently, such as via a vending machine or e-commerce. Also, direct marketing offers advantages via mass media advertising, where advertisers can budget for a broad scope of direct marketing activities (for instance, interacting with consumers at sponsored events, social media, mail or Email sent directly to a consumer, a phone call, online shopping, online chats with consumers, or in a personal selling conversation). Another advantage is that direct marketing is measurable and easily integrated with other forms of integrated brand promotion such as advertising or sponsorship.

4. Define database marketing and identify its purposes.

Database marketing is a type of direct marketing that relies on customer databases to facilitate more personalized communication or messages to market a product or service. A marketing database is a natural extension of a mailing/Email internal list but includes information about individual customers and their specific preferences and purchasing patterns. A marketing database is an extension of an internal mailing list with additional information about individual preferences and behavioral patterns, allowing organizations to identify and focus efforts on their best customers. This database can help in recognizing and reinforcing preferred customers for building loyalty, as well as for cross-selling opportunities and for gaining information about how to attract new customers. However, many consumers are uneasy about privacy issues related to marketing databases.

5. Identify the privacy concern that is associated with database marketing and direct marketing.

Customers understandably want privacy about their personal information, and unless they have consciously given opt-in permissions to be marketed to, customers expect and deserve privacy. Companies need to address the privacy concern and meet the laws as well as maintain ethics about consumer information privacy. Companies can address concerns about privacy via two premises of database marketing. One, a goal for developing a marketing database is to get to know customers so an organization can offer products and services that better meet their specific needs with relevant offerings.
Two, a marketing database is about meaningful customer relationships and it is crucial to maintain trust and not to collect personal information and sell it without consent.

6. Overview the media applications associated with direct marketing.

Direct mail and telemarketing are commonly used in executing direct marketing programs, as well as low-cost alternatives such as social media, Email, and text messages. Because the advertising done as part of direct marketing programs typically requests an immediate response from the customer, it is known as direct response advertising. Television, newspapers, magazines, and radio are also used for direct response by offering a chat feature on their website, toll-free number, or social media engagement to facilitate customer contact.

7. Identify the role of direct marketing and personal selling in closing sales.

Personal selling is the use of one-to-one communication and persuasion for the purpose of selling; traditionally via face-to-face communications, now personal selling has emerged to include personal chats, video sessions, calls, and other ways to communicate in a more personal manner with a consumer as it relates to a sale or service. Personal selling can be B2B (selling to a business representative) or B2C (selling to a consumer for personal or household use). Organizations seek synergy through a consistent and compelling message delivered through multiple advertising and IBP media, often supported and reinforced by well-trained sales personnel. The sales force plays a critical role in the process because they are responsible for closing the sale while also ensuring customer satisfaction. Organizations can plan for personal selling in the form of order taking, creative selling, system selling, and the missionary salesperson. Salespeople can play a critical role in customer relationship management for building long-term bonds with customers.

Key Terms

cost per inquiry (CPI)
cost per order (CPO)
creative selling
cross-selling
customer databases
customer relationship management (CRM)
direct mail
direct marketing
external lists

General Data Protection Regulation (GDPR)
hybrid commerce
internal lists
junk mail
mailing list/email list
marcom manager
marketing database
missionary salesperson
netiquette

opt-in marketing
opt-out
omnichannel
order taking
personal selling
RFM analysis
spam
system selling
telemarketing

Endnotes

1. Bob Stone, *Successful Direct Marketing Methods* (Lincolnwood, IL: NTC Business Books, 1994), 5.
2. The discussion to follow builds on that of Stone, *Successful Direct Marketing Methods*.
3. Davey Alba, "YouTube TV Goes Live in Google's Biggest Swipe at Comcast Yet," *Wired*, April 5, 2017, https://www.wired.com/2017/04/youtube-tv-review.
4. Harsh Taneja, "The Myth of Targeting Small, But Loyal Niche Audiences," *Journal of Advertising Research* 60 (3), Oct. 2019, 239–250.
5. Chun-Wei Chang and Jonathan Z. Zhang, "The Effects of Channel Experiences and Direct Marketing on Customer Retention in Multichannel Settings," *Journal of Interactive Marketing* 36 (November 2016), 77–90.
6. The historical data here were drawn from Edward Nash, "The Roots of Direct Marketing," *Direct Marketing Magazine,* February 1995, 38–40; Cara Beardi, "Lillian Vernon Sets Sights on Second Half-Century," *Advertising Age,* March 19, 2001, 22.
7. Allison Cosmedy, *A History of Direct Marketing* (New York: Direct Marketing Association, 1992), 6.
8. Burçak Ertimur and Gokcen Coskuner-Balli, "Brands Expressing Compassion and Care through Advertising," *Journal of Advertising* 50, no. 3, 4 June 2021, 230–239.
9. Ibid.
10. Daniel Klein, "Disintegrated Marketing," *Harvard Business Review,* March 2003, 18, 19; Michael Fielding, "Spread the Word," *Marketing News,* February 15, 2005, 19, 20; Michael Fielding, "Direct Mail Still Has Its Place," *Marketing News,* November 1, 2006, 31, 33.
11. Edward Nash, "The Roots of Direct Marketing," *Direct Marketing Magazine,* February 1995, 38–40.
12. Betsy Brock, Samantha C. Carlson, Molly Moilanen, and Barbara A. Schillo, "Reaching Consumers: How the Tobacco Industry Uses Email Marketing," *Preventive Medicine Reports* 4 (December 2016), 103–106; Michael Sebastian, "Camel Cigarettes Return to Magazine Advertising After Five Years," *Advertising Age,* May 31, 2013, http://adage.com/article/media/camel-cigarettes-return-print-ads/241818.
13. See, for example, Dan O'Shea, "Why Apple Pay's Move Online Means More Drama in the Payments Space," *Retail Dive,* June 30, 2016, http://www.retaildive.com/news/why-apple-pays-move-online-means-more-drama-in-the-payments-space/421482.
14. Nikki Gilliland, "Seven Retailers That Use Live Chat to Improve Customer Service," *E-consultancy,* March 17, 2017, https://econsultancy.com/blog/68898-seven-retailers-that-use-live-chat-to-improve-customer-service.

15. Erik Modig and Micael Dahlen, "Quantifying the Advertising-Creativity Assessments of Consumers versus Advertising Professionals," *Journal of Advertising Research* 60, no. 3, 29 Mar. 2019, 324–336.

16. Micael Dahlen et al., "Advertising 'on the Go': Are Consumers in Motion More Influenced by Ads?," *Journal of Advertising Research* 60, no. 4, 25 June 2019, 417–425.

17. Ailsa Kolsaker, Dirk Görtz, and David Gilbert, "Making Sense of Metaphor: The Impact of Target-Group-Specific Headlines in Direct Mail," *Journal of Marketing Communications* 22, no. 1 (2016), 56–82.

18. Michael Bush, "Why Harrah's Loyalty Effort Is Industry's Gold Standard," *Advertising Age,* October 5, 2009, 8.

19. Bernard Marr, "Big Data at Caesars Entertainment — A One Billion Dollar Asset?" *Forbes,* May 18, 2015, https://www.forbes.com/sites/bernardmarr/2015/05/18/when-big-data-becomes-your-most-valuable-asset/#1e1e20701eef.

20. Thorin Klosowski, "The State of Consumer Data Privacy Laws in the US (And Why It Matters), *The New York Times,* September 6, 2021, https://www.nytimes.com/wirecutter/blog/state-of-privacy-laws-in-us/.

21. Ira Teinowitz and Ken Wheaton, "Do Not Market," *Advertising Age,* March 12, 2007, pp. 1, 44.

22. Jennifer Levitz and Kelly Greene, "Marketers Use Trickery to Evade No-Call Lists," *The Wall Street Journal,* October 26, 2007, A1, A14.

23. Data & Marketing Association, "What is the Response Rate from Direct Mail Campaigns," May 21 2021, https://dma.org.uk/article/what-is-the-response-rate-from-direct-mail-campaigns.

24. Maddie Shepherd, "Direct Mail Statistics You Should Know," *Fundera,* December 16, 2020, https://www.fundera.com/resources/direct-mail-statistics.

25. Scot Ganow, "Privacy Law Basics: 'SPAM, SPAM, SPAM, SPAM,' CAN-SPAM Act of 2003," *Lexology,* November 7, 2016, http://www.lexology.com/library/detail.aspx?g=61183d6d-1c6f-496c-b6a4-dc54031a944e.

26. Len Shneyder, "Holiday Email Best Practices: Avoiding the Spam Filter," *Advertising Age,* October 26, 2016, http://adage.com/article/digitalnext/holiday-email-practices-avoiding-spam-filter/306437.

27. Maureen Morrison, "Consumers Balance on Verge of 'Offer Anarchy,'" *Advertising Age,* February 13, 2012, 24.

28. Jodi Mardesich, "Too Much of a Good Thing," *Industry Standard,* March 19, 2001, 85.

29. Ruth P. Stevens, "Managing Email Addresses in B2B," *Quality Digest,* April 3, 2017, https://www.qualitydigest.com/inside/management-article/managing-email-addresses-b2b-040317.html#.

30. Anjala S. Krishen, Robyn L. Raschke, Angeline G. Close, and Pushkin Kachroo. "A power-responsibility equilibrium framework for fairness: Understanding consumers' implicit privacy concerns for location-based services." *Journal of Business Research* 73 (2017): 20–29.

31. Data drawn from https://www.consumer.ftc.gov/articles/national-do-not-call-registry-faqs#:~:text=Companies%20that%20illegally%20call%20numbers%20on%20the%20National%20Do%20Not,up%20to%20%2443%2C792%20per%20call.

32. Thomas Mucha, "Stronger Sales in Just 28 Minutes," *Business 2.0,* June 2005, 56–60; Elizabeth Holmes, "Golf-Club Designer Hopes to Repeat TV Success," *The Wall Street Journal,* January 30, 2007, B4.

33. Jack Bulavsky, "As Seen on TV Items Popular in Retail Outlets," *Las Vegas Review-Journal,* October 8, 2016, https://www.reviewjournal.com/life/home-and-garden/as-seen-on-tv-items-popular-in-retail-outlets.

34. Carmine Gallo, "Ten Reasons Why the Apple Store Was Never a 'Store,'" *Forbes,* August 25, 2016, https://www.forbes.com/sites/carminegallo/2016/08/25/ten-reasons-why-the-apple-store-was-never-a-store/#5f237b8376b5.

35. Sam Frizell, "What Car Salesmen Are Going to Disney to Learn," *Time,* February 18, 2015, http://time.com/3677476/chevrolet-disney-world.

36. Tom Beaman, "BMW Shoppers Want Dealership VIP Treatment—and Get It," *Ward's Auto,* December 2, 2016, http://wardsauto.com/dealer/bmw-shoppers-want-dealership-vip-treatment-and-get-it; Doron Levin, "BMW's Genius Move Is from Apple's Playbook," *Fortune,* November 26, 2014, http://fortune.com/2014/11/26/bmw-genius.

37. Buduo Wang, Angeline Close Scheinbaum, Siyan Li, and Anjala S. Krishen, "How Affective Evaluation and Tourist Type Impact Event Marketing Outcomes: Field Studies in Experiential Marketing," *Journal of Advertising* (2021): 1–16. (forthcoming; https://doi.org/10.1080/00913367.2021.1909516).

Public Relations, Influencer Marketing, and Corporate Advertising

In this chapter, we will give you a balanced perspective of marketing for the fundamentals of buzz building, influencer marketing, and sponsored events as PR strategies while building capacity in PR to strengthen a brand's overall IBP tool kit (see Exhibit 18.1). PR and buzz building have never been more relevant as social media influencers are becoming more mainstream in business. Public relations and corporate advertising are exciting topics to conclude our examination of advertising and integrated brand promotion (IBP).

Public relations (PR) brings to life the idea of "buzz building" for a brand that is increasingly popular in marketing today. PR can be used to activate social media/influencer marketing, engage mainstream media, highlight celebrity spokespersons, bond with a community, or stage a branded experience via event marketing/event sponsorships. PR also helps clean up messes when things go wrong. Public relations has progressed beyond its traditional role of managing goodwill or "relations" with a firm's many publics, which can take the form of damage control in the face of negative publicity or a corporate crisis. PR entails elements of corporate communications, influencing, and image management in times of noncrisis as well as crisis.

A related topic in this chapter—influencer marketing—will emphasize public relations activities as a dedicated brand-building agenda in a digital and social media environment. Influencer marketing, as a special case of public relations, focuses on individuals or groups who can help foster and cultivate positive conversations about a brand. In this era of social media, blogs, and digital and mobile communications among consumers, a firm can monitor, understand, proactively influence, and better respond to what influencers and consumers are saying about its brands.

In this last chapter, we will also cover corporate advertising, which typically uses media to communicate a broad-based message that is distinct from product-specific brand building. Corporate advertising contributes to the development of an overall image and reputation. As consumers are becoming increasingly informed and sophisticated, they are also demanding

Exhibit 18.1 ▶ Public relations, influencer marketing, and corporate advertising are key elements in an IBP strategy.

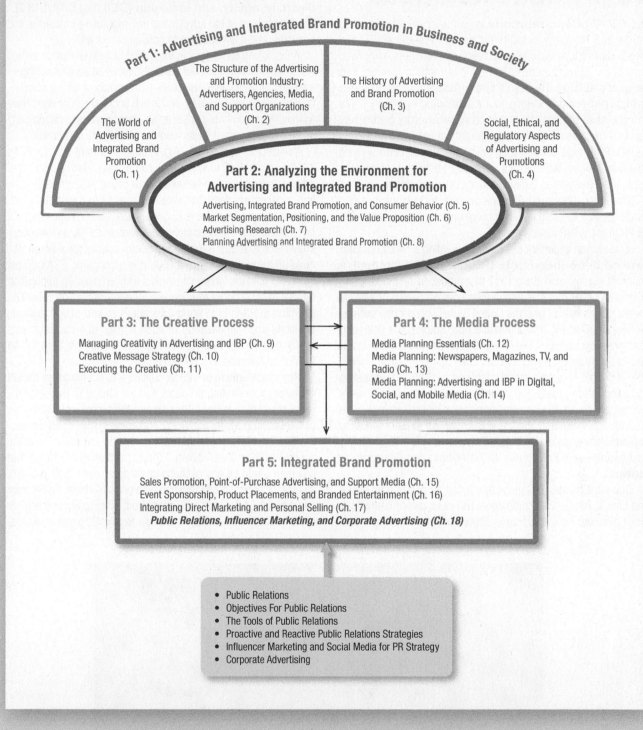

a higher standard of conduct and ethics from the companies they patronize. When a company has established trust and integrity, it is much easier to build productive, long term relationships with consumers.

18-1 Public Relations

The role of **public relations** is to foster goodwill among a firm and its many constituent groups ("publics"). These constituent groups include customers, stockholders, suppliers, employees, government entities, citizen action groups, and the public at large. The firm's public relations function seeks to highlight positive events like outstanding quarterly sales and profits (targeting stockholders) or noteworthy community service programs (targeting government entities and the general public). PR is also used strategically for damage control when adversity strikes, whether it's a product suspected of causing harm, a spokesperson behaving badly or an employee accused of mistreating customers. In addition, new techniques in public relations have fostered a bolder, more aggressive, proactive role for PR in many IBP campaigns.

PR is also an important tool for implementing prosocial **public service announcements (PSAs)**. The **Ad Council,** a nonprofit organization since 1942 that produces, distributes, and promotes public service announcements on behalf of various sponsors, has helped give the United States social icons such as Woodsy the Owl, McGruff the Crime Dog, Smokey the Bear, and effective prosocial copy like "A mind is a terrible thing to waste" (anti-drug messaging) and "Friends don't let friends drive drunk." The Ad Council has more recently focused on COVID-19 pandemic and vaccination messaging. Advertising agencies eagerly work without pay on Ad Council campaigns because staff members are motivated to make a difference. *It is important to use marketing and advertising expertise for good purposes, and to help society and people—not just to add to the bottom line financially in business.*

Traditionally, the Ad Council has relied on donated ad space and time to run its PSA campaigns. However, recent campaigns like *Love Has No Labels* have attracted corporate sponsors (official partners) including Bank of America, Google, Johnson & Johnson, State Farm, and Wal-Mart. This allows the Ad Council to broaden its reach in communicating the importance of **diversity, equity, and inclusion (DEI)** (see Exhibit 18.2).[1] DEI is important in the advertising and marketing industries and agencies, and it is important to consumers as well.

Antismoking campaigns in the United States have since shifted to antivaping campaigns, but PSAs also focus on social smoking—the habit of occasionally smoking with friends or with a cocktail. Consumer behavior research notes that social smokers don't have an identity of a smoker per se, so an agency can help debunk any myths about vaping or social smoking as both are dangerous.

Besides anti-vaping/smoking, another important topic for PSAs is against reckless driving, impaired driving, and/or distracted driving as these selfish behaviors can cause indescribable pain and unnecessary death to those they may hit in their path. A last important topic for PSAs is in domestic violence awareness. As an example of a domestic violence awareness PSA, an influencer known for makeup shocks her social media fans when her makeup tutorial turns into a PSA. It is a shocking PSA against domestic violence, where she makes a covert makeup application tutorial to teach how to cover up face injuries or bruises. The intention of PSAs is to bring awareness to and action towards solutions and minimization of such horrific and sad problems we have in society. See Exhibit 18.3 for an example from the Ad Council on the pandemic related PR communications.

Any macro–micro or ethical conflict a direct marketer should consider for marketing products that are shown to be unhealthy (e.g., cigarettes) is important for the third-ranked sustainable development goals for our world, according to the United Nations. See Exhibit 18.4, where the third goal is for our planet to enjoy "good health and well-being." Direct marketing initiatives that can help reinforce any of these goals along with their product, service, or nonprofit benefits can help generate trust. Again, trust and a general sense of "goodness" from a company or marketer is the backbone for healthy customer relationship management.

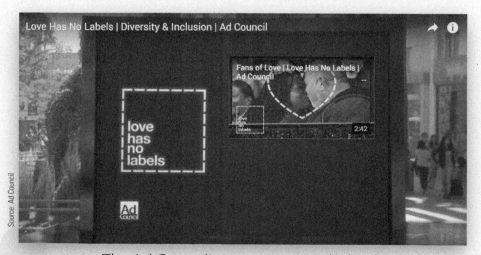

Source: Ad Council

Exhibit 18.2 ▶ The Ad Council's *Love Has No Labels* ad promoting inclusion and diversity attracted tens of millions of YouTube views and was the first PSA ever to win an Emmy Award.

18-1a Public Relations, Social Media, and Brand Conversations

There are many forces at work that support a growing role for PR activities as part of advertising and IBP campaigns as PR joins with social media to help spark brand conversations. Even governments are investing in public relations to boost their "brands" in the global marketplace: China alone spends an estimated $10 billion annually to portray the country in the best possible light.[2] In the United States, more than $11 billion is invested each year in public relations.[3] We have evolved to a commercial world where TV shows feature stories about marketing, stand-up comics perform skits about shopping routines and brand strategies, and documentaries like Beer Wars, with Budweiser playing the villain, make for **antibrand entertainment**. Antibrand entertainment is content that pokes fun at itself, doesn't mention the product, or uses some other seemingly unmarketable device to attract attention to a brand. It may seem counterintuitive; but when done creatively, it can work, especially with millennials and GenZers.[4] Modern times reflect a brand-obsessed world with an element of an antibrand culture.

Source: Ad Council

Exhibit 18.3 ▶ The Ad Council is known for their prosocial messaging and public service announcements, ranging from Smokey the Bear for fire prevention and also COVID-19 prevention and response messaging.

Source: UNITED NATIONS

Exhibit 18.4 ▶ The United Nations has some important goals for our future; notice how many of them relate to health and consumption. As such, it is our responsibility as leaders and influencers and marketers to think through these goals and how their business relates to them.

Consumers are increasingly in control in this brand-obsessed world, using tools like **vlogs** (video blogs), Snapchat, Instagram, Pinterest, Facebook, YouTube, Twitter, TikTok and whatever new digital, social, or mobile media tool will be invented next. It's a world in which marketers must monitor the brand buzz and become part of brand conversations in an effort to rescue, reinforce, or revive their brands. Mass media advertising has never been about dialogue, whereas digital/social/mobile media offer great opportunities to include firms in the conversation, tell a story, shape consumer attitudes, and develop brands or corporate images. No wonder global firms like Marriott maintain social media centers on several continents to plan new content, monitor consumers' brand conversations, and respond in real time. "We've bent over backwards for it to be fun and engaging without the promotions plastered all over the place," says the senior director of global creative and content marketing.[5]

Even though marketers have always believed that the most powerful influence in any consumer's decision is the recommendations of friends and family, they have never known exactly what to do about it. Some clues about what to do were provided by Malcolm Gladwell in his bestseller *The Tipping Point*, wherein he makes the case that people he labels as "mavens" and "connectors" are critically important in fostering social epidemics. The key idea here is that these mavens and connectors can be located, and if you give them useful information or interesting stories about your brand, they may share it with their personal networks, whether in person or with clicks, taps, or swipes.

People talk about brands. The challenge is to give them interesting things to talk about, things that bring a firm's brand into the conversation in a positive way and generates positive word of mouth. **Word of mouth (WOM)** or, when digital, **electronic word of mouth (eWOM)** is the process of encouraging consumers to talk to each other about a firm's brand or marketing activities. Word of mouth—whether in person or via digital, social, or mobile media—can be a powerful influence on a consumer's intentions to buy a brand, especially if the information comes from someone with close social ties to that consumer.[6] For example, consider the ritual played out during every Super Bowl, when the victorious team pours a cooler of Gatorade over the coach's head. This began as a spontaneous celebration, and now Gatorade makes the most of it in social media (see Exhibit 18.5). In addition to congratulatory dunking posts on Twitter and other media, Gatorade invites consumers to "dunk" themselves using a sponsored Snapchat lens. These IBP activities deliver hundreds of millions of impressions and get consumers talking about Gatorade.[7]

Hilton Worldwide offers another example of getting your brand into the day-to-day conversations of key consumers. The company enlisted PR specialists to help gain attention for the opening of its Conrad New York Hotel. Hilton was a sponsor of the prestigious Tribeca Film festival, using the event as a way to showcase its new property. Hilton brought in the "Pop-Up Conrad Concierge" (a mobile service facility) to various film festival locations around New York City. Using the PR agency's digital social intelligence system, Hilton monitored brand conversations across several social media sites and filtered them by location and event attendance. Then, the Pop-Up Conrad Concierge team appeared with Conrad-branded umbrellas and snacks for consumers waiting in line—a creative example of engaging the consumer with the brand.[8]

In today's digital and interactive marketplace, a brand builder needs to take a proactive stance in influencing at least some of those conversations. It takes a strong team effort to ensure integration, and research indicates that PR expertise needs to be well represented as part of any contemporary marketing, advertising, and IBP team.[9] This

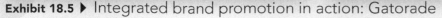

Exhibit 18.5 ▶ Integrated brand promotion in action: Gatorade
Gatorade engages sports fans during the Super Bowl by highlighting the ritual dunking of the winning coach and offering a Snapchat lens for consumers to virtually dunk themselves. *What objectives might Gatorade set for IBP activities related to this highly publicized dunking ritual?*

Source: PepsiCo

is a way to achieve synergy, and it requires internal and external specialists working closely together to create and deliver communications. "If you have the idea at the center, all platforms are necessary to amplify that idea above and beyond paid media," says the CEO of McCann Worldgroup. **Chief marketing officers (CMOs)** are often in charge of marketing strategy, and they would be wise to lean in on PR. "More and more CMOs are recognizing the power and importance of PR, and I'm seeing more practitioners in the field being involved in integrated campaigns and that's dramatically accelerated PR's pace."[10]

18-1b Public Relations and Damage Control

An important part of public relations is **crisis communications**, or how to communicate and respond with the public and stakeholders in times of problems, crises, or tragedies. Some of the top crises in 2021 included misinformation related to COVID-19, Facebook's whistleblower, and Peloton's treadmill crisis. Specifically, Facebook (renamed Meta) remains with negative public attention for some of their business practices that have shown misinformation, lack consumer privacy, and issues for user's mental health; the book "The Dark Side of Social Media: A Consumer Psychology Perspective" outlines some of these concerns.[11] Corporate renaming and bad PR are often related, as a smart PR strategy is to consider a new brand identity to help build trust after a major crisis, or series of **brand transgressions** (when a brand does something wrong and trust is lost). Frances Haugen, the whistleblower who used to work at Facebook, and impending Congressional hearings bring some details of nefarious business practices and outcomes of social media to the spotlight. Relatedly, with the pandemic, there was and is a lot of false or misleading information around the virus and related consumer behavior on social media and otherwise respected journalistic outlets alike; this is a problem because source credibility is on the line.[12] This speaks to the importance of responsible journalism, reporting, and social media as well as how PR professionals can help in branding. It is also important for CEOs to exhibit leadership in and out of times of crisis.

Another brand related crisis happened with Peloton, the bike and exercise equipment company. There were injuries and even a fatality associated with their Tread+ treadmill, and the CEO made a mistake in their response to the **Consumer Product Safety Commission's (CPSC)** request that the Tread+ be recalled. The Federal Trade Commission as well as the CPSC aim to have pro consumer stances, and the decisions and recalls they put out have valuable implications for research as well.[13] It is important for all CEOs to be responsive and to not minimize consumer harm associated with crises related to their brands. As both Facebook and Peloton's experiences demonstrate, sometimes a little damage control is needed (and sometimes a lot is needed—such as a rebrand). Advertising "won't die" but it is constantly evolving, and it is co-existing more and more with PR.[14] Public relations has always been a crucial contributor in that PR serves a damage-control role that no other promotional tool can. Peer-based advertising literacy information and sponsored vlogs are suggested ways to help the industry and brands overcome some problems.[15] Other ways to help offer helpful information to consumers includes **pre-roll advertising** (ads before a social media video or other content) or **text disclosures** (sending product- or service-related disclosures or important information to consumers via their phones). Such public relations problems can arise either from an organization's own activities or from external forces completely outside its control.[16] A good PR practitioner can have strategies, such as with sponsored blogging and brand related-digital engagement to help maintain or restore brand image.[17]

As many brands (including human brands) have learned, consumers are more informed and more connected than ever, so the bad news travels faster and lingers longer.[18] This bad news can take many forms, and there are more examples to consider how they used PR for damage control. For Chipotle Mexican Grill, the bad news was a series of high-profile food-safety problems that resulted in dozens of people becoming ill. Sales stalled for months as the restaurant chain sought to recover by focusing advertising and IBP messages on fresh ingredients, food safety practices, and flavor.[19] Johnson & Johnson walked into a PR firestorm by suing the Red Cross (that most revered of helping organizations) for logo infringement.[20] That's a hard case to win in the court of public opinion, and it was perhaps a self-inflicted wound for J&J. Companies need to learn how to handle the bad news. No company is immune to needing to work on their image. Even though many public relations episodes must be reactive, a firm can be prepared with public relations materials to conduct an orderly and positive relations-building campaign with its constituents.[21]

Amazon is an example of a company that invests in PR via promoting their corporate goodwill, which can be both altruistic and a good way to offset other PR issues the brand has had. Amazon's PR team does not report directly into marketing (they have marketing and PR separate, which is rare for large companies) and has over 500 public relations employees worldwide. See Exhibit 18.6 for Amazon Job's overview of their PR and communication, and how that unit of the company is "telling our story."

To fully appreciate the potential of public relations, we will next consider the objectives and tools of public relations and basic public relations strategies.

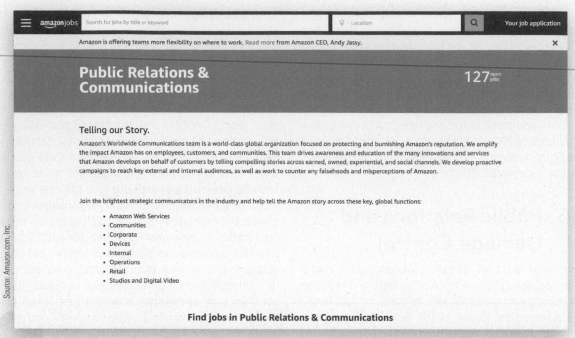

Source: Amazon.com, Inc.

Exhibit 18.6 ▶ Amazon has a unit in Public Relations and Communications, and these jobs are shown on the Amazon Jobs website as integral in how they tell the brand story.

18-2 Objectives For Public Relations

Even though reacting to a crisis is a necessity, it is always more desirable to be proactive. The key is to have a structured approach to public relations, with a clear understanding of the PR objectives. Within the broad guidelines of image building, damage control, and establishing relationships with constituents, it is possible to identify six primary objectives of public relations:

■ *Promoting goodwill.* This is an image-building function of public relations. Industry events or community activities that reflect favorably on a firm are highlighted. When Hilton provided movie festival attendees with umbrellas and snacks while waiting in line to attend film screenings, goodwill for the brand was no doubt enhanced.

■ *Promoting a product or service.* Press releases, events, or brand "news" that increase public awareness of a firm's brands can be pursued through public relations. Large pharmaceutical firms such as Pfizer issue press releases when they discover new drugs or achieve FDA approval. Likewise, Starbucks champions sustainable coffee production and encourages consumers to learn more, as in Exhibit 18.7. Starbucks has been working for years to develop and apply a comprehensive set of environmental, social, and economic guidelines for the ethical and sustainable growing of coffee. Its management believes that coffee produced in a responsible way helps foster a better future for farmers and a more stable climate for the planet.

■ *Preparing internal communications.* Disseminating information and correcting misinformation within a firm can reduce the impact of rumors and increase employee morale. For events such as reductions in the labor force or mergers of firms, internal communications can do much to dispel rumors circulating among employees and in the local community.

■ *Counteracting negative publicity.* This is the damage-control function of public relations, as discussed earlier. The attempt here is not to cover up negative events but rather to prevent the negative publicity from damaging the image of a firm and its brands.

■ *Lobbying.* The public relations function can assist a firm in dealing with government officials and pending legislation. Industry groups also maintain active and aggressive lobbying efforts at the state and federal levels, as well as lobbying the European Union and other international groups. Google, Microsoft, and other tech giants actively lobby the European Commission regarding important issues such as data protection and privacy practices.[22]

■ *Giving advice and counsel.* Assisting management in determining what (if any) position to take on public issues, preparing employees for public appearances, and helping management anticipate public reactions are all part of the advice and counsel function of public relations. This includes preparing top management for decisions that might have to be made to avert or defuse a crisis, when every moment counts.

COFFEE
Beans Blends Brewing

MENU
Drinks Food

COFFEEHOUSE
Music Wi-Fi Community

RESPONSIBILITY
Ethical Local Global

عربي   Customer Service   Find a Store   Search Keyword

Starbucks™ Shared Planet™

Tweet   +1   Like   2   Pin it

Starbucks™ Shared Planet™ is our commitment to do business in ways that are good for people and the planet.

It's our commitment to purchase only the highest quality, ethically sourced and responsibly grown coffee. To reduce our own environmental footprint and fight climate change. And to give back to the neighborhoods and communities we're a part of. Thanks to the customers who buy our coffee, together we are able to make – and make good on – these commitments on a truly global scale.

Acting Responsibly

We've always been committed to doing business responsibly and conducting ourselves in ways that earn the trust and respect of our customers and neighbours – from creating a great workplace to ensuring our customers have access to nutritional information on our products. Starbucks™ Shared Planet™ means focusing on the core areas where we have the biggest influence – ethical sourcing, environmental stewardship and community involvement.

Above all, Starbucks believes in engaging, collaborating and openly communicating with our stakeholders. Since 2001, one way we've tried to do this is by producing a Global Responsibility Report that details our efforts to do business responsibly.

Starbucks™ Shared Planet™ Progress

Ethically Sourced Coffee

Learn more about Ethically Sourced Coffee

Susan Van Etten

Exhibit 18.7 ▶ Starbucks actively promotes economic and social responsibility as a core brand value with the way the firm sources its coffee supplies.

LO 3

18-3 The Tools of Public Relations

There are several means by which a firm can pursue the objectives just cited. The goal is to gain as much control over the PR process as possible and integrate its public relations efforts with other brand communications.

18-3a Press Releases

One important tactical tool is the press release. Indeed, a narrow view of public relations envisions the PR department writing press releases and working with key contacts in traditional and digital media to get them interested in the release, with the hope that a story of some kind will follow. Having a file of information that makes for good news stories puts the firm in a position to take advantage of press coverage. The following are some typical categories of information that make for a good story:

- New product launches
- New scientific discoveries
- New personnel
- New corporate facilities

- Innovative corporate practices, such as energy-saving programs or employee benefit programs
- Annual shareholder meetings
- Charitable and community-service activities
- New sponsorship and partnership agreements

The only drawback to press releases is that a firm often doesn't know if or when the item will appear in the news. Also, journalists are free to edit or interpret a news release, which may alter its intended message. To help minimize unintended outcomes, it's critical to develop working relationships with editors or bloggers from publications the organization deems important to its press release program. Another key technique is to reach audiences directly via social media and corporate website posts. General Electric, for example, has a specialized website (www.gereports.com) and specialized Twitter account (www.twitter.com/GE_Reports) to communicate corporate and product news (see Exhibit 18.8). This helps the company get its message out exactly as it is designed.

As with most communication endeavors, know your audience. The retailer Target felt strongly enough about cultivating relationships with journalists that it relocated one of its PR specialists from Minneapolis to Phoenix to cultivate local-media relationships there and in other western U.S. markets.[23] Maui Beverages caught the attention of key journalists in a positive way when it planned a tropical

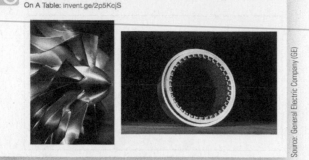

GE Reports ✅ @GE_Reports · Apr 12
GE Is Building A CO2-Powered Turbine That Generates 10 Megawatts And Fits
On A Table: invent.ge/2p5KcjS

Source: General Electric Company (GE)

Exhibit 18.8 ▶ General Electric posts information and images reflecting the content of press releases on its GE Reports Twitter account and website.

theme party for food and beverage writers during an industry conference. Not only did Maui Beverages increase its visibility with this key group, it quickly received substantial media coverage to boost its brand.[24]

Although public relations should not be defined by the press release, knowing how to write and release a press release is an important skill set. Press releases are especially vital to community building and event marketing. In the following example of a community and sport event press release, notice how the content showcases the value of the event to the sponsor, brand, athletes, and, most importantly, to the community. Here, Jackie Tyson of Peloton Sports, shows an example of how to write one after a sponsored event:

SALT LAKE CITY, UTAH—Two months after the completion of the Larry H. Miller Tour of Utah professional stage race, event organizers confirmed that new records were set for economic impact, national audiences, and media coverage. A quantitative research study reveals that out-of-state spectators contributed $14 million in direct economic impact for the state of Utah. Tour organizers also confirmed that national television viewership almost doubled from last year, media impressions grew by nearly 50 percent and the Tour earned $8.5 million in publicity value.

"The Tour of Utah has enjoyed tremendous growth this year. Judging by the excitement of the crowds, the cycling fans who tuned in online and on FOX Sports Network, and the positive feedback from the key stakeholders, the Tour of Utah has a solid foundation in place for the future. It is great to hear partners like the Utah Sports Commission confirm that the Tour of Utah has become one of the largest sporting events in the state. The gears have already started turning for 2013," said Steve Miller, President of the Tour of Utah.

The research included measurement of economic impact, sponsorship awareness and spectator profiles related to the cycling event, which took place August 1–12, 2012. Data was collected by crowd intercept surveys at all start

and finish host venue locations during race week— Ogden, Miller Motorsports Park in Tooele, Lehi, Salt Lake City, Snowbird Ski and Summer Resort and Park City.

Dr. Angeline Close of Clemson University led a research team and collected and processed completed surveys during race week. They found that Tour fans stayed 4.3 consecutive nights for the event, and that 14 percent of the total attendance traveled from outside the state of Utah to watch the race. Of the estimated fans who traveled from out of state, the majority confirmed they visited Utah specifically to watch the Tour of Utah. The average daily expenditure for out-of-state spectators was calculated to be $353 per person, based on five factors: lodging, food /beverage, transportation, retail/ groceries, and other sightseeing/entertainment. A total of $12–14 million in economic impact was directly linked to out-of-state fans.

The method divided spectators into three distinct groups—out-of-state fans, Utah residents who traveled more than 50 miles to attend a stage, and local residents who wanted to watch the event. Only visitor dollars from out-of-state fans were tabulated in the final report, so that the analysis aligned in a similar fashion with other Utah sporting event studies conducted by the Utah Sports Commission, one of the Tour of Utah's top partners.

"Utah has a solid reputation for hosting some of the best international sporting events in the world, showcasing Utah as the State of Sport for winter and summer. The Larry H. Miller Tour of Utah has grown significantly in just the past two years and has become a centerpiece for summer, now one of the largest outdoor sporting events for our state," said Jeff Robbins, president and CEO of the Utah Sports Commission.

The Utah Sports Commission is focused on sport development to grow Utah's economy and leverage the state's world-class sports assets to enhance Utah's position in the global sports marketplace. In 2011–2012, the Sports Commission partnered with 44 world-class sporting events across the state. An estimated $1.8 million in funding was provided to sports events, resulting in an estimated $146 million in economic impact to the state of Utah. Twenty-seven of these events hosted also had a major national and international television component to them generating an estimated $46 million in media value to the state.

The Tour of Utah also generates solid exposure for Utah across multiple media channels. Media coverage of the 2012 Larry H. Miller Tour of Utah grew 49 percent from the year before, with an estimated 37.2 million media impressions and $8.5 million in earned publicity value. It is also the second year for national television coverage on FOX Sports Network and live webcasting to a worldwide audience. FOX Sports Network aired 12 hours of live coverage over the six days of racing, *reaching an average of 61 million homes. Live coverage was a significant factor in raising the number of households to 631,000 people who watched the race daily, an increase of 75 percent from the year before. The Tour of Utah web site received 113,000 visits during race week, with 362,530 page views. In addition, 64 percent of site visits viewed the Tour Tracker® component, which provided start-to-finish audio and video coverage of the race on the web site and with various mobile applications. The Tour Tracker® experience was viewed in 123 countries and had more than 10,500 mobile downloads.*

The Tour of Utah gained attention in its eighth year in 2012 for increased race mileage, more elevation gain, and stronger international field of competition. The race route covered 543 miles of diverse and mountainous terrain with 38,500 feet of elevation gain. Mileage increased 33 percent and vertical feet of climbing increased 25% from 2011, solidifying the event as "America's Toughest Stage Race™." Seven of this year's 11 professional teams competed at the Tour de France, including the BMC Racing Team, which featured 2012 overall Tour of Utah winner Johann Tschopp of Switzerland.

The Utah Sports Commission supports the Tour of Utah as it looks to expand in 2013 to the southern part of the state. An exploratory committee has received positive feedback from more than seven communities interested in hosting the multi-day stage race in Southern Utah. The Larry H. Miller Tour of Utah continues to be free to all spectators, making professional cycling one of the most unique professional sports in the world today.

Note that the press release covers the basic who, what, when, where, and why. A good press release for an event shows the economic impact on sponsors to help leverage their investment and attract future sponsors for the event. A sport press release should also include key athletes, teams, and, if postevent, the winners. Like a USP, the press release should end with something that makes the event unique; in this case, it is that it was a fabulous spectator event that is free! Note that a press release is often in a media outlet in a story-like manner. Yet a press release is distinct from a feature story—a related PR tool.

18-3b Feature Stories

Although a firm cannot write a feature story for a newspaper or any other medium, it can invite journalists to do an exclusive story on the firm when there is a noteworthy event. A feature story is different from a press release in that it is typically more controllable, detailed, and substantial. A feature story, as opposed to a news release, offers a particular journalist the opportunity to do a fairly lengthy piece with exclusive rights to the information for a certain period. Companies must have facts and interviewees available when the journalist is ready to research and write. During major events like industry trade shows, companies often have PR and communications experts on site to "pitch" features and provide details to journalists on deadline. Harman, which makes music systems for cars, sends a team of communications specialists to the annual Consumer Electronics Show, where they connect with media representatives and build relationships to encourage feature coverage during and after the show.[25]

18-3c Company Newsletters/ E-Newsletters

In-house publications such as newsletters (either printed or digital or both) can disseminate positive information about a firm through its employees. As members of the community, employees are proud of their firm's achievements. Digital or e-newsletters can also be distributed to important constituents in the community, such as government officials, the chamber of commerce, or the tourism bureau. Suppliers often enjoy reading about an important customer, so newsletters can be mailed and emailed to this group as well and shared on the company's website for convenient access by interested audiences.

18-3d Interviews and Press Conferences

Interviews with key executives or staged press conferences can be highly effective public relations tools. Often they are warranted in a crisis management situation. But firms also call press conferences to announce important scientific breakthroughs or explain the details of a corporate expansion or a new product launch. The press conference has an air of credibility because it uses a news format to present salient information. For example, Apple often holds press conferences when introducing changes or new products. It also makes executives and spokespeople available for interviews and to answer reporters' questions. In addition, Apple uses digital channels and audience events for its shareholder and analyst announcements.

18-3e Sponsored Events and Event Marketing

Event marketing and sponsoring events can also serve as an essential PR or community-building component for a brand. Sponsorships run the gamut from supporting community events, such as local USA Cycling races, to mega-events such as the Olympics or World Cup. At the local level, prominent display of the corporate name and logo offers residents the chance to see that an organization is dedicated to supporting their community. Further, event marketing offers VIP sponsors and their clients a special experience, often via luxurious skyboxes, dining, and gift bags exclusively for sponsors and friends. While market resistance may occur due to advertising, it is rare to not like event sponsors, as they make the event of your choosing more financially beneficial to the consumer—and provide value added in forms of products, entertainment, or coupons to try the product or service. Also, events add to the local economy, again making them good for communities by providing jobs and additional business for local hotels, restaurants, retailers, and other local service providers.

18-3f Publicity

Publicity is essentially free media exposure highlighting a firm's activities or brands. The public relations function seeks to monitor and manage publicity but obviously can never actually control what the media chooses to say or report. This lack of control was demonstrated earlier in the chapter with the examples of brand transgressions from Facebook, Peloton, Johnson & Johnson, and Chipotle. Politics is another walk of life—one where the tone of one's publicity can be hard to manage. Organizations (or politicians) need to be prepared to take advantage of events that make for good publicity and to counter events that are potentially damaging to their reputations. And you can be sure that human brands such as politicians running for office or holding prominent positions have a team of PR experts.

The appeal of publicity—when the information is positive—is that it tends to carry heightened credibility. Publicity that appears in conventional news media and official news websites of established media outlets like *The Wall Street Journal* assumes an air of believability because of the credibility of the media context. Consumers also view noncommercial vehicles such as certain blogs as independent sources of information.[26] The choice of where to aim for publicity depends, of course, on the target audience and the objective.

Nonbusiness organizations, such as schools and charities, often use publicity in the form of news and public-interest stories as ways to gain widespread visibility at little or no cost. When TV weatherman Al Roker visited Loyola University as part of a series of campus visits, the university went all out to make the most of the nationwide publicity. Cheering students and costumed team mascots greeted Roker during his visit. The university also organized a large-scale crab walk that earned it a spot in the *Guinness Book of World Records*. Loyola's vice president for marketing noted the extensive nature of the publicity, adding, "We're hoping a lot of prospective students and parents will be watching."[27]

But publicity is not always completely out of the company's control. For instance, during the Academy Awards, a bracelet worn by actress Julia Roberts caused quite a stir. After Roberts won the award for best actress, she stood smiling and waving to the cameras, and suddenly the whole world wanted to know about the snowflake design Van Cleef & Arpels bracelet that adorned her right (waving) wrist. What a lucky break for the designers? Not really. The whole episode was carefully planned by Van Cleef's PR agency, Ted, Inc. The agency lobbied hard to convince Roberts that the bracelet and matching earrings were stunning with her dress, knowing that if she won the Oscar, she would be widely photographed waving that pretty bracelet.[28] See Exhibit 18.9 for an example

Chris Weeks/Vetta/Getty Images

Exhibit 18.9 ▶ Julia Roberts is a celebrity who brought a lot of buzz when she wore a Van Cleets diamond bracelet to a major awards show. Often times, celebrities wear designer clothing and accessories for free (or are paid to wear them) as a partnership with the brand in order to bring buzz.

of this celebrity-based tactic, and the star showing the award and bracelet. Before social media influencers, such award show celebrity tactics were among the most successful way to influence in fashion.

LO 4

18-4 Proactive and Reactive Public Relations Strategies

Given the breadth of possibilities for using public relations as part of a firm's overall advertising and IBP effort, it's good to revisit the possibilities in simple terms. Public relations strategies can be categorized as either proactive or reactive. **Proactive public relations strategy** is guided by marketing objectives, seeks to publicize a company and its brands, and should serve to build goodwill (and buzz) for the brand. **Reactive public relations strategy** focuses on problems to be solved rather than on opportunities and requires a company to take defensive measures.

18-4a Proactive Strategy

In developing a proactive PR strategy, a firm acknowledges opportunities to use public relations efforts to accomplish something positive, as the "Tools of Public Relations" discussion revealed. Companies often work with their public relations firms in preparing a proactive strategy. In fact, analysts believe that marketers will increasingly turn to PR specialists as they seek to converge brand equity with corporate reputation.[29] As an example, the biotechnology industry is often the subject of much controversy in the press regarding genetically altered food and seed products. A prime example is Monsanto, portrayed as the evil empire in the documentary film *Food, Inc.* The advertisement in Exhibit 18.10 from the biotechnology industry attempts to

Biotechnology is helping him protect the land and preserve his family's heritage.

"I'm raising a better soybean crop that helps me conserve the topsoil, keep my land productive and help this farm support future generations of my family."
—Rod Gangwish, farmer

Biotechnology is helping Rod Gangwish to grow a type of soybean that requires less tilling of the soil. That helps him preserve precious topsoil and produce a crop with less impact on the land. Preserving topsoil today means a thriving farm for generations to come.

Biotechnology allows farmers to choose the best combination of ways to help grow their crops. It helps cotton farmers use fewer chemicals to protect their crops against certain pests. And, it's helping provide ways for developing countries to better feed a growing population. And, in the future, it can help farmers grow better quality, more nutritious food.

Biotechnology is also enhancing lives in other ways, helping to create more effective treatments for diseases such as leukemia and diabetes.

Biotechnology is helping create solutions that are improving lives today, and solutions that could improve our world tomorrow. If you're interested in learning more, visit our Web site or call the number below for a free brochure about biotechnology and agriculture.

COUNCIL FOR BIOTECHNOLOGY INFORMATION

good ideas are growing

1-800-980-8660
www.whybiotech.com

Council for Biotechnology Information

Exhibit 18.10 ▶ The biotechnology industry is taking a proactive PR approach to the controversies surrounding the industry and its processes.

take a proactive approach to dealing with the controversies by presenting a positive image and information. In this ad, the industry portrays itself as not only a protector of the land but also a protector of that most revered of all professions—the American farmer.

In many firms, the positive aspects of employee achievements, corporate contributions to the community, and the organization's social and environmental programs go unnoticed by important constituents. To implement a proactive strategy, a firm needs to develop a comprehensive public relations program. The key components of such a program are as follows:

1. *A public relations audit.* **A public relations audit** identifies the characteristics of a firm or the aspects of the firm's activities that are positive and newsworthy. Information is gathered in much the same way as information related to advertising strategy is gathered. Corporate personnel and customers are questioned to provide information. This information may include descriptions of company products and services, market performance of brands, profitability, goals for products, market trends, new product introductions, important suppliers, important customers, employee programs and facilities, community programs, and charitable activities.

2. *A public relations plan.* Once the firm is armed with information from a public relations audit, the next step is a structured plan. A **public relations plan** identifies the objectives and activities related to the public relations communications issued by a firm and integrated with the rest of the advertising and IBP plan. The components of a public relations plan include the following:

   a. *Situation analysis.* This section of the public relations plan summarizes the information obtained from the public relations audit. Information contained here is often broken down by category, such as product performance or community activity.

   b. *Program objectives.* Objectives for a proactive PR program stem from the current situation. Objectives should be set for both short-term and long-term opportunities. Public relations objectives can be as diverse and complex as advertising objectives. The focal point is not sales or profits per se. Rather, factors such as the credibility of product performance (i.e., placing products in verified, independent tests) and the stature of the firm's research and development efforts (highlighted in a prestigious trade publication article) are legitimate types of PR objectives. For example, Mattel's "Dads Who Play Barbie" campaign included a PR component highlighting the important relationship between fathers and daughters, based on academic research. Mattel wanted to spark discussion of how playing with dolls helps girls develop their imagination and tell stories and the fathers' role in encouraging their daughters' development.[30]

c. *Program rationale.* In this section, it is critical to identify the role the public relations program will play relative to all the other communication efforts—particularly advertising and community involvement—being undertaken by a firm. This is the area where an IBP perspective is clearly articulated for the public relations effort. For Mattel, PR was a vital IBP element complementing a campaign that included TV commercials, magazine feature articles, cinema advertising, and other communications. Showing fathers playing with Barbie attracts attention because it's an unexpected image—which only adds to the publicity possibilities.

d. *Communications vehicles.* This section of the plan specifies precisely what means will be used to implement the public relations plan. The tools discussed earlier in the chapter—press releases, interviews, newsletters, vlogs, websites—constitute the communications vehicles through which objectives can be implemented. There will likely be discussion of how to use press releases, interviews, and company newsletters and digital/social/mobile media to achieve objectives. Mattel's Barbie campaign included traditional media and social media, with the hashtag #DadsWhoPlayBarbie identifying campaign posts. A Super Bowl commercial generated widespread interest and viral sharing. Press releases referenced the academic research concerning the importance of father–daughter relationships. Two magazine exclusives provided in-depth coverage, prominently showcasing the Barbie brand along with the salient points. Mattel also planned contests and other IBP activities to engage consumers, resulting in even more publicity.[31] (see Exhibit 18.11).

Exhibit 18.11 ▶ Mattel's "Dads Who Play Barbie" campaign included social media posts inviting user-generated content and asking consumers to vote for their favorites.

e. *Message content.* Analysts suggest that public relations messages should be researched and developed in much the same way that advertising messages are. Focus groups and in-depth interviews are being used to fine-tune PR communications. For example, a pharmaceutical firm learned that calling obesity a "disease" rather than a "condition" increased the overweight population's receptivity to the firm's press release messages regarding a new anti-obesity drug.[32] And, in the new digital era, firms are keenly aware that the message content will likely be passed along through social media. One expert in PR strategy said, "Back in the old days, our agency would write a fantastic piece of content, like a white paper (a firm's position or strategy related to a situation) and think that was the end. Today audiences take that content and post it, comment on it and share and give it additional life."[33]

f. *Evaluation.* No plan for advertising or IBP is complete without specifics on how results will be measured. Decision makers need to know how the investment in PR paid off. In the case of Mattel, the plan called for counting the number of feature article placements, the number of media impressions, the number of social media views and subscribers/followers, and other measures indicating that members of the media, consumers, and influencers were receiving and sharing the messages.

A proactive public relations strategy has the potential for making an important supportive contribution to a firm's IBP effort. Carefully placing positive information targeted to potentially influential constituents—such as members of the community or stockholders—supports the overall goal of enhancing the image, reputation, and perception of a firm and its brands. Mattel, for example, was demonstrating the relevancy of Barbie as a toy to bring fathers and daughters together for fun with developmental purpose. "Through each communication touch point, our goal is to remind parents of the purpose and power of Barbie; that through open-ended play, storytelling, and imagination, girls can imagine everything they can become," explained Mattel's senior global communications manager.[34]

18-4b Reactive Strategy

A reactive PR strategy may seem like a contradiction in terms, but as stated earlier, firms must quickly implement a reactive strategy when events outside of its control create negative publicity. A delayed or inappropriate response can compound the situation. That's what happened to United Airlines. Two days after videos of police forcibly removing a passenger from a United flight went viral, the CEO finally accepted responsibility and publicly apologized to the passenger. "It's never too late to do the right thing. I have committed to our customers and our employees that we are going to fix what's broken so this never happens again," he said. Although the CEO continued to apologize from then on, the crisis had by then grown into a major PR problem for the airline.[35]

Coca-Cola was able to rein in negative publicity by acting swiftly after an unfortunate incident occurred in Europe. Seven days after a bottling problem caused teens in Belgium and France to become sick after drinking Coke, the firm acted quickly and pulled all Coca-Cola products from the market, with an apology from the CEO.[36] Coca-Cola's quick actions could not prevent negative consequences in terms of product sales. That would call for new marketing programs tailored to meet the needs of consumers on a country-by-country basis. The reactive PR program relied heavily on IBP strategies, including free samples, dealer incentive programs, and beach parties featuring sound and light shows, DJs, and cocktail bars with free Cokes to win back the critical teen segment.[37] In the end, it was a complete and integrated effort that restored consumers' trust and rebuilt the business across Europe.

Pepsi also has done reactive PR as a result of an insensitive and tone-deaf ad featuring Kendall Jenner. In the ad, Kendall Jenner hands a police officer a Pepsi during a protest related to the #BlackLivesMatter movement. The ad was offensive to many; and as a result, Pepsi reacted by removing the ad, apologizing to Kendall Jenner, and apologizing to the public.[38] Exhibit 18.12 shows a screen shot of the pulled ad; in general, one solution could be to have more diversity of all types in the room when such creative and/or advertising decisions and strategies are created.

It is difficult to organize for and provide structure around reactive PR. Since the events that trigger a reactive effort are unpredictable, a firm must simply be prepared to act quickly and thoughtfully. Two activities help firms implement a reactive public relations strategy:

1. *The public relations audit.* The public relations audit that was prepared for the proactive strategy helps a firm also prepare its reactive strategy. The information provided by the audit gives a firm what it needs to issue public statements based on current and accurate data.

2. *The identification of vulnerabilities.* In addition to preparing current information, the other key step in a reactive strategy is to recognize areas in which the firm has weaknesses in its operations or products that can negatively affect its relationships with important constituents. From a public relations standpoint, these weaknesses are called *vulnerabilities.* If aspects of a firm's operations are vulnerable to criticism, such as environmental issues related to manufacturing processes, then the public relations function should be prepared to discuss the issues in a broad range of forums with many different constituents. Leaders at Pepsi and other firms were taken somewhat by surprise when shareholders challenged their practices with respect to genetically modified foods. Even though the concern was among a minority of shareholders, there were enough concerned constituents to warrant a proxy vote on the issue.[39] Executives at these firms now understand that pursuing any form of genetically modified foods will always be one of their vulnerabilities.

Source: PepsiCo

Exhibit 18.12 ▶ Pepsi resorted to reactive public relations after its ad featuring Kendall Jenner at a protest giving a Pepsi to a police officer was overall shunned as offensive and inappropriate.

LO 5

18-5 Influencer Marketing and Social Media for PR Strategy

Public relations is a prime example of how a firm (or an individual) can identify and then manage aspects of communication in an integrated and synergistic manner to diverse audiences. Without recognizing public relations activities as a component of the firm's overall IBP communication effort, misinformation or disinformation could compromise more mainstream communications, such as advertising. The coordination of public relations into an integrated program is a matter of recognizing and identifying the process as critical to the overall IBP effort and, as always, getting the right set of players on your IBP team. Modern marketing managers feel that social media is a "sweet spot" for public relations. As one manager said, "Social media is recognized as a place for relationships—and that, historically and intrinsically, is the province of public relations."[40] As such, we illuminate that social media is being used for various PR strategies.

If public relations is the discipline devoted to monitoring and managing how people view us, then it can also be thought of as a discipline devoted to monitoring and managing what consumers are saying to one another about us. Moreover, as noted earlier in this chapter, consumers have become increasingly predisposed to talk about brands, both online and offline. Since we know they are likely to talk about our brands anyway, it seems prudent to follow the advice of Bonnie Raitt from her album *Luck of the Draw.* As Bonnie says (and sings) in her 1990s blues-rock hit: "Let's give them something to talk about!"

That basic idea, "give them something to talk about," underlies the evolution of an important communication discipline that we will represent under the general label of influencer marketing. As defined by Northlich, a leader in influencer marketing programming, **influencer marketing** refers to a series of personalized marketing techniques directed at individuals or groups who have the credibility and capability to drive positive word of mouth in a broader and more salient segment of the population. The idea is to give the influencer something to talk about. In addition, it is useful to distinguish between professional and peer-to-peer influencer programs. Both can provide one of the most valued assets for any brand builder—an advocacy message from a trusted source.

18-5a Professional Influencer Programs

Many consumers turn to professionals for advice and guidance about goods and services. Your doctor, dentist, neonatal nurse, veterinarian, auto mechanic, and hair stylist all have the credibility to influence product choices in their specific areas of expertise. In fact, word-of-mouth communications that result in brand referrals by influencers have a strong impact on new customers—much more so than traditional marketing techniques.[41] One of the points of influencer marketing is that it feels more personal especially with a **micro-influencer**, or an influencer, usually in a specific knowledge area, who has between 10,000-50,000 followers on social media followings; this is compared to **macro-influencers** that have at least 500,000 followers.[42] Then, there are A-list celebrities such as Jennifer Aniston. She, known for her healthy lifestyle, glowing skin, and glossy hair, has recently assumed the role of Chief Creativity Officer for Vital Proteins, a move certainly driven by her influencer status. Thus, one may be an influencer and a celebrity alike—but not all influencers are celebrities.

Take a look at the creative influencer campaign set up by Select Comfort for its Sleep Number bed targeting occupational therapists (OTs). OTs commonly receive promotional materials and products they could suggest to patients. If you are Select Comfort, you'd like the OT to encourage patients to have a look at the Sleep Number bed. The first step is to get that OT to try and use the bed themself. Thus, Select Comfort offers special promotions to encourage OTs to purchase Sleep Number beds for their own bedrooms. Next, the OT needs tools to follow through on their potential advocacy. Like most professionals, OTs belong to associations and subscribe to journals. Name and address files from such sources allow a company to start building an OT marketing database. Once an OT expresses any kind of interest in the Sleep Number bed, they are sent an advocacy kit. Some key elements of that kit are displayed in Exhibit 18.13. These materials include a demonstration video and "prescription pads" so the OT can write clients a recommendation for a Sleep Number bed. Marketers at Select Comfort cannot control what the OT says to her patient about the Sleep Number bed. But they can put materials in her hands that will make it easy for her to become an advocate, if they believe such advocacy is justified. That's the nature of influencer marketing.

> "
> *Influencer marketing refers to a series of personalized marketing techniques directed at individuals or groups who have the credibility and capability to drive positive word of mouth in a broader and more salient segment of the population.*
> "

Exhibit 18.13 ▶ Firms need to try to encourage key influencers to recommend the firm's brand. Here, Select Comfort, maker of the Sleep Number bed, provides an information kit to health-care professionals that includes a video and brochures that carefully document the product benefits. There is even a "prescription" pad that allows the therapist to put his or her recommendation in writing.

Think of influencer marketing as systematic seeding of conversations involving a consumer, the influencer, and the brand. Often, they are bloggers or vloggers who are market mavens and/or opinion leaders with large social media followings. Often, influencer programs are directed at professionals because professionals are experts in their field and, as such, are often implicitly influencers to other interested parties.

Professionals in any field of endeavor take their role very seriously, so influencer programs directed to them must be handled with great care. Several points of emphasis should be kept in mind when developing programs for professionals. First, their time is valuable, so any program that wastes their time will be a waste of money and not be implemented. However, tactics designed to encourage professionals to try the product themselves can be very valuable. Also important to note is that messaging with professionals needs to provide intellectual currency and help the professionals learn important benefits of the brand and potentially increase their perceived expertise with their clients. For example, health-care professionals' concerns will be better addressed through clinical studies than celebrity endorsements. Additionally, programs directed at professionals require a long-term commitment. For them to be advocates, trust first must develop, and

any marketer must show patience and persistence to earn that trust and consumer relationship.

18-5b Peer-to-Peer Influencer Programs

Peer-to-peer programs typically have a very different tone than programs for professionals. In peer-to-peer programs, the idea is to give influencers something fun or provocative to talk about. Think of it as an emphasis on "social currency" for peer-to-peer programs versus "intellectual currency" for professionals. A great guiding principle for peer-to-peer programs is "Do something remarkable" to get people talking about your brand.[43] Creating buzz about a brand or having a brand go "viral" in terms of consumer conversations are key peer-to-peer programs. Additionally, there is the process of cultivating "connectors" for a firm's brand. Let's examine these peer-to-peer phenomena in detail. See Exhibit 18.14 for an example of a peer-to-peer program from Bumble, who uses campus ambassadors to promote their online dating company so college students can inform or persuade their peers.

Source: Bumble INC.

Exhibit 18.14 ▶ Bumble, an Internet dating website and brand, works with campus ambadassors for peer-to-peer marketing initiatives.

Buzz and Viral Marketing

Two hot concepts in this area of peer-to-peer influence are buzz and viral marketing. Essentially, both of these refer to efforts to stimulate word of mouth involving key targets that might otherwise be impervious to more traditional advertising and promotional tools. **Buzz marketing** can be defined as creating an event or experience that yields conversations (buzz) about the brand. Buzz marketing occurs when a firm's marketing activities gain widespread media coverage and become a source of conversation in households, between friends, at work, or at school.

Buzz marketing can be face to face with traditional word of mouth and/or via digital channels such as social media for eWOM. As mentioned earlier, this is when consumers discuss brands, companies, or organizations in a positive or negative way on digital platforms (e.g., social media pages, website comments, etc.). A key difference between word of mouth and electronic word of mouth is that eWOM is often more visible (i.e., seen, heard, or read by more people) than in a traditional face-to-face conversation.

As noted in Chapter 14, *viral marketing* involves marketing to consumers via digital, social, or mobile media (e.g., via vlogs, TikTok, Facebook, Twitter, YouTube links, texts, etc.) or through personal contact stimulated by a firm marketing a brand. Viral marketing occurs when word of mouth in digital media reaches high levels of activity. If a consumer is excited about a new purchase, it is not unusual to see a comment show up

on Facebook or for a blast of tweets or texts go out to friends and relatives. Researchers have also noted that approximately 30 percent of online word of mouth is stimulated by traditional media—particularly consumers talking about TV ads they have seen recently.[44] One campaign that went viral is by Dove; it featured a forensic artist who drew sketches of real women based on their self-descriptions of their faces to him. He then compared those sketches to sketches he later made based on how others described them. It went viral, and as the screen shot of the YouTube page where a version is, there were already 67.5 million (now almost 70 million) or so views as you see in Exhibit 18.15. That is true viral status. The idea behind both buzz and viral marketing strategies is to target a handful of carefully chosen trendsetters or connectors as your influencers and let them spread the word.

Buzz and viral marketing both depend on high levels of contact among consumers; it is often the case that these programs are fielded in cities like New York, London, and Los Angeles, because that's where you find the trendsetters. Consider this scene at the cafés on Third Street Promenade in and around Los Angeles. A gang of sleek, impossibly attractive bikers pulls up and, guess what, they seem *genuinely* interested in getting to know you over an iced latte—their treat, no less! Sooner or later the conversation turns to their Vespa scooters glinting in the sun, and they eagerly pull out a pad and jot down an address and phone number—for the nearest Vespa dealer. The scooter-riding, latte-drinking models are

Exhibit 18.15 ▶ This Dove campaign about real beauty sketches went viral on YouTube, as you can see from the millions of views.

on the Vespa payroll, and they're paid to create buzz about the scooters by engaging hip café dwellers in conversation and camaraderie.[45] Vespa has gotten some good buzz for being featured in the Netflix show Emily in Paris, as the main character Emily drives a luxury brand version of the scooter while thriving as an American in Paris who works at a marketing firm. See Exhibit 18.16 for a photo of the Vespa 646 Christian Dior that has gotten buzz via celebrity and pop culture.

Exhibit 18.16 ▶ Vespa has a collaboration with top fashion designer Christian Dior for one of their scooters, and when it was featured on the Netflix show "Emily in Paris," it received a lot of buzz and interest in the product.

Publicity Stunts

Publicity stunts can be thought of as buzz builders, and there is nothing new about them. In 1863, P. T. Barnum orchestrated a wedding between two of his circus stars to boost attendance at the circus. The remarkable thing about this circus wedding was that the bride and the groom were both just three feet tall. P. T. Barnum knew how to create a buzz; he just didn't call it that. See Exhibit 18.17 for an example of creating buzz through an attention-getting stunt. As an example, the New Zealand cider brand Monteith pulled a stunt by putting twigs and sticks in their cases of hard cider. They did this purposely to try to get complaints by consumers so they can then show how the brand relates with nature. Overall, this stunt was to gain buzz and get consumers associating nature or natural with the cider brand.

There is a lot separating old-school publicity stunts from today's influencer marketing. For one, there is the level of experience and sophistication of technology, organizations, ad agencies and marketing professionals when it comes to assisting clients with influencer programming. For instance, Keller Fay has developed a tracking system that can estimate the number of word-of-mouth conversations taking place on a daily basis. And the Word of Mouth Marketing Association (WOMMA), cofounded by Andy Sernovitz, is a great resource for learning about the art and science of buzz building. Sernovitz's five keys for success with influencer marketing are featured in Exhibit 18.18.

Cultivating Connectors

Advertisers are interested in identifying and cultivating connectors for peer-to-peer marketing, connectors like Donna. Donna is an outgoing mom and works at a customer-service call center, where she knows about 300 coworkers by name. She likes to talk about shopping and lots of different brands. She always seems to have lots of extra coupons for the brands she likes, so much so that her coworkers call her the coupon lady. Donna is a connector, one of 600,000 that are enrolled in the Vocalpoint influencer program (see Exhibit 18.19), which was originated by Procter & Gamble.[46]

That's right, your chatty next-door neighbor, who seems to know everyone and loves to talk about their favorite brands in person and on social media, could be one of these highly coveted connectors with large social networks. Once a connector database is developed, it again becomes a matter of giving your connectors something to talk about. It is not always a simple thing to get consumers talking about a product like dishwashing detergent. P&G execs noted, "We do tremendous research behind it to give them a reason to care."[47] Just as with professional programs, you can't force someone to be an advocate for your brand. You can identify people who have big social networks, but they're not going to compromise their relationships with others by sharing dull stories or phony information. You must give them something interesting to talk about.

CRUSHED APPLE CIDER

Made from 100% freshly crushed New Zealand apples.

Source: DB breweries

Exhibit 18.17 ▶ The New Zealand brand Montelith pulled a notable publicity stunt when they purposefully put twigs in the cases of cider.

Exhibit 18.18 ▶ To generate buzz, five Ts are the keys: Talkers, Topics, Tools, Talking, and Tracking.

Talkers. Much like our point about connectors, Andy Sernovitz asserts that you have to find the people who are predisposed to talk about brands in general and/or your brand in particular. Often you need to be on the Internet to find these people. Find them and get to know them.

Topics. Next, of course, you have to give them something to talk about. This can't be a marketing message or a mission statement. There needs to be a mystery or a cool story or some breaking news that you are sharing to get people talking. Steve Jobs at Apple knew how to do this. He definitely had a knack for stirring up interest and conversation with his suspenseful product announcements and his implied promise that our next great thing is just around the corner.

Tools. Make good use of the tools that promote a viral conversation. You can post a story on a Web page and some will find it there, but in the end it just sits there. You put the exact same story on a blog and it's linkable, portable, built to travel across the Internet. Suddenly lots of people are sharing the story.

Taking Part. Stop thinking in terms of one-way communication; start thinking in terms of dialogue. If you want favorable word of mouth, you need to be part of the conversation, not ignore it. Dell was slow to take part in a conversation about problems consumers had getting service. Basically, they ignored the conversation. When blogger Jeff Jarvis had big problems with his Dell and couldn't get the company's attention, he coined the phrase "Dell Hell," which became a lightning rod for conversation about Dell on the Internet. You've got to be tuned in if you ever want to join the conversation.

Tracking. Word of mouth on the Internet is very measurable. With blogs, people write things down in full view. This is an opportunity for any company to know what people are saying about their brands and why they are saying it. Lots of companies are paying close attention to what consumers are saying about their brands. Even Dell is now among them.

Source: Andy Sernovitz, *Word of Mouth Marketing: How Smart Companies Get People Talking* (Chicago, IL: Kaplan Publishing, 2006); Piet Levy, "Tease Please," *Marketing News,* April 30, 2009, 6.

Exhibit 18.19 ▶ Vocalpoint gets influencers buzzing about brands by offering free samples and invitations to special events.

Developing connector databases, finding the conversation starters, tracking the buzz online and off—that's the new era of influencer marketing. And it doesn't hurt to have a little of the P. T. Barnum flair as part of the process either. An area that once was very mysterious, that is, word-of-mouth marketing, is becoming increasingly demystified and in some ways made more scientific. Firms like BzzAgent and Influentser are a logical outgrowth of this movement, with millions of consumers in their databases.[48] BzzAgent has recruited "agents" that are ready to build buzz for your brand. According to the firm's website, when you are a BzzAgent, you will tell others about products you like, try new products, and then "Get people talking by sharing your honest opinion through face-to-face conversations and online via sites including Facebook, Twitter and blogs. Remember to always disclose that you're a BzzAgent and to keep the spam in the can. Bzz is no place for excessive, repetitive, or unauthentic posts."[49]

Transparency in Buzz

One issue raised by the effort to cultivate connectors and influencers is the need to comply with all applicable laws and regulations and ensure transparency. When a brand supplies an influencer with free samples (or payment) in exchange for social media buzz, the Federal Trade Commission requires that this be disclosed. The influence agencies recognize the importance of transparency and communicate the rules to those in their databases. For example, here's what BzzAgent says: "BzzAgent works with advertisers who pay us to distribute their products to members of our network, or BzzAgents, to try for free. FTC guidelines require us to make it clear to our agents to disclose they received the item for free."[50] This rule applies whether the influencer is a teenager with a few dozen social media followers or a movie star with a million followers.

18-6 Corporate Advertising

Corporate advertising is not designed to promote the benefits of a specific brand but instead is intended to establish a favorable attitude toward a company as a whole. A variety of highly regarded and successful firms use corporate advertising to enhance the image of the firm and affect consumers' attitudes. This perspective on corporate advertising is gaining favor worldwide. Firms with the stature of Walmart, Amazon, and Target are investing in corporate ad campaigns. Exhibit 18.20 shows a corporate campaign for Elkay, a high-end manufacturer of sinks and other plumbing fixtures. Notice how this ad fits the description of corporate advertising perfectly. Elkay is not featuring any one of its products in particular. But rather this interesting and attractive ad is designed to draw attention to the Elkay name and the general nature of its product line.

18-6a The Scope and Objectives of Corporate Advertising

Corporate advertising is a significant force in the overall advertising carried out by organizations around the world. Billions of dollars are invested annually in media for corporate campaigns. Interestingly, most corporate campaigns run by consumer-goods manufacturers are undertaken by firms in the shopping-goods category such as appliance and auto marketers. Studies have also found that larger firms are much more prevalent users of corporate advertising than smaller firms are. Presumably these larger firms have broader communications programs and more money to invest in advertising, which allows the use of corporate campaigns. Apple is another company that has historically relied on corporate campaigns to support its numerous subbrands. The billboard in Exhibit 18.21 is a classic example of Apple's corporate campaign strategy. The brand logo and slogan for Apple appear, but no mention of product features is included.

Delight in everyday perfection.

ELKAY.
elkay.com
specialty collection sinks. Style that endures.

Exhibit 18.20 ▶ Firms often use corporate advertising as a way to generate name recognition and a positive image for the firm as a whole rather than any of its products in particular. Here, Elkay touts the company name rather than any specific product features.

Exhibit 18.21 ▶ Corporate image advertising is meant to build a broad image for the company as a whole. Here, Apple's "Think Different" slogan does just that.

With the proliferation of individual product types, Apple also prepares separate brand campaigns for its many products.

Magazines and television are well suited to corporate advertising, although as the Apple billboard demonstrates, other media can accomplish the task as well. Corporate advertising appearing in magazines has the advantage of being able to target particular constituent groups with image- or issue-related messages. Magazines also provide the space for lengthy copy, which is often needed to achieve corporate advertising objectives and the high-quality reproduction that can add a positive aura to a corporate campaign. Television is a popular choice for corporate campaigns because the creative opportunities provided by television can deliver a powerful, emotional message. IBM has long used both television and magazine ads (see Exhibit 18.22) in a corporate campaign designed to reaffirm its image as an innovator. Notice in this ad that IBM relies on featuring the futuristic vision of the firm's

Exhibit 18.22 ▶ IBM has felt that the company's image as an innovator is important in the face of competition from the likes of Apple and Samsung. This is one of the ads in a corporate image campaign designed to unify the image of the firm as a futuristic innovator with its technology.

approach to technological innovation—a very positive image for a corporate campaign. And of course, corporate advertisers use their websites (and sometimes microsites) as part of their corporate campaigns.

The objectives for corporate advertising should be focused. In fact, corporate advertising shares similar purposes with proactive public relations when it comes to what companies hope to accomplish. Here are some of the possibilities for a corporate campaign:

- to build the image of the firm among customers, shareholders, the financial community, and/or the general public,

- to boost employee morale or attract new employees,

- to communicate an organization's views on social, political, or environmental issues,

- to better position the firm's products against competition, and

- to play a role in the overall advertising and IBP strategy of an organization, providing a platform for more brand-specific campaigns.

Notice that corporate advertising is not always targeted toward the consumer. A broad range of constituents can be targeted with a corporate advertising effort, including investors, partners, suppliers, regulators and government officials, as well as other audiences.

18-6b Types of Corporate Advertising

Three basic types of corporate advertising dominate the campaigns run by organizations: image advertising, advocacy advertising, and cause-related advertising. Each is discussed in the following sections. We then consider green marketing, which can be considered as a special case of any of these first three.

Corporate Image Advertising

The majority of corporate advertising efforts focus on enhancing the overall image of a firm among important constituents—typically customers, employees, and the general public. When State Farm features its slogan "Like a good neighbor, State Farm is there," the goal is to enhance the overall image of the firm (not to promote specific State Farm insurance offices or agents or specific insurance offerings).

Bolstering a firm's image may not result in immediate effects on sales, but as we saw in Chapter 5, attitude can play an important directive force in consumer decision making. When a firm can enhance its overall image, it may well affect buyer predisposition in brand choice. Consider the way BNSF Railway polishes its image by sponsoring public television and

Exhibit 18.23 ▶ BNSF airs this corporate ad on public television to demonstrate its support and to remind viewers of its historic role in connecting the nation for economic development.

airing a 30-second corporate ad (see Exhibit 18.23). This ad associates the brand with the long and rich heritage of connecting the nation, starting in the early days of railroads and progressing to today's sophisticated systems for transporting goods to facilitate economic development. Corporate advertising shapes BNSF's public image and keeps the brand in front of business decision-makers who see the message.

Advocacy Advertising

Advocacy advertising attempts to establish an organization's position on important social or political issues. Advocacy advertising is meant to influence public opinion on issues of concern to a firm. Typically, the issue featured in an advocacy campaign is directly relevant to the business operations of the organization. Target's "What We Value Most Shouldn't Cost More" campaign launched with a focus on the company's commitment to promoting and highlighting brands owned and led by people of color. And Heineken promotes moderation in drinking to combat binge-drinking and to make moderate drinking seem not just acceptable but "cool." These advertising campaigns, which combines traditional and social media elements, ties directly to the companies' products while also addressing issues of social concern.[51]

Cause-Related Advertising

Cause-related advertising features a firm's affiliation with an important social or societal cause—examples are reducing poverty, increasing literacy, conserving energy, protecting the environment, and curbing drug abuse—and takes place as part of the cause-related marketing efforts undertaken by a firm. The goal of cause-related advertising can be to enhance the image of the firm by associating it with social issues of importance to its constituents; this tends to work best when the firm confronts an issue that truly connects to its business.

Cause-related marketing is becoming increasingly common. There are several reasons for this. First, research supports the wisdom of such expenditures. In a consumer survey conducted by Cone, a Boston-based brand strategy firm, 91 percent of respondents said they have a more favorable impression of companies that support good causes and also said they believed that the causes a company supports can be a valid reason for switching brands.[52] Other studies indicate that support of good causes can translate into brand preference with the important qualifier that consumers will judge a firm's motives.[53] If the firm's support is perceived as disingenuous, cause-related expenditures are largely wasted.

Businesses are increasingly embracing social responsibility to do the right thing and, in the process, set their brands apart, as discussed in the Chapter 1 definition of *purpose-driven marketing*. For instance, Whirlpool Corporation is a Habitat Cornerstone Partner and assisted in the massive rebuilding effort needed in the wake of Hurricane Katrina. Jeff Terry, who manages the program of donations and volunteering on behalf of Whirlpool, says of the experience, "The first time you do this work it will change your life."[54] Sure, Whirlpool's participation in this program brings the company a lot of favorable publicity, but its people's hearts also appear to be in the right place. That makes the program a win–win activity for everyone involved.

The range of firms participating in cause-related marketing programs continues to grow. Pedigree has built its dog food brand through a commitment to finding homes for orphan animals, with free food and grant support for rescue shelters.[55] Ralph Lauren, Apple, and Yoplait have products or partnerships that generate funding to support research for a breast cancer cure. The beer brand Stella Artois partnered with Water.org and promotes water conservation with in areas of desperate need through its limited edition product campaign. Nick at Nite funded an initiative called "National Family Dinner Day;" to advance the cause of families spending more time together, Nick at Nite networks ran the program by shutting off for the dinner hour on Nick at Nite Family Day to help make their point.[56] These examples illustrate the wide variety of programs that can be launched to support a cause.

Green Marketing

Green marketing refers to corporate communication efforts that embrace a cause or a program in support of the environment. Such efforts include Apple's product boxes being made out of recycled materials and the "Dawn Saves Wildlife" program sponsored by Procter & Gamble. General Electric and its "Ecomagination" campaign was another high-profile exemplar of this movement. In funding this corporate campaign, GE took the stance that it is simply a good business strategy to seek real solutions to problems like air pollution and fossil-fuel dependency.[57] These advertisers are demonstrating that going green can really be a great business strategy. Surveys show that environmental issues are of major concern to consumers, and a formidable segment is acting on this concern.[58] The green movement looks sustainable for some time.[59]

Yet some firms do use advertising and IBP to communicate misleading or questionable claims about goods or services having environmental benefits, a practice known as **greenwashing**. Consumers who suspect greenwashing can look for certification from groups like Green Seal and check on sites like EnviroLink to see who is really doing what to protect the environment. Here's

hoping that you too are getting on board the green bandwagon. It "ain't easy being green" due to conflicting societal (macro), corporate (meso), and individual consumer (micro) goals and preferences, but solid advertising, PR, and IBP can help persuade and reinforce the importance of more sustainable and greener consumption and lifestyles.[60] The future of advertising is bright, as are the various forms of marketing and social media for branding and image building.[61]

Summary

1. Explain the role of public relations (PR) as part of an organization's overall advertising and IBP strategy.

Public relations entails proactive and reactive brand or corporate communications that can foster goodwill among a firm and constituent groups such as customers, stockholders, employees, government entities, and the general public. Businesses utilize public relations activities to highlight positive events associated with the organization and stimulate brand conversations. PR strategies are also employed for damage control when adversity strikes. Public relations has entered a new era, as changing corporate demands and new techniques have fostered a bolder, more aggressive role for PR in IBP campaigns.

2. Detail the objectives of public relations.

An active public relations effort can serve many objectives, such as building goodwill and counteracting negative publicity. Public relations activities may also be orchestrated to support the launch of new products or communicate with employees on matters of interest to them. The public relations function may be instrumental to the firm's lobbying efforts and in preparing executives to meet with the press and the public.

3. Overview the tools of public relations.

The primary tools of public relations experts are press releases, feature stories, company newsletters, interviews and press conferences, and participation in the firm's event sponsorship decisions and programs, plus generating publicity.

4. Distinguish between proactive and reactive public relations strategies, and under-stand what they may entail.

When companies perceive public relations as a source of opportunity for shaping public opinion, they are likely to pursue a proactive public relations strategy. With a proactive strategy, a firm strives to build goodwill with key constituents via aggressive programs. The foundation for these proactive programs is a rigorous public relations audit and a comprehensive public relations plan. When public relations activities are used for damage control or crisis communications, the firm is obviously in a reactive mode, but organizations must be prepared to react to bad news. Organizations can use a public relations audit and identify inherent vulnerabilities so they are ready to react quickly and effectively in the face of hostile publicity.

5. Illustrate the strategies and tactics used in influencer marketing.

We know that consumers are predisposed to talk about brands, which is why marketers are pursuing strategies to proactively influence the conversation. Influencer marketing covers personalized marketing techniques targeting individuals or groups who have the credibility and capability to drive positive word of mouth among broader audiences. In professional programs, important gatekeepers like veterinarians or any type of health-care professional may be a focal point. In peer-to-peer programs, the key is finding the connectors and giving these influencers something meaningful or provocative that they will want to talk about, with buzz marketing and/or viral marketing. Advertisers should be transparent about relationships with connectors and influencers.

6. Discuss the applications and objectives of corporate advertising.

Corporate advertising is not undertaken to support an organization's specific brands but rather to build the general reputation of the organization in the eyes of key constituents. This form of advertising serves goals such as enhancing the firm's image, building credibility for products, boosting employee morale, communicating views on social or political or environmental issues, defending against competition, and supporting the organization's platform for brand-specific campaigns. Corporate ad campaigns generally fall into one of three categories: image advertising, advocacy advertising, or cause-related advertising. Green marketing refers to corporate communications that support an environmental cause or program.

Key Terms

Ad Council
advocacy advertising
antibrand entertainment
buzz marketing
cause-related advertising
chief marketing officer (CMO)
Consumer Product Safety Commission
   (CPSC)
crisis communications

diversity, equity, and inclusion (DEI)
electronic word of mouth (eWOM)
green marketing
greenwashing
influencer marketing
macro-influencer
micro-influencer
pre-roll advertising
proactive public relations strategy

publicity
publicity stunt
public relations
public relations audit
public relations plan
reactive public relations strategy
text disclosures
vlog
word of mouth (WOM)

Endnotes

1. Robert Klara, "How the Ad Council Turned the PSA into a Powerful Engine for Social Change," *Adweek,* March 21, 2017, http://www.adweek.com/brand-marketing/how-the-ad-council-turned-the-psa-into-a-powerful-engine-for-social-change.

2. "China Is Spending Billions to Make the World Love It," *The Economist,* March 23, 2017, http://www.economist.com/news/china/21719508-can-money-buy-sort-thing-china-spending-billions-make-world-love-it.

3. Data drawn from: https://www.statista.com/statistics/185472/estimated-expenses-of-us-public-relations-agencies-since-2005/

4. Stephen Brown, "Ambi-brand Culture," in Jonathan Schroeder and Miriam Salzer-Morling (Eds.), *Brand Culture* (New York: Routledge, 2006), 50–66.

5. Grace Caffyn, "Marriott Brings Its Social Media War Room to Europe," *Digiday,* July 25, 2016, https://digiday.com/uk/marriott-brings-social-media-war-room-europe.

6. Andrew M. Baker, Naveen Donthu, and V. Kumar, "Investigating How Word-of-Mouth Conversations About Brands Influence Purchase and Retransmission Intentions," *Journal of Marketing Research* 53, no. 2 (2016), 225–239.

7. Christopher Heine, "Check Out Gatorade's Super Bowl Snapchat Ad With Serena Williams," *Adweek,* February 7, 2016, http://www.adweek.com/digital/check-out-gatorades-super-bowl-snapchat-ad-serena-williams-169474/; Garett Sloane, "Gatorade Is Reprising the Super Bowl Dunk on Snapchat," *Advertising Age,* February 3, 2017, http://adage.com/article/special-report-super-bowl/gatorade-reprising-super-bowl-dunk-snapchat/307844.

8. Matthew Schwartz, "Directing Traffic at the New Branding Crossroads," *Public Relations,* November 12, 2012, C5.

9. Claire Stammerjohan, Charles M. Wood, Yuhmiin Chang, and Esther Thorson, "An Empirical Investigation of the Interaction between Publicity, Advertising, and Previous Brand Attitudes and Knowledge," *Journal of Advertising* 34 (Winter 2005), 55–67; Jonah Bloom, "With PR on the Rise, Here's a Refresher Course in the Basics," *Advertising Age,* May 11, 2009, 22.

10. Lindsay Stein, "How Public Relations Is Earning Its Place in 2016," *Advertising Age,* January 11, 2016, http://adage.com/article/cmo-strategy/public-relations-earning-place/302060.

11. Ted Kitterman, "Five Top Crises from 2021—and the Warnings They Offer for the Year Ahead, *PR Daily,* Dec 1, 2021, https://www.prdaily.com/5-top-crises-from-2021-and-the-warnings-they-offer-for-the-year-ahead/; Angeline Close Scheinbaum, ed. *The Dark Side of Social Media: A Consumer Psychology Perspective.* (New York: Routledge, 2017).

12. Breves, Priska Linda, Nicole Liebers, Marina Abt, and Annika Kunze (2019), "The Perceived Fit Between Instagram Influencers and the Endorsed Brand: How Influencer–Brand Fit Affects Source Credibility and Persuasive Effectiveness," *Journal of Advertising Research* 59 (4), 440–454.

13. Campbell, Colin and Pamela E. Grimm (2019), "The Challenges Native Advertising Poses: Exploring Potential Federal Trade Commission Responses and Identifying Research Needs," *Journal of Public Policy & Marketing* 38 (1), 110–123.

14. Micael Dahlen and Sara Rosengren (2016), "If Advertising Won't Die, What Will It Be? Toward a Working Definition of Advertising," *Journal of Advertising* 45 (3), 334–345.

15. Steffi De Jans, Veroline Cauberghe, and Liselot Hudders (2018), "How an Advertising disclosure alerts young adolescents to sponsored vlogs: The moderating role of a Peer-Based Advertising Literacy Intervention Through an Informational Vlog," *Journal of Advertising* 47 (4), 309-325.

16. Jeremy Kees and J. Craig Andrews (2019), "Research Issues and Needs at the Intersection of Advertising and Public Policy," *Journal of Advertising* 48 (1), 126–135; Nathaniel J. Evans, Mariea Grubbs Hoy, and Courtney Carpenter Childers (2018), "Parenting "YouTube Natives": The Impact of Pre-Roll Advertising and Text Disclosures on Parental Responses to Sponsored Child Influencer Videos," *Journal of Advertising* 47 (4), 326-346.

17. Christian Hughes, Vanitha Swaminathan, and Gillian Brooks (2019), "Driving Brand Engagement Through Online Social Influencers: An Empirical Investigation of Sponsored Blogging Campaigns," *Journal of Marketing* 83 (5), 78–96; Angeline Close Scheinbaum, "Digital Engagement: Opportunities and Risks for Sponsors: Consumer-Viewpoint and Practical Considerations for Marketing via Mobile and Digital Platforms." *Journal of Advertising Research* 56, no. 4 (2016): 341–345.

18. Pete Blackshaw, *Satisfied Customers Tell Three Friends: Angry Customers Tell 3,000* (New York: Doubleday, 2008).

19. Jessica Wohl, "Chipotle Seeks Laughs (and Distance From Food Safety Concerns) in Biggest Campaign Yet," *Advertising Age,* April 10, 2017, http://adage.com/article/cmo-strategy/chipotle-comedy-show-real/308580/; Austin Carr, "Recovery Efforts Stalled, Chipotle Faces Challenges That Go Well Beyond Food Safety," *Fast Company,* December 14, 2016, https://www.fastcompany.com/3066581/recovery-efforts-stalled-chipotle-faces-challenges-that-go-well-beyond-food-safety.

20. Jack Neff, "J&J Targets Red Cross, Blunders into PR Firestorm," *Advertising Age,* August 13, 2007, 1, 22.

21. Yanfen You, Xiao Jing Yang, Lili Wang, and Xiaoyan Deng, "When and Why Saying 'Thank You' Is Better than Saying 'Sorry' in Redressing Service Failures: The Role of Self-Esteem," *Journal of Marketing*, 84, no. 2 (2019), 133–150.

22. Peter Sayer and Loek Essers, "Google, Microsoft Among Biggest IT Industry Lobbyists at European Commission," *PC World,* June 25, 2015, http://www.pcworld.com/article/2940752/google-microsoft -among-biggest-it-industry-lobbyists-at-european-commission.html.

23. Natalie Zmuda, "Target Gets Local with On-the-Field Team of PR Pros," *Advertising Age,* February 13, 2012, 12.

24. Steve Olenski, "5 Publicity Stunts Your Brand Can Learn From," *Forbes,* September 23, 2016, https://www.forbes.com/sites /steveolenski/2016/09/23/5-publicity-stunts-your-brand-can-learn -from/#2ca84c6f511b.

25. "Outstanding In-House Team 2017," *PR Week,* March 17, 2017, http:// www.prweek.com/article/1427708/outstanding-in-house-team-2017.

26. Rodrigo Uribe, Cristian Buzeta, and Milenka Velásquez, "Sidedness, Commercial Intent, and Expertise in Blog Advertising," *Journal of Business Research* 69, no. 10 (October 2016), 4403–4410.

27. Tim Prudente, "Big Stage for Loyola: 'Today' Show Brings National Spotlight to Baltimore Campus," *Baltimore Sun,* March 29, 2017, http://www.baltimoresun.com/news/maryland/education/higher -ed/bs-md-ci-loyola-today-show-20170328-story.html; Megan Pringle, "Loyola Breaks Crab Walking Record during Rokerthon," *WBAL-TV 11,* March 30, 2017, www.wbaltv.com/article/loyola -breaks-crab-walking-record-during-rokerthon/9207158.

28. Beth Snyder Bulik, "Well-Heeled Heed the Need for PR," *Advertising Age,* June 11, 2001, S2.

29. Matthew Schwartz, "Directing Traffic at the New Branding Cross-roads," *Public Relations,* November 12, 2012, C5.

30. Kristina Monllos, "Why Barbie Wants to Show Dads Playing Dolls with Their Daughters," *Adweek,* March 13, 2017, http://www.adweek .com/brand-marketing/why-barbie-wants-to-show-dads-playing -dolls-with-their-daughters/; David Frederick, "Mattel Brings Dads into the Barbie Narrative," *PR Week,* April 14, 2017, http://www .prweek.com/article/1430630/mattel-brings-dads-barbie-narrative.

31. Kelly O. Cowart, "Daddy Dearest: The Influence of Paternal Invest-ment on Attitude toward the Advertisement," *Journal of Advertising* 49, no. 2 (2019), 202–212.

32. Geri Mazur, "Good PR Starts with Good Research," *Marketing News,* September 15, 1997, 16.

33. Julie Liesse, "Forecast for 2013: PR Pros' Predictions," *Public Relations,* November 12, 2012, C6.

34. David Frederick, "Mattel Brings Dads into the Barbie Narrative," *PR Week,* April 14, 2017, http://www.prweek.com/article/1430630 /mattel-brings-dads-barbie-narrative.

35. Erin McCann, "United's Apologies: A Timeline," *New York Times,* April 14, 2017, https://www.nytimes.com/2017/04/14/business/united -airlines-passenger-doctor.html.

36. Kathleen V. Schmidt, "Coke's Crisis," *Marketing News,* September 27, 1999, 1, 11.

37. Amie Smith, "Coke's European Resurgence," *Promo Magazine,* December 1999, 91.

38. Daniel Victor, "Pepsi Pulls Ad Accused of Trivializing Black Lives Matter," *New York Times,* April 5, 2017, https://www.nytimes .com/2017/04/05/business/kendall-jenner-pepsi-ad.html?_r=0.

39. James Cox, "Shareholders Get to Put Bio-Engineered Foods to Vote," *USA Today,* June 6, 2000, 1B.

40. Julie Liesse, "The Digital Sweet Spot," The PR Factor 2010, *Adver-tising Age,* November 29, 2010, S4.

41. Michael Trusov, Randolph E. Bucklin, and Koen Pauwels, "Effects of Word-of-Mouth versus Traditional Marketing: Findings from an Internet Social Networking Site," *Journal of Marketing* 73 (September 2009), 90–102; Chen Lou and Shupei Yuan, "Influencer Marketing: How Message Value and Credibility Affect Consumer Trust of Branded Content on Social Media," *Journal of Interactive Advertising* (2019) 19 (1), 58-73; Sapna Maheshwari, "Are You Ready for the Nanoinfluencers?" *The New York Times*, (Nov. 11, 2018) https://www.nytimes.com/2018/11/11/business/media /nanoinfluencers-instagram-influencers.html.

42. Kelly Ehlers, "Micro-Influencers—When Smaller is Better," *Forbes*, June 2, 2021, https://www.forbes.com/sites/forbesagencycouncil /2021/06/02/micro-influencers-when-smaller-is-better /?sh=314fec0c539b.

43. Michael Krauss, "To Generate Buzz, Do Remarkable Things," *Marketing News,* December 15, 2006, 6.

44. Simon Dumenco, "In Praise of the Original Social Media: Good Ol' Television," *Advertising Age,* May 17, 2010, 30; Ed Keller, "All Media Are Social: The Unique Roles of TV, Print and Online in Driving Word of Mouth," *MediaBizBloggers.com,* July 15, 2010.

45. Gerry Khermouch and Jeff Green, "Buzz-z-z Marketing," *Business-Week,* July 30, 2001, 50–56.

46. Robert Berner, "I Sold It through the Grapevine," *BusinessWeek,* May 29, 2006, 32–34.

47. Ibid., 34.

48. "Micro-influencers Are the New Field in Influencer Marketing," *Business Insider,* December 1, 2016, http://www.businessinsider .com/micro-influencers-are-the-new-field-in-influencer-marketing -2016-12.

49. Descriptions taken from the BzzAgent website accessed at www. bzzagent.com (accessed March 16, 2013).

50. Garett Sloane, "Now Everyday Instagram Users Face Complaints Over Breaking FTC Ad Rules," *Advertising Age,* December 1, 2016, http:// adage.com/article/digital/consumer-group-everyday-instagram -users-break-ad-rules/306960.

51. Michael Addady, "Why Heineken Is Encouraging People to Drink Less," *Fortune,* January 13, 2016, http://fortune.com/2016/01/13 /heineken-commercial/; Mark Sweney, "Heineken Ad Suggests Women Prefer Men Who Don't Drink Too Much," *The Guardian (UK),* January 13, 2016, https://www.theguardian.com/media/2016 /jan/13/heineken-ad-moderate-drinking.

52. Stephanie Thompson, "Raising Awareness, Doubling Sales," *Adver-tising Age,* October 2, 2006, 4.

53. Michael J. Barone, Anthony D. Miyazaki, and Kimberly A. Taylor, "The Influence of Cause-Related Marketing on Consumer Choice," *Journal of the Academy of Marketing Science* 28, no. 2 (2000), 248–262.

54. Ibid.

55. James Tenser, "The New Samaritans," *Advertising Age,* June 12, 2006, S–1, S–6.

56. Bob Liodice, "Ten Companies with Social Responsibility at the Core," *Advertising Age,* April 19, 2010, 88.

57. James Tenser, "The New Samaritans," *Advertising Age,* June 12, 2006, S–1, S–6; Natalie Zmuda and Emily York, "Cause Effect: Brands Rush to Save World One Good Deed at a Time," *Advertising Age,* March 1, 2010, 1, 22.

58. Mya Frazier, "Going Green? Plant Deep Roots," *Advertising Age,* April 30, 2007, 1, 54–55; Jack Neff, "Green-Marketing Revolution Defies Economic Downturn," *Advertising Age,* April 20, 2009, 1, 23.

59. Ali Tezer and H. Onur Bodur, "The Greenconsumption Effect: How Using Green Products Improves Consumption Experience," *Journal of Consumer Research* 47, no. 1 (2019), 25–39.

60. Aubrey Fowler and Angeline G. Close, "It Ain't Easy Being Green: Bridging the Gap among Macro, Meso, and Micro Agendas," *Journal of Advertising* 41, no 4 (December 2012), 119–132.

61. Hilde A. Voorveld, "Brand Communication in Social Media: A Research Agenda," *Journal of Advertising* (2019) 48 (1), 14-26.

Glossary

3Ps creativity framework Indicates creativity is fostered by three inputs: people, process, and place.

A

Above-the-line promotion Traditional measured media advertising: any message broadcast to the public through conventional means such as television, the Internet, radio, and magazines.

Absolute cost The unit cost or media vehicle cost.

Accessibility How easy (quick) it is to remember something.

Accessibility bonus A psychological phenomenon in which easily remembered brands are also believed to be more prevalent (common), more popular, and better.

Accommodation A mediating process that lies between the production and reception phases. Accommodation (and negotiation) are the ways in which consumers interpret ads, decoding what the source has encoded.

Account executive (AE) The liaison between an advertising agency and its clients; the nature of the account executive's job requires excellent persuasion, negotiation, and judgment skills in order to both successfully alleviate client discomfort and sell highly effective, groundbreaking ideas.

Account planner In an advertising agency, the professional who synthesizes all relevant consumer research and uses it to help the team design a coherent advertising strategy for a client's brand or product.

Account planning A system by which, in contrast to traditional advertising research methods, an agency assigns a coequal account planner to work with the agency team, analyzing research data related to a client's brand or product.

Account services A team of agency managers that identifies the benefits a client's brand offers, its target audiences, and the best competitive positioning, and then develops a complete promotion plan.

Account team A group of agency people comprising many different facets of the advertising industry (direct marketing, public relations, graphic design, etc.) who work together on a client's advertising, under the guidance of a team leader.

Action for Children's Television (ACT) A group formed during the 1970s to lobby the government to limit the amount and content of advertising directed at children.

Ad blocker Software that consumers install to prevent advertising messages from being visible.

Ad Council A nonprofit organization since 1942 that produces, distributes, and promotes public service announcements on behalf of various sponsors.

Advergaming Advertising and brand placement within video games.

Advertisement A specific message that an organization has placed to persuade an audience.

Advertiser Business, not-for-profit, or government organization that uses advertising and other promotional techniques to communicate with target markets and to stimulate awareness and demand for its brands. Also called *client* by agency partners.

Advertising A paid, mass-mediated attempt to inform, persuade, or remind.

Advertising agency An organization of professionals who provide creative and business services to clients related to planning, preparing, and placing advertisements.

Advertising campaign A series of coordinated advertisements and other promotional efforts that communicate a single theme or idea.

Advertising clutter An obstacle to advertising resulting from the large volume of similar ads for most products and services.

Advertising effectiveness A measure of how effective a particular ad or marketing approach is in meeting its goal.

Advertising plan A plan that specifies the thinking and tasks needed to conceive and implement an effective advertising effort.

Advertising response function A mathematical relationship based on marginal analysis that associates dollars spent on advertising and sales generated; sometimes used to help establish an advertising budget.

Advertising specialties A sales promotion having three key elements: a message, placed on a useful item, given to consumers with no obligation.

Advertising substantiation program An FTC program initiated in 1971 to ensure that advertisers make available to consumers supporting evidence for claims made in ads.

Advocacy advertising Advertising that attempts to influence public opinion on important social, political, or environmental issues of concern to the sponsoring organization.

Aerial advertising Advertising that involves airplanes (pulling signs or banners), skywriting, or blimps.

Affirmative disclosure An FTC action requiring that important material determined to be absent from prior ads must be included in subsequent advertisements.

Agency of record The advertising agency chosen by the advertiser to purchase media time and space.

Alternative evaluation A stage of the consumer decision process, where the consumer searches for and is simultaneously forming thoughts and opinions about possible alternatives (choices).

Antibrand entertainment Content that pokes fun at itself, doesn't mention the product, or uses some other seemingly unmarketable device to attract attention to a brand.

App ads An ad within a Web, tablet, or smartphone application (i.e., app) that is associated with a third party.

Appropriation The use of pictures or images owned by someone else without permission.

Attitude An overall evaluation of any object, person, or issue that varies along a continuum, such as favorable to unfavorable or positive to negative.

Attitude study A research method that measures consumer attitudes after exposure to an ad or measures attitudes about a company's product, as well as that of the competing brand.

Audience A group of individuals who may receive and interpret messages sent from advertisers through mass media.

Authenticity The quality of being genuine and natural, a powerful influence on brand loyalty.

Axis A line, real or imagined, that runs through an advertisement and from which the elements in the ad flare out.

B

Balance An orderliness and compatibility of presentation in an advertisement.

Barter syndication A form of television syndication that takes both off-network and first-run syndication shows and offers them free or at a reduced rate to local television stations, with some national advertising presold within the programs.

Behavioral intent Refers to essentially what consumers say they intend to do, but is not always a great substitute for actual consumer behavior.

Behavioral targeting The process of database development made possible by online tracking markers that advertisers place on a Web surfer's hard drive to track that person's online surfing and shopping behavior.

Below-the-line promotion A promotional effort that includes in-store promotions, coupons, dealer discounts, and product placement.

Benefit segmentation A type of market segmenting in which target segments are delineated by the various benefit packages that different consumers want from the same product category.

Between-vehicle duplication Exposure to the same advertisement in different media.

Big Data Term used to refer to massive data that have become available through social media where researchers find patterns in using computer algorithms. These data may include email surveillance and analysis, frames per second (fps) tracking, and capturing every single click, location, and words users of smartphones create as examples relevant to advertising.

Bill-back allowances A monetary incentive provided to retailers for featuring a marketer's brand in either advertising or in-store displays.

Blackletter A style patterned after monastic hand-drawn letters characterized by the ornate design of the letters. Also called *gothic*.

Blimps Ultralight aircrafts that go through the air with its own power and may serve as an advertising vehicle.

Blocking In the production stage of advertising where the director works with the on-camera talent and camera operators to practice the positioning and movement planned for the ad.

Blog Website frequented by individuals with common interests where they can post ideas, opinions, and personal experiences. Such sites have emerged as sophisticated (but not objective) sources of product and brand information.

Bounce rate The percentage of people who come from or go to another site after clicking on a website.

Brainstorming An organized approach to idea generation; for effective brainstorming, it is necessary to learn about the material in question beforehand, foster a safe environment free of destructive criticism, and openly discuss disagreements that may arise.

Brand A name, term, sign, symbol, or any other feature that identifies one seller's good or service as distinct from those of other sellers.

Brand advertising Advertising that communicates the specific features, values, and benefits of a particular brand offered for sale by a particular organization.

Brand ambassador A consumer who actively recommends a brand to others.

Brand awareness An indicator of consumer knowledge about the existence of the brand and how easily that knowledge can be retrieved from memory.

Brand communities Groups of consumers who feel a commonality and a shared purpose related to a consumer good or service.

Brand equity Developed by a firm that creates and maintains positive associations with the brand in the mind of consumers, building brand loyalty.

Brand extension An adaptation of an existing brand to a new product area; also known as *brand variant*.

Brand knowledge What a customer knows about a brand, which may take several forms such as a brand claim or a belief about the brand.

Brand loyalty A decision-making mode in which consumers repeatedly buy the same brand of a product as their choice to fulfill a specific need.

Brand managers A job title for the team members (or professional) responsible for developing and adapting the brand strategy for the target market.

Brand platform A core idea that frames an ambition or aspiration for the brand that will be relevant to target audiences over time.

Brand promise A statement of the key value of the brand. The promise to a brand makes to the consumer that may be implied via advertising.

Brand switching An advertising objective in which a campaign is designed to encourage customers to switch from their established brand.

Branded apps A mobile application that is branded, and some of which may feature advertising inside the app and/or encourage digital engagement.

Branded entertainment Embedding one's brand or brand icons as part of any entertainment property (e.g., a sporting event), blending advertising and IBP with entertainment in an effort to impress and connect with consumers in a unique and compelling way.

Branded experience The consumer experience itself in experiential marketing.

Branding The strategy of developing brand names so that manufacturers can focus consumer attention on a clearly identified item.

Budgeting The act of planning how much will be spent each period (month, quarter, year) and in what areas.

Build-up analysis A method of building up the expenditure levels of various tasks to help establish an advertising budget.

Business markets The institutional buyers who purchase items to be used in other products and services or to be resold to other businesses or households.

Business-market sales promotion Promotion designed to cultivate buyers from large corporations who are making purchase decisions.

Business-to-business As opposed to business-to-consumer, B2B refers to when companies sell or advertise to other companies or organizations.

Buzz marketing The process of creating events or experiences that yield conversations that include the brand or product advertisers are trying to sell.

C

Cable TV A type of television that transmits a wide range of programming to subscribers through wires rather than over airwaves.

Cause-related advertising Advertising that identifies corporate sponsorship of philanthropic activities.

Cease-and-desist order An FTC action requiring an advertiser to stop running an ad within 30 days so a hearing can be held to determine whether the advertising in question is deceptive or unfair.

Chain of needs Customer needs lead to products; new needs are created by the unintended side effects of modern times and new products; even newer products solve additional and even newer needs.

Channel grazing Using a television remote control to monitor programming on other channels while an advertisement is being broadcast.

Chief Executive Officer (CEO) Usually is the highest ranking executive of a business who is in charge overall of running the business.

Chief Financial Officer (CFO) The executive who is responsible for the financials and monetary aspects or investments of the firm.

Chief Marketing Officer (CMO) The executive who is in charge of marketing strategy.

Chief Technology Officer (CTO) The executive who is in charge of technology and networks.

Cinema advertising Includes ads that run in movie theaters before the film and other advertising appearing off-screen within a theater.

Classified advertising Newspaper advertising that appears as all-copy messages under categories such as sporting goods, employment, and automobiles.

Click fraud Occurs when a company's ads are clicked not by actual humans but by bots designed to mimic what Internet users do, causing the advertiser to overpay.

Click-through A measure of the number of page elements (hyperlinks) that have actually been requested (i.e., "clicked through" from the display/banner ad to the link).

Client/Sponsor The company or organization that pays for advertising. Also called the *sponsor*.

Cognitive dissonance The anxiety or regret that lingers after a difficult purchase decision.

Cognitive style The unique preference of each person for thinking about and solving a problem. Cognitive style pioneer Carl Jung proposed three different dimensions in which thinking differs: sensing versus intuiting, thinking versus feeling, and extraverted versus introverted.

Commission system A method of agency compensation based on the amount of money the advertiser spends on the media.

Communication test A type of pretest message research that simply seeks to see if a message is communicating something close to what is desired.

Community A group of people loosely connected by some common characteristic or interest; a community may share a sense of kinship and exert influence.

Comp A polished version of an ad.

Comparison advertisements Advertisements in which an advertiser makes a comparison between the firm's brand and competitors' brands.

Competitive field The companies that compete for a segment's business.

Competitor analysis In an advertising plan, the section that discusses who the competitors are, outlining their strengths, weaknesses, tendencies, and any threats they pose.

Concept test A type of developmental research that seeks feedback designed to screen the quality of a new idea, using consumers as the final judge and jury.

Consent order An FTC action asking an advertiser accused of running deceptive or unfair advertising to stop running the advertisement in question, without admitting guilt.

Consideration set The subset of brands from a particular product category that becomes the focal point of a consumer's evaluation.

Consolidated agency networks Large holding companies that consist of many agencies or marketing groups.

Consultants Individuals who specialize in areas related to the promotional process.

Consumer-based strategy A way of doing business and advertising that starts with consumer psychology; first, we understand consumers with respect to the product or brand and how they use it and then use the consumer insights to help build or redo the creative strategy.

Consumer behavior Those activities directly involved in obtaining, consuming, and disposing of products and services, including the decision processes that precede and follow these actions.

Consumer–brand relationship The affiliation between consumer and brand, meaning the consumer's emotional attachment to a brand or category.

Consumer culture A way of life centered around consumption.

Consumer–event congruity/fit When an event sponsor fits a consumer's image and sense of self.

Consumer-generated content (CGC) Advertisements and other content related to products or brands, created in part or completely by their end users.

Consumer insights Knowledge of how consumers think about, use, or otherwise view brands, good, or services within the context of their lives. These insights are typically derived through ethnographic methods.

Consumer markets The markets for products and services purchased by individuals or households to satisfy their specific needs.

Consumer-market sales promotion A type of sales promotion designed to induce household consumers to purchase a firm's brand rather than a competitor's brand.

Consumer packaged goods (CPG) Low-involvement consumer products, typically low-priced items such as paper towels, batteries, toothpaste, laundry products, and frozen or canned food.

Consumer Product Safety Commission (CPSC) An agency of the U.S. government that promotes the safety of consumer products by addressing injury risks, provides safety standards, and researches illness or injury that results from products.

Consumer sales promotion A type of sales promotion aimed at consumers that focuses on price-off deals, coupons, sampling, rebates, and premiums.

Consumer watchdog groups Groups of consumers or citizens who try and help bring attention and solutions to certain issues.

Consumerism The actions of individual consumers to exert power over the marketplace activities of organizations.

Content marketing Creating and posting relevant informational messages for target audiences online and on social media, accessible whenever targeted decision makers are considering a purchase.

Contest A sales promotion that has consumers compete for prizes based on skill or ability.

Continuity The pattern of placement of advertisements in a media schedule.

Continuous scheduling A pattern of placing ads at a steady rate over a period of time.

Conversion A process where consumers go on from trying a brand to buying it a second time.

Cooperative advertising (Co-op advertising) The sharing of advertising expenses between national advertisers and local merchants. Also called *co-op advertising*.

Copy-testing A form of copy research (evaluative research) aiming to judge the effectiveness of actual ads, for example, to see if consumers get the joke in the ad or retain key knowledge about the brand from the ad.

Copywriting The process of expressing the value and benefits a brand has to offer, via written or verbal descriptions.

Corporate advertising Advertising intended to establish a favorable attitude toward a company as a whole, not just toward a specific brand.

Corrective advertising An FTC action requiring an advertiser to run additional advertisements to dispel false beliefs created by deceptive advertising.

Cost-per-click (CPC) Digital advertising revenue model based on cost-per-thousand exposures.

Cost per inquiry (CPI) The number of inquiries generated by a direct marketing program divided by that program's cost.

Cost per order (CPO) The number of orders generated by a direct marketing program divided by that program's cost.

Cost per thousand (CPM) The dollar cost of reaching 1,000 members of an audience using a particular medium.

Coupon A type of sales promotion that entitles a buyer to a designated reduction in price for a product or service.

Creative abrasion The clash of ideas, abstracted from the people who propose them, from which new ideas and breakthroughs can evolve. Compare with *interpersonal abrasion*.

Creative boutique An advertising agency that emphasizes copywriting and artistic services to its clients.

Creative brief A document that outlines and channels an essential creative idea and objective guiding the creative team.

Creative message strategy The set of objectives and methods or tactics used to create and disseminate a relevant and resonating message (such as about a product, service, experience, or brand) to customers and potential customers.

Creative selling The act of assisting and persuading customers regarding purchasing decisions; creative selling typically involves products in which customers require extensive knowledge about the product before buying, such as specialty goods or higher-priced items.

Creative services A group that develops the message that will be delivered through advertising, sales promotion, direct marketing, event sponsorship, or public relations.

Creative strategy The creative team is guided by the creative brief in executing the creative strategy, or broad plan of the copywriting and art direction content.

Creative team The copywriters and art directors responsible for coming up with the creative concept for an advertising campaign.

Creativity The ability to consider and hold together seemingly inconsistent elements and forces, making a new connection; creativity is essential in the advertising world because successful marketing demands a constant seamless synthesis of the product and entirely different ideas or concepts.

Crisis communications Communicating with and responding to the public and stakeholders in times of problems, crises, or tragedies.

Cross-selling Marketing programs aimed at customers that already purchase other products from the company.

Crowdsourcing The online distribution of certain tasks to groups (crowds) of experts, enthusiasts, or even consumers.

Culture What people do—the ways they eat, groom themselves, celebrate, mark their space and social position, and so forth.

Customer databases All databases with customer information, customer lists, records of customer information and customer information collected and used by companies or their partners.

Customer relationship management (CRM) The continual effort toward cultivating and maintaining long-term relationships with customers; many companies have recognized trust and rapport are key elements to repeated sales and thus train their sales teams to emphasize each particular customer's needs rather than the bottom line.

Customer satisfaction Good feelings that come from a favorable post purchase experience.

Cyber-identity theft Having one's identity stolen by online or digital means.

D

Dailies Newspapers published every weekday; also, in television ad production, the scenes shot during the previous day's production.

Database agency Agency that helps customers construct databases of target customers, merge databases, develop promotional materials, and then execute the campaign.

Day-after-recall (DAR) A measure where ad elements such as jingles or slogans or logos are tested for recall the day after exposure.

Dayparts Segments of time during a television broadcast day.

Deception Making false or misleading statements in an advertisement.

Defamation When a communication occurs that damages the reputation of an individual because the information was untrue.

Delayed-response advertising Advertising that relies on imagery and message themes to emphasize the benefits and satisfying characteristics of a brand.

Demographic segmentation Market segmenting based on basic descriptors like age, gender, race, marital status, income, education, and occupation.

Demographics Descriptors of people or consumers such as their age, gender, or income, which help with target marketing.

Design The structure (and the plan behind the structure) for the aesthetic and stylistic aspects of a print advertisement.

Designer Specialist intimately involved with the execution of creative ideas and efforts.

Dialogue Advertising copy that delivers the selling points of a message to the audience through a character or characters in the ad.

Dialogue balloons A type of projective technique that offers consumers the chance to fill in the dialogue of cartoonlike stories, as a way of indirectly gathering brand information.

Differentiation The process of creating a perceived difference, in the mind of the consumer, between an organization's brand and the competition.

Digital footprint The trail of social media posts, videos, photos, status updates, and online information on a person, organization, or brand.

Digital/interactive agency Agency that focuses on using online, mobile, and social media for direct marketing and target market communications for clients.

Digital video recorder (DVR) A computer-like hard drive that can store many hours of television programming.

Direct mail A direct marketing medium that involves using the postal service to deliver marketing materials.

Direct marketing An interactive system of marketing that uses one or more advertising media or communication channels to affect a measurable response and/or transaction at any location.

Direct marketing agency Agency that maintains large databases of mailing lists; some of these firms can also design direct marketing campaigns either through the mail or by telemarketing. Also called a *direct response agency*.

Direct response Copy research method measuring actual behavior of consumers.

Direct-response advertising Advertising that asks the receiver of the message to act immediately.

Direct-response agency Also called **direct marketing agency**.

Direct-response copy Advertising copy that highlights the urgency of acting immediately.

Directory advertising Includes all the local phone directory and local business advertising books published by a variety of firms.

Display ads Advertisements placed on websites that contain editorial material.

Display advertising A newspaper ad that includes the standard components of a print ad—headline, body copy, and often an illustration—to set it off from the news content of the paper.

Diversity Differences in people (such as socioeconomic, racial, ethnic, geographic, academic or professional background, religions, beliefs, and sexual orientations).

Diversity, equity, and inclusion (DEI) The representation of and focus on having work environments and/or ads are diverse, fair, and that groups are included in/feel belonging in.

E

Earned media The incremental exposure that a brand earns through viral engagement and consumer interactions with the brand.

Economies of scale The ability of a firm to lower the cost of each item produced because of high-volume production.

Editorial and entertainment content Content in a website or magazine, for example, that is intended to inform educate or entertain consumers.

Effective frequency The number of times a target audience needs to be exposed to a message before the objectives of the advertiser are met.

Effective reach The number or percentage of consumers in the target audience that are exposed to an ad some minimum number of times.

Electronic word of mouth (eWOM) The process of encouraging consumers to communicate with each other about a firm's brand or marketing activities.

Embedded Consumption practices tightly connected to a context.

Emergent consumers A market segment made up of the gradual but constant influx of first-time buyers.

Ephemeral The content lasts for just a short time.

Ethics Moral standards and principles against which behavior is judged.

Ethnocentrism The tendency to view and value things from the perspective of one's own culture.

Ethnographic research Researchers observe and interview consumers in real-world settings.

Evaluative criteria The product attributes or performance characteristics on which consumers base their product evaluations.

Evaluative research Research on the actual ads or promotional language, finished or unfinished and is used to judge or evaluate ads and promotions, usually right before or after the ad is finalized (sometimes also referred to as copy research).

Event-planning agency Experts in finding locations, securing dates, and putting together a "team" of people to pull off a promotional event.

Event social responsibility An opportunity for (sports) sponsors to demonstrate good corporate citizenship, generate positive word of mouth, and boost both attendance and patronage intent.

Event sponsorship Providing financial support to help fund an event, in return for the right to display a brand name, logo, or advertising message on-site at the event.

Event sponsorship measurement Includes (but is not limited to) models and metrics on the following areas: event–sponsor fit, attitude, event social responsibility, sponsorship awareness, image transfer, affect transfer, brand meaning transfer, and sponsorship patronage (i.e., preference toward buying from the sponsoring brand).

Evoked set The set of brands that comes to mind when a category is mentioned.

Executive summary Typically two paragraphs to a page in length, it previews the most important aspects of the advertising plan/what the reader should remember about the plan.

Experiential marketing Marketing of and with the consumer experience.

Extended problem solving A decision-making mode in which consumers are inexperienced in a particular consumption setting but find the setting highly involving.

External facilitator An organization or individual that provides specialized services to advertisers and agencies.

External lists Mailing lists purchased from a list compiler or rented from a list broker and used to help an organization cultivate new business.

External position The competitive niche a brand pursues.

External search A search for product information that involves visiting retail stores to examine alternatives, seeking input from friends and relatives about their experiences with the products in question, or perusing professional product evaluations.

Eye-tracking system A type of physiological measure that monitors eye movements across print and online ads during research studies.

F

Fake news Could range from incorrect information that is inaccurate and attention getting without credible sources to completely made-up stories in general.

Federal Trade Commission (FTC) The government regulatory agency that has the most power and is most directly involved in overseeing the advertising industry.

Fee system A method of agency compensation whereby the advertiser and the agency agree on an hourly rate for different services provided.

Fieldwork Research conducted outside the agency, usually in the home or site of consumption.

First-run syndication Television programs developed specifically for sale to individual stations.

Flighting A media-scheduling pattern of heavy advertising for a period of time, usually two weeks, followed by no advertising for a period, followed by another period of heavy advertising.

Focus group A brainstorming session with a small group of target consumers and a professional moderator, used to gain new insights about consumer response to a brand.

Forgetting function Idea that people's forgetting is fairly predictable and seems to obey a mathematical function.

Formal balance A symmetrical presentation in an ad—every component on one side of an imaginary vertical line is repeated in approximate size and shape on the other side of the imaginary line.

Frame-by-frame test Copy research method that works by getting consumers to turn dials (like/dislike) while viewing television commercials in a theater setting, to assess response.

Free premium A sales promotion that provides consumers with an item at no cost; the item is either included in the package of a purchased item or mailed to the consumer after proof of purchase is verified.

Free-standing insert (FSI) A newspaper insert ad that contains cents-off coupons for a variety of products and is typically delivered with Sunday newspapers.

Frequency The average number of times an individual or household within a target audience is exposed to a media vehicle in a given period of time.

Fulfillment centers Centers that ensure customers receive the product ordered through direct mail.

Full-service agency An advertising agency that typically includes an array of advertising professionals to meet all the promotional needs of clients.

G

General Data Protection Regulation (GDPR) Europe's data privacy and security law that has requirements and laws for businesses and organizations with respect to personal and information privacy.

Geodemographic segmentation A form of market segmentation that identifies neighborhoods around the country that share common demographic characteristics.

Geofencing The ability to track consumers' locations within a certain geographic area via their smartphones.

Geographic scope Scope of the geographic area to be covered by advertising media.

Geo-targeting The placement of ads in geographic regions where higher purchase tendencies for a brand are evident.

Global advertising Developing and placing advertisements with a common theme and presentation in all markets around the world where the firm's brands are sold.

Government officials and employees One of the five types of audiences for advertising; includes employees of government organizations, such as schools and road maintenance operations, at the federal, state, and local levels.

Great Depression A period (1929–1941 for the United States) in which the vast majority of people in many countries suffered from a severe economic decline.

Green marketing Corporate efforts that embrace a cause or program in support of the environment. Green marketing is currently of particular importance, as the public is becoming increasingly aware and concerned about the urgency of environmental issues.

Greenwashing Using advertising and IBP to communicate misleading or questionable claims about goods or services having environmental benefits.

Gross domestic product (GDP) A measure of the total value of goods and services produced within an economic system.

Gross impressions The sum of exposures to all the media placement in a media plan.

H

Habit A decision-making mode in which consumers buy a single brand repeatedly as a solution to a simple consumption problem.

Hashtag A word or words followed by a # often used on social media to help organize and/or identify online content on a certain topic.

Headline The leading sentence(s), usually at the top or bottom of an ad, that attracts attention, communicates a key selling point, or achieves brand identification.

Heavy users Consumers who purchase a product or service much more frequently than others. Also known as *committed users* or *lead users*.

Household consumers The most conspicuous of the five types of audiences for advertising; most mass media advertising is directed at them.

Household penetration An example of a marketing plan sales objectives given as the number of homes that an ad or marketing effort gets to.

Households using TV (HUT) A measure of the number of households tuned to a television program during a particular time period.

Hybrid commerce A part of omnichannel strategy, where sales are done as a blend of in-person and online shopping or purchasing as customers have both digital and in-store channels.

Hyper-localism The process where people will get their global and national news from the Web but turn to local newspapers for items on sale at local stores.

I

Identity Who one perceives themselves to be.

Illustration In the context of advertising, the drawing, painting, photography, or computer-generated art that forms the picture in an advertisement.

Implicit memory measures Techniques used to obtain feedback that determines consumers' recognition of advertising, characterized by questions or tasks that do not explicitly make reference to the advertisement in question. The perceived advantage of this type of test is a more subconscious, unadulterated response.

In-depth interviews A form of qualitative research done with consumers that bring a deep understanding and are often used to supplement the findings from AIO research.

Industrial Revolution A major change in Western society beginning in the mid-18th century and marked by a rapid change from an agricultural to an industrial economy.

Industry analysis In an advertising plan, the section that focuses on developments and trends within an industry and on any other factors that may make a difference in how an advertiser proceeds with an advertising plan.

Inelasticity of demand Strong loyalty to a product, resulting in consumers being less sensitive to price increases.

Influencer marketing A series of personalized marketing techniques directed at individuals or groups who have the credibility and capability to drive positive word of mouth in a broader and salient segment of the population.

Infomercial A long advertisement that looks like a talk show or a half-hour product demonstration.

Informal balance An asymmetrical presentation in an ad—nonsimilar sizes and shapes are optically weighed.

In-house agency The advertising department of a firm.

Inquiry/direct response measures A type of posttest message tracking in which a print or broadcast advertisement offers the audience the opportunity to place an inquiry or respond directly through a reply card or toll-free number.

Institutional advertising Corporate advertising that takes place in the trade channel. This form of advertising is used most prominently by retailers.

In-store sampling A type of sampling that occurs at the point of purchase and is popular for food products and cosmetics.

Integrated brand promotion (IBP) The process of using a wide range of promotional tools that work together to create widespread brand exposure. It is brand focused.

Integrated marketing communications (IMC) The process of using promotional tools in a unified way so that a synergistic communications effect is created for a brand.

Interactive media Media that allow consumers to access games, entertainment, shopping opportunities, and educational programs, sometimes on a subscription or pay-per-view basis. Such media allow direct measurement of ad exposure and impact.

Interactivity Two-way communications that can feed off one another, an advantage of digital media.

Internal lists An organization's records of its customers, subscribers, donors, and inquirers, used to develop better relationships with current customers.

Internal position The niche a brand achieves with regard to the other similar brands a firm markets.

Internal search A search for product information that draws on personal experience and prior knowledge.

International advertising The preparation and placement of advertising in different national and cultural markets, outside the home market.

Interpersonal abrasion The clash of people, often resulting from an inability to regard idea feedback as separate from personal feedback, from which communication shuts down and new ideas get slaughtered. Compare *creative abrasion*.

Interstitial An ad that loads while you browse; they appear on a site after a page has been requested but before it has loaded and stay onscreen long enough for the message to be registered.

Involvement The degree of perceived relevance and personal importance accompanying the choice of a certain product or service within a particular context.

J

Junk mail Mail that perceivably has no benefit, is unwanted, and useless to the consumer.

L

Layout A drawing of a proposed print advertisement, showing where all the elements in the ad are positioned.

Lead time The time it takes to develop and place an ad.

Leveraging Any collateral communication or activity reinforcing the link between a brand and an event.

Libel Defamation that occurs in print and would relate to magazine, newspaper, direct mail, or Internet reports.

Life-stage A circumstantial variable, such as when a family's youngest child moves away from home, which changes the consumption patterns of the family.

Lifestyle research (AIO) Survey-based knowledge derived through questions about consumers' activities, interests, and opinions (AIO). It is used to help develop messages and target profiles of consumers.

Lifestyle segmentation A form of market segmenting that focuses on consumers' activities, interests, and opinions.

Limited problem solving A decision-making mode in which consumers' experience and involvement are both low.

Local advertising Advertising directed at an audience in a single trading area, either a city or state.

Local spot radio advertising Radio advertising placed directly with individual stations rather than with a network or syndicate.

Local TV Television programming other than the network broadcast that independent stations and network affiliates offer local audiences.

Location-based technologies Often associated with mobile; use geographical coordinates to determine where the person is and can synergize with digital advertising for nearby businesses.

Logo A graphic mark that identifies a company and other visual representations that promote an identity for a firm.

Long interview A one-on-one interview, as long as one hour, with a consumer in which the interviewer probes to get at deeper connections between brands, consumption practices, and consumers' real lives.

Long-copy email Copy written for an email message designed to offer the receiver incentives to buy the product and usually offers a link to a short-copy landing page.

Long-copy landing page Website copy designed to sell a product directly; the copy might equal the equivalent of a four- to eight-page letter to a potential customer.

Loyalty programs/Frequency programs A type of sales promotion that offers consumers discounts or free product rewards for repeat purchase or patronage of the same brand or company.

M

Macro-influencer A person who is paid or compensated to deliver messages or content about a brand and has at least 500,000 social media followers.

Mail sampling A type of sampling in which samples are delivered through the postal service.

Mailing list/email list A file of names and addresses that an organization might use for contacting prospective or prior customers.

Marcom manager A marketing communications manager who plans an organization's overall communications program and oversees the various functional specialists inside and outside the organization to ensure that they are working together to deliver the desired message to the customer.

Market analysis Complements the industry analysis, emphasizing the demand side of the equation, where an advertiser examines the factors that drive and determine the market for the firm's product or service.

Market segmentation The process of breaking down a large, widely varied market into submarkets that are more similar than dissimilar in terms of consumer characteristics.

Market share The percent of a market/industry's total sales volume earned or controlled by a company during a certain time period.

Marketing The activity, set of institutions, and processes for creating, communicating, delivering, and exchanging offerings that have value for customers, clients, partners, and society at large.

Marketing database A mailing list that also includes information collected directly from individual customers.

Marketing mix The blend of the four responsibilities of marketing—conception, pricing, promotion, and distribution—used for a particular idea, product, or service.

Markup charge A method of agency compensation based on adding a percentage charge to a variety of services the agency purchases from outside suppliers.

Materialism When people place particular emphasis on money and material goods.

Meaning What an advertisement intends or conveys.

Measured media Media that are closely measured to determine advertising costs and effectiveness: television, radio, newspapers, magazines, and outdoor media.

Media buying Securing the electronic media time and print media space specified in a given account's schedule.

Media-buying service An independent organization that specializes in buying media time and space, particularly on radio and television, as a service to advertising agencies and advertisers.

Media class A broad category of media, such as television, radio, or newspapers.

Media impressions Instances in which a product or brand is exposed to potential consumers by direct newspaper, television, radio, or magazine coverage (rather than the payment of these media as venues in which to advertise). The effectiveness of sponsorship spending is often judged by the comparison of media impressions to traditional media advertising, such as commercials.

Media kit A resource of information provided by a publisher to assist ad buyers, reporters, and media professionals who are seeking information on circulation, readership, subscribers, and prices to evaluate advertising opportunities.

Media mix The blend of different media that will be used to effectively reach the target audience.

Media plan A plan specifying the media in which advertising messages will be placed to reach the desired target audience.

Media planner An advertising agency (although on occasion an in-house person) with expertise in buying and scheduling media for ad placements.

Media planning and buying services Services related to media planning or buying that are provided by advertising agencies or specialized media-buying organizations.

Media specialist Organizations that specialize in buying media time and space and offer media strategy consulting to advertising agencies and advertisers.

Media vehicle A particular option for placement within a media class (e.g., People is a media vehicle within the magazine media class).

Members of a trade channel One of the five types of audiences for advertising; the retailers, wholesalers, and distributors targeted by producers of both household and business goods and services.

Members of business organizations One of the five types of audiences for advertising; the focus of advertising for firms that produce business and industrial goods and services.

Merchandise allowances A type of trade-market sales promotion in which free products are packed with regular shipments as payment to the trade for setting up and maintaining displays.

Message weight A sum of the total audience size of all the media specified in a media plan.

Microblogs Social networking services that enable users to post and read short messages, for instance, Twitter. Posters are restricted by the number of characters in the message.

Micro-influencer A person who represents a brand, usually having a specific knowledge area, who has between 10,000–50,000 followers on social media.

Micro-targeting Refers to the practice of delivering customized messages down to the individual level or near the individual level.

Mindshare brands Brands that are promoted and purchased largely through memory of the brand name and sometimes one simple quality or attribute.

Missionary salesperson A person who proactively contacts customers after a purchase has been made, in order to ensure customer satisfaction and foster goodwill, by asking if the customer has questions about the product, providing additional information, and checking to see if the customer's current needs have changed (and may present an opportunity for further sales).

Mobile applications (apps) The apps on a smartphone for the digital media platform.

Mobile marketing Directing advertising and IBP campaigns to consumers' mobile devices—smartphones and tablet devices.

Mobile sampling A type of sampling carried out by logo-emblazoned vehicles that dispense samples, coupons, and premiums to consumers at malls, shopping centers, fairgrounds, and recreational areas.

Monopoly power The ability of a firm to make it impossible for rival firms to compete with it, either through advertising or in some other way.

N

Narrative Advertising copy that simply displays a series of statements about a brand.

Narrowcasting The development and delivery of specialized television programming to well-defined audiences.

National advertising Advertising that reaches all geographic areas of one nation.

National Advertising Review Board (NARB) A body formed by the advertising industry to oversee its practice.

National spot radio advertising Radio advertising placed in nationally syndicated radio programming.

Native advertising An ad seemingly in its natural environment and part of the content such as a news feed.

Need state A psychological state arising when one's desired state of affairs differs from one's actual state of affairs.

Negotiation Along with accommodation, the ways in which consumers interpret ads, decoding what the source has encoded to reach an agreement of brand meaning.

Netiquette Online etiquette, or the customary code of behaviors and norms of online interactions or communications.

Netnography A research method to understand online communities or online cultures.

Network radio advertising Radio advertising placed within national network programs.

Network TV A type of television that broadcasts programming over airwaves to affiliate stations across the United States under a contract agreement.

New customer acquisition When a company or business gains a first-time client or customer, which is a goal for many companies especially when the new customer comes from a competitor.

New normal A term used often during the COVID-19 pandemic, to refer to a shift in behaviors and norms that goes beyond a temporary change, such as a shift toward working from home or ordering groceries online.

Niche marketing The practice of narrowly targeting a relatively small segment of a market in which the consumers are typically willing to pay a premium price for the brand.

Normative test scores Scores that are determined by testing an ad and then comparing the scores to those of previously tested, average commercials of its type.

O

Objective-and-task approach A method of advertising budgeting that focuses on the relationship between spending and advertising objectives by identifying the specific tasks necessary to achieve different aspects of the advertising objectives.

Off-invoice allowance A program allowing wholesalers and retailers to deduct a set amount from the invoice they receive for merchandise.

Off-network syndication Television programs that were previously run in network prime time.

Omnichannel The consumer has the choice of digital or in-store channels or both.

Online resistance An attitude or behavior against the digital movement at times. For some consumers, and for the authors as well, social networks are designed as a vehicle that connects us with people who have at one point graced our lives.

On-package sampling A type of sampling in which a sample item is attached to another product package.

Opinion leaders People who influence the opinions and behaviors of consumers.

Opt-in marketing When a customer or potential customer chooses to receive marketing communications from a company.

Opt-out When a customer or potential customer chooses not to receive marketing communications from a company; here the default would be where the company sends the messages and it is up to the customer to elect not to receive the messages.

Order The visual elements in an ad that affect the reader's "gaze motion" through the ad.

Order taking The practice of accepting and processing needed customer information for prearranged merchandise purchase, or scheduling services that a consumer will purchase once rendered. While their role in the transaction process rarely involves communicating large amounts of information, order takers must be able to answer customer questions and be accommodating and considerate.

Out-of-home media advertising The combination of transit and billboard advertising.

Owned media Brand assets or objects created within social networks by a particular organization, such as a Facebook page or an application.

P

Packaging The container or wrapping for a product; packaging serves as an important vessel for product information and user appeal, as it is often viewed by the customer in a potential buying situation.

Paid media Media that are paid for on social media or other media; advertisements that can be purchased on a social network or other digital platforms.

Paid search The process by which advertisers pay websites and portals to place ads in or near relevant search results based on key words.

Parallel layout structure A print ad design that employs art on the right-hand side of the page and repeats the art on the left-hand side.

Parity products Products with few major objective differences between brands—for example, paper towels and other low-involvement goods.

Pass-along readership People other than the primary subscriber who read a publication.

Pay-for-inquiry advertising model A payment scheme in which a media company gets paid by advertisers based solely on the inquiries an advertiser receives in response to an ad.

Pay-for-results A compensation plan that results when a client and its agency agree to a set of results criteria on which the agency's fee will be based.

Percentage-of-sales approach An advertising budgeting approach that calculates the advertising budget based on a percentage of the prior year's sales or the projected year's sales.

Personal selling The face-to-face communications and persuasions process, often used with products that are higher-priced, complicated to use, must be tailored to individual user needs, involve a trade-in, or are judged at the point of purchase.

Pester power The strong persuasive influence kids can have on an adult's purchases even when they have no money.

Phishing A form of email spam with which spammers try to entice Web users to enter personal information on fake websites that are forged to look like authentic sites such as a bank, the IRS, or other organizations that will get the email users' attention.

Physiological assessment The research interpretation of certain biological feedback generated from viewers who are exposed to an ad or IBP message, using brain imaging and other neuroscience techniques.

Pica A measure of the width or depth of lines of type.

Point A measure of the size of type in height.

Point-of-entry marketing Advertising strategies designed to win the loyalty of consumers whose brand preferences are still under development, in hopes of gaining their loyalty.

Point-of-purchase (P-O-P) advertising Advertising that appears at the point of purchase.

Pop-up/pop-under ad An Internet advertisement that appears as a website page is loading or after a page has loaded.

Pop-up/pop-under copy Copy to accompany pop-up/pop-under digital/interactive ads.

Position A brand's meaning relative to its competitors.

Positioning The marketer's attempt to give a brand a certain meaning and distinct place in the consumer's mind, relative to its competitors.

Positioning strategy The key themes or concepts an organization features for communicating the distinctiveness of its product or service to the target segment.

Post ads Ads in a social media post that tend to have higher relative response rates because they are within a consumer's post to their network of friends and friends of friends.

Pre- and post-exposure tests A form of marketing research that is done to measure attitude change by measuring attitudes before the person sees the ad or message and then again after they see it.

Predecisional distortion A psychological bias in favor of a brand that unconsciously weights incoming information in the direction of the favored brand. It is thought to be due to an emotional response to the brand.

Prelight In the production stage, which involves setting up lighting or identifying times for the best natural lighting to ensure that the shooting day runs smoothly.

Premiums Items that feature the logo of a sponsor and that are offered free, or at a reduced price, with the purchase of another item.

Preprinted insert An advertisement delivered to a newspaper fully printed and ready for insertion into the newspaper.

Preproduction The stage in the television production process in which the advertiser and advertising agency (or in-house agency staff) carefully work out the precise details of how the creative planning behind an ad can best be brought to life with the opportunities offered by television.

Pre-roll advertising Ads that are shown to consumers before a social media video or other content.

Price promotions A type of consumer-market sales promotion that temporarily entails a lower price, saving money, or other discount.

Price-off deal A type of sales promotion that offers a consumer cents or even dollars off merchandise at the point of purchase through specially marked packages.

Primary demand The demand for an entire product category.

Primary demand stimulation Using advertising to create demand for a product category in general.

Primary research A type of systematic discovery-seeking or testing when the researcher designs their own study and/or collects their own original research/data.

Principle of limited liability An economic principle that allows an investor to risk only his or her shares of a corporation, rather than personal wealth, in business ventures.

Principles of design General rules governing the elements within a print advertisement and the arrangement of and relationship between these elements.

Privacy seal Logo on certain websites that show the site has been endorsed or is a member of a third-party privacy endorser of privacy.

Proactive public relations strategy A public relations strategy that is dictated by marketing objectives, seeks to publicize a company and its brands, and is offensive in spirit rather than defensive.

Product placement The sales promotion technique of getting a marketer's product featured in movies and television shows.

Production facilitator An organization that offers essential services both during and after the production process.

Production services A team that takes creative ideas and turns them into advertisements, direct mail pieces, or events materials.

Production stage/shoot The point at which the storyboard and script for a television ad come to life and are filmed. Also called the *shoot*.

Professionals One of the five types of audiences for advertising, defined as doctors, lawyers, accountants, teachers, or any other professionals who require special training or certification.

Program rating The percentage of television households that are in a market and are tuned to a specific program during a specific time period.

Programmatic media buying Automatic buying of ads based on data such as online consumer behavior.

Projective techniques A type of developmental research designed to allow consumers to project thoughts and feelings (conscious or unconscious) in an indirect and unobtrusive way onto a theoretically neutral stimulus.

Promotion agencies Specialized agencies that handle promotional efforts.

Proportion The size and tonal relationships between different elements in an advertisement.

Psychographics A form of market research that emphasizes the understanding of consumers' activities, interests, and opinions.

Public relations A marketing and management function that focuses on communications that foster goodwill between a firm and its many constituent groups.

Public relations audit An internal study that identifies the characteristics of a firm or the aspects of the firm's activities that are positive and newsworthy.

Public relations firm Firms that handle the needs of organizations regarding relationships with the media, local community, competitors, industry associations, and government organizations.

Public relations plan A plan that identifies the objectives and activities related to the public relations communications issued by a firm.

Publicity Unpaid-for media exposure about a firm's activities or its products and services.

Publicity stunt A type of public relations that serves as a "buzz builder" that is crafted to get people talking or to get the brand on peoples' mind.

Puffery The use of absolute superlatives like "Number One" and "Best in the World" in advertisements.

Pull media A form of media where consumers go looking for the advertiser or advertising and thus "pull" the advertised brand toward them.

Pulsing A media-scheduling strategy that combines elements from continuous and flighting techniques; advertisements are scheduled continuously in media over a period of time, but with periods of much heavier scheduling.

Purchase A main objective of many ads or integrated brand promotions, where the consumer buys something.

Purchase intent A measure of whether or not a consumer intends to buy a product or service in the near future.

Pure Food and Drug Act A 1906 act of Congress requiring manufacturers to list the active ingredients of their products on their labels.

Purpose-driven marketing Marketing (including advertising and IBP) that helps the organization achieve its long-term social purpose.

Push media A form of media in which the brand is "pushed" at the consumer (rather than the consumer seeking it out).

Push strategy A sales promotion strategy in which marketers devise incentives to encourage purchases by members of the trade to help push a product into the distribution channel.

Q

Qualitative research Entails research that has data that is descriptive and entails phenomena that are observed rather than measured.

Quantitative research A form of systematic information gathering and analysis based on measures of quantities or numbers.

R

Radio networks A type of radio that delivers programming via satellite to affiliate stations across the United States.

Radio syndication A type of radio that provides complete programs to stations on a contract basis.

Ratings point A measure indicating that 1 percent of all the television households in an area were tuned to the program measured.

Reach The number of people or households in a target audience that will be exposed to a media vehicle or schedule at least one time during a given period of time. It is often expressed as a percentage.

Reactive public relations strategy A public relations strategy that is dictated by influences outside the control of a company, focuses on problems to be solved rather than opportunities, and requires defensive rather than offensive measures.

Rebate A money-back offer requiring a buyer to mail in a form requesting the money back from the manufacturer.

Recall tests Tests of how much the viewer of an ad remembers of the message; they are used to measure the cognitive residue of the ad. These are the most commonly employed tests in advertising.

Recognition In a test, when the audience members indicate that they have seen an ad before.

Recognition tests Tests in which audience members are asked if they recognize an ad or something in an ad. These are the standard cognitive residue test for print ads and promotion.

Regional advertising Advertising carried out by producers, wholesalers, distributors, and retailers that concentrate their efforts in a particular geographic region.

Repeat purchase A second purchase of a new product after trying it for the first time.

Repositioning Returning to the process of segmenting, targeting, and positioning a product or service to arrive at a revised positioning strategy, to address changing market or competitive conditions.

Resonance test A type of message assessment in which the goal is to determine to what extent the message resonates or rings true with target audience members.

Retargeting Serving consumers digital ads that are directly based on past online content they've clicked on.

RFM analysis An analysis of how recently and how frequently a customer is buying from an organization and of how much that customer is spending per order and over time.

Rituals Repeated behaviors that affirm, express, and maintain cultural values.

Roman The most popular category of type because of its legibility.

Rough layout The second stage of the ad layout process, in which the headline is lettered in and the elements of the ad are further refined.

S

Sales promotion The use of incentive techniques that create a perception of greater brand value among consumers or distributors.

Sampling A sales promotion technique designed to provide a consumer with a trial opportunity.

Sans serif A category of type that includes typefaces with no small lines crossing the ends of the main strokes.

Satellite and closed-circuit A method of transmitting programming to highly segmented audiences.

Script (television) The written version of an ad; it specifies the coordination of the copy elements with the video scenes.

Search Often refers to information search, or a stage in consumer behavior process where the customer seeks out information or a specific product or brand either online or offline.

Search engine optimization (SEO) Utilizing a search engine to a company's best advantage.

Secondary research Research when the researcher does not collect the data, but acquires it from another source.

Segment A portion of the market.

Selective demand stimulation Using advertising to stimulate demand for a specific brand within a product category.

Self-actualization The highest level of Maslow's hierarchy, where an individual strives for maximum fulfilment of individual capabilities.

Self-liquidating premium A sales promotion that requires a consumer to pay most of the cost of the item received as a premium.

Self-reference criterion (SRC) The unconscious reference to one's own cultural values, experiences, and knowledge as a basis for decisions.

Self-regulation The advertising industry's attempt to police itself.

Self-transformative Something or an experience that is used by the consumer to help create or transform their sense of self.

Serif The small lines that cross the ends of the main strokes in type; also the name for the category of type that has this characteristic.

Share of audience A measure of the proportion of households that are using television during a specific time period and are tuned to a particular program.

Share of voice Percent of the total advertising in a category (e.g., autos) spent by one brand (e.g., Ford).

Short-copy landing page Digital/interactive copy; a brand offer that may be accessed by a consumer through key word search and has the length and look of a magazine ad.

Single-source data Information provided from individual households about brand purchases, coupon use, and television advertising exposure by combining grocery store scanner data with TV-viewing data from monitoring devices attached to the households' televisions.

Site stickiness A digital marketing metric measured by how long a consumer stays on a website or page.

Situation analysis In an advertising plan, the section in which the advertiser lays out the most important factors that define the situation and then explains the importance of each factor.

Slander Oral defamation that in the context of promotion would occur during television or radio broadcast of an event involving a company and its employees.

Slogan/tagline A short phrase used in part to help establish an image, identity, or position for a brand or an organization, but mostly used to increase memorability.

Slotting fees A type of trade-market sales promotion in which manufacturers make direct cash payments to retailers to ensure shelf space.

Small print In advertising or marketing, it refers to the writing that is small and difficult to read, and is often challenged by customers as being unethical.

Social couponing Sites that give or sell price discounts under the condition that a set number of other consumers buy or download the deal.

Social listening An emerging research discipline that specializes in tracking conversations about brands on the Web, analyzing the data, and reporting various metrics, including numbers of people discussing a brand, sentiments expressed, and volume (how much conversation about a brand occurs in a given period), and so on.

Social meaning What a product or service means in a societal context.

Social media Highly accessible Web-based media that allow the sharing of information between individuals and between individuals and groups. Prominent examples are Facebook, Twitter, and LinkedIn.

Social media copy Language in social media communications that highlights a brand name or brand features.

Source The originator or creator of the content.

Spam Unsolicited bulk email sent to a large number (often millions) of personal and commercial email addresses.

Sponsor–event congruity/fit The degree to which consumers perceive the sponsor and sponsee as congruent in both image and function.

Sponsor spillover An earlier sponsor still may get "credit" for being the sponsor in the consumer's memory—even when a new brand is the sponsor.

Sponsorship activation Any collateral communication or activity reinforcing the link between a brand and an event is referred to as leveraging or activating a sponsorship.

Sponsorship articulation Integrated brand promotion that explains the event sponsorship.

Square root law The recognition of print ads increases with the square of the illustration.

Steering organization A group of expert advisors and professionals that help give direction and guide strategy and decisions on the brand or organization.

Stigmatized When someone's personal attribute is a source of devaluation in the marketplace or by other people.

Storyboard A frame-by-frame sketch or photo sequence depicting, in sequence, the visual scenes and copy that will be used in an advertisement.

Story construction A type of projective technique that asks consumers to tell a story about people depicted in a scene or picture, as a way of gathering information about a brand.

STP marketing For segmenting, targeting, positioning. A marketing strategy employed when advertisers focus their efforts on one subgroup of a product's total market.

Straight-line copy Advertising copy that explains in straightforward terms why a reader will benefit from use of a product or service.

Stratification (social class) A person's relative standing in a social system as produced by systematic inequalities in things such as wealth, income, education, power, and status. Also referred to as *social class*.

Subhead In an advertisement, a few words or a short sentence that usually appears above or below the headline and includes important brand information not included in the headline.

Subject matter expert A person who has extensive experience and/or knowledge about a specialty area, and are often used as sources in journalism or research.

Subliminal advertising Advertising alleged to work on a subconscious level.

Support media Media used to reinforce a message being delivered via some other media vehicle.

Sweepstakes A sales promotion in which winners are determined purely by chance.

Switchers A market segment made up of consumers who often buy what is on sale or choose brands that offer discount coupons or other price incentives.

Symbolic value What a product or service means to consumers in a nonliteral way.

System selling Selling a set of interrelated components that fulfills all or a majority of a customer's needs in a particular area.

T

Target To focus advertising and promotion effort upon a given segment or segments.

Target audience A particular group of consumers singled out for an advertisement or IBP campaign.

Taste A generalized set or orientation to consumer preferences.

Teaser email Copy written for an email message that is a short message designed to drive readers to a long-copy landing page where they can order the brand directly.

Telemarketing A direct marketing medium that involves using the telephone to deliver a spoken appeal.

Television syndication Either original programming or programming that first appeared on network TV that is then rebroadcast on either network or cable stations with pending distribution on the Internet.

Testimonial An advertisement in which an advocacy position is taken by a spokesperson.

Text disclosures When a company or organization sends product- or service-related disclosures or important information to consumers via their phones.

Thought listing (cognitive response analysis) A type of pretest message research that tries to identify specific thoughts that may be generated by an advertisement. Also known as *cognitive response analysis.*

Three-point layout structure A print ad design that establishes three elements in an ad as dominant forces.

Thumbnails, or thumbnail sketches The rough first drafts of an ad layout, about one-quarter the size of the finished ad.

Top-of-mind awareness A measure used by advertisers which is the first brand one can remember when asked to name the brands in a category.

Tracking studies Studies that document the apparent effect of advertising over time, assessing attitude change, knowledge, behavioral intent, and self-reported behavior. They are one of the most commonly used advertising and promotion research methods.

Trade journals Magazines and websites published specifically for members of a trade, containing highly technical articles.

Trade-market sales promotion A type of sales promotion designed to motivate distributors, wholesalers, and retailers to stock and feature a firm's brand in their merchandising programs.

Trade reseller Organizations in the marketing channel of distribution that buy products to resell to customers.

Trade shows Events where several related products from many manufacturers are displayed and demonstrated to members of the trade.

Transit advertising Advertising that appears as both interior and exterior displays on mass transit vehicles and at terminal and station platforms.

Trendspotting Identifying new trends in the marketplace.

Trial offers A type of sales promotion in which expensive items are offered on a trial basis to induce consumer trial of a brand.

Trial usage An advertising objective to get consumers to use a product new to them on a trial basis.

TV households An estimate of the number of households that are in a market and own a television.

Type font A basic set of typeface letters.

U

Unfair advertising Defined by Congress as "acts or practices that cause or are likely to cause substantial injury to consumers, which is not reasonably avoidable by consumers themselves and not outweighed by the countervailing benefits to consumers or competition."

Unique selling proposition (USP) A promise contained in an advertisement in which the advertised brand offers a specific, unique, and relevant benefit to the consumer.

Unity The creation of harmony among the diverse components of an advertisement: headline, subhead, body copy, and illustration.

Unmeasured media Media less formally measured for advertising costs and effectiveness (as compared to the measured media): direct mail, catalogs, special events, and other ways to reach business and household consumers.

Upfronts A period of media buying in which advertisers purchase time on network television a few months before (May) the new season of shows begin (September). They are thus bought "up-front."

User base The current customers who are using (or who have recently used/purchased your product or service).

User interface (UI) The point of human-computer interaction with a webpage, computer, website or app.

V

Value A perception by consumers that a product or service provides satisfaction beyond the cost incurred to acquire it.

Value proposition A statement of the functional, emotional, and self-expressive benefits delivered by the brand, which provide value to customers in the target segment.

Variety seekers Consumers who enjoy new experiences and switch brands or products for that reason, not necessarily for lower prices or another incentive.

Variety seeking A decision-making mode in which consumers switch their selection among various brands in a given category in a random pattern, often because they enjoy new experiences.

Vertical cooperative advertising An advertising technique whereby a manufacturer and dealer (either a wholesaler or retailer) share the expense of advertising.

Video on demand (VOD) A cable television service that enables subscribers to watch a selection of videos at any time.

Viral marketing The process of consumers marketing to consumers over the Internet through word of mouth transmitted through emails and electronic mailing lists.

Virtual identity This is how the consumer or brand uses images and text online to construct or showcase identity.

Virtual reality A newer technology that advertisers are using with computer models that allow a consumer to interact with 3-D visuals for an immersive, artificial experience.

Vlog A video-based blog.

W

Web 2.0 The progression of the Internet to interactive online communication, participation, and engagement.

Web 3.0 A stage of Internet progression which entails sites and e-services that use machine learning and artificial intelligence to interpret a Web full of data.

Within-vehicle duplication Exposure to the same advertisement in the same media at different times.

Word of mouth In marketing parlance, this is the process of encouraging consumers to talk or communicate with each other about a firm's brand or marketing activities.

Zaltman Metaphor Elicitation Technique (ZMET) A research technique to draw out people's buried thoughts and feelings about products and brands by encouraging participants to think in terms of metaphors.

Name/Brand/Company Index

Page references in **bold** print indicate ads or photos. Page references in *italics* indicate tables, charts, or graphs.

A

AAAA. *See* American Association of Advertising Agencies (AAAA)
AARP The Magazine, 282, 285
ABC, 32, *267,* 286, 290. *See also Good Morning America*
Absolut, **13, 189,** 278, **279**
   Animal, **14**
Accenture, 38, 46, 48
Action for Children's Television, 67, 88
Activision, 42
Acura's NSX, 18
Ad Council, 396, **396**
   Love has no labels, 396, **396**
   McGruff the Crime Dog, 396
   Rosie the Riveter, 61
   Smokey the bear, 396
   Woodsy the Owl, 396
Addady, Michael, 419
Adidas, 9, **9,** 15, 261, 355
Advertising Age, 194
Aetna Life & Casualty, 84
Aflac (American Family Life Assurance Co.), 170, **170**
Alba, Davey, 392
Alba, Jessica, 213
Albertson's, 329
Alderton, Matt, 141
Alfa Romeo, 264, **264**
Alibaba, 24
Allstate Insurance, *236*
   "You're in Good Hands with Allstate" campaign, 207, 236, *236*
Alphabet, 32
Always' "Like a Girl" campaign, 71
Amazing Race, The, 360
Amazon, 23, 24, 113, 130, 131, **131,** 286, **300,** 309
American Advertising Federation (AAF), *93*
American Airlines, **65**
American Association of Advertising Agencies (AAAA), 44, 70, *93,* 94
American Business Press, *93*
American Express, **7**
American Red Cross, 37
American Wine Association, *93*
AmerisourceBergen, 36
Anacin, 67
Anderson, Chris K., 318
Anderson, Wes, 280
Andrews, Travis M., 295

Ang Lee, 72
Animal House, 66
Ant-Man, 360
AP News Network, 290
Apple, 8, 12, 14, 21, 24, 34, 121, 135, **135,** 144, 156, 165, 212, 220, *267,* 338, 388, **389,** 414, **414**
   App Store, 158
   iPad, 34
   iPhone, 165, 169, 338
   iPod, 191, **191**
   Mac, 188
   MacBook, **212**
   MacBook Air, 212
   Pay, *15,* 21, 379
   "Think Different" slogan, **414**
   Watch, 8, **8**
Aquafina, 18. *See also* PepsiCo
Architectural Digest, 283
Armani, Giorgio, 137
Arm & Hammer, 114
Armstrong, Lance, 214
Artzt, Edwin L., 70
Association of National Advertisers (ANA), *93*
ATF. *See* U.S. Bureau of Alcohol, Tobacco, Firearms, and Explosives (ATF)
Atlanta, 282
AT&T, *267,* 287, 355, 375, 377
Audi, 360, 362
Avocados From Mexico, 268, **268**
Axe, 151, 313, 331, **332, 363.** *See also* Unilever
Ayer, Francis W., 56
Azfar, Rakin, 349

B

Baack, Daniel W., 202, 226
Bach, King, 363
Back to the Start, 363
Bacon, Jonathan, 51
Baileys, 157, **157**
Bain, Marc, 27
Bank Marketing Association, *93*
Bank of America, 286
Barajas, Joel, 162
Barnum, P. T., 57, 412, 413
Barthel, Michael, 294
Barton, Bruce, 59
Batra, Rajeev, 26
Baysinger, Tim, 295
Deaman, Tom, 393

Bean, L.L., 374
Beck, 239, **240**
Beef Industry Council, *236*
Beer, Jeff, 100, 203
Beer Wars, 397
Belk, Russell W., 318
Bellman, Steven, 50
Benefit Cosmetics, 300, **301**
Ben & Jerry, 16, 18
Bernbach, Bill, 65
Best Buy, 13, 373, **373,** 373, **373**
Best Roommate Ever, 363, **363**
Better Homes and Gardens, 282
Beverage, 151
Bhattacharyya, Suman, 294
Biles, Simone, 76, 216
Birchbox, 336, **336**
Birkner, Christine, 76, 100
Blendtec, 214, **215**
Blevins, Jason, 51
Blob, 62
Blomkamp, Neill, 72
BMW, 40, 72, 138, 231, **231,** *236,* 268, **310,** 354, 360, 389, **390.** *See also* Mini Cooper
BNSF Railway, 415–416, **416**
Body Alarm, **219**
Body-Snatchers, 62
Bond, Vince, Jr., 368
Boone County National Bank, 158
Borchardt, Debra, 125
Boston News Letter, 55
Boston Red Sox, 357
Bouche, Louis, **61**
BP, 21
Branchik, Blaine, 100
Braniff Airlines, **66**
B-Reel, 46
Brita, 363, **363**
Brock, Betsy, 392
Broitman, Adam, 76
Brunsman, Barrett J., 368
Budweiser, 54, 88, 172, 216, *236,* 397
Burger King, **68,** 69
Burnett, Leo, 65
Burrell, Thomas J., 67–68, **68**
   Burrell Advertising, 67
Business Wire, 314
Buss, Dale, 252
Butterfinger, 145, **146**
   "Bolder than Bold" campaign, 145, **146**
Byron, Ellen, 367
BzzAgent, 413

C

Cabela's, 381, 382
Cable News Network (CNN), 68, 290
    Airport Network, 287
Cadillac, 6, **7, 154,** 354
    "Dare Greatly" campaign, 7, **7**
Caesars Entertainment, 382
Caffyn, Grace, 418
Calderwood, Kathleen, 141
Calkins, Earnest Elmo, 56
Calkins, Tim, 100
Callaway Golf, 361
Calvin Klein, 220, **220**
    Eternity for Men, 260
    Obsession for Men, 260
Campbell's Soup, 12
Canon, *267*
Capital One, 353
Captain America, 360
Car and Driver, 283, **283**
Carter, Jimmy, 67
Castle Wholesalers, 13
Cave, Bryan, 102
CBS, 287. *See also Guiding Light*
    CBS All Access, 287
Center for Digital Democracy, 95
CFA. *See* Consumer Federation of America
    (CFA)
CFPA. *See* Consumer Finance Protection
    Agency (CFPA)
Chanel, 137, **137, 171,** 374, **377**
Chen, Jiemiao, 202
Chevrolet , 315
    Bolt EV, 32
    Trucks, *236*
Children's Advertising Review Unit, 90, *92*
Children's Food and Beverage Advertising
    Initiative, 88
Chipotle Mexican Grill, 363, 399
Chobani, 134, **134,** 135, 151
Choi, Candice, 349
Choi, Hojoon, 100, 226
Chun-Wei Chang, 392
Cimarron, 7
Cinelli, Melissa D., 100
Citi Bike, 128–129
Citizens Against Hunger, 37
Civil Aeronautics Board, 90
Cleveland Cavaliers, 357
Clow, Lee, 188, 189, 196
Coca-Cola, 15–16, 54, **54,** 61, **61, 67,** 95,
    121, 144, 205, 221, 329, 345, 3461,
    362, 378, **379,** 407. *See also* Dasani;
    Sprite
Coca-Cola Zero, 16
Cohen, Liz, 61
Colgate-Palmolive, 19, 114, 205
    Total, 19

Colorado (Tourism), 37, **37**
Comcast, 16, 46, **47,** 286, 287
Cone Communications, 416
Connolley, Kate Bertrand, 349
Conrad New York Hotel, 398
    "Pop-Up Conrad Concierge," 398
Constant Contact, 386
Consumer Federation of America (CFA), 95
Consumer Finance Protection Agency
    (CFPA), *91*
Consumer Reports, 95, 211
Consumer Value Products, 93
Consumers Union, 95
Coppola, Roman, 247
Cosgrave, Bronwyn, 252
Costco, 329, 336, 341
Coty, 40
Council of Better Business Bureaus, 88,
    90, *93*
Coupons.com, **333**
Cover Girl, 83, 223, **223.** *See also* Procter &
    Gamble (P&G)
Cox, Kate, 102
Craig, Edward, 294
Creating Minds (Gardner), 188
Crest, 114
Crisco, 364
    Crisco Cooking Talks, 364
Crispin Porter + Bogusky (CP+B), 197
Curry, Stephen, 213, 363

D

DAA. *See* Digital Advertising Alliance (DAA)
Dahlen, Micael, 26, 50
Daniels, Chris, 125
Dannon, *267*
Darden Restaurants, 256. *See also* Olive
    Garden
Daredevil, 360
Dasani, 16, 18. *See also* Coca-Cola
Davenport, Thomas H., 50, 274, 294
Davidson, Martin, 121, 125
Davis, Ben, 161
Davis, Bruce, 349
Dawar, Niraj, 141
DDB North America, 43
DDT, **63**
Deal, Jennifer, 203
Dean Foods, 346
De Beers, *236*
Dell, 413. *See also* Dell, Michael
Dell, Michael, 374. *See also* Dell
Deloitte & Touche, 38, 355
Dentsu, 38, 39
Deuze, Mark, 274
de Vries, James, 51
Diaz, Ann-Christine, 51
Dichter, Ernest, 62, 63

Digital Advertising Alliance (DAA), 95
DigitasLBi, 40
Direct Mail Marketing Association (DMMA), *93*
Direct Marketing Association (DMA), 94, 99,
    375, 383
Direct Selling Association, *93*
DirecTV, 287
DISH Network, 287
Disney, *267,* 270, 272, **287,** 311, 388, 389
Distilled Spirits Association, *93*
DKNY, 301
    "Be delicious" campaign, **302**
DMA. *See* Direct Marketing Association (DMA)
DMMA. *See* Direct Mail Marketing Association
    (DMMA)
Doland, Angela, 181
Domino's, 331, **331**
Donaton, Scott, 100
Doritos, 106, 107, 109, **111,** 111–113, **112,**
    120, 122, **123, 129,** 327, **327**
    Rainbows chips, **120**
Doritos "Boldest Choice" campaign, **111**
Dove, 83–84, **84, 128,** 151, 174, 410, **411**
    Dove Evolution, 174
Doyle Dane Bernbach (DDB), 65, **65**
Dr Pepper, 16
Drucker, Peter, 19
Druckman, Charlotte, 295
Dunkin' Donuts, 236
Dua, Tanya, 226, 317
Dupre, Elyse, 349

E

EA Sports, 327, **327**
Eaton, Dan, 27
eBay, 34, 282
Ebbinghaus, Hermann, 265
Ebony magazine, 67
Edensohr, Hannah, 294
Einstein, Albert, 188, 201
Electronic Arts, 313
Eliot, T. S., 188
Elkay, **414,** 414
Elle, 284
Elsen, Millie, 252
English Premier Soccer League, 355
EnviroLink, 417
Escort Radar, **283**
ESPN, 32, 286–288
Esrey, William T., 70
Essany, Michael, 161
Estée Lauder, 81
Esteves, Rosa-Branca, 181
E.T., 359
EU. *See* European Union (EU)
European Commission, 400
European Union (EU), 400
Exide, 16

F

Facebook, 6, 24, 29, 30–32, 37, 95, **177,** 267, **269,** 285, 300, 301–302, 305, 307, 311, 398. *See also* Instagram
Fairway Gourmet, The, 363
Fajardo, Tatiana M., 252
Fanta, 14, **146**
Fast Company, 283, **283**
Faull, Jennifer, 162
FCC. *See* U.S. Federal Communications Commission (FCC)
FDA. *See* U.S. Food and Drug Administration (FDA)
FedEx, 207, 221
Fiat , 6, 224
Fifty-Foot Woman, The, 62
Fight Club, 70
Fishing League Worldwide, 355
FNV (fruits 'n veggies), 213, **213**
Folgers, 130, **131**
Food, Inc., 405
Food Network Magazine, 282, 283, **284**
Food Technology, 13
Ford, 17, **18,** 34, **154, 236, 237,** *267,* 315, 335, **335**
    Mustang car, 17
    F-series Super Duty pickup trucks, 17
    Trucks, *236*
Fornell, Claes, 27
Fossen, Beth L., 318
Four Seasons hotel, 22
Fox Networks Group, 290. *See also Glee*
Frank, Thomas, 66, 121
Frankenheimer, John, 72
Frankel, Daniel, 50
Franklin, Benjamin, 374
Frauenheim, Ed, 203
Frederick, David, 419
Freud, Sigmund, 188
FTC. *See* U.S. Federal Trade Commission (FTC)
Fulgoni, Gian M., 102, 294, 319

G

Gallo, Carmine, 393
Gandhi, Mahatma, 188, 201
Ganow, Scot, 393
Garcia, Ahiza, 226
Gardner, Howard, 188
Garfield, Bob, 352, 360
Gatorade, 398
Gazdik, Tanya, 181, 275
Gebhart, Andrew, 295
Geico, 207, **207,** 210, **210**
Geller, Martinne, 181
General Electric (GE), 22, 401, **402,** 416
General Mills, 88, 95, 331
General Motors (GM), 3, 6, 32, 34, 116, **154,** 354

General Tire and Rubber Company, 341
Ghosh, Tathagata, 26, 50, 368
Gianatasio, David, 295
Gibson, Danielle, 319
Gijsenberg, Maarten J., 226
Gillette, *236*
Gilliland, Nikki, 392
Giorgio Armani, **137**
Glade, *267*
Gladwell, Malcolm, 398
Glee, 290. *See also* Fox Networks Group
Gneezy, Ayelet, 161
GoDaddy, 84
Godard, Frederic, 203
Godin, Seth, 386
GoldenEye, 360
Golden, Jessica, 102
Golden State Warriors, 357
Goldman, David, 226
Goodyear, 346
Google, 23, 24, 32, 95, 188–189, **189,** 209, 270, 307, **308,** 309, 312, 400
    AdWords, **23, 270,** 309
    Chrome, 32
    DoubleClick, 32
    Play tutorial, **189**
    Plus, 333, 362
Graeter's, **262**
Graham, Martha, 102, 188, 201
Green Seal, 417
Grewal, Dhruv, 50, 162
Grey Group, 35
Grimes, Roger A., 102
Gucci, 22, 217, 304, **304**
Guess, **217**
Guiding Light, 368. *See also* CBS
Guinness Book of World Records, 404
Gutenberg, Johannes, 374
Guttmann, A., 51

H

Handley, Lucy, 368
Hanssens, Dominique M., 162, 274
Harley-Davidson, 71, 113, 121, *236,* 240, **241**
Harley Davidson Owners Group (HOG), **72**
Harman, 403
Harper's Bazaar, 284
    #BlackLivesMatter movement, 407
Harrington, John, 51
Hawaii Visitors & Convention Bureau, 363
Hearst Media, 285
Head & Shoulders shampoo, 209, **209**
Hearst newspapers, 30
Heine, Christopher, 26, 349, 418
Heineken, 113, 354, 416
Heinz, 336, 360, **360**
    "Pass the Heinz" campaign, 360, **360**
Helm, Burt, 51

Hermes, 19
Hewlett-Packard (HP), 30
Hidden Persuaders, The, 62
Hilton Hotel, 127, **130,** 133
    Hilton Worldwide, 398
Hof, Robert D., 51
Holt, Doug, 121
Home Depot, 113, 329, 339
Honda, 84, 249, 311, 313
Hoover, 388
Hopkins, Claude, 56
Hotels.com, **190**
Hublot, 339, **340**
Huffington Post, 279, 314

I

IBM, 12, 14, 46, **64,** 144, 415, **415**
    Watson Ads, 12
IHOP. *See* International House of Pancakes (IHOP)
IKEA, 113, 149, **149**
Inärritu, Alejandro Gonzalez, 72
Infiniti, 7. *See also* Nissan
Instagram, 6, 31, **98,** 199, 220, 269, **269,** 299–303, 398. *See also* Facebook
Interactive Advertising Bureau (IAB), 309, 316
InterActiveCorp (IAC), 32
InterBrand, 136
International House of Pancakes (IHOP), 305
Interpretation of Dreams, The (Freud), 188
Iron Man, 360
Italian Job, The, 72, 360, **361**
Ives, Nat, 50, 294
Ivory, 54–56. *See also* Procter & Gamble (P&G)

J

Jardine, Alexandra, 50
JC Penney (JCP), 375
Jeep, 113, 311
Jenner, Kendall, 407, **407**
Jeopardy, 287, 360
Jessica Jones, 360, 362
Jing Zhang, 318
Jobs, Steve, 165
John, Elton, 349
John Hancock, 357
Johnson, Bradley, 50, 51, 274
Johnson, John H., 67
Johnson & Johnson, 14, 120, 399
Johnson, Lauren, 102, 162
Johnston, Melanie, 190
Jonze, Spike, 247
Jordan, Michael, 213
Jovan Musk, 260
Jung, Carl, 202
J. Walter Thompson (JWT), 59, 143

K

Kähr, Andrea, 102, 319
Kantar Media, 23, **24**
Kate Spade, 325, **325**
Katz, Jeff, 367
Katzenbach, Jon, 196
Kell, John, 100
Keller Fay Group, 412
Kellogg's, 168, 216. *See also* Special K
Kennedy, John F., 56
Kennedy, Rachel, 50
Kharpal, Arjun, 26
Kia, 8, 211, **211**
Kim, Jae-Eun, 141, 162
Kim, Kacy K., 100, 294
Kimberly-Clark, 95
KitKat, 168, **168**
Klara, Robert, 418
Koenigstorfer, Joerg, 100
Kotler, Philip, 141
Kraft, 88
Kraft Heinz, 336
Kroger, 281, 329
Kukar-Kinney, Monika, 125
Kulp, Patrick, 226
Kumar, V., 26
Kurkure, 168

L

Lagerfeld, 260
Lamar Advertising, **345**
Land Rover, 118
Lasker, Albert, 56
Lee, Spike, 247
Leo Burnett, 30, 65
Levi Strauss, 361
Lewis, Byron, 67
Lexus, 7, 359
Library of Congress, 90
Liedtke, Michael, 50
Lifebuoy, **58**
Liffreing, Ilyse, 318, 349
LinkedIn, 298, 300, 303, 311–313
Listerine, 58
L.L. Bean, 374, 376, **376, 380**, 383
Lobschat, Lara, 318
Lois, George, 192
"Look on the Light Side" campaign, **221**
L'Oréal, 83, **98**, 131, *236*
Lowes, 339
Luck of the Draw, 408
Lukovitz, Karlene, 182
Lululemon, 22
Luxottica, 22
Lynch, Jason, 275

M

Ma, Jingjing, 226
Mad Men, 63, 65, 360, **360**

Maheshwari, Sapna, 319
MailChimp, 386
Maltesers, 221, **221**
Manchester United, 355, **356**
Man Nobody Knows, The, 59
"Man Your Man Could Smell Like, The"
    campaign, 151
Mandel, Naomi, 124
Marriott, 96, 398
Mars, 221
Martex, 216
Martex Bath & Bedding, **216**
Martin, Roger, 203
Martín-Herrán, Guiomar, 51, 102
Maslow, Abraham, 81
MasterCard, 24, 231, **232**
Mattel, 405–406, **406**
    "Dads Who Play Barbie" campaign, 406, **406**
Maui Beverages, 401
Maxwell House, 54
Maybelline, 223, *236*
Mazda, 353, **354**
McAlister, Leigh, 50, 348
McCann, Erin, 419
McCann Worldgroup, 33, 399
McCracken, Grant, 122–123, 355
McDonald's, 10, 12, **23,** 36, **81,** 83, **85, 86,**
    88–89, 138, 220, 239, 240, 261, 328,
    353, 353
McGruff the Crime Dog, 396
McKinsey, 46
McLane Company, 93
Mediamark Research, *261*
Meek, Andy, 50
Mercedes-Benz, 388
Michelob Ultra, 214
Microsoft, 24, 34, 46, 144, 212, **212,** *267,*
    400. *See also* Gates, Bill
Miller Brewing, 33
Miller Lite, 33, 246, 247
    Beer, **247**
    "Can Your Beer Do This?" campaign, 246
Mini Cooper, 360, **361.** *See also* BMW
Minute Maid, 16, 207
Mishra, Saurabh, 100
M&M's, 334, **335**
Modern Family, 268
Mondelez International, 34, 177, 341. *See
    also* Ritz
Monllos, Kristina, 101, 125, 419
Monsanto, 405
Monster Energy, 355, **363**
Moreau, C. Page, 51
"Morning in America" campaign, **69**
Mortimer, Natalie, 141, 162
Moscaritolo, Angela, 141
Mosendz, Polly, 348
Motion Picture Association of America, *93*
Mountain Dew, 33, 121, 222
Mr. Clean, 207, **208**
Mukherjee, Ashesh, 226
Murray, Rheana, 227
Muzellec, Laurent, 368

N

NAB. *See* National Association of
    Broadcasters (NAB)
NAD. *See* National Advertising Division (NAD)
NARB. *See* National Advertising Review Board
    (NARB)
NASCAR, 17, 41, 362, **363**, 363
National Advertising Division (NAD), 92, *93*
National Advertising Review Board (NARB),
    67, 92–93, *93*
National Association of Attorneys General
    (NAAG), 92
National Association of Broadcasters (NAB),
    93, 94
National Breast Cancer Foundation, 357
National Broadcasting Company (NBC), 30,
    46, 80, 365
National Fluid Milk Processor Promotion
    Board, 20
National Geographic, 283
National Pancake Day, 305, **306**
National Retail Federation (NRF), 151
National Swimming Pool Institute, *93*
Nature Conservancy, 37
NBC. *See* National Broadcasting Company (NBC)
Neff, Jack, 50, 161, 226, 294, 368
Nenycz-Thiel, Magda, 50
Nelson, Jonathan, 203
Nestlé, 145–146
Netflix, 32, 46, 113, 286, **286**, 322
Network Alliance Initiative, 95
Newton, Cam, 213
New York Times, 259, 278
New York Yankees, 355
Ng, Alfred, 317
Nickelodeon, 46, 68
Nike, 15, 16, **17,** 30, 41, 188, 196, 213, 220,
    247, 267, 268
Nintendo, 40, *267*
Nissan, 352, 354. *See also* Infiniti
    Versa, 18
Nixon, Richard, 66
Nokia, 361
Nordstrom, 21, **21,** 23
North Face, The, 22
Northlich, 408
NPD Group, Inc., 151
NRF. *See* National Retail Federation (NRF)
Nudd, Tim, 251, 368

O

Ogilvy, David, 65, 252
Ogilvy & Mather, 65
Old Gold Cigarettes, **60**
Old Spice, 151. *See also* Procter & Gamble
    (P&G)
Olen, Helaine, 102
Olenski, Steve, 419
Olive Garden, 256. *See also* Darden Restaurants
Olmstead, Kenneth, 318

Omnicom Group, 30, 38, 39, 38–40
Oracle, 40, 46
O'Reilly, Lara, 51
Oreo, 168, 177, **177,** 182, 325, **326**
Organic, 40
Outback Queensland Tourism Association, 131
Outdoor Advertising Association of America, *93*

P

Palmer, Volney, 55
Pampers, 327, **364**. *See also* Procter & Gamble (P&G)
Panera, 11, **12,** 338
Pang, Kevin, 27
Parekh, Rupal, 51
Parent Is Born, A, 364, **364**
Parents, 283
Parmalat, 242, **242**
Partnership for a Healthier America, **213**
Patel, Neil, 51
Patel, Sahil, 27, 51
Pathak, Shareen, 51
Patrick, Danica, 84
Patrón Tequila, 85
PayPal, 379
Peacock, 16
Pedigree, 416
Peloton Sports, 402
Penn Railroad, **61**
Pennsylvania Gazette, 55
Peppercomm, 197
PepsiCo, 16, 18, 38, 41, **66, 72,** 88, 113, 121, 156, 205268 **268,** 269, 313, 346, **407**. *See also* Aquafina; Diet Pepsi
"Drink up, Rock Out" campaign, **72**
Perez, Sarah, 295
Perlstein, Josh, 348
Permission Marketing, 386
Petty, George, **60**
Pew Center, 151
Pfizer, 400
Pharmaceutical Manufacturers Association, *93*
Philips, 48
Picasso, Pablo, 188, 190, 201
Pinterest, 11, 31, 37, 96, 300, 301, 302, 305, 312, 313, 398
Pirelli Tires, 14
Pizza Hut, 302
Planters, 336, **337**
Pods, 62
Poggi, Jeanine, 295
Pokémon Go, 143, 329–330 **330**
Polo, **239**
Popeyes, 10, **11**
Porsche, **283**
Portland, 38
Powers, John E., 56

Prado Land Cruiser, 167
PRE Brands, 346
"Priceless" campaign, **231**
Prius Prime, 138
PR Newswire, 42, 314
Procter & Gamble (P&G), 18, 21, 29, **30,** 34, 36, 41, 44, 70, 72–73, 93, 95, 145, 151, 207, 216, 219, 287, 337, 359, **359, 364,** 412, 416. *See also* Cover Girl; Ivory; Old Spice; Pampers; Tide
"Thank You, Mom" campaign, **359**
Professional Bull Riders, 335, **335**
Progressive Grocer, 151
Progressive Insurance, 12
Promotional Product Association, 340
Promotional Products Association International, 340
Proprietary Association, *93*
Prudente, Tim, 419
Public Broadcasting Service (PBS), 363
Publicis Worldwide, 38, 39, **40,** 40

Q

Qatar Airways, 30, **30**

R

Radcliffe, Damian, 294
Radio Advertising Bureau, 290, **291**
Raitt, Bonnie, 408
Ralph Lauren, 22
Rea, Chad, 191
Reagan, Ronald, 69, **69**
Red Cross, 399
Reddi-wip, 264
Red Bull, 352, **353**
Reebok, 15, 266
Reeves, Rosser, 63, **64**
REI, **82**
Reichert, Tom, 217
Resor, Helen, 59
Resor, Stanley, 59
Retail-Me-Not, 314
Revlon, 42, 81
Richards, Katie, 227, 317
Rihanna, 121
Ritchie, Guy, 72
Ritz. *See also* Mondelez International Bits, 361
Roberts, Julia, 404
Roderick, Leonie, 348, 349
Rodriguez, Ashley, 295
Rodulfo, Kristina, 227
Roebuck, Alvah, 374
Rogers, Stuart, 62
Roker, Al, 404
Rosengren, Sara, 50
Rolex, 221, 354
Roth, Yefim, 319
Rubens, Paul, 102
Rucker, Derek D., 124

S

Saatchi and Saatchi, 69
Safronova, Valeriya, 100
Sahni, Navdeep S., 318
Salado Sales, 93
Samsung, 14, 135, **136,** 156, **415**
Sapient, 38
Saur, Abe, 368
Schaefer, Mark W., 51
Scheinbaum, Angeline Close, 317, 367
Schiefelbein, Jill, 275
Schmitt, Garrik, 50
Schonenberg, Fred, 101
Schreier, Martin, 50
Schultz, E. J., 141, 275
Schwindt, Oriana, 295
Scorsese, Martin, 247
Scott, Kendra, 118
Scott, Ridley, 247
Sears, Richard, 374
Securities and Exchange Commission (SEC), *91*
Seinfeld, 287
Select Comfort, 408, **409**
Sernovitz, Andy, 412
Shanker, Deena, 181
Shavitt, Sharon, 124
Sheldrick, Drew, 100
Sherwood, I-Hsien, 251, 368
Shields, Mike, 252, 295
Shinola, 221
Shneyder, Len, 393
Shoup, Mary Ellen, 349
Silber, Tony, 294
Singapore Airlines, 14
Sirius/XM satellite radio, 291
Sleep Number bed, 408, **409**
Slefo, George, 294, 318
Sloane, Garett, 419
Smith, Aaron, 318
Smith, Douglas, 196
Smith, Gerry, 295
Snapchat, 31, 31, 37, 86, 112, 301, 305, 313, 319, 398
Sony, 36, *267,* 361
Southern Living, 382
Southwest Air, **385**
Special K, 216. *See also* Kellogg's
Sprint, 70, 76
Sprite, 16. *See also* Coca-Cola
Sridhar, Shrihari, 51
Stanley, T. L., 226
Starbucks, 33, **33,** 130, 257, 302, 303, **303,** 330, **331,** 400, **401**
Star Trek: The Next Generation, 287
State Farm Insurance, 357
Stein, Lindsay, 418
Stravinsky, Igor, 188, 201
Subaru, 121, 200, **301**
Sugar Association, 92
Sullivan, Laurie, 51, 294
Sullivan, Luke, 251

Susko, Jenna, 275
Swant, Marty, 50, 318
Sweeney, John, 195, 196
Sysco Food Services, 13

T

Taco Bell, 189, **191**, 257
Tadena, Nathalie, 51, 182
Tag Heuer, 221
Tankovska, H., 50
Target, 12, 16, 21, 107, **109, 110,** 114,
    115, 116, **116, 118, 119,** 144, 337,
    338, 274, 401
    back-to-school campaign, **245**
TBWA, 38, 43, 278
Team One Advertising, 192, **192**
Ted, Inc., 404
Ted Bates, **63**
TeleBrands Inc., 388
Terlep, Sharon, 161
Terry, Jeff, 416
Thibodeau, Ian, 275
Thompson, Anne Bahr, 136
Tide, 55, 114, 144, **144, 145,** 153, 216, 327.
    See also Procter & Gamble (P&G)
Tiffany & Co., 83, **83**
TikTok, 9, 29, 31, **32,** 314
Tipping Point, The, 398
Tode, Chantal, 226
Tour of Utah, 402–403
Toy Manufacturers Association, *93*
Toyota, 22, 33, 132, **133,** 138, 167, 181
    Prius, 22, 138
Travel & Leisure, 283
Trejos, Nancy, 141
Trickling Springs Creamery, 20
Tropicana, 136
Troy, Terry, 27
Twitter, 10, 29, 96, 235, 267, 298, 300, **301,**
    312, 398, 398, 401
Tylee, John, 75
Tyson, Jackie, 402
Tzuo, Tien, 294

U

Udi's Gluten Free , **169**
Un-Dead, The, 62
Under Armour, 15, 223–224, **224**
    "Rule Yourself" campaign, Michael Phelps,
        177, 223–224, **224**
Unilever, 12, 14, 19, 83, 145, 151, 168. *See
    also* Axe
United Airlines, 216, 406
United Way, 37

University of Georgia Bulldog, 304
University of Texas Longhorn, 304
Uniworld, 67
UPS, *267*
Uribe, Rodrigo, 50, 161, 317
U.S. Army, 40, 72, 361
USA Today, 259, 266–267, 273, 279, 300
U.S. Brewers Association, *93*
U.S. Bureau of Alcohol, Tobacco, Firearms,
    and Explosives (ATF), *91*
U.S. Census Bureau, 12, 131, 133
U.S. Centers for Disease Control and
    Prevention, 218
U.S. Congress, 60
U.S. Federal Communications Commission
    (FCC), *91*
U.S. Federal Trade Commission (FTC), 67,
    88–90, *90,* 383, **383,** 413
U.S. Food and Drug Administration (FDA), *91*
U.S. Postal Service (USPS), *91*
U.S. Tennis Association, 355
US Weekly, 282

V

Valvoline, 377, **378**
Van Cleef & Arpels, 404
Vans, 132, **132,** 418
Vaughan, Kelly, 141
Verizon, 36, 377
Vespa, 410–411, **411**
Viacom, 46
Vicary, James, 62
Victor, Daniel, 419
Vietnam Airlines, 360
Visa, 7, 23, **24,** *236,* 364, **385**
Vogue, 282
Voleti, Sudhir, 141
Volkswagen (VW), **65, 144, 145,** 216
Vranica, Suzanne, 50

W

Wakabayashi, Daisuke, 319
Waldorf Astoria, 127
Walgreens, 329
Walker, Rob, 141
Wall Street Journal, The, 273, 275, 279, 280,
    387
Wal-Mart, 329, 343, 396
Walt Disney Co., 32, 36, 92, 270, 389
Warby Parker, 379, **379**
Warhol, Andy, 66, **85**
Warner-Lambert, 67
Washington Post, The, 279
Watson, Elaine, 141

WBA. *See* World Bunco Association (WBA)
Weather Channel, 361
Webber, Liz, 226
Wedel, Michel, 161
Wegert, Tessa, 51
Weiser Lock, 339
Wells, Mary, 65, **66**
Wells Fargo & Company, 83, **84**
    "When Two Accounts Become One"
        campaign, **84**
Wells Rich and Green, 65
Westwood One, 290
Whirlpool Corporation, 416
White Castle, 361
Whitehawk, Christine, 161
Wilbur, Kenneth C., 295
Wilker, Deborah, 367
Wilson, Bill, 367
Wilson, Marianne, 348
Wine Institute, *93*
Wingfield, Nick, 318
Wisdom of Teams, The (Katzenbach and
    Smith), 196
Witchel, Alex, 295
Wohl, Jessica, 275, 418
WOMMA. *See* Word of Mouth Marketing
    Association (WOMMA)
Wong Kar-Wai, 72
Woodside, Arch G., 162
Woodyard, Chris, 50
Word of Mouth Marketing Association
    (WOMMA), 412
World Bunco Association (WBA), 357
World Wide Fund for Nature (WWF), **20**
WPP plc, 38–39

Y

Yan, Ruiliang, 27
Yoplait, 416
Young, James Webb, 59
YouTube, **21,** 31, **31,** 37, 109, 130, 174,
    223, 269, 285, 300, 302, 305, 398,
    410, **411**

Z

Zappos, 305, **305,** 338, 374
Zenetti, German, 26, 162, 275
Zenith Media, 275
Zhang, Bo-Lei, 181, 317
Zielske, Hubert, 265
Zindagi Na Milegi Dobara (You Only Live Once)
    (Bollywood film), 363
Zumda, Natalie, 51

Subject Index

Page references in **bold** print indicate ads or photos and key terms. Page references in *italics* indicate tables, charts, or graphs.

3Ps creativity framework, **201**

A

Above-the-line promotion, **258**
Abrasion, 199
Accessibility, **113**
Accessibility bonus, **114**
Accommodation, **11**
Account executives (AE), **193**
Account planner, **43**, 159
Account planning, **159**
Account services, **43**
Account team, **197**
ACS. *See* American Community Survey (ACS)
Action for Children's Television, **67**
Activities, interests and opinions (AIO), 132, 144
Ad blocker, **71, 72**
Administrative services, 44
Advergames, 313
   and video games, 313–314
Advergaming, **313**, 361, 365. *See also* Video game advertising
Advertisements, **9**
   brand meaning through, 144
   comparison, 211–212
   consumer behavior influenced by, 88
   deceptive elements of, 89
   direct response, 158, 384, 387
   display, 307–308
   diversity in, **84**, 86
   humor in, 152, 216–217
   IBP utilizing, 8–9, **9**
   interstitial, 308
   meanings transmitted by, 121–122, *122*, **122**
   minorities portrayed in, 63–66, 67
   in newspapers, 55
   offensive, 84–85
   pop-under, 307
   pop-up, 307
   principles of design in, 239
   with product placement, 221
   radio formats of, 234–235
   sales estimations from, 158
   self-parody in, 70
   social meaning through, 22
   social media, 307
   stereotypes in, 82–83
   target audiences of, 12
   television copywriting for, 232–233
Advertisers, **36–37**

agency relationships with, 45
categories of, 36–37
commercial data sources to, 151
consumer memory and, 152
consumption and, 66
focus groups used by, 144–146
IBP role of, 37–38
media decisions of, 278
message placement coordination of, 365
packaging promotional benefits to, 346
Advertising. *See also* Corporate advertising; Developmental advertising; Digital advertising; Interactive media; Magazine advertising; Mobile marketing; Point-of-purchase advertising; Print advertising; Radio advertising; Social media; Television advertising
   advocacy, 416
   aerial, 345
   affects happiness and general well-being, 80–82
   audiences for, 12–14
   and authenticity, 122
   brand, 21
   brief history of, 53–55
   broadcast, 234–235
   as business process, 14–20
   campaign, 9–10
   cause-related, 416
   to children, 87–88, 90
   cinema, 346
   classified, 281
   clutter, 281
   communication process, 10–12
   competition influenced by, 21
   consumer response to, 328
   consumers educated by, 79–80
   controversial products, 88–89
   cooperative (co-op), 14, 281, 339
   corporate image, **414**, 415–416
   corrective, 92
   and creativity, 82–84
   culture-reflected in, **61, 62**
   defining, **8**
   delayed response, 20–21
   directory, 346
   direct response, 20, 158, 384, 387
   display, 281
   economic influence of, 21–22
   effect on prices, 21–22
   effect on values, 22
   eras of, 55–74

   ethical aspects of, 87–95
   focus on, 10
   global, 14
   IBP and, 3–4
   industrialization era of, 55–56
   institutional, 21
   international, 14, 167
   investments, 259, *259*
   language of, 12, 87
   local, 14
   in marketing mix, 15–19
   mass media and, 55
   mass mediated, 8
   media budgets on, 245–246
   national, 14
   objectives, 276–277
   organizations, 38–42
   out-of-home media, 345–346
   plan, 165–179
   politics and, 68–71
   reaching consumers through, 4
   and rebellion, 121
   reflects society's priorities, 82
   regional, 14
   regulatory agents and, 90–92
   regulatory aspects of, 89–95
   revenue from, 19
   sales promotions, **326**
   and self-regulation programs, *93*
   social aspects of, 79–87
   society and, 56–74
   stereotypes in, 82–83
   structure of, 34–36, *35*
   subliminal, 64, 85
   target audiences of, 48
   technology influencing, 28–31
   on television, 69
   with traditional media, 6–7
   transit, 345
   truth in, 87
   types of, 20–22
   unfair, 89
   in United States, 344
   vertical cooperative, 89–90
   video game, 361
   visuals in, 238
Advertising agencies, **38–42**
   advertisers relationships with, 45
   advertising planning role of, 164–165, 168
   African-Americans and, 67
   agency of record and, 272
   associations and, 93–94
   compensation of, 44–45

441

Advertising agencies, (*Continued*)
  creativity and, 192
  defining, 38
  founding of, 55
  historical context used by, 168
  in-house, 40
  promotion agencies in, 41–42
  research methods and, 142
  services of, 42–44
  types of, *38*, 38–42
  of United Kingdom, 70
Advertising campaign, **10**
Advertising clutter, **114**–115
Advertising plans, 164–165, **165**
  advertising agencies role in, 164–165,
    168
  advertising planning role of, 178–179
  budgeting and, 178–179
  competitor analysis used in, 169
  components of, **166**
  evaluation of, 178
  execution of, 177
  industry analysis used in, 168–169
  in Integrated Brand Promotion, 177
  market analysis used in, 169
  objectives of, 169–173
  situation analysis and, 166–169
  strategy in, 176
  time frames in, 173
Advertising/promotion industry
  advertising agencies in, 38–42
  agency compensation in, 44–45
  agency services in, 42–44
  external facilitators in, 45–46
  feelings/emotions interests of, 155
  interactive media influencing, 70
  persuasion used in, 8, 87, 210
  recall/recognition tests used in, 152–153
  research of, 142–143
  resonance tests of, 155
  self-regulations in, 92–94, *93*
  structure of, **35**
  technology influencing, 28–31
  tracking studies used in, 157
Advertising research firms, 45
Advertising response functions, **174**
Advertising specialties, **334**
Advertising substantiation program, **91**
Advertorials, 215
Advocacy, 212, 364
Advocacy advertising, **416**
Aerial advertising, **345**
Affective association, 215–218
Affirmative disclosure, **92**
African-Americans, 67, **68**, 120
Agency of record, **272**
Agency services, 42–44
Aided recall, 153

AIO. *See* Activities, interests and opinions
    (AIO)
Alcohol consumption, 88
All-in-one single source data, 159
Allowances, 339
American Civil War, 54
American Community Survey (ACS), 150
  all-in-one single source, 159
  cable television in, 286
  computer models, 271
  internal company sources of, 150
  single source, 159
AM radio, 290
Anxiety advertisements, 219
App ads, 4, 34, **307**. *See also* Mobile
    marketing
Appropriation, **98**
Approval process, 236–238
Art direction, 238–246
  design in, 239
  illustration in, 238–239
  in interactive media, 244–245
  layout in, 243
  print production typography and, 244
  in radio, 234–235
  in television, **247**
Art directors, 7, 43, 64, 229–230
Attention, clutter and, 114–115
Attitude study, **155**
Attitude(s), **115**
  consumer's brand, 155
  copy research and, 155
  decision-making involving, 115
  testing of, 216
Attorney general, 92
Audience, **11**. *See also* Consumers; Target
    audiences/segments
  categories of, 12–14
  defined, 12
  geography and, 14
  headlines attracting, 231
  interactive media and, 235–236
  interest, 282–283
  of magazine advertising, 285
  profiling, 144
  research profiling, 144
  selectivity, 282, 288
  share of, 289
  of television advertising, 289
Authenticity, **361**
  and advertising, 122
  and brand, 9
Automated media buying, 271–272, 277,
    307–308. *See also* Programmatic
    buying
Automobile racing, 17, 362–363
Average-user testimonial, 214
Axis, **242**

B

Baby boomers, 63
Badao, 167
Balance, **240**
Banner ads, 281, 307–308
Barter syndication, **287**
Behavioral retargeting, 309
Behavioral targeting, **95**
Belgium, 407
Below-the-line promotions, **258**
Benchmarks, 176
Benefit segmentation, **132**–133
Benefits
  of event sponsorship, 357–358
  packaging promotional, 346
  of products, 108
Berlin Wall, 69
Better Business Bureau (BBB), 92, 93
Between-vehicle duplication, **263**
Bids, 248
Big data, **150**, 261, 309
Bill-back allowances, **339**
Billboards, 344–345
Blackletter, **244**
Blocking, 248
Blogs, **32**, 92, 302, 303. *See also* Microblogs,
    Social media
Body copy, 231–232
Bonus, accessibility, 114
Boycotts, 95
Brainstorming, **199**
Brand, **15**
Brand advertising, **21**
Brand ambassador, **109**
Brand awareness, **170**
Brand buzz, 410, *413*
Brand communities, **121**
Brand conversations, 397–399
Branded entertainment, **72**, 72, 268–269,
    362–365
  approaches to, 268–269
  automobile racing and, 362–363
  future of, 364–365
  in IBP, 350–352
  with product placement, 72, 222,
    268–269
Branded experience, **357**
Brand equity, **16**
Brand extension, **16**
Brand heroic, 238, **239**
Branding, **54**
  advertising and cultural, 121
  point-of-purchase, 206
Brand loyalty, **16**
  among consumers, 16
  building, 7, 15
  decision-making mode with, 113

event sponsorship and, 357
through emotional appeal, 113
Brand platform, **138**
Brand promise, **138**
Brands, 15, 120. *See also* Integrated Brand
    Promotion
    advertisements giving meaning, 144
    attracting attention to, **326**
    awareness of, 7
    building of, 363
    celebrity endorsements of, 92
    consumer attitudes of, 155
    consumer relationship with, 268–269
    consumers co-creating, 71
    consumers influenced by, 408–409
    core, 400
    core values of, **401**
    crowdsourcing building, 33–34
    demographics/strength of, *261*
    differentiation of, 17–18
    emotional connection with, 187–188
    equity of, 16
    event sponsorship/leveraging of, 359
    extension of, 16
    free media exposure of, 404
    image and visibility, 304–306
    image/language and, 220
    image of, *15,* 16, 220, **414–415**
    implicit memory measures and, 153
    integration, 365
    introducing/expanding, 16
    loyalty, 16
    marketing of, 55
    meaning, 144
    message strategy/recall of, 205–208
    names, 206–209
    online community for, 71, **72**
    positioning of, 18
    proliferation of, 329
    promoting, 258–259
    purchases of, 331
    recognition tests and, 153, **154**
    social context for, 238
    social meaning of, 22, 221–222
    social media and, 135, 300–306
    success of, 7
    switching, 172
    value, 232
    variant, 16
Brand switching, **172**
Brand value, 324
Brand variant, **16**
Brand virtual identity, 303–306
Brazil, 14
Broadcast advertising, 234–235
Broadcast media, **47**
Budgeting. *See also* Costs
    advertising plans and, 173–176
    approval, 246

for budget dollars, 365
competition in, 365
evaluation in, 178
execution, 177
media, 245
modifying in, 176
objective-and-task approach in, 174–175, *175*
percentage-of-sales approach in, 173–174
response models in, 174
share of voice in, 174
strategies, 176
television advertising, 247
Build-up analysis, **175**
Bulk emails, 386
Business gifts, 340
Business markets (business-to-business).
    See also Retailers
    consumer markets and, 133
    creative selling in, 389
    defining, **133**
    point-of-purchase advertising and, 343
    sales promotions in, 340–341, 343
Business-market sales promotions, **325**
Business organizations, members of, 12–13
Buyer's remorse, 110
Buying services, 271–273
    and media planning, 43–44
Buzz marketing, **410–413**

C

Cable television (CATV), **286**
Campaign, 9–10, 12, 71. *See also*
    Advertisements, Advertising
CAN SPAM Act, 96
Capital, 53
Capitalism, 53
Cast, 248
CATV. *See* Cable television (CATV)
Cause-related advertising, **416**
Cease-and-desist order, **91**
Celebrities, 114
    endorsements, 92
    testimonials, 212–214, 387–388
CGC. *See* Consumer-generated content (CGC)
Chain of needs, **58**
Channel grazing, **289**
Chaos Scenario, 352
Children. *See also* Youth culture
    advertising to, 87–88, 90
    demographic segmentation and, 131
    privacy concerns of, 90
Children's Online Privacy Protection Act
    (COPPA), 90
Children's Television Act, 88
Cinema advertising, **346**

Claim-recall, 152–153
Classified advertising, **281**
Click fraud, **313**
Click-through, **311**
Clients, 8, **36**
Closed-circuit television, 287
Clutter
    advertising, 281
    and attention, 114–115
    magazine, 284
    media, 32–33, 329
    television, 289
Cognitive dissonance, **110**
Cognitive residue, 152
Cognitive response analysis, **152**. *See also*
    Thought listings
Cognitive style, **199**
Cold War, 61
Color (in illustrations), 238–239
Commercial sources, 151
Commission system, **44**
Commitment, 188, 209
Committed users, 128
Communications. *See also* Language; Peer-
    to-peer communications
    audience interpretation of, 12
    clutter and, 11
    consumers interpreting, 11
    integrated marketing, 22–24
    internal, 400
    model of mass-mediated, 10–12
    sales objectives with, 172–173
    technology, 68
    vehicles for, 406
Communication test, 151–152
Communism, 61
Communities, 71, **72**, **120**
Comp, **243**
Company e-newsletters, 403
Comparison advertisements, **90**, 211–212
Compensation, 44–45
Competition
    advertising's influence on, 21–22
    clutter and, 284
    regulations and, 90
    sales promotions influencing, 332
    sampling and, 335–336
    strategies for, 331–332
Competitive fields, **134**
Competitive media assessments, 266
Competitor analysis, **169**
Comprehensive layout, 243
Computers, models from, **270**, 271
Concept testing, **144**
Connectors, 412–413
Consent order, **91**
Consideration set, **109**
Consultants, **45**

Consumer-based strategy, **185**
Consumer behavior
    advertisements influence on, 88
    community influence on, 120–121
    consumption stages in, 106
    cultural values influencing, 106
    data about, 381
    defining, **106**
    ethnicity and, 119–120
    of families, 118–119
    gender influence in, 120
    politics influencing, 120
    psychographics and, 132
Consumer–brand relationship, 111
Consumer culture, **56**
Consumer-event congruity/fit, **358**
Consumer Finance Protection Agency (CFPA), *91*
Consumer-generated content (CGC), **71**, 245
Consumer insight, **143**
Consumerism, **95**
Consumer markets, **133**, 324, 330–338.
    See also Household consumers
Consumer-market sales promotion, 324
Consumer organizations, 95
Consumer package goods (CPG), **106**, 113
Consumer perception, 17
Consumer publications, 282–285
Consumers
    advertising educating, 79–80
    advertising reaching, 4
    attitude studies of, 155
    brand attitudes of, 153
    brand influence on, 408
    brand loyalty among, 16–17
    brands co-created by, 71
    brands emotional connection with,
        187–188
    brands relationship with, 268–269
    communications interpretation by, 11
    control, 31–32
    creativity attracting attention of, 186–187
    culture influencing, 115–117
    decision-making process of, 108–110
    embedded consumption practices of, 149
    frame-by-frame testing of, 155
    household, 12
    information search of, 108–109
    memory of, 152
    message strategy persuading, 208–215
    perceptions of, 17
    persuasion and, 208–215
    postpurchase evaluation of, 109–110
    privacy protection of, 95–96
    purchases of, 109
    as regulatory agents, 95
    resonance tests of, 155
    response testing of, 158
    sales promotion response of, 327–328

    as social beings, 115
Consumer sales promotion, **41**
Consumer virtual identity, 303
Consumption
    advertisers and, 66
    alcohol, 88
    consumer behavior stages in, 107–110
    embedded practices of, 148
    gender and, 120
    materialism and, 82
    in society, 85
Content marketing, 5, **48**
Contests, 97, *97*, 314, **334**–335
Continuity, **264**
Continuous scheduling, **264**
Controversial products, 88–89
Conversion, **109**
Cooperative advertising, **14**, 281, 339
Coordination, 365
Copy approval process, 236–237
Copy research, 151–157
    attitude changes and, 155
    cognitive residue in, 152–157
    developmental, 237
    evaluative criteria in, 151, 237
    politics in, 151
    recognition tests and, 153
    research and, 143–157, 237
Copyright infringement, 98
Copy strategy, 177
Copywriting, **229**
    approval process in, 236–237
    art directors and, 229–230
    for broadcast advertising, 234
    challenges to, 232
    dialogue in, 231
    for digital media/interactive media,
        235–236
    for print advertising, 231–232
    for radio, 234–235
    slogans/taglines used in, 236–237
    for television, 232–233
Corporate advertising, **21**, 414–417
    magazine/television using, 415
    objectives of, 414–415
    types of, 415–416
Corporate image advertising, **414**, 415–416
Corrective advertising, **92**
Cost-per-click (CPC), **307**
Cost per inquiry (CPI), **380**
Cost per order (CPO), **380**
Cost per thousand (CPM), **266**
Costs
    of magazine advertising, 285
    of newspaper advertising, 281
    of radio advertising, 291
    of sales promotions, 340
    of television advertising, 249, 287
Coupons, 96, 314, **332**–333, *332*

CPI. *See* Cost per inquiry
CPM. *See* Cost per thousand
CPM-TM. *See* Cost per thousand target
    market (CPM-TM)
CPO. *See* Cost per order (CPO)
Creative abrasion, **199**
Creative boutiques, **39**–40
Creative brief, **197**, *198,* 229, *230*
Creative directors, 43, 200, 230
Creative revolution, 63–66
Creatives
    in advertising business, 188–189
    lifestyle research of, 144
    message strategy and, 209, 211,
        217–218, 219, 222
    science conflict with, 195
    social media challenge to, 228
Creative selling, **389**–390
Creative services, **43**
Creative teams, **229**, 230
Creativity, **187**, **189**–191
    across domains, 187–191
    advertising agencies and, 194–195
    in the business world, 190
    and caution, 190–191
    commitment in, 188
    consumers attracted by, 186–187
    creative team and, 229
    defining, 187
    fostering, 199
    framework for, 201
    importance of, 186–187
    management conflicts with, 192–196
    marginality and, 188
    opportunities, 281
    process, 191–196
    stifling, 201
    team collaboration, 196–200
    through team, 199
Credibility, 280
Crisis communications, **399**
Cross-selling, **382**
Crowdsourcing, **3**
Cultural branding, advertising and, 121
Cultural capital, 118, **119**
Cultural movements, 222–223
Cultural revolution, 63, 121
Culture, **56**
    advertising reflecting, **60–61**
    consumer, 55
    consumers influenced by, 115–116
    international advertising and, 167
    rituals in, 116
    youth, 69
Current Population Survey, 150
Customer relationship management (CRM),
    45–46, **390**–391
Customers
    alienating, 341

direct marketing response of, 387
satisfaction, **110**
Cyber-identity theft, **311**

D

Dailies, **55**
Damage control, 399–400
DAR. *See* Day-after-recall (DAR)
Dark side of digital, social, mobile media, 311–312
Data
  about consumer behavior, 380
  big data, 150, 261, 309–310
  for demographics, 380
Database agencies, **41**
Database marketing
  applications of, 382
  mailing lists in, 380–381
  privacy concerns in, 382–384
Day-after-recall (DAR), 153, 208
Dayparts, **292**
Deception, **87**, 89
Decision-making
  attitudes involved in, 115
  with brand loyalty, 113
  in teams, 197
Defamation, **98**
Delayed-response advertising, **20**
Demographic(s)
  brand strength and, *261*
  data for, 380
  newspaper readers and, 280
  segmentation by, **131**, *261*
Demonstration, 214
Design, **238**
Designers, **41**
Design firms, 41
Design principles, 238–239
Design thinking, 144
Developmental advertising
  audience profiling in, 144
  commercial sources in, 151
  concept testing in, 144
  design thinking in, 144
  field work in, 149
  focus groups in, 144–146
  government sources in, 150
  IBP research and, 143–149
  internal company sources in, 150
  projective techniques in, 146–148
Developmental copy research, 237
Developmental research, 150
Dialogue, **231**
  balloons, **146**
  in copywriting, 231
Differentiation, **17**–18

Digital advertising, **38**. *See also* Email, Interactive media, Internet, Mobile marketing, social media
  and online search, 307
  types of, 307
Digital billboard displays, 345
Digital footprint, **130**
Digital/interactive agencies, **40**, 46
Digital media, 6–7, 235, 244
  advantages of, 310–311
  privacy issues of, 310–311
Digital video recorders (DVRs), **289**
Direct mail, **385**
Direct marketing, 314, 384–388
  advantages of, 378–380
  challenges of, 388
  customer response to, 387
  defining, **372**
  direct mail in, 385
  email in, 385–387
  evolution of, 374–377
  history of, 372–374
  milestones of, *375*
  privacy and, 95–96
  regulation issues with, 95–96
  telemarketing in, 387
  uses of, 374–377
Direct marketing agencies, **41**
Directors
  art, 7, 43, 64, 229–230
  creative, 43, 199, 230
  of television advertising, 43
Directory advertising, **346**
Direct response, **157**, 158
  copy, 231–232
Direct response advertising, **20**, 158, 384, 387
Direct-response agency, **41**
Direct response copy, **231–232**
Display advertising, **281**
Display/banner ads, 281, **307**
Distribution, 338
Distributors, 36–37
Diversity, **84**, 86
Do Not Call Registry, 96, 383, 387
DVRs. *See* Digital video recorders (DVRs)

E

Earned media, **300**
E-commerce, 314
  regulation issues with, 95–96
Economies of scale, **19**
Economy, 21–22, 63
Editorial houses, 246
Education, 117, 131
Effective frequency, **262**
Effective reach, **262**
Effective search, 262

Electronic word of mouth (eWOM), **398**
Email, 45, 314, 385–387
  bulk, 385
  in direct marketing, 385
  marketing strategies, 96, 234
Embedded consumption practices, **149**
Emergent consumers, **130**
Emotion, 114
Emotional appeal
  brand loyalty through, 113
  emotional appeal in, 231–232
  in print advertising, 231–232
  research and, 151
  truth in advertising and, 87
Emotional benefits, 113, 138
Emphasis, 242–243
Employees, 13
Endorsements, 92
Ephemeral, 302
Episodic memory, 114
E-revolution, 70
Esteem needs, 81
E-tail, Integrated Brand Promotion (IBP) and, 309–310
Ethics, **87**–89, 365. *See also* Controversial products; Dark side; Greenwashing; Privacy
Ethnicity, 119–120
Ethnocentrism, **167**
Ethnographic research, **149**
Evaluation, advertisement plan and, 178
Evaluative copy research, 151, 237
Evaluative criteria, **109**
  in copy research, 152, 237
  of IBP, 151
  for products, 109–110
Event-planning agencies, **41**
Event social responsibility, **354**
Event sponsorship, **352**
  benefits, assessment of, 357–358
  brand leveraging in, 359
  brand loyalty and, 357
  guidelines of, 358
  in IBP, 353–359
  measurement, **356**
  spot for, 356
  users of, 354–356
Evoked set, **205**
Evolution
  of advertising
    1800-1875, 55–56
    1875-1918, 56–57
    1918-1929, **57**, 57–59, **58–60**
    1929-1941, 59–60
    1942-1960, 60–63, **60–66**
    1960-1972, 63–66
    1973-1980, 66–68
    1980-1992, 68–69
    1993-2000, 70–71
    2000-present, 71–73

Evolution (*Continued*)
  pre-1800, 55
  of direct marketing, 374
Execution, 177
Experiential marketing, **352**, 352
Expert spokespeople, 213
Exposure, to ad, 23, 152, 153, 155, 156, 260,
    263, 267, 281
Extended problem solving, **111**–112
External facilitators, **45**–46
External lists, **380**
External position, **18**
External search, **109**
Eye-tracking systems, 156, **157**

F

Fair Credit Reporting Act, 90
Fair Packaging and Labeling Act, 90
Fake news, **303**
Families, 63–64, 118–119, 416
Fashion, advertising and, *122*
Fear-appeal advertisements, 218
Feature stories, 403
Federal Communications Commission (FCC)
    advertising regulation of, *91*
    Do Not Call Registry and, 96
    sales promotions and, 341
Federal Trade Commission (FTC), **67**, 90, *91*
    Do Not Call Registry and, 96
    legislative mandates of, 90–92
    regulatory programs of, 91–92
Federal Trade Commission Act, 60
Feel-good advertisements, 215–216
Fee systems, **44**
Feminism, 67
Fieldwork, **149**
Fifty-Foot Woman, The, 62
Films, on Internet, 222, 359
First-run syndication, **287**
Flighting, **264**
Flowchart, for media planning, *271*
FM radio, 290
Focus groups, **144**–146
Fonts, type, 243
Food and Drug Administration (FDA), *91*
Forgetting function, **265**
Formal balance, **240**
Frame-by-frame tests, **155**
Free premium, **334**
Free-standing inserts (FSI), **281**
Frequency, **262**
Frequency-marketing programs, 382
Frequency programs, **338**, 341
FSI. *See* Free-standing inserts (FSI)
Fulfillment centers, **41**
Full-service agency, **39**
Functional benefits, 138

G

Gender, 116, 118, 120
Geodemographic segmentation, **381**
Geofencing, **95**
Geographic scope, **260**
Geography
  magazine's selectivity of, 288
  newspaper's selectivity of, 279–280
  segmentation by, 131
Geo-targeting, **260**
Gift cards, 336
Global advertising, **14**
Globalization, advertising and, 14
Goodwill, 400
Government officials/employees, **13**
Government regulations, 90–95
Government sources, 151
Great Depression, **59**–60
Great Recession, 71–73
Green marketing, **416**
Greenwashing, **417**
Gross domestic product (GDP), **21**
Gross impressions, 263, **263**
Gross rating points (GRP), 263, **263**
GRP. *See* Gross rating points (GRP)

H

Habits, **112**–113
Hard-sell ads, 211
Headlines, **231**
Heavy users, **128**
Historical context, 168
Household consumers, **12**
Households using television (HUT), **289**
Humor
  in advertisements, 152, 216–217
  strategic implications of, 217
HUT. *See* Households using television (HUT)
Hyper-localism, **282**
Hyper-localism newspaper, 281

I

IBP. *See* Integrated brand promotion (IBP)
Identity, 119
Illustrations, **238**
  art direction with, 238
  color in, 238
  formats in, 238
  visuals and, 238–249
Image
  advertisements, 220, **220**
  brand, *15,* 16, 221, **414**
  corporate, **414–415**, 415, **416**

IMC. *See* Integrated marketing
    communications (IMC)
Implicit memory measures, **153**
Incentives, 338
Increasing income inequality, 117
Individualism, 197
Industrialization era, of advertising, 55–56
Industrial revolution, **53**–54
Industry analysis, **168**–169
Inelasticity of demand, **19**
Influencer marketing, **408**–413
Infomercials, **41**, 214–215
Informal balance, **240**
Information overload, simplification and, 114
Information search, 108–109
Informercials, 387–388
In-house agencies, **40**
Inquiry/direct response measures, **157**
Inserts, 281
Institutional advertising, **21**
In-store sampling, **336**
Integrated Brand Promotion (IBP)
  advertisements used in, **9**, 9–10
  advertisers role in, 38
  advertising and, 3–4
  advertising plan in, 178
  branded entertainment in, 350–352
  defined, **8**–9
  developmental advertising research and,
      143–148
  digital media used in, 6
  and e-tail, 309–310
  evaluative criteria of, 152
  event sponsorship in, 353–359
  product placement in, 350–352, 359–362
  synergization, 313–316
Integrated marketing communications (IMC),
      22
Interactive communication, 312
Interactive media, **46**, **70**
  art direction/production in, 244
  audience and, 235
  copywriting for, 235–236
Interactivity, 311
Internal company sources, 150
Internal lists, **380**
Internal position, **18**
Internal search, **108**
International advertising, **14**, 167. *See also*
      Globalization
International Social Survey Programme, 150
Internet. *See also* Digital advertising, Digital
      media, Interactive communication,
      Mobile marketing, Social media,
      Web 2.0
  films on, 222, 359
  IBP strategies with, 298–299
  and mobile radio, 290–291

online community on, 71, **72**
radio, 290–291
self-regulation of, 95
social networking on, 267–268
strategies, 298–299
Interpersonal abrasion, **199**
Interstitial ad, **308**
Interviews, 403
long, 149
Inventions, 55
Inventory, 331, 334, 338
Involvement, 110–111

J

Jingles, 207, 208
Junk mail, **385**

K

Knowledge, 154

L

Language, 13
of advertising, 12, 87
brand image and, 220
cultural revolution and, 64
in radio advertising, 234
Latinos, 119
Layout, **243**
Leadership, 197
Lead users, 128
Legal issues, 341
Legislative mandates, of FTC, 90–92
Leverage, **359**
LGBTQ (lesbian, gay, bisexual, transgender, queer) consumers, 64, 83, 119
Libel, **98**
Life-stage variables, **119**
Lifestyle research, **144**
Lifestyles, 79, 132
Lifestyle segmentation, **132**
Lighting, 238, 248, 344
Limited liability, principle of, 54
Limited problem solving, **112**
List enhancement, 381
Lists, external/internal, 380–381
Lobbying, 400
Local advertising, **14**
Local spot radio advertising, **291**
Local television, **287**
Location-based technologies, 302
Logos, **41**
Long interview, **149**
Long-copy email, **235**
Long-copy landing page, **235**

Lotteries, 88, 342
Love and belonging needs, 81

M

Madison & Vine in IBP, 222
Magazine advertising
corporate advertising and, 415
costs of, 285
future of, 285
Magazines, 282–285
advantages of, 282–284
clutter in, 284
disadvantages of, 284–285
future of, 285
special interests in, **283**
top advertisers in, **283**
Magnetic Resonance Imaging (MRI), 155, *156*
Mailing lists, **380**
Mail sampling, **336**
Management, 192–196
Manufacturers, 36, 340
Marcom manager, **388**
Marginal analysis, 174, *175*
Marginality, 188
Marketing, **15**. *See also* Database
Marketing; Direct Marketing;
Mobile marketing
advertising in, 15–20
brand buzz in, 410–411, *413*
of brands, 54
content, 5
database, **380**–382
email, 45, 96, 235
frequency, 382
green, 416
influencer, 408–413
integrated communications, 22
mobile, 5, 315–316
niche, 134
point-of-entry, 130
PRIZM, 131
purpose-driven, 416
strategies, 127
viral, 315, 410–411
Marketing mix, *15,* **15**–20, 21
Marketing research services, 43, 45
Market analysis, **169**
Market niche, 134
Market segmentation, **17**–18, 128–133
Markup charges, **44**
Maslow's hierarchy of needs, 81, *192*
Mass media, 55, 86
Mass mediated advertising, 8
Mass-mediated communications, 10–12
Materialism, 79, 81–82, **116**, 195
M-Commerce, 315–316. *See also* Mobile
Marketing

Meanings, 10–12, **22**, 115, *122,*
121–122
Measured media, **258**
Media. *See also* Digital media; Interactive
media; Radio; Social media;
Support media; Television;
Traditional media
advertiser's decisions on, 278
budgets, 266
buying, 43–44, **271**, 277, 307
class, **260**
clutter, 32–33, 329
competitive assessment of, 266
digital, 235–236, 244–245
efficiency, 266–267
flowcharts, *271*
impressions, **357**, 362
mass, 55, 86
measurement, 5, 178, 289, 358
mix, **260**
mobile, 34
objective, 260–265
organizations, 46
planning and buying services, 43–44
planning model, 269–271
plans, 177, **260**
proliferation, 32
social, 31–32
specialists, 40–41
spending, 272, *273*
strategies, 260–265, 278–285
types in social media, 300–301
unmeasured, 259
vehicles, **260**
Media-buying service, **272**
Media organizations, 35, 94
in advertising/promotion industry, 46
competitive media assessments, 266
efficiency in, 266–267
multiplatform, 32
Media planner, **229**
Media planning, 177, 229
brand promotion spending in, 256–257,
259
buying services and, **43**–44, 270
computer models for, 271
flowchart for, *271*
forgetting function, 265
GRP in, 263, **263**
media strategies in, 260–265
message weight and, 262–263
spending in, 256–257, *259*
Media specialist, **40**–41
Members of a trade channel, **13**
Members of business organizations, **12**
Memory, 152
Merchandise allowances, **339**
Mergers and acquisitions, 90

Message content, 406
Message impressions, 263
Message placement, 365
Message strategies, 204–224
    affective association in, 215–218
    anxiety inducing advertisements, 218–219
    brand image in, 220
    brand recall in, 205–208
    consumer persuasion in, 210–215
    creatives and, 209, 211, 217–218, 219
    fear-appeal advertisements in, 218
    objectives/methods in, *206*
    social/cultural movements in, 222–223
    social meaning in, 221–222
    transformational ads in, 223–224
Message weight, **262**–263
Metaphors, 147
Microblogs, 302, **303**
Micro-target, **261**
Mindshare brands, **107**
Minorities, 63–66, **68**
Missionary salesperson, **389**
Mobile applications (apps), **302**
Mobile marketing, 5, 34, **315**–316, 343
Mobile sampling, **336**
Monopoly power, **90**
Movies, 360–361. *See also* Branded
        entertainment; Product placement
MRI. *See* Magnetic Resonance
        Imaging (MRI)
Multiplatform media organizations, 32
Music. *See also* Jingles
    branded entertainment and, 222
    radio advertisements and, 234–235
    suppliers, 246–249

N

NAICS. *See* North American Industry
        Classification System (NAICS)
Narratives, **231**
Narrowcasting, **288**
Narrowcasting programming, 288
National advertising, **14**
National Advertising Division (NAD), 92–93
National Advertising Review Board (NARB),
        67, 92–93, *94*
National spot radio advertising, **291**
Native advertising, **307**
Needs
    creating, 81
    esteem, 81
    love and belonging, 81
    Maslow's hierarchy of, **81**, *192*
    physiological, 81
    products satisfying, 108
    recognition, 108
    safety, 81
    self-actualization, 81
Need state, **108**

Negative publicity, 400
Negotiations, **11**
Netnography, **150**
Network radio advertising, 290, **291**
Network television, **285**
Neuroscience, 155–156, 218
New media. *See* Digital media; Interactive
        media; Mobile marketing; Social
        media
Newspaper advertising
    advantages of, 280
    categories of, 281
    costs of, 280
    disadvantages of, 281
Newspapers
    demographics and, 280
    early advertising in, 56
    future of, 281–282
    geographic selectivity of, 280
    segmentation and, 281
Niche marketing, **134**
Normative testing, 151
Normative test scores, **151**
North American Industry Classification System
        (NAICS), 133
Not-for-profit organizations, 12, 37

O

Objective-and-task approach, **174**–175, *176*
Objectives
    of advertising plans, 169–173
    of corporate advertising, 414–415
    of media, 260–265
    in message strategy, *206*
    of public relations, 400–401
    sales, 172–173
Offensive advertisements, 84–85
Off-invoice allowances, **339**
Off-network syndication, **287**
Omnichannel strategy, **374**
Online communities, 70, **71**
Online media. *See* Digital media; Internet;
        Interactive media; Social media
Online resistance, **312**
Online search, digital advertising and,
        307–309
On-package sampling, **336**
Opinion leaders, **121**, 409
Order, **242**
Order taking, **388**
Outdoor signage, 334
Out-of-home media advertising, **345**–346
Oversaturation, 364
Owned media, **300**

P

Packaging, **346**
Paid media, **300**

Paid search, **308**–309
Parallel layout structure, **242**
Pass-along readership, **283**
Pay-for-inquiry advertising model, **282**
Pay-for-results, **45**
Payout time frame, 175
Peer-to-peer communications, 408, 409
    connectors in, 412–413
Percentage-of-sales approach, **173**
Perceptual space, 18
Permanent long-term displays, 342
Personal growth, 197
Personal selling, **388**
Persuasion
    advertising/promotion using, 8, 87, 210
    consumers and, 210–215
    fear-appeal advertisements influencing,
        218
    information and, 16
    personal selling using, 388
    strategic planning triangle and, 138–139,
        139
    subliminal, 63–64
Phishing, **96**
Photo sharing sites, 302–303
Physiological assessment, **155**–156
Physiological needs, 81
Picas, **244**
Picture completion, 146
Plan, advertising 165–179
Podcast advertising, 234–235
Point, **244**
Point-of-entry marketing, **130**
Point-of-purchase advertising, **329**, **342**
    branding and, 207–208
    defining, 342
    objectives of, 342
    sales promotions with, 341
    trade/business markets and, 343
    types of, 342–343
Point size, 244
Politics
    advertising and, 70–71, 86–87
    consumer behavior and, 120
    publicity and, 404
Pop-under ads, **307**
Pop-up ad, **307**
Pop-up/pop-under copy, **235**
Positioning, **18**. *See also* STP marketing
        (segmenting targeting-positioning)
    benefits, 138
    repositioning and, 135–136
    strategies in, 127, **137**–138
    themes in, 137
Positive realism, 67, **68**
Post ads, **307**
Postproduction, 246–249
Postpurchase evaluation, 111–112
Potential ad impressions, 263
PPC. *See* Pay-per-click (PPC)
Predecisional distortion, 113

Preindustrialization era, of advertising, 55
Prelight, **248**
Premium offers, 96, 334
Premiums, 96
Preprinted inserts, **281**
Preproduction stage, **246**–249, *247*
Press conferences, 403
Press releases, 401–403
Price-off deals, **333**–334
Price orientation, 341
Prices, 21–22
Pricing flexibility, 19
Primary demand, **88**
Primary demand stimulation, **20**
Principle of limited liability, **54**
Principles of design, **239**–240
Print advertising. *See also* magazine
        advertising; newspaper advertising
    copywriting for, 231–232
    design principles in, 239–240
    headline purpose in, 231
    recognition tests used in, 153
    strategic planning in, 278
    subheads in, 231
Print production, 244
Privacy, 95–96
    children and, 90
    concerns of, 382–384
    consumer protection concerning, 95–96
    cross, 382
    direct marketing and, 95–96
    public relations problem of, 98
    regulation issues on, 98
    on television, 98
Privacy seal, **312**
PRIZM (potential rating index by zip
        marketing), 131
Proactive public relations strategy, **405**
Problem solving, extended/limited, 111–112
Production
    facilitators, **45**–46
    houses, 246–249
    in interactive media, 244–245
    post/pre, 246–249, *247*
    print, 244
    of radio advertising, 234–235
    services, **43**
    stage, **248**
    television advertising timetable for, 249
    television costs of, 249, 288
Product placement, 72, **359**–362
    activity report of, 222
    advertisements with, 222
    branded entertainment with, 222,
        268–269
    challenges of, 361–362
    consumers and, 365
    ethics, 87
    future of, 364
    in IBP, 350–352
    movies with, 360–361

on television, 97, 360
in videogames, 361
Products
    benefits of, 108
    controversial, 88–89
    need satisfaction with, 108
    relevant evaluative criteria of, 109–110
    with social meaning, 120–121
Professionals, **13**
Program ratings, **289**
Programmatic media buying, **271**–273, 277,
        278, 288, 313. *See also* Automated
        media buying
Projective techniques, **146**–148
Promotion agencies, 38–44, **41**
Promotional benefits, 346
Proportion, 242, **242**
PSA. *See* Public service announcements
Psychographics, **132**
P. T. Barnum era, of advertising, 56–57
Publicity, **404**
    and public relations, 314
Public relations, **396**–407
    brand conversations and, 397–399
    damage control in, 399–400
    firms, 41
    negative publicity and, 400
    objectives of, 400–401
    plan, 406
    privacy problem of, 98
    proactive, 405–406
    publicity and, 314
    reactive, 387, 406–407
    regulatory issues in, 98
    strategies in, 404–407
    tools of, 401–404
Public relations audit, **405**
Public relations firm, **42**
Public relations plan, **405**
Public service announcements (PSA), 8, 396
Puffery, **87**
Pulsing, **265**
Purchases, 109
    intent in, **171**
    new brand, 331
    repeat, 330–331
Pure Food and Drug Act, **56**
Purpose-driven marketing, **416**
Push money, **339**
Push strategy, **338**

Q

QR codes, 301, **302**
Quantitative benchmarks, 173

R

Race, 116, 119–120, 131, 142
Radio

advertising emergence in, 60
AM/FM, 290
copywriting for, 59–60, 234
internet, 291
local spot, 291
national spot, 291
network, **290**, 291
satellite, 291
selectivity, 292
syndication, **290**
types of, 291
Radio advertising, 290–292
    advantages of, 291–292
    audience of, 292
    categories of, 290–291
    cost of, 291
    disadvantages of, 292
    formats of, 234
    future of, 292
    guidelines to, 234–235
    language in, 234
    music and, 235
    types, 291
Ratings points, **289**
Reach, **261**–262
Reactive public relations, **405**, 407
Reason-why ads, 210–211
Rebates, **337**
Rebellion, advertising and, 121
Recall tests, **152**–153
Recession, 59–60, 71–73
Recognition, **153**
Recognition tests, 153
Regional advertising, **14**
Regulations
    in advertising, 89–95
    agents involved in, 90–95
    competition and, 90
    consumers enforcing, 95
    direct marketing/e-commerce issues with,
        95–96
    e-commerce, 95–96
    FCC advertising, *91*
    FTC, 91–92
    government, 90–92
    industry self, 92–94
    internet self, 95
    product placement issues and, 97–98
    public relation issues and, 98
    sales promotion issues with, 96–98
    state, 92
Repeat purchases, **172**, 330–331
Repetition, 206–207
Repositioning, 18, 135–136
Research. *See also* Copy research;
        Neuroscience
    account planning *versus,* 159
    advertising, 142–143
    advertising agencies and, 142–143
    advertising firms for, 45
    attitude changes and, 154–155

Research. *See also* Copy research;
  Neuroscience (*Continued*)
  audience profiling and, 144
  copy research and, 143–157, 237
  developmental advertising and,
    143–149
  feelings/emotions and, 155
  focus groups and, 144–146
  government sources and, 150
  international advertising and, 167
  marketing services of, 43, 45
  media planning models for, 269
  in memory, 152
  physiological changes and, 155–156
  services, 260, *261,* 270
Resonance tests, **155**
Response models, 174
Retailers, 329, 338
Retargeting, **309**
Return on investment (ROI), 70, 134, 158,
    328, 362
Revenue generation, 19
Revolution
  creative, 63–66
  cultural, 63, 121
  industrial, 53–54
  sexual, 63–64
RFM analysis (recency, frequency and
    monetary), **382**
Riding the boards, 344
Rituals, **116**
Roaring Twenties, 57
Robinson-Patman Act, 90, 96
ROI. *See* Return on investment (ROI)
Roman fonts, **244**
Rough layout, **243**

S

Safety needs, 81
Sales
  advertisements estimation of, 158
  budgeting and, 173
  communications in, 172–173
  creative, 389
  future, 341
  objectives, 172–173
  personal, 388
  system, 389
  trade, 36
Sales force, 172, **389**
Salesperson, **389**
Sales promotion agencies, 41
Sales promotions, 96–98, 314
  in advertising, **326**
  in business markets, 325, 340–341, 343
  competition influenced by, 331–332
  consumer-market, 324, 330–338
  contests/sweepstakes in, 314
  costs of, 341

coupons in, 332–333, *333*
  defining, **324**–325
  growth in, 327–330
  in IBP, 324–325, 331–332
  importance of, 226–227
  point-of-purchase, 342–343
  rebates in, 337
  regulation issues with, 96–98
  repeat purchases from, 330–331
  risks of, 341–342
  in trade channels, 338–340
  trade-market, 41, 325, 343
Sales-training programs, 339
Sampling, **335**–336
Sans serif fonts, **244**
Satellite, 287
Satellite radio, 291
Satellite television, 287
Science, 195
Script fonts, **246**
Scripts, **246**
Search, **308**–309
Search engine optimization (SEO), **308**–309
Securities and Exchange Commission (SEC),
    91
Segment, **127**
Segmentation, 17–18. *See also* STP
    marketing; Target audiences/
    segments
  benefits, 132–133
  demographic, 132–133, *261*
  geodemographic, 131, 381
  geography, 131
  lifestyle, 131
  market, 127–133
  newspapers, 279
  strategies, 279
  target, 129
Selective demand stimulation, **20**
Self-actualization needs, 81
Self-liquidating premiums, **334**
Self-parody, 70
Self-reference criterion (SRC), **167**
Self-regulation, **92**
Semantic (word) memory, 113–114
Sentence completion, 146
SEO. *See* Search engine optimization (SEO)
Serif fonts, **244**
Service firms, 36
Sets, 248
Sex-appeal advertisements, **60**, 217–218
Sexual revolution, 63–64
Share of audience, **289**
Share of market, 174. *See also* Share of voice
Share of voice, **174**. *See also* Share of market
Shoot, in production, **248**
Short-copy landing page, **235**
Single-source data, **159**
Situation analysis, **166**–167, 405
Slander, **98**

Slice-of-life advertisements, 221
Slogans/tagline, 207, 208, **236**
  classic company, *236*
  copywriting using, 236
Slotting fees, **339**
Social anxiety, 219
Social aspects of advertising, 79–87
Social context, for brands, 149, 239
Social couponing, **314**
Social meaning, **22**, 221–223
  of brands, 221–223
  products with, 121
Social issues. *See* Cause-related advertising;
    Ethics; Green marketing;
    Greenwashing; Privacy
Social media, **31**–32, 300–303. *See also*
    Blogs; Digital media; Interactive
    media; Microblogs; Mobile
    marketing
  advantages of, 311
  advertisement, 307
  as brand management tool, 304–305
  categories, 302
  creatives challenged by, 229
  definitions, 302
  information in, 312
  Madison & Vine in, 222
  media clutter and, 32–33, 329
  media types in, 300–302
  newspapers and, 281–282
  platforms and disclosure, 312–313
  privacy issues of, 312
  sales promotions in, 324–325
  sampling as, 335–337
  spending on, 34–36
  and web 2.0, 316–317
Social media copy, **235**
Social movements, 222–223
Social networking, 267–268
  websites, 302
Society
  advertising and, 56–74
  consumption in, 85
  families in, 63–64, 118–119, 416
  gender in, 116, 120
  materialism in, 81–82
  race in, 119–120
  stratification in, 116–117
Software firms, 46
Source, **11**
Spam, **96**, 385
Sponsor-event congruity, **358**
Sponsors, **8**
Sponsor spillover, **353**
Sponsorship activation, **359**
Sponsorship articulation, **355**
Square root law, **265**
SRC. *See* Self-reference criterion (SRC)
Standard of living, 57, 79, 80. *See also*
    Economy

State regulations, 92
Stereotypes, 82–83
Store traffic, 338–339
Storyboard, **232**–233, 246, **247**
Story construction, **147**
STP marketing (segmenting targeting-positioning), **127**
    marketing strategies with, 127
    strategic planning triangle in, 138–139, **139**
    target segments prioritization in, 133–135
Straight-line copy, **231**
Strategic planning triangle, 138–139, **139**
Strategies. *See also* Message strategies
    in advertising plans, 178
    budgeting, 176
    for competition, 331–332
    copy, 177
    email marketing, 96, 235–236
    humor and, 217
    IBP, 298–299
    marketing, 127
    media, 260–264
    in positioning, 127, 137–138
    in public relations, 404–407
    push, 338
    segmentation, 128, 281
Stratification, **116**
Subheads, in print advertising, **231**
Subliminal advertising, **62**
Supply-demand equation, 168
Support media, **343**–345
    billboards in, 344–345
    directory advertising and, 346
    outdoor signage in, 344–345
    out-of-home advertising in, 345–346
    packaging and, 346
Sweepstakes, 87, 96, 97, 314, **334**
Switchers, as target segment, **129**–130
Symbolic value, **22**
Syndicated television, 287
Synergy, 9, 22, 172, 196, 197, 268, 276, 279, 298, 315, 338, 358, 399
System selling, **389**

T

Taglines, 236
Target, **127**
Target audiences/segments, **12**, 36, 48, 127, 135–138. *See also* STP marketing (segmenting targeting-positioning)
    of advertisements, 11
    by benefits, 132–133
    brands and, 350–351
    definition of, 12
    by demographics, 130–131, *261*
    by geography, 131
    by lifestyles, 132

    media objective of, 260–265
    prioritization of, 133–135
    stereotypes and, 83
    usage patterns/commitment levels of, 128–129
Taste, **117**–118
Teamwork, 196–201
    brainstorming in, 199
    creative abrasion in, 199
    decision-making in, 197–198
Teaser email, 235
Technology. *See also* Computers; Digital media; Internet; Mobile marketing; Programmatic buying; Social media; Web 2.0
    advertising/promotion industry influenced by, 30–34
    communications, 68
    e-revolution and, 70–72
    mass media influenced by, 55
    of physiological assessment, 155–156
Telemarketing, 95, **384**, 386
Telephone Consumer Fraud and Abuse Prevention Act of 1994, 96
Television. *See also* Cable television; Traditional media
    advantages of, 287–288
    advertising recognition tests for, 153–154
    art direction in, 246
    cable, 286
    categories, 286–287
    closed-circuit, 287
    clutter, 289
    copywriting for, 232–233
    dayparts, 292
    disadvantages of, 284–285
    future of, 285
    households, 285
    local, 287
    measuring audiences of, 289
    network, 285–286
    production costs in, 288
    product placement in, 98, 359–360
    satellite/closed-circuit, 287
    social, 290
    strategic planning, 285
    syndicated, **287**
    using visuals, 232–233
Television advertising, 69
    advantages of, 287
    art direction in, **247**
    budget approval in, 246
    categories of, 285–286
    corporate advertising and, 414
    cost of, 248–249, 288
    disadvantages of, 288–289
    guidelines to, 233–234
    length of, 265–266
    power of, 285
    preproduction stage of, 246–249

    production costs of, 248–249, 288
    production timetable for, 248
Testimonials, 92, **212**–214, **213**
Testing
    attitude, 216
    concept, 144
    normative, 151
    recall, 152–153
    recognition, 153
    resonance, 155
Thought listings, **152**
Three-point layout structure, **242**
Thumbnails, **243**
Time frames
    in advertising plans, 173
    in build-up analysis, 176
    payout, *175*, 176
Top of mind, **205**
Top-of-the-mind awareness, **109**, **170**
Tracking studies, **157**
Trade allowances, 96–97
Trade channel, members of, 13
Trade channels, 13, 338
Trade journals, **13**
Trade-market sales promotions, **41**, 325, 339
Trade resellers, **36**
Trade shows, **340**
Traditional media, 276, 277
    advertisers decisions of, 278
    advertising with, 6–7
    future of, 278
Traffic managers, 44
Transformational advertisements, 223–224
Transit advertising, **345**
transparency in buzz marketing, 413
Trendspotting, **143**
Trial offers, 335 336, **336**, 340–341
Trial usage, **171**
Truth in advertising, 87
Truth in Lending Act, 90
TV households, **289**
Type fonts, **244**
Typography, 244

U

UGC. *See* User-generated content (UGC)
Unaided recall, 153
Unfair advertising, **89**
Unique selling proposition (USP), **208**
United States, 62
United States Postal Service (USPS), *91*
Unity, **242**
Unmeasured media, **259**
Upfronts, **272**
Urbanism, 54
Usage patterns, 128, 133
User-generated content (UGC), 245, 299
USP. *See* Unique selling proposition (USP)

V

Value, **23**
    brand, 232, 324
    proposition, **138**
    symbolic, 22
Variety seeking, **112**–113, 129
Vendor co-op programs, 339
Vertical cooperative advertising, **89**–90
Video game advertising, 361
Video games, 361
    and advergaming, 313–314
Video on demand (VOD), **286**–287
Video sharing websites, 303
Viral marketing, **315**, 410–411

Virtual identity, **303**
    consumer and brand, 303–304
Visuals. *See also* Illustrations
    in advertising, 238
    element, **242**
    illustration and, 238–244
    television using, 232–233
VOD. *See* Video on demand (VOD)

W

Web 2.0, 71, **299**–300, 311. *See also*
    Internet; Technology
Web/tablet/smartphone TV, 287
Wheeler-Lea Amendments, 60, 90
Wholesalers, 35–36

Within-vehicle duplication, **263**
Women, stereotypes and, 83
Word-of-mouth, 32, 311, 324, 370, 408, 412,
    413
World War I, 57
World War II, **60–61**, 60–64

Y

Youth culture, 63, 66

Z

Zaltman Metaphor Elicitation Technique
    (ZMET), **147**, 220